Antiques

Antiques

An Encyclopedia of the Decorative Arts
Edited by Paul Atterbury

Foreword by Sir Hugh Casson Director of the Royal Academy

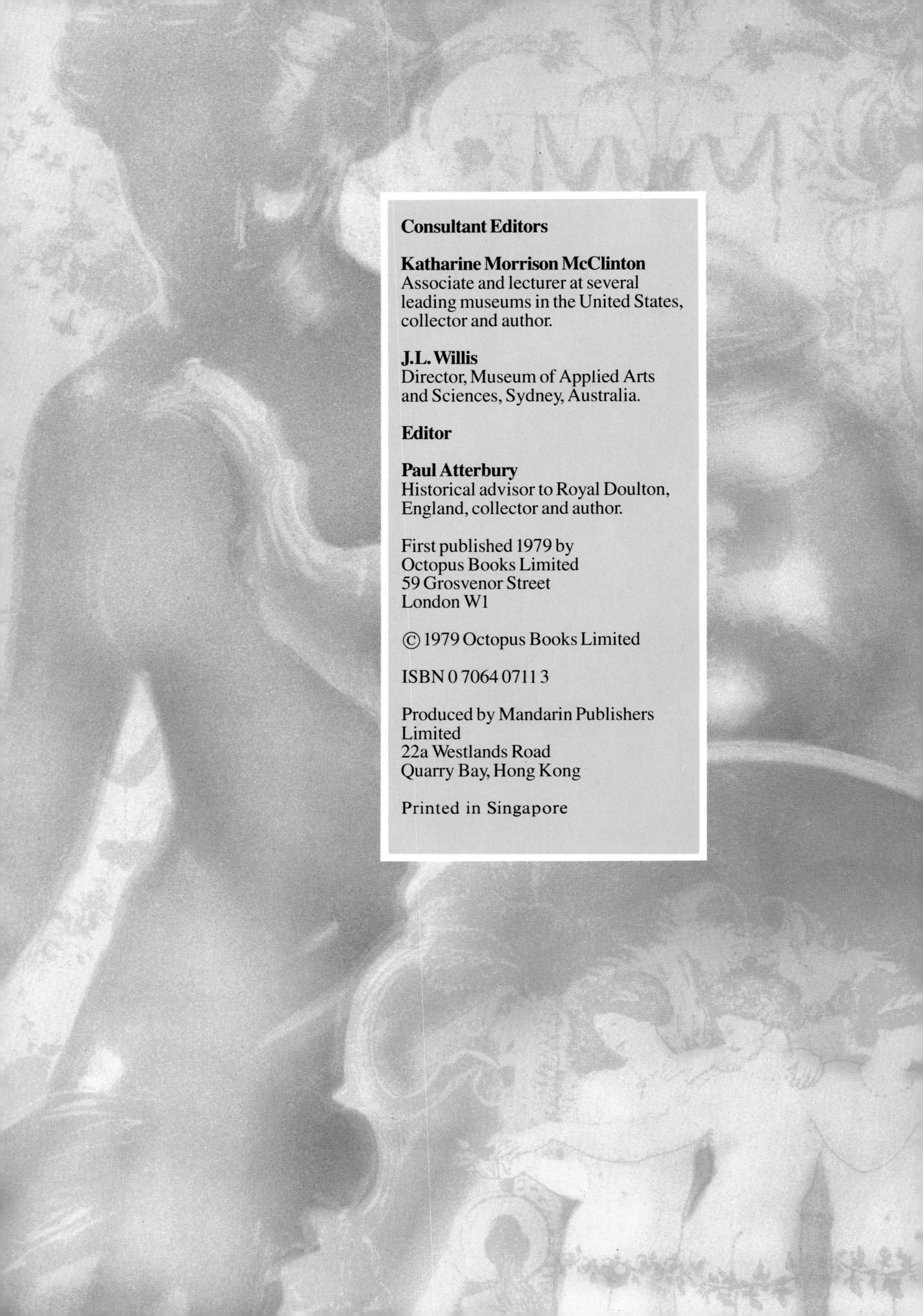

Consultant Editors

Katharine Morrison McClinton
Associate and lecturer at several
leading museums in the United States,
collector and author.

J.L. Willis
Director, Museum of Applied Arts
and Sciences, Sydney, Australia.

Editor

Paul Atterbury
Historical advisor to Royal Doulton,
England, collector and author.

First published 1979 by
Octopus Books Limited
59 Grosvenor Street
London W1

© 1979 Octopus Books Limited

ISBN 0 7064 0711 3

Produced by Mandarin Publishers
Limited
22a Westlands Road
Quarry Bay, Hong Kong

Printed in Singapore

Contents

Contents

Acknowledgements

The publishers would like to thank the following individuals and organizations for their kind permission to reproduce the photos in this book:—

Actualit 379 below; American Museum in Britain, Bath 50 below, 52 below, 172 below right; Antique Porcelain Company 103 below; Paul Atterbury 75, 112 right; Australian Information Service, London 377 above and below; Bavaria-Verlag 222 below, 374–375; Bennett Collection 272 below; Bennington Museum, Bennington, Vermont 93 above left, 106 left; John Bethell 43; Bethnal Green Museum (photo by K. Jackson) 42 right; Bildarchiv Foto Marburg 22 right, 235 below; Bodleian Library 293 left; Bonhams Auctioneers and Valuers 166 above, 166 below, 167 above and below; Boston Museum of Fine Arts (M. and M. Karolik Collection) 13; Brighton Art Gallery and Museum 238 below; Bristol City Art Gallery 134–135, 136 left; British Museum 121 above, centre and below, 130, 140 left, 152, 187, 230, 233 left; Brooklyn Museum 28 left; Campbell Collection, Campbell Museum, Camden, N.J., U.S.A. 88–89; Carmen Collection (photo by Angelo Hornak) 349; Carter Nash Cameron Ltd. 114, 138, 204 above left, 291, 292, 293 above right, 294 below (Brooklyn Museum) 105 right, (Hanley Museum and Art Gallery, Staffordshire) 89, (Maxwell Joseph Collection) 58 above, (Metropolitan Museum of Art, Gift of Mrs. Winthrop Attwell) 208 above, (Victoria and Albert Museum) 60 left, (Henry Francis du Pont Winterthur Museum) 199 above, 204 below; Christie, Manson and Woods Ltd. 196 left and right, 198 below, 201, 219 below, 236 above, right, 272 above, 318 right, 321 above right, 366 above; ©Cilag-Chemie Schaffausen, (photo by U. Leibacher, Beringen, Switzerland) Frau P. Rychner Collection 342; Clandon Park, Guildford 29; Conway Library, Courtauld Institute of Art 219 above; Cooper-Bridgeman Colour Library 15 below, 21, 22 centre, 24, 36–37, 45 right, 56–57, 79 left, 104 left, 141 below, 164 below, 171, 180 above, 189 above and below, 206 left, 225 below left, 234 right, 242 above, 244 right, 280, 307 above, 320 above, 324, 344, (Allingham Park, Shrewsbury) 334, (American Museum in Britain, Bath) 301 below, (Ashmolean Museum) 200–201, (Bethnal Green Museum) 128 left, 209 above, 343 above, (Birmingham Museum) 241 right, (N. Bloom and Sons) 165 right, (British Museum) 116 left, 120, 299 above, 318 left, (Christie, Manson and Woods) 80 below right, 100, 155 left, 158 right, 168, 169 above, centre and below right, 173, 174 above, 175, 204 above right, 231 right, 232 left and right, 253, (City Museum of Sheffield) 202 right, (Clandon Park, Guildford) 97 above and below, (Clockmakers Company Collection, London) 316 left, (A. Derlam Collection) 77 above, (Editions Graphiques) 106 right, 188, 209 below, (Gabriella Gross Collection) 147, (Guildhall, London) 316 right, (Hakim and Sons) 170 below, 172 above right, (Celia Johnson Collection) 53, (Kenwood, London) 336 below, (Leeds City Art Gallery) 79 right, (Lady Lever Gallery) 49 above right, (London Museum) 341 above, (Dr. John McMaster, Cambridge) 304 right, (Musée des Arts Décoratifs) 198 above, 203 above, (Museum of London) 120, 341 above, (National Trust, Lord St. Oswald) 33, (S.J. Phillips) 194 right, (John P. Raison) 103 above, (Sloane Collection) 154, (Sotheby Parke Bernet and Company) 183, (Stourbridge Glass Museum) 136 right, (Tower of London) 273 left, (Trinity College, Oxford) 194 left, (Victoria and Albert Museum) 10–11, 22 left, 32, 40 above, 41 above, 42 left, 48, 57, 58 below, 76, 77 below, 80 left, 81, 85, 104 right, 105 left, 126 left, 182, 183 below, 192 right, 197, 206 right, 237 right, 240 above, 260, 276, 301 above and below, 339 below; Corning Museum of Glass, Corning, New York 143 below; Graham Findlayson endpapers; Reproduced by permission of the Syndics of the Fitzwilliam Museum, Cambridge 87 left and right; Fotomas 298 above, John Freeman Group (British Museum) 299 below, 300 left, 330 below; Phillippe Garner 145 centre; Giraudon 98 left, 144 above centre and right, 370 below, Goldsmiths Hall 199 above, Gunshots 254 below, 256 left and right, 257, 264, 265, 273 right, 277 below; Sonia Halliday 124, 125 left and right; Hamlyn Group Picture Library (Mollo Collection) 254 above; Robert Harding Associates 169 below left, 172 left, 174 below, 224, 376 below; Heirloom and Howard Ltd. (photo by Angelo Hornak) 78 left; Cecil Higgins Museum, Bedford 126 right, 127, 129 right, 132 above right, and below, 141 above; Holbourne of Menstrie, Bath 134 left, 140 right; Michael Holford 148–149, 176, 177 above and below, (British Museum) 180 below, 300 right, (Science Museum) 310–311, 329 above, 351 above, 354 above, (Victoria and Albert Museum) 178 above, 181, 338 below right, (Sir Isaac Wolfson) 179; Angelo Hornak 18 above, 37 above, 60 right, 61, 63 above, 65 below, 99, 101, 110, 113 below, 129 left, 137 below right, 144 below centre, 191, 221, 225 below right, 243 left, 248–249, 274 above and below, 279, 281, 282, 317 above left, 370 above, 371 below left, 374 centre left and below left, 378 above and

below, (Mary Bellis, Hungerford) 234 left and centre, (Bethnal Green Museum) 45 left, (Christie Manson and Woods) 319 right, (Editions Graphiques) 165 left, (Avril Hart) 144 left, (Imperial War Museum) 306 below, (Jensen, London) 205 right, (John Jesse) 247, (Martins-Forrest Collection) 44 right, (R. McCrindell Collection) 345 above, (National Trust) 18 above, 237 left, (Ca. Rezzonica Venice) 27 above, (Tower of London) 281, (Town Clerk, Bury St. Edmunds) 315, (Victoria and Albert Museum) 45 centre, 52 above, 108 above left, 111 left, 245, 246, (Waterways Museum) 111 right, (Willet Collection, Brighton Museum) 92; Illustrated London News (photo by Angelo Hornak) 308 above; Ironbridge Gorge Museum Trust 284–285; Kennedy Galleries, Vigo Street, London W.1. (photos by Malcolm Robertson) 62, 63 below, 65 above, 66 right and left, 67, 70, 71; A.F. Kersting 220, 371 above, 372 below, 374 above left, 376 above; Kodak Museum 296 left, 297 left and right; Kosta Boda 146 below; Kungl. Husgeradskammaren 222 above; Kunstindustrimuseet I Oslo 54; James Mackay Collection 308 below, Mansell Collection 228 above left, 228–229, 259, 338 below left, 341 centre; Martin Brothers 112 left; MAS 44 left, 215 left and right, 216–217, 235 above; David C. Mitchell, British Matchbox Label and Booklet Society, (photo by P.J. Gates) 309; Dr. Med. R. Horgenthaler, Harpo Lyng photo Zurich 343 below; Museum of the City of New York 41 below, 341 below; Museum of London 88 left; Museum of Modern Art, New York 46 right and below; National Army Museum 251, 261 above and below right, 262, 263 left and right, 271, 278 above and below, 282 above, 283 above and below; The National Trust 19 above, 34 above, 371 below right; National Museum of Ireland 233 right; National Museum of Wales 108 below left, 241 left; W.K. Neal 274 centre, 277 above; Old Salem Inc. 243 right, Orrefors, Glassbruk Sweden 146 above; Walter Parrish International (Museum of the History of Science, Oxford) 331; Carl Patterson 356–365; Peabody Museum of Salem 327; Percival David Foundation of Chinese Art 78 right; S.J. Phillips 159 below; Photo Meyer 225 above; Pilkington Glass Museum 118 left and right, 119, 128 right, 131, 132 above left, 135 right, 139 right, 142 left; Pitt-Rivers Museum 335, 336 above; Prague Museum of Applied Art 139 left; Raymonds Photographic, Derby 223; Rijksmuseum 20 right; Malcolm Robertson 314 left, 317 right and below left, 320 below, 321 below right, 323 above, 325 above and below; Royal Doulton Tableware Ltd. 108 above right and below right, 109; Royal Scottish Museum 133; Salmer 372 above, 379 above; Scala 24–25, 96, 217, (Pitti Palace, Firenze) 72–73; Science Museum 321 left, 329 below, 330 above, 332 below, 348 above and below, 352 above and below, 354 below, 355 above and below, (photo by Derek Witty) 351 below; Nicholas Servian FIIP, Woodmansterne Ltd. 213; Ronald Sheridans Photo Library 192 left; Mrs. Edwin Smith 240 below; Sotheby Parke Bernet and Company 16 left, 17 above and below, 19 below, 26, 31, 46 left, 47, 94, 113 above, 151, 153, 155 right, 156, 157 above, 159 above, 160, 161 left and right, 162, 164 above and below centre, 208 below, 314 right, 366 below, 367 above centre and below, 368 above, centre and below, 369 above and below; Steuben Glass 145 left and right; Stourbridge Corporation 137 below left; J.T. Van Riemsdyck 346, 347; Victoria and Albert Museum 15 above, 16 right, 28 right, 30 above, below left and right, 34 below, 38, 49 below, 50 above, 51, 55, 64, 69, 80 above right, 83 right, 84, 86, 93 below left, 95 left and right, 98 right, 127, 137 above, left and above right, 142 right, 143 above, 157 below, 158 left, 178 below, 193, 202 left, 203 below, 231 left, 236 above left and below, 238 above, 239 above and below, 252 above right and below right, 261 below left, 266, 268, 269 above, 287, 294 above, 304 left, 313, 318 centre, 323 below left and below right, 339 above, 345 below, (Michael Holford) 338 below right, (Angelo Hornak) 49 left, 82, 107, 293 below, 306 above, 307 below, (Dereck Witty) 20 left; Roger Viollet 373 above and below; Albert de Visscher, Brussels 328, 332 above, 333; Reproduced by permission of the Trustees, Wallace Collection, London 18 below, 27 below, 39 right, 83 left, 242 below, 244 left, 319 left; Wartski (photo by Angelo Hornak) 164 above centre; Wedgwood Museum, Barlaston 93 right; Weidenfeld and Nicolson Ltd. 68; Weinreb and Douma Ltd. 302, 303 above and below; Whitbread and Co. Ltd. (Overlord Tapestry Trust) 59 above and below; Henry Francis du Pont Winterthur Museum 35, 36 above left, 37 below right; Yale University Art Gallery 39 left, 40 left.

Picture research by: Phillippa Lewis, Juliette Scott.

Illustrations by Michael Strand.

The pubishers would like to thank Kennedy Carpets & Kelims, 9a Vigo St., W.1, for allowing photography of the carpets on pages 66–71.

8

Foreword

'Have nothing in your house,' wrote William Morris, 'except what you know to be useful or believe to be beautiful'. Simple, high-minded advice from a simple, high-minded man, that has, I suppose, been consistently (and rightly) ignored through the centuries by all those rich enough to have any choice in the matter. How strange that so warm-hearted and passionate an artist should underestimate so completely the influence of social processes, and dismiss the crucial power of, for instance, the images and symbols of heroes, artefacts, language, which give shape to our physical and mental landscape.

Convenience and function can never, of course, be discarded – they are essential weapons in the struggle for existence – but there are always good emotional reasons for surrounding ourselves with 'unfunctional' or, indeed, 'unbeautiful' objects. Comfort, for instance, has never historically been an important ingredient of the chair. In ancient Egypt, and in parts of Africa still, a chair is a symbol of nobility, not something to sit on.

Our sense of beauty too, far from being absolute, is continually being diverted by social pressures and cultural shifts. Recently it has received a positively explosive charge from television and package tours, from pop music, universal jeans and the rag bag of revivalism. 'An Apartment,' wrote Robert de Montesquiou, 'is a mood,' – a form of personal expression. In a period of impermanence and obsolescence – in objects as well as relationships – these moods seem to succeed each other with bewildering speed. It is not surprising, therefore, that in such turbulent tides, we seek reassurance in the marker buoys of ritual and tradition, in familiar forms and recognizable objects and, above all, in the beautiful achievements of the artists, designers and craftsmen of past centuries.

It is the purpose of this book to present and consider these works, not in isolation (as so often happens in museums), but truly as part of the society and social attitudes of their times, so that they can be more properly understood. Although devised by acknowledged experts, this survey can be approached at many different levels of knowledge and experience. It is hoped, that by studying these pages, the general reader and the amateur collector will join the historian and the scholar in identifying and interpreting the fascinating complexity of references and sub-codes that form the background to this rich and comprehensive study. As in everything else, the more we know, the more we will be rewarded.

Sir Hugh Casson
President of the Royal Academy

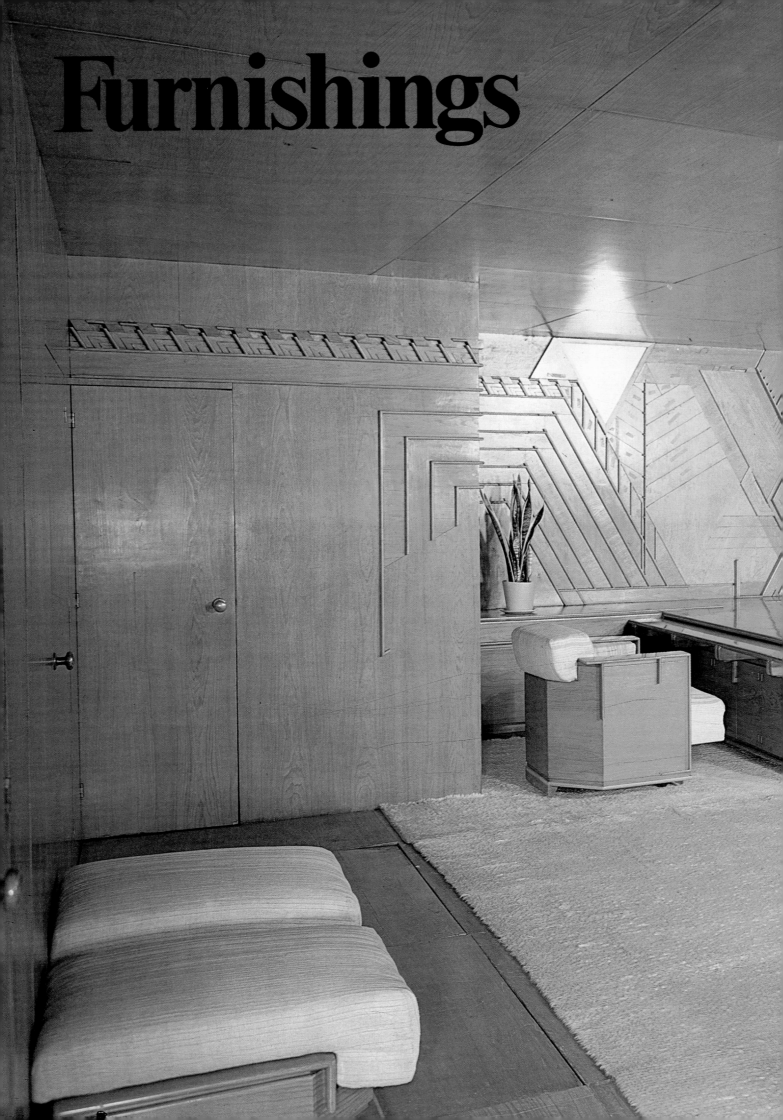

Furnishings

The development and change in interior design from one period to another involves many factors that are not typical of antiques as a whole. Some of these, such as size, permanence, function, methods and materials of construction, help to determine changes in style in a very direct manner. However, perhaps more important is the totality of interior design; any interior is composed of a number of closely related elements, many of which lose some of their significance when removed from their original context. It is therefore necessary to see furniture, carpets and textiles as part of a related pattern of stylistic change and development.

Furnishings are often dependent upon architecture, taking their styles from contemporary building and interior design. On a grand scale, an architect would produce a design for a total scheme, including not only the structure, exterior and interior details of the building, but also all its related equipment, such as furniture, carpets, tiles, wallpapers, light fittings, fireplaces and door furniture. This approach was common in the 18th century, and is perhaps typified by the work of Robert Adam, but it is not unusual to find it in later periods: obvious examples being Mackintosh, Pugin, Gaudi, Le Corbusier and Frank Lloyd Wright. On a lesser level, many architects and interior designers have designed furnishings, often without a specific location in mind, but conceived broadly within the confines of interior design. At the same time, many furniture and carpet designers have consciously attempted to follow architectural principles of style and structure. Thus, many 18th century cabinet makers were able to establish their reputations without actually making very themselves. Designers such as Chippendale and Sheraton simply produced and published designs which in themselves were enough to affect the development of style. It was left to their followers to make the actual pieces.

The nature of style in furnishing was also influenced by its changing role. In the Middle Ages, pieces were made to be transportable because of the unstable and transitory nature of society, but by the late 17th century, furnishings had become a fixed part of a domestic interior, and an inseparable part of the architecture. Although such large-scale fixed interiors continued to be produced until the 19th century, they became less absolute during the latter part of the 18th century. The increasing mobility of society, frequently for reasons of pleasure, demanded smaller, more adaptable pieces that could be moved from house to house, a pattern that has continued until today virtually unchanged. This mobility was also encouraged by the increasing availability of exotic items imported from abroad, which reflected the taste of the owner rather than their location. Since the 19th century, furnishings have generally been more flexible in their use, a pattern that has also affected the development of style.

Function has also been instrumental in determining the nature of style in furnishing more than in other fields. Most furniture is made to be used and so has a clearly defined set of criteria to be fulfilled. All periods have produced their share of fantastic objects, but even the more bizarre fantasies, such as cotton reel or stags' horns chairs, or Dali's Mae West couch, still perform their basic function. Totally useless furnishings are quite rare and normally exist only in some other field, such as sculpture. Although tapestries ultimately became fine art objects, their size and structure were permanent reminders of their original role as providers of warmth and insulation.

Economics have also played a considerable role. Frequently, furnishings have been created and used to reflect the wealth and status of their owner, either by size, or by complexity of ornamentation and detail, or by the materials used. Generally furnishings are technically quite simple in structure, requiring readily available skills, materials, tools and equipment. All the skill is expressed by the style and finish. It is this finish that reflects the wealth of the owner, the status of the designer and the craftsman and the awareness of the styles of the period. It is also this finish which enables collectors to date and identify items, aided to a lesser extent by a knowledge of materials and techniques.

Furniture perhaps declares its style more obviously than any other kind of antique, and style is created by the skill of the cabinet maker or craftsman. Most inevitably work in wood, and take great pleasure in exploring the full potential of the material and its many different species and qualities. The choice of woods available to the craftsman has therefore often helped to determine the style. Until the 17th century he had to rely on sturdy, readily available woods such as oak, rich in strength and colour, but limited in its decorative qualities. Changes in the social role of furniture and the demand for lighter pieces encouraged the development of techniques such as veneering, which in turn brought about the dominance in Europe of walnut and other fruit woods. In the 18th century the expansion of overseas trade brought about an increasing import and so use of exotic woods such as mahogany and rosewood. At the same time the increasing choice of materials for decoration, such as ivory and lacquer, radically altered the appearance of furniture on all levels of the market.

During the same period, the cabinet maker increasingly combined his talents with those in other fields, such as metalworkers, gilders and engravers, to produce a new type of furniture that appealed greatly to the new aristocratic and merchant classes. In the 19th century, the general availability of all sorts of exotic materials encouraged the cabinet maker to produce furnishings that expressed an eclectic and extreme approach to style in which craftsmanship was dominant. More recently, the exploration of new materials such as aluminium, steel, plastics and paper has affected furniture styles. The use of these has been provoked in part by the dramatic increases in the costs of traditional materials and craftsmanship, and partly by a more temporary attitude to furnishings.

However, relative permanence is a feature of most furnishings. Even allowing for wear and tear, a well-made piece in normal use can be expected to survive its maker and original purchaser by several decades or even centuries. This means that many pieces, although reflecting precise styles, can still achieve a dateless quality that makes them suitable for a great variety of environments. The continual popularity of 18th century pieces is partly explained by their now being old enough to be beyond fashion, and so have become universally accepted as expressions of 'good taste'. On the grandest level, this relative permanence encouraged governments to sponsor state manufacture in order to reduce the costs of imports and to develop new skills, while on a lesser one it allowed styles to filter down through the market, prolonging indefinitely their popular life. The grand novelties of avant garde designers were imitated, first by the important trade manufacturers, secondly by provincial craftsmen, and ultimately by country makers whose use of a style may actually be so far behind the mainstream of design development that they manage to stop it ever finally going out of fashion. This process also ensures that the collector can choose from a range of items far greater than actually implied by the known life of the style in historical terms, and at a greater range of prices. This has encouraged him to buy antique furnishings for their own sake, confident that they will fit into any style or environment, regardless of the period that inspired their original creation.

A fine example of the cabinet maker's art, this painted side chair with a back of delicately carved peacock feathers dates from c. 1795.

Furniture

Milestones in the history of furniture

mid-15th century	Gothic forms characterized the few pieces of furniture found in Europe.
mid-16th century	Italian Renaissance decorative style spread northward.
17th century	Italian and Flemish Baroque styles influenced furniture forms throughout Europe.
1667	*Manufacture Royale des Meubles de la Couronne* established at Paris.
1688	Publication in England of Stalker and Parter's *Treatise of Japanning, Varnishing and Guilding* marked the popularity of Oriental styles.
c.1715	Regence style introduced in France.
c.1740	Rococo style achieved great popularity in France and England.
1758	Robert Adam returned to England from Italy and introduced neo-classical style.
1850–90	Classical, Gothic, Renaissance, Rococo and other revival styles swept Europe and North America.
1893	Art Nouveau style originated in Belgium and France.
1919	Walter Gropius established the Bauhaus School at Dessau.
1926	Dutch designer, Mart Stau introduced the cantilever chair.

The network of spectacular Gothic cathedrals that sprinkled the 15th century European landscape with towers, pinnacles, statuary and spires, manifested the wealth and strength of the main force of internationalism in the Middle Ages, the Christian Church. Commerce also united European societies, but although mercantile exchange, ecclesiastical splendour and courtly extravagance, all helped shape interior styles in the late medieval period, they in no way provided the degree of domestic comfort taken for granted today.

Throughout Europe, common houses generally consisted of a single room only, and their stark furnishings revealed a low standard of living. Even in rich aristocratic establishments, interiors were likely to be more showy than comfortable. European nobility constantly moved among their various estates, and as they travelled they took with them the sparse furnishings. The dominant features of late medieval furniture were necessarily those of adaptability and easy transport.

This furniture reflected, in miniature, the Gothic architectural style. This was possibly connected to Arabic sources, and was related to the earlier, northern Romanesque style of the 9th and 10th centuries. Characterized by pointed ogival arches, cusps, tracery and stylized flame-like carving, the Gothic mode flourished in northern Europe from the 13th to the 15th centuries. The imposing fabric of cathedrals, such as Nôtre Dame, with sculpture and stained glass executed on a large scale, provided a pictorial medium for presenting the Biblical text to a world that lacked printing and literacy.

Ecclesiastical furniture followed this style, echoing on pews and misericordia such features as tracery, arcades and Biblical figures and scenes. Domestic furniture shared the same ornament, and by the 15th century also included the profile 'romayne' heads derived from Italian Renaissance interpretations of Roman coins, and the Flemish-inspired linenfold panelling.

Gothic furniture was sparse. Chairs, chests and tables that date from before the 15th century are rare; hangings were the real furnishings of medieval interiors, and it was the collection of tapestries, velvets, silks and leathers that dominated rooms with their presence and colour. These materials, many produced in Italy and Spain, far outweighed the status and worth of the wooden pieces they dwarfed. Sets of elaborate textiles, called *chambres* in medieval French inventories, together with metalwork, were the most ornate of the decorative arts. The rich wall fabrics of the Coronation Room of Queen Jeanne of Burgundy were embroidered with 1,321 parrots and the ducal coat of arms. The poor building insulation that made these hangings necessary also popularized the footstools that kept feet off cold floors. Also heavy tapestries almost totally cloaked medieval beds.

Even in wealthier homes, rooms were not assigned exclusive functions, and the few pieces of furniture that each house contained were moved according to necessity. Life often centred around a large hall which accommodated eating, entertainment and casual socializing. Such halls generally included a long high table for the manor family; this table, and the rows of tables set beneath it at right angles, were taken apart into their component trestles and planks at the end of meals and removed to make way for whatever activity was to follow.

Etiquette required that high tables, four-poster state beds, and princely seats be elevated on a dais. Canopies were hung above the same pieces, and even children's cradles and press cupboards that displayed collections of plate were similarly distinguished.

In addition to being easily dismantled, furniture of the late Middle Ages tended to be plain and serviceable. The woods most often used were oak, walnut and pine. Construction methods progressed from the crude, hollowed-out tree trunk chests of early medieval England to assemblages of wood planks, and finally to the more durable panel-and-frame construction, introduced possibly in Flanders towards the end of the 14th century.

The chest was the most common piece of furniture in the Middle Ages. It was used to store bridal dowries, to transport belongings, to safe-guard valuables such as books and imported spices, as well as to sit on. Italian Gothic chests were often gilt and were generally uncarved, being painted with religious scenes. French chests were carved with Gothic arches, tracery and figures. Those from Spain were often leather-covered, and bound with iron. During the Renaissance, chests developed domed tops, possibly to facilitate their fixture to animals when being transported.

The most elaborate chairs of any establishment were reserved for the head of the household, although benches and other seats may have been available to others.

In general, Gothic interiors were equipped with few of the accoutrements of easy living that the following centuries would introduce. The sharp contrast between the minimally comfortable furniture that people used, and the ostentatious and expensive embellishments displayed in the rooms around them, only began to diminish during the Renaissance.

The Renaissance

In the 15th century the Gothic style began to wane. The flamboyant and perpendicular Gothic exhausted itself in its final stages. It gradually gave way throughout Europe to Renaissance influences which had originated about two centuries before in Italy, where the Gothic mode had never been completely established. There, a turn towards humanism in religion in the 13th century transformed the medieval preoccupation with religious salvation into a glorification of man and the world. Simultaneously, the papacy and the rigid feudal system declined, favouring aristocratic and mercantile families such as the Medici, Gonzaga and Sforza, who embraced the new age of expansion, exploration,

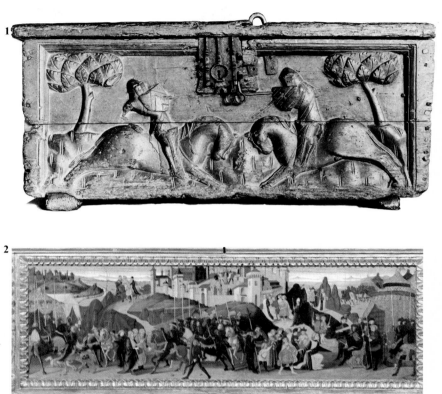

technical advance and unprecedented wealth.

Their patronage fostered a revolution in European thought and art, which originated in Florence. It fast spread to the rest of Italy and gradually permeated northern Europe. Revived studies of classical architecture, arts and literature revitalized antique principles, manifested in the corporeal realism of paintings such as Giotto di Bondone's fresco cycle at the Arena Chapel in Padua, and in the classical proportions of buildings such as Filippo Brunelleschi's Pazzi Chapel at Santa Croce, Florence.

The resurrection of classical architectural forms and concepts brought with it a profusion of acanthus leaves, griffins, urns and other details taken from ancient villas and temples, introducing a repertoire of motifs that would appear on furniture for centuries to follow.

Rivalries of patronage and artistic display among aristocratic families resulted in the building of expensive palaces and villas in Italy and elsewhere. These villas disseminated the Renaissance style, attested to the new social stability and demanded the production of new and finer furnishings.

Early Renaissance interiors continued to be draped with brightly-coloured textiles, but as the period progressed it saw the introduction of a variety of new furniture forms, which increased in abundance everywhere. At first, classical ornaments were merely added to traditional Gothic furniture. Gradually, however, although the types of woods used remained

1 Plank construction, rectangular shape, and front panel ornament are characteristic features of surviving medieval chests. This 14th century French coffer is decorated with a scene of two tilting knights. The simple, heavy carving is typical of oak. Massive iron locks protected such chests from being opened by anyone but their owners, whose most valuable possessions they would have contained; this lock is of a later date than the chest. (Victoria and Albert Museum, London).

2 Prominent painters often decorated Italian cassoni with religious or narrative compositions, or scenes of pageantry and pomp. This panel is from the gilded and painted Nerli cassone, produced in the late 15th century in Florence. The persistence of classical Roman motifs is seen in the leaf border. (Courtauld Institute Galleries, London)

largely unchanged, Renaissance architecture, painting and sculpture led to the application of classical architectural motifs and naturalistically carved animals, figures and foliage. Italian and French chests of the 15th and 16th centuries often combined elements such as Gothic arcades and religious figures with classical columns and cornices.

Furnishings and interior decoration developed from the classic restraint of the early Renaissance to an increasing opulence during the 15th and 16th centuries. Walls were hung with cloths of gold, Italian silks and velvets, imported oriental carpets, Spanish leathers, and tapestries woven with mythological and Biblical scenes. Artists such as Sandro Botticelli and Domenico Ghirlandaio frequently executed wall frescoes of allegories, hunting scenes, landscapes with birds and animals, and architectural views.

Wooden wainscoting, often with contrasting marble panels or intarsia (inlaying or marquetry) decorations, also covered room walls. Coffered and panelled ceilings, such as Leonardo da Vinci's gold and azure stellar composition in the ballroom of the Castello at Milan, were colourfully painted.

These interior schemes, opulent in themselves, contained collections of paintings, sculpture, silver and gold plate, manuscripts, musical instruments and maiolica. Furniture was still scarce, but increasingly refined. Italian Renaissance woodworkers ornamented their walnut cabinets, beds, chairs and other pieces with rich carving and marquetry.

The Italian *cassone*, box-like and painted in earlier periods, developed into an architecturally-schemed chest with strong cornice and base, classical pilasters and panels, and ornaments of arches and refined classical mouldings.

The *cassapanca*, a form of chair derived from a chest with back and sides, eventually became the honoured seat of the head of an Italian household. It was fitted with cushions and often raised on a dais, as were the carved or inlaid throne seats, with panel-backs and canopies, found in patrician ceremonial apartments. *Sgabello* stools, with narrow triangular backs, were carved and inlaid. The folding, easily-transported X-shaped *Savonarola* chair was upholstered with leather or fabric. Cabinets acquired the friezes, pediments and columns of Renaissance architecture; their front panels were often inlaid with intarsia *trompe l'oeil* scenes which themselves depicted open-doored cabinets with contents or architectural vistas revealed. Four-poster beds with canopies of rich velvets, silks and tapestries, were often gilt and raised on a dais. Large tables, with vase-shaped end supports joined by stretchers, were frequently covered with tapestries or exquisite lace, as were the *credenze*, or side-boards, that developed during the 15th century.

The flourishing court of Renaissance Spain eagerly adopted the decorative elements that Italian craftsmen introduced to the already unusual *mudéjar* style, a medieval form which had resulted from the amalgamation of Arab, African and Mediterranean influences, and which was characterized by geometrical interlaces, polygons, stars and foliage motifs. In furniture, *mudéjar* derived much of its effect from the native materials, so varied and exotic by northern European standards, – cypress, orangewood, chestnut, walnut and poplar – and from the increasing imports of rare metals and semi-precious stones from the Spanish American colonies.

The many-drawered Spanish *hembra* evolved into the elaborate *vargueno*, a writing desk on a stand containing tiny, brightly-painted and gilt drawers, columns, doors and carvings.

The *sillone de frailero*, which superseded an

1 Subdivision, miniaturization, and diverse materials add delightful variety to this 16th century Spanish vargueño on stand. Drop fronts often provided writing surfaces for these cabinets. (Sotheby's, London)

2 This design for two beds appeared in Paul Uredeman de Vrie's *Verscheyden Schrynwerck* (Various Cabinetwork) published in Amsterdam in 1630; the blocky proportions and heavy details are characteristic of his style.

earlier X-shaped seat derived from Italy, was square and solid, with horizontal, sometimes curved arms. Large decorative brass nails attached the leather to the back and seat, and a hinged stretcher pierced with a geometric ornament joined the legs. The characteristic Spanish table, with a thick walnut top projecting above a frieze of small carved drawers, also came into use during the Renaissance, when it acquired ironwork stretchers shaped as symmetrical S-scrolls. Furniture legs in general tended to be boldly turned with spheres, rings and balusters.

In Northern Europe, where oak was commonly used, the Netherlands led in the adoption of Renaissance forms, disseminating the style to Germany, Scandinavia and England through circulated prints such as those by Cornelis Floris (active in the 1550s), who introduced Renaissance scrolled ornament and grotesques to the Low Countries and Germany in mid-century. Engravings by Hans Vredeman de Vries (1527–c.1604) and his son Paul (1567–c.1630) accelerated the dispersion of northern Renaissance design.

Around 1580 in Antwerp, de Vries published a pattern-book showing strong Italian Renaissance and Mannerist influence in his designs for four-poster beds, tables, chairs, cupboards and other furnishings. The cornices, caryatids, pilasters, arches and other architectural details illustrated in these plates were to be as important for northern European furniture production as his depictions of scrolls, spindles, figures, heavy strapwork and gem-shaped bosses.

Late Renaissance joined cupboards of the Netherlands, particularly those of Antwerp, were characterized by this heavy style. Set on bun feet, they had panelled doors ornamented with rectangular mouldings and separated by pilasters or consoles. Turned supports of spheres, blocks and balusters, the latter often fluted, appeared on Flemish stools, benches, chairs, tables and beds, often joined by similarly turned stretchers.

In Germany, prints executed by Albrecht Dürer (1471–1528), Peter Flötner (c.1485–1576) and the de Vrieses, circulated Renaissance-inspired forms and motifs which furniture-makers had widely adopted by the mid-16th century. Engravings by Lorenz Stöer (active 1555–c.1620) popularized designs for the inlay and marquetry ornament of tables and cabinets, with involved and complicated perspective views that included overgrown architectural ruins, strapwork, rollwork and odd polyhedral forms such as dodecahedra.

3 Late 16th century South German chests were often decorated with carvings and marquetry work, depicting foliage, animals, half-figures, and grotesques; this composition was assembled from natural and green-stained woods. The architectural components of columns, arches, and pediments reflect the dissemination of Renaissance influences from Italy. (Sotheby's, London)

4 Superb craftsmanship and intricate detail distinguish this section of the chest illustrated below. Interlaced strapwork often appeared in German Renaissance ornament. (Sotheby's, London)

4

3

1 Hardwick Hall, in Derbyshire, England, was built in 1591–97 for Elizabeth, Countess of Shrewsbury, 'Bess of Hardwick.' The house contains this 16th century English chest, carved with the initials 'GT' possibly referring to either George or Gilbert Talbot, the 6th and 7th Earls of Shrewsbury. The decoration consists of architectural carvings, ill-proportioned as they often were in northern Europe, and marquetry. (Hardwick Hall)

2 This architecturally-schemed walnut French cupboard, inlaid with plaques of veined marble, dates from the second half of the 16th century. Henri II style cupboards were often ornamented with mythological figures; those carved on the lower doors represent Venus and Diana. The upper doors, which hide eight small shelves and a green silk lining, were probably recarved in the 19th century; the oval cartouches bear the arms of Queen Isabella II of Spain, who fled to France in 1868. (Wallace Collection, London)

3 Large-scale acanthus leaves, gadroons, and strapwork enliven the large oak bed located in the Crimson Room of Montacute House, Somerset, England, begun in 1588 by Sir Edward Phelips. The headboard of the bed is carved with the coats of arms of King James I, Henry, Prince of Wales, and Frederick V, the Elector of Palatine, who came to England in 1612, the probable date of the bed. The room was originally hung with tapestries. (Montacute House, Somerset)

4 This Chinese Kuei, or cupboard, from the late Ming period (1368–1644), is constructed of hardstone, rosewood, and padouk-wood, with ornament of teak, jade, stained ivory, and mother-of-pearl. Cupboards such as this often served as wardrobes; smaller ones contained books, hats, and other items. (Sotheby's, London)

In the conservative and more commercially isolated north, stylistic changes occurred more slowly; pieces were heavily formed and enriched with massively carved figures and ornament. Gothic vestiges, such as linenfold ornament on cupboards, lingered well into the mid-16th century.

Application of classical architectural motifs to French furniture forms in the first half of the 16th century created the bold, vigorous François I style. Tables carved with griffins and grotesques, beds with baluster posts and pictorial hangings, and panelled chairs, benches, stools and cupboards exhibited the initial ripples of Italian influence in their ornament and form. In the second half of the century the integrated, more independently French Henri II style developed, shaped largely by the engravings of architecture and furniture executed by the designers Jacques Androuet du Cerceau (*c.*1520–*c.*1584) and Hughes Sambin (*c.*1520–*c.*1601). Architectural details, fruit and foliage, caryatids and lion, ram and eagle forms ornamented the heavily carved *armoires* and tables of this period. These also appeared on the characteristic four-doored cupboard in two stages, which was often carved with figures and crowned by a broken pediment.

The school of Fontainebleau combined the styles of du Cerceau, Sambin, and the Italian craftsmen imported by François I and Henri II to decorate the palace of Fontainebleau in the Renaissance manner.

French furniture craftsmanship in the second half of the century showed increasing mastery and refinement of the techniques of carving, dovetailing and joinery.

In England, the prospering wool trade and the sale of monastic lands after Henry VIII's dissolution of the monasteries in the 1530s led to a national proliferation of manor houses, reaching an extreme form with 'prodigy' houses such as the magnificent Longleat in Warminster, begun in the 1560s. These stately homes were enlarged and multiplied in Elizabeth I's reign, when the expense of entertaining the Queen's entourage, and of improving features that her critical eye might find defective, led to more than one devious scheme to keep her away.

The geometric gardens and curious plans of these buildings, some shaped as their owner's initials (as was the ornament often carved on the furniture they contained), expressed the Tudor delight in intellectual curiosities.

Many English beds, cupboards and refectory tables resembled the massive and bulbous forms illustrated in Flemish and German pattern-books, especially those of Hans Vredeman de Vries. English pieces were generally joined of oak, with turned stretchers and legs that occasionally dominated design, as in the wholly-turned bobbin chairs with triangular seats. Various local woods were combined in the geometric patterns, chequering, and strapwork inlaid into gate-leg tables, beds, chairs and the pilasters that commonly divided the oak wainscoting of room walls.

The English court cupboard was highly

3

4

decorative itself, with bright paint, applied bosses and spindles and ebony inlay. Chairs with panelled backs and arched crests were carved with strange conglomerations of Tudor roses, Gothic linenfold ornament, dates and grapes, pomegranates and foliage. Grotesques, stumpy figures, and other motifs ornamented tables, beds, benches and X-shaped chairs.

The Baroque

The Baroque era followed the inspired humanism of the Renaissance with inflated statements of pomp, power and splendour. During the 17th century, the institutions of the Church in Italy, the state in France, and the small courts of Germany, spawned materialistic monuments to their own glory in architecture and fine and decorative arts.

In Italy, papal families such as the Barberini, Pamfili, Aldobrandini and Borghese constructed elaborate villas, and filled them with works of art and expensive furnishings. At Versailles, the association of Louis XIV with the sun-god Apollo required the development of an interior setting not quite of this earth.

Initiated by Gian Lorenzo Bernini, the Baroque architectural and sculptural style retained classical elements, but took liberties with principles of symmetry and restraint. Columns became twisted, sculptured figures contorted, carvings expressive and exuberent. Baroque interiors achieved striking effects through a colourful welding together of architecture, sculpture, and painting, which dazzled the eye with splendour and variety. Rising numbers of wealthy merchants, bankers and newly-aristocratic families resulted in a refinement of rules of etiquette and ceremony in order to define rank rigidly. The villas of princes, cardinals and courtiers were replete with devices that filtered and arranged guests and residents to exclude those of lower rank from the more intimate courtly gatherings. Private audiences were held in cabinets and closets, small rooms richly decorated with fine furnishings, hangings, crystal, porcelain and paintings.

Rank determined access to the 'public' *levées* and *couchers* of heads of state, princes and nobility in state bedrooms, where elaborately hung beds were generally enclosed inside alcoves or behind ceremonial balustrades. Rank also determined the allocation of seats; ornate, gilded throne chairs in Italy and elsewhere were reserved for heads of household and state, and progressively less imposing chairs and stools were used according to social position. In Spain, ladies were relegated to floor cushions.

In France, privileged women received in bed, and guests sat on cushions in the *ruelle*, or alley, beside them. Fixed positions of most furniture pieces emphasized the formality of Baroque interiors. Chairs generally lined room walls, and were put back in place there by servants after use.

Intended to impress, these palatial interiors were lined with Turkish tapestries, Genoese cut velvets, Lucchese silks, and Spanish embossed and gilt leathers that were exported throughout

1 This English lacquered
cabinet, about the period of
King Charles II (1660–85),
reflects the style of early
English reproductions of
Oriental lacquered designs,
and may have been in-
fluenced by Stalker and
Parker's Treatise of Japanning in 1688. The silvered
stand, carved with cherubs
and acanthus leaves, cap-
tures the Baroque feel for
contrasts.
(Victoria and Albert
Museum, London)

Europe. Ceilings and walls were painted with
brilliant frescoes; and self-glorifying messages
were not uncommon. Gilding of ceiling panels
and wall ornaments became increasingly fashionable throughout this period.

Although still relatively scarce, Baroque
furniture took on the proclamatory aura of the
pompous fittings around it. Carved sconces,
guéridons, and chandeliers provided glittering
supports for candles, and their gilded surfaces
were reflected in cascades of light by decorative
mirrors in elaborate carved frames.

In Italy, large villas such as the Ca' Rezzonico

portedtables, beds, chairs, stools and cupboards.
Carved dolphins, eagles, shells, putti and grotesques were combined with volutes, dense
scrolling and foliage, and placed beneath seats or
slabs of marble to form chairs or tables.

Gilded chairs with outstretching arms and
velvet upholstery were carved with broad,
ribbon-like forms which twisted and furled to
incorporate putti and foliage. Decorative console
tables were carved by sculptors such as the Venetian Andrea Brustalon (1662–1732) in vigorous
compositions of animals, blackamoors, shells
and figures. As all over Europe, these side tables

2 The designs of the Huguenot Daniel Marot were in-
fluential in the Netherlands,
France, and England. His
style is reflected in this walnut chair, made in the North
Netherlands in about 1700.
The bold acanthus carvings
characterize the 17th century Flemish baroque; the
serpentine lines look forward to the Queen Anne
style, which followed later in
England. (Rijksmuseum,
Amsterdam)

in Venice housed suites of state apartments, including galleries, libraries, dining rooms and
salons, all decorated with hangings, gold galloons
and fringes, lacquerwork, and ivory and marble
wainscoting. The furnishings of these rooms were
objects of sculpture and art, rather than comfort.
Produced by leading contemporary artists, scale,
exaggerated style and cost precluded casual use.
The private family apartments located above the
show rooms of the *piano nobile* were furnished
very simply.

Baroque furniture was bold, vigorous, and
sculptural. Naturalistic carving in high relief sup-

were often crowned with mirrors and flanked by
candelabra or guéridons. The meticulous, rich
pietra dura works of the *Opificio delle Pietre Dure*,
established by Ferdinando I de' Medici in 1599,
were incorporated into cabinets produced
throughout Europe.

Features of the Italian Baroque reached
France during the reign of Henry IV, who established craft workshops in the *Grand Galérie du
Louvre* on the example of the Florentine ducal
manufactories. Aided by cardinals Jules Mazarin
and Armand Jean de Richelieu, who wished to
establish a national style, Louis XIII continued

to promote the emulation of Italian and Flemish achievement in the decorative arts.

In 1661 Louis XIV acceded to the throne, and in 1667 Jean Baptiste Colbert, his minister of arts, founded the *Manufacture Royale des Meubles de la Couronne*, known as the Gobelins after the workshops previously established in 1622. Under the directorship of the artist Charles le Brun, and stimulated by the personal interest extended by Louis XIV, the Gobelins workshops developed into flourishing collaborative manufactories, in which designs of le Brun, Jean Bérain (1638–1711), and Jean le Pautre (1618–82) were completed by craftsmen contributing diverse skills and talents. Among the most prominent were Jacques Caffieri (1678–1755) and André Charles Boulle (1672–1732).

The French Baroque incorporated the exuberance and lavishness of Italian designs, forms and ornamented carving into a more restrained and classical style. Rectilinear gilt upholstered sofas, day-beds and chairs were made at the Gobelins along with other furnishings for the palace at Versailles. Tall, imposing cabinets, bureaux, and commodes were covered with floral marquetry, or the delicate interlacing compositions of contrasting tortoiseshell and brass popularized by Boulle's superb craftsmanship. Heavy ormolu mounts of mythological scenes, masks, lions and acanthus leaves appeared on tables and case pieces.

The Revocation of the Edict of Nantes in 1685, and the great reductions in Gobelins' output which the government imposed for economic reasons, forced many craftsmen to leave France. The designs of Huguenot emigré Daniel Marot (1663–1752) proved especially important in the dissemination of the Louis XIV style.

In the United Netherlands the expanded enterprises of the Dutch East India Company brought wealth to the rising class of maritime merchants, who patronized painters, silversmiths and furniture craftsmen. Dutch 17th century interiors were lively and colourful, decorated with checkerboard marble floors, tapestries, portrait paintings, chandeliers and upholstered furniture. Furniture was gilded, crisply carved, painted, lacquered in the oriental manner, and faced with figured veneers. Portuguese and Spanish Baroque influence inspired boldly turned legs and uprights, scrolled feet and caned backs and seats. The tall, straight backs of settles, chairs and daybeds, painted black or gilt, or plain walnut, were richly carved with Flemish strapwork, putti and grotesques.

The naturalism of the Dutch 17th century still-life school, and of sculptor Artus Quellin, were reflected in floral marquetry and inlay compositions executed by craftsmen such as Jan van Mekeren and Dirk van Rijswijk of Amsterdam.

An influx of craftsmen from Germany and Belgium popularized expensive furniture of ebony; *witwerkers* worked in soft white deal and pine, producing painted pieces for less wealthy purchasers. The tall, double-doored *kas* often had a flat, bold cornice and arched panels separated by pilasters or twisted columns. Tables stood on tapering or spiral-turned legs often with the curves of the apron echoed in the stretchers.

The designs of Daniel Marot, who became Minister of Works to William of Orange after leaving France, popularized ornamented volutes, strapwork and grotesques, and features such as curved chair backs, diagonal stretchers and tapering legs.

Of enormous influence on the Dutch and English furniture crafts at this time were the rare and highly fashionable foreign specimens brought from the Orient in East India Company cargoes. In both countries, oriental cabinets

3 Chinese 'Coromandel' lacquered screens, featured incised decorations which followed contemporary Chinese painting styles. In Europe, screens such as this were occasionally split through the middle, so that both sides could be used as veneer. Believed to date from about 1700, this screen suggests European export market design; the figures wear western dress, including tall hats. (Christie's, London)

raised on silvered or gilt stands displayed porcelain treasures, and lacquered furniture was especially sought after.

Known in the Orient since the last centuries B.C., lacquer was used to cover boxes, leather armour, bows, chests, household utensils, baskets, earthenware, incense-burners and furniture. The grey resinous sap of the *Rhus vernicifera* tree, *urushi* in Japanese or *ch'i-ichou* in Chinese, was utilized because it hardens, develops a gloss and turns black upon exposure to air. Dyes were added to produce coloured lacquer, and the purified *urushi* was applied in about thirty separate coats.

Various lacquer treatments were used including 'Coromandel' lacquer, with incised and coloured designs; raised designs with mountainous landscapes; mother-of-pearl inlay; and Japanese *maki-e*, in which the design was formed of sprinkled gold particles on a black ground.

Imported screens were cut up and inserted into European cabinets, secretaires, mirrors and tables, often with total disregard for the cohesion of the oriental scheme. In Amsterdam, before 1610, a guild of Dutch lacquerworkers existed, and pieces were made at about the same time in London and Copenhagen. Although the craft suffered a decline in the mid-17th century, it became increasingly popular in England after the publication in 1688 of Stalker and Parker's *Treatise of Japanning, Varnishing, and Guilding* which provided essential information for professionals. Publications in the following century raised the craft to a level of a fashionable pastime in England, inspiring accomplished ladies to entertain themselves at lacquer-making parties.

Foreign influences permeated England after the Restoration. Early in the century heavy oak pieces still persisted. Jacobean gate-leg and draw tables, presses, benches, and chests were ornamented with carved Renaissance foliage and mouldings, grotesques, strapwork, and spindles and bosses. Chests-of-drawers, faced with geometric panels which were ornamented with ebony mouldings as well as mother-of-pearl inlay, appeared about the middle of the 17th century.

The wide-scale rebuilding programme that followed the Great Fire of 1668 made great use of walnut, and also popularized the classical interior architectural style introduced to England by Inigo Jones (1573–1652) after the example of the Italian Renaissance architect Andrea Palladio. The Flemish style carvings of Grinling Gibbons (1648–1720), appointed Grand Carver to Charles II, initiated a school of highly delicate and realistic carvings, which decorated tables and painting frames such as those in the Carved Room at Petworth House, Sussex, with putti (chubby, naked boys), fruits, flowers, vegetables and birds.

The accession of William and Mary in 1689 brought Dutch craftsmen to England. Carved black, gilt and occasionally silvered chairs and day-beds reflected the Flemish Baroque style, as did the rectangular forms, marquetry and figured veneers, spiral-turned legs, and curved stretchers of cabinets, stands, and tables. An intricate, lacy form of marquetry known as 'seaweed' developed in England, possibly from the examples in tortoiseshell and metal of André Charles Boulle.

1 16th-century English oak armchair, with panel back, rectilinear form, and Gothic linenfold and Renaissance foliate carving.

2 17th-century English X-shaped armchair, with velvet upholstery, gold fringe, and brass studd ornament.

3 17th-century English armless 'Farthingale' chair, probably designed for ladies wearing Farthingales (hooped skirts).

4 English William and Mary style chair, about 1690, painted black, with turned stretchers and supports, curved crest, and Netherlandish carved ornament.

5 Chair in the style of Daniel Marot, about 1717, with curvilinear form and legs, and pierced splat.

6 English chippendale style armchair, mid-18th-century, with shaped crest rail with ears, pierced splat, and light foliate and *rocaille* carving.

7 Armchair in the French Louis XV style, mid-18th century, revived in the 19th century, with curvilinear form and floral Rococo carving.

8 French Louis XVI armchair, mid-late 18th century, with oval back, fluted tapering legs, and Neo-classical ornament.

9 American Hepplewhite style shield-back chair, about 1795, with swag ornament and delicate tapering legs.

10 American windsor armchair, late 18th century, with curved crest and arm rails, turned supports, and shaped wooden seat.

11 English 'Egyptian'-style Regency armchair, about 1806, with monopodia legs and paw feet.

12 American Gothic-revival sidechair, about 1841.

13 'Art Furniture' chair by C. R. Mackintosh, about 1900 (Scotland), with slender, streamlined form.

14 Cantilevered chair by Marcel Breuer, 1928 (Germany) with continuous tubular steel support.

15 'Tulip pedestal' chair of plastic and aluminium by Eero Saarinen, about 1956 (Finland), with integrated, continuous form.

Richly hung state beds, such as the one at Knole in Sevenoaks, Kent, with fabric woven with silver threads, were the prized features of the best 17th century manor houses. They were draped with silks, damasks, brocades, crewel embroidery, mohair and gold cords and fringes.

The production of long-case clocks also became an increasingly important industry in England. As in Dutch examples, they were often enlivened with colourful floral marquetry and small classical or twisted columns on the hoods, and were frequently used to display pieces of oriental porcelain.

The accessories that made life comfortable in European courts, cities and provinces filtered very slowly across the Atlantic, where architec-

tural and decorative styles emerged in much simplified forms often decades after having dictated European fashion.

Small houses, generally with a maximum of two rooms and a large fireplace, were standard in the colonial settlements of the American east coast until after the mid-17th century. Sparsely furnished, these homes reflected the austere conservatism of religious emigrés, such as the Puritans, and the simple lifestyle of a settlement economy. The essential furniture they contained was serviceable, sturdy and simple, although frequently colourfully painted.

The northern Baroque idiom surfaced in North America in about 1675. Until then colonial furniture continued to be made in the Renaissance style, based on Dutch, German, English or French prototypes, according to the ethnic character of the region in which it was produced. Joining and turning were used for construction; as in Europe, oak predominated, but pine, maple and cherry were sometimes used. Chests formed of six planks and painted with stripes existed side by side with more solidly joined panel-and-frame examples, the latter carved with anglicized classical ornament, such as pilasters and arches, or lunettes enclosing broad acanthus leaves. This ornament showed regional variations.

Bulbous, fluted baluster uprights, showing the influence of Hans Vredman de Vries, appeared on presses and court cupboards executed in the English Jacobean manner with knob pulls, 'ebonized' spindles and bosses, chequered inlay, colourful paint and carved figures. Toward the end of the century walnut gained favour, and veneers and dove-tails, together with new pieces such as chests-of-drawers, were introduced.

Immigrants and imports took the primarily Flemish William and Mary Baroque style to America through English intermediaries. American highboys, lowboys and tables were veneered simply with rich walnut burls. European forms including cabinets with convex top drawers and arched panels, and tables and flat-topped highboys with curved stretchers and aprons were adopted, as were carvings of Flemish-style strapwork on day-beds and chairs.

Germany also received the Baroque late in the century, but there the style became rigid rather than relaxed. The small courts of Germany's many principalities translated the already exaggerated ceremonial Baroque in dazzling statements of pomp and grandeur. Yielding to Italian influence and then to the example of Versailles during the first half of the 18th century, court rivalries inspired palaces such as Pommersfelden, Charlottenburg and Belvedere, in which state rooms and suites were lavishly decorated with mirrors, marquetry panels and collections of porcelain.

Engravings of court interiors and furniture designs by Paul Decker, J. J. Schübler, Joseph Furttenbach and Friederich Unteutsch, circulated widely along with pattern-books of designs showing the French influence of Daniel Marot, Bérain, and le Pautre. Unteutsch's *Knorpelwerk*, designs of masks and other ornaments disseminated a taste for soft, earlike forms. Especially successful in silver, this 'auricular' ornament was also carved on walnut chairs and cupboards. Engraved and embossed silver furniture was made in Augsburg and Nuremburg, where collectors' cabinets, with miniature drawers and architectural details, were executed in silver, gold, painted glass, boxwood, ivory, and precious stones. In Eger, now part of Czeckoslovakia, similarly rich cabinets were faced with mythological or biblical scenes, executed in wood and intarsia in low relief.

For the Brandenburg court, Gerard Dagly produced a refined imitation of ornamental lacquer on various grounds, those on white suggesting oriental porcelain.

Elaborate as these palatial interiors may have

1 Sturdily built and frequently cheerfully decorated, English 17th century oak armchairs generally had straight backs and rectangular seats. Carved ornament, and the unrounded arms and stretchers seen here, were also often characteristic. This chair is in the style of the period of King Charles I. (Mary Bellis Antiques, Hungerford)

2

been with their halls and state rooms sparkling with gilt mirrors and silver, the Baroque style that the Germans embraced well into the 18th century had begun to decline in other European centres. There, loosened political, social and artistic attitudes had sparked off the more animated Rococo.

2 The rich and elaborate compositions assembled in the Florentine workshops of the Opificio delle Pietre Dure, established in 1599, were painstakingly produced and internationally renowned. This table incorporates lapis lazuli; it is 175 cm in diameter, and took 13 years to complete. It was begun in 1837.
(Palatine Gallery, Florence)

Rococo

The accession of Philip of Orléans as French Regent upon the death of Louis XIV in 1715 marked the beginning of a transition from the unaccommodating formalities of the Baroque towards the more casual lifestyle we enjoy today. The migration of the French court from Versailles to Paris, where aristocrats and the *bourgeoisie* began to refurbish their town-houses elaborately and with great concern for style, ushered in an age which focused unprecedented attention on comfort in private life.

In France especially, rooms became smaller; throughout Europe, social hierarchies were more relaxed and entertainment more intimate. Rising standards of living and the expansion of the middle classes made the ceremonies of the Baroque *passé*, and removed the complicated network of symbols of rank that had been incorporated into everyday social behaviour and interaction.

The release from Baroque court circles, which had been primarily preoccupied by the immediacies of their own pomposity, sparked off in the 18th century a series of quests for the exotic, the whimsical and the refreshing. These yearnings were satisfied in the fine and decorative arts by such light-hearted schemes as Jean Honoré Fragonard's painting of *The Swing*, and the tapestry scenes of the *Loves of the Gods*, woven after François Boucher's example at the Gobelins manufactories.

Continuing trade heightened European taste for things oriental, from tea and porcelain tea-services to the lacquered trays and tables that went with them. In France, comfortable *salons*, where ladies of the *ancien régime* conducted conversations between dandies and *philosophes*, were increasingly fitted through the century with small and serviceable pieces of elegant furniture. Walls were hung with tapestries, silks, or velvets, or wainscoted with fluidly-moulded panels painted in combinations of colours, such as mint green, pale pinks and yellows.

The softening of the rectilinear Louis XIV style was initiated by the designer Jean Bérain and the craftsman André Charles Boulle, with the influence of the Regent's own architect A. J. Oppenord (*c.*1639–1715), the architects Robert de Cotte (1656–1735) and Pierre le Pautre, and the designers Nicolas Pineau (1687–1757) and Jacques Caffiéri (1678–1755).

After the turn of the century, Bérain replaced his earlier scrolling designs with lighter, linear arabesques and fanciful *singeries*. Chairs, tables, bureaux and commodes assumed serpentine lines, stretchers became fluid and were gradually discarded; and chairs became lower. Rich ormolu mounts highlighted the curves of cabriole legs, the edges of drawers and the tops of tables, commodes and bureaux. On the elegant, increasingly curvaceous commodes of Charles Cressent (1685–1768), the edging around drawers gradually disappeared, giving way to large compositions spreading over the lacquer or marquetry design of the façade.

The engravings of Juste Aurèle Meissonnier

1 English Palladian Furniture was grandly conceived. This gilded console table, formerly in the collection of the Dukes of Leeds at Hornby Castle, Yorkshire, probably dates from about 1730. Carved with large-scale motifs in the bold style of William Kent, it is topped with red and green veined Derbyshire marble. (Sotheby's, London)

(1695–1750) led the early designs of the *Régence* into the exuberant asymmetries and curvaceous naturalism of the Rococo, or Louis XV style. Derived from the lively, cave-like, and sometimes aquatic decorations inside Italian landscape grottoes, Rococo compositions were characterized by illogical combinations of the peculiar *rocaille* scroll, C- and S-curves, shells, foliage, branches and animals, water and flame motifs, and even Chinese figures. Commodes, tables, cabinets and beds assumed fluid shapes. Ormolu mounts became more swirling and elegant, and delicately carved flames and sprays of foliage emphasized the curves of knees, elbows, edges and crests.

These French forms, and the French Rococo ornamental vocabulary, were extremely influential throughout Europe, where chairs and other pieces in the relaxed Louis XV manner were made well into the century in Spain, Portugal, Italy, North America, and elsewhere.

The supple, undulating forms created by Daniel Marot, Jean Bérain, and the French

Régence permeated England during the reign of Queen Anne (1702–14). Characterized by curvaceous lines and ornamental restraint, Queen Anne style furniture asserted the first truly English style. As a thriving national economy encouraged more building on the part of landed gentry and middle-class merchants, increased demand for interior furnishings was met by unprecedented standards of skill among London cabinet-makers.

Balanced curves and straight lines gave chairs cabriole legs, vase-shaped splats, horse-shoe shaped seats and undulating backs which followed the sitter's profile. Walnut, and later mahogany, was applied in highly figured veneers to cabinets and tables, or sparingly carved with shells, masks or foliage on the crests, knees and rails of chairs. 'Seaweed' marquetry, japanning on red ground, and judicious touches of gilt coated the flat surfaces of tables, chests-of-drawers, day-beds and settees. Feet were carved as hooves, hairy paws, trifids and oriental inspired claw-and-ball.

Secretaires and architectural cabinets with
arched or mirrored panels were crowned by
swan-neck or double-arched pediments, often
with ornamental finials. Of Netherlandish origin,
these curving pediments were to find extreme
expression later in the century on Dutch Rococo
case pieces, when curves alternated with horizontal plinths on which porcelain rarities were
displayed.

The architecture and furniture of William
Kent (1689–1748) promulgated a heavy, Baroque
style based on Italian architectural sources, and
especially on the Renaissance work of Vicenze
architect Andrea Palladio. However, the softer
forms of the Queen Anne style persisted, and
various elements characteristic of it appeared on
furniture well into the century.

In the Netherlands, Portugal and Spain,
Queen Anne characteristics such as cabriole legs,
shell motifs, claw-and-ball feet, and vase-shaped
chair splats were translated into local styles.

The Queen Anne style was adopted in colonial
America in the early 1730s, when flourishing

2 Eighteenth century Venetian craftsmen decorated
furniture with lacca, a particularly Italian interpretation of Oriental lacquer
work, comprised of floral
schemes. Carved and gilt
wood mouldings enliven
the lacca composition and
fluid Rococo curves of this
bombé commode, in the
Palazzo Rezzonico, Venice.
As in the preceding baroque
era, Italian Rococo com-
modes were frequently ac-
companied by complemen-
tary mirrors with ornately
carved and gilt frames.
(Palazzo Rezzonico, Venice)

3 The architect and decorator Jean Bérain, born in
Lorraine in 1637, was one of
the major initiators of the
French Rococo style. Ap-
pointed Dessinateur de la
Chambre et du Cabinet du
Roi in 1674, Bérain designed
royal celebrations, firework
displays, ballet costumes,
and interiors for the King
and other clients. Bérain's
scrolling arabesques and
singeries – lively compo-
sitions with monkeys and
fanciful figures – were executed on furniture in marquetry work of contrasting
tortoise-shell and brass.
This cabinet, possibly made
in the workshops of the
master André Charles
Boulle (1642–1732), shows
Bérain's whimsical style in
the ornamental marquetry
fantasy of the doors.
(Wallace Collection, Lon-
don)

1

Regional differences in furniture-making were sharpened as craftsmanship developed in each area, and immigrant tastes and traditions expressed themselves. Chair splats were shaped with distinguishing silhouettes, those from Dutch settled New York broader than those from English-settled Massachusetts. The spaces between splat and stiles on Philadelphia chairs resembled birds with bold, inward-curving elongated beaks; the curves of Philadelphia Queen Anne style seats tended to inflect more than seats found on chairs made elsewhere. New York claw-and-ball feet were square in form, while those from Massachusetts characteristically featured raking claws. The cabriole legs of many southern pieces were almost straight. Stretchers generally disappeared during this period, although they tended to persist on Massachusetts pieces, typical of furniture forms produced there.

In mid-century, the French Rococo caught on in England, inspired largely by the engravings of H. F. Gravelot and by improved peace-time relations with France. In England the cave-like *rocaille*, and the cult of the picturesque that accompanied it, became popular along with ornaments suggestive of the romantic Gothic and the tantalizing Orient, and the three styles occasionally merged together. As in France, private rooms were made increasingly comfortable by pieces such as small desks, candlestands, fire-screens and work-tables. The most fashionable Rococo interiors featured curvaceous gilt panels, or wall hangings of oriental paper or silk. William Chambers travelled to China in 1749, and in 1757 published his *Designs of Chinese Buildings, Furniture, and Dresses*. Publications by designers and craftsmen such as Thomas Chippendale, Thomas Johnson, Matthew Darly, Matthias Lock, Robert Manwaring, and William Ince and John Mayhew, popularized fanciful furniture along with ordinary forms. Their most exuberant Rococo designs were characterized by asymmetrical ornament and whimsicalities. Unpublished cabinet-makers, such as John Linnell, and William Vile and John Cobb, were equally forceful exponents of the mid-century style.

Cabinets, book-cases, long-case clocks and commodes for the most part retained the basic forms of the preceding Queen Anne period, but many pieces assumed the serpentine shapes and swelling anthropomorphic *bombé* of the French Louis XV style. Gilding and japanning remained in vogue. Twisted girandoles resembling branches, and pier-glasses assembled from C-curves, waterfalls and *rocailles*, captured the effect of rustic naturalism. Increasingly available mahogany, but also pine and gesso, lent itself especially well to crisp depictions of Chinese dragons and pagodas, cusps and pointed Gothic arches, and stylized scenes of peasants, windmills and donkeys.

Many of the chair designs published in Chippendale's *Director* of 1754 had broad square seats, projecting scrolled ears, and animalistic cabriole legs. Settees formed of repeated chair

1 Architectural elements including swan-necked pediments and fluted pilasters were among the features that colonial American cabinetmakers borrowed from buildings and pattern-books to adorn highboys during the Queen Anne and Chippendale periods. Pad feet, cabriole legs, elaborate brass escutcheons, and carved ornaments – including shells, fans, and cartouches – appeared on furniture of both styles. This mahogany highboy is characteristic of Massachusetts craftsmanship. (Brooklyn Museum, New York)

2

2 Matthew Darly's etched design for a garden chair made of roots, plate 86 in his *New Book of Chinese Designs*, was published in London in 1754, with an obscure artist named Edwards. Darly's asymmetrical chair, naturalistic both in its resemblance to live roots and in its anthropomorphic personality, is one of the most fanciful examples of the 'rustic' aspect of the English rococo. The affinity for naturalism persisted for some time. In 1765, Robert Manwaring published designs for rural chairs for summer houses in his *Cabinet and Chairmaker's Real Friend and Companion*, noting that the chairs should be formed of 'rude branches, or limbs of trees.' If properly painted, Manwaring promised, the chairs would 'look like nature.'

trade in the major mercantile centres of Boston, Philadelphia, New York, Newport and Charleston encouraged a desire for large, comfortable and fashionable mansions. Classical architectural details appeared on buildings from the Carolinas to New Hampshire. Houses such as Westover, in Virginia, reflected elements of the English Palladian style, which reached the colonies through such publications as W. Salmon's *Palladio Londinensis* published in 1734, and James Gibbs's *Book of Architecture* of 1728.

Columns and pilasters, swan-neck pediments, and finials filtered on to highboys, long-case clocks, and even the fragile frames of pier-glasses. The favoured woods of walnut, maple, cherry and pine, and increasingly mahogany, were sparsely highlighted with carved shells or foliage, and occasionally offset with inlay in such forms as stars, or with gilded shells on tables, highboys and lowboys. Slender cabriole legs, horse-shoe shaped seats, and feet carved as pads, trifids, and claw-and-balls, imitated English fashions long after they had fallen from favour in England. Highboys and secretaires, fronted with doors with arched panels, contained tiers of drawers and pigeonholes. Easy chairs, corner chairs, candlestands, piecrust tea tables on tripod legs, and fire-screens, all became more popular.

3

backs were occasionally carved with bamboo-like supports and oriental frets; beds in the Chinese manner, with fantastic dragons perched atop the corner posts, were fashionable but unusual extravagances. Light, gilded seats with serpentine silhouettes in the Louis XV style were common; most seats were upholstered with rich floral needlework, velvets, or silk damasks.

The influence of the English Rococo was far-reaching. Contemporary printed designs travelled across the Atlantic, were thrown back to France, and reached as far north as Denmark, where chairs showed *Director*-type pierced splats, set between straight wide stiles. The Rococo style characterized by Chippendale's less exotic engravings permeated American design in about 1755.

In America, the Rococo emerged as a distinctly restrained version of the European style: interiors were hardly as fanciful as their European counterparts, and drawing room walls were ornamented with architectural pediments and rectangular panels rather than gilt cartouches, in a persistence of the Palladian style. Japanning was popular, especially in Boston, but in America the fantastic cult of *chinoiserie* never crystallized into carved mahogany dragons. The Gothic revival struck no chord in American tradition, and the stylized rustic scenes favoured by mid-

century English and French aristocrats could hardly have been adopted as refreshing in a nation which was still in the process of developing vast expanses of wilderness.

Because examples reached the colonies largely through pattern-books, some American Rococo carving is flat rather than sculptural, especially on Boston pieces. Queen Anne forms such as arched pediments, classical details, and claw-and-ball feet were retained, and Rococo ornaments and variations added to them.

The superior craftsmanship of Philadelphia cabinet-makers, such as Benjamin Randolph and the English immigrant Thomas Affleck, produced well-proportioned highboys with swan-neck pediments, flame finials, sculptural carvings of foliage and figures, and sculptured busts and cartouches held above the broken pediments. Scroll pediments carved with Philadelphia-style open lattice-work may be found in the cherry highboys from Connecticut executed by Eliphalet Chapin, who worked for some time in Philadelphia.

Some case pieces of Boston, where John Cogswell worked, exhibit the only *bombé* forms found in the colonies; mirrored panels with ogee-curve borders are also found on cabinets made there. The cabinets and chests-of-drawers from the Townsend-Goddard cabinet-making family

3 English 18th century craftsmen preferred mahogany because of the crispness it lent to carved ornamental detail. These mahogany settees, of about 1755, incorporate pagoda roofs, typical of the motifs suggestive of Chinese design that appeared on English furniture in mid-century. The arches beneath the arms are in the Gothic mode, another element of contemporary style. The small cabinet of about 1750 rests on a stand carved with Chinese-style fretwork. The set, now in the Prince Regent's Room at Clandon Park, Surrey, formerly belonged to the great connoisseur-collector, Mrs David Gubbay. (Clandon Park, Surrey)

1

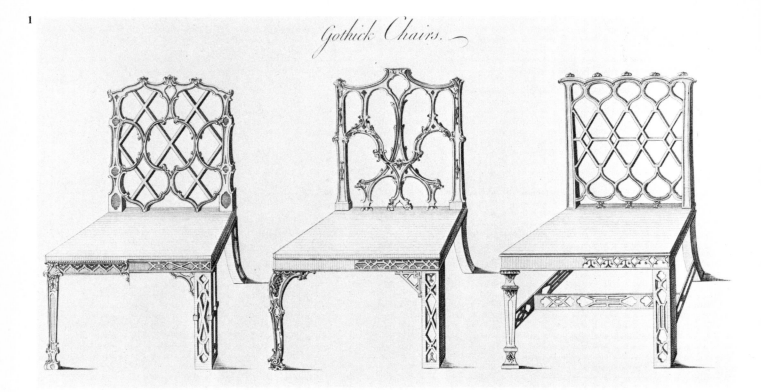

Gothick Chairs.

1 These chairs, whimsical amalgams of Gothic, Rococo, and Chinese styles, appeared as plate 22 in the first and second editions of Chippendale's Director in 1754 and 1755.

2 Designs for furniture in conservative, more traditional styles also appeared in Chippendale's Director. This drawing by Chippendale for a mirror dates from about 1750.

3 The lace-like assemblages of C-curves, sprigs, and water motifs in these designs for two mirrors, of about 1750 and perhaps by Chippendale, characterized the French and English Rococo.

of Newport, Rhode Island, were exceptional pieces of workmanship, with undercut claw-and-ball feet, undulating concave and convex shells, and smoothly executed block fronts.

Tables were of many forms, including Pembroke and fold-top card-tables. Serpentine card-tables from New York had rectangular candle supports at the corners and gadrooning on the aprons. Small Philadelphia bird-cage tables, with tilting tops, stood on fluidly curved tripods. Upholstered seats included sofas with sinuous rails and straight 'Marlborough' legs, easy chairs with cartouches carved on the cabriole legs, and local variants of chairs copied from the publications of Chippendale, Manwaring, and Ince and Mayhew. More primitive forms, such as the brightly painted chests and cupboards of German and Dutch settlements in Pennsylvania and New York, continued to be made in provincial areas.

In Italy, where the landscaped grotto was a long-established source of ornament, the Rococo at times took on an extreme lightness, with chairs and tables resting on shapely cabriole legs comprised of reversing C-scrolls. Delicate effects of underground rock-like growth were achieved in the crisp, crustaceous carvings on the edges of

techniques combined with established traditions; the compositions of Piedmont craftsman Pietro Piffetti were especially ornate.

The inclinations towards pompous display among the multitude of small German states produced the palace of Frederick the Great, at Sanssouci, that of Max Emanuel at Munich, and courts elsewhere such as at Würzburg and Frankfurt. The furnishings of these interiors reflected the refinement of traditional German cabinet-making techniques, such as marquetry, and the introduction of foreign influences by Parisian-trained designers such as François Cuvilliés.

German wall panelling also echoed the graceful ormolu or gilt ornaments and the characteristically exaggerated *bombé* forms of the commodes, console tables, and velvet-upholstered seats beneath them.

The swelling form, a peculiarly German expression of the Rococo, had great influence on furniture produced in the Scandinavian countries. There, *bombé* commodes and serpentine cabinets were covered with marquetry and crossbanding much as they were in Germany, as seen in pieces produced by Mathias Ortman of

4

4 English card-tables such as this mahogany example, in the style of the George II period, inspired many imitations in the North American colonies, where card playing reached the peak of its popularity around the time of the Revolutionary War. The serpentine shape, cabriole legs, claw-and-ball feet, and acanthus and gadroon ornament characterize English high-style pieces of the period. The folding tops of these tables were often fitted with baize, as this one is; the square projecting corners served as candle-stands. (Sotheby's, London)

legs, backs, and skirts of tables and chairs. Carved shells, lion masks, and naturalistic foliage appeared alongside elements of *chinoiserie* such as peasant figures. Curvaceous gilt structures ornamented with flames, foliage and waves, supported console tables with serpentine marble tops, and framed Muranese pier-glasses.

In Italy, foreign influence was strong, although Italian Rococo furniture was not as varied, comfortable, or well-constructed as that produced in England or France. Marquetry work was especially skilled in Milan, where German

Copenhagen and Lars Bolin of Sweden. Organic, bulbous forms also appeared in the extremely broad commodes, secretaires, and cabinets of the Dutch Rococo. These flatter translations often had wide, chamfered corners, with central orna-

1

mental cartouches at the apron and pediment;
although the drawers of German *bombé* commodes extended to the serpentine edges, on
Dutch pieces the drawers remained rectangular,
with veneered strips filling the gap to the undulating side.

German palatial rooms, decorated with japanning or marquetry work, often contained complementary furnishings, such as collections of porcelain, or cabinets ornamented with marquetry
and parquetry arrangements. Abraham and
David Roentgen, of Neuwied, executed elaborate examples of woodworking with scenes of
perspectives and architectural ruins, and compositions of figures and foliage. Their work was
to be of especial influence in Paris, where the
Louis XVI style soon began to take shape.

Neo-classicism

The Rococo style reached its peak in Europe in
the late 1750s. Meanwhile, the discoveries of
Herculaneum and Pompeii just before mid-
century had intensified the already popular vogue
for continental grand tours among English and
French scholars, young gentlemen, and dilet-
tanti, who mixed with native scholars and artists
at academies and societies in Italy, and inaugur-
ated the classical revival. The aesthetic rivalry

between the Italian Giovanni Battista Piranesi
and the German Johann Joachim Winckel-
mann, who defended the supremacy of Roman
and Greek civilization respectively, sparked off
an increased interest in classical architecture and
art.

In England, the Scottish-born architect
Robert Adam (1728–92) returned from Italy and
Europe in 1758. His publication in 1763 of the
Ruins of the Palace of Diocletian at Spalatro
added to the growing number of volumes of engravings of classical ruins which circulated
among aristocratic subscribers who were continually redecorating their homes during the 18th
century according to passing fashion. Other
publications included Robert Wood's *Ruins of
Palmyra* of 1753, and the *Antiquities of Athens* of
1762, by James 'Athenian' Stuart and Nicholas
Revett.

By the early 1760s Robert Adam had established himself as the pace-setter and leading
exponent of the new 'neo-classical' architectural
and decorative style, derived from free combinations of the grotesques, arabesques, and classical
ornaments of antique and Renaissance Italian
interiors, and from lively French designs such as
those of Bérain. While the earlier English Palla-
dians had applied the exterior accoutrements of
classical architecture to their rooms, Adam's
lighter schemes were based on the interiors of
domestic Rome and Pompeii.

Creating effects of gaiety and movement,
Adam covered his walls with colours and a
repertoire of delicately interpreted classical
ornaments arranged on ceilings, walls, friezes,
and decorative door and window frames. Adam
designed and refurbished entire buildings, har-
monizing and co-ordinating to the minutest
detail the schemes of ceilings, carpets, walls,
furniture, and even in one celebrated case the
ornament of a lady's gold watch band to be worn
in a certain room. The refined motifs he introduced, including anthemions, palmettes, rinceaux, griffins, bay leaves, and peltoid shields,
appeared repeatedly with minor modifications
within any given room, creating a unified decorative effect. Adam's total schemes also dictated
the placement of furniture, as in the chairs which
echo the wall ornament in the Etruscan Room at
Osterley Park in Middlesex. This is one of several
rooms Adam designed in an 'Etruscan' style with
terracotta and black ornament derived from
Greek vase painting.

The furniture Adam fitted to these rooms was
often executed by John Linnell or Thomas
Chippendale. Although it followed no classical
examples, it suggested the antique through
architectonic forms, straight lines, and classical
symbols. Semi-circular commodes, mosaic-
topped rectangular side-tables, and chairs with
lyre, anthemion, and oval backs stood on tapering straight legs. Adam's smooth, flat surfaces
were enlivened by contrasting marquetry compositions, and inset roundels and placques
painted in the style of Angelica Kauffmann,
paralleled by the Sèvres plaques, painted panels,
and marquetry work found in French Louis XVI

furniture and later popular on pieces from Italy, Spain, Germany and the Netherlands throughout the neo-classical era.

Although many contemporaries found his mature style finicky, the influence of Adam's example at all stages of his career was pronounced possibly because of the charm it captured. Contemporary English and European architects and craftsmen, such as James Wyatt, continued to adopt elegant rectilinear forms, classical motifs, and a lightened approach to interior design. The

and the rectangular panels of flat facades and sides were articulated by ormolu borders. A widespread delight with mechanical devices spawned a variety of complicated combination forms equipped for such varied uses as writing, eating and sewing. Those of Oeben and Riesener were particularly cleverly mechanized, typifying Louis XVI restraint by enclosing a potentially ungainly variety of components, such as springing drawers and dishwarmers, inside smooth surface facades.

2

taste for delicacy and attenuation persisted even in the scrolling rinceaux and half-figures of the early 19th century neo-classical works of the Turin carver Giuseppe Maria Bonzanigo.

In mid-century neo-classicism was on the ascendance in France as well, where C. N. Cochin, the Comte de Caylus, and others were busily attacking the Rococo as frivolous. Decorative styles derived from French studies of the classics in Italy were gradually popularized by such designers as the Marquis de Marigny and patrons such as Mesdames du Pompadour and du Barry, in their collections at Versailles and Louveciennes. Craftsmen such as Gilles Joubert (1689–1775), Antoine Foulet (*d*.1775), Jean François Leleu (1729–1807), Jacques Dubois (1693–1763), and the Germans Jean François Oeben (1720–1763), Jean Henri Riesner (1734–1806), Adam Weisweiler, and Guillaume Beneman, largely shaped the Louis XVI style.

Chairs, sofas and canapés such as those designed by Georges Jacob (1739–1814) had square or oval backs, straight fluted uprights and rails, and tapering legs. Case pieces such as secretaires *encoignures*, and chests-of-drawers assumed neat, compact forms made more serviceable by castor feet. The straight lines of the tops and sides were emphasized by ormolu friezes and consoles,

Although it remained unusual, the fashion for mechanical devices in furniture spread through Europe to the Netherlands and elsewhere, expressing itself in such pieces as the combination desk-table-chair of the Italian Giovanni Socchi, of about 1810.

Oeben, who managed one of the most flourishing Parisian workshops, produced pieces in a transitional style with studiously naturalistic floral marquetry and cube patterns, but died before the Louis XVI style reached its peak. Floral and picturesque marquetry with classical motifs characterized the early, more truly neo-classical work of Riesener, but soon after he became *ébéniste ordinaire du Roi* in 1773, he began to produce simpler geometric patterns, and frets enclosing flowers.

Pierre Gouthière (1732–*c*.1813) created delicate, jewel-like bronze mounts comprised of goats, vines, and cornflowers and roses, Marie Antoinette's favourite flowers. Sèvres porcelain trays and panels were incorporated in commodes and tables increasingly after about 1760 by Weisweiler, Martin Carlin, and others. Towards the end of the century, English-inspired carved mahogany chairs became popular, and plain furniture also showed contemporary English influence. Furniture sheathed in the tortoise-

2 The English designer Robert Adam's commodes and tables were often topped with Neo-classical compositions such as this, in which geometric shapes appeared as cameos and the curves of strings of bellflowers, husks, or pearls. The palmettes and leaf forms in the outer border band are borrowed from classical antiquity. Thin lines, sparse ornament, and delicate treatment of motifs were features of Adam's mature style; he designed this pier-table, one of a pair, for the Saloon in Nostell Priory, Yorkshire, in 1775. The gilt table that supports the inlaid marble top is carved with Neo-classical ornament. (Nostell Priory, Yorkshire.)

1 Pembroke tables were popular in England around the 1780's. Thomas Sheraton, who published the *Cabinet-Maker and Upholsterer's Drawing Book* (1791–94), said that they probably derived their name from the woman who first suggested and ordered one; this may have been a Countess of Pembroke. This Pembroke table, decorated with satinwood marquetry and fitted for games, is located in the Morning Room at Clandon Park, Surrey, England. It probably dates from the very early 1780s. (Clandon Park, Surrey)

2 These designs by George Hepplewhite for Pembroke tables, dated 1787, appeared as plate 62 in the 1788, 1789, and 1794 editions of his *Cabinet-Maker and Upholsterer's Guide,* published in London. The geometrical forms and shapes, tapering square legs, and ornamental motifs are elements from the earlier, more spirited phase of English Neo-classicism. However, the overall design is more economical. Veneers cut in geometric shapes, and placed against contrasting backgrounds, became popular in North America during the corresponding Federal period, as did the use of thin bands of contrasting veneers as decorative edging. American craftsmen also adopted such devices as the rosettes and classical urns seen here, and the flowers inlaid in the table legs.

shell and brass marquetry popularized by Boulle was considered collectable even during the 18th century, when craftsmen such as Etiènne Levasseur continued to produce it.

The elements of the Louis XVI style were dispersed throughout Europe, where cabinet-makers such as Andries Bongen of Amsterdam produced neo-classical marquetry compositions, and Giuseppe Maggiolini of Milan sheathed his Louis XVI-style forms with marquetry ornament and decorations.

The dissemination of the Adam style led in England to a second phase of neo-classicism, more accessible to the middle classes because of its use of less costly materials. Pattern-books such as George Hepplewhite's *Cabinet-Maker and Upholsterer's Guide* and Thomas Shearer's *Cabinet-Maker's London Book of Prices*, both of 1788, and Thomas Sheraton's *Cabinet-Maker and Upholsterer's Drawing Book* (1791–94), popularized straight legs and tall light forms derived from Adam's designs. This reductionist form of classicism abandoned Adam's vocabulary of neo-classical motifs for simplified ornamental schemes comprised of large areas of figured veneers similar to those made fashionable on the mahogany fall-fronts of Louis XVI secretaires.

Sheraton, Hepplewhite, and Shearer popularized a variety of light forms such as ladies' work tables with silk bags, serpentine-front commodes, tambour desks, and cabinets with doors of bronze latticework backed by pleated silk. The backs of settees and chairs were carved with Prince of Wales feathers and classical motifs such as swags and urns.

The purified neo-classicism of England and France returned to invigorate Italian design, and filtered from there to craftsmen in Portugal and Spain. Light, rectilinear chairs with tapering slender legs, were produced as local interpretations of Hepplewhite and Sheraton designs in Italy and Iberia late in the century.

Louis XVI influence surfaced in Italy in the lyre and oval-shaped backs of chairs, which were caned or upholstered in velvets and striped damasks as in England and France, and in the fluted or spirally-turned straight legs of frequently parcel gilt chairs and side-tables. Marble-topped semicircular tables and commodes, with gilded friezes ornamented with fluting, guilloches, and plaques, exhibited the architectonic preferences that Adam had refined. Other Italian chairs and tables preceded by decades the French Empire style, with elements such as sweeping S-curved arms, curved rear legs, Egyptian hieroglyphics and monopodia, and the horizontal placement at the centre of chair rails of symmetrical, classical foliate motifs in ormolu.

Neo-classical Spanish chairs had straight rails and stiles and oval or arched rectangular backs in the Louis XVI style; their legs often combined vestiges of Baroque capping with French flutes and tapering forms. Chairs with lyre backs and round seats, and caned examples with concave-sided interlaced trapezoidal backs, showed Italian influence. Rectangular console or side-tables, carved or inlaid with attenuated classical ornament, occasionally stood on legs of sweeping S-curved form. Vitruvian scrolls, acanthus leaves, masks, and rinceaux appeared on drop-front desks, commodes, tables and beds.

Portuguese furniture revealed similar ripples of influence. Delicate English-inspired chairs and settees with tapered legs and fluted front rails were ornamented with classical plaques and roundels; marble-topped commodes, semi-circular side-tables, and *bureaux à cylindre* reflected the Louis XVI manner.

The federation of the American colonies upon the adoption of the Constitution in 1789 established, in American eyes, a republic sufficiently blessed with democratic principles to bear an association with ancient Rome. At the same time the geometric rationalism of Robert Adam's neoclassical style reached the United States in published pattern-books of engravings by Hepplewhite, Shearer, and Sheraton.

Just as Thomas Jefferson would have found appeal in the classical example of Palladio's geometrical Villa Rotunda for his residence at Monticello, American craftsmen were attracted to the purities of geometry and classicism that these later English designs evoked.

After about 1790, geometric forms and surface ornament began to appear on the most fashionable American furniture. Tables and commodes with semi-circular plans were made by John and Thomas Seymour of Boston and the Townsends of Newport. Veneered ovals and circles, bordered with narrow strips of crossbanding that emphasized their geometricity, were set in rectangular fields of contrasting colours on the facades of secretaries produced in Salem, Baltimore, and elsewhere.

Chests-of-drawers had restrained serpentine facades and simple bracket feet, and the legs of sofas, chairs, side-boards and tables were tapered, slender and straight. The moulded glazing bars on the upper portions of secretaries from Baltimore, Massachusetts, Charleston and elsewhere were arranged in compositions of ovals, circles, and diamonds and squares.

American cabinet-makers also adopted a collection of classical ornaments in more specific allusions to the civilizations of Rome and Greece. Allegorical figures were painted in black and white *verre églomisé* panels on Baltimore furniture; the Boston Seymours inlayed desks with completely flattened *trompe-l'oeil* pilasters; sparingly applied paterae, bell-flowers, eagles, shields, and busts all alluded to the classics.

The carved vine leaves and cornucopias that Salem architect-craftsman Samuel McIntyre applied to his mahogany sofas and chairs similarly reflected the national optimism that pervaded federal America.

Clocks and mirrors were adorned with brass sphere or urn finials, quarter-columns, and gilded eagles. Case pieces such as bookcases became increasingly light, and women's secretaries and work-tables, of delicate proportion and ornament, were introduced. Tea-tables, card-tables with folding tops, Windsor chairs, four-poster beds, and chests-of-drawers on bracket, turned or brass paw feet, all took on the restrained dignity of the Federal period.

The shapes and ornaments of French and English neo-classical interior and furniture design, including arabesque wall panelling, rectilinear forms, tapering legs, ormolu mounts and mouldings, and geometrical and pictorial marquetry compositions, were also adopted in Scandinavia, the Netherlands and Germany. However, local traditions distinguished these renditions.

As in the Rococo era, the Scandinavian royal court favoured European styles, and recruited talent from abroad; the Swedish craftsman George Haupt worked in England with William Chambers before returning home. Erik Ohrmark in Sweden, Nicolas Henri Jardin and Joseph Christian Lillie in Denmark, and Lillie in Norway produced furnishings showing Louis XVI

3 The American counterpart of the ladies' exquisitely light work tables that French and English craftsmen produced in the late 18th century were small, delicate, and elegantly veneered. Their utility was often enhanced by silk workbags and castors. This mahogany and maple worktable was made in Boston in about 1800. (Henry Francis du Pont Winterthur Museum, Delaware)

and Adamesque characteristics.

In the Netherlands, Andries Bongen and Carel Breytsspraak assimilated the French and English use of marquetry and veneer on restrained neo-classical forms.

German neo-classicism was best expressed in the internationally famed work of David Roentgen, who produced musical boxes, toys, and mechanized furniture with hidden drawers. Roentgen perfected a marquetry technique in which he depicted ribbons, flower baskets, and other motifs with extraordinary realism by using a variety of woods of different colours, rather than burning, to simulate shadows and depth.

The publication in 1802 of the *Voyage dans la Basse et Haute Egypte*, a collection of drawings by Baron Vivant-Denon, who had accompanied Napoleon on his excursion to Syria and Egypt in 1798–1801, heightened the interest in Egypt that Napoleon's campaign had itself generated.

Interiors designed by Napoleon's architects, Charles Percier (1764–1838) and Pierre Fontaine (1762–1853), including those at the Tuileries and the Château de Malmaison, and pieces produced by makers such as F. H. G. Jacob-Desmalter and L. F. and P. A. Bellangé, developed the Empire style. This drew on Greek, Roman, and Egyptian sources, and became popular from England and North America to Germany, Italy and Spain.

This grand, imperial style achieved much of

1 Windsor chairs were light, strong, and serviceable, popular in wealthy and common homes alike in the late 18th century. Their turned components were easy to produce in large quantities. They were generally painted green or black. This chair was made by the craftsman Thomas Hayward, of Charlestown, Massachusetts.

2 Most of the furniture in this Baltimore, Maryland drawing room of the Federal era was made in the American south; the two Martha Washington armchairs and the small kettlestand are from New England. The cylinder-fall writing table and bookcase, of mahogany, satinwood, zebrawood, and ebony, was probably made in Baltimore about 1790. (Henry Francis du Pont Winterthur Museum, Delaware)

3 Shirley Plantation, at James River, Virginia, home of the Hill-Carter family for nine generations, was founded in 1613. The two-story kitchen dates from the 18th century.

4 Painted chairs were stylish and popular in America around 1801, the possible date of this chair of soft maple. Probably made in Philadelphia, the chair may be one of a set of chairs delivered to John Derby by John Stille Jun and Company of Philadelphia in 1801. Derby's brother, Elias Hasket Derby, placed an order in 1796 for '24 Oval Back Chairs, Stuff'd Seats covered with Hair Cloth . . .' with the Philadelphia Firm of Joseph Anthony and Company. (Henry Francis du Pont Winterthur Museum, Delaware)

3

4

1

its effect through massive forms and rich ornament. Although an ornate, propagandistic style, it derived great dignity from its clear forms and classical restraint. Motifs such as eagles, lions, caryatids, griffins and sphinxes, taken from Roman, Greek, and Egyptian antique examples, appeared on furniture as ornaments and supports. Tables with monopodia legs, gilt eagle supports, or lion's paw feet, elegant sofas and 'sleigh' beds with sweeping S-curved arms and endboards, and klismos and curule chairs, presented classical motifs on a much larger scale than in earlier classical styles. Rich woods such as mahogany, gilt carving, and ormolu mounts of anthemions, stars, and medallions, characterized Empire furniture.

The English version of this style, known as the Regency, lasted from about 1790 to 1830, when the vogue for relics of antiquity popularized furniture ornamented with sphinxes, griffins, classical mouldings, and other Empire style elements.

Although it reached its peak early in the 19th century, the Empire style represented merely one phase in the evolution of the classical style that would take place in the course of the century, when a variety of past idioms would be continually reinterpreted and renewed.

The Nineteenth Century

Much of the spirit of the 19th century may be summed up as a growing nostalgia in the face of the machine age. Throughout Europe and North America, change continued with populations increasing, economies expanding and cities burgeoning. In the course of the century, automobiles, electricity, photography and skyscrapers were to appear.

Internationally, the much-enlarged middle class rose to a point of unprecedented social domination. Change and advance were adopted more quickly in the 19th century, as railroads, widely circulated publications, and increased international commerce made communications and international cross-fertilization of ideas more rapid. Technological and scientific developments improved health and hygiene, provided new degrees of comfort and wealth, and introduced mass production.

At the same time, the century's innovations altered established orders and eroded long-standing traditions. Standards of quality, especially in production – and rarity that individual craftsmanship had guaranteed – gave way to the economies, ubiquities and machine-made finishes of mass production. Proliferating factories turned out articles of domestic comfort in great quantities, and put money in the pockets of the masses who manufactured them.

The resulting demographic shift saw, for the first time, a population in which a bourgeoisie class with an enormous disposable income was the most powerful sector. Its emergence allowed the production on a large scale of items far below the standards of style and workmanship that a discriminating élite had exacted in the previous century in procuring articles of aesthetic merit. Throughout the century, the defenders of the survival of that discriminating taste rejected innovative products and styles. Past styles were revived and old objects sought out in successive waves of revival fashions, producing an extraordinary eclecticism in interior design and architectural styles.

Of great importance in the development of 19th century design was the series of international exhibitions, launched by the Great Exhibition of the Works of Industry of All Nations, held in London in 1851, largely a result of the efforts of Albert, Prince Consort, and proponents of good design such as Henry Cole (1802–83), publisher of the *Journal of Design*.

Six million people attended the London exhibition, which was housed in the Crystal Palace, a structure designed by Joseph Paxton and made of glass and cast-iron, a strong testimony itself to progress. This and other exhibitions, which followed at intervals into the 20th century, accelerated the dissemination of innovations, and similarly internationally spread current stylistic fancies.

The rise in demand for furniture, and the simultaneous adoption of technological developments, contributed to changes in the organization of furniture production and in the construction of furniture itself.

In an age that delighted in inventions however quixotic, numerous mechanized processes were perfected to improve the production of articles of interior decoration. Machines wove carpets and printed wallpapers and textiles in increasing quantities. In furniture manufacture, new devices were able to mould, plane, mortise, cut frets, slice veneers, rough out carving, laminate, drill and shape.

1 Plate 56 of George Smith's *Household Furniture*, published in England in 1808, showed a design, dated 1804, for a chair in the Egyptian style. It inspired this armchair, probably part of a set made in 1806 for Frome Abbey, Frome, England. Painted black and gilded, the chair captures the boldness of Regency period furniture. The stars, half-palmettes, monopodia and animal heads were among the ornaments borrowed from classical antiquity and Egypt at the time. (Victoria & Albert Museum, London)

2 Chairs with Grecian Cross fronts appeared in the 1808 Supplement to the London Chair-Maker's and Carvers' Book of Prices; it was probably after this that 'Grecian cross' legs began to be used on New York furniture. This sofa of about 1810–15, possibly by the New York craftsman Duncan Phyfe (1768–1854) is an elegant, atypical example, standing on one pair only of crossed legs. Antique forms and ornaments inspired the English and American Regency styles; the crossed legs were borrowed from the Roman curule chair. The carved paw feet, drapery swags, and reeds tied with ribbon bow are other elements taken from antiquity. The carved reeding, which conforms to the tapering and swelling of the arms, legs and rails, is an example of excellent craftsmanship and integration of design. The sofa is of mahogany, with caned back seat and sides. (Yale University Art Gallery New Haven, Connecticut)

In America, the New York firm of Henry Belter produced pieces by means of a laminating process in which layers of wood were steamed into curves with the use of moulds.

The first popular piece of furniture to be produced in mass quantities was the simple English Windsor chair, made by firms such as Webb and Bunce of London. The shortcomings of mass production would spur passionate protests among reformers, and ultimately provoke the formation of an arts and crafts movement which championed medieval traditions of hand craftsmanship.

More significant than changes in methods of execution were alterations within the furniture craft. In the mass-assemblage factories that the end of the century would see, craftsmen's contributions were confined to the completion of only one part of the whole piece. Moreover, furniture came to be designed by architects rather than by craftsmen themselves.

Far more consequential was the introduction of cast-iron, which spread from England before the mid-19th century, and because of its durability was widely used in North America in a variety of styles for beds, chairs, garden furniture and small decorative pieces. Brass beds, with light, decorative endboards, were also popular. Chairs of bent wood, introduced by the German Michael Thonet in the 1850s, presented innovations of design and concept that would not be advanced upon until the early 20th century.

The taste for the exotic, which showed itself in an extreme form early on in John Nash's Hindu-Chinese confection, the Royal Pavilion at Brighton, which he constructed from 1815–21 for the Prince Regent, continued throughout the century. Turkish-style decors, with Persian tiles, hangings and cushions, were not infrequent choices for smoking rooms. Indian furniture, exhibited at the International Exhibition of 1851, was imported to England in great quantities; and oriental ornament enjoyed wide popularity. However, although Japanese examples would greatly influence the wallpaper and textiles of William Morris's arts and crafts movement late in the century, none of these modes played a dominant role in shaping the century's interior design. They did, however, offer refreshing respites from the more standard styles.

Although never surfacing in a pure form, geometric preferences provided much of the basis of furniture designed by Gothicists, including William Butterfield and William Burges. The arts and crafts school would eventually produce furniture formed of simple geometric forms and shapes.

Naturalism, another thread that pervaded the Victorian era, permeated the Gothic style with figures and foliage, the Rococo with scrol-

2

3

3 Adam Weisweiler worked in David Roentgen's furniture workshop at Neuwied before coming to France, where he produced elegant furniture in the Louis XVI style. Weisweiler's incorporation of Sèvres porcelain plaques added lightness and colour to many of his pieces. The The interlaced stretchers and tapering feet of this drop-front secrétaire à abattant are also characteristic of his style. The porcelain plaques, painted with pastoral scenes, may be of a later date than the rest of the piece. The secrétaire is veneered with thuya-wood, satinwood, and purplewood; inside, the drop front is set with gilt and tooled green morocco leather. (Wallace Collection).

The evolution of interior decorating shops, which bought furnishings wholesale from suppliers and profered hangings, upholstery, furniture and all the other necessities of room decoration, meant that except for the most affluent, the previous close collaboration of client and craftsman in interior decoration came to an end. This severing of the relations, which was traditionally so essential to the furniture craft, accounted for a great deal of the diminution in status of furniture itself. Instead of being commissioned works of decorative art, they became ready-made decorative objects, bought like other necessities.

About 1830 papier-mâché furniture appeared in England, and although it continued to be fashionable until the 20th century, it never caught on as a major design innovation. Tables, trays, chairs and other pieces incorporated the material, which was often ornamented with mother-of-pearl inlay, gilt, and painted floral designs, but generally coated with imitation oriental lacquer.

ling acanthus, the aesthetic movement with oriental flowers, and then achieved its ultimate expression in organic forms of the Art Nouveau.

The dichotomy between expensive and elegantly styled furniture and cheaper versions was to remain throughout the century. Another contrast was the coexistence of several different styles, each of which underwent major modifications. Both middle-class preferences and the persistence of neo-classicism were crystallized in the German Biedermeier style, expounded by designers such as the neo-classical architect Karl Friedrich Schinkel of Berlin, and others including Josef Danhauser and Michael Thonet.

Biedermeier furniture was unpretentious and informal. Round tables, secretaires and commodes with flat façades and recessed arches, broad beds and sofas with arms and endboards shaped as swans' necks or cornucopias, were covered with flat veneers that displayed the natural beauty of mahogany, walnut and cherry.

Throughout Europe and North America, neo-classicism was favoured during the century, managing to survive the vigorous competition of the Gothic revival which superseded the classical mode at times.

In England, buildings such as the British Museum of Sir Robert Smirke (1823–4) and C. R. Cockerell's Ashmolean Museum at Oxford (1839–41) paralleled the neo-classical work of Schinkel in Germany and Benjamin Latrobe in

America. Publications such as George Smith's *Cabinet-Maker and Upholsterer's Guide* (1826), Peter and Michael Angelo's *The Practical Cabinet-Maker* (1826), and Mésangère's *Album*, championed this late classical mode.

After about 1815, massive mahogany furniture with carved ornament formed with chunky

proportions became 'internationally popular. Known as 'fat classical', furniture in this style was characterized by heavy twist turnings, fattened classical columns, lush, bulging acanthus leaves, and thick, tightly wound scrolling ornament. This more stodgy translation of classicism was reflected by French chairs with backs carved as large, thick-leaved palmettes, Biedermeier case pieces with classical ornament and blocky proportions, Italian furniture made by Paolino Moselini, Giuseppe Cairoli, and Pelagio Pelagi, and American examples by Duncan Phyfe and Joseph Meeks & Son.

Although elements of a Renaissance revival had surfaced as early as the 1851 Exhibition, this interpretation of classical sources gained great popularity only in the late 1860s and early 1870s in England, Italy, America, Austria, and elsewhere. This revival often reflected the Renaissance as it had been translated centuries earlier into various national modes. German pieces recalled the squareness of Hans Vredeman de Vries; French Renaissance style furniture incorporated decorative elements typical of du Cerceau's Henri II cabinets.

Towards the end of the century, rising political nationalism, and the increasing vogue for amassing great collections of antiques, resulted in reproduction styles which revived historical national furniture forms. In England, neo-Georgianism again renewed the neo-classical idiom. In America, colonial furniture became newly fashionable after about 1870, especially in New England.

Simultaneous with 19th century classicism, various antiquarian styles evolved, generally presumed to be based on national medieval examples of furniture but often drawing more on architectural ornaments and forms. The Gothic mode had long been a popular alternative decorative and architectural style in Europe. Horace Walpole's Strawberry Hill at Twickenham, England (1749–77), was a Gothic folly of monumental scale, and even Robert Adam had worked in the Gothic style.

Unlike the purified geometricity of classical styles from Greece and Rome, European Gothic images and forms smacked of local history, were steeped with the medieval humanism of the familiar and local Gothic cathedrals, and provided a picturesque retreat from the galloping advance of modernism.

Publications such as E.J. Willson's *Specimens of Gothic Architecture* (1821–23), Edward Blore's *Monumental Remains* (1826), Henry Shaw's *Specimens of Ancient Furniture* (1836), preached the merits of the Gothic style. Other exponents were Batty Langley, A. W. N. Pugin, the Italians L. F. Basoli and Alessandro Sidole, and the French architect and furniture designer Eugene Viollet-le-Duc.

In Scotland, the *Waverley Novels* (1814–32) of Sir Walter Scott, who filled his home with relics from antiquity, heightened nostalgia for the medieval in England.

1 This sideboard, of American black walnut, tulip, and American black ash, was made in New York in about 1850–60.
It was inspired by the heavy Renaissance styles of northern Europe.

2 A.W.N. Pugin's *Gothic Furniture in the Style of the 15th Century*, published in London in 1835, included this design for a Gothic bookcase. The same volume illustrated beds, tables, seats, and other pieces, including a reading task, prie dieu, and cheval screen, all in the Gothic mode.

The Gothic revival was reflected internationally in the furniture of designers and makers such as Franz Xavier Fortner, Johann Wilhelm Vetter, the firms of Kimbel and Leistler of Germany, and the Italian Pelagio Pelagi. Others were Aimé Chénavard and P. A. Bellangé of France, Joseph Meeks & Son of New York, and the talented English carvers W. G. and W. H. Rogers.

In England, and to a lesser extent in North America, an Elizabethan furniture style, which combined Elizabethan, Jacobean, and Caroline forms, was favoured in the 1830s and 1840s, when Elizabethan interior schemes were popularized through publications by Robert Bridgens, J. C. Loudon and Joseph Nash.

Country houses with Tudor towers, windows and patterned chimneys were built, and interiors were fitted with oak wainscoting, Glastonbury style chairs, beds and draw tables carved with Jacobean and Elizabethan strapwork and bosses, and chairs with spiral-turned uprights modelled on Caroline forms. The latter were imitated in America, along with chairs modelled after Daniel Marot. In Germany, where the Gothic style had reached a high point in cathedrals such as that at Cologne, country houses with medieval interiors were also built.

Though not necessarily any more archaeologically correct, interiors in the Gothic revival style purported to be true to their name. William Burges, Norman Shaw, and Augustus Welby Northmore Pugin (1812–52) were among the leading English exponents of this style, and designed furniture with Gothic arches, colonettes, trefoils and other medieval motifs.

Pugin, a devout Roman Catholic who championed the Gothic as the only acceptable Christian style, advanced Gothic design in such publications as *The True Principles of Pointed or Christian Architecture* (1841) and *An Apology for the Revival of Christian Architecture in England* (1843). Pugin designed Gothic style furniture characterized by thick, sturdy oak members, ogival arch-shaped supports, and naturalistic foliate carving. His best-known work was the interior of the Palace of Westminster in London, in which he integrated form and ornament in an unparalleled rendition of the Gothic. Pugin's meticulous designs Gothicized the Westminster rooms down to the smallest detail, from ribbed ceilings, panelled walls, tiled floors and carpets, to metalwork, fire-dogs, carvings and furniture.

In the United States, Alexander Davis (1803–92) designed Gothic interiors for Lyndhurst and Ericstan in New York, and supplied them with tables, chairs, and other oak furniture with crockets, finials, cusps and quatrefoil. Alexander Roux, John Jelliff and other cabinet-makers produced American Gothic furniture.

In the mid-19th century, a reformist, and

3 Rich, dense ornament adorned John Henry Belter's furniture. The elaboration of ornamental carving on this laminated rosewood sofa, made by Belter in New York between 1856 and 1861, characterized much of his furniture, but he produced pieces in various styles. (Museum of the City of New York).

4 Papier-mâché furniture was generally decorated with japanning and gilt ornament and mother-of-pearl inlay, as is this English chair from the mid-19th century. The backrail and splat are of papier-mâché; the rest of the chair is of wood. (Victoria and Albert Museum, London)

more archaeologically correct approach to the Gothic style, was adopted in England by architects and designers, including Pugin, William Burges, William Butterfield, G. E. Street, and Charles Bevan. The art furniture movement, which preceded the aesthetic movement that eventually evolved into the Art Nouveau style, grew from the work of Bruce Talbert, Sir Henry Cole, Christopher Dresser, T. E. Collcutt, William Godwin, and Thomas Jeckyll.

such as the Century Guilt founded by A. H. Mackmurdo, the Art Workers' Guild founded by C. F. A. Voysey, and the Guild of Handicrafts founded by C. R. Ashbee in England, and societies and guilds of Arts and Crafts in Minnesota, Boston, Chicago, and New York forwarded various interpretations of the arts and crafts movement. The work of Mackmurdo, Voysey, Mackay Hugh Baillie Scott, and the Glasgow designer Charles Rennie Mackintosh

1

2

1 The English arts and crafts movement placed great emphasis on tradition in design. Philip Webb based this piece on an old chair from Sussex. It was produced by the arts and crafts firm of Morris and Company from about 1866; this example, of ebonized wood, retains its 'Bird' pattern woollen upholstery. The chair has an adjustable back. (Victoria and Albert Museum, London)

2 The German Richard Riemerschmid (1868–1957) designed simple forms in the Art Nouveau style. In 1899 he included this oak chair, upholstered in leather, in the music room he exhibited at the Dresden Exhibition of Decorative Arts. (Bethnel Green Museum, London)

Drawing on Japanese and Gothic sources, these designers produced furniture in the 1860s and 1870s that was simple and decorative, making use of light forms, flat surfaces, and dark woods, incorporating richness in carved and applied ornament, stoneware and painted panels.

Pugin's writings, which preached integrity, propriety, and functionalism in design, were of great importance to Burges and William Morris.

Morris's arts and crafts movement created a style of furniture which, although not necessarily as identifiably Gothic as Pugin's pieces had been, was meant to be medieval in conception. The firm of Morris, Marshall, Faulkner, and Co., founded in 1861 and renamed Morris & Co. in 1875, adopted as its essential principles the tradition of hand craftsmanship in construction, and considerations of simplicity, utility and necessity in design. Creating a decorative style that was ornate, highly patterned, and colourful, Morris's firm produced wallpapers and textiles with stylized flat foliage, flowers, fruit and birds, and somewhat heavy furniture with rectilinear forms and broad members.

Beginning in the 1880s, craft organizations

looked forward to the Art Nouveau style. Mackintosh's tall, straight-backed chairs and slender cabinets, like the uncomfortable, blocky furniture designed by the American Frank Lloyd Wright whom he influenced, was rectilinear and rigid, but his fluidity of form and attenuated proportions anticipated the Art Nouveau.

The revival of French 17th and 18th century styles, often termed 'Louis XV' no matter which era was represented, permeated 19th century interior design internationally, providing the decorative schemes for middle-class homes, hotel lounges and palatial suites. Revitalized in about 1835 in England, the Louis XV style was embraced by the French Emperor Louis-Napoleon Bonaparte in mid-century, and gave way later in both countries to the more restrained Louis XVI mode. Publications including George Smith's *Cabinet-Maker and Upholsterer's Guide* of 1826 paved the way for a Rococo revival. In Vienna, the Thonet firm and Karl Leistler produced Rococo revival furnishings; in the course of the century, Pössenbacher in Munich, Anton Bembé in Mainz, Giuseppe Cima and Alessandro Sidoli of Milan, J. P. F. Jeanselme and

Guillaume Grohé of Paris, William Smee, Collard & Collard, Dowbiggon & Co., of London, J. & W. Hilton of Montreal, Prudent Mallard of New Orleans, and Alexander Roux of New York turned out 19th century renditions of Louis XIV, Rococo, and Louis XVI designs.

It was the modernization of these old styles, more than the seeming confusion about which style was which, that most significantly characterized their 19th century renditions. Antiques were adapted to suit current taste; misinterpretations of Rococo pattern-books occasionally led to exaggerated asymmetries that 18th century designers would never have intended. Rooms were generally more crowded and casual than they would have been in the previous century.

The invention of coil springs and deep-button upholstery led to the production of large, over-stuffed sofas and easy chairs, and although these Louis style seats were shaped as three-pronged pinwheels or other sequences of curves, to a certain degree they lost the lightness and delicacy of 18th century design.

Balloon-back chairs with cabriole legs and lightweight fly chairs, meant to be moved about easily, were innovations of this style, as was the use of papier mâché by the Englishman Charles Bielefiled to produce Rococo ornaments, and the substitution of putty for wood by G. Jackson and Son of London for their ornamental mouldings. John Belter of New York made great use of his lamination process to produce beds, sideboards, chairs, and other rosewood pieces that were highly carved with flowers and foliage in a naturalistic Rococo style.

Art Nouveau

Emerging at the very end of the century, the Art Nouveau style produced furniture which, light, ornamental and organic in conception, was hardly as ponderous as the blocky pieces of the contemporary arts and crafts movement. These were as heavily formed as they were laden with social significance.

Representing the first major break from the traditions that had shaped so much of 19th century design, the Art Nouveau style flourished from about 1893 to 1910. Its dominant feature, curvilinearity, originated from sources as varied as the Japanese prints that enjoyed wide circula-

3 This room in William Morris's house in Hammersmith Terrace, London is decorated in his typical style. The ornate, highly patterned wallpaper and textiles complement the heavy furniture.

tion in the West at that time, the French Louis XV and XVI styles, and the flowing, organic decorations on recently popularized Minoan pottery. In the pictorial world, the English artist Arthur Rackham illustrated fairy tales with delicate etchings of attenuated figures and sinuous tangled trees. The architects Victor Horta in Brussels and Antoni Gaudi in Barcelona created buildings and furniture characterized by swirling undulations suggesting underwater or plant growth. Horta's celebration of line and light surfaces seen in his combination of glass and cast-iron at the Hôtel van Eetvelde of 1895, was shared by Louis Comfort Tiffany of New York, who in the 1880s began to produce lamps, vases and other furnishings of iridescent glass, which hinted at organic movement and growth with their swirling forms and naturalistic motifs such as dragonflies.

Similarly, Art Nouveau furniture was characterized by swirling lines and attenuated shapes,

and suggestions of such light, natural forms as curved growing plant stems. Although not a unified international movement, the flowing tendencies of the Art Nouveau style were expressed by European furniture designers including the German Richard Riemerschmird, the Italians Carlo Bugatti and Pietro Fenoglio, the Belgian Henry van de Velde, and the Frenchmen Hector Guimard, Emile Gallé, Pierre Chareau, and Louis Majorelle. These designers generally achieved decorative effects through a careful integration of form and surface ornament; rich woods, such as cherry, walnut and mahogany

were flatly carved with decorative rounded panels, whiplash curves and swirling ormolu mounts.

The work of Louis Majorelle was exceptionally successful; the cabriole legs he used show the influence of earlier Louis styles, but the attenuated, stretched shapes of his desks and cabinets exhibit a greater freedom and lightness. The rounded, slightly trapezoidal panels and drawers of pieces by Jacques Gruber, and the flowing continuity of line joining crest rail and stiles in the chairs of Pierre Chareau and Sue et Mare, similarly manifested the natural integration of form that defined the Art Nouveau style.

Although the style declined soon after the turn of the century, its very occurrence freed designers from the series of revivals into which the preceding era had been bound. The qualities of lightness, tensile strength, and integration of ornament and form it embodied foreshadowed the approach to furniture that 20th century designers would take.

The Modern Era

The era that would dismiss the swirls of the Art Nouveau style for the streamlined rationality of machine-age design also witnessed the Art Deco style, which shared some qualities of each. At the turn of the century, European interest in Indo-Persian exotica was aroused by the displays at the Asian Pavilion of the International Exhibition in Paris in 1900, and was heightened by the publication of a French translation of the *Tales of the Arabian Nights*.

1 Antonio Gaudí's bizarre, anthropomorphic buildings included the spectacular Casa Milá at Barcelona, of 1907, with its fluid, rippling facade. This Art Nouveau style armchair, of veneered mahogany, is one of a set of six Gaudí designed (c.1898–1904) for the boardroom of the Casa Calvet, also in Barcelona. (Museo Gaudí, Barcelona)

2 Art Deco furniture was characterized by combinations of geometric forms and bright, lively ornament. Carlo Bugatti's rectangular cabinet is inlaid with metal and brass; the leather mirror frame is decorated with a painted floral design. Bugatti, who exhibited work at the 1902 Turin Exhibition, designed furniture that showed elements of oriental, Art Nouveau, and Art Deco styles. The figure is by Chiparus. (Martins Forrest Collection)

3 Japanese design and flowing plant forms comprised much of the inspiration of the Art Nouveau style, influencing the work of Emile Gallé and other designers. In 1899, Gallé exhibited furniture at the Paris Universal Exhibition; he created glassware, furniture, and ceramics in the Art Nouveau style. This firescreen by Gallé, of 1900, is made of wood. The curving ornament merges with the outlines of the form of the firescreen itself, capturing the organic fluidity of Art Nouveau design. (Bethnal Green Museum, London)

4 Gerrit Rietveldt (1888–1964), a member of the Dutch De Stijl group from 1919–1931, designed his Red-Blue Chair in 1917–18. This version, produced by G.A. van de Groeneken 'Het Goede Meubel', De Bilt, Holland, in 1919, appeared in the De Stijl magazine the year it was made. In 1923 it was shown at the Bauhaus Exhibition at Weimar. The De Stijl group preferred compositions of planes and lines in which primary colours, white, and black were used. Rietveldt's separation of seat, back, legs, and arms initiated the search for weightlessness and abstraction. (Victoria and Albert Museum, London)

5 The design for this chair, based on a suggestion by the Surrealist artist Salvador Dali (*b.*1904) was drawn by Edward James of West Dean, England. Arthur English produced the chair in 1936 of French walnut and leather. Dali's paintings juxtaposed forms and images in combinations meant to conjure up the subconscious experiences of dreams. Dali said that a chair should be 'the supreme spectre of style.' (Owned by Edward James)

3

The Art Deco style was launched by the erotic, sensuous and spectacularly exotic productions of the *Ballets Russes* which, beginning with such dazzling displays as R. and S. Delaunay's *Cléopatre* in 1909, drew its ornamental schemes at first from the lingering Art Nouveau style, and then increasingly from Russian, antique, and Far Eastern sources.

Designed by such artists as Leon Bakst, A. Benois, and Alexander Kolovine, the rich and colourful decors and costumes of subsequent productions, including *Scheherezade* and the *Afternoon of a Fawn*, enchanted and enraged the Parisian élite. Meeting success also in Rome, London, and Monte Carlo, the *Ballets Russes* inspired a decorative style that relied for its effects on sumptuous, rich textiles and Ottoman affectations such as tapestries and opulent floor cushions.

In Paris, the firm of Poiret, and its branch the *Atelier Martine*, designed costumes and interiors

4

that closely paralleled those of the *Ballets Russes* stage, pronouncing a stylistic dogma that balanced rich materials with simple forms.

Shaped by designers such as Josef Hoffman (1870–1956) and Koloman Moser (1868–1918) of the Viennese Secession Movement, and by other artists including Eileen Gray, Andre Groult, Edgar Brandt, J. E. Ruhlmann, A. A. Rateau, Ambrose Heal, and E. W. Gimson, the Art Deco interior style combined highly decorative surface treatments with simple geometric forms, the latter foreshadowing the reductionism of the era that was to follow.

Cabinets, chairs, mirrors and tables designed by Heal, Gimson, and Hoffman showed almost classical principles of restraint and geometricity in form. Stained woods, boxwood, ebony, mother-of-pearl, shagreen, and lacquer covered these simple shapes, as did sparingly applied line ornament. Though cheerful, fresh, and often sparkling with colour, Art Deco ornament took on a similar restraint and geometric order. Furniture was inlaid with geometric shapes, small panels containing flowers, clustered discs, or layered arcs, or surfaced with plain lacquer or geometric compositions of such materials as lacquer and eggshell.

Elements such as disc-like flowers shown frontally, simplified unserrated leaves with thick, straight veins, and flat carvings of birds, figures and clouds, reflected the stylization of contemporary architectural sculpture, which was similarly executed in low relief.

The delight in surface texture and ornament that the Art Deco movement embraced was eschewed by the less productive, though seminally influential, de Stijl school of Holland in the first several decades of the century. Formulated in 1917 by the writer, painter and architect Theodore von Doesburg, the painter Piet Mondrian (1872–1944) and others, the movement sought to strip all superfluous decoration from essential forms, and to dissolve these forms into abstractions.

In the decorative arts, the most important product of this school was the chair designed by architect Gerrit Rietveld (1888–1964), commis-

5

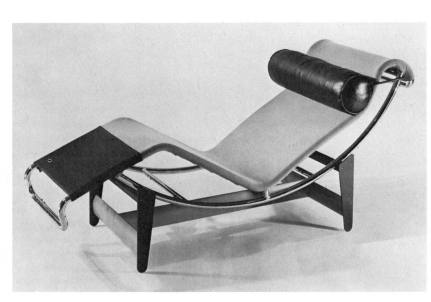

aesthetically pleasing, giving the appearance of industrial manufacture, for which each object was meant to be suited.

In addition to creating a wealth of fresh, clean new designs, the Bauhaus initiated the use of tubular steel in furniture, and also developed furniture that was easily stacked.

At the Bauhaus, Marcel Breuer created a series of chairs based on the Rietveld example. The first few of these followed the *de Stijl* model closely; the fifth, known as the 'Wassily' chair of 1925, was constructed of nickel-plated steel tubing, and transformed the rigid Rietveld precedent into a lightweight, airier structure, with arms and legs formed of continuous, pleasing lines of tubing, and arm, back and seat supports formed of flexible, supple leather or canvas.

This construction allowed for the first time an avoidance of the visual clutter that chair legs had traditionally imposed on interior design. The chair also paved the way for the revolutionary 'cantilever' form chair, which was first developed in 1926 by the Dutch designer Mart Stam, in his attempts to create furniture that was light, mobile, and simply and perfectly scaled to the human body. Mies van der Rohe developed the similar 'MR' chair in the same year, and in 1928 Breuer perfected his own cantilever chair which, consisting of a rectangle of tubing bent sinusoidally, achieved maximum bounce, lightness, and fluidity of form. Fitted with back and seat of canvas, leather, caning, or vinyl upholstery, this chair has since been popularized internationally. Breuer also made use of the light, tensile qualities of steel tubing in his designs for glass-topped tables, which similarly expressed the simple beauty of structural form with their continuous linear supports.

Mies, whose pioneering work in glass-sheathed skyscrapers initiated an entire new phase of modern architecture, designed the German Government Pavilion at the Interna-

sioned with the request that it be based on the furniture of American architect Frank Lloyd Wright. Although singularly uncomfortable, and thus never made in large quantities, the chair reached European designers through the *de Stijl* magazine, in which it was published in 1919. The chair also appeared at an exhibition at the Bauhaus school of design in Germany in 1923, where some of the most progressive decorative artists of the era saw it.

The Bauhaus school was founded in 1919 by Walter Gropius, who designed the building that housed it in Dessau. The school attempted to approach modernity rationally and to embrace it fully, by welding high quality design with innovations in technology, materials and efficiency. The Bauhaus adherred to the precepts of the international style architect, Le Corbusier, who prescribed the clear presentation of pure geometric volumes and shapes. The school produced furniture, ceramics, and other items in a style that was simple, functional, streamlined and

1 An ornate centre table *c.* 1905 attributed to Carlo Bugatti, one of the leading Italian furniture designers of the time. The motifs used to decorate the piece show some of the themes which influenced Bugatti's work.

2 The 'Wassily' chair designed by Marcel Breuer in 1925. Following the precepts of the Bauhaus, of which he was a member, Breuer was one of the earliest designers to realize the potential of tubular steel in the making of furniture.

3 Although primarily an architect, Le Corbusier also designed furniture. This chaise longue, dating from 1927 follows the clean, uncluttered style which was the hallmark of his architecture.

tional Exhibition at Barcelona in 1929, and the Tugenhadt House in Brno in 1930. Simple forms. flat planes, screen-like walls, and rich materials characterized these interiors, for which he also designed two extremely significant 20th century chairs: the Barcelona chair and the super-streamlined Brno cantilever chair.

In the wake of these examples other designers have created furniture with steel frames – from Le Corbusier and others in the late 1920s, to the Danish Poul Kjaerholm, the Italian Claudio Salocchi, and the Finnish Antti Nurmesniemi in very recent years. The firm of Thonet, which with its bent beechwood furniture of the 19th century had provided a prototype for bent steel construction, produced a great quantity of such furniture which was exported throughout Europe.

Beginning in the late 1930s, Danish furniture designers such as Borge Mogensen, Kaarl Klint, Mogens Koch, and Hans Wegner began designing chairs which, relying on the natural beauty of curvaceously sculpted wood, were light, and fluid, often with caned seats, sweeping crest rails, and slightly undulating back uprights. Swedish Finnish, Swiss, and Italian designers similarly incorporated a light, linear approach to furniture design.

In the 1930s, Alvar Aalto adapted the use of plywood to the construction of furniture. In 1931, Aalto designed a chair with a sinusoidal seat-back comprised of a piece of bent plywood

rather than metal. This tendency was furthered by the American designer Charles Eames, who designed chairs with continuous curved surfaces, first with Eero Saarinen in 1940 using moulded plywood, and then by himself in 1948 using glass fibre-reinforced plastic.

The invention early in the century of latex foam meant that upholstery could be preformed into strong, shaped curves. Plastic furniture, with smooth continuous surfaces enclosing backs, seats, and sides of chairs or curving gently from table into central leg into round base, was designed in a light, fluid style by Eero Saarinen in the 1950s.

These modern furniture pieces are not found in middle-class houses even today, although cheap mass production is more efficient than ever. Wall-to-wall carpeting, built-in cabinets and drawers, and other innovations have had their effect on modern interior design. As in preceding centuries, past styles persist along with the most progressive, and most homes are likely to include antiques, attractive reproductions of old styles, and generally useful but stylistically homogenized pieces, in eclectic collections of styles. Rather than new stylistic forms, it is changes in standards of living that have probably most affected interior design today.

The unprecedented informality in domestic life, increasing 'furniturization' of such technological devices as televisions, radios, air conditioners and refrigerators have made their mark. And reduced dependence on servants for cleaning, the constant availability of electric lighting, improved insulation and heating systems, and such new materials as laminated boards, thermoplastics, acrylics, vinyls, and linoleum, have altered interior design far more drastically than any of the innovations that the rapid stylistic changes of a century ago could have wrought.

Some designers preferred to use the natural colours and textures of wood, as a relief from the man-made industrial materials. This trend was particularly marked among the Scandinavian designers in the late 1930s. In England Heals achieved a high reputation as manufacturers of furniture by leading designers, such as this daybed after a design by Marcel Breuer, c. 1935–40.

Textiles

1 The Syon Cope is one of the most famous examples of Opus Anglicanum. It is embroidered with scenes from the life of Christ, saints, angels and heraldic devices and was probably made between 1300 and 1320.

2 An English stumpwork mirror frame dating from the third quarter of the 17th century. It is divided into 10 sections and worked with some of the favourite subjects of the period: a king and queen (possibly, Charles II and Catherine of Braganza), animals, fruit, flowers and (below) a mermaid, in brilliant colours and a variety of stitches and applied motifs.

Embroidery – the embellishing of fabric with stitches – was already a well-established craft in 16th-century Europe. For several centuries professional embroiderers had been among the most respected of craftsmen, their art linked with that of the illuminator. Most of them, at least in England and France, were organized into powerful guilds which, by maintaining high standards of workmanship and by protecting the interests of the embroiderers, helped to ensure the high standing of the craft.

It was customary for the royal courts of Europe to employ professional embroiderers to work heraldic insignia and all kinds of furnishings. The church was also a lavish patron, and although some work was done in monasteries and convents, the best and most valued was made by professional specialists. From early on 'the labours of the distaff and needle' were considered of prime importance for ladies all over Europe, and spinning, weaving and fine needlework formed an important part of every girl's education prior to her marriage.

In the medieval period the finest of all embroidery was the ecclesiastical work produced in England. Opus Anglicanum, as it was called, was worked with coloured silks and couched gold and silver threads, and the designs – of saints, angels and heraldic motifs – have close parallels in the manuscript illumination of the time. Opus Anglicanum was exported to Europe on a large scale, and although France, Germany and Flanders produced embroidered vestments of a similar style. their quality rarely matched the fine work which came out of the ateliers of London and East Anglia.

Although the emphasis in 14th and 15th century Europe was on ecclesiastical embroidery, there was at the same time a growing use of domestic embroidery. Woven tapestries, for example, were of importance in furnishing the draughty castles and houses of the rich, and embroidered bed hangings were also invaluable in the cold winters of northern Europe.

3 A Stuart period casket embroidered in coloured silks. Caskets of this kind were often worked by young girls to show off their skills in needlework.

4 A linen sleeve worked in silk with blackwork embroidery. The stitches include stem stitch and speckling.

flowers, fruit and animals worked in black silk on linen. Sometimes, gold and silver threads were introduced for richer effect. Blackwork is said to have originated in Spain, where it developed from Moorish work. It soon became popular for collars, caps, cuffs, shirts and other clothing.

While Italy, France and Flanders excelled in the production of lace and tapestries, England reigned supreme in the realms of domestic embroidery. English ladies covered bed-hangings, cushions, wall panels and, of course, costumes, in a profusion of flowers, birds, butterflies and animals worked in wools on canvas, or silks on linen. They took their designs from woodcut

There was an increasing use of embroidery for costume and personal adornment. Much of this, whether it took the form of fine linen undergarments or the embroidered and bejewelled purses for which France was famous in the 15th and 16th centuries, was done domestically as well as by professional and religious embroiderers.

The upheavals of the Reformation as well as outbreaks of bubonic plague took their toll and effectively ended the great days of church embroidery, but by the 16th century needlework was already taking on a new emphasis. It was now based firmly on a secular footing in the courts of royalty and in the homes of the rich, who adorned themselves and their furnishings with an increasingly exotic array of embroidered fabrics and lace.

Blackwork was a form of embroidery widespread in the 16th century but which died out early in the 17th. It consisted of all-over designs of trailing tendrils and leaves interspersed with

illustrations in newly available books, from herbals and increasingly, as the century wore on, from books of designs especially published for embroiderers. These came from the presses of Italy, Switzerland, France, the Low Countries and England, and continued to be used by many generations of domestic embroideresses.

This habit – which was universal – of using favourite old designs for embroidery, makes dating extremely difficult, and in the absence of other evidence like a date or supporting document, embroideries are notoriously hard to place within 50 years or so.

A 16th-century development was the working of samplers as a method of recording stitches and designs. The earliest 'exemplars', as they were called, are generally worked in coloured silks on linen and they must have provided invaluable reference material at a time when embroiderers' design books were still rare and expensive. Often they formed long strips of material and were clearly added to over many years.

1 A detail from an English crewel work curtain worked in coloured wools on linen and cotton. It dates from the mid-17th century.

2 A sampler worked by an 11-year old American girl from Newport, Rhode Island in 1774. She has used mainly satin and cross stitches to create a colourful variety of figures, animals, birds, flowers and alphabets.

cases they provide an impressive record of individual performance.

In time, however, design books became more widely available and fewer adult embroideresses made samplers for their own use. Although they continued as part of the educational curriculum for girls they soon became debased into exercises 'in neatness and perseverance'. They showed fewer and fewer different stitches until by the 19th century they were nearly always worked entirely in cross-stitch. As well as an alphabet and sometimes the child's name, age and the date, they included motifs such as flowers, animals, houses and birds and, nearly always, a pious verse. The whole picture – for this is what the sampler had become – was generally surrounded by a decorative border and was clearly designed to be framed and hung up for all to see.

The later 17th century in England was remarkable for its vibrant pictorial embroidery. The period after Charles II's restoration in 1660 was one of unashamed luxury, colourful splendour and sensual excesses of all kinds, and the extravagance of the time is reflected in the array of late Stuart needlework pictures, mirror frames, caskets and keepsakes which have survived to the present day. Some were embroidered in coloured silks in the flat, while others were done in three-dimensional stumpwork, with figures, flowers, fruits and other motifs raised and padded; details of costume-like collars and cuffs were frequently semi-detached and made of needlepoint lace. Although many of the designs were biblical – the Finding of Moses, Esther and Ahasuerus and the Judgement of Solomon were among the favourites – the figures all wear elaborate Stuart costume. In the background fanciful castles, huge caterpillars, birds, butterflies, cows, lions and flowers, mostly taken from the popular design books of the time, jostle for space with total disregard for the rules of proportion. Their colourful naivety is charming, and the stitchery, often punctuated with sequins and seed pearls, is breathtaking.

Meanwhile, across the Channel, the French were enjoying an even more glittering period under Louis XIV. As in England and Holland, the exotic imports of the East India companies stimulated both household and sartorial fashions and gave the French, in particular, a taste for richly embroidered silks. Louis XIV himself had a huge band of embroiderers working for his entourage at Versailles, and anybody who was anybody spent vast sums of money on lace and embroidery for their clothes. Some even sent materials to China to be embroidered with oriental motifs.

The chain-stitch embroidery known as tambour work, another Chinese import, was a favourite occupation with French needlewomen from the end of the 17th century, and the habit spread to other countries, especially England, in the mid-18th century. On the whole, the best French embroidery was done by professionals. Many of these were Huguenots and after the Revocation of the Edict of Nantes in 1685 a great number of them fled to England, Germany,

By the later years of the 17th century, the making of samplers had become part of the needlework education of young girls, who would often make several – perhaps a coloured sampler of stitches, motifs and alphabets, a whitework sampler showing cut and drawn work and embroidery suitable for household linen, and finally an embroidered picture or casket in which she was able to display her most flamboyant skills. Until well into the 18th century samplers were a rich source of stitches and designs and in many

Switzerland and Holland where they soon set up successful workshops. Ironically, a proportion of their embroideries found their way back to France.

Louis XIV's minister, Colbert, himself a mercer's son, worked hard to establish France's pre-eminence on all fronts, and especially in the textile industry. As well as encouraging French lace and tapestry he helped to promote linen manufacture at Cambrai, Valenciennes, St Quentin and Lille. Most important of all – for it was probably the most successful – the silk industry of Lyons became supreme in the late 17th century. The colourful garlands of flowers woven on rich cream grounds were as luxurious as any embroidered materials, and they soon became fashionable for the best-dressed people all over Europe.

One of the major influences exerted by East India Company imports of printed cottons and chintzes was, surprisingly enough, on the wool-embroidered bed hangings so essential to keep out winter draughts in northern Europe and America. Again, these were mainly the province of the domestic embroideress, who worked the bed-curtains and valances – the pelmet-like hangings round the roof of a four-poster bed – in coloured crewel wools on a linen or cotton ground. Her designs for these crewel or Jacobean embroideries, worked in long and short, chain and stem stitches with French knots and a variety of fillings, were frequently taken from oriental originals.

The Tree of Life pattern was much favoured. In this, a swirling tree laden with improbable fruit and flowers springs from a rocky base. Among and beneath its branches hover birds of paradise and all kinds of animals – lions, squirrels, stags, rabbits and insects – which were usually taken not from oriental sources but from the needlework pattern books which had been in current use for most of the century.

In the late 17th century, life in the American colonies was beginning to grow less spartan than it had been in the days of the early settlers, and with increasing comfort came an emphasis on domestic embroidery. American wool work hangings were at first confined to repeating motifs worked in a single colour, but by the end of the 17th century these had progressed to colourful crewel embroideries similar to those made in northern Europe.

Americans, as well as Europeans, used knotted pile Turkey work for covering cushions, chairs and other furniture in the late 17th century. Carpets and rugs of Turkey work had originally been imported to Europe from the Near East by the East India companies, and they soon became popular for their hardwearing properties and colourfulness. They were made by pulling wool through canvas or coarse linen stretched on a loom and then cutting it to form a pile. The technique lent itself to formal geometric designs and heraldic motifs in bright colours and was soon made on a commercial scale in Europe. Like many professional crafts, it was also done by persevering ladies at home, and in America,

Turkey work was more often done domestically than by professionals.

The bed, always the most important piece of furniture in a house, was given the most lavish – and usually the most expensive – attention. Sometimes it had hangings of home-made crewel embroidery or festoons of silk, or velvet decorated with gold and silver threads by the professional upholsterers of London and Paris. By the early 18th century furniture in general was becoming more refined and comfortable with an increasing use of decorated fabrics for upholstery. Velvets, silks and damasks were extensively used, but many chairs, stools, settees, screens and even card tables were covered with embroidery.

3 French brocaded silk made in Lyons in the early 18th century. This panel is woven with exotic chinoiseries which were extremely popular during this period.

Sometimes, designs were worked in crewel wools on linen, but more often, especially as the 18th century progressed, wool or silk on canvas was favoured. This either took the form of bold 'Florentine' patterns in flame stitch, or figurative designs in tent and cross stitches. Often, they conformed to the oriental fashion with Chinese figures, pagodas and exotic trees and birds, but by the early 18th century the influence of the Dutch flower painters was bringing a new naturalism to all kinds of decoration. Vases of flowers were inlaid into furniture and worked on canvas for chairs, and flower designs were clearly among the most popular by the 1720s and 1730s. Whole sets of chairs were sometimes covered with fine

were arranged in deliberate groupings in drawing rooms. They would have been too much even for the most indefatigable of needlewomen, and besides, they were much more suitably clad in the delicate striped or flower-sprigged brocades, light-coloured damasks or gaily printed chintzes which became more and more widely available. Women contented themselves with knotting fringes and weaving braids for trimming their furniture.

Throughout the 18th century both men's and women's costume was lavishly embroidered. The rich employed professional craftspeople to work flowers, in sprigs, garlands, trailing patterns, bunches and festoons on their clothes, to quilt

1 A profusion of cabbage roses and other flowers worked in Berlin wools on canvas.

1

2 Detail from an American patchwork quilt worked with compass motifs in blue, green, red and yellow printed cottons on a white ground. It was probably made about 1830–40 in Pennsylvania.

stitchery and evidence of these mammoth undertakings – which often kept the ladies of a household employed for years – can still be found in old country houses.

Many furniture embroideries were probably worked in silks or in wool with silk highlights, but because of its fragility compared with the robustness of wool, much silk embroidery has perished, leaving the almost certainly false impression that wool was the most favoured embroidery material. In France, where after the Revolution special workmen were employed to unpick embroideries, very little 17th or 18th century needlework in any material has survived.

Comfortable upholstered chairs covered with embroidery or rich velvets continued to be fashionable until the craze for Neo-classicism began to sweep through Europe in the 1760s and '70s. After that, the 'best' houses had rows of elegant but much less comfortable chairs ranged round the edges of rooms. Sets of settees and stools

2

3

3 A late 18th century needle-work picture of Una and the Lion embroidered with coloured silks, mostly in satin stitch, with water-colour details.

their petticoats and to beribbon plainer materials. Coloured silks, metal threads and jewels were used for the most sumptuous, while those who chose not to employ embroiderers wore equally beautiful gowns and waistcoats of flower-be-decked brocade.

In the furnishing of houses too, the domestic embroideress continued to work fine household linens and particularly bed coverings, and here the Americans were pre-eminent. In North America, where the winters are particularly cold, crewel embroidered coverlets continued to be made throughout the 18th century, whereas in Europe they had become unfashionable by mid-century. A form of looped embroidery in wool on woollen cloth was also used for coverlets, mainly in New England, from the 1720s until the early 19th century.

It was more usual in America than elsewhere for women to dye and spin their own embroidery yarns and to weave cloth, and many of them also printed their own cottons with stencils or wood blocks. Cotton bedcovers with home-printed designs in red, green or yellow, and often quilted, are not an unusual find, and they mostly date from the 18th and early 19th century. Quilting, the technique by which a thick layer of material is sandwiched between two thinner ones and bound by patterns of running stitches all over the surface, was used a great deal to conserve warmth. Candlewicking and embroidery in white on white were also used for American bed-spreads of this period. The most celebrated American quilts, however, are undoubtedly those decorated with appliqué or patchwork.

Printed cotton chintzes were imported into America in the 18th century, but they were ex-tremely expensive and were at first luxuries con-fined to the rich. It was soon realized that if the printed designs were cut out and appliquéd on to a background material, the chintzes could be used much more economically, and it was not long before appliquéd chintz quilts gave way to patchwork in which even smaller pieces of material were stitched together, side by side, to make colourful patterns.

Some American quilts are a combination of patchwork and appliqué and their range is endless, probably because every girl was expected to make several quilts before she married, and it was also customary for quilts, made through the joint efforts of several women (at 'quilting bees'), to be given as presentation pieces.

The different patchwork patterns were given names–Puss-in-the-Corner, Dutchman's Puzzle, King David's Crown and Lincoln's Platform are typical, and these often varied from region to region. Some of them recorded historic figures or events while others are simply quaint. Few give any clue to dating, any more than the materials used in patchworks, since these were often already old when they were put into a quilt.

Another point of interest in American weaving and embroidery is the wide range of discernible national styles. America was colonized by immigrants from almost every country in Europe, and just as they all took with them their own national characteristics, so they took their textile skills, needlework patterns and embroidery techniques. Whereas dating American needlework accurately is almost impossible, it can often be attributed to a specific region, colonized by a particular national group, on the basis of its European stylistic roots.

Among late 18th century gentlewomen, whether in America or Europe, there was a definite tendency towards maximum effect in the minimum of time where decorative needlework was concerned. The developing machine age was already giving people a taste for speed, besides changing the entire face of textile manufacture, and women were no longer happy to persevere for years on a single project like the embroidering of a set of chair covers or the panels of a screen. Instead, they turned to smaller items, such as panels for tea caddies and trays, firescreens and pictures. These they stitched with gentle and refined designs of shepherds and shepherdesses, rustic views, flowers and wistfully romantic scenes from Goethe's *The Sorrows of Werther* or Sterne's *Sentimental Journey*, in coloured silks on a silk or satin background.

Designs were copied over and over again and most of them were available 'off the peg'. The faces of figures, skies and other details were nearly always painted in watercolours, and contemporary magazine advertisements recommended shops selling embroidery designs complete with the silks for working them.

Interesting variants of the late 18th and early 19th century silk embroideries were the 'printwork' pictures done entirely in black, grey and dark brown silks. They were made in imitation of the fashionable prints of the time, and must have been exceedingly monotonous to work. Some pictures of the same period were embroidered as mourning pieces, and these are occasionally worked partly in human hair – presumably that of the deceased. In America, these printwork or

1 Portrait of a lady in court dress, possibly Princess Elizabeth of Denmark, Duchess of Brunswick (1573–1626). She is wearing a magnificent collar of stiffened Venetian lace – the height of fashion in the early 17th century.

'etching' embroideries were known as 'engraved' work and were very popular.

By the 1820s a new craze had gripped needlewomen, who were more and more intent on speed and colourful effects. In the early years of the 19th century a German printseller called Phillipson had begun to sell hand-coloured needlework designs on squared paper, and they were eminently suitable for working on canvas with the soft wools of Saxony. The designs – and the wools – spread very rapidly to France, Spain, England and America, where thousands of women spent hours each day working chair and footstool covers, bell-pulls, slippers, braces, card cases and all conceivable trifles with garish flowers, parrots, animals and even whole scenes from old master paintings. Some were highlighted with beads. By mid-century the beads were obtainable in the same variety of brilliant colours as the wools. Other designs included 'plush' stitched features in which a section of the design, for example a bird or a rose, was worked in a looped stitch and then cut to form a pile, giving a three-dimensional effect. In spite of occasional variations of canvas stitchery, tent stitch was by far the most usual for Berlin wool work, or 'zephyrs' as it was called in America (after the yarn used in it).

After the mid-19th century, Berlin wool work began to lose its pre-eminence, at least in 'artistic' circles. A new movement, aimed at encouraging a more inventive approach to embroidery design

2

Lace

Lace was the most luxurious and, in its heyday, the most expensive of textiles. During the 16th, 17th and 18th centuries the rich spent vast fortunes on lace and the less rich expended more on it than prudence should have allowed. However, lace was considered the ultimate embellishment for fashionable attire, and fashion was a more respected ruler then than it is now.

In the 16th century the ruff was considered the ideal vehicle for showing off fine laces, and these were heavily starched until the fashion for more flowing lace collars and ruffles crept in at the beginning of the 17th century. Handkerchiefs, aprons, caps, dresses, coats, baby clothes and even gloves and shoes were trimmed with lace, and the wealthy had lacy household linens. Church vestments were embellished with lace.

In the 18th and 19th centuries ladies carried lace parasols and fans, babies were draped in lace christening robes, brides were married in lace veils and the dead were buried in lace shrouds. Lace was probably at its height in the late 17th century when extravagance knew no bounds, even though several countries placed restrictions on the import and the wearing of lace.

Technically, there are two kinds of lace: needlepoint and pillow. Needlepoint lace (or needlemade as it is also called) is derived from cut and drawn thread work and is made with a single thread and a needle using embroidery stitches, and particularly buttonholing.

and re-introducing many of the stitches which had all but disappeared from the needleworker's repertoire, was already afoot by the 1860s. Known as art needlework, its ideals were fostered in England by William Morris and Edward Burne-Jones, and the movement found its vehicle in the Royal School of Art Needlework, founded in 1872. Its objective was 'restoring . . . ornamental needlework to the high place it once held among the decorative Arts'. Its members were mainly impoverished gentlewomen and its patrons were almost invariably titled. Much of the work was designed by such artists as William Morris, Edward Burne-Jones and Walter Crane.

The Royal School of Art Needlework was most influential in America, where similar schools were set up in major cities in the 1870s and 1880s. The Royal Irish School of Art Needlework, established in Dublin in the 1870s, helped to popularize the new ideas all over Ireland. Other movements took root in Europe and by the end of the 19th century there was a noticeable merging of styles. This common ground, embodied in Art Nouveau, was manifest more in textile design than embroidery which, largely because of the relentless development of industrial technology, was relegated and remains a minor accomplishment. The design of machine-made fabrics, on the other hand, has continued to attract artists of high calibre, and it is probably in this field that one should look for the best examples of modern textile achievement.

2 Detail of a Valenciennes lace lappet dating from the second half of the 17th century.

Pillow lace (often known as bobbin lace) is made by weaving and plaiting many threads together. For convenience the threads are wound on bobbins (or, in the early days, small animal bones – hence the technique's other name, bone lace) and the pattern is formed by twisting the threads round pins stuck into a firm pillow.

A third kind of lace, derived from fishing net decoration, was a form of embroidered net. Known as filet lace it achieved prominence much later, at the beginning of the 19th century, when machine-made nets were becoming available. This machine-made net ground was embroidered by lace-makers and could be of extremely fine quality.

Italy was probably the first country to produce lace on a commercial scale, although some form of lace is known to have been made in ancient Coptic and Peruvian cultures. Certainly, needlepoint and bobbin laces were being made during the 15th century in Italy, and by the 16th thriving industries were established in Venice, Florence, Genoa, Milan, Naples and other Italian cities. A great deal of it was being exported, especially from Venice, in answer to the rapidly growing fashion for lace in other European countries.

Flanders was also a front-runner in the development of lace-making techniques and in the expansion of the industry in the 16th century. The main centres were Antwerp, Binche, Bruges, Brussels and, later, Ghent, Mechlin and Ypres.

As consumers, the French were among the most extravagant buyers of lace and some time during the 17th century numbers of Venetian lacemakers were enticed to France to start a new industry. They were eminently successful, and by the beginning of the 18th century a large proportion of the population was engaged in lacemaking, mainly round Alençon, Argentan, Arras, Chantilly, Lille and Valenciennes.

Italian lacemakers introduced their craft to Spain, where laces made with gold and silver threads became a speciality and were exported to the rich people of other countries on a large scale. Spanish lace also took influence from the Low Countries which were a Spanish dominion until the end of the 16th century.

A large number of French protestants were engaged in the lace industry and after the Revocation of the Edict of Nantes in 1685 hundreds of them swarmed eastwards, setting up successful lace industries in many other centres. The main beneficiaries of this Protestant lace-making influx were Germany and Switzerland. Indeed, Dresden, in Germany, had been a major lace-making centre since the 16th century, and the pulled thread whitework known as Dresden work which evolved during the 17th century was to become popular all over Europe and America in the 18th century.

Few of the English laces matched the best continental products either in quality or quantity, and the wealthy continued to favour the unsurpassed laces of Brussels, Mechlin, Chantilly, Valenciennes and other continental centres. However, one form of needlepoint lace, known

as Hollie point, was peculiarly English. It was used a great deal for insertions in baby clothes in the 17th and 18th centuries, and much of it was made by skilled amateurs. Indeed, cut and drawn whitework was very much part of an accomplished needlewoman's repertoire, and many progressed to lace-making proper. It is not unusual to find needlepoint fillings in 17th and 18th century samplers.

Much later, the 19th century machine-made nets took some of the effort out of lace-making, and a great many ladies included it, along with tatting and crochet, in their 'fancy work'. Amateur lace-making in the late 19th century was widespread – patterns were published in magazines and needlework books – but the quality was generally coarse compared with 18th century work.

Tatting and crochet, which gave lacy effects with less skill and effort, were especially popular during the 19th century. Both have a long history and were practised intermittently in different parts of Europe from the 16th century. Tatting is done with a shuttle, crochet with a hook, and both techniques enjoyed a revival in the 19th century for working collars, flounces, doilies and all kinds of edgings and embellishments.

During this period several professional lace industries were started in Ireland, mainly by philanthropic gentlewomen who attempted to relieve unemployment and poverty among the country people. However, the invention of lace-making by machinery (pioneered at the beginning of the 19th century by the Englishman John Heathcoat) had already debased and cheapened the craft. Demand for the expensive hand-made laces of the continent diminished as soon as it became possible to buy the cheap and showy products of the lace machines. The fine laces which for centuries had been so keenly sought had had their day.

Tapestry

During the Middle Ages, when buildings in northern Europe were cold and draughty, tapestries hung round walls were an invaluable source of insulation as well as decoration. They were among the most valuable and treasured possessions of royalty, nobility and the church (few others could afford them). In the case of a landowner who habitually moved from castle to castle they were taken down and rehung wherever he went.

Tapestries are by definition woven, not worked, and it is a mistake to refer to tent-stitched canvas embroidery (or petit point) as tapestry, however much it might seem to imitate a woven pictorial effect. Technically, tapestries fall into two categories: high warp (or *haute lisse*) woven on a vertical loom and low warp (*basse lisse*) made on a horizontal one. Low-warp tapestries are generally smaller – the method is ideal for objects such as rugs and cushion covers, whereas the large hangings which made the factories of Flanders and France famous were almost all made on high-warp looms. In any assessment of European tapestries,

1 A Gobelins tapestry illustrating the *Marriage of the King*, woven between 1673 and 1680.

2 A mid-15th century Alsatian tapestry from a series depicting the Labours of the Months. This one shows harrowing and sowing.

Flanders must take pride of place. French centres and particularly the Gobelins factory, also rank high, but most of them, like those of other countries, owed much to Flemish expertise.

It was during the 14th and 15th centuries that some of the most important series of hangings were woven, generally for the church or royal patrons. Apart from these large and costly projects, many tapestries depicted biblical stories such as that of Esther and Ahasuerus or David and Bathsheba; history, heraldry, legend, allegory and moral subjects were popular, and so were scenes of hunting and country pursuits. The flower-strewn verdures of what were called *mille-fleur* tapestries are among the most charming survivors of the late medieval period.

The Gobelins factory was set up in Paris in the mid-15th century by a family of famous dyers from Rheims. From the beginning they employed Flemish weavers and the venture was highly successful. After the 17th century, Gobelins excelled even the Brussels factory in technical expertise and fineness of design, and probably through its extensive royal patronage has become the most famous of all tapestry factories. Under Louis XIV the title *Manufacture de la Couronne* was conferred and from about 1690 the factory became crown property.

Among other French tapestry factories were those of Fontainebleau, Beauvais, Fulletin and Aubusson. Beauvais, established in 1664, is

2

famous for its illustrations of La Fontaine's **1**
Fables (early 18th century) and other secular
subjects of great charm and refinement, some of
them designed by Boucher.

There were tapestry establishments in Switzerland (where Basle was the centre of production),
Denmark, Sweden and Russia. In Italy, Flemish
weavers had set up workshops in Ferrara,
Florence, Siena and other cities in the 14th century, but the most famous, the Barbarini factory
in Rome, was not established until 1665.

A royal tapestry factory was set up in Madrid
under Philip V of Spain. At first the output consisted mainly of copies of French and Flemish
tapestries, but later, during the 18th century,
artists such as Goya were commissioned to make
designs and the factory produced some fine and
original work.

In England, there had been tapestry workshops during the medieval period, especially in
London. But England's chief contribution to
tapestry weaving was the high quality wool she
produced. This was not only used in England for
large quantities were exported, especially to
Flanders, to be used in the tapestry workshops
of the continent.

2

From 1557–1614 a certain William Sheldon
produced a unique series of tapestry maps from
his factory in Warwickshire. However, the most
famous English tapestry establishment was the
Mortlake factory, set up under James I with
weavers from Bruges and Brussels. Most of its
early output consisted of copies of Flemish
designs, and the palaces of Windsor, Hampton
Court, Whitehall, Nonesuch and Greenwich
were all hung with Mortlake tapestries. Charles I
continued to patronize the factory: he purchased
the Raphael cartoons and had them copied at
Mortlake with borders designed by Van Dyck.
After the Civil War, the factory became royal
property. Unfortunately, no amount of royal
patronage was proof against the financial difficulties. By the end of the 18th century almost
none of the English factories remained. It was
not until the late 19th century that the art of
tapestry weaving was revived, as part of the arts
and crafts movement. William Morris set up his
Merton workshops in 1881 to carry out his own
designs and those of Rossetti, Burne-Jones,
Maddox-Brown and Walter Crane.

In 1893 a New York businessman set up
America's first tapestry workshop, and it survived until 1912. Others, also in New York, were
in production in the early 20th century.

1 A Mortlake tapestry,
dating from the late 17th
century, showing the month
of September.

2 *Angeli Laudantes* designed
by Edward Burne-Jones in
the 1870s and woven by
Morris and Company.

The Overlord Embroidery will undoubtedly become an 'antique of the future' comparable in workmanship and historical interest with the Bayeux Tapestry. It was commissioned in 1968 to commemorate the invasion of Normandy – Operation Overlord – in World War II.

It consists of 34 panels, each 2.4 × 0.9 metres (8 × 3 ft), totalling 82.9 metres (272 ft) in length. Twenty ladies of the Royal School of Needlework took five years to complete this remarkable monument.

3 Panel 26 shows American troops moving inland and arresting the first prisoners.

4 Detail of panel 30, showing the British and Canadian capture of Caen about a month after D-day.

3

4

Oriental carpets

Milestones in the history of carpets

c.500 B.C.	The Pazyryk rug was placed in a Scythian burial mound in the Gornai Altai ditrict of Siberia. It was discovered in 1947 by R. D. Rudenko.
c.500 A.D.	The 'Spring of Chosroes' carpet was woven of silk, precious stones and gold and silver thread.
13th century	Date attributed to Seljuk rugs found in the mosque of Alaeddin in Konya.
late 14th century	Fragment of Turkish carpet found in Fostat.
1539–42	The Ardebil Carpet was woven with an inscription including the date.
1499–1574	The Safavid period in Persia was the golden age of Persian art when some of the finest Persian carpets were woven.

1 2

1 The Ardebil carpet in the Victoria & Albert Museum. This carpet measures 34 ft 6 in × 17 ft 6 in, and was knotted with approximately 320 knots to the square inch. According to the inscription in the panel at the top of the field which reads: *I have no refuge in the world other than thy threshold, My head has no protection other than this porchway; The work of the Slave of this Holy Place.* Maqsud of Kasham, 946 A.H.
The part of the carpet containing this inscription was knotted in the year 946 of the Arab Hegira, which accords with the Christian date of 1540. This carpet is the result of careful work in using one of the two carpets discovered in the mosque at Ardebil to repair the other. The finished piece was bought by the V & A Museum in 1893 for the sum of £2,500. Today it is priceless.

2 Another dated rug, this time the date is 1314 A.H., which works out at a date just before the turn of the century. This is a Kazak prayer rug from the Caucasus, and is obviously woven by nomads, evidenced by the bad shape and the heavy abrash or change of colour in the field.

3 A rug from the Moghan area of the Caucasus, just above the border with Persia. The hooked and stepped polygons covering the field are typical of this type; note the great variation in the size of the reciprocal trefoils at the side of the field. Second half of the 19th century.

During recent years antique Caucasian rugs have exerted a greater appeal to connoisseurs than was hitherto the case. Prayer rugs or namazliks are not so dominant as they are in the Turkish group, though quite a large number occur from time to time, particularly in Daghestans. In general, Caucasian rugs are very colourful, and therein lies their appeal. All Caucasians are made with a Turkish knot.

Kazak The largest group is undoubtedly the Kazak, wherein there are a number of subdivisions which are generally ignored by most collectors, with the exception of Chelaberds, often called 'Eagle Kazaks', which are really from the Karabagh area and Bordjalous.

Kazaks, in general, are woven from thick lustrous wool with a longer pile than most other rugs, and the texture is sturdy and usually fairly coarse, with knotting varying between 6.5 and 14 sq cm (42 to 90 sq in). Colours are strong, and include green, red, blue, yellow, white and brown, and the drawing of the designs is clear-cut and vigorous. Warp and weft are both of wool; the weft, usually dyed red or brown, crosses two, three or even four times between every two rows of knots.

Patterns are very varied, ranging from extreme simplicity with large areas of solid colour bearing disjointed motifs to several large medal-

one, two or three sunburst patterns that give a wild and untamed effect. Borders are usually in the 'crab' pattern.

Shirvan Equally as numerous as Kazaks are the antique Shirvans, but usually they are very different in styling, design and texture. Knotting varies from 8.75 to 22.25 to the sq cm (56 to 144 sq in) and the rows of knots have a slightly wavy appearance from the back, which is not ridged. Colours are mostly blue, red, ivory, with some yellowish tan and occasionally green, and the designs mostly tend to be a number of angular medallions occupying the centre of the field, with the remainder of the space filled with small unrelated motifs as in the manner of nomad rugs.

There are many other designs to be found in this group however, both in field and border, but by far the commonest border design is the leaf-and-wineglass.

Soumak Currently very popular, but rapidly becoming scarcer, are the flatweave Soumaks, a form of kelim with loose ends of weft threads hanging at the back, and the design on the surface effected in a flat chain stitch, while there are also separate weft threads additional to those employed in creating the design. The field usually contains three or four large diamond-shaped medallions stretching the full width of the field, with flattened octagons in their centres and in the

lions of different colours on a ground filled with small motifs. Borders are small in comparison with the remainder of the rug. The main stripe can vary from the most common 'crab' pattern, to the leaf-and-wineglass, or the reciprocal sloping latch hook, or consist of rows of stylized rosettes.

The so-called 'Eagle Kazaks' have similar wool, but the whole of the field is occupied by

triangular areas remaining at the sides of the medallions. The main colours employed are blue, red, brown, a little yellow and some ivory, and the warp and weft are both of wool.

Daghestan Although less frequently encountered than the Shirvans, the Daghestan rugs are very popular with collectors. They have a short pile, which gives an incisive clarity to the designs, and they are some of the firmest textured rugs in the

1

1 Typical Daghestan prayer rug from the Caucasus. The trellis arrangement of the field containing stylized floral forms is very characteristic, as is the 'running dog' border. The field most usually has the brilliant white ground as this, although other colour grounds are occasionally seen.

Caucasian group. Both prayer rugs and other types of rugs are encountered, the only difference in their treatment being the inclusion of a geometrical *mihrab*.

The field and spandrels are covered with the same design, which is usually a diaper pattern in which the diamond shapes carry a very highly stylized small floral spray, the whole designed in blue, red, ivory, green and yellow on an ivory ground. The main border stripe is usually composed of a series of triangular shapes in contrasting colours.

Knotting varies from coarse, at 8.75 knots, to fine, with 28 knots to the sq cm (56 to 180 sq in). Unlike Shirvans, the rows of knots at the back look straight.

Khila (Baku) At one time these rugs were more often called Baku, but today's opinion comes down on the side of Khila, although they come from the Baku area. They are different from all other Caucasian rugs in colouring and in design. The colour is duller and not so vivid, and consists of dark and light blue, shades of brown, yellow and tan and black. The main design – and the most usual – is a long narrow field carrying two or more rhomboidal medallions delineated by stepped outlines, with the corners of the field matching the medallions. If several medallions are present, they are set on larger rhombs in a

contrasting colour, the intervening half rhombs matching the inner medallions.

The main ornamentation consists of larger boteh or cones which cover the field and are very heavily ornamented and of a strong rectangular form. Knotting is on the coarse side, varying from 6.5 to 15.25 to the sq cm (42 to 99 sq in) and the texture is fairly firm.

Derbend Mostly on the coarse side, with knotting varying between a mere 4.5 and 16.75 to the sq cm (30 and 100 sq in). However, there are few to be found at the finer end of the scale, representing the earlier productions. There are two or three shoots of wool weft between every two rows of knots. Warp is usually wool, though frequently brown goat hair was used. Designs are varied, often with the field occupied by a number of medallions, sometimes filled with small stepped rhombs and similar devices. Usually, there are three border stripes, but more in the older and finer pieces. The main colours are red, blue, brown and ivory, with a little yellow and green.

Chichi These rugs are nearly always in small sizes, and the fields are covered with either horizontal or diagonal rows of small stepped polygons in differing colours. The most distinctive feature, however, is the main border stripe, which consists of alternate rosettes and diagonal bands which have been squared by the addition of stylized trifoliate forms. Colours are rich, and include light and dark blue, red and ivory, with a little yellow, green and brown. Texture is fairly firm, with knotting varying from 8.75 to 18.50 to the sq cm (56 to 120 sq in), the back being flat and not ribbed.

Talish These rugs are always long and narrow, and have an air of character; they are not very common. The most characteristic feature is the main border stripe which is invariably composed of a large rosette alternating with four tiny squared rosettes arranged in a square. Both the rosettes and squares appear in a variety of colours. The field, always long and narrow, is usually blue, often plain, though there might be one or two small rosettes capriciously placed in any position on the field. Very occasionally, the field is covered with eight-pointed stars arranged in a diaper pattern. Texture is rather loose, and knotting coarse, around 16.50 to the sq cm (100 sq in).

Kuba From the Kuba district comes a great variety of designs and styles, and this also includes the border designs. Nevertheless, they are not difficult to place, having silky wool, fine ordered patterning with a rather Persian styling and motifs that are not disjunct, and a general air of sophistication.

Knotting varies from 6.5 to around 18.5 to the sq cm (42 to 120 sq in), with a fairly closed look on the back, with very little of the warps showing, yet the overall texture is rather loose. Patterns may closely follow the Shirvan medallion type or, on the other hand, they may consist of refulgent star shapes arranged in horizontal and diagonal rows, in differing colours, in glowing colours. Again, they might borrow formal-

2

3

2 A typical Perepedil design with the *Wurma* or ram's horn design on a dark blue ground, and a fine example of a 'bracket' or 'chain' border. Quaint animals and stylized flowers fill the spaces of this fine rug from the second half of the 19th century.

3 A Caucasian Shirvan rug with the field occupied with characteristic flattened octagonal medallions with the remainder of the field filled with small disjunct forms. The main border stripe of serrated leaf forms is much used in the Caucasus. Late 19th century.

ized rosettes and other devices from other areas, but arrange them in their own fashion.

Borders often are of the rosette and bracket type, and usually with three border stripes. But there are many other main stripes, a popular one being of alternate diamond-shaped rosettes and four serrated leaves arranged in a quadrangular form. Colours are rich, with medium and dark blue, red, ivory, sable brown, green and yellow.

Lesghi Lesghi rugs are sometimes mistaken for Shirvans, but generally the large eight-pointed medallions occupying the field are flatter than those of Shirvan, and the corners at the diagonals where the straight lines intersect have arrowhead forms. Generally, there are more colours in Lesghi rugs, with red, blue, ivory and green predominating, and some tan and yellow. Texture is firm though the knots may be as few as 5.5 to the sq cm (36 sq in), but they may also range up to around 16.5 (100 sq in).

Gendje These rugs, which often resemble Kazaks, are much more loosely woven, so that by no means have so many survived to become antiques. In the Gendje there may be as many as four to eight shoots of red weft between every two rows of knots and the warps are visible from the back, and may be of wool or goat-hair. There are no designs that are typical, and this also applies to the borders.

Karabagh These rugs are woven in an area adja-

1

1 An extremely characteristic rug from the Fereghan plain, with practically every part of the design conforming to the accepted pattern for this type of rug. The 'turtle' motif of the main stripe of the border is very typical, as are also the cut–off corners of the field, the pole medallion on a shaped field, and the closely spaced version of the Herati which covers the remainder of the field. This is a classic example of Fereghan weaving of the late 19th century.

cent to the Persian border, and the Persian influence is very apparent in the flowing type of design, especially in the borders, which may consist of a wavy vine and floral arrangement. The reds of these rugs are very characteristic, having a marked pinkish tendency not seen in any other Caucasian pieces, while the indigo blues are almost black. Medium and light blues are also used, though somewhat sparingly, and ivory white and yellow. Occasionally there is green colour.

In the field the patterns tend towards the use of medallions, which can be either lightly or heavily ornamented. Knotting tends to be coarse, varying from 6.5 to 16.5 to the sq cm (42 to 100 sq in), while the texture is loose. The warp is wool and is not very apparent from the back of the rug, which has a ribbed appearance. The weft is also of wool, which is sometimes dyed red, and there are typically two shoots between every two rows of knots in these rugs.

Persian Carpets

Although many of the oldest antique carpets and rugs come from Persia, generally speaking there are fewer antiques from this group than there are from Turkey and the Caucasus. There are, however, possibly more fine 'old' pieces to be found than in any other group – and these now command extraordinarily high prices.

Fereghan Within this group there are two main types – in one the field is covered with an all-over pattern, and in the other a pole medallion is set upon a shaped field of plain colour and the corners covered with a closely packed all-over design.

In the first type the most common design is the Herati, so called because it was very common in rugs from Herat. It consists of a central quadrant with a rosette in the centre, from the corners of which palmettes spring. From the sides of the quadrant stalks extend with curved serrated leaves. This pattern is repeated all over the field, so closely set that it almost obscures the ground colour of the carpet. When the Herati pattern is used there are usually small cut-off corners to the field.

Less frequently seen is a repetitive form of the Gul-i-Hinnai pattern – a design based upon the henna plant, with light coloured flowers. There are a few variations from these patterns, but they are rarely encountered.

The most common border design is the well-known 'turtle' style, which is really a palmette with an extension on either side at the top which gives the impression of a turtle with flippers. These are alternatively reversed and joined together by dainty tendrils and vines. Most frequently the borders have an almond green ground which has been attacked by the dye used so that the border is embossed against the green ground. Other borders used are generally based upon a vine and rosette combination.

Colours used are a deep indigo blue and red, with some light blue, green, yellow and ivory. Texture is firm, and knotting varies from coarse with 8.75 knots to the sq cm (56 sq in) to fairly fine with up to 36.25 (234), the knots being Persian. Warp and weft are made of cotton.

Ispahans It is normal to refer to antique carpets from this area as Ispahans, and modern products as Isfahans. Both types demonstrate superb workmanship, the antique types going back to late 16th and early 17th centuries when Isfahan was the newly created capital of Shah Abbas.

The most usual design is, appropriately, the Shah Abbas, which consists of intricate scrolls and arabesques terminating in palmettes. In the very old pieces cloudbands were often introduced. Borders were wide, with large palmettes and other floral and foliate motifs. In the 16th century the motifs were small and the design well balanced, but with time the designs became larger. Usual colours were a red field with dark blue border, though occasionally a blue field turns up with a dark green border. Touches of ivory and yellow were also used. Almost all the pieces from this period are large carpet sizes.

Warps and wefts are mostly cotton, though wool was also used; sometimes cotton and wool were twisted together. The Turkish knot is used, varying from 7.5 to 19.5 knots to the sq cm (48 to 126 sq in). The texture is firm and the back flat.

2 Ispahan rugs in the antique sense are rare, and many of the 16th and 17th century specimens were Indo-Ispahans where the dark blues had a very slight green tendency. Designs usually had the field covered with a tracery of leaves and vines with palmettes, with a medallion and corners of a complementary design as shown in this later piece. Within this set framework it is surprising how much variation could be obtained while still conforming to the overall style.

3 A rare and unique example of a Karabagh rug from the Caucasus with a magnificent main border stripe consisting of rosettes alternating with birds in a number of different colours set against a light ground, the bird forms and rosettes being echoed in the field. The guard stripes carry a Caucasian 'running dog' motif, while the inner border is formed of an s-chain. This rug is the work of nomads as can be gathered from the in-fill of any spare space with disjunct floral forms.

1 and **2** A very characteristic Sehna rug from the Kurdistan area of Persia, with its field covered with rows of boteh, each of which is delineated with a diamond sharp clarity achieved by very fine knotting and extremely close shearing. The narrow border is also typical, and the sides are usually overcast with silk. Between the boteh the spaces are covered with an exquisitely delicate floral tracery which can better be appreciated in the enlarged detail photograph on the right.

3 A truly delightful example of a Qashqai rug woven by the women of that nomadic tribe which roams the southwestern area of Persia. Triple medallion designs are common in this type, with the remainder of the field covered with a profusion of disjunct motifs including highly stylized floral and geometric forms, animals and Trees of Life. Careful examination will reveal that, although the overall pattern appears symmetrical, it is in fact not truly reciprocal in arrangement of detail, and this is most marked in the change of background colours in the corners. The soft flocky wool imparts an almost silken lustre to the rich ruby red and deep indigo blue which characterize these weavings.

Kashan The weavers of Kashan produced an astonishing number of excellent pieces of tight stout weave and superb designing. However, after the 16th and 17th centuries there appear to be no representative pieces until the 19th century.

The later pieces are all well designed with the fields filled with flowing foliate designs in rich ruby reds, shades of blue, green, ivory, yellow, and a characteristic light brown. The outer guard stripe of the border almost invariably consists of a reciprocal trefoil or more rarely a sawtooth pattern, while the secondary guards carry a flower and tendril pattern.

Texture is extremely firm and the Persian knots very fine, varying from 39.75 to 74.5 to the sq cm (256 to 480 sq in) the weave being so tight that the sides often curl under. Warps are usually cotton, and the fine cotton wefts are normally

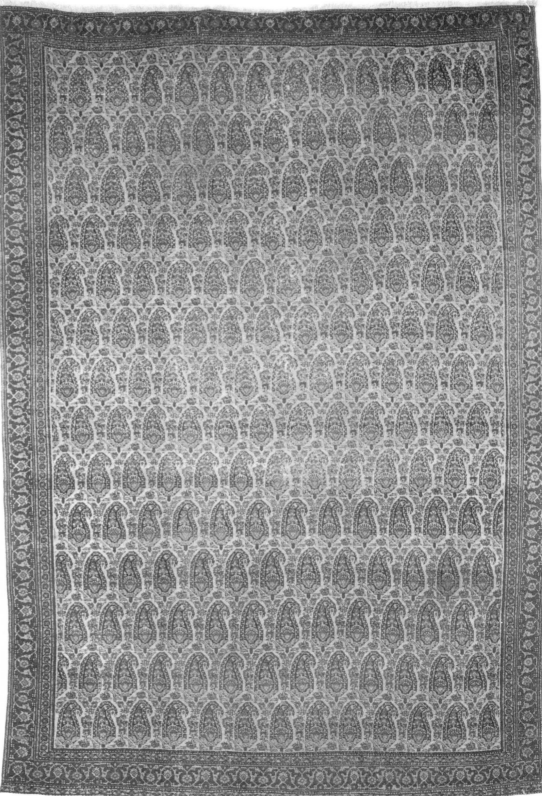

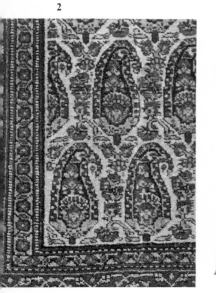

dyed blue giving the back of the rug a charac- 3
teristic blue appearance.

Sehna Most rugs from Kurdistan are stout and
heavy but Sehna produces some of the lightest,
thinnest rugs in all Persia. The workmanship is
superb. Unlike most weavers, those of Sehna
only use one shoot of weft between every two
rows of knots and this shows up on the back
with a quincunx appearance, and also leads to a
very characteristic feel of roughness when the
hand is rubbed over the back of a Sehna rug.

Designs are mostly small all-over diaper patterns, using the *boteh* or cone design, small floral
designs, and the Herati pattern. Some of the
older pieces have a medallion on which a further
smaller medallion is superimposed, both covered
with small repeated motifs. Borders of only three
stripes and occasionally just two are the rule, the
main stripe mostly being of the 'turtle' type on a
yellow ground. Knotting is fine, varying between
20.25 and 74.5 to the sq. cm (130 and 480 sq in),
and is almost invariably in the Turkish knot.
Warps are generally cotton and the overcasting
in wool, but sometimes the warps are of linen or
silk and the overcasting at the sides silk, usually
in a purple shade.

Tabriz This is one of the greatest weaving areas
of Persia and has produced many fine pieces.
This area, like most of Western Persia, used the
Turkish knot, and knotting varies from medium,
at 18.5 to the sq cm (120 sq in), to very fine at
68.25 (740). Many silk rugs and even silk carpets
have been produced here, and these may still be
found.

There are no really typical designs of this area,
for the weavers copied anything, but the workmanship is good. Many of the patterns are of the
medallion and corner type, and the drawing is
good. In both wool and silk products the red has
a typical brick tone which helps to distinguish
this type, the other main colours being blue and
ivory, though a great number of subsidiary
colours are employed.

Heriz Rugs from this area are noted for their
stout construction, the Turkish knotting varying
from a mere 4.5 to the sq cm (30 sq in) up to a top
of 18.5 (120). Designs are extremely geometric,
hard and angular, with no suggestion of softening. All are carried out in light blue, red, yellow,
reddish-brown, green and ivory, and usually a
little black. Both warp and weft is white cotton,
with two shoots between every two rows of
knots, the weft showing at the back of the rug.
Heriz rugs are rather more square than most
Persian carpets.

Kirman Unlike many of the modern products,
antique Kirmans are attractive pieces, beautifully made and designed, with lovely soft colourings, including characteristic rose red and rose
pink. Designs are very varied, covering such
styles as floral designs, medallion and corner,
hunting carpets and figured rugs, all depicted
with charm and delicacy, and with very naturalistic drawing.

The weavers of Kirman used more colours in
their rugs than almost any other type, as many as
15 appearing in one rug. In addition to rose red

and rose pink there may also be green, yellow,
brown, ash grey, ivory and shades of blue. The
Sehna knot is used, with anything from 18.5 to
62 to the sq cm (120 to 400 sq in), giving a very
firm texture. Warps are cotton, while the fine
wefts are usually wool, often dyed blue. The
main border stripe is always floral in character.

Shiraz Rugs from this area were and are made
from a soft flocky wool which is semi-translucent
and imparts a brilliance to the colours that
enrich the appearance of the whole rug. Unfortunately the wool was not very hard wearing, and
antiques from this area are usually well worn.
Most of the pieces that come on the market today
are from the latter half of the 19th century.

Owing mainly to tribal differences, designs

1

vary, for they are the product of nomads, and the motifs are the usual disjointed agglomeration typical of nomads. In the finer qualities the arrangement of the motifs is more regular and also more balanced. Typically there is an extra chequered border at either end of the rug. Sometimes the field design may consist of vertical or diagonal rows of boteh in differing colours. Sides of the rugs are invariably overcast with a two colour effect or in short lengths of different colours. Warps are of wool or of goat hair, and the weft is wool, usually dyed red. Texture is loose. Both Persian and Turkish knotting occurs, according to the sub-tribe producing the rug, and there are from 8.75 to 22.25 knots to the sq cm (56 to 144 sq in).

Joshaghan The Joshaghan area has produced many fine pieces in the past, and the most common design covers the field with small diamond-shaped panels in a diaper pattern, each panel being enlivened with small floral motifs, the main colours being dark indigo blue and red with the addition of green, yellow, brown and ivory.

1 A Basrah Ghiordes prayer rug from Asia Minor from the second half of the 19th century. The shape of the mihrab or arch of the field is typical Ghiordes, and the spandrel ornamentation of the Basrah type. Another characteristic of Ghiordes weavings is the quadrangular arrangement of the stylized floral forms making up the main border and the guard stripes.

There is usually a small diamond-shaped medallion in the centre bearing a similar design to the field, while the corners are cut off with narrow saw-toothed lines. The main border stripe is usually floral, often arranged in a rather quadrangular form.

Knotting varies between 8.75 to 21.75 Turkish knots to the sq cm (56 to 140 sq in). The back is slightly ribbed, and the texture on the firm side. The warp is cotton, and the weft is wool usually of natural colour but sometimes dyed red or brown.

Bidjar These rugs are noted for their stoutness, both in substance and in wearing qualities. They have stout wool warps and the weavers pull the knots so tightly when knotting that one warp thread encircled by the pile is pulled behind the other, doubling the thickness of the back. This gives a fabric feeling as firm as a board, so firm indeed that they should never be folded, only rolled. Wefts, too, are of wool, which is fairly coarse and usually dyed red.

Designs vary, often consisting of a central medallion and corners set on a plain field, or a field covered with a lattice bearing small floral forms. The field may be covered with sprays of roses, well drawn, or may consist of a hotchpotch of flowers, and animal and human forms. Colours are a rosy red, light and dark blue, ivory, yellow, green and brown.

Meshed These carpets mostly have a medallion set in a field covered with floral traceries, but the most characteristic thing about them is the peculiar reds with a slight purple tinge that local dyers produce. There are two types of Meshed: those tied with the Persian knot being known as Farsibaff (which literally means 'Persian knot'), and the finer pieces tied with the Turkish knot and termed Turkbaff, the latter being of far stouter construction and commanding higher prices.

Texture is fairly firm, and the weave is medium, the knotting varying between 15 and 31 to the sq cm (96 and 200 sq in). Apart from the purplish red, there are also blues, green, yellow and ivory.

Turkish Carpets

Among antique rugs, probably the most interesting and colourful group are those made in Turkey – mostly in Asia Minor – in the 17th and early 18th centuries. At that time, the finest of the Turkish products rivalled all but the very best of Persian weavings, and the rugs of Ghiordes, Mudjar, Ladik and Konieh, for example, are still eagerly sought by connoisseurs and collectors, to say nothing of the lovely little Melas rugs which are available in an infinite variety.

Most of the Turkish production was in standard rug sizes, with the exception of the Oushak area, which mostly produced standard carpet sizes, and an occasional Ghiordes. So-called Sparta carpets (a corruption of Isbarta), and the similar but more finely-knotted Sivas, were of a much later period and were more of a commercial product. All Turkish rugs are knotted with the Turkish knot.

Ghiordes The best known of all Turkish weavings, the Ghiordes at its finest is a magnificent rug, rivalling the best in Persia. Examples exist covering several centuries and, even today, pieces from the 17th and 18th centuries still come on to the market. In the namazliks or prayer rugs the arch is very typical in form, rather suggesting a Pathan turban, with flat shoulders rising steeply to a point, from which a lamp is suspended. In later forms, this could also be a vase or basket of flowers. Often, in later pieces, there is a form of pilaster inside the edges of the field, acting as supports for the shoulders of the arch. The remainder of the field is plain, but the spandrels above the *mihrab* or arch are closely covered with tracery or angular foliate forms. There is a great variety of main border stripes, but they are invariably squared off in quadrangular forms, except when, possibly through intermarriage, the main border stripe from nearby Kulah is

adopted (see below).

Knotting varies from coarse 8.75 to the sq cm (56 sq in) to fine 29.75 to the sq cm (192 sq in). The coarser pieces are of a looser texture, with wool or silk warps, though cotton was sometimes used in later pieces. The main colours used include a rich red, dark green, ivory and deep blue.

Kulah The village of Kulah produces a much looser fabric than Ghiordes, and the *mihrab* is the flattest of all the Turkish prayer rugs. The field is almost invariably decorated, usually with vertical rows of flower heads, and the spandrels are covered with small repetitive designs.

Red, blue, a mid-green, ivory and yellow are the main colours used, and there is never any clashing of colours. Texture is loose, with two weft threads between every two rows of knots, the knotting varying between 5.5 and 18.5 to the sq cm (35 and 120 sq in). The border stripe con-

2 This fine 18th century piece has the characteristic low pitched mihrab of the Kulah prayer rug. Mostly the border consists of several narrow stripes bearing tiny floral forms at intervals, but here the weavers have borrowed from the neighbouring Ghiordes weavers by using a quadrangular arrangement of forms which are set into squares by being woven in slightly different colourings, more clearly observed in the top border. The colouring of Kulah rugs is usually rather dull and insipid.

1

1 A classic example of a
Yamout *khatchli ensi* made
by the Yamout tribeswomen
for use as a tent door
hanging, and also as a
prayer rug, hence the term
ensi. The word *khatchli*
means a cross and refers to
the 'cross' in the design
which divides the field into
four. The arch which
denotes that it is a prayer
rug is in the panel above the
field, and in some cases is
almost concealed in the
top border, while in others
there may be from three to
five arches above the field,
although there is no added
significance in the greater
number. The y-shapes in the
quarters of the field are
characteristic of the type,
as also are the bracket forms
in the outer border. It is
also quite usual for the skirt
at the foot of the rug to be
of a different colour from
the rest of the rug, though
this is not an invariable
practice. The serrated
diamond devices which
cover the skirt are again
typical Yamout
ornamentation. These rugs
originate in Russian Central
Asia, to the east of the
Caspian Sea, and the shapes
in the inner border show
some affinity with motifs
which appear in the rugs
of the Shirvan area from
the western shores of the
Caspian.

sists of several narrow stripes about 2.5 cm (1 in) in width in alternate contrasting colours, each bearing minute floral forms at regular intervals.

There are quite a few rugs other than prayer rugs in this category, mostly like a double-ended namazlik, having an identical arch at either end of the field.

Konieh There is a wide variety of design in this group in almost every part. Borders may vary from several narrow stripes to an exceptionally wide main stripe that is rather too wide for the rest of the design. Positioning of the prayer arch or *mihrab* also varies a great deal, and the fields are rarely plain, mostly bearing small stylized floral forms.

The *mihrab* is stepped and often small latch-hooks project from these steps into the spandrel, which is also covered with small designs similar to those of the field. Two threads of red wool wefts cross between each two rows of knots, and

the backs of these rugs are less ribbed in appearance than most Turkish rugs. Knotting is coarse, varying between 4.5 and 12.5 to the sq cm (30 and 80 sq in) and texture is reasonably firm.

Melas Although these rugs are characterized by a soft strawberry red, and the designs have an artless simplicity, they offer the widest scope of design in all the rugs in the Turkish group. The variety of design is almost endless, yet there is rarely any hesitation in ascribing a rug to the right category. Generally, the *mihrab* is charac-teristic in that it is sharply waisted with an angu-lar indentation on either side before the arch ascends at about 45 degrees to meet in the centre. The indentations are often filled, with the excep-tion of a small dividing line, with a triangular piece of the same colour as the field.

Despite this, the rule is broken as often as it is observed. In some namazliks the field may be only a long narrow panel running the centre of the rug with a tiny arch at the top, while the rest of the field may be covered with an assortment of designs or even more, shorter vertical panels.

Rugs other than namazliks are quite common, but the variety of invention in design is bewildering. Knotting is coarse, varying from 4.5 to 14 to the sq cm (30 to 90 sq in) and there are usually four weft threads of fine red wool between every two rows of knots.

Ladik These lovely and colourful rugs may still be found in the auction rooms, though the older pieces are often in bad shape. The *mihrab* generally has a triple arch of which the centre one is higher than the others, while the field is usually a rich red or pale blue. Below the field is a deep panel with a row of reciprocal vandykes from which depend a downward pointing row of stems with leaves ending in what look like pomegranates. These are very characteristic, as are the main border stripe which usually consists of alternate conventionalized rosettes and Rhodian lilies. Colours are mainly red and a lightish blue enlivened by a typical canary yellow, with a certain amount of green and brown. Texture is on the firm side, with from 14 to 24 knots to the sq cm (90 to 156 sq in). The back is ribbed.

Oushak The carpets of Oushak were some of the first oriental carpets to be seen in the West. 2 There are a good number of examples of these weavings from the 16th and 17th centuries, either in designs with large rounded medallions or with star-shaped medallions. There are also 'bird' Oushaks and examples with the Tamerlane motif of three dots superimposed over two tiny wavy bands, both used as repetitive patterns on a white or ivory field. Some prayer rugs are to be found but they are not so numerous as other types. The principal colours are red, blue and green, and the texture is very loose, while knotting is coarse, varying from as little as 2.5 to a top limit of around 11 to each sq cm (16 to 72 sq in). Warp and weft are of wool, the weft being dyed red.

Makri Sometimes referred to as Rhodian. These stoutly woven rugs are knotted from thick, lustrous wool of excellent quality, and 18th and 19th century pieces can be found in superb condition, but they are very rare. Like the rugs of Bergama they are rather squarer in format, but they are distinctive in that the field may be divided into one, two or three vertical panels in strongly contrasting colours, each panel carrying a number of disjunct motifs in bright colours.

Ground colours of the panels are usually red, blue and green in rich depth, with a lot of golden yellow and white. The back is not ribbed, and the knotting is coarse, varying between 5.5 to 12.5 to the sq cm (35 to 80 sq in) giving a fairly loose texture. There is a web at both ends, and usually a flat two, three or four cord selvage in bright mid-blue at the sides.

Mudjar The Mudjar is a rare type that is a joy to find, with borders like tessellated tiles, each tile a different colour from that of its neighbours. Colours include mauve, blue, green, red, pink, yellow and ivory. The arch is steeply stepped with three or four lines in differing colours out-

lining the arch which ends with a vandyke, with disjunct ornaments – often including water jugs – in the spandrels. Above the *mihrab* is a shallow panel carrying a row of vandykes terminating in arrow heads.

Texture is loose and the weave fairly coarse, with from 6.5 to 16.75 knots to the sq cm (42 to 108 sq in). There are two shoots of wool weft between each two rows of knots, the weft being dyed red or brown. Warp is also wool.

Kir-Shehir Like the Mudjar prayer rugs, the *mihrab* is steeply stepped, ending in a vandyke, with the arch delineated by several parallel rows of coloured lines, but there the similarity ends. In the Kir-Shehir, stylized carnations extend into the centre panel from all round the sides, and there are usually carnations projecting into the sides of the field and spandrels, while the panel above the *mihrab* usually carries a cloudband and rosette design. There are two main border stripes characteristic of this type, one of which consists of sprays of flowers arranged in quadrangular form in different colours, while the other consists of quadrangular arrangements of stylized lilies alternating with cypress trees.

2 Little has been said about kelims, but they are very much part of the way of life throughout the East, acting all kinds of roles—wrappings for all manner of things, hangings for the walls of tents, horse covers, floor coverings, prayer mats, and a host of other uses. They are flat woven pieces, with the pattern formed by the warp threads. As colours must turn back on themselves, this imposes restrictions on designs as long straight down lines would result in long gaps appearing in the finished fabric, hence the use of 'fringe' effects to enable down lines to be broken up so as to give stability to the whole.

Ceramics & Glass

Ceramics and glass are commonly linked together because they share one essential feature, namely that they are formed by the conversion of earth into a rigid and permanent material through fire. The discovery of this transformation process is shrouded in myth and legend, but it was certainly known in prehistoric times. As a result, ceramics and glass have both played an important part in man's development as a social animal.

Ceramics is a broad term, encompassing domestic and ornamental pottery and porcelain, architectural materials such as bricks, tiles, refractory and sanitary wares, and technical products, which include insulators, electrical equipment and the ranges of specially developed high temperature ceramics used in the aerospace industry. The interests of the collector are understandably limited to domestic and ornamental ceramics, although there is an increasing awareness of the decorative qualities of wall and floor tiles and similar architectural wares. The term 'glass' also includes a variety of materials. Apart from the obvious domestic and ornamental items that appeal to collectors, there are the materials produced for windows and packaging and an equivalent range of highly specialized technical glass, particularly for the electrical and chemical industries.

The development of domestic and ornamental glass and ceramics has been affected primarily by three factors, the technical, the socio-economic and the artistic. Of these, the first is probably the most important. The making of ceramics and glass, even in their most primitive forms, requires a control of technology. The basic materials, clay, water, sand, have to be collected together and organized into a usable form. The potter has to shape his wares on the wheel, or by coiling, or by modelling and moulding, in such a way that they can withstand handling, decoration and firing. Similarly, the glass maker has to control his molten material precisely, in order to shape it either by blowing or casting. The firing of any ceramic item, even the humble building brick, is a complex process requiring control over temperature, firing time and atmosphere. Subsequent decoration by glazing, cutting, painting or printing, requires an even more advanced technology. It is remarkable that such complex technologies were mastered so early in the development of civilization. It is only necessary to look at Egyptian glass or Chinese porcelain to see how little an advance has been made in the last 1,000 years compared with the advances in almost all other areas of technology.

However, if the basic processes have altered little, there have been many changes in the style and scale of production. These changes have generally been the direct result of advances in technical control over materials and processes. During the 16th and 17th centuries European potters were limited to basic earthenwares and stonewares, with a finite number of methods of decoration. They were aware of the gulf between their products and the imported Chinese porcelains, but were not able to bridge it because they lacked both the technology and the materials. Adequate deposits of the special clays needed for the commercial production of porcelain were not exploited until the 18th century, or rather their significance was not understood until then. Improvements in clay bodies and glazes were often inspired as much by the need to make wares non-porous as by an increasing sophistication in demand.

In the field of glass, the technical changes were less significant because the basic manufacturing principles did not alter. However, the scale of production was radically affected by new machinery and techniques. Changes outside the immediate field were also influential. The ceramic and glass industries were revolutionized by the application of steam power and the related machine tools that accompanied it. New methods of transport such as canals, railways and steamships opened new markets previously inaccessible to manufacturers. Many of these external changes were closely related to changes in social and economic patterns. Increased production was dependent upon the existence of a public able to afford the products. Ceramics and glass could only replace wood and metal for general domestic use when they could be made with sufficient consistency of quality, quantity and price. Changes in table manners and eating habits encouraged the production of wares not previously required. All the equipment designed for use in the drinking of chocolate, coffee and tea could not exist until the drinking of these liquids had become an established social habit. On another level, tableware reflects the wealth and habits of the period that produced it; a 19th century dinner service would be far too large for general use today and would contain a number of items that no longer have any relevance.

Much of the development of European and American ceramics was based on the need to imitate Chinese porcelain, which was imported into Europe in vast quantities until the end of the 18th century. Delftware, creamware, white salt-glazed stoneware and soft paste porcelain were all conceived and marketed as substitutes for Chinese wares, which both reflected the demand for the original and determined the style of the copies. However, Europe did not really develop an adequate substitute until the Chinese export trade stopped completely in the 1790s. The need to satisfy this vast new market rapidly provoked the development of bone china, the best European answer to oriental porcelain in terms of consistency, reliability, cheapness and ease of manufacture. The widespread adoption of bone china in England was also closely related to the development of the china clay deposits in Cornwall.

Collectors of ceramics and glass, today as in the past, tend to concentrate on the artistic aspects of their field, and pay little attention to the technical and economic factors that actually determined the shapes and styles of the objects they collect. It is important to see any item as the product and reflection of its period, but this applies more to ceramics than to any other field of applied arts. Ceramic design is generally wholly derivative, and is based either on revived versions of earlier styles or on reflections of contemporary artistic movements. Even the studio potters, with their blunt rejection of the repetitiveness of industrial design, have done little more than replace the revival of sophisticated

styles with the revival of the primitive. It is important to remember always the sources that have influenced potters and glass makers; such as the influence of metal shapes on tableware design, the uses of woodcuts and engravings as inspiration for both 17th-century slipwares and 18th- and 19th-century transfer-printed wares, the rediscovery of Greek and Roman art in the late 18th century, the impact of ancient Egypt in the early 19th century and again in the 1920s following the opening of Tutankamen's tomb, and the continuing awareness of the desire for oriental styles which simply reflects the dominance by the Far East of the whole field of ceramic production. It is also useful to consider ceramics and glass as adjuncts to architecture and interior design, for they have no real independent existence. Designers of ceramics and glass are therefore frequently at the far end of the chain of inspiration, and are dependent upon the fashions that rule the market place. A producer of tableware or ornaments has to reflect contemporary styles if he wants to stay in business, and so has to concentrate on the development of factory, rather than individual style.

The collector on the other hand tends to be fascinated by the individual, and so pursues a designer, decorator or factory in isolation. As a result he often fails to see the importance of pieces in reflecting a period as a whole. The work of a particular decorator is generally far less important than the reasons for his working in a particular style. After all, the decoration of glass and ceramics is rarely more than an applied skill requiring little or no actual artistic ability. To collect ceramics and glass without a broad understanding of their period is to take them out of context and thus to miss the greater pleasure in seeing them as part of a grand pattern of artistic and stylistic development. To concentrate on who made the piece, rather than why and how, is to misunderstand the whole nature of ceramic design.

The development of ceramics and glass is presented on a chronological basis, to show their dependence upon technical and economic factors. The influence of technology upon style was considerable, and so it is necessary to have a broad understanding of the processes involved. The ceramic section is divided into pottery and porcelain because the two materials have tended to follow independent patterns of development. On the level of style they relate more closely, and reflect the changing artistic movements that swept across Europe from the Middle Ages to the present day.

Ceramics

Milestones in the History of Ceramics

c.1900 B.C.	Egyptian wall-paintings from a tomb at Beni Hasan show a potter's turntable in use.	**1757**	Robert Hancock, started producing the necessary copper-plates for the Worcester porcelain company, enabling them to decorate their porcelain with on-glaze enamel, or underglaze-blue printed designs.
1465–87	During the reign of the Chinese Emperor Ch'eng Hua, the Chinese potter perfected the technique of applying overglaze enamel colours to hard-paste porcelain.	**1759**	Josiah Wedgwood established his own factory at Ivy House, Burslem, Staffordshire.
1575	The production of the first soft-paste porcelain, started in Florence.	**1768**	William Cookworthy started the first production of a hard-paste porcelain in England at Plymouth, Devon.
1710	The Royal Saxon Porcelain Manufactory of Augustus Rex, Elector of Saxony, King of Poland, established at Meissen, near Dresden. The first production of hard-paste porcelain in Europe.	**1772**	Following the discovery of deposits of china-clay (kaolin) at Saint Yrieix, in the Limousin, France, in 1768, a regular production of hard-paste porcelain was started concurrently with soft-paste at the Sèvres factory.
1743	Charles IV, King of Sicily, founded the soft-paste porcelain factory at Capodimonte.	**1780**	English potters started to produce an earthenware called 'Pearlware'. A pale cream-coloured opaque body covered with a bluish-tinted glaze, intended to to imitate porcelain.
1743	The Italian hard-paste porcelain factory at Doccia, near Florence, began to decorate some of their wares with underglaze-blue transfer-prints, probably taken from engraved wood-blocks.	**1800**	Josiah Spode II used china-clay, china-stone and calcined bone, to produce the now popular English ceramic body, bone-china.

There are very few ceramic bodies and techniques associated with the art of the potter which were not originally introduced by Chinese craftsmen, and even with advanced knowledge of science and technology the present-day potter only rarely achieves the perfection seen on the wares produced by the Far Eastern potters of earlier times.

From the late Neolithic period, about 2000 B.C., potters in Northern China were producing fine, boldly shaped jars for tomb furnishing which were usually formed by the 'coiling' technique and decorated with vigorous designs in red and black clay slips on a buff-toned burnished earthenware body. The slip is clay reduced to a liquid batter, and used for making, coating or decorating pottery. Primitive feldspathic glazes were occasionally used during the Chou dynasty (10th–3rd century B.C.) but it was from the early years of the Han dynasty (206 B.C.–A.D. 220) that the low-fired earthenwares were made to serve a more practical purpose by the addition of a lead-silicate glaze, sometimes tinted green or brown with metallic oxides. During these early years higher-fired stonewares were produced with a 'tight-fitting' olive-green feldspathic glaze, often inspired by the form and decoration of contemporary bronzes. These stonewares were improved when finer pottery shapes were made during the Six Dynasties period (A.D. 265–589), and are known as 'Yüeh' wares.

During the T'ang dynasty (A.D. 618–906) many fine achievements were made in China in

all artistic fields, aided primarily by an increase in trade with Central and Western Asia. Ceramic tomb wares still provide the majority of surviving examples of the potters' art; and these may well be inferior to those made for court use, which have only rarely survived. It was during these years that the popular yellow-and-green toned glazes were so widely used; referred to today as 'egg and spinach'.

It has long been considered that it was during the late years of the T'ang dynasty that the Chinese potter made his greatest discovery – a

1 It was during the Han Dynasty (106 B.C.–A.D. 220) that considerable use was made of a lead-silicate glaze. This cylindrical jar is one of two types made for tomb-furnishing and is of rather poor quality pottery. The form is also seen in bronzes of the same period and is called a *lien*. The example shown does not have a lid but some similar jars have a cover moulded with a group of hills, intended to represent the Mountains (or Islands) of the Blest, which feature in the mythology concerning Taoism.

These 'hill-jars' or 'hill-censers' are often supported on three feet moulded in the form of bears. The lion mask and ring is also copied from the bronze versions.

method of producing a white, translucent body, referred to today as a hard-paste porcelain. This was made by fusing China-clay (kaolin) and China-stone (petuntse), at a temperature of about 1,350°C/2,462°F. China-stone was used to produce a tight-fitting clear glaze, which could be fired together with the body.

Porcelain of this type was considered to have been made by the 9th century, but the National Palace Museum in Taiwan now claim that true porcelain was being made in China as early as the Wei and Tsin states (A.D. 220–420) and that recently more of these early wares have been discovered, although the earliest porcelains exhibited in the museum are of the Northern Sung dynasty (A.D. 960–c.1127). These include the fine imperial wares of the *Ting, Ju, Kuan, Ko,* and *Chün* kilns. The most beautiful wares made during the Sung dynasty (A.D. 960–1279) rely primarily upon their shape and fine glazes rather than painted or applied decoration, styles which were to become so popular during the Ming dynasty.

Equally worthy of note are the heavily potted wares with moulded or carved decoration under a greyish-green celadon glaze, made during the Yüan dynasty (A.D. 1279–1368). During this time the country was under the power of the Mongols, following the successful onslaught of Kublai Khan.

It was some time during the early 14th century that the Chinese potter began to use the metallic oxide of cobalt as an underglaze-blue decoration, a technique and colour that was later to be used

2 The hard-paste porcelain dish, shown on the right, was made in China during the early years of the 15th century and shows a much more formal style of blue-and white decoration than that seen on the wares of the previous century.

The plate illustrated on the left was made at Isnik (Western Anatolia), and is of a type made from the second quarter of the 16th century. They are of a white earthenware decorated here in blue, under a clear thin glaze.

At one time they were wrongly attributed to the Isle of Rhodes.

3 Among the most admired of all Chinese porcelains are the celadon glazed vessels from the kilns of Lung-ch'üan, in the Chekiang province. They are of the Southern Sung period. This example is from the 14th century.

The Lung-ch'üan are famous for their unique translucent glazes of light bluish-green tones.

These baluster-shaped vases with short, narrow necks are known today as *mei p'ing.*

1 From the late 17th century it became very fashionable for Europeans to collect large amounts of Chinese porcelain. These collections often included complete services decorated with the family coat-of-arms. The large dish seen here was made in about 1722 for Thomas, created Lord Trevor of Bromham in 1711.

The arms are those of Trevor impaling Weldon; he married Anne, daughter of Robert Weldon.

2 Among the most famous of all the porcelain in the Sir Percival David Collection is this fine vase painted in underglaze-blue. It is one of a pair, 25 inches (63 cm) high and they are the only known pieces of fully documented blue-and-white Chinese porcelain. They are dated 1351.

Each vase bears a long inscription on the neck, revealing that, in 1351, they were given, together with an incense burner to a temple of a minor deity. Hu-Chingi. It is also recorded that the donor, Chang Wên-chin, lived in a town only 70 miles away from Ching-tê Chên.

It is rather rare for a mark or inscription to give the actual year of manufacture and is usually only to be seen on wares made for presentation to a temple.

throughout Europe up to the present day. This new form of decoration continued into the succeeding Ming dynasty (A.D. 1368–1644) with very little change, and the porcelain factories in the city of Ching-tê-chên multiplied and flourished, producing wares not only for the court but also for the Near East. Many examples can be seen today in the Topkapi Sarayi Palace in Istanbul.

From the time of the reign of the Ming Emperor Hsüan Tê (A.D. 1426–35) it became a common practice to add a 'reign-mark' in underglaze-blue. This form of mark must not necessarily be accepted as indicating the date of the piece; many marks of earlier periods were often added, some to deliberately confuse, but others merely as a mark of veneration, indicating similarity to wares made in outstanding periods in the history of Chinese porcelain.

An exciting new range of enamel colours, fused to the surface of the glaze, were first successfully used during the reign of the Emperor Chêng Hua (A.D. 1465–87). An underglaze-blue outline was sometimes used together with delicate translucent colours, a style referred to as *tou-ts'ai* (contrasted colour).

Although trading with Europe began as early as the mid-16th century, it was not until the late years of the Ming dynasty that blue-and-white porcelain was imported by the Dutch in quantity. It was during the Ch'ing dynasty that Emperor K'ang Hsi (A.D. 1662–1722) recognized the value of porcelain as an export. During his reign facilities were made available to other European countries to trade through the port of Canton. This prolific trade in porcelain and other commodities continued unabated during the following reigns of the Emperors Yung Chêng (A.D. 1723–35) and Ch'ien Lung (A.D. 1736–95). Genuine reign-marks are rarely to be found on wares made during the reign of K'ang Hsi, whereas a four-character mark, instead of the customary six, is invariably an indication of 19th century, or even later, work.

Many French terms are today used by writers, collectors and dealers to indicate various enamel palettes, such as *famille verte* (green family) in which tones of green tend to dominate the reds, yellow, purple, black and blues. These colours were frequently applied direct on to the body of the ware, rather than upon the glaze; the technique is referred to as 'enamel on the biscuit'. The colours of the *famille noire* (black family) include a thick brownish-black enamel, usually overpainted with translucent green, a palette also usually applied 'on the biscuit'.

From about 1720 the Chinese made use of the European rose-pink enamel, giving the further term *famille rose*. Opaque white was used with chloride-of-gold to achieve tones ranging from pale pink to deep crimson.

Today, some of the most popular Chinese wares with the more modest collector are those specially made during the 18th century and decorated to the customer's requirements with armorial arms or European scenes. Wares of this type continued to be made into the 19th century,

often for the American market. The erroneous term 'Chinese Lowestoft' is now rarely heard for these 'Chinese Export Porcelains'.

Korea

Excavations have revealed that Korean potters were producing grey stoneware vessels and figures for burial purposes during the Silla kingdom (*c*.57 B.C.–A.D. 935), but it was in the reigns of the Koryō kings (A.D. 918–1392) that many fine porcellanous stonewares were produced, with celadon glazes, including the then unique technique of inlaying black and white clays into the grey toned clay body, the whole being covered with celadon glaze.

The coarser wares of the Yi dynasty (1392–1910) showed a bold originality, much admired by todays studio potters. Iron-brown and copper-reds were often applied to sturdy porcelain forms, and these sometimes acquired a greater charm due to lack of temperature control and the partial burning away of colours.

Japan

Although many original pottery forms were produced in Japan as early as the 2nd millenium B.C., it is the later red-clay *haniwa* burial figures of about A.D. 300–600 which present-day collectors of Far Eastern ceramics find entrancing. Their figures of humans, animals or buildings

3 The porcelain made during the reign of the Emperor Wan Li (1573–1619) tends to be of a poorer quality clay than used during the previous reign of Chia Ching. The under-glaze blue decoration on this garden seat includes a finely painted dragon, symbolic of the Emperor.

It was during the reign of Wan Li that so many wares were made for export to Europe via the vessels of the Portuguese, who were trading from 1514.

only those considered aesthetically suitable for such a dignified ceremony. Certain areas and potters are today recognized as being outstanding for the creation of these essential wares, where perfection was not necessarily a requirement. The province of Bizen produced wares of heavy, coarse brownish-red stoneware during the 17th century. The similar coarse and partially glazed stonewares of Iga and Shigaraki were also in demand.

Wares of this type are not always readily accepted by today's European ceramic collectors as having any aesthetic appeal, whereas the finer brown-glazed stonewares made in the Satsuma province during the 17th and 18th centuries can

were placed upon the large burial mound, showing at times a distinct resemblance to those made by primitive tribes of Africa.

The growing popularity of the 'Tea Ceremony' (*chanoyu*) gradually changed from an aid to meditation to a cultured social habit, and by the 16th century notable 'tea-masters' were in need of the various utensils involved. No ordinary table-wares would suffice, they demanded

4 The Korean potters had been making hard grey stonewares for burial purposes from about 57 B.C., but it was in the Koryo period (918–1392) that so many fine wares were made from a porcellanous stone-ware with black and white clay inlaid designs in under a celadon glaze.

more readily be appreciated as fine examples of the Japanese potter's art. Perhaps the best known of all Japanese tea-wares are those of low-fired earthenware, known as 'Raku', a form of ware made by a generation of potters dating back to the early 16th century. Especially beautiful are the hand-moulded forms with soft lacquer-like glazes in black, red or yellow.

It was only during the latter part of the 19th

1 This fine large dish dates from the second half of the 16th century, a class which at one time was thought to have been made on the island of Rhodes, but now attributed to the potters of Isnik, in Western Anatolia. The body is of a low-fired, coarse grained, siliceous type, upon which the red, green and blue colours are applied under a fine transparent glaze. Wares of this type were copied a great deal during the 19th century, by such potters as Cantagalli of Florence.

2 Very few Islamic wares have survived from the early 13th century to the present day in such fine condition as those found in about 1940 at the site of the medieval town of Gurgan, known today as Awdan-Tepe, near Gunbad-i Qabus.

Many examples, such as this fine Persian ewer, painted in brownish lustre were seemingly buried by the owners at the time of the Mongol raid in 1221, but the town and the inhabitants were destroyed and slain. It is suggested that some of the lustre wares found were made in nearby Ravy, Kashan or Sava.

3 It was not until the early years of the 17th century that potters in Japan began to make a hard-paste porcelain from the clays found at Arita. This large jar is painted in a range of enamel colours referred to as Kakiemon, a style attributed to a family of Japanese potters named Sakaida, but given the nickname of Kizaiemon 'Kakiemon' after making an ornament in the form of a persimmon (*kaki*) for the Lord of Nabeshima. This jar dates from about 1670.

century that Western scholars began seriously to seek knowledge of the comparatively short history of Japanese porcelain. There appears to be little doubt that porcelain similar to that produced in neighbouring China for so many centuries was not made in quantity until about 1620. It was made in a town now known as Arita, which is where the necessary deposits of clay were first located; it is still a source of ceramic materials today.

During the last decade documents have come to light confirming the name of Ri Sampei as the Korean potter responsible for the beginnings of porcelain manufacture in Japan. He worked at Tangudani (The Valley of the Long-nosed Goblins), near Arita, in the province of Hizen.

The earliest Japanese porcelain had much in common with contemporary Korean wares, decorated in underglaze-blue or covered with a celadon glaze, occasionally left in the white. The time was ripe in Japan for the creation of fine porcelains, not only to meet the demands of the local lords, but also to provide wares for the Dutch East India Company. During the troubled times in China in the mid-17th century, this

company for trade relied primarily on the porcelains of Japan, though these were very costly in comparison with the wares of China.

It was during the second half of the 17th century that the potter Sakaida 'Kakiemon' introduced a distinctive style of polychrome enamel decoration, which was later imitated by many major European factories.

In the late 17th and 18th centuries Europe became well acquainted with the rather cruder Japanese porcelains, decorated in underglaze-blue and iron-red enamel with gold. Most of these porcelains were erroneously termed 'Imari' due to such wares being shipped from the seaport of that name when en route to Europe by way of Nagasaki. Many very poor examples of these so-called 'Imari' wares only date from about 1860, when Japan began to flood Europe with their exports.

Islam

Collectors of early Islamic pottery are few. Those decorative wares which are today available have in almost every instance been reconstructed from fragments, often recovered from the sites of early rubbish tips. There have been rare finds of pots buried for safety because of fear from invaders, remaining unclaimed until recent years. Fragments of Chinese imported wares, together with local wares, were excavated on the site of the Mesopotamian city of Samarra.

The Islamic potter was soon to create more original styles of decoration, and although unable to locate the materials essential for the manufacture of porcelain, their fine earthenwares provided ideal grounds for beautifully applied designs in various coloured clay slips and metallic oxides, including lustre.

The technique introduced by the Mesopotamian potter in the late 9th century which was to have such influence in Europe, was the application of a glaze made both white and opaque by the addition of tin-oxide, providing a white porcellanous surface, suitable to receive the limited range of colours offered by the metallic oxides known at that time. Colourful wares in this new style were created in the form of Chinese T'ang period pottery and Islamic metalwork.

The skill of these same Near Eastern potters

being used by the Mesopotamian potter at a much earlier date, during the 9th century. The Chinese are known to have obtained much of the cobalt used during the Ming dynasty from Iran.

Many of the Persian wares made during the 17th century in the style of Ming blue-and-white porcelains were used to fulfil orders placed by Dutch traders, who were having difficulty trading with China during their years of internal strife. Wares of this type were still being made during the 19th century.

4 Among the many fine examples of Turkish pottery made at Isnik are the tiles, which have survived to this day as wall decorations in many Turkish mosques and palaces.

The tile shown is painted in blue, turquoise and green and dates from about 1520–50. The painting and body is the same as that on the slightly later dish shown opposite.

By the middle of the 17th century, there was a great decline in both the quality and quantity of such wares.

4

to achieve a beautiful 'mother-of-pearl' lustre in a wide range of metallic tones can still be seen today on many surviving wall-tiles in mosques and palaces, painted in a wide variety of geometrical, human or animal forms, the latter often showing a Picasso-like quality in the simplicity of line.

Blue-and-white wares are usually thought to have originated in China, where porcelain was being decorated with designs in underglaze-blue from about A.D. 1300, but this same cobalt was

Until comparatively recently the term 'Rhodian' was wrongly applied to a class of pottery made in Turkey from the 15th century at Isnik in Western Anatolia. These same wares are often wrongly classed as 'tin-glazed'; they are actually made from a rather low-fired white siliceous body, upon which the high-temperature metallic oxides are painted under a thin transparent glaze. The earliest class, decorated with flowing arabesques and flowers in cobalt blue, date from the last quarter of the 15th century.

The later and more prolific group was made from the mid-16th century until the start of the 18th century. These examples usually show beautiful naturalistically painted flowers.

1

Among the later classes of ware more likely to be encountered by collectors are 18th and 19th century earthenwares made in Kütahya, where potters catered primarily for Armenian and other Christian groups in the Ottoman Empire. Kütahya potters produced a fine white earthenware, painted in a variety of high-temperature blues, greens and yellows, under a clear glaze, made in forms which often showed a relationship to more familiar European table-wares.

A type of peasant-pottery which often baffles the new collector, is that made during the 18th and 19th centuries in Chanak Kale, in the Dardenelles. The smaller ewers in the form of animals (like cow-creamers) have at times been mistaken for the Astbury-Whieldon type, made in Staffordshire during the mid-18th century. Larger bulbous bodied jugs, or pitchers, with animal-like pourers and rope-handles are more easily recognized and appear to have been exported to many areas.

It was not until the 19th century that two unsuccessful attempts were made in Istanbul to produce a white translucent porcelain. The wares were of a poor quality and could not compete in any way with the exports of the Far East or the prolific and cheap English earthenwares, which were being exported in great quantity.

Spain

The early influence of the Near Eastern potters was first seen in Europe during the occupation of the southern regions of Spain by the Moors. As early as 1154 Arabic writers were telling of the fine 'gold-coloured pottery' which even at that early date was being exported to many neighbouring countries. By the early 14th century lustrewares from Malaga were reaching as far afield as England.

These early Hispano-Moresque wares showed clearly in their decoration the influence of pottery formerly made at such centres as Rayy and Kashan in Persia, and Raqqa in Syria, but in form the Spanish wares were generally more robust in every respect. Many of the pieces were decorated in both blue and 'gold' lustre, the blue being fired at the same time as the rather poor quality white tin-glaze. After firing, the fine thin film of silver or copper oxides to form the lustre were applied, then subjected to a final firing in a low-temperature reduction kiln.

Knowledge of the so-called 'Malaga work' was soon to spread to neighbouring areas, including Granada and Manises, near Valencia. One of the best known and oft-illustrated example of Manises workmanship is the fine large conical bowl in the Victoria and Albert Museum, London, decorated with a stylized Portuguese sailing ship, seemingly riding upon the backs of four large fish. It is interesting to note that the practice of painting upon the entire ground with what sometimes appears to be quite irrelevant patterns, is a device that was continued into the 17th century by the English Staffordshire potters when decorating their 'slip-trailed' dishes.

Hispano-Moresque table-wares were very popular with some of the great Italian families, whose coat-of-arms they often bore, usually upon a tediously painted background of small leaves and flowers, sometimes within a gadrooned pattern.

One of the most common shapes was the cylindrical drug-jar, with a narrow 'waist', usually with an out-turned lip to retain a cord to hold a parchment-type cover; the so-called *albarello*. The form originated in the Near East and was later made by almost every European country engaged in the manufacture of tin-glazed wares for the use of the apothecary.

In 1492 the Moors were finally expelled from Spain by Ferdinand and Isabella, but the production of Hispano-Moresque type pottery was to continue in southern Spain to the present day, when the wares are produced for the tourist trade. By 1500 the demand was for lighter and more practical table-wares, and this resulted in the technique of press-moulding being introduced. This made possible the production of shapes previously made only by silversmiths, including ewers, goblets and salvers.

The middle of the 15th century saw Seville as the centre for an interesting ceramic technique which again originated in the Near East. Coloured tin-glazes were kept from intermingling by first incising the design into the prepared clay form, the outline was then filled with a preparation of manganese and grease which acted as a barrier between the colours, a procedure known as *cuerda-seca* (dry-cord). During the first half of the 16th century this same technique was used for the decoration of wall tiles.

Some excellent tin-glazed earthenwares were produced at Alcora from about 1727. Decorative plaques and tablewares were painted in high-temperature colours, often after the designs of Jean Bérain. Similar designs were later used at the French factory of Moustiers, by Joseph Olerys, who was a painter at both factories.

2

3

3 The maiolica dish depicting the Triumph of Aloyone, is dated 1533 and signed by the Urbino painter, Francesco Xanto Avelli da Rovigo. Many paintings by this painter can be traced to copies or adaptations of engravings by such artists as Raphael, Baccio Bandinelli and Il Rosso. His palette usually included a predominating yellow and reddish-toned orange and his figures invariably looked a little plump. He was trained in the workshops of Ferrara and Faenza. His signatures, usually in full, together with an indication of the scene depicted are a great help to the student.

2 Some of the finest painting to be seen on Italian maiolica can be attributed to the painter Nicola Pellipario, a native of Casteldurante, where he painted the dish shown in about 1525. The name 'Ramazotta' is thought to be either Armaciotto Ramazzoti or Melchiorre Ramazzotto, the Bolognese *condottieri* who served respectively under Emperor Charles V and with the Papal Forces in the 16th century.

From the last quarter of the 18th century fine sculptured figures were produced at Alcora, which might be mistaken for French or Italian pieces.

Italy

The earliest forms of Italian tin-glazed earthenware, or *maiolica*, which date from the 11th–12th centuries, were very primitive, painted primarily in brown, yellow and green on a poor quality white ground. These rare examples, the result of excavations as far apart as Sicily and central North Italy, are hardly likely to be encountered by the average collector.

Italian maiolica was at the peak of production from the late years of the 15th century until the middle of the 16th century. Italy had already established a superiority over the Western world in the art of fresco and *tempera* painting, an art confined primarily to the adornment of churches. The humble potter was soon to treat his pottery as an artist did a canvas, introducing forms which were to offer wide scope to his brush and palette. Indeed, it has been acknowledged that the colourful painted maiolica gave a much truer record of the art of the period than many better known Italian paintings, which over the centuries had suffered damage and been subjected to considerable restoration.

From about 1450 Florence had become a major centre of the pottery industry, producing fine bold forms decorated in a rich palette, sometimes referred to as 'severe', due to their similarity to metal shapes. A much more common class of ware being made in Florence at this time was again being made for the apothecary. The large drug-pots decorated in a thickly applied dark blue with a purple outline are often referred to as 'oak-leaf' jars, due to their having painted backgrounds of highly stylized leaves, somewhat similar to those of the oak. The broad strap-like handles to these larger drug-jars often displayed

the badge of the hospital for which they were made.

The last quarter of the 15th century saw Faenza as the major centre for the manufacture of Italian maiolica, having in turn great influence upon the productions of such other areas of distribution as Siena and Deruta. The painting on the early Faenza wares was usually very distinctive, consisting of strong deep blues, purples, drab orange, with bright yellows and greens. The occasional use of heraldic arms or dated signatures of painters sometimes enables a precise date to be given, such as on the service made for Matthias Corvinus, King of Hungary, whose arms are coupled with those of Beatrice of Naples, his bride of 1476. Workshops can only rarely be dated by a recognized mark, such as was used at the Casa Pirota of the Pirotti family.

Some of the most beautiful painted maiolica was made at the Cafaggioli pottery near Florence, a workshop catering exclusively for the needs of the household of Pierfrancesco de 'Medici, a member of a younger branch of the family. Similar fine painting in the so-called *istoriato* style is seen on the wares produced at Casteldurante, in the Duchy of Urbino, painted in many instances by Nicola Pellipario, whose signature on wares made at other centres indicates his nomadic travels.

Two further centres of note are Deruta and Gubbio. The Gubbio workshops of Giorgio Andreoli specialized in the application of a brilliant ruby-coloured lustre. This factory remained active in the family until 1576. Deruta, in Umbria, started to produce wares with a brassy-yellow lustre from about 1500, but the fine quality rapidly deteriorated from about 1530. From the late years of the 19th century, the lustres of Deruta have been imitated, in a poor manner, by Cantagalli of Florence, who uses a broadly painted cockerel in blue as his mark.

One of the most imitated styles of Italian maiolica consists of arabesque figures on a white ground. Wares of this type were at one time referred to by collectors as 'Raphael wares', due to their similarity to the Raphael paintings in the Loggie of the Vatican. The finest examples in this much-copied fashion were produced originally in the workshop of Orazio Fontana in about 1565.

It was during the middle years of the 16th century that Italian potters appear to have become increasingly acquainted with Chinese porcelain, the result being to leave the thick white tin-glaze with little or no decoration whatever, a form of ware (*bianchi*) which quickly found favour abroad.

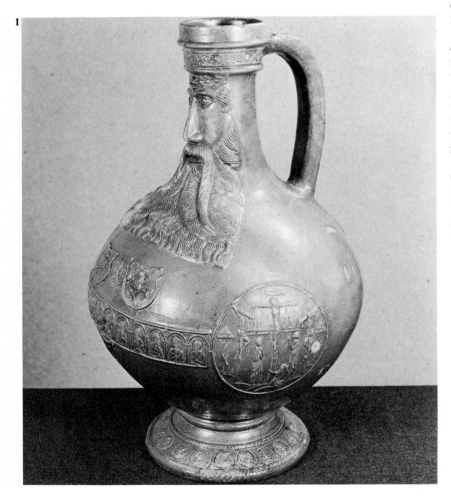

1 Salt-glaze stoneware has been consistently manufactured in Germany since the late 16th century. Early examples do not usually bear a recognized factory mark. This jug, which is 19½ inches high, was made about 1575.

The manufacture of tin-glazed wares were to continue in Italy during the 17th century with many new innovations and further centres of distribution. The Montelupo workshops of Tuscany decorated their wares with coarsely painted figures of soldiers and other characters in contemporary costume. Sicily was no longer to rely on wares made elsewhere. Palermo and other centres began to produce good quality examples inspired by their 16th century imports. The Gentile and Grue families of Castelli introduced new styles of landscape painting in delicate tones of high-temperature colours which were to inspire other potters throughout Italy, well into the 18th century.

Along the northern Ligurian shores of Italy further prolific centres developed during the 17th century, with Genoa as a major centre, as it remains to this day. Their familiarity with Chinese blue and white porcelain is apparent in their preference for decorating solely in blue.

Tin-glazed wares in the new Rococo styles were made at many Italian workshops, nearly all decorated in the usual range of high-temperature colours until the second half of the 18th century. Then, in common with other European countries, the low-fired enamels were fused to the previously fired glaze, which was primarily to counter the new threat of popular porcelain to their trade. Faenza, Doccia, Savona and Naples were all engaged in the manufacture of wares decorated in this new colourful fashion, which in fact had a comparatively short life.

The popularity of English cream-coloured earthenware was soon to affect the demand for tin-glazed wares throughout the Continent, it was a question of the Continental potters either going out of business or taking up the manufacture of comparable wares. During the 19th century some extremely good quality creamwares were made in Italy at Le Nove and Naples, much in the styles of the Leeds Pottery.

Germany

Despite the popularity of tin-glazed earthenware, the use of a clear lead-glaze over the natural coloured clay bodies was to continue throughout Europe and had by the 16th century reached a very high standard. But wares of this type were to take second place in Germany to salt-glazed stoneware, a development which took place towards the end of the 14th century.

Stoneware has all the advantages of a hard-paste porcelain, merely lacking the colour and the quality of translucency. Due to the high content of silicic acid, the material vitrifies at a high temperature and although a glaze is not essential, the appearance and texture were improved by throwing common salt into the kiln at the peak firing-temperature. The resultant close fitting glaze was often coloured an attractive brown by the previous application of a clay slip rich in iron.

The earliest of these wares were probably made at Siegburg, in the Rhineland, where the tall slender jugs, known as *Jacobakennen* were made as early as 1400. Wares from the 16th century can sometimes be identified by the initials or signatures of such well known Siegburg potters as Knütgen, Symons, Flack or Oem, all of whom were engaged in producing a wide variety of well designed vessels, including the tall cone-like tankards (*Schnellen*), or the long-spouted ewers (*Schnabelkanne*), wares usually decorated with moulded or carved relief decoration. Examples of these stonewares are sometimes seen with English silver-mounts.

A form of Cologne wares which appear to have been exported to England in quantity from the 16th century are the rotund bottles, varying in size, with a bearded mask applied in high relief upon the neck. These are the so-called 'Bellarmine' (*Bartsmannskrug*), and similar wares were made by the English potter John Dwight of Fulham from about 1672.

The most colourful of all German stonewares are the early 17th century tankards made at Kreussen, they are of a dark-brown salt-glaze, decorated with brightly painted enamel figures of the Apostles, the Planets, the Electors of the Empire, or hunting-scenes, the decoration has a great deal in common with that seen on the contemporary glass made in both Germany and Bohemia. A further form peculiar to the Kreussen potters is a square or octagonal flask with a metal screw-stopper (*Schraubflashen*). In the latter part of the 17th century Freiberg, in Saxony, was producing a class of stoneware

of the 16th century by the German stove-maker Hafner, very little use appears to have been made of tin-glaze and it was early in the 17th century before Hamburg became well-known as a faience centre, specializing in blue-painted jugs decorated with the heraldic arms of well-known local families. Their dishes were invariably painted in imitation of Chinese blue-and-white porcelain of the Wan Li period (1573–1619).

By the third quarter of the 17th century faience was being made in both Hanau and Frankfurt of a quality to rival the Delftware of Holland, both often using an additional clear lead-glaze to achieve a brilliance akin to that of porcelain. Hanau and Frankfurt faience was sometimes

2

2 It was towards the end of the 14th century when German potters started to produce fine salt-glazed stonewares. The production of any stoneware calls for a clay which is rich in silicic acid and when fired at a high temperature, forms a very hard and non-porous body, which does not necessarily require a glaze for practical purposes. The advantage of a salt-glaze is that the glaze can be fired together with the body and the texture of the ware is greatly improved.

Common salt is thrown into the kiln at the peak firing temperature. The soda then combines with the silica and alumina in the clay, providing a thin, colourless glaze, which at times justifies the term 'an orange-peel' textured glaze. The technique was probably first discovered in Hessen.

The salt-glazed stoneware jug illustrated was made in Siegburg during the 15th century and is known as a *Jakobakanne*. They are always very slender and can often be seen in use in contemporary paintings.

decorated with hand-carved patterns, sometimes picked out with black, white, red or blue enamel colours, often geometrically precise to a degree of becoming dull.

The manufacture of salt-glazed stoneware has continued in Germany to the present time, but usually confined to those made from a grey-bodied clay, decorated with a very bright high-temperature blue. Early German stonewares did not normally bear a recognized factory-mark and collectors should note that the mark of an impressed jug within a triangle, denotes the work of S. M. Gerz I, who only started making such pieces in 1857.

Apart from the tiles made from the beginning

used by well-known outside decorators (Hausmaler) as a ground for fine enamel painting. From the mid-17th century until at least the second quarter of the 18th century, the work of fine painters such as Schaper, Faber, Rössler, Helmhack, Heel and Schmidt, may often be recognized.

During the 18th century some very beautiful Rococo-fashioned faience was produced at Stockelsdorff, Schleswig-Holstein. Much of the fine painting was of a quality usually seen only on porcelain and generally attributed to Abraham Leihamer, who worked about 1773. The collector should also be aware of the colourful class of peasant-ware faience, boldly painted in

1 From the early 17th century tin-glazed earthenware (*fayence*) was being made at Kreussen, often in the form of the earlier stonware.

At about the same period the potters of Hamburg were also producing a range of tin-glazed vessels, often decorated with a coat-of-arms.

From the early 1660s a wide variety of wares and patterns were being made at Hanau, but the finest wares of this period are those made from 1666 at Frankfurt; a manufacture which appears to have catered for some of the wealthier families in the city.

Due to the influence of Chinese porcelain, the majority of Frankfurt fayence was decorated only in high-temperature blue and was often given a second, clear lead-glaze to acquire a porcellanous brilliance. The pattern on the dish shown owes a great deal to the decorations seen on the porcelains of the Wan Li period.

high-temperature colours at Kellinghusen in about 1830.

The Netherlands

There appears to be good evidence that Italian-type maiolica was being produced in Bruges during the 15th century, but no examples of this work appear to have survived or can be clearly identified. By the beginning of the 16th century there is ample proof that Italian potters were well established in Antwerp, a centre which was to become the 'nursery' for potters who were to take the craft to many other European areas.

It is very difficult for anyone other than the specialist to identify the rare Netherlandish wares made in Italian styles. The colours often appear harsher and the painting cruder – this is certainly so with the Antwerp copies of the Urbino 'grotesques' painted on a white ground. By the end of the 16th century Antwerp had ceased to be a pottery centre of any importance, but knowledge of the technique survived, resulting in the city of Delft becoming one of the most prolific centres for the manufacture of the so-called 'Delftware' for a minimum of at least one hundred years.

It was not until 1609 that Holland, together with six other provinces of the Northern Netherlands, first became independent of Flanders and the Duchy of Burgundy. This date roughly coincides with the period when the country first became acquainted with vast quantities of Chinese hard-paste porcelain, which was being imported by vessels of the Dutch East India Company. These were the wares which were going to inspire the Dutch potters in their endeavours to create similar wares in their tin-

glazed earthenware. Their pottery became finer. They endeavoured to completely cover all surfaces with a fine white glaze, and their cobalt blue painting was finely applied in the Wan Li porcelain style. Usually, a second clear glaze was applied, at a separate firing, over the tin and decoration, to impart a porcellanous brilliance.

Delft was ideally situated as a trading centre for this new industry. Waterways were readily available, giving access to the sea-routes for the importing of raw materials and exporting of the finished wares. The industry was given a further boost during the third quarter of the 17th century, when there was a decline in the Dutch brewing industry, due to competition from England. Many breweries were vacated, only to be speedily taken over as premises by 'Delftware' potters, who in many instances adopted the name of the former occupier. This resulted in such potteries as 'The Golden Flowerpot', 'The Rose', 'The Hatchet' and 'The Peacock'.

Unlike the English potters engaged in the making of tin-glazed earthenware, the Dutch usually marked their wares with registered factory-marks. However, the marks of the finest potters can often be seen on very inferior 19th century wares, the most common being the 'AK' monogram of Adrianus Kocks, who was working at 'The Greek A' factory from about 1686.

The earliest occupant of 'The Greek A' factory was Samuel van Eenhorn, whose 'SVE' monogram can sometimes be seen on beautiful reproductions of Chinese porcelain made between 1674–86. The decoration of the finest Delft can often be recognized by their use of a finely painted manganese-purple or dark blue outline to the design, into which the paler colour-washes are added – a technique called *trek*, which is rarely used elsewhere.

Eenhorn's successor at 'The Greek A' factory, Adrianus Kocks, is probably the name most commonly associated with the finest Delftware. His best known works the large sets, as designed by the Dutch court architect, Daniel Marot. These include the pagoda-like tulip-vases, and were intended for the apartments of Queen Mary II in the Water-Gallery at Hampton Court. Similar sets can be seen at Chatsworth, the stately home of the Duke of Devonshire in Derbyshire and at Dyrham Park, Gloucester, maintained by the English National Trust.

Porcelain, such as the Dutch were importing from Japan, also inspired other fine potters, including Rochus Hoppesteyn, who was working at 'The Young Moor's Head' in about 1690. Wares bearing the initials 'RHS' were often further decorated with gold, a rich red pigment and a bright green enamel. Probably one of the most common, yet genuine marks seen on Dutch Delftware is that of a stylized bird's claw, used originally from 1662 by Cornelis van der Hoeve, who produced some good wares in the Chinese manner. The wares made from the late 18th century until the factory closed in 1850 are very poor quality in every respect.

'The Rose' factory was in operation from 1662–1775, and their blue-and-white plates

painted with scenes from the New Testament made a welcome change from the masses of Delft inspired by Far Eastern porcelain.

It was the Delft potters who first introduced the five-piece garnitures, intended for the decoration of high chimney-pieces or the tops of cupboards. The set comprised three covered jars, of Chinese form, and two beakers, with flaring mouths. This form was quickly taken up by the Chinese potters when producing wares for the European market and later produced by several 18th century European porcelain factories; usually on a smaller scale.

The Delft potter of the early 18th century turned his attention to Chinese porcelain other than the popular 'blue-and-white'. Several factories made wares in imitation of the black-ground *famille noire* or Far Eastern lacquer, both of which were extremely popular in Europe.

The new collector of Dutch Delftware should train his eye to recognize the more recent wares, where the bright blue decoration appears to have been applied to a previously fired tin-glaze, resulting in a 'pen-like' precision to the painting. Today in Holland wares for the tourist are often referred to as 'Delft', when they are in fact merely produced by applying underglaze-blue decoration to a white earthenware body, the whole being covered with a transparent lead-glaze.

One cannot discuss Dutch tin-glazed wares without referring to their prolific manufacture of wall-tiles. Those made during the 17th century were usually quite thick and decorated in colour with fruit and flowers with distinctive corner motifs. Tiles of the late 17th century and early 18th century were only about 6 mm ($\frac{1}{4}$ in) thick

and 12.5 cm (5 in) square, and favoured biblical illustrations, ships, sea-monsters, mounted warriors or men-at-arms, sometimes inspired by well-known engravings, painted in either blue, manganese-purple or a combination of both. There is quite a lucrative business in Holland today in the manufacture of 'tiles for the tourist', often deliberately 'crazed' to suggest age.

The Dutch imported great quantities of English salt-glazed stonewares and cream-coloured earthenwares, which were usually left in an undecorated state, ready for enamel decoration to be added on arrival in Holland. There was also a small production of poor quality creamware made in Holland for the home market, but few could compete with the quality and low cost of the English exports.

Scandinavia

Small, but important, productions of tin-glazed wares were made at several centres in Scandinavia, including Sweden, Denmark, Schleswig-Holstein and Norway. These were started in most instances by potters who had acquired their knowledge elsewhere in Northern Europe.

The first undertaking in Sweden was at Rörstrand, near Stockholm. The company was started in 1726, but had little success until nearer the middle of the century, when the majority of their wares were decorated in blue or the attractive Italian technique of *bianco-sopra-bianco*, where a white pigment is applied over a tin-glaze which had been tinted to a pale blue or green. Towards 1760 the full palette of enamel colours were being used and before the end of the decade Rörstrand wares were being decorated with some

2 This fine tulip-vase was made at Delft in Holland in about 1700. Their finest work of this type was made between about 1650 and 1710. It appeared to have been the aim of the Delft potters to make their wares look as similar as possible to the original blue and white porcelain. This vase intended for displaying blooms of the tulip is of a more original type and is similar to the work attributed to Adrianus Kocks.

3 Flemish potters were at work in London producing tin-glazed earthenware as early as 1571, but during the 17th and early 18th centuries the manufacture spread and many potters set up in Lambeth, Southwark, Brislington, Wincanton, Bristol, Liverpool, Lancaster and Dublin.

Bowls, of various sizes, were made at many of these centres, but some of the finest were made at Liverpool during the first half of the 18th century. The bowl illustrated is from the famous Glaisher Collection, in the Fitzwilliam Museum, Cambridge and is inscribed Success to Great Britain, Safe may she stem the turrant of the Main, with great success and safe return again. A. STAFFELL.

1

were usually more appropriate to the finer materials of porcelain.

Other factories at Criseby and Eckernförde were started during the 1760s, but the factory producing some of the finest Scandinavian faience was that at Kiel, under J. S. F. Tännich, whose wares made up until about 1768 are considered to have equalled those of Strasbourg. But later, under Johann Buchwald, there was a marked decline in both quality of material and

2

2 Tin-glazed earthenware was made at Marieberg, in Sweden, from about 1760.

The factory was founded by J. L. E. Ehrenreich, who was formerly the Court Dentist.

1 This English tin-glazed earthenware dish (English Delftware) is the earliest recorded example with an English inscription. It is dated 1600 and the scene is thought to represent the Tower of London. This dish was probably made at Aldgate, London.

attractive transfer-prints. Many of their forms were highly original and included large trays made to fit as tops of tea-tables. During the last quarter of the century the Rörstrand production of tin-glazed earthenware gave way to the more practical English-type creamware.

From 1760 the Marieberg factory, started by J. L. E. Ehrenreich, produced some beautifully enamelled wares, but again the demand for creamware was such that the faience production was abandoned and in 1782 the factory was taken over by Rörstrand.

Denmark's claim to fame in the ceramic field is associated with the porcelain of Copenhagen, but during the second quarter of the 18th century the Store Kongensgade factory, under the direction of Christian Gierløf, produced a wide range of useful wares, including a punch-bowl in the form of a bishop's mitre. Their decoration was generally restricted to the limited range of high-temperature colours.

The rival factory of Peter Hoffnagel at Østerbro, Copenhagen, was producing many typical Scandinavian forms, decorated in blue and manganese-purple from about 1763.

The decoration of the faience made at Schleswig from about 1758 was somewhat limited due to the monopolies previously granted to other undertakings. Their most common palette consisted of a brownish-manganese together with a grey-green, and their Rococo forms

choice of decoration and palette.

During the 1760s a successful production of faience was conducted by Peter Hoffnagel at Herrebøe, where the painting was primarily of high-temperature blue and manganese, applied to extreme Rococo forms.

Great Britain

The term English Delftware is rather an inappropriate one, since Flemish potters were pro-

3

3 This 'blue-dash charger' was made in London around the middle of the 17th century, when decoration with stylized fruit and foliage became popular.

ducing tin-glazed earthenware first in Norwich, East Anglia, and later in London by about 1570 – nearly half a century before Delft achieved fame. The production of Jacob Jansen (or Johnson), and other Flemish potters, centred first around Aldgate, in London, neighbouring Southwark becoming a further popular area in the early 17th century. Lambeth, Brislington, Bristol, Wincanton, Liverpool, Lancaster, Glasgow and Dublin were all to become well-known centres of production. All were noticeably within easy reach of the coast, enabling the necessary Cornish tin to be transported by sea. Recent excavations of some early sites have made attributions to specific areas more accurate than has formerly been possible.

Plates or dishes decorated with paintings of reigning English monarchs are very popular with collectors but are also very expensive to acquire. Such dateable wares are ideal indicators to the forms of border decoration, profiles, and so forth, in vogue at a certain period, but the facial likeness to the characters could hardly have met with the approval of the individuals. The majority of the dishes made before the end of the 17th century had a clear glaze applied to the reverse, to economize on tin, and they usually have a small undercut foot-rim, which could retain a cord for hanging purposes. The popular term 'blue-dash chargers' refers to the blue painted strokes around the rim. 'Dish' would in most cases be a more accurate description than 'charger'.

The early English and Flemish potters were actively engaged in making a variety of wares for the use of the apothecary, including wet and dry drug-pots, and pill-slabs. The simply decorated ointment-pots could well have been made in either the Low Countries or England.

The popularity of the tulip, and its association with Holland, is seen on many dishes made in the last quarter of the 17th century, the style of painting often having much in common with the early Isnik dishes of Turkey. Unlike most of the Continental faience potters, the British counterpart used only high-temperature colours – blue, green, manganese-purple, yellow and sometimes a poor quality red. The only exception here being the enamel transfer-prints applied to the Liverpool tiles by a firm of printers known from about 1763 as Sadler & Green.

Among the most desirable British tin-glazed wares are tea-wares, which are extremely rare; flower-bricks, a brick-shaped vessel with perforated top; puzzle-jugs, with fretted designs around the neck. The late wares illustrating Lunardi's balloon ascent of 1784, which took place at Moorfields, near the Lambeth factory, are among the class of pieces sought by todays collectors, even when in poor condition.

Due to the fragile nature of the material and the consequent difficulties of transportation by road, the early potter catered primarily for his immediate neighbourhood. But by the middle of the 17th century, the area we now know as Stoke-on-Trent, in Staffordshire, had become recognized as an important pottery centre, with Burslem known as the 'Mother of the Potteries'

or sometimes the 'Butter-pot Town', due to the large production of red earthenware jars made for the local farmers for conveying their butter to market. These same potters could, when the occasion arose, produce what might well be termed 'English Peasant-Pottery'. Dishes or drinking vessels which were decorated by trailing clay-slips of contrasting colour on to the body of the unfired ware, their designs appearing at times to have been suggested by contemporary needlework.

Wares of a similar type were also made at Wrotham, in Kent, and in the London area, where the decoration often including such pious inscriptions as 'Watch and Pray'. All these low-fired earthenwares were covered with a thick lead-glaze, which often had disastrous effects upon the health of the potter.

It was in 1672 that John Dwight set up a factory in Fulham, London, for the production of salt-glazed stoneware or 'Stoneware vulgarly called Cologne Ware'. Dwight's main production was of German style wine bottles made to the order of specific inns. There is little doubt that he was also occupied in carrying out experiments concerned with the manufacture of Chinese-type porcelain, which at that time was still only being produced in the Far East. Some of his fine mugs of about 1680 are so finely potted, that despite being made of stoneware, they do show a slight amount of translucency by transmitted light.

Two further important potters working in England during the late 17th century were John and David Elers, born in Utrecht and Amster-

1 The 17th century potter in Staffordshire was usually engaged in making everyday requirements for the kitchen or farmhouse, but when the occasion arose he was prepared to make more fanciful slip-trailed earthenwares. The name particularly associated with such examples of the English potter's art is that of Thomas Toft, whose dishes were usually decorated with a tight trellis-pattern and are often commemorative.

2 One of the most famous names in the history of English ceramics is John Dwight (1637–1703). In 1672 he took out his first patent concerned with his manufacture of salt-glazed stoneware. Bottles of the type shown can be surely identified by the discovery of the various metal stamps he used to produce the relief decorations 'sprigged' on to many of his pieces.

These stamps were found on the factory site.

1 Soft-paste porcelain decorated in the Chinese manner, made in London about 1750.

2 Bone-porcelain miniature cup, incised 'R'. Bow, about 1752.

3 Bone-porcelain cup, with 'heart-shaped' terminal to handle. Bow, about 1762.

4 Bone-china, made at Derby during the Bloor period, about 1830.

5 Hard-paste porcelain, New Hall factory, Staffordshire; 1790–1803.

6 Sèvres-type handle used at Pinxton, Derbyshire, 1796–99.

7 Soft-paste porcelain of Billingsley period, Pinxton, 1796–99.

8 Soft-paste porcelain, Longton Hall, Staffordshire, about 1756.

9 Soft-paste porcelain, with reeded decoration, Longton Hall, about 1755.

10 Soapstone porcelain, made at Worcester during Flight period, 1783–93.

11 Soapstone porcelain, produced at Caughley, Shropshire in about 1785.

12 Bone-china, one of eight handles used at the Rockingham factory, Yorkshire, 1830–42.

13 Bone-china, made by John Davenport at Longport, Staffordshire, 1815–25.

14 Bone-china, produced at Davenport's factory in about 1820.

15 Bone-china, manufactured by John Davenport between 1830–37.

16 Bone-china coffee-cup, made by Davenport between 1850–55.

17 Bone-porcelain, made at Lowestoft, Suffolk, about 1768.

18 Soft-paste porcelain, produced at Duesbury's factory, Derby, 1785–90.

19 Bone-china, John Rose's factory, Coalport, Shropshire, 1836–40.

20 The so-called 'Porringer' form, used by Spode in about 1810.

21 Hard-paste porcelain, made at the New Hall factory, Staffordshire, 1782–87.

22 Gadrooned-edge cup, produced at Spode's factory in about 1822.

23 Bell-shaped cup, made at Spode's factory from about 1819.

24 Cup in art deco design made by Shelley in about 1933.

1 There are very few wares made in Staffordshire during the eighteenth century which are of a type that can be said to indicate the work of one part potter; it is therefore only safe to refer to a 'type'. The three small figures are referred to as 'Astbury' type, the name of a potter, John Astbury of Shelton, who is known to have made many small figures, usually in a brown clay decorated with white and often tinted with the limited range of metallic oxides.

2 The figures of a stag and doe are covered in a rich brown glaze, which was considered in America to resemble closely the glaze used on the English pottery made at the Rockingham factory, in Swinton, Yorkshire.
The factory of C. W. Fenton at Bennington, Vermont, made many wares covered with this glaze, and many figures of various animals which, though usually cruder, are undoubtedly based on Staffordshire models.
They date from the mid-19th century.

dam. They claimed they acquired their knowledge concerning stoneware while on the Continent of Europe. The name of Elers is best associated with high quality red stoneware, which they may have been making while working for Dwight at Fulham, but which they were definitely producing at Bradwell Wood, Staffordshire, from about 1693.

From about 1720 Staffordshire and Yorkshire potters were producing salt-glazed stoneware which had been considerably improved by the addition of white Devonshire clay and calcined flints. Apart from 'thrown' tablewares, they also made a large variety of novel forms, such as teapots in the form of houses or camels by the slip-casting method (pouring watered-down clay into hollow plaster of Paris moulds). Other forms of decoration included rubbing cobalt into incised decoration (scratch-blue) and enamel painting.

The early Staffordshire lead-glazed slipwares were soon to be similarly refined to provide wares suitable for the popular beverage tea. The name of John Astbury of Shelton is today used to describe the mid-18th century wares and figures involving the use of applied or trailed clays in contrasting colours as a means of decoration. Similar wares are known to have been made by many other English potters. The name of Thomas Whieldon is similarly used to describe the variegated glazes acquired by the application of various high-temperature oxides under a fluid lead-glaze, which was again a technique used by many other potters during the same period.

Before becoming a Master Potter, Josiah Wedgwood (1730–95), was in partnership with Thomas Whieldon from 1754–59. Wedgwood is known throughout the world for his large production of blue-and-white jasperwares, made from about 1775, during the time he was in partnership with Thomas Bentley (1769–80), but in his earlier years Wedgwood produced some

beautifully moulded lead-glazed wares, often aided by the modeller William Greatbatch.

If fired at a lower temperature and then covered with a refined pale yellow lead-glaze, the body of salt-glazed stoneware can be used to produce cream-coloured earthenware. A primitive creamware was being made as early as 1720, but credit is given to Josiah Wedgwood for improving this body to such perfection that he was patronized by Queen Charlotte. His 'Queen's Ware' was in world-wide demand. He produced the famous 'Frog' service for Catherine II of Russia which is now in the Hermitage, Leningrad.

It was Wedgwood's aim to convert a rural craft into a great industry, and this he achieved. Fortunately, some contemporary potters continued to make wares in the traditional manner. Foremost was the Wood family of Burslem, who are best known to collectors for their figures, many of which were modelled by the nephew of Ralph Wood, Enoch Wood. Ralph Wood died in 1772, but the production continued under his son and grandson. The early wares were decorated with lead-glazes which had been previously coloured with high-temperature oxides, resulting in a much more orderly finish than the figures of Whieldon type.

Recent research has proved that a very large production of creamware and other ceramic bodies associated with the Staffordshire potteries was also taking place during the second half of the 18th century in Yorkshire, including the Leeds Pottery, which started about 1770.

Porcelain
Prior to about 1710 the only true porcelain being produced in the world was that of the Far East, but experiments were started in Italy, concerned with the manufacture of an artificial, or soft-paste porcelain, during the second half of the 16th century. This was the Medici porcelain.

The early Florentine wares were made be-

4 Although the English potter, Josiah Wedgwood, made a great variety of ceramic bodies, he is, without doubt, best known for his large production of 'jasper' wares, often made as exact replicas of early Greek wares. This blue jasper vase with white applied relief decoration, was called by Wedgwood 'The Apotheosis of Homer'. It was modelled by John Flaxman.

4

tween 1575–87, for what would appear to have been the personal requirements of the Grand Duke Francesco I de Medici. The artificial porcelain body was produced from a white-firing clay, together with a high percentage of frit (glass). The existing pieces, which now number about 60, are almost all decorated solely in underglaze-blue, with the occasional manganese outline, often showing firing faults.

There appears to have been no further serious attempts to produce porcelain of any type in Italy until 1720, when Francesco Vezzi, of Venice, was aided by the renegade Meissen arcanist, C. K. Hunger, to produce a good quality hard-paste porcelain with clays obtained from Saxony. The factory closed in 1727 when supplies of the necessary clays were halted.

The wares produced during the seven years of activity were extremely good, primarily table-

3 Josiah Wedgwood made a great variety of ceramic bodies, but without doubt the most popular was his fine cream-coloured earthenware, or Queen's ware, which he perfected in 1763. He described the ware as 'a species of earthenware for the table, quite new in appearance, covered with a brilliant glaze . . . and consequently cheap'.

wares of designs obviously inspired by contemporary silver, usually decorated in strong enamel colours with a variety of subjects including Italian Comedy figures, heraldry, or *chinoiseries*. Cups and saucers were made with relief prunus decoration in the style of the 17th and 18th century Chinese Fukien province wares.

A further Venetian factory was started in 1764 by Geminiano Cozzi, whose early forms and decoration showed very little originality, the hard-paste material being very grey, but the production of both table-wares and figures was seemingly large and pieces marked with a distinctive form of anchor in red enamel are by no means uncommon in Europe.

The factory started at Doccia, near Florence, by the Marchese Carlo Ginori in 1735, is still active as the Richard-Ginori concern. The early porcelain is often referred to as *masso bastardo*, a grey-toned hybrid porcelain, which at times was hidden under a tin-glaze to make the ware appear more suitable for Far Eastern type decoration. Their early tea-wares were Baroque in style, with snake-like spouts and high-domed lids, but Doccia might well claim to be the earliest factory using transfer-printed underglaze-blue decoration. The coarse prints suggest the use of an engraved wood-block, rather than the English-type copper-plate.

Some of the finest quality soft-paste porcelain was produced between 1743–59 at the factory of Charles of Bourbon, situated in the grounds of the Palace of Capodimonte, near Naples. When Charles succeeded to the throne of Spain in 1759, his porcelain factory was moved to Buen Retiro, near Madrid. The only mark ever used at both Capodimonte and Buen Retiro was a fleur-de-lys, in blue, gilt or incised, never a crowned 'N' as commonly supposed. The later mark was used at The Royal Naples Factory established in 1771, but was used during the 19th century at Doccia and also on the late 19th century porcelains of Ernst Bohne of Rudolstadt in Thuringia.

A further Italian factory whose wares are worthy of comment is that of Le Nove, near Bassano. Pasquale Antonibon began experiments as early as 1752, but little success was achieved before 1781, when the concern was leased to Francesco Parolin, and later to Giovanni Baroni, closing in 1825. The early wares had much in common with those of Cozzi, but from about 1780 decorated wares were produced from a fine white porcelain, with gilt decoration comparable in style and quality to that used at Sèvres.

Germany and Austria

Until at least 1770 the porcelain fashions in Europe were dictated by those of China and Japan. These wares were imported into Europe in increasing quantities, and dominated popular taste until the rise of first of Meissen, then Sèvres.

For many years a great deal of wealth was spent in the purchase of Far Eastern porcelain for use at the court of Augustus II, Elector of Saxony, King of Poland. In order to try to remedy this vast expenditure, Count von Tschirn-

haus was given the task of researching into the mineral wealth of Saxony, in an effort to produce the necessary materials for the manufacture of a true porcelain and fine glass, which at that time was only being made in Bohemia. From 1704, Tschirnhaus was assisted in his experiments by a young alchemist, Johann Friedrich Böttger, who claimed to possess the secret of producing gold

1

from a base metal. Their first combined success was to produce a hard fine-grained stoneware, which could be ground and polished in the manner of a semi-precious stone. This red stoneware had the appearance of the Chinese Yi-hsing ware, usually used to produce the teapots for the European market. Some of Böttger's lower-fired red wares remained porous and so were given a dark-brown glaze, with added gold or lacquer decoration.

Tschirnhaus died in 1708, leaving Böttger to take all the credit for the production of a form of white porcelain, resulting in the establishment in 1710 of the Royal Saxon Porcelain Manufactory, in the Albrechtsburg fortress at Meissen, 12 miles from the city of Dresden. The early Meissen porcelain was made from the white-burning China-clay (kaolin) from Colditz, near Zwickau, and a calcareous flux in the form of alabaster. It was in about 1718 that the correct material of China-stone (petuntse) was put to use, resulting in the Saxon hard-paste porcelain being an even whiter ware than that made in the Far East.

The early white porcelains produced prior to the death of Böttger, in 1719, were mostly inspired by contemporary metalwork, sometimes from the designs of the court silversmith, Irminger. The figures were often modelled after the 17th century prints of Jacques Callot's grotesque dwarfs, who were a favourite subject in the early 18th century, when there was a morbid curiosity in those suffering from various unattractive physical afflictions.

The year 1720 marked a further milestone in their success, being the time Johann Gregor Höroldt was introduced to the factory by the disloyal kiln-master, Samuel Stölzel. He persuaded Höroldt to leave the services of Du Paquier at the early rival porcelain factory of Vienna. Within two years, the influence of Höroldt was

clearly seen in their improved decoration. A new range of vivid enamel colours was used in a wide variety of patterns, including copies from engravings telling of Far Eastern travel, and far more original *chinoiseries* – fairy-land fantasies based on the Court and social life of China (Höroldt's original sketches still exist).

The new enamel colours were also used to depict stylized Oriental flowers. These were wrongly termed 'India flowers', as they were developed from paintings on late 17th century Chinese porcelain brought to Europe by the vessels of the East India Companies. These Oriental flowers were replaced in about 1740 with naturalistic flower paintings, often inspired by the engravings of recorded botanists. Between 1725 and 1730, harbour-scenes and landscapes were also extremely popular and many are attributed to the painters J. G. Heintze and C. F. Herold.

In 1727 Gottlieb Kirchner was appointed as the first Chief Modeller, his earliest creations being the life-size figures of animals, as requested by Augustus for the furnishing of his Japanese Palace. Kirchner was soon to be overshadowed by the more famous modeller J.J. Kaendler, who was appointed in 1731. Kaendler excelled not only in decorative figures for table decoration but in designing other large heavily modelled table-wares, including the famous Swan Service for Count Brühl, who was appointed Director of the factory following the death of Augustus II in 1733. This was a post he retained until he died in 1763.

By 1738 Kaendler had produced a wide variety of small porcelain figures based upon characters featured in the traditional theatre of Italian Comedy, made to *wander among groves*

of curled paper . . . (Horace Walpole, 1753). **3**
These figures were far more animated when
placed upon the simple mound bases of the
Baroque period, but by 1750 the more ornate
bases, in the now popular Rococo styles, seemed
to arrest their movement.

The Meissen factory was occupied by the
troops of Frederick the Great of Prussia at the
start of the Seven Years War of 1756–63 and by
the end of hostilities the porcelain factories of
Europe were looking towards the French factory
of Sèvres for fresh inspiration. Meissen was
never to fully recover from this disaster, but
during the so-called 'Marcolini' period of 1774–
1814, novel shapes were produced in the Neo-
Classical taste. But porcelain was not an ideal
body for such fashions, which were inspired by
the early Grecian wares excavated at Herculaneum and Pompeii.

The success of the Vienna factory was due
entirely to the disloyalty of the Meissen gilder,
Hunger, and the kiln-master, Stölzel, who in
1719 deserted Meissen in order to help Du
Paquier produce a good quality hard-paste
porcelain in Austria. The factory was taken over
by the State under Empress Maria Theresia in
1744. It remained under State direction until
1784, when the concern came under the manage-
ment of Konrad von Sorgenthal, eventually
closing in 1866. The unmarked wares of the Du
Paquier period were mostly decorated in original
chinoiseries and Baroque versions of the popular
leaf and strapwork designs (*Laub-und-Bandel-
werk*).

The table-wares of the State period showed
very little originality and owed much to Meissen.
However, the figures tended to have a slightly
prettier and more doll-like quality, a charm often
lacking in the bold and sometimes harsh work of
Kaendler.

By the mid-18th century all the materials

and techniques concerning the manufacture of
hard-paste porcelain were no longer a secret,
and those possessing the knowledge were well
paid by heads of other German States to part
with their knowledge. Johann Josef Ringler;
who obtained the secret at Vienna by 'courting'
the Director's daughter, is known to have helped
in the establishment of at least six other factories.

The collectors of German porcelain are fortunate in that nearly all the major 18th century
factories adopted a recognized factory-mark,
which was usually applied to the base of the
wares in underglaze-blue. Without this aid,
attribution to a particular concern would in
most instances be very difficult.

Höchst, making porcelain from 1750, adopted
as their mark a six-spoked wheel; often reproduced on 19th century wares made elsewhere.
Their early figures, attributed to the hand of
Simon Feilner, are of a rather coarse porcelain,
with a milky-white glaze, but their table-wares
were beautifully painted with flowers, landscapes
or *chinoiseries*, with fine quality gilding.

By 1752 Duke Carl I of Brunswick was spon-
soring a factory at Fürstenberg, where some
good figures are attributed to the hand of Simon
Feilner, but the table-wares tended to be extremely fussy. The Fürstenberg factory continues
to the present time, still using a version of the
original letter 'F' as their factory-mark.

1 This famous porcelain
room was created between
1757 and 1759 as a *sallotino*
for Queen Maria Amelia. It
is now in the Palace of
Capodimonte, near Naples.
It is 18 ft by 14 ft (5.5 m by
4.25 m), and 14 ft (4.25 m)
high and must rank as one of
the greatest works in soft-
paste porcelain.

2 Much of the fame of the
Meissen factory is due to the
modelling skills of J. J.
Kaendler, who was the
Modell-meister from 1733.
'The Greeting Harlequin' is
typical of the Italian
Comedy figures he created
from about 1738.

3 Among the finest hard-
paste porcelain figures made
during the Rococo period
are those created by Franz
Anton Bustelli, who was
chief modeller at Nymphenburg from 1754–63. These
two Italian Comedy figures
portray Donna Martina
and Octavio.

A further factory still in production today is that of Berlin, started in 1761 by J. C. Gotzkowsky and purchased by Frederick the Great in 1763. Many skilled workers were recruited from Meissen, and their early wares, which relied primarily on fine painting, are most attractive and original. The mark remains a sceptre in blue.

Paul Hannong established the porcelain factory at Frankenthal in 1753, having had to abandon his production at Strasbourg due to the monopolies enjoyed by Vincennes. Hannong's early wares tended to be fashioned in the contemporary French styles of Vincennes and Sèvres, but lacked the quality of the fine French soft-paste. The factory passed into the hands of the Elector Carl Theodor in 1762 and continued until 1800. The original moulds are being used today at the Nymphenburg factory, Bavaria.

wares of this Ludwigsburg factory can at times be easily recognized by a rather off-white clay, but mention must be made of a charming series of miniature groups, modelled by J. J. Louis. There are several characters in a scene, such as men playing dice, tailors at work and inn scenes, all of which show great depth of detail.

France

From the mid-17th century various East India Companies had been bringing Far Eastern porcelain into Europe in increasing quantities. In consequence, there was little incentive for potters of other countries to spend time and money trying to produce a similar type of porcelain. It was eventually left to a few French potters already engaged in the production of *faience*, to make an artificial or 'soft-paste' porcelain.

While one must accept Kaendler as the outstanding modeller during the Baroque period, there is little doubt that Franz Anton Bustelli, who worked at Nymphenburg from 1754, was the master of Rococo porcelain sculpture. His models clearly indicate by their carving and postures that he had been trained initially as a woodcarver. Some of his best work is seen in the form of centrepieces for the table, where the entire group appears to be stirring in a placid wave-like motion. The Nymphenburg shield is still used as a factory-mark on modern wares produced from early moulds.

The factory, patronized originally by Duke Carl Eugen, was established in 1758. It cannot be said that they flourished, as the workers were at times compelled to accept their wages in 'seconds' (faulty wares) which they in turn had to sell. The

The wares supposedly made by Louis Poterat of Rouen after he had been granted a patent in 1673, are very difficult to attribute with any certainty. However, some collectors consider a limited number of examples of a thin glassy paste, decorated in an inky underglaze-blue and with the mark A.P. to be the work of Poterat.

Records concerning early porcelain made at Saint-Cloud are more readily accepted. Pierre Chicaneau, another *faience* maker, appears to have passed on his knowledge of the manufacture of soft-paste porcelain to his son and widow before he died in 1678. The widow later married Henri Trou and the factory was continued by their descendants until 1766.

The beautiful creamy-toned soft-paste porcelain of Saint-Cloud was necessarily rather thickly potted and left either in the glazed 'white' state or decorated in underglaze-blue with the so-called *lambrequin* designs, as seen on Rouen *faience*. Moulded scale patterns, probably suggested by the artichoke, were very popular, and handles of vessels were usually of square or rectangular section. Many saucers had a raised ring to locate the foot of the cup. This so-called *trembleuse* feature was probably first introduced at Saint-Cloud.

Saint-Cloud also produced a wide range of table-wares, snuff-boxes, cane-handles, and so on, decorated in the bright enamel colours and gilding in the Japanese 'Kakiemon' style.

The early French soft-paste porcelain factories rarely showed a profit, and it was only by the interest and generosity of wealthy patrons that they were able to survive. This was certainly so with Chantilly, the factory established by Louis Henri de Bourbon, Prince de Condé, in 1725. The production was directed by Ciquaire Cirou, who almost certainly acquired his knowledge at Saint-Cloud.

The Prince de Condé possessed a very large collection of Japanese porcelain, which was to inspire early Chantilly decorators to use so many 'Kakiemon' designs, but such polychrome decoration did not show to advantage on creamy-toned porcelain. Therefore, the majority of pieces decorated in the Japanese taste were given a white opaque glaze.

Following the death of the Prince in 1740, more original styles in French taste were introduced, including a wide range of flower decoration. These designs were later to be taken to the Vincennes factory by the Chantilly workmen, Gilles and Robert Dubois, who helped to establish the factory in 1738.

Chantilly is best known to the collector for the wares made from about 1770, when the decoration consisted almost entirely of sparse floral sprays in underglaze-blue, the much copied 'Chantilly sprig'. The original mark of a French hunting-horn was used during the 19th century by other Chantilly potters making wares in a hard-paste body in the earlier 18th century styles. Samson of Paris also made hard-paste reproductions of the early wares, decorated in the 'Kakiemon' manner.

Some of the most beautiful soft-paste porcelain ever to have been produced was that made at Mennecy. The factory of François Barbin was started in Paris in 1734, under the patronage of the Duc de Villeroy, whose initials 'D.V.' were used as a mark. From 1748 until 1773 production continued at Mennecy, from which time a further move was made to Bourg-la-Reine, where the factory finally closed in 1806.

The beauty of Mennecy wares was undoubtedly due to the simplicity of form. The glaze is well described as having a 'wet' appearance, and probably illustrates better than any other soft-paste porcelain how the enamels tend to fuse into the glaze, rather than lie upon it, as seen with hard-paste. The figures of Mennecy are especially charming and were obviously intended as table decorations, which can be enjoyed from any viewpoint. The popular groups

of child musicians were almost certainly inspired by the paintings of François Boucher. Many of the later Mennecy figures were left 'in the biscuit' and had a lot in common with the contemporary English Derby figures.

It is fortunate for todays collectors that the French porcelain factories did not have access to the necessary clays for the production of a hard-paste porcelain until 1769. Instead, they relied upon fine quality soft-paste, such as first seen at Mennecy and then at Vincennes, and we have some very beautiful wares as a result.

The first experiments concerned with the production took place in 1738 in a royal château at Vincennes, on the eastern border of Paris, under the direction of a financier, Orry de Fulvy. He was aided by Gilles and Robert Dubois, who claimed to have acquired the necessary know-

ledge while employed at Chantilly.

It was not until about 1745, when a further Chantilly worker, François Gravant, was engaged, that any real success was achieved. He was aided by other outstanding artists and craftsmen. Precise dating of early Vincennes is difficult, the royal double 'L' cipher was adopted as a mark from the beginning of production, but by no means consistently, and it was not until 1753 that a letter 'A' was enclosed within the cipher. That was the start of an alphabetical dating system (A = 1753, B = 1754, C = 1755, and so on), which continued until 1793.

It was from the Vincennes period that most of the well applied ground colours, including *bleu lapis, jonquille* and apple-green, were so beautifully applied. There was also superb engraved gilding used as borders to reserves painted with

1 The French potter, Bernard Palissy, set up his pottery at Saintes in about 1542, from which time he produced a wide range of earthenwares decorated with glazes coloured with the full range of high-temperature metallic oxides. This large, oval dish depicts the allegory of *Fecundity*. Palissy's wares were imitated a great deal during the 19th century.

2 The French *faience* makers did not try to make their wares look like Chinese blue-and-white porcelain, as did the Dutch. This helmet-shaped ewer, after the silver which it was intended to replace, was a very popular form and shows the very elaborately painted style referred to as *lambrequin*. It was made in Rouen in about 1710.

3 Among the most beautiful of all soft-paste porcelains were the pieces made at the French factory at Saint Cloud from about 1690 until 1766. Their tablewares were necessarily rather heavily potted, but the rare figures, which were usually left in the white, date from about 1740, when naked boys playing around rocks seem to have been a most popular subject.

1 Among the many original shapes introduced at the soft-paste porcelain factories of Vincennes and Sèvres, is the *vase hollandais*, also referred to as a *jardinière éventail*. This example is decorated with the ground-colour of *bleu céleste*, which was first used in 1752, and so might well be seen without a date-letter, a system of marking which was not started until 1753.

polychrome enamel floral sprays, scenes after Watteau or Boucher, birds, or chubby cupids. Among the most prolific articles produced at Vincennes were porcelain flowers, which can at times be seen as part of a bocage, used as a background to Meissen figures on *ormolu* mounts. In 1754 plans were put in hand to rehouse the porcelain manufactory in a new building at Sèvres, between Versailles and Paris, eventually occupied in 1756.

The move to the new factory coincided with the occupation of Meissen by the Prussians and marked the start of a period during which the French soft-paste was to surpass that of the Saxon concern in every respect. However,

Sèvres was far from successful financially and in 1759 the factory was purchased by Louis XV, from which time it was heavily subsidized as part of the royal estate.

Much of the beauty of Vincennes and early Sèvres porcelain was due primarily to the simplicity of decoration, allowing large areas of the fine white surface to be seen to advantage. From the late 1760s there was a tendency to apply enamels and gilding to the entire surface, which resulted in a loss of the sense of fragility. From about 1750 it was realized that some of the ground colours were too intense and various methods were introduced to break up the large areas with various gilt patterns, including

cailloute (pebbling), *vermiculé* (wormlike) or *oeil-de-perdrix* (partridge-eye), which were all very successful. Recent research into the archives of the factory has proved that several terms used over a long period are inaccurate, for example, the rose-pink introduced in 1757 was recorded as simply *rose*, never *rose Pompadour*.

The first porcelain figures made at Vincennes were glazed, but from about 1752 it became fashionable to leave the porcelain 'in the biscuit'. Some of the finest miniature statuary of this type was modelled by Etienne-Maurice Falconet, who was trained as a sculptor. He worked as a modeller at Sèvres from 1757 until 1766, when he went to Russia, where French porcelain was in great demand. In about 1788 the Empress Catherine II ordered a 740 piece service, decorated with her monogram 'E II' (Ekaterina II). Tea drinking played a large part in the social life of the French court, and nobility, and services for the enjoyment of the drink were made in quantity, including cabaret services, which had the pieces necessary for 'tea-for-two'. They were often made to be carried in fitted travelling cases.

Experiments concerned with the manufacture of hard-paste porcelain following the discovery of kaolin (China-clay) at Saint Yrieix near Limoges were successful by 1769 and in 1772 true porcelain was in regular production, although soft-paste was also made in limited quantities until the end of the century.

Following the death of King Louis XV in 1774, both the quality and quantity of the wares rapidly declined, caused to a large degree by competition from the newly established Paris factories. Due to the patronage of members of the royal family, these were permitted to make certain classes of wares previously reserved for the Sèvres factory alone.

The royal porcelain factory was taken over by the new revolutionary regime in 1793 and the mark of the royal cipher was replaced with the 'R.F.' monogram (*République Francaise*), which was used until about 1800. During these seven years very few pieces of any great importance were made, other than those with decoration including revolutionary emblems, sometimes applied together with newly introduced ground colours. These new colours were intended to imitate tortoiseshell and semi-precious hardstones.

Belgium

François Joseph Peterinck was granted a privilege in 1751 by the Empress Maria Theresia to establish a porcelain factory at Tournai, where some very good quality soft-paste porcelain was made until the time of the founder's death in 1799, when the factory passed into the Bettignies family. The Bettignies are better known for their 19th century reproductions of Sèvres, Saint-Cloud, Chantilly, Sceaux and Chelsea.

The best known Tournai pattern is said to have been introduced in 1787 to decorate a service for the Duke of Orleans. The naturalistic bird-painting is based on drawings made by Buffon for his 1786 publication *Natural History*.

Because Peterinck engaged some English workmen, there is frequently a distinct similarity to the porcelains of Derby and Worcester. This is especially so with the 'biscuit' figures, and positive attribution can be extremely difficult as there are no factory-marks. The Tournai models would be slightly earlier than those of Derby and probably modelled by either N.-J. Gauron, who previously worked at Mennecy, or Joseph Willems, who was working at Chelsea for many years before modelling for Tournai from 1766.

Holland

The Dutch, who excelled in the manufacture of tin-glazed earthenware, were less successful with porcelain and produced few wares which were entirely original.

The earliest production of hard-paste porcelain in Holland was that started by an Irishman, Daniel MacCarthy, at Weeps near Amsterdam, in 1757. The raw materials were obtained from Germany, and resulted in a fine white body, but the decoration of flowers, landscapes and 'exotic' birds was very stilted and lacked the naturalistic colours seen on the contemporary German porcelains.

In 1771 the Weeps concern was purchased by Johannes de Mol, who moved the operation to Oude Loosdrecht, near Hilversum, where further good, but dull, wares were produced with the aid

2 This hard-paste porcelain plate, showing a view of Saint Cloud, is of early 19th century date and is from the large collection of continental porcelain of this period which was once the property of the Duke of Wellington and is now exhibited in his former London home, Apsley House.

Although hard-paste porcelain was being used at Sèvres from about 1772, the more admired soft-paste was also used until about 1800.

1 Although a limited range of soft-paste porcelain figures and a few documented cream-jugs were made at Derby from about 1750–56, it was in 1756 that William Duesbury founded a factory, which he advertised as 'Derby or the second Dresden'. Many of his early models were spoiled by an over-blued glaze, which was intended to give a 'hard-paste' look to his wares.

This treatment seems to have been stopped in about 1760 and the chalky white soft-paste can be seen to advantage.

The centrepiece shown dates from between 1760 and 1765. The shell-shaped dishes were intended for a variety of delicacies. Derby wares of this period were unmarked.

2 During their early years, the Chelsea porcelain factory looked towards the Saxon factory at Meissen for many of their designs. In consequence, there are many Chelsea tablewares created to resemble animals, birds, fruit or vegetables. The sale catalogue of the 'Chelsea Porcelain Manufactory' of 1755, lists many such interesting forms as shown, sometimes described as Two fine large cabbage leaves and two fine large melons for desart (dessert) or Two small fig-leaves, and two fine cabbage lettuces, for desart.

Chelsea porcelain was of the highest quality in the so-called 'red-anchor' period, between about 1752 and 1758, when many of the wares were marked with a small, red, enamel anchor.

These small tureens were usually sold in lots of two or four, in most cases with matching stands.

of the arcanist L. V. Gerverot. Following the death of Mol in 1782, the factory was moved yet again by the new owners to Oude Amstel, where production continued under the direction of the German, F. Däuber. The next move, made in 1809, was to Nieuwer Amstel, where the manufacture of good table-wares in the French Empire style continued until the factory closed in 1820.

The factory established at The Hague in 1776, by Anton Lyncker, remained in his family until 1790. The wares again showed very little originality, other than some excellent painting by Leonhardus Temminck in the style of Boucher, often featured on tea-wares. The mark of The Hague was a stylized stork with an eel in its beak, but because porcelain made elsewhere was often decorated by the Lynckers, the original under-glaze-blue mark of such factories as Höchst, Ansbach, Meissen or Tournai are often seen to be overpainted in enamel with the stork-mark.

Denmark
Despite attempts being made to establish a porcelain factory in Copenhagen from as early as 1730, there is little evidence of any real success being made until 1759, when Louis Fournier, who had previously worked at Vincennes and Chantilly, produced a good quality soft-paste porcelain, usually fashioned after French or German table-wares of the period. It was unfortunate that the material proved to be uneconomic and production was halted in 1765.

It was in 1775 that a successful production of a hard-paste porcelain was achieved under the ownership of F. H. Müller, who engaged skilled painters and modellers from major German factories. This concern was taken over in 1779 by the King of Denmark, when the Royal Danish Porcelain Factory was established. The earliest wares were of a greyish-toned body and often decorated with underglaze-blue versions of Meissen designs. It was at Copenhagen that yet another famous service was again associated with the Russian Empress Catherine II, but upon completion the *Flora Danica* service of nearly 2,000 pieces was acquired by the King. The decoration, on the neo-Classical styled service, consisted of botanical specimens from G. C. Oeder's *Flora of the Danish Kingdom*. The painter was J. C. Bayer from Nuremberg.

From about 1780 an increasing number of 'biscuit' porcelain figures were produced, again often inspired by those of France or Germany. After 1835 the Royal Danish Porcelain Factory started their now famous production of figures based on the work of the sculptor Thorvaldsen.

Sweden
In 1759, as in Denmark, a successful production of soft-paste porcelain was started on the estate of Marieberg, on Kungsholmen in Stockholm, by the German dentist J. L. E. Ehrenreich, but almost immediately the newly erected factory was burnt down and no further porcelain was made at Marieberg until 1766. Then the Frenchman Pierre Berthevin produced wares which, if unmarked, are difficult to separate from those

made in France, at Mennecy; this is certainly true of the little covered ice-cream cups.

Following the departure of Berthevin in 1769, the charming soft-paste porcelain was abandoned in favour of a poor quality hybrid hard-paste, which was improved upon in about 1777, when Jacob Dortu, from Berlin, made some excellent hard-paste table-wares in the manner of Sèvres and Berlin, which had now become a far more fashionable factory than Meissen. Production ceased in about 1782.

Great Britain
The British potters were comparatively late starters in the field of porcelain manufacture, but in this respect it must be remembered that unlike the majority of their Continental rivals, they were only rarely subsidized by royal or noble patronage and so were entirely dependent upon the commercial success of their undertakings.

The early factory of Chelsea, managed by the Flemish silversmith, Nicholas Sprimont, was an exception, recent research having proved that Sir Everard Fawkener, Secretary to the Duke of Cumberland, was involved with the factory on a financial basis. In common with many other European factories of the mid-18th century, Chelsea looked first to Meissen for their inspiration, and then from about 1756 to Sèvres.

The period from 1745–70, during which time the Chelsea factory remained independent under Sprimont's direction, is usually discussed under four periods, named after the marks usual at certain dates. From 1745 to about 1749 wares were often marked with a small triangle, and during this 'triangle' period the majority of the wares echoed the form of Sprimont's earlier silver. In about 1749 the quality of the paste was improved, permitting a larger range of table-wares to be made, often marked with a small moulded anchor on an oval tablet, hence 'the raised-anchor' period, which continued until about 1752.

It is generally agreed among todays collectors that the Chelsea wares and figures made between 1752–58 were the finest they produced. During this period, when the mark was a small red enamel anchor (red-anchor period), some very fine figures were modelled by Joseph Willems, again mostly inspired by Meissen. Naturalism at the table also extended to the wares and various vessels were modelled to resemble animals, birds, fruit or vegetables.

During the 'gold-anchor' period, from about 1758–70, the small scale figures of about 16 cm (6½ in), previously used for table decoration, were replaced by large ungainly figures, often with a background of bocage and suitable only for side-table or cabinet decoration. During this same period the table-wares were fashioned in an exaggerated Rococo style as popularized originally at Sèvres.

The slightly later production at Bow catered for the less wealthy customer, and by about 1747 a soft-paste porcelain, including calcined animal bone, was being used to produce large quantities of cheap and durable wares, primarily decorated

1

pletely erroneous term 'Chinese Lowestoft'.

The Lund and Miller factory, started in Bristol in 1748, was probably the first English factory to produce a porcelain body containing the material soap-rock, or steatite. There is difficulty in identifying their early unmarked wares as the factory was taken over in 1752 by the newly established Worcester concern, under the famous Dr. Wall.

The new ingredient produced a ware which had almost all the advantages of a true porcelain and the proprietors claimed their products could withstand the temperature of boiling water and so be less liable to crack.

Both Bristol and early Worcester concentrated on blue-and-white, although by about 1756 Worcester were also making some beautifully decorated wares in delicately applied enamelled colours. Worcester was one of the first English porcelain factories to decorate their wares with enamel and underglaze-blue transfer-prints, many from the copper-plates engraved by the master Robert Hancock, who had previously worked at the Battersea enamel factory.

Towards 1770, Worcester began to attract several fine painters who had previously worked

in the Chinese fashion of underglaze-blue. By about 1750 many Bow wares were being decorated in enamel colours, often inspired by the Japanese 'Kakiemon', the Chinese *famille rose* or the German naturalistic flower-painting.

2

Bow figures were also of a type which would have particular appeal to the mid-18th century Londoner. Popular actors and actresses, such as Henry Woodward and Kitty Clive, were depicted in recognized roles, and national heroes including General Wolfe and the Marquis of Granby, were made in quantity, together with such characters as Bacchus or figures symbolizing the Four Seasons or the Elements. The early wares of Bow were comparatively simply made, but nevertheless possessed a distinct charm which is lacking in later wares, when both table-wares and figures became very clumsy, with loud and poorly applied enamelling.

The new collector may well be forgiven for confusing some examples of Bow with those made at the small Suffolk factory at Lowestoft, established in 1757 and continuing until about 1799. It is said that one of the proprietors, Robert Browne, actually obtained employment at the Bow works in order to learn the secrets of the production. Until about 1768 almost all the Lowestoft wares were decorated in underglaze-blue, and these examples are in great demand today. Many of the later wares were decorated in enamel colours in *chinoiseries*, a style of decoration that was probably responsible for that com-

over by Robert Bloor in about 1812 and closed in 1848.

William Cookworthy, a chemist, eventually produced a hard-paste porcelain at Plymouth, Devon, in 1768. Although it was near the source of the raw materials of China-clay and China-stone, the undertaking was moved in 1770 to Bristol, probably because of the difficulty of recruiting competent potters. It remained in production until 1781. The early Plymouth wares were often badly fired, probably due to difficulty in controlling the high temperatures, but from 1774 when Richard Champion, one of the original partners, assumed control, his claim to produce wares with the hardness of Dresden and the elegance of Sèvres, was well justified. Some extremely fine tea services were made in Neo-classical styles.

1 The early American settlers relied primarily upon wares imported from England for the finer table-wares, but from the early 17th century, the English colony of Jamestown, Virginia, were hoping for four 'potters of earth' to arrive from England. There is also evidence of early potting in both New York and Massachusetts. The archeological evidence suggests that these early potters were all engaged in the manufacture of rather coarse red clay wares, often decorated with clay slip or a white or buff tone.

Despite the fact that English earthenwares were being imported into the U.S.A. in vast quantities during the early years of the 19th century, there was still a large production of the traditional American red-wares, such as this dish and water-carrier.

2 The Four Continents, produced at Plymouth under William Cookworth but made from moulds brought from Longton Hall.

for Sprimont at Chelsea. From about 1768 their wares were rather heavily decorated, often with the famous underglaze-blue applied as scales, leaving reserves for enamel decoration, of flowers, birds or *chinoiseries* in rich gilt scroll-work frames. Worcester is the only English porcelain factory to have survived to the present day with an unbroken history.

Other English porcelain factories were soon to acquire knowledge of soapstone and gain access to the material, which was quarried in Cornwall, in the West of England. Caughley, the factory Thomas Turner established in Shropshire in 1772, produced a very good quality soapstone porcelain, decorated in a wide range of pattern, both in underglaze-blue and enamel colours. At least four major Liverpool factories made a similar class of ware, but the decoration was restricted mainly to underglaze-blue.

During the mid-18th century the only porcelain factory in Staffordshire to survive for several years was at Longton Hall, where a glassy soft-paste porcelain was made from 1749–60. Due to the high content of frit (glass), their early wares were subject to high kiln-losses and were often misshapen, but these difficulties were seemingly overcome by about 1755. Then some simple but highly original figures were produced, together with many table-wares, often of naturalistic form. Some Longton Hall mugs, and other wares, were decorated at Liverpool by the firm of Sadler & Green with enamel transfer-prints.

William Duesbury, who was formerly an independent pottery and porcelain enameller in London, established a porcelain factory at Derby in 1756, an undertaking he likened to 'a second Dresden'. The finest wares produced at Derby were made from the time Duesbury took over the Chelsea factory. During this so-called 'Chelsea-Derby' period (1770–84) many well designed and tastefully painted table-wares were produced in the Neo-classical styles. It was on Derby wares that the fine naturalistic flower-painting of William Billingsley first appeared, alongside the painting of Zachariah Boreman, who excelled in the painting of landscapes of the Derbyshire countryside. The factory was taken

In 1781 a group of Staffordshire potters purchased the unexpired years of Champion's patent for the manufacture of hard-paste, and so gave birth to the now popular New Hall factory, where a hard-paste body, with a rather soft glaze, was used to produce a wide range of useful wares until about 1812. Then in common with most other factories making porcelain, they started to produce bone-china, as introduced by Josiah Spode in about 1796, when China-clay and China-stone became legally available to any British potter for translucent ware.

America

Early American colonists could ill afford, or have any use for, decorative table-wares. Just as 17th century English potters primarily catered for the farming community, so in 18th century

America the potters were producing 'redware' or 'stoneware' vessels for cooking or storage; but when the occasion arose, they too were able to apply their skills to fashion more decorative items. Plates or platters, various sized bowls, some suitable for tea drinking, and a wide range of jugs or pitchers, were made more attractive with brushed, 'splashed' or trailed clay slips of contrasting colours. New England archaeologists have found evidence of a wide range of wares, which has enabled the collector to readily distinguish between pottery made in America from that imported from England. Porringers in the form of a large shallow cup with a single 'steadying' handle, were used at the table for multiple foods, together with mugs of tall cylindrical form.

Towards the middle of the 18th century, the American potters, many of whom had migrated

from Staffordshire, became aware of the dangers of using glazes with a high lead content. As a result there was an increased manufacture of salt-glazed stoneware, of a type which had much in common with the early German Rhenish vessels, rather than the fine white body of mid-18th century Staffordshire. There was little encouragement for the American potter to try to improve upon the quality of these humble wares, for from the last quarter of the 18th century masses of white earthenware was being exported from England at a price American craftsmen could not possibly match, despite efforts to produce both tin-glazed and cream-coloured earthenware.

Due to the importation of Chinese porcelain, the demand for the more expensive and vulnerable English blue-and-white soft-paste was very

low. However, many wares such as Nankin China mugs and salt cellars went to America by way of England, as there was no direct trading taking place between America and China before the American Revolution.

3

3 An earthenware pottery was established in Bennington, Vermont by a Captain John Norton on 1793. It was later in the history of this factory that C. W. Fenton gained enough knowledge to enable him to set up his own concern in 1847, partly staffed by English potters from Staffordshire. Many of his wares were glazed in a brown mottled manner, considered to resemble the earthenwares made at the Rockingham factory, Yorkshire, England, during the second quarter of the 19th century. Despite the fact that Fenton patented a very fine flint enamel glaze in a variety of high-temperature colours in 1849, the factory was unable to compete with the English imports and closed in 1858.

Similar glazes can be seen on this originally formed water-cooler, made by this Bennington factory.

Attempts have been made by many researchers to find proof of the type of porcelain said to have been made by the Savannah potter Andrew Duché, who according to William Stephens, Secretary to the Colony of Georgia, was making 'translucent' wares as early as 1741. This would pre-date any documented English porcelain. South Carolina also appears to have attracted potters from England. In 1770 John Bartlam was advertising the opening of 'A China Manufactory and Pottery' to be staffed by 'the proper-hands' from England. A contemporary pottery in the same area was also advertising for fine clays, which were probably required for the manufacture of creamware.

The most important finds concerning 18th century American ceramics were made at Philadelphia, where excavated fragments identify at least 20 examples of the soft-paste porcelain made by Gouse Bonnin and George Morris. These identified pieces include baskets, sauce-boats, cups and saucers, sweetmeat dishes and covered jars. They are decorated in underglaze-blue, having a great deal in common with English porcelains made at Bow, Derby and Worcester. It was a pity that this venture only lasted from 1770–72.

During the first half of the 19th century various types of earthenware were being produced by several potters in the Philadelphia and Trenton areas. These included some admirably printed wares of English type, made by the American Pottery Company of Jersey City. Jugs of 'Parian' type porcelain, with moulded relief decoration and patterns 'pirated' from the English manufacturers, were in great demand. They are known to have been made by the United States Pottery at Bennington, Vermont, and E. and W. Bennett of Baltimore, Maryland.

Also popular during the mid-19th century were vessels with a rich, dark-brown glaze, so-called 'Rockingham', a fashion catered for by many American factories. The American 'Rockingham' glaze differs from that associated with the English factory at Swinton, Yorkshire, by having a thicker and mottled appearance. These American Rockingham wares had much in common with *majolica* ware. This was popular both in America and England. Glazes coloured with high-temperature oxides were applied to wares moulded in relief. The colours usually included 19th century pinks and crimsons derived from chrome.

From about 1826 some very good quality hard-paste porcelain was made in Philadelphia by William Ellis Tucker and his various partners. Jugs, or pitchers, tea sets and dinner services were well decorated with flower paintings and monochrome landscapes, together with fine gilding. Many such pieces have so much in com-

1 Pottery in America followed a similar pattern of development as in Europe, but it was mostly condensed into the 19th century. This jar in saltglazed stoneware was made at Bennington in about 1855, although the simple style and primitive decoration belongs really to the 1750s.

2 In the late 19th century American pottery came into its own, and American art pottery of this period was frequently more advanced and imaginative than its European rivals. The pottery run by Artus van Briggle produced these two matt-glazed Art Nouveau style vases in the early 1900s.

mon with the contemporary French porcelains, that positive attributions can only be made by reference to pattern-books preserved in the Philadelphia Museum.

Art Pottery did not really become popular in the United States until after the 1876 Centennial Celebration, from which time Cincinnati, Ohio, became the centre for this new taste. This attracted many art potteries, including the Rookwood Pottery, which was the only one to survive beyond 1890. Mrs. Maria Longworth Nichols, a well-to-do Cincinnati socialite, was primarily interested in the creation of finely designed wares, rather than establishing a commercial success. Aided by friends skilled in the appropriate arts, Mrs. Nichols succeeded in producing a wide variety of most interesting effects on wares. These wares were in great demand from 1880, when the first kiln-firing took place, until 1941, when the firm became bankrupt. The early years were very unprofitable, but by 1889 Rookwood Pottery was well established and a wide range of artistic wares were being produced. These included some very original underglaze painting, under the direction of William Watts Taylor, who moved the production to larger premises in 1892. By 1900 the Rookwood Pottery was the foremost American art pottery.

Zanesville, Ohio, was also a popular centre for the manufacture of art pottery. The foremost concern was the Lonhuda Pottery, originally located at Steubenville and purchased by Samuel Weller of Zanesville as an addition to his existing factory. Their wares had a great similarity to those of Rookwood and included various fruit, flowers and figures painted in coloured slips on a

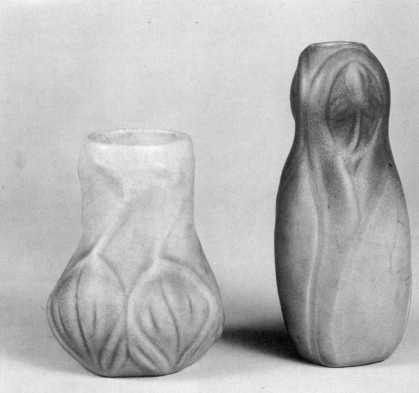

dark ground and covered with a brilliant glaze. **3**
Some of their pieces were painted with characters from the works of Charles Dickens, the English author. However, such ill-fitting decoration under a matt glaze is not very successful.

There is great similarity in some of the matt-glazed forms made by the Grueby Faience Company of Boston, Massachusetts, and those of the Martin brothers, working in London at about the same time. They both seemed to be inspired by the leaf forms, which played such a large part in the *Art Nouveau* decorative art in many European countries.

British porcelain

During the early decades of the 19th century, the entire ceramic industry of Europe was dominated by the prolific output of British pottery, porcelain and bone-china.

John Rose, who had established a factory mainly devoted to the manufacture of porcelain at Coalport, Shropshire, in about 1797, was to flourish and in turn absorb the concerns of neighbouring Caughley (1799) and later two Welsh factories, Nantgarw and Swansea (*c*.1820). Coalport is now part of the Wedgwood Group and is still in operation in Staffordshire.

There is still a little confusion concerning the wares made at Caughley by Thomas Turner between 1796–99 and those made by John Rose, who after his purchase continued in production until about 1815, when he transferred the entire manufacture to Coalport. Further difficulties also arise because quite a lot of Turner's Caughley wares were decorated independently by Robert Chamberlain at Worcester. Also, in the early 19th century John Rose was supplying the London decorator Thomas Baxter with 'Coalport White China'. Therefore, attribution is usually best verified by form rather than decoration.

Most early Coalport porcelain is unmarked, but pattern numbers can be a useful guide. Progressive numbers 1–1000 were used from about 1805–24, after which fractions were used. This resulted in 2/1 to 2/999 being applied to wares made between 1824–38, reaching as high as 8/1–8/1000. The later numbers are usually accompanied with a recorded and datable factory-mark. During the middle of the 19th century Coalport produced some fine quality reproductions of Sèvres porcelain, sometimes complete with mark!

It had long been the ambition of the painter William Billingsley to produce a fine porcelain. He left Derby in 1796 to establish a factory at nearby Pinxton, financed by John Coke. The limited production consisted primarily of tablewares, very much in the same styles as those of Derby. Sometimes they were decorated with pleasing landscapes by Billingsley himself, in the manner of Zachariah Boreman of Derby. Due to lack of expected profits, Billingsley moved on in 1799 to become an independent decorator, but Pinxton continued in a modest way until 1813. Pinxton used some distinctive handles on their vessels and cups, which are a useful identification

3 One of the most florid styles in English ceramics was the Rococo revival of the 1830 and 1840s, when the most extravagant styles of the 1740s were reproduced. This flower-encrusted coalport pot pourri vase of about 1840 is a typical example. Similar vases were produced by many English companies, including Minton, Spode and Rockingham.

aid to the collector.

Having found a new financial backer, Billingsley started to produce a beautiful, but costly, soft-paste porcelain at Nantgarw, near Cardiff in South Wales, in 1814. However, within the same year he was compelled to transfer the manufacture to the Swansea pottery of L. W. Dillwyn. There, Billingsley and his son-in-law, Samuel Walker, were forced to make a more stable porcelain, with a so-called 'duck-egg' translucency. In 1817 they returned to Nantgarw to restart their original factory. Stylistically, the early wares of Billingsley had much in common with French porcelain of the Empire Period, but a large amount of Nantgarw porcelain was ruined by the over ornate decoration added in London by the decorators employed by the china dealers Mortlocks of Oxford Street.

Josiah Spode was born in 1733 and at the age of 16 years he was apprenticed to Thomas Whieldon. In 1770 he was sufficiently experienced to take over the pottery of William Banks, for whom he had previously worked. He became a Master Potter, establishing a major ceramic factory which has flourished to the present day. The son, Josiah Spode II, first produced bone-china in about 1800, taking William Copeland

into partnership in 1805. William Spode, the grandson of the founder, died in 1829, and in 1833 William Taylor Copeland and Thomas Garrett became joint proprietors until 1847. From that time the company has been associated

with the Copeland family, although now part of the Carborundum group of Companies.

The name of Spode is probably best known among collectors for the large production of earthenware decorated with underglaze-blue transfer prints, often illustrating subjects taken from published engravings. Josiah Spode II used

1 English porcelain finally came of age in the early 19th century with the development of bone china and related bodies. Highly prized by collectors today are the products of the short-lived Welsh Nantgarw pottery, which produced this elegant covered dish and stand in about 1820.

2 Bone china, with its whiteness and translucence, was frequently used to reproduce the Sèvres and Meissen products of the 18th century. This fine vase and cover in Sèvres style was made by Minton in about 1850.

3 William Billingsley, an itinerant china decorator, trained at the Derby factory before working for a number of early 18th century English potteries. He specialized in flower painting. This plate is a typical example of his work.

4 Parian porcelain, a fine white unglazed modelling material named after the white marble from Paros, was first produced in the 1840s. It was a huge success at the Great Exhibition of 1851, and was made by many companies throughout the second half of the century. This wall bracket in French style was made at the Minton factory in about 1855.

5 Many French artists came to work in the English ceramic industry, including L.M. Solon, who came from Sèvres to Minton in 1870. He developed the *pâté sur pâté* technique of decoration, a very costly and time consuming process of sculpting the decoration in successive layers of liquid clay. These vases date from about 1875.

5

fine bone-china to produce a wide range of tea and dessert services and many good quality decorative wares. He managed to survive trading difficulties resulting from the Napoleonic Wars better than many of his rivals. It has been suggested that Spode's stone-china was being made as early as 1805, after having acquired the patent From W. & J. Turner, but factory records indicate the material was not introduced until about 1813.

A further important name in the field of 19th century English ceramics is that of Thomas Minton, born in Shrewsbury in 1765. Minton was first apprenticed to Thomas Turner at

Caughley, to learn the art of engraving copper-plates for the making of transfer-prints. It is said that he was involved in the early version of the so-called 'Willow' pattern, as seen on Caughley. He later worked as an engraver in London and after marrying returned to Stoke where he engraved plates for other potters, including Spode.

Minton's business flourished and in 1793, at the age of 28, he became a partner in a pottery. By 1796 he had built his own factory, where he first appears to have concentrated on the manufacture of blue-printed earthenware, soon to be

patterns which would normally be associated with such contemporary potteries as Spode, Miles Mason, New Hall and Pinxton.

Many bone-china figures and ornamental wares previously considered to be the work of Coalport, Derby or Rockingham, have been confirmed by the pattern-books to have been made by Thomas Minton and his son Herbert, who was in control from 1836. Herbert Minton took John Boyle into partnership from 1836–42, after which he was joined by Daintry Hollins and Colin Minton Campbell in 1842 and 1849 re-

1 During the Victorian period a vast range of portrait figures, chimney ornaments and flat-backs were produced by Staffordshire potters. These simple, naive models reflected popular events and figures, such as Grace Darling, depicted on the example illustrated.

followed by cream-coloured earthenwares of the Wedgwood type and bone-china. By 1810 Thomas Minton was producing wares in almost the entire range of ceramic bodies being made in Staffordshire at that time, although the production of bone-china was halted between 1810–24.

Recently, identification of many of Minton's unmarked wares made between 1810–24 has been made easier for the collector through the surviving pattern-books. These show not only the form, but a wide variety of original printed, painted and gilt designs, in addition to many

spectively. Herbert Minton died in 1858, by which time the company had 1,500 employees.

Today, Minton continues in production as part of the Royal Doulton Tableware Group.

A wide range of commonplace earthenware had been produced at Swinton, Yorkshire, from the mid-18th century, but the Rockingham factory is best known today for the fine porcelain made by the Brameld family from 1826. Many so-called Rockingham porcelains were beautiful. However, they were so expensively decorated that profits were small and despite financial aid

2

from Earl Fitzwilliam closure became necessary in 1842.

For many years a large number of bone-china figures, table-wares and decorative pieces have been attributed to this factory, without the benefit of any evidence. But recent research has enabled present-day attributions to be more accurate. It has, for example, been proved beyond all reasonable doubt that Rockingham made no figures of small 'shaggy' poodles or pastille-burners in the form of little cottages or other buildings. The adopted 'griffin' mark (in red enamel from 1826–30, and in puce from 1830–42) was not used consistently and sometimes is seen only on a single item of a service. The collector should note that any pattern number exceeding about 1570 definitely indicates the work of another factory making similar wares.

The Artist-Potter
During the late decades of the 19th century most major industrial potteries were influenced by Japanese taste. Thereafter, designers turned to either the old traditional patterns in vogue during the earlier years of the century, or the simple functional designs made in Berlin, Vienna, Paris, Milan, the various Scandinavian factories and especially England. In Great Britain, the ideas of Keith Murry are seen on Wedgwood wares of the 1930s, clearly indicating that formerly the designer was an architect working with a rule and compass.

It is fortunate that during this same period many skilled potters preferred to use clays as a new means of expressing personal feelings towards their craft. Today, many artist-potters are creating the antiques of the future.

The earliest evidence of the artist-potter obviously under the influence of the Near and Far Eastern potter was seen in the work of the Frenchman Théodore Deck (*d.* 1891), who opened a studio in Paris in 1856 and continued to produce beautiful painted earthenwares in the Islamic manner until he became Director of

Sèvres art department in 1887. While Deck is best known for his painting, Ernest Chaplet, who was working at Bourg-la-Reine in the 1870s, later specialized in glaze techniques and produced a wide range of unique effects on both stoneware and porcelain. They often equalled the glazes of the Chinese potter. Similar beautifully glazed stoneware was made in France by Adrien Dalpuyrat during the last decade of the 19th century. His contemporary, Auguste Delaherche, who produced some fine glazed stonewares, sometimes decorated in *sgraffiato*.

2 The movement towards art and studio pottery started during the 1860s in France, lead by artists such as Theodore Deck (1823–91) who introduced new techniques and styles of ceramic decoration, many based on oriental and Islamic models.

3 Popular Victorian pottery included the famous barge teapots, made primarily at Meacham in Leicestershire for sale to the families who lived and worked on the canal narrow boats. Many examples carry the name of the original owner.

The French artist-pottery movement was particularly evident during the 1920s and 1930s, when many original and interesting wares were produced by George Serre, Jean Besnard, Jean Mayoden, René Buthaud and Paul Beyer, the latter reviving the technique of salt-glazed stonewares.

The vogue for artist-pottery was soon to be seen in other European countries, especially Germany, where some interesting shapes and techniques were produced around the turn of the century by such potters as Herman Mutz of Altona. He was strongly influenced by Japanese ceramics and his son Richard also made some interesting stonewares in Berlin, often decorated with attractive 'flowing' glazes. These glazes appear to be suddenly 'frozen' from their liquid state. They were also very successfully applied by Julius Scharvogel, who was working in Munich in about 1900.

1

tory, Stig Lindberg at Gustavsberg, Harry Stålhane at Rörstrand and Toini Muona at the Arabia factory, Helsinki, Finland.

The first wares which may well be termed artist-pottery in England, were similarly sponsored by industry. The factory of Doulton, in Lambeth, London, had been in production since 1815 and their wares consisted of domestic and industrial salt-glazed stonewares. In 1871, students of the Lambeth School of Art were invited to work at the factory to choose jugs and vases to the shape required and to apply their original decoration. This was usually incised, carved or applied in a range of browns, blues and greys. The artists were then required to sign their work. Today, the individual work of such former students as Hannah Barlow, George Tinworth and Frank Butler is in great demand.

Salt-glaze stoneware was also the preference for the now famous Martin brothers, who from 1873 were working at Fulham, London. Later they moved to Southall on the western outskirts of London. Walter and Edwin Martin were trained at the Doulton studios, but much of their work was decorated with floral forms inspired by Japanese taste which enjoyed much popularity following the London International Exhibition of 1862.

It was in 1872 that William de Morgan started a workshop in Chelsea, London, where he specialized in the painting of tiles and pottery in lustres of the greens and blues seen on so much

1 The studio pottery movement that started in France spread to England during the 1870s. The Martin Brothers made their highly individualistic saltglazed stoneware from 1873, working first at Fulham and later at Southall. They combined many styles, including Gothic and Japanese.

2 A large studio was established at the Doulton factory in Lambeth in the 1870s. Here many art school-trained designers pursued their own ideas, including Hannah Barlow who developed a style of drawing on the unfired clay. She specialized in animal subjects, such as this vase made in 1880.

Following the First World War, there was a revived interest in Germany and the works of many potters active during the 1920s are to be seen in public and private collections. Foremost of this school was Bontjes van Beek, a naturalized German of Dutch descent, who was extremely successful with his finely glazed stonewares in the styles of the Chinese Sung period. Since 1946, artist-potters have been working in both East and West Germany. The work of Ingeborg and Bruno Asshoff, working in Bochum in the 1960s, was highly original. They produced many simple shapes as a ground for some most unusual 'bubbly' glazes.

The artist-pottery movement in Scandinavia was quite strong by the 1880s, when Thorwald Bindesbøll was creating decorative earthenware in Denmark. Most Scandinavian potters of the earlier period seemingly preferred the lower-fired earthenwares to stoneware, and often relied more upon applied decoration than original glaze effects. This was certainly so with Herman A. Kähler of Naestved, Denmark, who had great success with metallic lustres.

The division between the artist-potter and the ceramic industry is not so marked in Scandinavia, due to many factories providing the facilities for the artist-potter to experiment and create individual work. This was in addition to using his talents in designing for a greater production of wares made industrially. This practice has been a great asset to such fine potters as Axel Salto at the Royal Copenhagen Porcelain Fac-

2

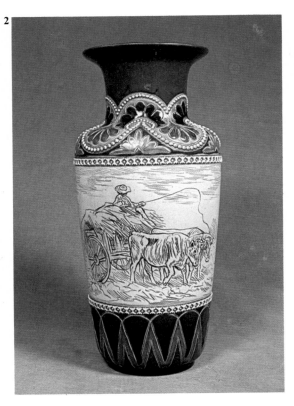

4 During the 1920s and 1930s the European potteries became dominant again, inspired partly by the Paris Exhibition of 1925 which launched the Art Deco style. These pieces were made by the Belgian pottery Keramis during the late 1920s.

Persian pottery of the 15th–19th centuries. De Morgan's work was quickly appreciated and it became necessary for him to employ more staff, including the painters Charles and Fred Passenger and Frank Iles.

3

Few of these early artist-potters were completely responsible from start to finish for the work they were involved with. Possibly the first true artist-potter was the world renowned Bernard Leach, who was initially trained at the Slade School of Art to be a teacher of drawing and etching. Leach then spent about 11 years in Japan where he received training as a potter under a Japanese master. He then returned to England accompanied by a Japanese potter, Shoji Hamada. Together they established a pottery at St. Ives in Cornwall. Leach and Hamada worked together, using all locally obtained ma-

3 The range of English art and studio pottery is shown by these examples, from left to right, a reduction-fired flambé jar and cover made at the Ruskin Pottery in about 1905, a Royal Doulton *Chang* vase, about 1925, and a vase and jardinère designed by William de Morgan and painted with bright colours and lustre glazes in Islamic style, 1888–1900.

terials, from which they produced a wide variety of wares, including Japanese style stonewares and traditional English slip-trailed wares.

Many now famous English potters worked at some period during their training at St. Ives, where Leach ran his pottery on a community basis. This enabled them to produce many modestly priced and readily saleable wares, while allowing them to create original and personal work. Michael Cardew, Nora Braden and Katherine Pleydell-Bouverie all owe a great deal of their success to the knowledge gained from the master, Bernard Leach.

4

Glass

Milestones in the history of glass

c.3100 B.C.	Beads of blue glass stamped with name of King Menes (3100–3038 B.C.) found in Egypt.
1500 B.C.	First small glass vessels appeared in Egypt and Syria.
c.1 A.D.	Glass blowing with an iron blow tube invented.
680	Glassmakers from Gaul called to Britain.
1291	Venice established glass industry on Island of Murano.
1500	Venice developed Cristallo, a clear, colourless glass.
1567	Italian and Lorraine glassmakers taken to England.
1575	Jacopo Verzelini granted a patent by Queen Elizabeth I to make glass in the manner of Murano.
c.1600	Caspar Lehman of Prague applied rock crystal cutting techniques to glass.
1608	First American glass made by settlers in Jamestown.
1615	Use of wood fuel forbidden in England and coal furnaces introduced.
c.1670	Bohemian glassmakers developed lime potash glass, a clear and robust glass metal suitable for wheel engraving.
1673–6	Ravenscroft developed lead crystal glasses.
1688	Lucas de Nehou invented a method of casting and rolling glass at Tours La Ville.
1695	St Gobain glass factory established.
1739	Caspar Wistar established first successful American glassworks in Salem county, New Jersey.
1773	Plate glassworks established at Ravenhead in England.
1827	American patent established for revolutionary designed glass pressing machine.
1864	Establishment of the Union Centrale des Arts Décoratifs in Paris led to the public recognition of the works of Emile Gallé and Eugène Rousseau.

Glass is a product of earth and fire, the result of fusing silica (sand) with an alkaline flux (soda), and a small quantity of limestone to harden the mixture. We tend to think of it as only man-made, but glass occurs naturally in the guise of a number of minerals, such as tektites (also termed moldavites), Lybian desert glass and Darwin glass. These are glassy pebbles found in many parts of the world and are thought to be the weathered remains of prehistoric meteorites. Another form of natural glass, utilized by earlier civilizations in toolmaking, is obsidian – a material of volcanic origin and produced by the rapid cooling of viscous lava. Quartz is pure silica and all types of quartz are related to natural glass. However, nearest in appearance to the man-made product is rock crystal, named from the Greek *crystallos* = clear ice. Mined in areas all over the world, it has long been cherished as a precious material suitable for all kinds of arte-facts. Stone cutters (lapidaries) delighted in working with this substance, and the technique of rock crystal cutting presents one of the most important aspects of glass decoration.

Glassmaking Techniques

Glasshouses will obviously be located where raw materials are accessible and of satisfactory quality. In Mediterranean regions, the essential soda would be obtained from certain types of seaweed although, if necessary, some raw materials could be procured from a distant source. The forest glasshouses would replace the soda of southern tradition by potash derived from wood-ash. The quality of sand – the source of silica – is of great importance to the glassmaker since impurities affect the glass colour and finality. A most important addition to the glass batch is cullet, waste pieces of glass which used to be collected by children and poor families who sold them back to the glasshouse. To form the glass frit (*frittare* – to fry), the cullet and raw materials are ground, ready for melting in the furnace. Glass is a supercooled liquid. It has no crystalline structure and passes into a viscous fluid on heating, without a definite melting point. Three stages are required for heating the frit, beginning with placing it into the melting pot, a preheated refractory crucible which stands in the furnace. The resultant viscous mass is then ready for the refining stage, during which the pot melt is increased to a maximum heat of $1,600°C$, when the frit becomes a thin liquid containing air bubbles which give off undesirable gases and water vapour. Impurities rising to the surface are skimmed off with the ladle. Lastly, the frit must be cooled so that by returning to its former viscosity it will be suitable for working at a temperature of about 700 to $800°C$.

It may now be shaped by blowing, moulding, pressing or casting and will remain ductile for about 20 minutes. If a longer working time is required, the mass can be kept pliable by brief refiring at the furnace mouth. This procedure is also used to polish the finished glass – the so called fire polish. To reduce internal stresses which may result in the glass cracking or break-ing, the shaped article must be placed into a special annealing oven or lehr, at a carefully controlled temperature.

By the 18th century, the slightly elliptical glasshouse with its enormous chimney cone had become a familiar landmark. An English Act of Parliament decreed that to enable waste smoke to drift away, glasshouse chimneys were to have a height of at least $15.24 m$ (50 ft), and some were built much taller.

Glasshouse pots are made by hand and need special treatment, having to remain in a heating chamber from four to eight months before being tested for additional periods at very high tem-peratures. Nevertheless, these pots are service-able only for a period of up to three months at most, because glass attacks the clay. Potsetting is one of the most hazardous tasks even under modern factory conditions. The men receive special pay for this work and there is a tradition of free beer as well.

The glassmaker's tools and techniques are as old as Christianity, although glass was probably made at least 4,000 years ago. The blowpipe made its appearance about the first century A.D. It is a tube made of iron, with a thickened end to gather the glass metal and is protected at handl-ing points by a wooden covering. The lump of glass, termed the paraison, may be taken from the pot with the blowing iron or an iron rod, the pontil. The pontil is used for drawing out the glass and leaves a rough mark where broken off, the so-called pontil mark. Both small and large shears are used for cutting off parts such as rims, and pincers and a wooden lipper are needed for shaping.

The rake and ladle are used for skimming off impurities from the frit. These tools are sus-pended from the arms of the master blower's chair – a short bench with flat and slightly slop-ing long arms, developed during the 17th cen-tury. The term chair also refers to the team of glassmakers working together – the gaffer, or master blower, and his assistants called the servitors and footmen, usually three or four in number. An important glassmaker's requisite is the marver, a polished iron slab for rolling, smoothing or shaping the paraison, and also used for embedding applied decoration in the glass surface.

Advances in technology have enabled greater control in glass manufacture, guaranteeing a larger percentage of perfect output, although the production method remains basically un-changed. Diamond and wheel engraving can now be applied with electrically-powered tools. Mass produced polishing is achieved by placing the glass objects in an acid bath; and acid etching, although applied in earlier times and popular-ized during the 19th century, is now utilized in the fields of decorative, domestic and industrial glassmaking. Sandblasting, too, is a modern in-novation, although it is a variant of the abrasive technique.

Engraving, either by hand tool or copper wheel, and wheel cutting will always represent the pinnacle of the glass decorator's art. Unlike any other decoration it highlights the refractive property of the material.

Gilding and enamelling can be applied either cold, when life expectancy is short, or permanently fused to the glass surface.

Because of impurities contained in the raw materials, glass will not be entirely colourless, unless decolorized by addition of certain substances, the most common being manganese dioxide. Additions of metallic oxides result in glass of all possible colour shades.

pattern. Since metal contracts when cooling, the rod could be extracted quite easily and the remaining core cleaned out. Handles and foot are applied separately.

Cored vessels represent one of the most delightful facets of the early glassmaker's art. Turquoise and yellow colours dominate; later, almost all colours were applied.

Certain other techniques for shaping glass were available to early craftsmen. Casting glass in open or closed moulds was a logical step,

1 This fragment is from the bottom of a flat-bottomed bowl decorated in gold with painted details. The basal disc shows half figures of a husband and wife – Orfitus and Constantia. Between them stands a small figure of Hercules, emphasizing the couple's paganism. The bowl is Roman and dates from the 4th century. The diameter is 104 mm.

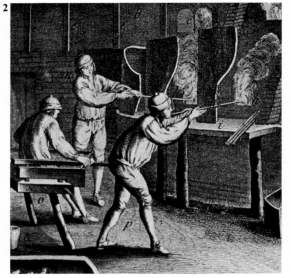

The Ancient World

Glass, as an independent material, made its appearance some time during 3000 to 2000 B.C., although man had prior knowledge of this substance in the form of vitreous glazes. On the basis of newly excavated material, it is now thought that glassmaking originated in western Asia rather than in the eastern Mediterranean littoral. Hollow glass in larger quantity appears for the first time in Egypt from about 1500 B.C.

Early glass centres were favourably situated in the Tigris–Euphrates region, the coastal and river areas of Egypt and along the Phoenician coast in the cities of Sidon, Tyre and Acco. The colourful glass pastes and enamel inlays of Egyptian artefacts bear witness to an abundance of fine raw materials.

The first hollow glass consists of small vessels produced by the core technique, whereby the required form is pre-shaped over the end of a metal rod, the diameter of which corresponds to the required orifice of the vessel. The form is made of clay or straw and sand, probably held together by a cloth bag. The glass mass, ground from larger pieces and reheated frequently to allow satisfactory fusion, is contained in a small crucible into which the glassmaker places his metal dipstick and trails threads of glass around the preformed core until it is covered.

After reheating and marvering smooth, the vessel was frequently decorated by application of contrasting coloured glass threads, which could be combed with a special tool to create a feather

since it was similar to existing techniques of metal and pottery working. Larger vessels and small ornaments could be produced by making a glass paste from powdered fragments and fusing it in the mould. In the mosaic glass technique, the vessel, usually a large open bowl, is built up from slices of coloured glass laid next to each other over a mould forming the shape, and covered by an outer mould. When fused and released from the moulds, the vessel surfaces are ground smooth. Mosaic plaques and millefiori glass made from slices of multi-coloured glass rods are produced in a similar manner.

Egyptian artisans were able lapidaries and it is not surprising that they applied their craft to glass. There are reasons to suppose that large glass blocks were transported from their place of manufacture to regions where facilities for glassmaking were not available. This may account for glass objects of similar colour and texture found over widely dispersed areas. Such raw glass blocks were often cut and ground to form a variety of objects.

From about 1200 to 700 B.C., Egyptian glassmaking fell into a decline due to a number of political events and disasters. From the 9th century B.C., the main centres on the Syrian coast and in the Tigris–Euphrates region may have been of Phoenician origin or Phoenician influenced. Phoenicia owned a great fleet of trading ships and Phoenician-made beads and glassware found their way to the most Northern parts of the world.

When cored vessels reappeared about 700 to 600 B.C., they had changed drastically in character, and display four distinct design forms: the aryballos, a globular flask with everted rim, short neck and two miniature handles with finials, applied from under the rim to the shoulder; the alabastron, a cylindrical vessel, rounded at the base with short neck and wide, flattened rim and two short handles applied below the shoulder; the oinochoe, a miniature one-handled jug with pinched-in (trefoil) lip and splayed out foot; the

Roman rule. The so called muzzines, bowls of agate glass made in imitation of semiprecious stones, were still popular during the early 2nd century, and are frequent finds on Roman service sites.

The momentous discovery of blowing glass by means of the iron blowpipe is thought to have occurred during the early years of the first century A.D., and in one sweep transformed the material from luxury to domestic use. Pliny ascribes the invention of glass to Phoenician

2 Glassblowers at work by the furnace 'glory holes'. To protect their eyes from the flame and heat, the glass-workers wore a shield fixed to a band around their heads.

3 Various processes of glassmaking are shown; such as heating the glass and adding the cullet, marvering it on a metal slab (the marver) placed on the gaffer's chair, blowing into a mould, rolling and cutting off the surplus from the pontil rod. Shears and pincers are clearly shown hanging from the side of the glassmaker's chair, and the assistant servitor or footman is prepared to take the paraison off from the blow iron onto the pontil.

amphorisk of baluster shape, a longish cylindrical neck with handles of the same length and a pointed base ending in a knop or minute disc shaped foot.

Cored vessels are small, between $2\frac{1}{2}$ to 5 in, rarely larger, and were used as containers for perfumes and ointments. Those which were not provided with a foot were either strung up by the handles or rested on specially made stands of metal or glass.

With the coming of Alexander industry flourished and a great centre was established in the new founded Egyptian city of Alexandria, where the finest luxury glass was produced by workmen who had immigrated from centres in the Middle East. Asiatic glassmakers brought techniques of colouring, moulding, cutting and engraving. Fine glass seals and glass cameos of many different shades are representative of the excellent workmanship of the new Hellenistic glass industry, and formed part of the luxury ware exported during the first centuries of

traders. Irrespective of whether this is true, it does seem that the new technique of blowing must be credited to the glassmaking centre of Sidon, on the Phoenician coast, and this is borne out by the character of the first blown vessels. These are small flasks and ewers in the shape of fruit, especially bunches of grapes and dates, and figurative vessels, particularly single or double head flasks, the latter representing the god Janus. Green or brownish colours are frequently seen in this early group of glasses, which are known as relief glasses.

The new discovery spread quickly and soon Eastern and Hellenistic craftsmen set up workshops for glassblowing in the western domains of the Roman Empire.

Much of the early blown glass is a replica of pottery and metal ware of the period, and in the same way as Roman artisans and factories stamped their products with their own mark, so the early glassblowers incorporated a personal stamp or name in the mould.

The Roman Empire

At the end of the first 150 years of Roman expansion, the Empire stretched from Britain to Africa and from Spain to the Black Sea. Stable and prosperous conditions, particularly during the first 150 to 200 years of Roman rule, encouraged trade and industry. Glassmakers from Mediterranean centres followed in the wake of the Legions, and began to establish glasshouses throughout suitable areas of the western domain the vast Roman Empire.

Glass made during the period of Roman occupation is frequently termed Roman glass, even though it may have been produced by Syrian gaffers in the Rhineland or a Hellenistic workshop in Gaul. Because of the difficulties in obtaining the vital raw materials, large quantities of glass, especially luxury ware, were imported from Syria, Alexandria and Rome, and it is often impossible to determine the provenance of a piece of Roman glass.

Gold sandwich or *fondi d'oro* glasses present a specialized technique already known to Alexandrian glassworkers who established workshops in Antioch and brought their gold glass to Syria. The method involves placing patterns in gold leaf between two layers of clear glass. In the earlier Syrian pieces the gold pattern usually covers the entire area, up to a defined rim, and there may be additional cut decoration applied to the outer vessel. Gold sandwich glass reaching western territory was probably made in Italian workshops. The majority of gold sandwich glass was discovered in catacombs in the vicinity of Rome.

The earliest free blown Roman glass are the so called tearbottles, club formed vials 2–5 inches (5.1–12.2 cm) in length. Mainly funerary finds,

1 Unguentarium of green tinted metal composed of two joined tubes held together and decorated by a festoon of spiral and zig-zag glass threads, which also serve to strengthen the vessel. Found in Syria, this flat based vessel dates from the 1st to the 3rd century. The height is 112 mm.

2 Syrian one-handled flask in green glass metal. Mould-blown in the style of the Ennion school, the decoration consists of a design of garlands, columns and swirls. The multi-ribbed handle rises from the shoulder of the circular body and is attached below the lip rim of the neck.

3 Snake-thread flask in pale green clear glass, slightly weathered with a short, squat stem reasting on a circular foot. Both stem and foot have been applied separately. The body is decorated with applied snake coils, flattened and nicked, the neck encircled by a thin glass thread.

they supposedly serve as receptacles for mourners' tears, but more likely are used as unguentaria, containing perfumes and ointments. Domestic vessels, glass bangles, beads, finger and earrings are common in Roman graves. They may not be elaborate, but provide one of the most spectacular features associated with ancient glass – the iridescence.

Iridescence or weathering is the result of long exposure to damp earth and air, and the glass surface attacked will become scaly and flake off. Although this disease is not progressive, with prolonged exposure the vessel may deteriorate to the point of disintegration. However, the striking scintillating rainbow effect of the glass surface caused by chemical reaction of the weathering process is irresistible to the collector of Roman glass, who will not be deterred by the high prices currently asked.

Roman glassmakers ably exploited the new technique of mould blowing. An attractive and individual group are the Eastern inspired glasses by the maker Ennion and his circle. Mould blown vessels of this group from Sidon and Cyprus are decorated with early Christian symbols, naturalistically patterned freezes, Greek inscriptions, circus scenes and human figures. Inscriptions usually denote the makers name with added slogans or wishes. Dating from the first century, these pieces probably represent almost the earliest glasses signed by their makers. Ennion's branch subsidiaries sprang up quickly in many parts of the Roman West. Most of these related vessels come from Gallic and Rhenish provinces, and British settlements such as Colchester. Few were produced in Italy.

The unmistakeable influence of Syrian gaffers is seen in the group of free-blown glass decorated by applied snakelike threads of opaque colour. These vessels, with or without handles or in the shape of ewers, have their counterparts in the Eastern hemisphere, but were produced in quantity in 3rd century Rhineland. The late W. A. Thorpe aptly refers to this group as Snake Thread (Rhine) Ltd.!

On functional lines, several factories produced the practical Roman round or rectangular jar and bottle, an industry which flourished from the late first century. These bottles were largely produced in south eastern Gaul and frequently bear a makers mark, the name of Frontinus occurring repeatedly. By the late 2nd century attractive vessels emerged, decorated with applied trails and spirals, and during the 3rd century tall jugs with elegant handles became popular. Fragments with painted decoration have been discovered, although never complete, but other finds included dishes and bowls decorated by shallow cutting and engraving. The most consummate *tour de force* must be attributed to the lapidary, and cameo cutting, was expertly carried out in Alexandrian workshops.

During the 3rd and 4th centuries, an astonishing cutting technique evolved which has never been equalled. This is applied in the Vasa Diatreta, a mould-blown, thick, ovoid or bucket-shaped vessel, which may be monochrome or cased in layers of coloured glass. The coloured casing is so manipulated by the cutter that a contrasting coloured network of delicate pattern surrounds the glass body, held only by some remaining struts. The upper half of these so-called cage cups is usually encircled by an inscription, undercut in the same manner. Figurative cage cups reminiscent of oriental ivory carving are related to this technique.

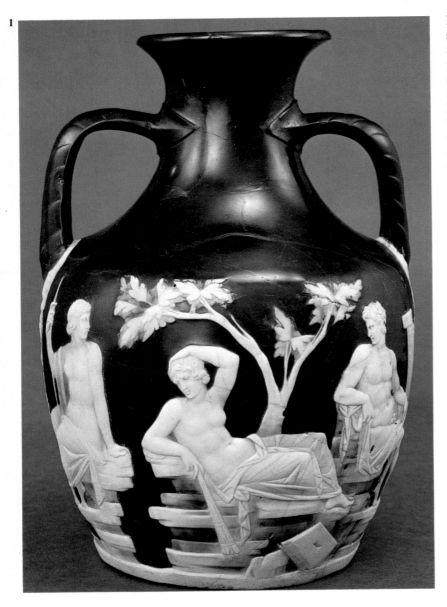

known as *Waldglas*, or in France and the French speaking Lowlands as *verre de fougere*, was of a green or greenish blue colour, as well as of a pale amber tone, depending on local raw materials. The medieval slump or, in glassmaking language the empty ages, had affected Western Europe by the 8th century. The church, which in the eras that followed encouraged and subsidized the arts and architecture, forbade the use of glass vessels for ritual purposes. The foreign elements introduced by Roman colonization in the form of successful competition by Eastern artisans and merchants resulted in persecution and deprivation of oriental and semitic glassworkers and any flourishing of a native glass industry was doomed.

Pre-Islam and Islamic Glass
Not until the 4th century was the Christian religion adopted in Rome. By this time, the Empire's financial burden had become enormous. Apart from the difficulties of maintaining order and prosperity throughout a vast territory, the army met increasing difficulties in beating back hordes of barbarians which threatened to weaken – and eventually overran – the frontier lines.

In A.D. 324, Constantine I came to the throne to rule his great Empire. Christianity was adopted as the official religion of state and Constantine built himself a new capital, Byzantium, from which to rule. This split of East and West predestined the division of the Empire. In the Western part, isolated forest glasshouses produced simple, poor quality domestic glass, under hazardous conditions. In the East, however, glassmaking continued almost undisturbed under the protection and new affluence of Byzantium and her rulers. Craftsmen were encouraged by special privileges. Under Theodosius II (A.D. 408–450) glassmakers were exempt from all taxes.

Worship of the new religion was expressed by the erection of new temples, and the Byzantine basilica in all its shining splendour required equally sumptuous adornment, which survives to this day in the golden and colourful brilliance of the mosaic pictures decorating walls and ceiling, and made of millions of coloured glass cubes, the tesserae. This aspect of mosic art inspired the manufacture of coloured glass windows, representing a large section of glass manufacture. Stone and plasterwork consisted of a tracery of naturalistic patterns with the voids filled by small pieces of coloured glass.

Most of this attractive work was destroyed as a result of Leo III's iconoclastic movement in A.D. 726. This occurrence, as well as the sack of Constantinople in 1204 during the fourth crusade may be a valid reason for the scanty survival of Byzantine glass, despite a prolific industry. Some pieces of green, wheel-cut glass in the form of cups and dishes are still to be seen as part of the treasure of St Marks in Venice. This greenish glass colour is responsible for travellers' tales of enormous objects cut from single huge emeralds. The hexagonally shaped Sacro Catino cup at Genoa was originally thought to have been

1 The Portland Vase is the finest example of Roman cameo glass – a cobalt blue amphora, cased with opaque white in which the design is cut in relief. The vase is blown, possibly into a mould, and appears to have been cut by the wheel.

2 This colourless mosque lamp is enamelled and gilded, decorated with a Naskh script dedication. It dates from 1330–45 and is Syrian.

3 This 5th century drinking horn was found in Bingerbrück in Germany. It is blown and curved with applied nine fold horizontal spiral trail and continuous sloping trail.

4 12th century Islamic beaker with a relief cut with linear elements. Details of the design are filled in with engraved hatched lines. Height 140 mm.

Glass in Medieval Europe
By the 5th century, a fair number of glasshouses established themselves in the Seine–Rhine areas, largely with the help of Syrian glassmakers. Important centres were situated in the Lorraine, in Trêves, Picardy, Cologne, Mainz, Namur and Liège. This fusion of Northern concept and Eastern know-how and artistic inspiration resulted in the emergence of a characteristic glass style, which dominates the product of all glassmaking areas in the Roman domain. Freeblown vessels with applied trails or blobs, cone beakers and drinking horns with patterns of applied threads, vases and bowls with trails applied in a diamond pattern – the 'nipped diamond waies' and finally the intricate claw beaker, were the results of glasshouses affected by the still present but diminishing influence of Rome. The accent at this time was on domestic, rather than luxury glassware, and the 6th and 7th century glasshouses produced a metal of liquid greenish colour prevalent in forest regions where wood- or plant-ash was used as the source of potash alkali, and knowledge of decolorization was non-existent. This forest glass comonly

carved from a single emerald, and a solid emerald table on three golden feet, plundered by the Arab commander Musa (*c.*710–20) from Toledo, was most likely made of nothing else but Byzantine glass, sumptuous though it must have been.

In A.D. 634 the Byzantine forces succumbed to Moslem invaders and by A.D. 750 a huge Arab empire from Turkestan through Armenia, Syria, Persia, Arabia, Egypt, the North African coast and Spain had been created, embracing all important Eastern glassmaking centres. Despite the mixed elements which made up the Islamic population, a distinct Islamic style had evolved by the 10th century. Due to religious ethics, the decoration was initially confined to the ornamental, non-figurative style. Geometrical wheel-cut patterns of ovals and diamonds typify 9th and 10th century glass found in Persia.

A unique group decorated by masterly relief cutting are the so-called Hedwig Glasses, named after St Hedwig, patron saint of Poland and Silesia who died in 1243 and supposedly the owner of one of these vessels, still preserved in Wroclaw.

An innovation, also thought to have originated in Egypt, is lustre surface painting, whereby a metallic colour pigment was applied and fired to form a lustrous film.

Islam's greatest contribution to glass art consists of exquisite and imaginative enamelled decoration. This technique was carried out in three stages. At first, the ornamental pattern was applied in gold leaf and fired. During the second stage the design was traced in red enamel and again fired. Lastly, the design was filled in with coloured enamels and once more returned to the muffle kiln for firing.

Islamic enamel is usually translucent, except for white, which is opaque. The main centres for this technique were Raqqa (*c.*1170–1270), Aleppo (1250–65) and Damascus (1250–1400). Glassmaking in Raqqa declined with the city's destruction by the Mongols in 1259.

Aleppo enamelling work is of a more imaginative and refined character than the Raqqa product, partly due to the gradual relaxation of Islamic laws toward figurative representation. Musicians, hunters, birds, beasts, flowers and trees in elaborately traced cartouches with trefoil decoration are associated with Aleppo workshops. The celebrated 'Luck of Edenhall' (Victoria and Albert Museum), a finely enamelled flared beaker, can most certainly be associated with Aleppo workmanship.

Rich, small-scale enamelling is one of the features of Damascene glass decoration. The Saracene mosque lamps with overall gilding and enamelling, and elaborate inscriptions in stylized Naksh script created a fashion for glass *à la façon de Damas*, and many specimens have found their way into European collections. During the late 19th century, the French glass artist Joseph Brocard recreated a number of enamelled glass pieces which are almost exact copies of Damascene mosque lamps and vessels.

Characteristic friezes of animals and flowers with the added emblem of the Chinese Lotus

2

indicate the influence of invading Mongols. When Tamerlane invaded Damascus in 1400 and deported all artisans to Samarkand, the glass industry did not survive. A revival took place much later with the aid of Murano workmen, and the best product came from 18th century Shiraz glasshouses, with the typical blue coloured rosewater sprinkler as its most elegant representative.

4

3

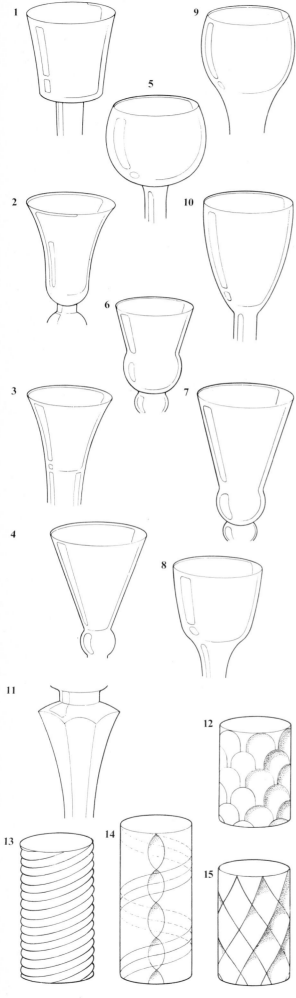

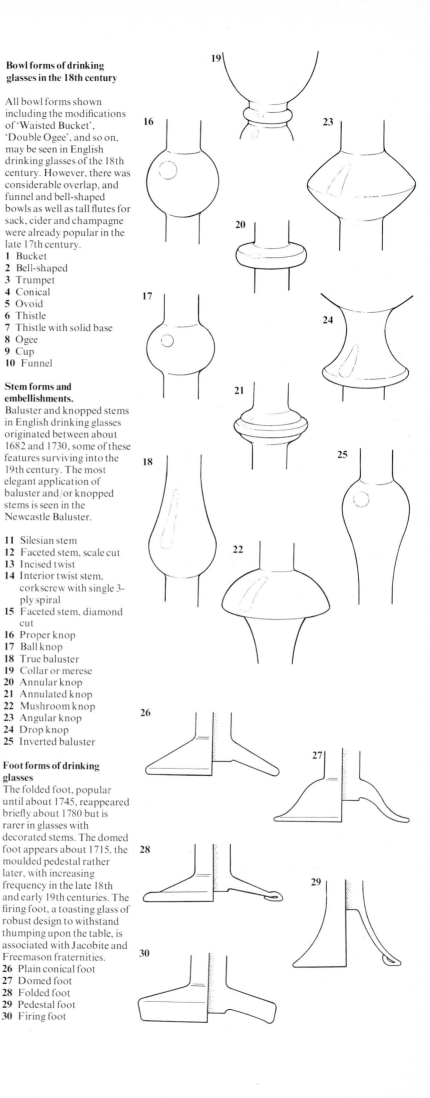

Bowl forms of drinking glasses in the 18th century

All bowl forms shown including the modifications of 'Waisted Bucket', 'Double Ogee', and so on, may be seen in English drinking glasses of the 18th century. However, there was considerable overlap, and funnel and bell-shaped bowls as well as tall flutes for sack, cider and champagne were already popular in the late 17th century.

1 Bucket
2 Bell-shaped
3 Trumpet
4 Conical
5 Ovoid
6 Thistle
7 Thistle with solid base
8 Ogee
9 Cup
10 Funnel

Stem forms and embellishments.

Baluster and knopped stems in English drinking glasses originated between about 1682 and 1730, some of these features surviving into the 19th century. The most elegant application of baluster and/or knopped stems is seen in the Newcastle Baluster.

11 Silesian stem
12 Faceted stem, scale cut
13 Incised twist
14 Interior twist stem, corkscrew with single 3-ply spiral
15 Faceted stem, diamond cut
16 Proper knop
17 Ball knop
18 True baluster
19 Collar or merese
20 Annular knop
21 Annulated knop
22 Mushroom knop
23 Angular knop
24 Drop knop
25 Inverted baluster

Foot forms of drinking glasses

The folded foot, popular until about 1745, reappeared briefly about 1780 but is rarer in glasses with decorated stems. The domed foot appears about 1715, the moulded pedestal rather later, with increasing frequency in the late 18th and early 19th centuries. The firing foot, a toasting glass of robust design to withstand thumping upon the table, is associated with Jacobite and Freemason fraternities.

26 Plain conical foot
27 Domed foot
28 Folded foot
29 Pedestal foot
30 Firing foot

Window Glass

Window glass has a long and varied history, and we know that some glass panes were already used in Roman buildings, although we have no exact knowledge of their purpose.

Two techniques of window glass production were available to early glassmakers. The Crown glass method was practised by Normandy glassmakers; a glass bubble is blown to the required size, then cut open, transferred to a pontil and freely rotated with frequent reheating at the furnace mouth. Great dexterity is necessary in this technique, and the result is a large, circular, thin and wavy pane of glass with the bulls eye at the centre. This is cut out and resealed with a blob of glass.

The Broadsheet technique was employed by Lorraine, and Bohemian glassmakers. An elongated bubble is blown and the ends cut off to form a hollow cylinder which is then slit open with a hot iron, and the opened cylinder placed in a flattening oven for reheating and flattening.

A technique of casting large panes of glass was perfected in 1688 by Louis Lucas de Nehou, who established his factory in 1695 at St Gobain, still one of the largest glass factories. In 1773 a plate glass works was established at Ravenhead in Lancashire. The building is still in existence and is owned by Pilkington Brothers, who have revolutionized sheet glass manufacture with their float glass process.

A window tax to aid revenue was levied in England in 1696 and repealed only as recently as 1851, although it was replaced by a tax on inhabited houses.

The casting of large glass panes also encouraged the mirror industry. The early mirrors of polished stone and metal were eventually replaced by mirrors of glass, backed with thin sheets of metal, which were later substituted with a coating. There are references to the use of mirrors in Venice before 1500, and before the development of casting glass mirror glass was produced by the broadsheet technique.

With increasing use, mirrors were decorated in every form and style applicable to glass. They were painted, engraved, bevelled, framed stylishly in metal, wood, gesso, glass and mirror glass. By the 18th century, the looking-glass had become a fashionable piece of furniture.

Stained and Painted Glass

From Byzantium and the Eastern church came the inspiration of coloured panes of window glass, appearing as early as the 9th century in Italy. The stained-glass window, however, is the great achievement of Northern glaziers.

Around the year A.D. 1000, several groups of glass painters were active, mainly within the confines of monasteries. We have precise descriptions of the staining, painting and making of glass windows at this early period, thanks to the invaluable work of Theophilus, the Helmershausen (Paderborn) monk, who supplies detailed information on all aspects of glassmaking in the second volume of his work *Diversarum Artium*

Schedulae of the 11th century.

The technique of producing stained glass has not changed during the centuries. The glass painter presents his design in actual size, marking all colours and leads. The glass is cut to shape by drawing the outline with a hot iron and dropping water on this design. The glass cracks and can then be broken as required. The diamond cutting tool did not come into use in window glass manufacture until about A.D. 1500. A notched, spanner-like tool, the grozing iron, was used for any additional cutting.

The glass, coloured in the batch – also termed potmetal – is painted with a low viscosity mixture prepared from copper oxide (later replaced by scale) and powdered glass. This mixture, called Schwarzlot, is also used to obtain shading or blackening, and other ornamental effects are obtained by scraping or abrasion. The painting is fused to the glass surface by annealing and the pane inserted into the prepared calmes (*calamus* = reed), and the strips of lead are then soldered at the corners and cemented.

The naturalistic design pattern of early stained-glass windows produces the effect of an oriental carpet. These concepts were soon swept away, and in the late Gothic window realistic pictorial-and-figurative representation merges with the architectural dimension of the period. It is thought that the earliest surviving stained-glass windows are those of Augsburg cathedral, with figures of the prophets dating from the mid-11th century. Glaziers from the Continent brought the craft to England, working on the windows of great cathedrals such as Canterbury, York and Lincoln.

Windows can be dated by the design style, not only of the figures but also of the type of border and its decorative geometrical pattern. In the 12th century, the central figure no longer stands alone, but is surrounded by a framework of separate cartouches, representing the entire sequence of the chronicle. During the 13th and 14th centuries stained-glass art flourished in a wealth of brilliant colour. The design achieves greater freedom, incorporating trees and leaves and certain naturalistic patterns. The industry expanded and became organized, each workman specializing in a particular field.

The 14th century invention of the yellow stain, a silver nitrate film which was applied to the glass surface and annealed, was exploited to produce colour tones from light brown to yellow and brilliant orange, and a bright emerald green when applied to panes of pot metal blue.

By 1500, a further colour, *eisenrot* (iron red) was developed and intricate colour effects were achieved by overlaying or grinding away colour films. The 16th century brought a great change in concept and treatment. The style of design becomes broader and richer, the window assumes the role of backcloth to a painting, and the application of enamels to glass paved the way for the metamorphosis from stained window to painted glass picture.

This developed into a small art and the finest work of this type was produced during the late

This is a Swiss stained
[glass] roundel representing
[the] dream of Jacob's ladder,
[whi]ch fills the upper two-
[third]s. The lower third part
[show]s an inscription: *Heer*
[Joh]*an Jacob Hediger und*
[Fra]*w Maria Elisabet*
[Kei]*serin sein Gemalin* with
[mem]orial plate and the date
[168]5. Besides this example,
[the] Church of St Michael
[whi]ch stands in Nostall
[Par]k in Wragby, Yorkshire,
[En]gland, contains much
[for]eign glass.

16th and the 17th century, particularly in
Switzerland with designs by great artists such as
Holbein, Burkmair and Urs Graf. Small commemorative panels were popular gifts, larger
glass panes accommodated a single design,
heraldic motifs and symbols were represented in
brilliant translucent enamels. Eventually these
gave way to opaque paint, lead surrounds were
dispensed with, and with the rococo taste the
glass picture had arrived. Now, however, the
picture looks at us from behind the glass, a
technique which required the painting process to
be applied in the reverse order on the back of the
glass panel. The highest artistic level is achieved
in the glass painting produced by the Augsburg
school from the late 17th and 18th century. The
theme remains religious, with representation of
popular saints or biblical events. The opening up
of eastern trade routes resulted in a growing
interest in oriental art, and the western drawing
room in the new Chinese Chippendale or rococo
style would have been incomplete without the
focal point of a splendid looking-glass, frequently
embellished by Chinese mirror painting of great
charm.

Glass pictures fall into several categories,

picture decorating the fashionable 19th centu[ry]
drawing room. For these pictures, engravings [of]
well known paintings are used and the inked pa[per]
transferred onto the back of the glass. Opaq[ue]
colours are then applied in a reverse proces[s.]
Silhouettes form another charming group [of]
great popularity during the *Biedermeyer* an[d]
Victorian periods. A revival of a type of Zwi[s-]
chengold glass technique using gold and silv[er]
foil is misnomered verre eglomisé, after th[e]
French 18th century picture and mirror frame[r]
Glomy. In actual fact, Glomy's speciality lay i[n]
applying a surround of black colour bordere[d]
with gold, onto the back of the glass protectin[g]
the picture, usually a coloured engraving or [a]
miniature, and particularly effective in th[e]
framing of silhouettes.

At the other end of the scale are the man[y]
small craft centres producing naive pictures [of]
saints, which found their allotted niche not onl[y]
in the home of the peasant but also in th[e]
bourgeois atmosphere of the town house, muc[h]
as the icon did in Eastern Europe.

With the pre-Raphaelite school of paintin[g]
came a renewed interest in the stained glass an[d]
mosaic picture, and most of this work is c[...]

Venice

After the fall of Damascus and the decline of the Islamic industry, a new element was prepared to fill the void, and for almost 250 years the development and flowering of the European glass industry was determined by the monopolistic aspirations of that great maritime power, the Republic of Venice. Just as under the auspices of Roman domination, glassmakers trod the path of the Roman Legions and brought their knowledge to all corners of the great Empire, so it was that the Italian glassmakers, with notable dedication, took to the road and began to establish or re-establish glassmaking centres in suitable areas throughout Europe.

Although there had been active trade in glass during previous centuries, it is only now that we see the dawn of a commercialized glass industry. This was due both to the practical genius of the glass artist and the commercial acumen of a number of able personalities.

The great church of St Marks provides an instant link between East and West, and indeed was originally planned as a Byzantine basilica. As late as 1159, Venetian artisans were employed on the mosaics, and this craft was carried on in centres such as Rome and Siena. Venice became

the nucleus for the manufacture of hollow glass, and in 1291 the entire industry was transferred to the nearby island of Murano. This was as much in the interest of safety to prevent conflagration as in the interest of secrecy to prevent any leakage of Venetian glassmaking techniques. Furthermore, it was intended to force buyers to purchase only direct from Venice.

The Murano glassworkers were strictly controlled and heavy punishment awaited the man who was tempted to accept employment elsewhere and was caught leaving the island; nor was he always safe from the long arm of Venetian vengeance on foreign soil. Nevertheless, inducement was great, and many glassworkers did escape to foreign lands. In addition, the rival industry at Altare, composed of French and Flemish workmen, imposed no such laws and even encouraged journeys abroad.

The revival of enamelling techniques was one of the earliest consequences of the newly established industry of Murano, and from Venice the art spread to all parts of the continent where it has been practised ever since, without interruption.

The earliest Venetian enamelling is found on deep-coloured Gothic-style tazza and goblets or

2 This stained glass from Canterbury Cathedral in England, 'Adam Delving' is the second figure of the genealogical series. It now occupies the central position in the lowest row of figures in the great west window. A 19th century copy is now found in its original position – the lower part of the far west clerestory window on the north side of the choir. The window dates from about 1174.

3 This stained glass – 'Annunciation' by Edward Burne-Jones is at Castle Howard, Yorkshire, England. It was made in 1874–5. The late 19th century saw a great revival in the art of stained glass and several of the Pre-Raphaelite painters were active in designing coloured windows and glass panels as well as mosaics.

1

standing cups with outsplayed foot, together
with applied, crenellated or gadrooned trail
around the base of the cup. These mid-15th
century vessels were frequently made to commemorate certain events, and a marriage cup
would portray the groom and bride. The
Berovieri family, distinguished glassmakers and
decorators, are credited with this type of work.
A special feature of early Venetian enamelling
and gilding is a scale-like pattern and the application of bright colour dots.

The greatest Venetian development was the
rediscovery, *c.*1500, of decolorizing agents, resulting in the production of a colourless, transparent glass metal, the cristallo. To retain its

2

clear property, cristallo had to be blown fairly
thin, and although brittle it was exceptionally
pliable, a joy to the gaffer who exploited this
sometimes to the point of absurdity. A distinctive style emerged, resulting in graceful airy
shapes and exaggerated winged glasses with
applied handles, writhing and snake-like, and
sometimes in a clear strong blue colour contrasting well with the colourless body of the vessel.
Finials and handles were often additionally
manipulated by pinching flat with a patterned
tool, and rims were crenellated and wavy.

A significant development was the *latticinio*
or lace glass technique. This most decorative
glass effect is achieved by embedding opaque
white enamel threads in a clear matrix, produced
by blowing clear glass into a mould lined with
canes of opaque white glass. The canes adhere to
the colourless glass mass and the paraison is then

manipulated to form a variety of patterns, the *tour de force* being the true criss-cross filigree net (Netzglas). The whole is then covered with a layer of clear glass, and the filigree pattern is truly embedded. Alexandrian colour techniques were successfully revived in the late 16th and 17th century. *Schmelzglas*, a process by which glass of several colours are allowed to fuse and run into each other in a natural stone design in imitation of various agates, is found in graceful forms of Grecian-inspired urn or ewer shapes. It was revived during the 19th century in several countries and particularly by another Italian, Salviati.

One of the most practical inventions of the Italian gaffer is the folded foot. The glassmaker needed a firm base for his vessel and by folding the soft glass under to obtain a foot rim of double thickness, this was achieved. This important innovation was quickly adopted elsewhere, and the folded foot was still applied to glasses of the 18th century.

Ice or crackle glass was another Italian invention but was only short lived. It was produced either by brief quenching of the hot glass bulb in water, which caused numerous fissures on the surface (which could then be reheated and blown to requirement), or by rolling the glass bulb in powdered glass fragments which adhere to the warm glass, and then further blowing and reheating to obliterate sharp edges. This last method was revived in 19th century France and named *brocs à glaces*. Contrary to the fanciful shapes of plain blown *façon de Venise*, ice glass is of sturdy, more down to earth design – beakers, standing cups – with added decoration applied in the form of gilt lion masks and glass pearls.

All these processes are seen in glass produced in Netherland glasshouses such as Antwerp and Liège, where Altarist and Venetian glassmakers had settled. It is therefore frequently impossible to distinguish between *façon de Venise* made on Italian or Flemish soil.

Little colour was introduced in the making of *latticinio*, but it does occur with pink and blue filigree canes, more frequently so in glass made outside Italy. While the Italian *latticinio* technique inspired the English 18th-century enamel twist stem, the Italian (hollow blown) baluster stem was equally adopted by foreign glasshouses. Cold gilding, cold enamelling and diamond engraving, mostly of the light, hatched type, was a popular form of Venetian glass decoration.

With the opening of Eastern trade routes, Venice too commenced production of milk-glass in imitation of the newly imported porcelain. During the 18th century, the Miotti glasshouse in particular responded to the latest fashion with drinking vessels and table-ware in milk-glass (*lattimo*), decorated with exquisite enamelling in bright colours and in black or sepia. By this time, however, Venice had lost her monopoly of the glassmaking industry and this was taken over by Bohemia and England. Each was very different in its concept, but both produced glass of excellent quality and design.

Several factors had contributed to this transition. The European glass industry had grown so successful that there was a decrease in glass imports from Venice. Spain and the Netherlands had developed into maritime powers due to the discovery of new trade routes by way of the Cape of Good Hope, and Venice was losing her supremacy on the seas. There was still a demand for mirrors and chandeliers, but a new invention pushed aside the fragile Venetian cristallo – the invention of a sturdy glass metal capable of supporting decorative treatment by deep cutting and engraving, gilding and enamelling by annealing. Bohemia and England shared this success – one with a potash-lime glass composition, the other with the sparkling lead crystal.

1 Façon de Venise goblet dating from the late 17th or early 18th centuries. It is an elaborate winged glass (Flügelglas or Schlangenglas) with an interlacing colour twist stem and honey-comb pattern bowl. It was made in the Netherlands.

2 This Venetian or Lowlands tall latticinio vase dates from the late 16th century. The enamelling of scattered insects is unusual and is possibly a device to disguise small glass defects.

3 This Milchglas beaker with enamelled decoration comes from Venice and dates from 1740. Due to a flourishing trade with the East, glasshouses soon attempted the manufacture of opaque white glass in imitation of Chinese porcelain. The most famous of Venetian glassfactories to produce milchglas was that of the Miotti family, and their pieces were frequently decorated to please the tourist trade.

In the 19th century, Antonio Salviati developed a commercial revival of 17th century Venetian techniques. The most interesting art glass, however, was produced in the 20th century in the studios of Paolo Venini and Ercole Barovier. After a number of earlier associations, Venini established his own factory at Murano. His achievements lay in the development of texture and surface effects, in the early stages similar to some of Tiffany's work in the United States, but later he adopted a distinctive design based on the exploitation of colour glass with shapes of elegant simplicity. Association with gifted designers, architects and professional artists coupled with excellent craftsmanship and good taste marks

1 This colourless glass goblet in façon de Venise, with elabroate coloured stem and pink and red applied flowers, dates from 1869. It was made by Salviati and Company in Murano, who imitated successfully many of the early techniques and copied about 70 pieces from the British Museum collections.

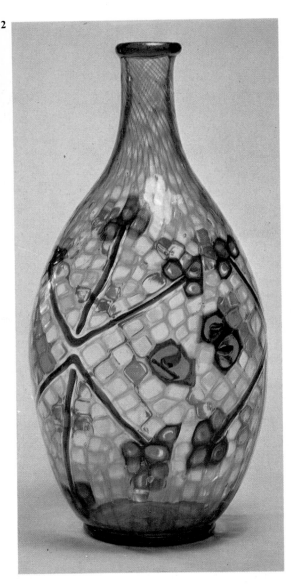

2 Millefiori vase made by Salviati about 1895. It is decorated with yellow 'millefiori' flowers on purple stems with fused millefiori slices in various colours.

Venini's work as the outstanding product of modern Italian glassmaking.

During the 1920s, Ercole Barovier, a descendant of the renaissance glassmaking family of Beroviero, made some original pieces in his desire for unusual colour glass effects. The company exists today as Barovier and Toso, very much catering for the tourist trade, but they have also developed a range of lightweight glass, well designed and of gentle colouring, which is original enough to stand apart from the popular Murano product. If signed, Venini's glass is marked with the full name and the addition of 'Murano'. Barovier and Toso use labels, but specially designed pieces carry the artist's signature.

The Netherlands

Roman, Merovingian and the common *Waldglas* produced into the 15th century in the Netherlands differed little from glass found or produced elsewhere in Europe. The uses of these glass objects were in the first instant domestic – flasks, bottles, drinking cups and a limited quantity of window glass were 15th century products. By the 17th century the applied blobs found on Rhenish beakers had developed into the fashionable raspberry prunt, a clever idea which allows a firm grip on a slippery glass. The *Krautstrunk* (cabbage stalk), a large beaker covered with pointed prunts, and the *Passglas*, a tall beaker ringed with applied trails of glass at measured distances and passed around the company with each man emptying the glass to the next ring, enjoyed great popularity.

Flemish 17th century still-life painters have provided an exemplary record of glass forms which were in popular use. Venetian and Altarist glassmakers brought with them all the important developments of their native industry. The elegant flute glass with a short baluster stem is certainly Venetian in origin, but this does not quite apply to that most famous of Rhenish drinking glasses, the *Roemer*, although a related form may be seen in the sketches (1667–72) accompanying John Greene's orders for Murano glass.

The *Roemer* developed from a prunted beaker into a goblet with a large, ovoid-shaped bowl, hollow cylindrical stem set with raspberry prunts, and a spreading foot of spirally wound glass. The early accidental pale green tint was deliberately retained, and an outsize version often appeared as an imposing table centrepiece.

The most notable glass centres were Antwerp, Liège, Brussels, Beauwelz, s'Hertogenbosch and Middleburgh. We know that glassmakers joined these centres not only from Italy, but also from France and Germany. Netherland factories became so prolific that at one stage glass was exported to Venice. In 1585, Antwerp was taken by Spain, but the centres at Liège and Brussels carried on.

Towards the late 17th century glass decoration assumes a new perspective with the emergence of outstanding engraving and cutting techniques exploited with brilliant ingenuity by Dutch craftsmen. Italian inspired engraving techniques seem at first somewhat stiff and unyielding, especially on portrait glasses made to order, but a cursive, calligraphic engraved decoration does appear to have been a purely Netherland technique. The innovation of accomplishing a design in the technique of diamond stippling in the manner of mezzotint engraving produced an effect of exquisite beauty hitherto unknown in glass decoration.

These supreme Dutch glass artists were mainly well-to-do amateurs who frequently signed their work with initials or full name and this, coupled with perhaps some engraved verses, brings a personal charm to this group of Dutch glass. A number of these engravers were women. Anna Roemers Visscher (1583–1651) of Amsterdam introduced fruit, plant and insect forms into the calligraphic design, in the best manner of still-life painting. She is also one of the earliest stipple engravers we know of; one of her glasses incorporating cherries is dated 1664. Anna's sister, Maria Tesselschade Roemers Visscher (1595–1649), and Anna Maria Schurman (1607–78) worked in a similar style. The giant *Roemer* was admirably suited for this type of decoration, which was frequently of a commemorative nature. The best known of these calligraphic engravers is probably Willem Jacob van Heemskerk (1613–92), a wealthy cloth merchant.

Fruiting vines, flowers and figures of dancing peasants in the Italian engraving technique were a speciality of Willem Moleyser. The globular

its most satisfying form in the Newcastle Baluster as produced by the Newcastle factory of Dagnia – an Altarist family.

The brilliance, whiteness and softness of lead metal combine to make English glass a perfect foil for the Dutch engravers, and as early as 1680 the Bonhomme factory at Liège attempted glass *à la façon d'Angleterre*. By the mid-18th century some good English-style glass was produced, though lighter in weight due to smaller lead con-

4 Flask in blue glass with calligraphic engraving in diamond point made by Willem van Heemskirk. The inscription reads *De Liefde zy ongeveinst*. The round pontil mark is signed 'Willem van Heemskirk AE. 73 A° 1686'. The height, without a mount, is 220 mm.

3

4

3 The so-called 'Daumenglas' is a thumb glass with finger grips in the form of applied milled rings. This example, from Germany or the Netherlands, dates from the 17th century.

long-necked Dutch bottle was greatly favoured by engravers, and was made in green and blue, as well as in a colourless metal. The best known stipple engravers are Frans Greenwood (1680–1761) of Dordrecht, and David Wolff (1732–1798). Wolff glasses, with their delightful treatment of children in formal dress, putti among clouds, commemorative portraits and allegorical designs accentuate the charm of Rococo art. Wolff applied his techniques almost exclusively to English glasses. *Façon de Venise* had gone out of fashion and glass *à l'Anglais* was favoured by most engravers. This was due to the great development of a brilliant English lead glass, seen in

tent. The new, thicker glass responded well to the growing demand for wheel engraved decoration in which the Dutch were supreme. One of the greatest exponents of this technique was Jacob Sang of Haarlem, whose work may be seen in the Victoria and Albert Museum, and other important collections.

A new factory, the Royal Dutch Glassworks, was established at Leerdam in 1765. This was re-established in 1878 with the aim of improving the quality of Dutch glass and expanding the industry to curtail imports from Belgium. A small glassworks was founded in Maastricht in 1834 by Petrus Regout, a descendant from the Italian glassmaking family of Rigo. Leerdam, as a meaningful glass factory, did not come into its own until after 1915, when the director, P. M. Cochius, decided to engage two enterprising designers, Berlage and de Bazel. This was the beginning of a great new development at Leerdam, which had been bypassed by the Art Nouveau movement. A new designer, Andries Dirk Copier, who had studied glass techniques after his traineeship at the Utrecht school of graphic art, became the moving spirit of the factory. He joined Leerdam at 16 as designer and in 1923, after the departure of one of the most gifted artist designers, Chris Lebeau, was made artistic director. Lebeau had initiated the Unica Studio at Leerdam and Copier extended the Unica glass ware and the Serica series to represent a range of studio glass which was desired by private collectors for its exciting and original treatment.

In the early 1920s, monumental, sculptured shapes with heavy cutting in clear coloured and colourless glass followed the designs of Berlage and de Bazel. Copier was interested in using both colour and blowing techniques to exploit the properties of the metal. Bubbles, inclusions, plain heavy and thin blown glass with perhaps one added colour effect, and glass forms inspired by early eastern or oriental glassmakers fascinate him. Today, a number of excellent young designers – including Lanooy, Valkema, Meydam, and Brigitte Altenburger – have been engaged by Leerdam to produce glass at studio level.

Signatures vary greatly, sometimes they enclose the initials of the designer within a right-angle, sometimes they spell out in full the Unica and Serica studio products with Copier's name added, or the initials of the designer are added to form a geometric pattern.

The British Isles

There is evidence that Glaziers from Gaul were called to Britain as early as A.D. 680. Glassmaking families from Normandy and the Lorraine found satisfactory sites for their craft in the forest areas of Surrey, Sussex and Kent, and when the fuel supply became exhausted moved to Gloucestershire, Staffordshire and other suitable regions. Laurence Vitrearius (the 'window glass maker') settled at Dyers Cross in the Chiddingfold district of the Weald at about 1226, and by 1240 was making glass for the Abbey at Westminster. The old glasshouse sites in the

Weald yield fragments which concur with Continental glass made during this period – bottles, beakers and cups of yellow or greenish metal of inferior quality. The industry concentrated on making window glass, though the best was still imported from the Continent. Laurence's son, William 'le verrier', carried on by producing

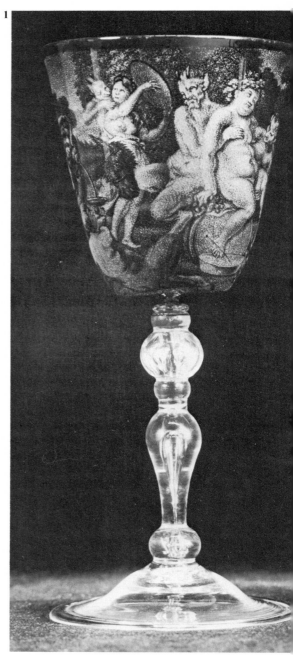

1 This colourless glass goblet with an oviform bowl on a stem enclosing ornamental air bubbles, was made in England, possibly at Newcastle-upon-Tyne. The bowl is stipple engraved with a bacchanal scene and includes a diamond-point inscription of verse. It is signed by Frans Greenwood of Dordrecht, Holland and dates from about 1750. Its height is 242 mm.

hollow glass and in 1300 Chiddingfold received a Royal Charter.

Between 1350–57, John le Alemayne supplied window glass for St Stephen's Chapel, and also produced some 'cuppis to drinke', but elegant table glass came from Venice.

By 1567 Jean Carré had arrived from the Lorraine by way of Antwerp and commenced making window glass by the Lorraine method under licence. Several Continental glassmaking families had already settled in England. The

Schurterres in the 14th, the Peytowes in the 15th, and in the mid-16th century the famous Huguenot families of Tyzack (du Thisac), Henzey (de Hennezel), Tittery (de Thietry) and Hoe (de Houx) arrived to lay the foundation of the Stourbridge glass industry.

Carré obtained his licence for making *cristallo*

2

à la façon de Venise at Crutched Friars Hall, a glasshouse which apparently was already in existence in 1564 or 65, though seemingly not particularly efficient. Carré therefore sent for Venetian craftsmen, among them the great glassmaker Jacopo Verzelini, who supposedly arrived in London from Antwerp in 1571. There are sources which indicate that he may already have arrived in 1565 and initiated the manufacture of Venetian *cristallo*, and this opens an interesting field of speculation as to the merits of Jean

Carré's role in the manufacture of *cristallo* at this early period. Suffice to say that in 1572, after Carré's death, Verzelini was the master of the Crutched Friars glasshouse, and in 1574 he obtained a Royal Patent from Elizabeth I to manufacture Venice glasses for a period of 21 years.

Of the dozen or so glasses associated with Verzelini today, about nine can be attributed to his London glasshouse. The earliest, dated 1577, is in the Corning Museum, New York. Typical features are the stem with hollow mould-blown knop or bulb, bowl of ample size, and of clear, faintly greenish or greyish metal. Diamond engraving in the hatched Italian style is associated with Anthony de Lisle who had come to England from the 'Dominions of the King of France' and applied for citizenship in 1597. A lozenge motif on the bowl and sometimes foot, scrolls, floral sections, friezes of trees, stags and hounds and commemorative inscriptions seem typical of de Lisle's work. Occasionally, Verzelini's glasses are decorated by enamelling or gilding, but this has worn badly. Glasses made at the same period in Hall, in the Tyrol, are in some instances so similar to Verzelini's work that they might have been produced in his glasshouse, and bear testimony to the communication and exchange between glassmakers throughout Europe.

Despite malicious acts by jealous glass merchants and importers, Verzelini led the industry until his retirement in 1592, and thus initiated the era of monopolies. Sir Jerome Bowes held the monopoly until 1604, when the licence was sold from one profiteer to another.

In 1632, a patent was granted to Sir Robert Mansell (1573–1656), a dynamic personality who, in spite of fierce competition and countless deliberately engineered setbacks which lost him a fortune, succeeded in the establishment of a commercial glass industry. In 1615, the famous 'Proclamation Touching Glasses' prohibited the use of wood fuel, and the necessity of utilizing coal effectively created a large industry in the Tyneside region, and brought about the evolution of crystal glass. By the mid-17th century a bottle industry had emerged, and at the end of the century the onion shape replaced the shaft and globe model. A hundred or so years later the bottle neck had grown taller, the shoulder less pronounced, and we see the development of the shape we know today. Bottles with applied glass seals bearing names, initials, crests and dates are desirable collectors' items. One of the earliest intact specimens is the Northampton Museum shaft and globe model, dated 1657.

The first Charter granted to the Company of Glaziers (The Glass Sellers' Company) by Charles I in 1635 was revived in 1664, as the Worshipful Company of Glass Sellers.

By 1660, the monopoly had passed from Mansell to Charles Villiers, Duke of Buckingham (1627–88), who made great efforts to improve trade and started a mirror production at his Vauxhall plate glasshouse. The famous Exeter and Scudamore flutes are attributed to

2 This colourless goblet with round funnel bowl has an elaborately cut stem incorporating five knops. The foot is plain. The bowl is inscribed *Vriendschap* (friendship) upon an aerial ribbon. Beneath the inscription, two elegantly clad boys, one wearing an oriental hat, are about to drink from a goblet at a table in a garden of trees and shrubs. On the ground beneath the table stands a typical onion-shaped wine bottle. The Dutch diamond stippled engraving is ascribed to David Wolff and dated about 1775. The glass is English and was probably made in Newcastle-upon-Tyne. The height is 210 mm.

Buckingham's workshops, and it seems that his glass was good, if of rather thin metal.

The increasing demand for glass, which caused a ban on Venetian imports to be lifted, encouraged the Glass Sellers Company in their researches for a more durable and resistant glass metal. The consequence was the flint (lead) glass developed by George Ravenscroft (1618–81). Crizzling, a defect due to excessive alkaline content and resulting in deterioration and eventual disintegration of the glass was not entirely overcome until about 1685, but Ravenscroft, who had established his glasshouse at the Savoy in 1673, was in May 1674 granted a 7-year patent to manufacture his crystal glass produced by the addition of oxide of lead. An experimental glassworks at Henley-on-Thames was subsequently set up and by June 1676 The glass Sellers' Company announced that most of the faults had been eliminated. In 1677 Ravenscroft pronounced his success by applying the Ravens Head Seal to his finest specimens. At its best, his glass was of heavy metal with excellent refractive properties, of clear and watery limpidity, fusing at lower

form a single or several spirals within the stem. By the mid 18th century the mixed air and enamel twists, the opaque white and colour twist glasses establish the English product as one of the greatest achievements in glassmaking history, and a delight for the collector.

The most elegant vessel is the Newcastle Baluster, tall and graceful with plain or twist stems, knopped, with enclosed tears and generous bowl – an ideal foil for the art of the Dutch

1 English lead-glass posset pot with vertical mould-blown ribbing. It was made in George Ravenscroft's Savoy glasshouse and bears the raven's head seal applied to the base of the swan-necked spout. There is a high kick in the base and very slight crizzling. The height is 95 mm and it dates from about 1677–8.

3

temperature than the Venetian cristallo and without the brittle surface hardness. Decorative effects were achieved by gadrooning, vertical ribbing, 'nipped diamond waies' and attractive rope handles applied to ewers, posset pots, flasks, roemers and so on.

The baroque influence seen in glasses with covers decorated by finials of crowns and crosses, elaborate stems and wrythen bowls, declined by the last decade of the 17th century and heralds the great period of English drinking glasses. Aided by the new variety of available beverages, the 18th century drinking glass emerges in all possible shapes and sizes imaginable. The stem received the greatest attention. The enclosed airtwist spiral (1730–70) was probably derived from the accidental and later deliberate 'tear', an elongated airbubble, cleverly manipulated to

2 A candlestick with air twist stem upon a domed and folded foot. It was made in England in about 1755–60.

3 This heavily crizzled jug in soda metal dates from the early Ravenscroft period – about 1674. Several of these jugs have survived and all are more or less ornately decorated with frilling, gadrooning and 'niptdiamond waies'.

4 Amen glass with drawn trumpet bowl and tear drop in the stem is engraved in diamond point with a crown, the cipher IR and RI entwined and verses of the Jacobite hymn concluding with the word 'Amen'. Consequently, these glasses, which belong to the group known as Jacobite glass, is designated 'Amen Glasses'. Only about 20 such glasses are known to be in existence and a few of these are dated 1747 and 1749.

engravers. The drawn trumpet, where bowl and stem are drawn from one piece and the foot applied, is one of the earliest drinking glasses already produced in the 17th century. A characteristic of the Lynn and Norwich factories are glasses with bowls manipulated by the gaffer to show horizontal 'corrugate' rings. Rarely do we find the famous folded foot in glasses after the middle of the 18th century. Most characteristic is the plain conical foot which should rise toward the centre and have a circumference at least equal to that of the rim of the glass.

Commemorative glasses represent the most fascinating group for the collector. Jacobite glasses referring to the rebellions of 1715 and 1745 are usually well engraved with pertinent symbols, the rose for Stuart, the thistle for Scotland, flowers for initials, Fiat – may it

happen, Redi or Redeat – may he return. The rare Amen glasses, engraved with verses of the Jacobite Anthem, portrait glasses picturing the Young Pretender, Irish glass commemorating the ascent of the House of Orange and glasses of William II interest fall into this group. Coinciding with this phase are the Privateering or nautical glasses. Coins enclosed in stem or foot of the glass are not always a true indication of the age of the vessel, which must be judged on its own merits.

The Glass Act of 1777–78 doubled the duty on lead glass and taxed the enamel necessary for producing white and colour twists. The consequence was the disappearance of this attractive decoration and the establishment of English glassmakers in Ireland which was not affected by the restrictive English tax regulations and had

133

been granted freedom of trade.

The best known Irish factories, Waterford, the Cork Glass Company, the Waterloo Glass Company, and Edwards Belfast, were founded by or with the help of English glassmakers or merchants. The years 1780–1825 are often referred to as the Anglo-Irish period, and the absence of restrictions allowed the manufacture of a heavy, dark glass metal which permitted deeper and more generous cutting of sometimes

however, no proof that all the gaily coloured glass objects, rolling pins, walking sticks and friggers (these were made 'at the end of the day' from left over glass remnants) came from the Nailsea factory.

The most gifted representatives of a Rococo style in glass decoration were William Beilby Jr (1740–1819) and his sister Mary (1749–97) who worked for the Dagnia-Williams glasshouse at Newcastle. This meant of course, that they had

1 This Irish preserve jar of heavy crystal is elaborately cut. The square base is moulded. It dates from about 1790.

available to them the finest glass made at that period. Most Beilby glasses have enamel twist stems, and range from small drinking glasses to large goblets with a generous bucket bowl. Wine glasses decorated in white enamel with fruiting vines are favourite subjects, but there are also Rococo landscapes with figures and animals. Magnificent heraldic decoration in polychrome enamel is found on impressive goblets and bowls, almost exclusively made to order. Signatures are present on important pieces.

The work of the decorator James Giles (1718–80) was directly influenced by the Adam style. He confines himself largely to gilding, decorating opaque white as well as coloured cut glass with elegant classical designs of garlands, birds, pheasants, grasses and bushes.

The work of Michael Edkins (1733–1811) is associated with colourful enamelling on opaque white glass produced in the Bristol area soon after 1750 in imitation of porcelain, and aptly expressed in delicate *chinoiserie* motifs. Edkins also produced much of the fine gilding on Bristol blue glass made at the Non-Such Flint

superb quality. Decanters were manufactured in large quantities by all Irish factories and are frequently marked on the base.

In 1788, John Robert Lucas, William Chance and Edward Homer founded the Nailsea factory near Bristol. To beat the tax they bought cheap cullet from Bristol's 'white' glasshouses and produced attractive dark green glass objects applied with fused-on enamel chips of various colour, or band and spiral patterns. There is,

Glass Manufactory of the Jacobs family. This glassworks was active between 1775 and c.1815 making fine blue glass table-ware decorated with non-figurative classical motifs.

Gilt decoration of a more rustic charm was produced by William Absolon of Great Yarmouth between 1790 and 1810. Absolon specialized in decorating souvenir ware of blue and white glass.

Two Scotsmen influenced by Neo-classicism were James Tassie (1735–99) and his nephew William (1777–1860), who resurrected the fashion for cameos with glass paste portraits and medallions. Apsley Pellat's (1791–1863) process of *cristallo-ceramie*, whereby a refractory material fusing at higher temperature than glass was moulded into medallions or reliefs and enclosed in a transparent glass matrix, was a technique known and exploited in the manufacture of scent flasks, beakers and paperweights, particularly in France.

The repeal of the Glass Excise Act in 1845 and the 1851 Great Exhibition created a new activity

3 This square cut perfume bottle is 140 mm high, with cristallo-ceramie enclosures: one showing George IV as a Roman emperor facing left; a profile of Queen Charlotte; a dove bearing a sealed letter; and a scene of Windsor Castle. Within the stopper is a cristallo-ceramie medallion of Cupid leaning upon a pillar with the inscription

Garde a Vous beneath.

It was made in England by Apsley Pellatt at his Falcon Street glasshouse in Southwark. In 1820, Pellatt was granted a patent of 14 years duration for his cameo incrustation or 'cristallo-ceramie' process.

The coronation of George IV took place in 1821 and this may possibly be a commemorative piece.

Stourbridge and Birmingham revived millefiori techniques for the production of paperweights, ink bottles, tumblers and doorknobs from the mid-19th century.

American pressed glass techniques reached England after 1830 and resulted in attractive novelty ware, especially slag glass, so termed because of the deliberate addition of waste material from metal foundries. The prettiest colour is light blue, other shades are purple,

2 This pair of opaque white glass vases with polychrome enamelling show chinoiserie motifs within Rococo cartouches. Opaque white glass was the response of glassmakers to the imports of Chinese porcelain. It was made in South Staffordshire about 1790.

in the glassmaking industry, with interesting results. Richardsons of Wordsley contributed with fine colour enamelling and acid etching. William Fritsche and Frederick Kny, two Bohemians, produced remarkable engraving in the rock crystal style at Stourbridge. John Northwood I (1836–1902) became the first glassmaker to produce cameo glass in the classical style with his replica of the Portland Vase. An entire school of cameo cutters and engravers was formed in the Stourbridge industry with a number of gifted artists: Alphonse Eugene Lecheverell at Richardsons, Joseph Locke (1846–1938), John Northwood II (1870–1960), Joshua Hodgetts (1857–1933) of Stevens and Williams, and the gifted Woodall brothers, George (1850–1925) and Thomas (1849–1926) of Thomas Webb, who financed the best artists with the result that 19th century cameo glass is described as Webb's Cameo glass, even if produced elsewhere. Signatures are frequently present. English cameo work usually shows the relief in opaque white glass on delicate natural shades from brownish yellow to orange and green, and on a distinctive midnight blue base.

glass of internationally high standard.

A revival of stippling techniques has extended the work of the engraver Laurence Whistler to a highly individual dimension, with tremendous influence on contemporary glass decoration. In a different vein, the glass engraving of New Zealander John Hutton produces a powerful impact of almost three dimensional effect as seen in his figures on doors and panels at the Shakespeare Centre Stratford-on-Avon and at Coventry Cathedral. Organized exhibitions by the Guild of Glass Engravers and other associations encourage appreciation and interest in these fine achievements.

1 This pair of green glass decanters with mushroom stoppers and gilt labels was probably made at the Bristol Non-such Flint Glass Manufactory of Isaac Jacobs in about 1790. It was decorated with gilding by Michael Edkins who was prolific in work of this type for the Jacob's glasshouse.

2 A cameo glass vase with a white relief on smoky grey-blue, made by George Woodall. The Woodall brothers worked in a team of about 70 craftsmen in Stourbridge, financed by Webb and Company and were nephews of the enameller Thomas Bott. George was one of the most gifted artists in the technique of cameo carving and much of his work is signed. This piece dates from about 1900.

3 This bottle-green door-stop or paperweight encloses three flowers built up in tiers, one growing from the centre of another. These were made in large quantities from clear bottle-glass. The interior silver bubble effect was achieved by tracing the desired pattern on the marver with a sprinkling of chalk, pressing the pre-shaped heated glass upon it and covering the whole with a second gather of glass. The action of heat on the chalk creates a gaseous film of tiny bubbles. These weights were produced over a long period and in most bottle-making areas. This one is possibly from Stourbridge and dates from the mid-19th century.

cream, white, black and marbled effects, applied in patterned ware in the shape of urns, lattice plates, jugs, dogs, mugs, obelisks, candlesticks, boots and more rarely portraits with inscriptions. The factories mainly associated with slag glass manufacture are: Sowerby's Ellison Glassworks at Gateshead (marks: moulded peacock's head; between 1872–83 diamond-shaped registration mark indicating date), George Davidson and Co. of the Teams glassworks at Gateshead (marks: lion overlooking rampart, facing right), and Greener and Co. of Wear Glassworks Sunderland (mark: lion facing left, bearing halberd).

Powell of Whitefriars produced eye-catching colour glass with a revival of glass *à la façon de Venise* in skilfully manipulated shapes. A more original development were the sometimes harsh and uncompromising forms of *avant garde* designers such as Christopher Dresser (1834–1904) and George Walton at the Glasgow factory of James Couper and Sons. Their streaky glass often bubbly and with aventurine inclusions named 'Clutha' (cloudy) was frequently produced for Liberty's, mounted in pewter or silver designed for the Tudric and Cymric range. If signatures are present, initials or the full name of the designer are included. From the early 1920s John Moncrieff in Perth produced a series of attractive glass, the so-called 'Monart' ware, in a variety of bright colours and shaded with marble-like streaks. It is still made today.

Many of the Stourbridge factories have survived, such as Webb Corbett, Steven Williams, and Thomas Webb and Sons. Wedgwood have taken over the Lynn Glassworks production, now Wedgwood Glass, and Powell's are now manufacturing as Whitefriars Glass. Many excellent artists design glass for the modern factories and the establishment of first-rate training centres for glassmaking and design such as the departments at the Stourbridge School of Art, the Edinburgh College of Art and the Royal College of Art in London has resulted in art

Bohemia and the German-speaking Lands
Slovakia, Silesia, Moravia and Bohemia are the areas involved in Czech glassmaking. In common with the medieval Rhenish product, the greenish bubbly *Waldglas* appears in traditional forms. The beaker with applied prunts – '*Nuppenbecher*' appears in various modifications: the '*Igel*' (Hedgehog) with prickles, and the tall *Krautstrunk* (cabbage stalk) covered with pointed prunts in circular arrangement. The antique sprinkler emerges as the *Angster* or *Kuttrolf* with bulbous body and long, slightly inclined neck which may consist of several twisted glass tubes. The *Maigelein* (a low cup) still appeared in the 15th century. Common vessel forms are the *Humpen*, a tall cylindrical glass of giant proportion, the *Passglas* as already mentioned, and the *Stangenglas*, of narrow cylindrical form with applied hollow foot.

With the expansion of the German mining

4 Made by Powell and Son, Whitefriars, London, this chandelier in Anglo-Venetian style is ornamented in ruby and green glass. It dates from about 1865.

5 Goblet with diamond point engraving in stipple and line, 'The Mausoleum' by Laurence Whistler is signed and dated 1960. The glass was made by James Powell and Son Ltd. The height is 265 mm and the diameter of the bowl is 130 mm.

6 These Clutha glass vases were designed by Christopher Dresser for the avant garde firm of J. Cooper and Sons, Glasgow. The two outer vessels are marked with the acid etched initials C. D., the centre vase is signed only with the manufacturer's name. They date from between 1890 to 1895.

4

5

3

6

industry, fuel costs rose steeply and in the 16th century a number of small glasshouses and individual glassmakers moved to Bohemia and Silesia where conditions were more favourable. The big landowners and nobility were quick to realize the advantages of possessing large tracts of forest land. They began to set up glasshouses on their estates, attracting glassmakers and their families by granting special privileges – a development parallelled in France.

Baroque and Rococo prosperity, the support by the Church of artisans and artists, and the monastic activities of winemaking and ale brewing all encouraged an expansion in drinking glass manufacture. This in turn proliferated enamelled decoration of a most fascinating kind

1

which flourished particularly during the 17th and early 18th centuries. Scenes from the domestic and political life of the nobility and of influential artisans or tradesmen, biblical subjects, representation of the 'Seven Ages of Man', the double-headed eagle (Reichsadler) with armorial shields of all embracing lands, and entire families and family trees are enchantingly represented in a refreshing rustic style. Emblems of Trade Guilds and scenic representations, as for instance the Ochsenkopf, a mountain in the Fichtelgebirge, frequently have added inscriptions and permit facile identification. Small beakers, straight or everted at the rim, decorated with brightly enamelled heraldic motifs are usually ascribed to Saxonian manufacture.

Cutting and engraving is Bohemia's great contribution to glass art. The revival of this craft is attributed to Caspar Lehman (1570–1622), lapidary to the art-loving Rudolf II at the court of Prague. Visiting Italian artisans recalled the work of Cellini with their artefacts in rock crystal and precious stones, and Lehman was inspired to transfer rock crystal cutting techniques to the medium of glass. The brittle Venetian soda glass was quite unsuitable for lapidary work, and it is a remarkable achievement that Lehman did succeed in his objective although a robust potash-lime glass was not developed in Bohemia until about 1670. A splendid armorial beaker of 1605 showing allegorical figures engraved in a broad stylized fashion at the Industrial Art Museum of Prague is the only piece signed by Lehman's hand. The Victoria and Albert Museum is in possession of an engraved panel attributed to this artist. In 1609 Lehman was granted a monopoly for glass engraving which passed to his pupil George Schwanhardt (1601–67), who left Prague for Nuremberg during the 30 Years' War. Schwanhardt's innovation consisted of imparting a bright polish to some of the matt engraved sections of the glass, resulting in a livelier representation.

A talented school of glass engravers sprang up in Nuremberg with Schwanhardt's sons George and Henry, H. W. Schmidt and Hermann Schwinger (1640–83) as some of the most gifted. The finest engraving is usually applied to the typical *Nürnberg Deckelpokal*, a tall covered goblet of thinnish metal with a knopped or hollow baluster stem, or both, interspersed by several pairs of flat collars or mereses, an unmistakable feature. Signatures of engravers are frequently present.

Johann Schaper (1621–70), a Nuremberg decorator of both glass and china, produced work in a different genre but of equally high standard. His distinctive technique consisted of delicate enamelling in *Schwarzlot* of landscapes and figures in black or sepia, often seen on glasses so much his own that they are called Schaper glasses – cylindrical beakers on three flattened ball feet. The same medium is employed by Ignaz Preissler (c.1675–1733) who, together with his son, worked for a rich Bohemian landowner, Count Kolovrat. Preissler, however,

1 Reichsadlerhumpen – enamelled in colour with the arms of the electors and portraying the double-headed eagle of the Holy Roman Empire with the imperial orb on its breast. This was a very popular emblem and is also found in the form of diamond point engraved decoration. This piece is German and is dated 1650.

already expressed the Rococo taste of his period with *chinoiserie* motifs set within garlands and foliage, hunting scenes and vivacious small figures. His *Schwarzlot* is often augmented by gilding and red enamel.

Soon after 1700, Bohemian cutters were able to utilize waterpower to drive their lathes. The mechanized engraving techniques were then applied to the new, robust potash-lime glass which permitted high and low relief cutting in the manner of rock crystal engraving.

The Lauensteiner Hütte was apparently the first to apply Ravenscroft's invention of lead glass, but this was not very successful and several surviving pieces are affected by crizzling. Some Lauenstein glasses are signed under the

by substituting gold with less costly metal oxides such as copper. The Kassel glasshouse was particularly fortunate in having the services of a great glass engraver, Franz Gondelach (*c.*1663). Gondelach was made lapidary to the Court and several of his glasses are decorated with portraits of his protector or other nobles in high and low relief techniques. An eight-pointed star under the base is associated with this engraver's work.

From 1720 to 1745 *Zwischengold* glass techniques were successfully revived in Bohemian workshops and possibly also produced in monasteries. This is a form of decoration whereby gold foil, engraved with a fine needle and sometimes highlighted in brilliant red or green lacquer, is enclosed between two walls of glass, the outer

2

3

2 Humpen with an enamelled representation of the glassworks at Zeilberg, presented to Caspar Steiner of Volpersdorf by Christian Preussler. The Preusslers were an important glass-making family and owners of the Zeilberg glassworks. It is Bohemian and dates from 1680.

3 Zwischengoldglas – a faceted beaker decorated with a scene of a chamois hunt in gold leaf between bands of acanthus in silver leaf. The base medallion shows a huntsman returning through the forest with his kill, in gold leaf upon a red lacquer ground.

Bohemian Zwischengold glass consists of two vessels, one fitting perfectly into the other. The design is etched with a needle on gold or silver leaf applied to the surface of the inner vessel, sometimes augmented by coloured lacquer. A colourless resin between the two walls serves as an adhesive. The join is usually about 1 cm below the rim. The inner vessel has a rim of double thickness which forms a lip and joins perfectly on to the outer glass. The vessels fit tightly inside each other and to avoid trapped air the base of the outer vessel is cut out and replaced last. The base of the inner vessel is frequently decorated.

This example from Bohemia dates from about 1735.

base with a lion rampart (*Lauenstein = Löwenstein =* lions stone) and the cipher C for Calenberg – the locality of the factory.

Work of high quality and individual character was produced at the Potsdam factory which employed the gifted engravers Gottfried Spiller (*d.*1721) and Martin Winter (*d.*1702). Potsdam specialized not only in fine engraving but also experimented in colour glass and produced a lovely deep blue and deep green. The factory was founded in 1674 by the Elector Frederick William of Brandenburg, who engaged a very able chief chemist, Johann Kunckel (1630–1703). By 1679 Kunckel had developed his famous gold ruby glass, by a very expensive, difficult and secret process. Much later, a similar effect was achieved

surface of which is usually additionally decorated by facet cutting. The majority of existing *Zwischengold* glass takes the form of faceted beakers, but the technique was also applied to bowls and covered goblets.

At Gutenbrunn in Austria, Joseph Mildner (1763–1808) developed a most distinctive variation with medallions or miniature portrait panels of enamel or painted on parchment enclosed within the wall of the vessel. These medallions usually carry the name of the sitter and the date on the obverse. Occasionally a little poem is added – Mildner had a penchant for poetry and created his own.

An individual form of glass decoration in a raised enamel technique was produced by

Johann Friedrich Meyer of Dresden (1680–1752). The most delicate and exquisite glass decoration, however, was the technique of transparent enamelling, inspired by stained glass methods. Several of these artists frequently dated and signed their work. One of the most influential was Samuel Mohn (1762–1815) of Dresden, who specialized at first in silhouette portraits on porcelain and on glass, and then turned to transparent enamelling, representing a variety of subjects including panoramic views of landscapes and cities. His son Gottlob Samuel Mohn (1789–1825) settled in Vienna where his work influenced one of the most prolific artists, Anton Kothgasser (1769–1851). Kothgasser's panoramic views are usually found on that most typical of *Biedermeier* vessels, the *Ranftbecher* – a plain flared beaker with cogwheel base, further enhanced by an all-over yellow stain. Followers of these artists are Hoffmeister of Vienna and Carl v. Scheidt in Berlin, among others. Subjects include floral decoration, romantic figures and verses of dedication, characters from playing cards and animal fables.

The most interesting developments in colour glass mark this phase of Bohemian glassmaking. A fluorescent green or yellow was achieved by the introduction of small quantities of uranium or vitriol to the glass batch. This technique was developed by Josef Riedel of Dolny Polubny in

1 A covered beaker made from ruby glass with silver gilt mounts with an Augsburg silver hall-mark. The sides are wheel-engraved with foliage, birds and fruit. The cover is similarly engraved. The finial is in the form of a silver gilt female figure with a cornucopia. This example from Southern Germany or Nürnberg dates from the late 17th century and is 215 mm high.

2 A Bohemian ruby cased wineglass, candlestick and tumbler show popular Rococo scroll motifs and forest scenes. They date from the mid- to late-19th century.

Northern Bohemia and the colours named *Annagrün* and *Annagelb* after Riedel's wife Anna. Uranium glass was produced between 1830–1848.

One of the most ingenious glassmakers of the *Biedermeier* period was Friedrich Egerman (1777–1864) of Novy Bor. Apart from his successful pinkish red, and gold topaz, stains, he developed a most interesting simulated stone glass akin to Venetian *Schmelzglas*, the so-called *Lithyalin*. This *Lithyalin* glass resembled marble, and though made in several colour shades was largely produced in a deep red. This marbled

glass was applied either as an overlay on transparent coloured glass, or used as an opaque glass mass, decorated by most sophisticated cutting which exploited the marble pattern in an inimitable technique. Egerman signatures are extremely rare.

A solid opaque black glass was patented by Count Buquoy, *c*.1820 and in sympathy with the classic revival in the arts was christened *Hyalith* glass. Pleasing classical forms were applied with fine gilding of flowers and insects and *chinoiserie* motifs. Similar decoration is seen on some of Egerman's products, and it is quite likely that the same artists were employed. *Hyalith* is very brittle with little heat resistance and not much has survived.

Rococo exuberance and the glitter of the Empire had been swept aside by the grim realities of the Napoleonic wars. The emerging *Biedermeier* style, at first necessarily frugal, developed along asthetic and still Neo-classic lines as expressed in furniture and furnishings of this period. The romantic and intimate character and the preference for pastel shades of blue, pink and alabaster white is echoed in *Biedermeier* glass. Workmanship is of high standard and this applies to all aspects of the arts and crafts. The finest engraver of this age was probably Dominic Biman (1800–57) of Neuwelt. His specialities were portrait glasses and portrait medallions, executed to order for visitors to the famous spas which had become so popular. The engraved work of K. Pfohl (1826–94) is especially memorable for its spirited representation of horses.

Red or amber overlay spa glasses were produced in great quantity. At first of good quality, they degenerated by the end of the century into poor copies of what they had been, with shoddy colour stain or lacquer and insipid engraving by acid etching. A new upsurge came with the *Jugendstil* or Art Nouveau, largely due to the efforts of Louis Lobmeyr of Vienna, industrialist and glass designer, who brought together the best Czech and Austrian artists to resume glassmaking on an individually inspired artistic level. Lötz Witwe at Klostermühle, Austria, created Tiffany-inspired lustre glass of great originality as well as exploring a number of other techniques under the direction of Max von Spaun. Bakalowitz Söhne, Adolf Meyers Neffe, the Harrach glassworks, Josef Pallme König, and Ludwig Moser & Söhne (the last three still exist), were the most important factories producing art glass. In Germany the glassworks of Count Schaffgotsch' Josephinenhütte, and the Württembergische Metallwarenfabrik, both operating today, made important contributions to glass development into our age. In 1904, the glass factory at Zwiesel set up an influential school for glass techniques.

The glasshouse Köln-Ehrenfeld was established in 1865 but ceased production in 1931. A noteworthy aspect of this factory is that they made a range of excellent facsimiles of medieval and renaissance glasses.

Today, Czechoslovakia once more takes a leading role, particularly in the manufacture of chandeliers, colour glass and excellent cut and engraved work produced at the old centres of Kemnicky Senov and Haida, the design schools and Lobmeyr factories, and at the Prague Arts and Crafts College with work by Joseph Drahanovsky.

France

Glassmaking was introduced into Gaul under Roman occupation and post Roman-period glass closely resembles the greenish and yellow-brownish objects found elsewhere. During the 12th century, glazier settlements were in existence in the region of Poitou and immigrant glassmakers gathered, intermarried and created future generations of glaziers. Analogous with Bohemia, the feudal system encouraged the setting up of glasshouses in the forest regions, in Provence and Normandy.

By 1490 the French glassmakers had obtained the right to style themselves *gentilhommes verriers*, a title applying equally to the real and impoverished nobility turned glassmaker. Numerous Huguenot nobles adopted glassmaking and in 1746, forty of these Gascon *gentilhommes verriers* perished on the gallows for their beliefs in the principles of the reformation. Rare surviving 16th-century goblets and chalices show attractive enamelling and a style of design which is clearly Venetian-influenced.

In the 1660s, one of the most able French glassmakers, Bernard Perrot (or Perrotto) inherited the monopoly for supplying glass in the Loire area and the work produced at his Orleans glasshouse is both charming and original. A large number of mould blown beakers, flasks and scent bottles were made in transparent and opaque white, blue and amber glass, showing recurring motifs of hearts, fleurs-de-lys, small figures and sun or moon faces. Perrot also produced an attractive marbled glass and in 1662 developed a process for casting; about that time he began to use anthracite fuel for his furnaces.

A vastly different glass concept is expressed in the so-called *verre filé de Nevers*. This refers to miniature models and grotesques of religious or comic character, made at the lamp by provincial glass enamellers from the late 16th century onward. Nevers figurines are made from hollow blown, very thin glass threads (*verre frisé*), usually wired with copper and placed on a stand of *verre filé* or arranged in groups. Domestic glass was largely imported from the Lowlands, England and Bohemia, and not until 1764 when the glasshouse of Sainte-Anne at Baccarat was established by the Bishop of Metz, was a French glass industry founded. In 1822, the company emerged as the Compagnie des Cristalleries de Baccarat. The agate and opaline manufactured during the first half of the century was followed by developments of colour glass and the application of excellent cutting and engraving from 1867. Baccarat too, produced a fine green and yellow fluorescent glass metal, the *cristal dichroide*. George Bontemps, one of the most imaginative of French glass designers exploited Venetian techniques at Choisy Le Roi (1823–48)

resulting in the manufacture of the paperweight, produced by various French factories.

The first Baccarat millefiori weights appeared in 1846, and if dated will be so from 1846–49 inclusive, the last year being the rarest. Dates are preceded by the initial B. In 1848 Baccarat started production of the *sulfures*, enclosing flowers, animals or fruit, and paperweights in the *cristallo-ceramie* technique, the so-called *sulphides*. Baccarat weights are frequently additionally decorated by cutting and a star cut base, and enclosure techniques are also applied to beakers.

The factory of St Louis, founded in 1767, produced paperweights which may be dated between 1847–9 with added initials SL. Snake and reptile weights are a speciality of this factory.

A distinct feature of paperweights made at the Clichy factory are swirl patterns, and some Clichy weights are marked in the pattern with the initial C. Table glass, vases and decanters were made by all these factories, and during the late 19th and early 20th century came up with well designed, pressed glass which was on occasion partly coloured, simulating overlay glass; a signature is present in the mould. Modern Baccarat is always signed in full.

During the third quarter of the century, a new development in glass art emerged, combining historic techniques with naturalistic design. The

3 These four vases in iridescent colour glass with interesting trailed decoration, are unsigned. The Austrian firm of Joh. Lötz Witwe at Klostermühle, and the Bohemian glasshouse at Steinschönau and Kosten of Josef Pallme König, have produced specimens of this type. These date from 1900.

4 'Porcelaine en verre' glass figure from a pair made at Nevers, France during the 18th century. These delightful figures of enamelled glass should not be confused with the popularly known 'verre filé de Nevers', small colourful figures made of threads of glass similar to 'pâté de verre'.

leader of this Art Nouveau movement was Emile Gallé (1846–1904), designer of ceramics, furniture and glass, and the inspiring force of the Ecole de Nancy. During the various phases of Gallé's creative style, decorative techniques were carried out with incredible virtuosity. Enamelling, gilding, cutting, engraving, acid etching, cameo carving, sandblasting, colour fusion and incrustation were applied in profusion. Gallé's early works, his *verreries parlantes* and *vases de tristesse*, are imbued with poetic spirit and lyricism. His later revival of cameo glass techniques influenced by the decorative treatment of Chinese snuffbottles in particular, made a tremendous impact and resulted in a real mechanization of cameo carving processes. The consequence was a commercial, factory-produced product which nevertheless did not exclude the development and exploitation of ingenious studio glass techniques on the highest artistic level.

Some fine results were achieved by several of Gallé's close followers: Daum Frères of Nancy, Muller Frères of Lunéville, St Louis-Münzthal (signatures Arsale for *Argental* = Münztal), De Vez (real name Camille Tutre de Varreux) of Stumpf, Touvier, Viollet and Cie.; Schneider (signed Schneider, also Le Verre Francais). Legras of Pantin. Gallé signatures are of incred-

1 Stoppered bottle, heavily carved and with an inlaid bubble effect made by Maurice Marinot. From Barsur-Seine, it dates from 1929.

2 Two vases of flattened form, incised and enamelled with fish and plants by Eugène Rousseau. It was shown at the Paris Exhibition of 1878. dates from about 1884–9. vase is iridescent, light example dates from about 1900.

ible versatility and on good pieces in close sympathy with the general style of the decor.

Of the highly gifted individual artists mention must be made of Eugène Rousseau 1827–91 and his pupil E. Leveillé, who experimented successfully with crackleglass and inlay techniques; Joseph Brocard (*d.* 1896) who revived Islamic style enamelling, and the group of artists who worked in *pâte de verre*: H. and J. Cros, F. Décorchement, H. Dammouse, G. Argy-Rousseau, Alméric Walter, G. Désprét and perhaps also Georges de Feure, a successful illustrator, designer of furniture, furnishing materials, theatre decor and ceramics. In principle, the *pâte de verre* technique consists of pulverizing

glass, adding a binder, placing it into moulds and cooking it in the kiln. Signatures are always present.

The work of René Lalique (1860–1945) brings us well into the modern age. A highly successful jeweller turned glassmaker, his first commercial success was the result of scent bottles produced for Monsieur Coty. His individual opalescent milky and frosted glass creations are moulded, and consequently mass produced. Embellishments by lacquer-type enamelling are particularly effective when they do occur, colour glass is more rare and in general Lalique relies for effect on form and texture. Lalique was one of the first artists to exploit the architectural possibilities of the glass material by creating doors, chandeliers, and fountains. The firm today makes high quality crystal glass, and still produces pieces in earlier mould designs. After Lalique's death, the initial R. is omitted from the signature.

The studio glass of Maurice Marinot (1882–1960) is the result of artistic concepts which produce striking effects. Glass masses treated by a combination of deep acid-produced incisions and inlaid colours and air bubbles have a compelling vitality, and this approach is echoed in contemporary studio glass. All Marinot's glass is signed.

America

The first attempts at glassmaking in America were introduced by English settlers in 1608 at Jamestown, Virginia, an event still commemorated there with the sale of blown glass souvenirs. The earliest successful venture came with Caspar Wistar's glasshouse, established in 1739 in Salem County, Southern New Jersey. Wistar's free-blown glass is characterized by applied decoration of trails, bird finials, prunts and blobs eventually developing into the (South Jersey) lily pad motif. Wistar's glass was clear, in pretty colours of aquamarine, olive green, amber, brown, blue and colourless. The factory ceased manufacture in 1780.

In 1763 Henry William Stiegel, a German-born iron worker appeared on the glassmaking scene. He rebuilt his father-in-law's iron works, named it Elizabeth Furnace, continued to prosper, and consequently invested in glassmaking first at Elizabeth Furnace and then at Manheim, Pennsylvania. Stiegel manufactured mainly table glass and flasks, both in mould-blown patterns – the daisy in a diamond design is associated with this factory – and with enamelled decoration of birds, flowers, hearts and inscriptions in the Continental rustic manner. In 1774 the company went bankrupt and Stiegel, after his release from a debtor's prison, died in 1785.

Since both Wistar and Stiegel employed foreign workmen and imported foreign glass, it is difficult to distinguish with certainty between American and foreign products but it seems reasonable for the decoration to have been applied in America.

The third glassmaker to have made his mark on the 18th century American scene was John

Frederick Amelung from Germany, who established an ambitious undertaking near Frederick, Maryland. The New Bremen Glassmanufactory, so named after Amelung's home town, employed some 300 workmen at its peak, mostly German and English. Without doubt, Amelung's glass is the finest made at that period. The high standard of Rococo-type engraving and the harmonious lines of free-blown goblets, flasks and tumblers testify to foreign workmanship. A further product was pattern moulded glass in attractive clear colours. After a number of misfortunes, the factory closed in 1795. The workmen were absorbed by other factories, in particular the New Geneva Glassworks founded in 1797 by a Swiss, Albert Gallatin.

By the early 19th century, several New York state glasshouses produced a South Jersey style in pleasant shapes and colours, and by 1815 about forty glasshouses were in operation in various parts of America, making bottle and window glass.

The war of 1812 and the blockade by the English encouraged home manufacture and by 1840 at least thirty glasshouses produced tableware. English, Irish and French and a little later Bohemian techniques made their mark on the new industry. The Pittsburgh Glass Manufac-

glass knobs were taken out by Bakewell in 1825, and by the New England Company in 1826. The designer of the metal moulds must be considered the real artist in this glassmaking process. Early American pressed ware is usually of fine quality lead glass, and the utilization of three-part moulds encouraged more elaborate designs. By the 1850s, three-quarters of American glass output consisted of pressed ware. Between 1825–50 the new process was exploited to the full with a very distinctive design, the 'lacy', a pattern with a stippled background which gives the appearance of delicate embroidery or textile. Because of the growing intricacy of these patterns, the moulds had to be exceptionally well made and heated, prior to being filled with a fluid glass metal. 'Lacy' was made in coloured as well as milky opalescent and colourless glass. The pattern variations are almost limitless and even detailed study cannot always ensure definite attribution to one factory or another. The publication *American Glass* by H. and G. S. Mckearin (New York 1941, Crown Publishers), will be very helpful to the collector of 'lacy' ware.

Favourite objects are the charming salt cellars in Rococo and Empire style, and the small cup plates of about 75–100 mm (3–4 in) in dia. Patriotic slogans and emblems were popular

4

3

3 A group of 'lacy' pressed glass made by the New England Glass Company. Between 1827 and 1850, several factories, in particular the New England Glass Company (1818–1888) and the Boston and Sandwich Glass Company (1825–1888), produced the so-called 'lacy' glass obtained by small dots in the mould which gave a stippled appearance rendering an overall lacy effect. It was produced in clear colourless and coloured glass and some of the smaller items, such as salt cellars are of a very attractive design and most collectable.

4 A bucket-shaped beaker blown from a two-piece mould. The metal is pale green and bubbly, and the decorative design consists of an arcade with ribbed pillars beneath a frieze of honeycomb pattern, and emblems of a prancing unicorn beneath a star, three fleurs-de-lys, and a sun in splendour. This glass with its motifs is typical of the work produced at the Orleans glasshouse of Bernard Perrot during the later 17th century.

tory, established by Benjamin Bakewell and Edward Ensell from England in 1808, continued trade under various names. In 1817, a group of businessmen purchased the defunct Boston Porcelain and Glass Company and began trading in 1818 as the New England Glass Company. The most dynamic of these partners, Deming Jarves (1790–1869), established his own glasshouse at Sandwich, and in 1826 this was incorporated as the Boston and Sandwich Glass Company.

The perfection of a pressing machine by means of which molten glass was pressed into any desired shape revolutionized the American and European industries. Patents for pressed

elements in pressed glass design. Pictorial and historical pocket flasks were produced from at least 1780 in a variety of colours, and include the charming group of violin bottles and the Jenny Lind bottles. Factory marks occur frequently on moulded glass but not automatically so, and numerous amalgamations and name-changes of smaller American glasshouses need patient research.

By the mid-19th century, renewed Continental influence caused the appearance of some delightful and well made paperweights. Floral bouquets or miniature fruit resting on a *latticinio* bed were the speciality of the Sandwich Glass Company and the work of a Frenchman, Nicholas Lutz,

The last quarter of the 19th century brings a spontaneous emergence of 'art glass', and with it a vogue for shaded colour glass. This fashion appears to have been introduced with the so-called Amberina glass, shaded amber to ruby red, a creation by the former Stourbridge glass artist Joseph Locke and patented in 1883. Another Englishman, Frederick S. Shirley, followed suit with his Burmese glass – a pale yellow to pink – patented by the Mount Washington Glass Company and manufactured under licence by Thomas Webb in Stourbridge. Colour shades became more and more exuberant with exotic names: Pomona, Peachblow, Maize, Coral Wild Rose. Glasshouses vied with each other in a profusion of novelty and art glass manufacture. The Mount Washington Glass Company and Hobbs-Brockunier and Company are perhaps the most prominent from the collector's point of view, with the Durand Glass Company a close second.

In 1864, William Leighton of the Wheeling Glass Factory in West Virginia developed a lime soda glass as a cheaper substitute for lead crystal. This was disastrous for some of the glasshouses producing high quality lead glass and they were forced to cease manufacture. When the New

fort Tiffany and Company, Associated Artists, and in 1880 Tiffany patented his iridescent glass – the 'Favrile'. Tiffany's interest extended to glass exploitation techniques recalling ancient processes of iridescence and corrosion, and re-created these effects by exposing his glass to metallic oxide fumes or by adding certain substances to the glass batch. His iridescent colour creations made an enormous impact on glass art everywhere, and iridescent glass was soon produced by most good and artistic glass factories. Signatures vary from the full name to initials only, or perhaps the trademark 'Favrile'. Tiffany produced a number of artefacts, small boxes, and lamps. He had produced stained-glass windows and screens as early as 1872 and applied this experience to the production of most fascinating lampshades. The factory closed in 1932.

In 1903 Frederick Carder of Stevens Williams (Stourbridge) and Thomas G. Hawkes founded the Steuben Glass Works. At first influenced by the work of Gallé, Lalique and Tiffany, they succumbed to popular concepts of novelty glass with the creation of *Aurene, Verre de Soie, Moss Agate, Jade Glass, Rouge Flambé.* Glassmaking by the *cire perdue* technique was a particular hobby of Carder's. In 1918, the firm was taken

England Glass Company finally closed down in 1888, the factory's agent, Edward D. Libbey moved the Company to Toledo Ohio where cheaper gas was available, and took over the Charter in 1890, with Joseph Locke still as leading glass artist. The Libbey Glass Company is now a division of the Owens-Illinois Glass Company.

In 1962, the Toledo Museum of Art initiated the formation of a glass workshop with Dominic Labino as advisor. Labino, a director of the Industrial Glass Research Company, is the creator of some of the most subtle and exciting colour glass today.

The greatest innovator in American Art Nouveau glass was Louis Comfort Tiffany (1848–1933), son of a fashionable jeweller. The company was established in 1878 as Louis Com-

1 This is an interesting vase by Daum in the Art Deco style of the 1920s. The wrought iron mount is by Louis Majorelle, one of the most important personalities of the Nancy school.

2 This vase is by Emile Gallé with a conventional Art Nouveau style mount. It dates from about 1884–9.

3 French paperweights produced during the second quarter of the 19th century. The top one is a Baccarat bouquet weight with a pansy; the centre one is a St Louis millefiori weight; the bottom one is millefiori on latticinio from Clichy.

over by the industrial Corning Glassworks, and in 1933 was incorporated as Corning's artistic division under the direction of Arthur A. Houghton, with the co-operation of Jack Gates and Sydney Waugh. Steuben have developed a particularly brilliant and soft crystal which lends itself to the more individual glass sculptures, a unique facet of Steuben today which establishes the factory as the leading American crystal glasshouse. Signatures are present in full, and specially designed pieces may carry a date and the name of the artist.

Spain

A distinct Spanish glass style was slow to develop because the industry was exposed to both Eastern and Western influences. Rustic type of decoration, reminiscent of Syrian work, is expressed by fanciful shapes and prunted, pinched or trailed embellishment. Venetian inspiration, predominant during the 16th century, resulted in exquisite enamelled work in characteristic colours of white and green, with added gilding—doubtless also Islam-influenced—and blown glass vessels in *latticinio* techniques. Typical domestic products are oil lamps and wall fonts, and certain table-ware—the *cantir* (a water can

resembling a footed teapot), the *almorrata* (a sprinkler), and the *porron* (a long-spouted wine carafe).

In 1728, the Royal Factory of La Granja de San Ildefonso was established by Catalan glassmakers. Glass production was almost exclusively for the Royal Palace and workmen were engaged from all over Europe. The characteristic late 18th century product are vessels with engraved and firegilt decoration, as well as enamelled decoration of a rather provincial style with flowers and garlands. Milk glass and coloured glass, sometimes with a mottled effect, was another feature of this factory.

Little figures similar to *verre file dé Nevers* were made in Spain from the 16th century onward.

Scandinavia

Although there was early knowledge of glass-making in Scandinavia, the first factory to operate in the Danish Norwegian kingdom was established in 1741, at Nøstetangen, Norway. German and English glassblowers were engaged and native workmen sent abroad to learn the craft, resulting in glass analogous with the prevailing Anglo-Venetian style.

4 A vase made by Emile Gallé in greenish-blue, semi-transparent glass. The dragonfly modelled in sepia glass with jewelled eyes, was a subject greatly favoured by the artist and is seen in some of his finest pieces. This one was made in 1903 and is 285 mm high.

5 The inlay and cutting of this blue and pink cologne bottle by Frederick Carder is reminiscent of the work of Marinot. Carder, at Stevens and Williams from 1881 to 1902, went to the United States and founded the Steuben factory at Corning in 1903, together with Thomas G. Hawkes. He was an extremely versatile glassmaker and experimented with a great variety of techniques. This piece dates from about 1935.

6 This Tiffany 'favrile' glass vase is iridescent, light brown with maroon inlaid swirls and ribbed waist. This example dates from 1900.

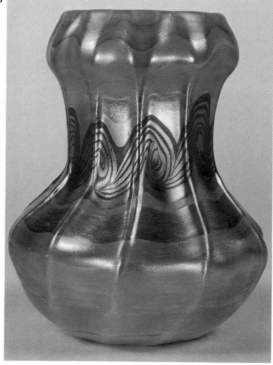

7 This Gazelle Bowl was designed by Sidney Waugh. It is a blown bowl resting on a cut base and engraved with a frieze of 12 leaping gazelles. Represented in a number of museum collections, the bowl was first made in 1935 and has been commissioned over 50 times. The height is 171 mm and the diameter 165 mm.

In 1676, Giacomo Scapitta founded the Swedish Kungsholm Glasbruk factory at Stockholm and supplied the glass for the Royal Household. Table glass and chandeliers in Venetian-influenced blown glass were produced in these factories. By 1757 two further glasshouses operated in Norway – Hurdals Verk specializing in crown glass manufacture and enamelled glass in small quantity, and Hadeland producing bottle glass. During the later 18th

1 These two wine glasses with drawn trumpet bowls and folded feet were made at the Kosta factory during the 18th century. The one on the left is engraved with a crown above the initials N. L. L. and the year 1765. The other is also engraved with a crown and a motto within a cartouche.

On the right is a free-blown, covered two-handled dish. The cover has an elaborate finial. It was made at Boda in the late 18th century.

2 This bowl and vases in amethyst coloured crystal in a free-blown functionalist style were designed by Edward Hald of Orrefors, Sweden. They were made in 1942.

century, some fine German engravers decorated glass at Nøstetangen: Heinrich Gottlieb Köhler working in a Rococo style, and Villas Vinter.

The Empire and *Biedermeier* periods accounted for pretty colour glass in pastel shades, predominantly blue and opaque white, of pleasing popular design. The Royal cipher is frequently engraved or enamelled on glasses and decanters, but is no reliable indication of date of manufacture.

Modern Scandinavia has probably made the greatest contribution to contemporary glass art. The Swedish factory of Kosta, founded in 1742, works in both old and contemporary styles, with designs which are sensitive and exciting. The most original developments took place at Orrefors (est. 1889) Sweden, with their *Graal* and *Ariel* glass. *Graal*, first made in 1916, is an extension of Gallé's cased glass technique in a more realistic mood with a fluid pattern which becomes smooth, where Gallé employs relief cutting. *Ariel* glass was developed about 1930, and consists of a complicated technique whereby the glass artist produces encased air spaces to fill an arranged pattern which has been sandblasted into the glass body. The method is applied in plain and colour glass, and when augmented by a contrast coloured glass inlay is exceptionally effective. Orrefors' reputation is largely due to the work of first rate and imaginative designers such as Simon Gate and Edward Hald. Signatures vary, Orrefors or 'Of' for the factory, with initials or name of the artist on individually designed pieces.

Hadelands Glassverk in Norway contributes with glass of sensible form and refined colour, and a genre of novelty ware – animals, eggs, and so on, decorated by engraving of fine quality.

Finland, too, makes an interesting range of domestic and art glass in the factories at Riihimäki and Karhula-Ittala, established during the late 1920s.

Russia

The first glasshouses in Kiev and Kostroma were destroyed in the early Christian era, and at the time when European artistic development expanded and flowered with the upsurge of the renaissance, Russian cultural and artistic life lay barren under Mongol occupation. In 1637, a Swede, Elias Koet, established his Dukhaninsky factory near Moscow and in 1668 set up another at the Tsar's summer residence at Izmailova, employing Venetian glassblowers. These factories proved inadequate and by the early 18th century Peter the Great's factory at Sparrow Hill was in production. After he had created St Petersburg as his capital, he moved the Imperial Glassfactory nearer, setting up two glasshouses at Yambourg and Zhabino for the manufacture of domestic and chemical glass, window panes, lanterns and mirrors. In 1735, the factories were moved once more, but after 1770 production ceased.

Glass was still made for the court at Schlüsselburg which was amalgamated with the Imperial Porcelain Manufactory in 1792. Under Elizaveta

1

2

Petrovna some interesting mosaics were created by Professor M. V. Lomonosov, but since glass was made almost exclusively for the Court any real progress was doomed to failure.

Fine glass with enamelling and gilding in the Rococo tradition was made at the Bakhmetev factory, established in the 1760s, and elegant early 19th century commemorative goblets, set with painted medallions and expertly cut, must be attributed to this glasshouse. The Imperial factory at St Petersburg also produced colour and milk glass, but during the Adam and Regency periods grand chandeliers, torchères, vases, mirrors and table glass, cut and ormulu mounted, differed little from the luxury glass of Versailles and Potsdam.

Fine quality as well as domestic moulded glass was a successful product of the Mal'tsev factories, who made some poor attempts at Bohemian colour techniques. Colour glass on a much higher level was made in the late 19th century during the last phase of the Imperial Glass Factory with a decorative style inspired by national folk art. Impressive colour glass goblets, carafes and vases with thickly applied gilding and enamelling recall the rich, byzantine ornateness of Old Russia.

From the 1920s, glass is used extensively and monumentally in Russian architecture, but great strides have been made in studio art glass produced by gifted young Soviet glassmakers, with special emphasis on glass sculpture and colour experiments.

Bakhmetev ceased production during the Revolution and is now resurrected under the name Krasniy Gigant – Red Giant. Bakhemetev signatures are quite rare, but the St Petersburg Imperial factory mark frequently appears as S.P. Burg – not an individual signature but an abbreviation for St Petersburg. After the amalgamation with the Imperial Porcelain Factory signatures are identical with porcelain marks, carrying the relevant Royal Cipher. Mal'tsev domestic ware has a moulded signature surrounding the double-headed eagle.

China

Fundamentally, the Chinese craftsman regarded glass not as a material in its own right, but as an additional media to which existing artistic techniques could be applied. A similar approach is apparent in Japanese glass art, but mention must be made of a late 19th century group of vases in which glass is used in a *plique-à-jour* technique.

It is surprising to note that while Chinese porcelain may be delicate and paper-thin, Chinese glass is heavy, thick walled, smooth of texture and oily to the touch. Edges are usually ground. Glassmaking was certainly known in China since the fourth century, but blowing techniques were only introduced a century or so later. The Peking factory came under Royal Patronage in 1680 and made clear and opaque glass in many colours, with a preference for a rich midnight blue and a bright yellow.

Crizzling is still present in some 18th century glass, but striking effects were achieved in techniques akin to rock crystal and jade carving. Exquisitely coloured and cut overlay glass vases, bowls and miniature snuff bottles dating from the Ch'ien Lung period (1735–95) have found no equal to this day and inspired Emile Gallé in his concept of glass techniques.

Throughout history glassmakers have attempted to overcome the difficulties of producing red glass, which needs special firing, particularly if it is to have transparency. Kunckel in the 17th, Meyer Oppenheim of Birmingham in the 18th and Egerman in the 19th century succeeded in this technique. Chinese glassmakers have pro-

3

duced an opaque red glass of an unusual dark crimson colour, the so-called *sang-de-boeuf*, a term also applied in pottery glazes. It is very likely that the experimental red glass produced at the St Petersburg Imperial factory was influenced by Chinese techniques, and Fabergé used this deep crimson type of stone glass which he termed *Purpurine* most effectively in his artefacts.

While modern Japan is now producing some quite outstanding work in the field of art glass, China seems to rely on early decorative techniques and the glass quality still leaves a great deal to be desired.

3 This covered vase of bluish transparent glass metal is richly enamelled and gilded with decorative motifs in the Byzantine style. It was made at the Russian Imperial Glass Factory and signed in gilt under the base with the initial 'A II' for Alexander II (reigned 1855–81). It dates from about 1870 and is 260 mm high.

Decorative Pieces

Decorative items in general, and jewelry in particular, are quite distinct from the other sections in this book. The reasons for this are related to their form and function, to their largely ephemeral nature, to their intrinsic value and to their role in determining social strata. Decorative items are also often quite useless, a feature that increases rather than diminishes their attraction. Yet, they are often able to express powerful extremes of emotion and indeed, by their very nature, have been created to play important roles in the continual conflicts between whole societies or individual human beings, particularly in the war between the sexes.

The main quality of most decorative items is that they are formed of intrinsically valuable materials – precious metals such as silver, gold or platinum, precious or semi-precious minerals and rare natural materials such as ivory, jade, shells, pearls and amber. The skill of the craftsman is only important in the way the materials are handled for, while this skill can increase the overall value of the object, it can never destroy the value altogether. Most items can be broken down into their component parts and still be sufficiently valuable to warrant their being worked again into a new form.

The products of jewellers, goldsmiths and silversmiths therefore, have a tendency to be highly reflective of changes in fashion. A piece of glass, furniture or porcelain cannot be unmade and reformed and so, once made, they are final statements of particular fashions or periods. A decorative item is, on the other hand, impermanent and so, however magnificent its structure and form, it can always be remade into something different.

In many cases, intrinsic value has limited the chances of survival from one age to another. The Spaniards in South America destroyed most Inca jewelry and metalwork because they were only interested in the base value of the materials used. Similarly, Renaissance jewelry is scarce today because its styles did not appeal to later generations. The 17th and 18th centuries required jewelry that was both more complex and abstract in structure, and less imaginative in design.

The chances of survival of individual pieces were also affected by changes in the social roles that decorative items were called to play, because most were made to reflect the status of the original owner or user. On one level they had to express the level of wealth, on another the awareness of style and fashion. It would thus have been unthinkable for a person of style in the 18th century to wear Renaissance jewelry, for its straightforward workmanship and cabouchon stones would have suggested both poverty and a lack of fashion. It was not until the 19th century that historicism became accepted as an important source of fashion, and the products of the past were given any serious consideration. Large collections of decorative items were more likely to survive from one age to another because collectively they represented the power, wealth and status of an individual or society. Thus, the destruction of the Inca jewelry was expressive of the Incas' destruction as a race; by the same token, the capture in time of war of the enemy's state treasury or crown jewels would have a devastating effect on his morale as well as on his finances. That the emotive value of some objects can be far greater than their actual worth was demonstrated recently by the furore that surrounded the return of St Stephen's Crown to the Hungarian people after its long exile in America.

In this sense, decorative items may not be useless because they can acquire over a period of time strong symbolic or religious significance. An obvious example is the great social value imposed upon sacred items such as reliquaries, the mere sight of which can control whole civilizations. More straightforward is the wedding ring, a simple object with a social and symbolic power far grater than its actual worth. This power is broken when the ring is no longer associated with a particular person, and it then reverts to the basic value of the materials involved in its making.

Decorative items thus frequently draw their power from direct association with individuals or societies. In this way they can resemble costume, something shapeless and meaningless until brought to life by contact with a human body. When seen simply as decorative and valuable objects, their symbolism and power is only indirect. However, when displayed in context on the body, their more subtle roles become apparent. They can determine the rank, wealth and status of the wearer, but their main power is a sexual one. The display of jewelry is often an expression of the sexual status of the wearer, and individual pieces can be very expressive of the language of pursuit, conquest, rejection and submission. In this way, they also determine clearly the roles to be played by men and women, for male jewelry, however ornate and decorative, would never be confused with its female counterpart. It is, in fact, an interesting reflection of the state of our society today that women are now often prepared to wear masculine jewelry, as they adopt a more dominant role that used to be the prerogative of men.

Decorative items can therefore be useful guides to the history of fashion, for they are so closely related to its general pattern of development. They can reveal thereby, not only the history of style, but also the more significant changes in social behaviour. Collectors today are often aware of this and so can buy and use antique decorative items for many reasons, among which the obvious investment factor is not always the most important. The intrinsic value is generally taken for granted, and so the buyer today can concentrate on the more interesting social and symbolic values. These latter values also make decorative items distinct from other branches of antiques, for they ensure a universal appeal and interest based not on style, but on the eternal nature of symbolism itself.

The reverse side of the French gold pendant shown on page 153. It is decorated with champlevé enamels and dates from the second half of the 16th century.

Jewelry

Milestones in the history of jewelry

c.1450–1550	The Renaissance liberates the jeweller, allowing him to develop his art.
c.1500	Discovery and subsequent colonization of the Americas yielded large quantities of gold and gems.
c.1640	'Rose diamond' style of cutting invented.
c.1675	George Ravenscroft developed 'flint glass' ideally suited to the production of paste gemstones especially in imitation of diamonds.
c.1700	Vincenzo Peruzzi developed the 'Brilliant-cut' diamond.
c.1800	'A jour' settings (open-backed) appeared.
c.1849	Large deposits of gold discovered in California. Large deposits were also discovered later in Australia and the Transvaal (1884).
1851	Great Exhibition in London formed a useful forum for European jewellers. Exhibitions in Paris were soon to follow.
c.1868	Spectacular diamond deposits discovered in South Africa.
c.1900	Synthetic stones appeared on the market.
c.1905	Platinum used extensively for settings.

1 The Swan badge of enamelled gold is probably French and dates from the mid-15th century.

2 This magnificent enamelled gold pendant, representing the sacrifice of Abraham, is French and dates from the second half of the 16th century.

Good jewelry of any period speaks to us in many ways: it says much of the designer's love of precious materials; it betrays the manufacturer's skills with metals, enamels and stones; it shows, very often, an attempt to express in miniature a notion of perfection; it also says a great deal about the person who purchased it and wore it, and about the society in which he or she lived. Jewels were designed not only to be admired from a distance, but also to be handled, and the collector or enthusiast is always limited if his knowledge is restricted to viewing pieces behind glass in a museum or shop.

To handle a piece of jewelry is to experience it's particular charm, it's own special magic; the magic that early craftsmen imbued in all their work. Pick up a fine 17th-century pendant and turn it over: the illusion is not immediately shattered, but sustained through fine modelling and engraving; there is no façade behind which the supports, struts and scaffolding may be plainly seen. Jewels were designed to be viewed in the round, like a piece of sculpture.

Primitive societies recognized this mystical element in jewelry and buried pieces with their dead; talismans and amulets to serve the owner in the afterlife. With the advent of the Christian epoch, however, this custom was to die out; as a result we know more about the jewelry of classical Greece and Rome than about the medieval period.

Another major contributor to the scarcity of early examples lies within the jewels themselves: the materials used in jewelry have three major elements in common: first, and perhaps principally, beauty; secondly, rarity; and thirdly, durability. It is this last element, the durability of the materials, which allows the continual reworking and remodelling to follow the vagaries of fashion and taste, that has spelt destruction for so many early and fine examples of the art.

The wind of revolution that blew through all the arts in Europe during the 15th century also had a dramatic effect on jewelry. For the first time the jeweller was able to emerge from the Goldsmiths Guilds, where he had been confined throughout the Middle Ages to the manufacture of liturgical objects under the patronage of the Church, or jewels commissioned by princes or noblemen, and to develop his art alongside his colleagues in painting and sculpture. Indeed, the new style evident in jewelry of this period may be partly attributable to painters and sculptors such as Verrochio, Pollaiuolo, Brunelleschi and Botticelli, many of whom started their careers in the goldsmith's workshop.

Jewelry, thus freed from the constraints of the Church, was allowed to develop freely and become a perfect expression of individual taste; a means of personal expression that was to prove indispensible to the display of prosperity of the emergent mercantile classes. Exploration and trade overseas was already adding to the materials available to the artist craftsman; this,

the only direct link with Greece and Rome was through the revival of the glyptic art (the technique of carving and engraving hardstones) with the result that many classical cameos were copied, imitated, and incorporated into rings, brooches and pendants. Jewellers also borrowed certain decorative motifs from the antique—the arabesques and scrollwork that Raphael had popularized through his decoration of the loggie at the Vatican, and the grotesques inspired by the frescoes discovered in the 'grottos' of the Baths of Petrus.

combined with the general increase in wealth evident throughout Europe, accounts for the extraordinary number of jewels which survive even today, testifying to the ostentation and splendour of the time.

Unlike painting and sculpture, Renaissance jewelry was not a rediscovery and celebration of classical Greece and Rome, rather it borrowed from these sister arts, especially sculpture, to develop a pictorial vocabulary of its own. It is likely the general techniques of goldworking had survived since the classical period, but there were very few pieces available for study. Perhaps

The emphasis during this period was upon harmony of design and craftsmanship rather than a display of wealth. This is not to say that stones were unpopular, rather they were incorporated into a design for their chromatic value and emphasized through the subtle use of coloured enamel and elaborate settings. The most common type of cutting of this period is the table-cut, where, as the name implies, the stone was roughly faceted so that it displayed a flat top, though many coloured stones remained *en cabochon*, like a pebble. Settings were generally of a square, pyramidal design with the top edges

1 One of Holbein's pendant designs, early 16th century.

2 Two late 16th century enamelled pendants; (left) representing St George and the dragon; (right) a bust of Minerva, probably South German.

3 This fine, Italian enamelled pendant in the form of a mermaid, the torso a baroque pearl, is probably Florentine and dates from the third quarter of the 16th century.

lapped over to retain the stone, very often with the additional ornament of imitation claws. Foil was generally used behind the stone to add the colour and brilliance the roughly faceted stone lacks. The jewels themselves were nearly always pictorial in design, or at least contained pictorial elements drawn from the wide range of subject matter which the new literature had made available. These included subjects taken from classical mythology, romance and heroic poetry, as well as medieval symbolic images such as the 'pelican in her piety', and, of course, the mythical unicorn.

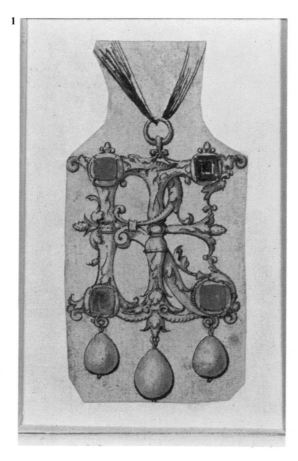

Perhaps the most original type of jewel to be created during this period was the hat badge or *enseigne*, which derives from the medieval pilgrim sign, and was quickly adopted to display the taste and individuality of the wearer through the choice of subject matter. Many of the contemporary portraits illustrate quite clearly how the jewel was worn. The most notable perhaps, are those by Francois Clouet, Bartolommeo Veneto and Holbein.

The signet ring served the same purpose as the *enseigne* in exhibiting the personality and individuality of the wearer. These were often set with an intaglio of either contemporary or classical manufacture, or engraved with a device, monogram or cipher to act as a seal. Other rings were more elaborate, often richly enamelled and with caryatid supports to the high collet, or set with portrait cameos or miniatures. Diamonds were used in the natural octahedral form so that the

point of the stone protruded from the collet, allowing the owner to use it as a scribe on glass. Rings were also used to celebrate certain events: the most attractive are those connected with betrothal or weddings, most notably the *fede* ring where the bezel is formed by a pair of hands clasping a heart or gemstone. Mourning rings were also popular, the shanks engraved with skeletons, the bezels set with death's heads or coffins. Contemporary portraits indicate how liberally rings were worn, gracing every finger, even the thumb, and very often the first and second joints as well.

Necklaces were worn in profusion and were generally of exceptional length, encircling the throat several times and cascading over the bodice. Many different types were often worn together, contributing to the opulent effect; chains of plaited wire had survived in popularity since the Middle Ages, and were augmented by more elaborate designs incorporating plaques and cartouches enriched with enamelled grotesques and arabesques and set with various gems. Pearls strung into long 'ropes' are also evident in the portraits of the time, and were often hung in festoons at the middle of the bodice from a central brooch.

The most significant jewel during the Renaissance, holding pride of place, is undoubtedly the pendant, and it is in this form that the finest examples of the jeweller's art are to be found, many achieving the stature of miniature sculpture. By the beginning of the 16th century, the subject matter of the greater part of these jewels was almost exclusively pictorial or involved in the portrayal of figures in one form or another, often within an elaborate architectural frame. Noted exceptions are the designs by Hans Holbein, the celebrated court painter of Henry VIII. His work mainly emphasizes the use of precious stones for their own sake in an essentially non-figurative composition with the sole addition of coloured enamel and engraving.

The ability to attribute a jewel to a particular country is very rare with pieces made during this period. Holbein was not an artist craftsman, but merely produced designs which were then executed by a goldsmith, probably Hans of Antwerp. This trend was being carried out in the rest of Europe as jewellers issued pattern books of engraved designs which were gradually circulated from country to country.

The infiltration of Renaissance taste and ideals from Northern Italy into the rest of Europe evoked a hunger for the new jewelry in the rising affluent courts of France, Germany, England, the Low Countries and Spain. Benvenuto Cellini, perhaps the archetypal Renaissance artist craftsman, himself worked for a time under the patronage of Francois I in France; while in Germany, Nuremburg and Augsburg quickly established themselves as great centres of the goldsmith's art; the latter centre claiming Vergil Solis (1514–62) whose widely published designs were extremely influential. Other worthy designers are: Androuet Ducerceau, Daniel Mignot, Etienne Delaune, and Theodore de Bruy.

The formidable wealth that Spain was to enjoy through the colonization of the Americas, and the vast quantities of gold and precious stones thereby made available, rendered the Spanish court an important patron too, importing designs and designers from the rest of Europe. As the 16th century progressed and the High Renaissance gave way to the elaborate ornamentation and excesses of Mannerism, so jewelry quickly adapted to the new taste and fashion. Designs for pendants in particular reflected the peculiarly bizarre nature of all ornament at this time as, gradually, the link with

painting and sculpture was abandoned in the search for more and more exotic motifs. Mythology remained a major source of inspiration, but interest also lay in the fabulous creatures such as mermaids and mermen, nereids and hippocamps. The large, misshapen baroque pearl, previously thought unsuitable for jewelry, was seized upon to suggest the bodies of such creatures, the figure completed in richly enamelled goldwork.

No element of the composition was left unembellished, or any surface left plain and unenriched with coloured enamels or stones. Dress

faceted. By 1640 experiments in Holland had led to the development of the 'rose' diamond, a vast improvement on previous styles, which at last released much of the true brilliance of the stone. In this cut, the flat-bottomed crystal has a concave surface covered with 16 or 24 triangular facets. Coloured stones, too, benefited from the improvement in cutting techniques, with the result that gems are rarely found *en cabochon* after the middle of the 17th century.

The new emphasis on stones rather than goldwork and enamel has, however, had an unfortunate outcome: succeeding generations must have coveted the gems more than the settings, for relatively few pieces of good 17th century jewelry have survived the melting pot compared with the products of the previous century.

Enamelling also flourished during this period, though in a different style, indeed some of the finest examples of this type of decoration are to be found in the 17th century. The general trend was towards the use of enamelling to enrich and enhance the settings of the stones themselves, rather than to be an essential feature of the design. Watch and miniature cases are an obvious exception, and it is in this form that the enameller excelled; early designs incorporate the moresque decoration so popular during the previous century, combined with elaborately interlaced tendril scrolls and strapwork motifs, executed in light-coloured enamel *en silhouette* against a dark background; occasionally the effect was reversed, a dark decoration against a light background, through the use of niello. Perhaps the most important of all the designers of silhouette enamels is Jean Toutin, who was working in Châteaudun during the first decades of the 17th century.

Designs for predominantly gem-set jewelry showed a departure, in spirit and motifs, from the Mannerist style. The Baroque love of naturalistic ornament evident in all the arts, especially ceramics and furniture, was quickly adopted in jewelry as well; brooches and pendants were soon designed as elaborate foliate scrolls, buds and flowerheads often supporting several pear-shaped drops, the whole richly set with various gems, often in peapod-like settings. The reverse of the mount was delicately engraved.

Enamelwork, too, found inspiration in leaves and flowers as a source of decorative motifs. By the second half of the 17th century, designers such as Petitot, Vauquer and Légaré had perfected the technique of painted enamel, where the medium is applied in the manner of paint on to an enamelled ground of uniform colour, usually white though occasionally pale blue, yellow or black. Through this technique, which allows a far greater degree of delicacy than the more common *champlevé* process, flower designs achieved a naturalism and beauty hitherto unknown and seldom rivalled. A further innovation was to model the leaves and flowers in relief by building up contoured layers in the enamel ground; in some instances, the ground was cut away leaving the enamelled blooms alone, and thereby adding even greater realism.

1 A fine jewelled collar with pearls and seven enamelled ovals and central pendant dating from the late 16th or early 17th centuries

2 This gold, enamel and gem-set pendant in the form of a cupid with a bow is German or Flemish and dates from about 1600.

3 Gold miniature case decorated with black and white champlevé enamels en silhouette; French, in the style of Michel le Blon, it dates from about 1620.

This type of naturalistic flower decoration found its way on to most items of jewelry, not only the pendants and watch cases already mentioned, but also rings, necklace links, earrings and the immensely popular *aigrette*; this last jewel, a hair ornament, which usually took the form of a spray of flowers or feathers richly set with cluster of stones, seems to have been *de rigeur* at all ceremonial occasions. Sadly, few have survived other than in engravings.

In dress design, the profusion and mixture of patterns and motifs that characterized the late 16th century was gradually abandoned for a

1 A large stomacher brooch, or *crochet*, in gold, set with emeralds and decorated with enamel flowers; Spanish, mid-17th century.

2 Necklace of different coloured topazes and rose diamonds; Spanish, 18th century.

as the pre-eminent gemstone. Indeed, colour was generally avoided during this period; this is reflected in the fact that diamonds were generally set in silver, gold being reserved for coloured stones. The emphasis on stones at the expense of workmanship meant that jewelry became gradually more and more expensive, placing it even further out of the reach of all but the privileged few. As a result, the market in imitation materials boomed. Since diamonds were so popular, attention was particularly directed towards the production of a cheap substitute. Many materials were used including rock crystal and good quality paste, the most famous of which was invented by a German, Stras, working in Paris. His name has become synonymous with paste jewelry in France. In Switzerland, where the wearing of diamonds was forbidden, marcasites, rose-cut crystals of iron pyrites, enjoyed great popularity, as indeed they did in England and France as well, the popularity spanning the following century, too.

Another diamond imitator which, like marcasite, was to become fashionable in its own right was faceted high-carbon steel; the process is generally supposed to have been discovered in Birmingham, England, but suffered the severe drawback of being prone to rust. Coloured stones and pearls were more successfully imitated in paste, but semi-precious gems were common as well; among these lowly stones the most popular were turquoise, citrine, agate, cornelian and garnet. Gold itself was the subject of many imitations, the most successful being the famous alloy of copper and zinc invented by

more luxurious and dignified style in rich silks and brocades exemplified in the portraits by Van Dyck. The jewels themselves, rather than tending to be lost among the plethora of decoration and ornament, as was the case in the previous century, focused the attention glimmering with rich colour; many jewels were worn *en parure*, with matching brooch, pendant and earrings.

These basic trends towards naturalistic designs and emphasis on stones rather than enamel were to be continued after 1700, but with added fervour so that, by the middle of the century, jewelry had become almost exclusively involved with the setting and display of gems, enamel rarely being incorporated into the design except in Spain.

The rose diamond, so popular during the 17th century, was soon superseded by the 'brilliant' cut discovered by a Venetian, Vincenzo Peruzzi, around 1700. This new style of cutting was a major contribution in establishing the diamond

Christopher Pinchbeck in the early years of the 18th century.

France remained the arbiter of taste throughout the period, but the Rococo style that held such a sway over the decorative arts during the mid-century, especially in France, had little effect on jewelry design other than in the decoration of watch cases and objects of vertu. Corsage ornaments such as spray brooches achieved a greater and greater degree of naturalism and informality; to these was added a fashion for bows and loops of ribbon and lace, notably the large sévigné brooches, (named after the French letter-writer) which had sprung up during the latter half of the 17th century. These brooches were often worn *en parure* with a pair of pendant earrings of *girandole* design, each in the form of a pendant with three drops, the longest at the centre. Designs incorporating feathers and feather scrolls are also frequently found during this period, especially in aigrettes. All these ornaments were essentially vehicles for the display of gemstones; the famous chatelaine however, perhaps the most characteristic jewel of the period, which supported not only watches but also keys, etuis, miniature notebooks and seals, was rarely set with fine stones, it's decoration relying on the fine working of gold and gilt metal often with the addition of painted enamel plaques.

Male jewelry was largely confined to buttons and shoe buckles. There are still many good examples in existence designed for both ceremonial and day-to-day wear; the former would invariably be set with diamonds, the latter with imitations such as paste and cut-steel. Rings, too, were favoured by both sexes; apart from signets and clusters, perhaps the most distinctive design of the period is the giardinetto, where the bezel is in the form of a pannier of flowers.

The second half of the century showed a great revival in enthusiasm for mourning jewelry; perhaps most typical are the pictorial pendants produced in large numbers during the last two decades. These were usually oval- or marquise-shaped (a sort of pointed ellipse), and contained a sepia miniature drawn from the current iconography of urns, weeping willows, broken monuments, angels, doves, and so on; part of the composition was usually executed in minute strands of hair taken from the deceased, and the reverse of the mount was invariably inscribed and dated.

The neo-classicism, inspired in many ways by the French Revolution, brought with it a renewed interest in cameos – an interest which had been waning since the Renaissance. The difficulty and expense of producing cameos in hardstone led to a serious quest for suitable substitutes. The relatively soft shells of certain large molluscs, when carved, closely resemble sardonyx cameos, and the process became increasingly popular during this period, although it was almost certainly also known during the Renaissance. In Britain, large numbers of substitutes were manufactured in paste and ceramic, most notably perhaps the well-known plaques pro-

duced by the Wedgwood factory as well as the paste copies of antique gems popularized by James Tassie.

In France, the conscious imitation of Imperial Rome was brought to a head when Napoleon became emperor during the first decade of the new century. His empress, Josephine, quickly re-established a taste for lavish jewelry display; this was made possible by Napoleon's recovery of many of the crown jewels which had been sold or broken up during the early years of the revolution. The new designs were essentially classical pastiches using

3 An interesting memorial pendant, set with a grisaille miniature of a mourner grieving beneath a weeping willow, while the spirit of the departed flies from the tomb, bearing a banner inscribed, *affection weeps, the heaven rejoices*, dated about 1797

4 Four silver buttons, set with white and opaline pastes; English, late 18th century.

such motifs as eagles, Greek-key patterns and laurel wreaths, combined with a reassertion of coloured stones, especially emeralds and sapphires, and the widespread use of cameos. Diadems, hair combs and *épingles à cheveux* were especially popular, the hair drawn up on top of the head away from the ears.

This neo-classical influence was present in most items of jewelry during the first decades of the century; it was arguably most effective in the iron jewels produced in Germany during the latter years of the Napoleonic wars. The Prussian government had appealed to the wealthy to donate their jewels to the war effort; in return they were given necklaces, brooches

1

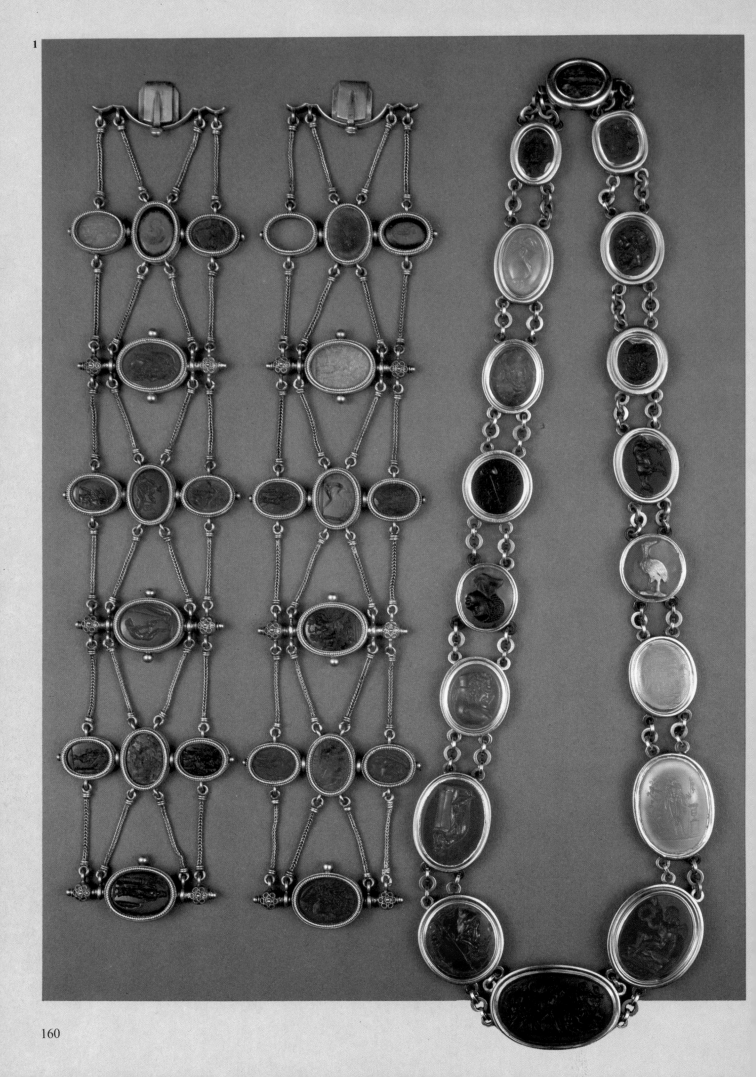

pendants and earrings in a delicate cast-iron-work, lacquered black, and frequently stamped on the reverse with a motto such as *Gold gab ich für eisen*, followed by the date of the donation. Iron jewelry continued in popularity well into the second half of the century and Rouen became a great manufacturing centre; the technique adapted itself particularly well to the gothic tracery motifs of the 1840s.

Jewelry suffered far more from the vagaries of fashion during the 19th century and became, as a result, immensely eclectic. By the late 1820s neo-classicism had burnt itself out and the poor jeweller was at a loss for new inspiration and motifs. What he could not conjure up afresh he sought in past styles and designs, borrowing from a procession of sources: among these, the romantic gothic, popularized through Walpole's novels and the architecture of Pugin and Burgess, was an important influence during the 1840s and is best illustrated by the knights, angels and gargoyles that decorate the jewelry of Froment-Meurice and Jules Wiese.

If the gothic jewelry was largely fantasy, the classical jewels produced during the 1860s were not: makers such as Castellani, Melillio and Brogden, who had all profited by the immense quantity of previously unknown pieces yielded through excavations at famous sites like Herculaneum and Pompeii, were involved in a re-working of Etruscan and Hellenistic jewelry that was both intelligent and faithful to the originals. Another important source of inspiration was the jewelry of the Renaissance, especially the designs of Holbein. In England, Carlo Giuliano and firms like Phillips of Cockspur St., London, seized on these designs as a vehicle for their superb enamelling skills. Carlo Giuliano, in particular, established an almost unrivalled reputation as an enameller during the 1870s, operating from a shop in Piccadilly, the reputation being continued by his sons working in

1 Cameo and intaglio jewelry was popular at the beginning and towards the end of the 19th century. The necklace on the right, about 1810, shows the use of the 'Roman' setting so popular at the time. The pair of bracelets, made during the closing years of the century, illustrate a more consciously 'classical' style with the liberal use of corded wire, filigree and beadwork.

2 A gold brooch, set with a five banded agate cameo of the young Bacchus. The mount, signed with two entwined 'Cs' is by Castellani, about 1860.

3 A collection of late Victorial jewels: (Top) Gold pendant decorated with enamel and set with opals and diamonds, signed 'C & AG', by Giuliano, about 1900. (Left, second row) Gold pendant, enamelled and set with rubies, diamonds and pearls, signed with the monogram 'CD' beneath the Prince-of-Wales feathers; by Carlo Doria, about 1870. (Centre, second row) Brooch in moonstones, rubies and rose diamonds, signed 'C.G.'; by Giuliano, about 1870. (Right, second row) Gold pendant, enamelled and set with peridots and pearls, signed 'C.G.'; by Giuliano, about 1890. (Third row) Gold brooch, enamelled and set with diamonds and chrysoberyls, signed 'C.G.'; by Giuliano, about 1890. (Bottom left and right) Pair of gold earrings, designed as oil lamps, enamelled and set with pearls, signed 'C.G.'; by Giuliano, about 1890. (Bottom centre) Gold brooch, set with crysoprase and rose diamonds, signed 'C.G.'; by Giuliano, about 1890.

'Holbeinesque' and 'archaeological' styles.

The grand exhibitions that took place in Paris and London during the second half of the century had an enormous effect on the spread of new motifs and designs drawn from myriad sources. For example, the Great Exhibition in London in 1851 showed that the fashion for all things Egyptian had had an effect on jewelry design as well: attention had been directed to the area through the excavations in the Nile valley, and the approaching completion of the Suez Canal. Similarly, the Paris Universal Exhibition of 1867 showed evidence of the French involvement in Algeria by the appearance of jewels designed around the knots and tassels common to North African dress. Other new designs were less successful; the battery-operated kinetic hair ornaments that appeared in the same exhibition are a good example.

Other jewelry of the period was less innovative. Spray brooches remained a popular vehicle for the display of diamonds and achieved a high degree of naturalism and informality; this was augmented by the mounting of some of the flowerheads *en tremblant* on a watch spring, so that the bloom literally trembled with the wearer's every move. Many of the brooches show great botanical accuracy; perhaps most attractive are those produced by Froment-Meurice during the 1840s, the leaves highlighted with translucent green enamel.

Less important items of jewelry tended to suffer from the Victorian flippancy and sentimentality; this latter element was responsible for the great fervour for mourning jewels, a habit especially seen in Britain. Many of them were particularly grisly and macabre. Even items that were not specifically involved with the commemoration of the dead frequently had provision for a hair compartment. Indeed, in some cases, jewels were fashioned entirely from the hair of the deceased person.

Birds and insects were fashionable too, ranging from the delicate doves of the traditional Normandy St Esprit pendants, to grotesque lizards and cockroaches. Birds were also a common motif of the mosaic and intarsia brooches widely exported from Rome and Florence respectively, and popularized through the medium of tourism.

Male jewelry was restricted to signet rings, watch fobs and chains, and tie or stock pins. It is really only in the latter group that designs show imagination; illustrated by the enamelled skulls, with articulated jaws operated by a drawstring, characteristic of the romantic gothic of the 1840s, and the golfclubs, whips and horseshoes produced during the last quarter of the century with the fashion for sporting jewelry.

The general appetite for jewelry, which increased dramatically during the 19th century and which spread to most social classes, was greatly served by the production of machine-made pieces, especially in Britain, Germany and Austria. Settings and components stamped out of sheet metal and assembled by hand are common throughout most of Europe from the mid-century onwards; the process was soon adopted in America, too, as a means of producing jewels

Diamond stomacher brooch, designed as a spray of wild roses, signed L. Pierret and dated 1832, Rome.

quickly and cheaply, though at first to predominantly European designs. Originally the process was reserved for gilt metal jewelry but was quickly applied to precious metals as well, largely as a result of the formidable increase in gold resources through discoveries in California, Australia and South Africa.

Towards the end of the century there was a gradual reaction against the ostentation and pondorousness of the previous 50 years. Diamond jewelry, in particular, shows a gradual lightening and increasing delicacy of design, very often looking to the Louis XVI style of decoration, especially in ormolu furniture-mounts, in swags, garlands, and ribbon bows. The technical excellence of the diamond jewelry during the last decades of the century and the early 1900s has seldom been surpassed, and benefited greatly from the immense quantity of diamonds that were being mined in South Africa after 1868, together with the use of platinum for the settings, a metal which combines good working qualities without tarnishing.

Fine examples of this technical excellence are the products of the Fabergé workshops in Russia. The firm is characterized by an immense attention to detail and a careful choice of materials, specializing in *objets de fantaisie* as well as hardstone sculptures and jewelry. Perhaps the most famous articles that the firm produced are the jewelled Easter eggs which were manufactured every year from 1882 and given by the Czar as presents to his wife.

In Britain, the move away from the excesses of the Victorian era in all the decorative arts is largely attributable to the crusading work of William Morris, whose firm, Morris & Co., had been set up as early as 1861 in an attempt to re-affirm the importance of craftsmanship and integrity to design. In jewelry this meant a reaction against the display of wealth through gold and precious stones to which the art had been confined since the late 16th century; instead the arts and crafts designers favoured silver and enamel set with agates, moonstones, mother-of-pearl and peridots. By 1900, several craft workshops had been set up in Britain, perhaps the most famous of which was the Guild of Handicraft founded in 1887 by C. R. Ashbee. It is difficult to view arts and crafts jewelry without being conscious of an odious comparison with the Art Nouveau jewellers in France and Belgium. The essential difference between the two is that, in England, the craft ethic had largely attracted designers with no sophisticated technical knowledge of manufacturing techniques; their products, as a result, generally fell below the standards of workmanship achieved by most commercial firms. Ironically, the style only enjoyed commercial success when it was applied to mass-manufacturing processes through firms like Liberty's and Murrle, Bennett; the very processes against which the designers had originally reacted. Among the arts and crafts jewellers who worked for Liberty's are Archibald Knox, Arthur Gaskin and Bernard Cuzner.

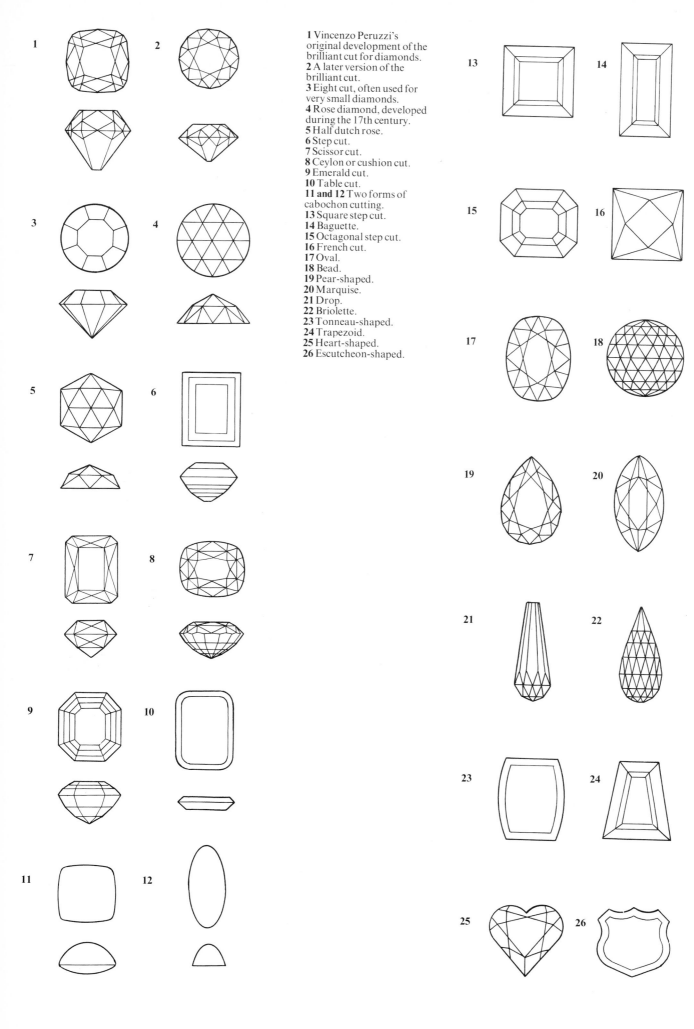

1 Vincenzo Peruzzi's original development of the brilliant cut for diamonds.
2 A later version of the brilliant cut.
3 Eight cut, often used for very small diamonds.
4 Rose diamond, developed during the 17th century.
5 Half dutch rose.
6 Step cut.
7 Scissor cut.
8 Ceylon or cushion cut.
9 Emerald cut.
10 Table cut.
11 and 12 Two forms of cabochon cutting.
13 Square step cut.
14 Baguette.
15 Octagonal step cut.
16 French cut.
17 Oval.
18 Bead.
19 Pear-shaped.
20 Marquise.
21 Drop.
22 Briolette.
23 Tonneau-shaped.
24 Trapezoid.
25 Heart-shaped.
26 Escutcheon-shaped.

Jewelry

The Art Nouveau jewellers, on the other hand, had generally served long apprenticeships before embarking on the new style. This is especially clear in the work of Renée Lalique. A greater innovator who revolutionized both design and the use of materials, his name has become synonymous with Art Nouveau jewelry in France. Many influences can be traced from Japanese art to gothic and celtic motifs, the characteristic forms being attenuated scrolls and bud motifs, intertwining creepers, insects such as dragonflies and butterflies, and human figures. Materials were often mixed and include horn, tortoiseshell, ivory, steel and copper as well as stones like opal, peridot and moonstone, combined with a love of *plique-à-jour* enamel; a technique which allows the light to pass through the enamel, achieving an effect like a stained-glass window. In America, the style had been adopted by Tiffany's, producing a large number of jewels of extremely high quality of workmanship and design, and contributing to the house image popularized by their famous lamps and favrille glass; proof, if it were needed that Europe did not have a monopoly of good taste. Art Nouveau continued to be popular up until the First World War, but gradually lost the inventiveness and originality that characterized the early years of the style.

The war caused a considerable disruption in the development of jewelry. By 1920, naturalistic motifs had been almost totally abandoned for a more abstract, geometrical style employing contrasting colours and materials; a style that we now call Art Deco. This change followed the fine arts away from representation, as impressionism gave way to cubism.

The years between the wars were ravaged by quickly changing fashions. Hair styles are just one example of this, and had a great effect on the types of jewels worn: just after the war, the 'bob' was all the rage, bringing with it a taste for hair clips and combs of every description, but, with the arrival of the 'eton crop' in 1925, clips and combs were to become redundant, and in their place there arose a fashion for earrings, many of which assumed

1 Emerald, sapphire and diamond brooch, designed as a peacock's plume. Dated about 1890, it is French, unsigned but probably by Boucheron.

2 Aquamarine and diamond lozenge-shaped brooch by Fabergè. (Wartski).

3 Art Nouveau silver brooch, the head in opalescent glass, by Lalique, about 1900.

4 Choker in gold, rubies and enamel by P. Wolfers, Belgium, about 1899.

immense proportions. Certain major influences on jewel design of the period shine out from among the rest; among these are Hollywood, and the immense sway over public taste exerted by the cinema; the Russian ballet, especially the design of Leon Bakst; Egypt, largely as a result of the excavations of the tomb of Tutankhamun.

Such fine jewels as were produced at this time (and they were certainly not numerous) were largely confined to famous houses such as Cartier, Boucheron, Van Cleef & Arpels, Lacloche, Mauboussin, and Tiffany. Characteristic of the period is the combination of contrasting precious and semi-precious materials in the same piece, and a love of primary colour; most common are jade, coral, onyx, and matt crystal in combination with diamonds. White metals were favoured rather than yellow and red golds and surfaces were generally highly polished.

The mass-manufacturing techniques begun a century before, were perfected during the 1920s and 1930s, greatly aided by the developments in metalplating, and in the production of synthetic and imitation stones. As a result jewelry ceased to be the prerogative of the affluent, and was soon worn by all social classes; those who could not afford the real thing were able to buy an effective and realistic substitute instead. Costume jewelry designed to be short-lived, answered the problem presented by the rapidly changing tastes and fashions.

Germany and Czechoslovakia were particularly successful in the manufacture of cheap, mass-produced jewels, maintaining a high standard of finish; the industry even survived the depression years, which spelt doom for so many small jewelry enterprises.

Viewed as a whole, the years leading up to the Second World War seem to represent a decline in the belief in jewelry as a means of artistic expression. The art schools of the 1960s, however, were to prove that it was merely a slumber.

5 Pendant earrings in jade, onyx and diamonds, by Boucheron, Paris, about 1920.

6 Necklace in diamonds and enamel by Tiffany, New York, about 1870.

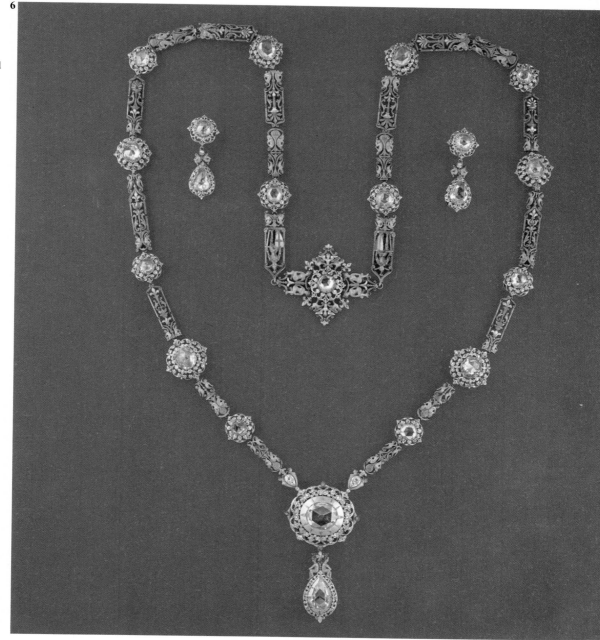

Objects of vertu

As with Renaissance jewels and works of art in enamel and gold, the task of establishing the country of origin for many gold boxes and small objects remains baffling. By the second half of the 18th century, most gold boxes were made in France, the main centre of *objects of vertu*, and bear hallmarks and makers' marks, but neither the English nor the German articles were normally marked and the problems of attribution are very often insoluble. The development of a purely national style in this field was made difficult by the arrival of foreign craftsmen in centres such as London, Dresden and Amsterdam. Another cause for this was the influx of foreign, particularly French, engraved designs for these objects, which the local goldsmiths copied, often quite slavishly. This section discusses examples of the various styles of European and American gold boxes and *objects of vertu* produced from the beginning of the 18th century and will give some idea of the various techniques employed by leading European and other goldsmiths.

Small receptacles for scent, snuff, pills and bonbons were not made in France before 1660. From the literature of the few countries where snuff-taking was well-established before this date, these appear to have been made of shell, horn and tortoiseshell, rather than of the costly materials used from the beginning of the 18th century. The first boxes which could vaguely be classed as works of the goldsmith's art were made as early as 1668.

After the death in 1715 of Louis XIV who disapproved strongly of snuff-taking, the official ban was lifted from the Court by Philippe d'Orleans during the Regence period which lasted until 1723. The production of small boxes began in Paris during this period. Most of the early boxes were of simple design, often in gold with the use of other materials for embellishment. They were very often in the form of scallop shells

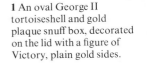
Objects of vertu is a term many people find mystifying. Although it is a definition well known among collectors, the meaning is often confused with the word 'virtue'. The expression is derived from the French word *vertu* and means a small object of beauty and rarity. In the 17th century, the word *vertu*, such as a 'Man of Vertu', meant that he had a particular interest in the fine arts. These objects help to provide an inkling into the elegant way of life in the 18th and 19th centuries.

Articles of a great many kinds were made and were in constant use during this period, such as *bôites-à-mouche*. These were boxes for holding patches, *bôites-à-rouge*, boxes for make-up, as well as many different types of receptacles for containing powder and comfits. Fine gold cases were also made for needles and wax, and called *Étuis-à-cire*. Other objects included boxes for powder, pills, also vinaigrettes for scent, seals, chatelaines for watches or étuis, cane and parasol handles, scent bottles, buckles and boxes.

These gold boxes were often called snuff boxes, although many were never used for snuff and were distinctive manifestations of the civilized life of the leisured rich in 18th-century Europe, just as pomanders for scent had been an indispensable accessory of the Renaissance courtier 200 years before. Gold boxes tend to be studied and discussed in isolation, whereas gold chatelaines and étuis are given their rightful place in the history of jewelry. Yet the designs for étuis and gold boxes were in many cases undoubtedly made by the same craftsmen. The gold box was as much a part of a gentleman's adornment as the buckles on his shoes, the rings on his fingers and the gold cane in his hands. In consequence, the gold box may best be studied as an extension of the goldsmith's craft in the field of jewelry.

3

3 A Battersea enamel
portrait plaque, transfer-
printed in puce with a profile
bust of William Augustus,
Duke of Cumberland, after
Ravenet; original gilded
frame; about 1755

4 A Swiss silver-gilt and
enamel singing bird box,
the top enamelled in *en plein*
technique with sprays of
flowers; mid-19th century.

or oblong shapes chased with reliefs and set with miniatures.

Boxes set with portrait miniatures were often made to be given by the King to visiting diplomats from abroad, the lids of these boxes being set with fine enamel portraits of the King and Queen and bearing the Royal Cipher and/or Coat of Arms. These miniatures were thought to have been painted mainly by Jean Petitot, who worked for the French Court from 1607 until his death in 1691. He was by far the most prolific painter of his time. Unfortunately, examples of his work set in contemporary boxes are not known to have survived, as these portraits were remounted by makers such as Adrien Maximillien Vachette at the end of the 18th century. However, their general style may be inferred from slightly later examples made by Daniel Govers, who worked exclusively for the Court of Louis XV, and others. Among his most important royal commissions was a box applied on the cover with a monogram of the King and Queen in rubies and diamonds on a tortoiseshell ground, the gold sides enriched with enamelled shells and the interior with a double portrait of Louis XV and Queen Maria Leszczynci. This box was not known to have been presented by the King until 1744, when it was given to a Swiss banker.

When leaving their posts many of the recipients of such diplomatic presentation gifts sold the articles back to the French Foreign Ministry, who re-used them at a later date, or if the style was by then unacceptable melted them down for the materials. By the 1730s, the effect of the Rococo movement was reflected in the design of bijouterie with such objects as boudoir clocks, scent flagons and all manner of small boxes. The first Rococo designs by Juste-Aurèle Meissonier, who lived from 1693 to 1750, displayed asymmetry, for nothing that could be

gracefully curved was left straight. Although many larger domestic objects such as candelabra in ormolu survived from this period, it is sad that few truly Rococo boxes remain.

Repoussé is the word used to describe a technique of decorating the metal, where the surface is pressed forward in relief with matted tooling in the sunken areas to give more emphasis to the raised parts. This type of repoussé decoration was England's main contribution in the field of valuable *objects of vertu*. While these Rococo articles were being produced in London, utilitarian wares were being produced in the English Midlands. The Georgian enamellers who fused enamel on to copper to make hand-painted and transfer-printed wares often imitated the more costly bijouterie of the London and Continental goldsmiths. The first factory producing this enamel work was founded at Battersea by Stephen Theodore Janssen in 1753 with two partners, Brooks and Dalamain, who were dropped from the firm after its first year of establishment. Although this venture was artistically brilliant, it suffered from commercial instability and in 1756, three years after it was founded, it was declared bankrupt. The other main factories were at Birmingham, Bilston, Liverpool and Wednesbury. These factories produced many fine enamelled wares, usually of a flamboyant nature, for many of these factories were in direct competition with the successful steel toy trade of their neighbours in Wolverhampton. Birmingham and Liverpool were the only factories that imitated the decoration of the earlier factory at Battersea and it can only be supposed that many of the engraved plates were bought from the York House factory at Battersea when the latter was sold.

4

Later boxes produced in England for the most part emulated French designs, or alternatively rigidly interpreted Neo-classical designs of Robert Adam and used, in many cases, similar colourings. In France in the late 1740s, receptacles for snuff and bonbons changed shape, new fashions came in and enamel appeared as one of the salient elements. At first it was used primarily to embellish floral motifs such as flowers and birds on grounds of mother-of-pearl and lacquer. Among the most attractive examples of this style were those decorated with shells, elaborate flowers and exotic birds, the designs being raised on gold and then enamelled in naturalistic colours. These objects were among the most outstanding and distinctive ever produced.

The Royal Manufactory of porcelain at Sèvres had begun to reproduce imitation flowers in porcelain in 1748. These were apparently first ordered by Madame de Pompadour to surprise her royal lover by presenting him with a mass of summer flowers in mid winter. In ornament, it was a sign of the return to nature that was to become manifest everywhere.

Among the makers most accomplished in this technique was Jean-Francois Breton in the early 1750s. In the Corbeille of Marie-Joseph of Saxe, who was married in 1747, there was included a box decorated with a hawthorn spray with enamelled leaves and diamond flowers. Others were decorated with fruit as well as flowers in a similar manner. The demand for articles decorated in this fashion soon greatly exceeded supply and an alternative was produced in the form of cagework bijouterie. This meant that the object could be more easily produced and a particularly popular model could be almost mass-produced in its various component parts. Occasionally, the retailer, who was not strictly allowed to do so, fitted his own panels of decoration into these cagework mounts.

These panels were often of Oriental lacquers and mother-of-pearl or under glass miniature paintings. Under Guild Law, it was illegal to replace them, but it was a rule that must have been frequently contravened. Dutch subjects had been in vogue since 1738 with peasant scenes after Teniers, and subjects were often taken from the painted interiors so characteristic of Dutch

4 A Swiss enamel gold and diamond butterfly snuff box; Geneva, about 1810.

FACING PAGE: Top: German gold mounted agate scent bottle and snuff box in the form on a monkey; about 1750.
Second row: Louis XV enamelled gold boxes; Paris, 1749 (left) and 1757 (right).
Third row: (left) Stroganoff box, said to have been given by Catherine the Great to Count Stroganoff; Russian, About 1780. (right) Louis XV Mother-of-Pearl and gold box; Paris 1744.
Bottom: Louis XV enamelled gold box; Paris 1764

1 Louis XV gold and enamel snuff box by Louis Roncel; Paris 1766.

2 Louis XV gold and enamel snuff box by Louis Philippe Demay.

3 Cut crystal scent bottles in Chelsea porcelain casket.

1

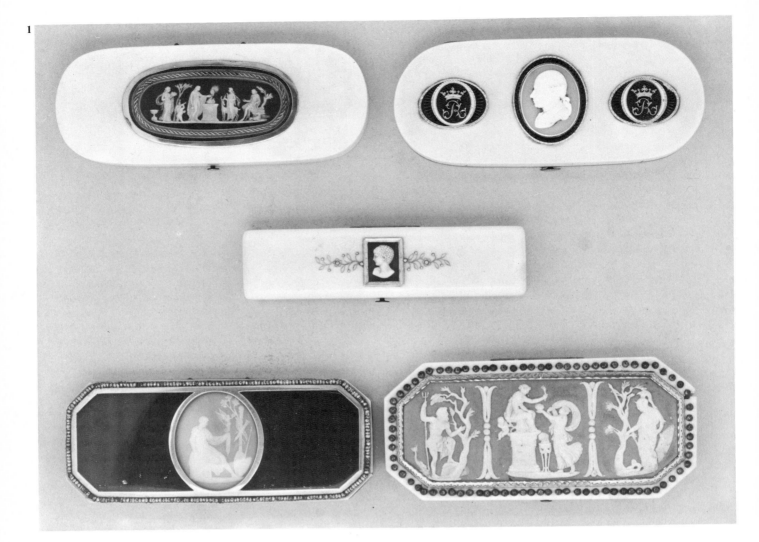

2

painting. However, there is no doubt that this fashion was partly motivated by commercial rather than artistic reasons. During the height of its popularity, the French philosopher and author Diderot exclaimed: "I prefer rusticity to affectation, I would give ten Watteaus for one Teniers". However, the fashion went out after 1760 as it no longer corresponded with current French taste.

Although scenes of this genre were popular with foreign craftsmen, Dutch boxes themselves generally lacked fine craftsmanship and the production of small boxes was restricted to those for tobacco which were very often made in materials such as wood, brass, tortoiseshell or silver. It is rare to find this type of box made purely in gold and the few that do exist date from the middle of the 18th century and are of oblong or cushion shape, the lids often chased or repoussé with classical or allegorical scenes and the remainder left undecorated. During the early 19th century, objects were produced in small numbers in gold and decorated with engine-turnings.

French goldsmith craftsmen working during the third quarter of the 18th century developed the technique of box-making with multi-colours of gold. Paris led the rest of Europe in this technique and none of those who emulated it at a later date, not even the Swiss, could reproduce

1 A group of ivory tooth-pick cases showing the use of enamel piqué work and Wedgwood plaques as decoration; made about 1780.

2 Swiss musical snuff box by J.L. Richter, enamel and gold, set with turquoises; 1800–10.

the sculptured effect that the French achieved in such perfectly balanced colours. This technique of decorating in variously coloured gold had been in existence for some time, but it did not fully come into fashion until the middle of the 1750s. The colour of gold could quite easily be changed by mixing it with other metals, the four basic colours being red, green, yellow and white.

Perhaps one of the greatest exponents of this technique, and also one of the greatest French boxmakers of the 18th century, was Jean Ducrollay. Much of his work dates from this period and although he used many other techniques, his multi-coloured gold articles display a sculptural quality unsurpassed during any later period. By the late 1760s the more fashionable bijouterie makers had restricted the use of four-coloured gold decoration to the more minor areas. From then the borders advertised this technique until the French Revolution. During the last quarter of the 18th century, there were predominantly two fashionable types of decoration used on boxes. In the first group, gouache miniatures under glass took the place of enamel panels. The second group consisted of portrait boxes, which had been made since Louis XIV's portraits had adorned the earliest presentation boxes, but now nearly all these small containers held items for *La Toilette* and were made in much cheaper materials and quite often produced in fairly large numbers.

The one artist whose work was almost exclusively mounted in gold, as an indication of his standing, was Louis Nicholas Van Blarenberghe (1715–94). His subjects included chateaux, pastoral scenes and townscapes. The late 1760s also brought about a further change in decoration in Europe, which reverted to the Greek influence in styles, not only in *objects of vertu* but also the interiors of buildings, furniture, fabrics and jewelry. The fashion became so popular that the elite would have been ashamed to appear in public without a receptacle that was not *à la grècque*. The flowers that had previously decorated these articles were now replaced with laurel wreaths and Greek key patterns. Gone, too, were the Rococo shapes, for from then on boxes were either oval, circular or oblong, quite often with the corners cut to allow the ends to be decorated with Grecian pilasters. While the enamelling changed in a more subtle way, with the inevitable scene from antiquity decorating the main areas of these pieces, others were decorated with plain translucent coloured enamel areas showing engine-turned grounds to advantage, producing a pleasing effect.

The pinnacle of Neo-classicism before the French Revolution can best be seen in the painted cameo miniatures by Jacques-Joseph de Gault, whose work was exclusively confined to reproducing classical bacchic friezes. The change in style during the 20 years preceding the Revolution in France can best be seen in the works of such makers as Joseph-Étienne Blerzy and Jean-Joseph Barrière.

Boxes and other *objects of vertu* produced between 1775 and 1791 fall into two distinct groups. The first group made use of bright distinctive coloured enamels with borders of green and red enamel foliage adorned with simulated jewels such as opals, pearls, rubies and sapphires. The other style was more to the Neo-Classical of English taste with the wide use of single-coloured panels. A goldsmith typifying the pre-Revolution period was Adrian Maximilian Vachette, who worked from 1779 to 1830. He made very successful use of materials of earlier periods, such as Oriental lacquers and miniatures by the artist Jean Petitot. His articles were always of a simple shape, often of tortoiseshell with covers or sides containing miniatures by 17th or early 18th century miniaturists. Many of his works were almost certainly made from dismantled objects, but his boxes of the early 19th century period were totally original, with portraits of Napoleon Bonaparte and other members of the Napoleonic Court.

Mention must be made of the thriving industry in Germany from the middle of the 18th century. Frederick II, in order to encourage active interest in the goldsmith's crafts, forbade the importation of the successful French goldsmiths' work into the country, although many of the styles used in Germany were adapted from the French originals of the day. The articles produced were generally of Baroque inspiration and were usually larger than the products they were copying. With its rich deposits of hardstones, Bohemia could provide a great number of types of quartz such as cornelian, bloodstone, jasper and rock crystal. Objects were produced in all manner of shapes and designs to attract

3 Etuis. Top: (left) French, engraved gold, 1725; (centre) English lapis lazuli mounted in gold, 1755; Bottom: (left) German, gold set with agate cameos, 1725; (right) French, malachite, 1795.

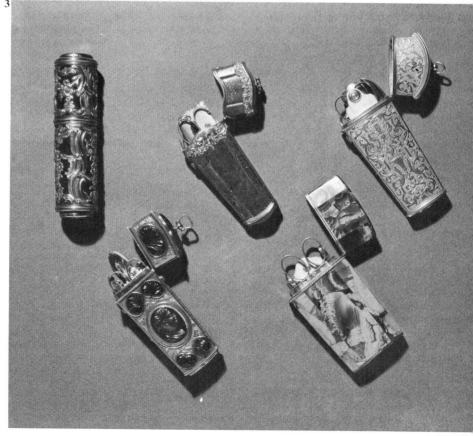

the collector who was doing the Grand Tour. The styles that predominated during the middle of the 18th century in Germany were those of carved work inlayed in hardstone and also the use of mother-of-pearl and other shells.

As well as hardstone and porcelain objects, enamel work on copper was also being produced and the earliest of the factories producing fine enamel work was that of Fromery, in Berlin. This factory must have been the most prolific of all the establishments making enamel wares in Germany in the 18th century. The work produced was easily distinguishable from that of its competitors because of the ornamentation on most of the articles produced by Pierre Fromery and his son, Alexander, who perfected the factory's individual style. They also mounted their work in gold and silver, whereas their contemporaries rarely did so.

The workshops of Augsburg, which had produced the most magnificent silver and gold wares in the 17th century, did not retain very much of their status in the production of *objects of vertu*, and from the late 1740s the only items produced were those of the Du Paquier factory,

many of which were only made to amuse, with painted enamel objects such as playing card boxes and shallow receptacles painted to simulate letters.

During the Seven Years War, 1757–63, there emerged enamel boxes and scent boxes with portraits of Frederick the Great and embellished with trophies of war and maps of his successful battles. This was a good way to spread propaganda for the Prussian cause. Although there were many centres in Germany producing bijouterie at this time, Berlin must have been the centre, making the most magnificent of all examples of the lapidary craft. These boxes were made for Frederick II, who designed many of them himself and who was also a great patron of the arts. Dresden also became prolific in the mining of quartz and the production of boxes and it emerged as the prime centre by the 1770s. Again appealing to the Grand Tourist, Johann Christian Neuber produced many fine examples with the use of classical hardstone cameos in the Italian manner – portrait miniatures and intricate patterns decorating the whole surface of the box in inlaid hardstones. These were very often

1 German enamel scent bottle with gold mounts; height 3¼ inches.

2 Enamel and gold Swiss snuff box bordered with plaques showing the regional costumes of 22 cantons.

3 Freedom boxes were presented to high officials when they were given the freedom or an American city or state.

1

2

3

numbered around the mounts and were usually accompanied by explanatory booklets describing the various hardstones. These charts were concealed in the base of the article and were revealed by means of a secret catch.

Among the centres in Europe embarking at this time on the manufacture of small *objects of vertu* were the Swiss, who in the 1770s successfully produced multi-coloured gold objects such as étuis for various materials and boxes for snuff and powder. The main decoration was classical-inspired and the use of columnar designs adorned with flowers and foliage often taken directly from French styles. This may be accounted for by the fact that many French craftsmen settled in Switzerland after the onset of the Revolution and at this time enamelling was a prominent factor in all Swiss articles. However, they did not quite achieve the quality obtained by the French goldsmiths. Enamel had been equally prominent in the decoration of Swiss watch cases in the second half of the 17th century, but it had been allowed to become extinct, as the exposed surfaces of the enamel very soon deteriorated in constant use.

The watches made in Geneva in the late 1780s made use of transparent enamel which served as a protective covering for painted surfaces, and this made the whole technique more viable, although enamel articles produced in Switzerland were generally unmarked, except where goldsmiths tried to imitate the earlier marks that the French had used, but this was always unsatisfactory as the date letter and Fermier Genérale marks rarely tallied. One of the reasons why the Swiss boxes bear pseudo-Paris hallmarks was because Geneva was under French rule during this period and wherever the French dominated, they tried to impose their hallmarking system. Signatures do appear on landscape paintings adorning these articles, the main enamellers in this medium at this time having been Jean Louis Richter (1766–1841) and David Etienne Roux (1758–1832).

Geneva, by the 1820s, was devoting much of its time to the manufacture of flamboyantly decorated and jewelled objects for the Turkish market, such as small enamel watches and clocks, singing bird boxes, zarfs (or coffee cup holders), gem-set bonbonnieres and scent containers. These items were in many cases over-decorated with emeralds, rubies or diamonds against vivid enamel grounds. It was not until the beginning of the 19th century that boxes produced by the Swiss enamellers developed a truly recognizable style of their own. These boxes were usually of a shallow oblong or oval shape with cut corners or scalloped effects and were painted in various colours with flowers, landscapes or lakeside scenes. These studies were often signed by the artist.

American boxes and *objects of vertu* are little known, but a few fine examples by such makers as Jacob Hurd are in a number of museums in America. The best known example is in the Museum of Fine Arts, Boston. It is engraved with a coat of arms and was presented to William

Dummer, Lieutenant-General, Massachusetts (1716–30). Other makers of Freedom Boxes (these were boxes presented when high officials were given the freedom of a city or state) include Charles Le Roux, who was the master goldsmith in New York and was apparently the only maker of Freedom Boxes from the period 1720–43. In the 1780s, Jacob Gerritse Langing was recorded as having made gold Freedom Boxes.

During the last quarter of the 19th century, simple engine-turned boxes for snuff and cachous were produced in fair numbers. Mexico City was also concerned during the latter part of the 18th century and the beginning of the 19th century in the making of small gold objects. In 1786, an Academy was founded there and staffed mainly by European instructor-craftsmen and the designs bear a very great similarity to European taste. The most interesting and original objects to be produced were boxes to contain cheroots. These boxes were of cylindrical shape with oval cross-section and flip-up lid decorated with multi-coloured gold garlands and foliate ornament and set with square or cushion-shaped diamond thumb-pieces. Objects produced in

4 Clock erected in a barbette supported by an elephant, Fabergé.

1 Tray by Fabergé, decorated with precious stones and enamel.

2 Spray of buttercups and cornflowers by Carl Fabergé.

Mexico were usually hallmarked and consequently dating of these pieces is fairly accurate.

By the 1820s, the fashion was turning from snuff-taking to other forms of indulgence, such as cigarettes and cheroots. In consequence, receptacles for containing these were devised by the goldsmiths of the day. From the onset of the Victorian period, and with the more severe styles of the following decades, there was little

demand for elaborate small boxes and associated objects until Peter Carl Fabergé revived and elaborated these *objects of vertu*. It was not until the Paris Exhibition of 1900 that Fabergé's objects became widely seen and admired outside the court of Imperial Russia.

Peter Carl Fabergé was the leading Russian goldsmith during the second half of the 19th century. The Fabergé family originated from Picardy and with many other Huguenot families fled from France following the Revocation of the Edict of Nantes in 1685 and later settled in St Petersburg, where they became Russian citizens. Peter Carl Fabergé was born on the 30th May, 1846. He was sent to study the goldsmith's craft and lapidary in all the main centres of Europe and on his return worked under the manager of his father's shop until 1870, when he was given the position as head of the entire concern at the age of 24. The same year, the 'English shop', which was run by two Englishmen called Nichols and Plincke who had run a fashionable jewellers in St Petersburg, was closed and the Court transferred their enthusiasm and patronage to the jewelry and objects produced by Fabergé. It was not until 1884 that Fabergé made his real breakthrough, when he produced a jewelled Easter egg, commissioned by Alexander III for his wife, Maria Feodorovna. This was the first Easter egg of its type to be made and during the reign of Alexander III and the last Czar, Nicholas II, 55 other eggs were produced.

The Easter celebrations, which were taken more seriously in Russia than in any other

3 Nephrite box and Russian Imperial Eagle by Fabergé

country in Europe, were more joyous and holy than Christmas. Easter was also the climax of the Orthodox Church Year and occasioned the lavish giving of presents. A great many more simple eggs than these costly objects given by the Czars were produced for presentation to the whole Court, often in porcelain and papier-mâché, as well as gold and enamel.

It was the success of these presentation gifts that inspired the Czar to grant a Royal Warrant to the Fabergé firm. Fabergé was undoubtedly the most prolific maker of fine objects during any period and as a craftsman and designer must be placed at the forefront of the 19th-century craftsmen reviving styles of previous periods, but his inspirations were mainly taken from French 18th-century originals and his designs were rarely totally original in all respects. Fabergé produced an enormous range of different objects, including cigarette cases, pill boxes, parasol handles, hardstone animals, snuff boxes, scent bottles, bell pushes, miniature frames, glue pots and stamp dampeners – all of which achieved great distinction in their own right. From 1900 until the outbreak of war in 1914, the Faberge workshops were still producing many fine objects to satisfy the demands of European royalty and nobility, but gradually the demand dwindled for such luxurious objects, as twinges of social conscience made themselves felt and the final blow was dealt by the Revolution. Fabergé escaped to Switzerland in the guise of a diplomat and he died two years later.

Apart from Fabergé, other silversmiths an goldsmiths, such as Khlebnikov, Ovtchinnikoff Sasikoff and co-operative groups, produced silver and enamel objects mainly in the old Russian style.

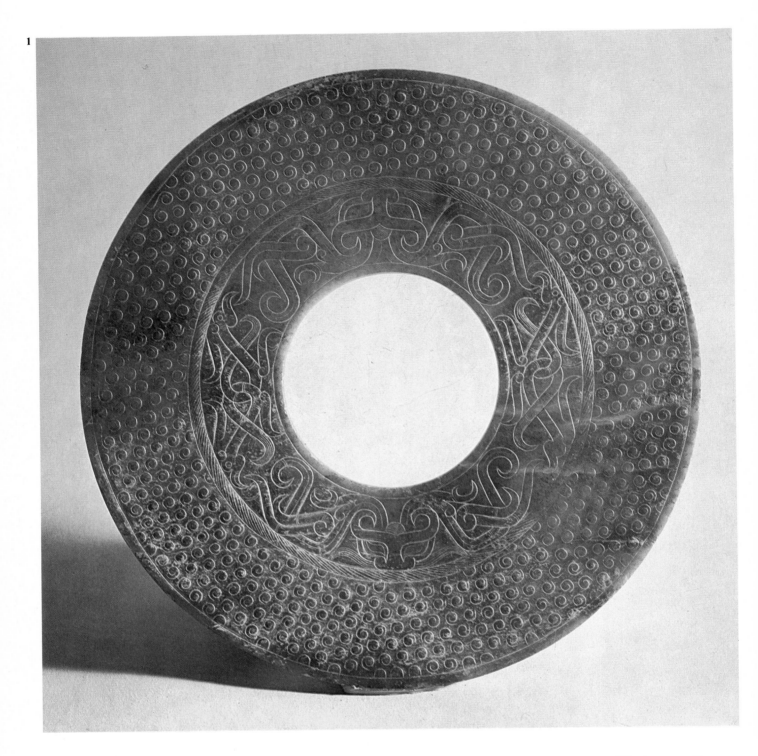

1 The jade disc with a hole, Pi, was the symbol of Heaven, the source of all light. In Shang royal burials the corpse was placed face down with a Pi disc on his back. In the Chou period the corpse was laid upon its back with the disc upon its chest.

Throughout Chinese history, until quite recently, jade, whose Chinese name *Yu* means 'beauty' or 'purity', was highly venerated. Magical and curative powers were ascribed to the stone and it was even thought capable of bestowing the gift of immortality. Although jade is found in the earth the Chinese did not believe that this was its origin; instead it was the essence of water, the concealed semen of the dragon or even the essence of Heaven. References to jade occur throughout Chinese mythology and thought; Taoist Immortals lived on jade; Jade Maidens attended the Queen Mother of the West; the

2 The shapes of this hind and stag indicate the influence of the peoples of central Asia upon China at this period. Central Asia was also an important source of jade for Chinese craftsmen.

3 The dagger axe, Ko, was used as an infantry weapon. These blades are of jade but Ko were also made in stone and bronze. In the Han period a bronze Ko was a badge of rank.

Jade Emperor of Heaven rules all other gods
and has power over this world and the next; the
'jade gate' is where the spine joins the skull.

Jade is not found in China proper and was
first brought to areas such as Kansu and Honan
in northern central China from the Lake Baikal
region of Siberia and later from the Sinkiang
mountains and around Khotan in central Asia.

The stone is extremely hard to work without
metal tools, yet Stone Age cultures in China used
polished jade for tools and for ornamental or
religious items such as plaques, rings and the
sacred *Pi* disc. During the Shang dynasty
(1600–1027 B.C.) jade was largely used for
ceremonial weapons, jewelry and musical instruments. Ceremonial knives and the blade of
the dagger axe, *Ko*, were made in jade and jade
axes were carried as sceptres by the kings. Jade
plaques carved as birds, fish and animals were
worn as pendants while jade chimes were used in
religious rituals.

In the Chou dynasty (1027–249 B.C.) the
use of jade in court ceremonial was recorded in
the *Chou-li*: the king or emperor held a jade
sceptre, *Chen-kuei*; courtiers held a jade tablet,
Kuei, against their mouth when speaking to the
emperor, and princes and court officials held
sceptres or tablets of jade carved in various
forms according to their rank. Three jade
objects *Pi*, *T'sung* and *Huang* (a half circle) were
included among the Six Instruments of court
ritual. In royal burials protective jade objects
were placed around the corpse: a *Kuei* sceptre
to the east, a tiger to the west, a *Huang* to the
north and a short sceptre, *Chang*, to the south.
A jade plaque carved in the form of a cicada, the
symbol of immortality, was placed in the mouth
and the orifices were sealed with jade plugs. Jade
tablets were also sent as signs of authority with
envoys carrying messages.

Jade carving was refined and developed about
500–200 B.C. with the introduction of iron
cutting tools and a rotary lap drill, which
allowed the production of hollow ware in jade.
Bowls, dishes for food and drinks, toilet boxes
and screens were added to the repertoire of
animal figures, as well as objects of personal use
– such as pendants, belt hooks, seals and sword
fittings. Ritual objects such as *Pi* and *T'sung* also
came to be used ornamentally.

Although more widespread in its use and
application jade still kept some significance and
the traditional lore about the symbolic use of
jade was recorded at the start of the Han dynasty,
about 200 B.C. This period saw the flourishing of
various philosophies and religions – the ancient
ancestral cult, Confucian ideals and prescrip-
tions and the more mystical but popular Taoist
ideas. Beliefs in the magical properties of plants,
wood and metals was prevalent. Jade, as the
produce of earth and water symbolized the
unified principles of Yin and Yang and both
form and colour symbolism were important.
Jade figures were used in sorcery and rainmaking
rituals, and were burned as sacrifices. Witches,
tao niu, made hollow statuettes in jade, clay,
paper or wood and gave them life by placing

models of human organs or a small living creature inside. Amulets and talismans were also made in jade. The most striking objects from this period are the jade suits of Prince Liu Sheng and his wife Tou Wan. These suits are made of jade plates sewn together with gold thread. The corpse was dressed in jade in the belief that this would prevent bodily decay.

Jade was also favoured elsewhere in Asia. In the 17th century the Mughal emperors of India had jade objects such as wine cups, made at their court. These were decorated by specialist engravers or *muhrkan*, and copied Persian styles. In prehistoric Japan grave goods included claw shaped beads, *magatama*, some of which were in jade, perhaps from Siberia. Jade was later used in Japan for netsuke, a kind of pendant fastened on one end of a cord.

'Yu' refers to both types of jade known as jadeite and nephrite. They are hard, brittle stones, difficult to differentiate, which resonate when struck. Nephrite is more fibrous and older objects tend to be made in this stone. In pure form both jadeite and nephrite are completely white, though these are rare and more usually some colouring is present. Spinach jade is a green form of nephrite with either black or gold flecks. The oldest jade objects are perhaps made in this colour. Jade also occurs in yellow, cream, grey, brown, cinnabar red, lavender and black. 'Mutton fat' jade has a lardish, greasy appearance, often with red spots, and was appreciated for its rarity. Jadeite was first imported into China in the 18th century from deposits in Upper Burma. *Fei-ts'ui* is the most valued type of jadeite and is either a brilliant emerald green colour, or white with brilliant patches of the same emerald green colour, resembling kingfisher feathers.

Carved jade is very difficult to date and value

1 Jade had meaning in many aspects of Chinese culture; the pattern of fibres in jade was known as Li, the principle of harmony and order. Jade was the essence of dragons which symbolized Heaven and its energies, the Emperor and his powers, the force of Yang; dragons were also steeds for the Immortals.

2 Flooding and water control were major concerns of the Chinese, who relied upon irrigation agriculture for their food supplies. Precious objects such as jades were therefore used to placate Ho Po or Ping I, Count of the River who ruled all the gods and spirits of rivers and streams.

3 Table screens were used by scholars to hold their scrolls in place.

for antique pieces were often later copied. Over the years the ritual significance of jade has been lost and more decorative items such as snuff bottles and screens have been made, but fine carving has persisted throughout China's history. Pieces from the Ming and Ch'ing periods are usually considered the finest jades, although work of very high quality is still being done in present day China.

and stone. Netsuke were in use in Japan from about the 14th century until the 19th century. In general Japanese craftsmen took their inspiration from China, and netsuke carvers were no exception. Some early netsuke were copied from Chinese seals, and were often carved in ivory with Chinese designs and called 'Chinese things', *karmono*.

Netsuke were used to carry a variety of

3

Netsuke

Traditional Japanese clothing consisted of robes and a sash. Small belongings such as a tobacco box or a seal case, *inro*, were suspended on a cord with a toggle or pendant, netsuke, fastened to the other end. The netsuke was pushed down through the sash to secure the object.

Early netsuke were probably made of natural materials – pieces of wood, bamboo, roots, horn

objects – medicine cases, writing cases, powder flasks, flint and steel, keys, chopsticks, small tea jars and drinking gourds. Some objects such as brush cases and compasses served in themselves as netsuke. The introduction and rapid adoption of smoking stimulated the production of netsuke and the majority were eventually used to carry pipes and tobacco boxes.

Smoking was introduced into Japan in the

179

mid-15th century but in 1603 the Shogun, Ieyasu Tokugawa, banned the practice. Then in 1605 the first tobacco plantation was established in Japan. However, further bans in 1607 and 1609 made tobacco cultivation a penal offence. In spite of these and other, even sterner measures, smoking continued to spread rapidly and was eventually adopted by the aristocracy. By 1639 smoking was part of the hospitality offered along with tea to guests.

Gentlemen, samurai, did not carry smoking equipment, nor did they smoke in public. Men of the lower classes – traders, farmers and labourers – did, and it was they who used netsuke to carry their smoking things, including metal netsuke to keep their pipe ashes alight until the next smoke.

The impetus to develop the craft of netsuke carving came from wealthy merchants in the early 17th century. Under the Tokugawa the merchant class was forbidden to carry swords, while at the same time the samurai were wearing increasingly decorative sword furniture. In order to compete, wealthy merchants commissioned more elaborate netsuke. The development of craftsmanship in sword furniture inspired in its turn an increase in the designs, material and quality of netsuke carving.

Before 1780 netsuke were the utilitarian side products of skilled workers in other crafts. Wood-workers of religious sculptures used their offcuts and musical instrument makers used the

2

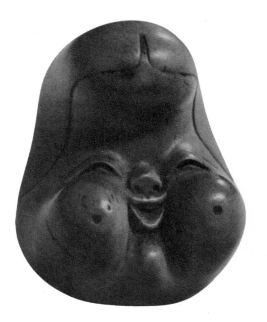

1 The distinguishing mark of a netsuke is the cord passage, himotoshi, which often runs through a corner of the piece. In older netsuke one end of this passage is larger than the other, to admit and hide the knot in the cord. In the manju type of netsuke the cord is fastened to the underside of the lid and passes out though a hole in the bowl.

1

2 In the 18th century netsuke were made from the waste products of other crafts; musical instrument makers, joiners, dentists and doll makers all carved netsuke; so did a few samurai and scholars as a pastime. Kabuki mask makers carved miniatures for use as netsuke and perhaps to advertise their trade.

3 Netsuke were worn by men only. Priests and scholars used netsuke to carry their seals and writing equipment. The lower classes used netsuke to carry their pipes and tobacco boxes. The best carvers of netsuke made them so carefully that they always hung with the 'face' side outwards, away from the wearer's body.

ivory remaining from a tusk after a *samisen* plectrum had been cut from it. Imported ivory was expensive and scraps were too valuable to waste. This shows in the typical shapes of ivory netsuke: triangular if the netsuke is taken from the outer layers of a tusk and pyramidal if carved from a tip.

In the late 18th century the demand for netsuke became so great that professional carvers became established, and over the next century produced the finest work in this genre. The best carvers lived in Osaka, Kyoto and Edo and sometimes became retainers on the staff of high ranking samurai, carving largely for their lord and his house. Most netsuke are unsigned while those that are often have the carver's nom

de plume rather than his real name. A surname is usually lacking since this was only held, along with the privilege of sword wearing, by those of samurai status.

The commonest material used for netsuke was boxwood, although other materials used were bone, teeth, metal, earthenware, porcelain, shells, nuts, and jade imported from China. Many of these materials were lacquered when carved into netsuke. An indication of the age of netsuke may be gained from the object and the carving style with older pieces showing a simpler carving style of fewer subjects. Late 18th century subjects including religious and mythical figures from poetry legends and proverbs, signs of the zodiac, masks and dolls. Some of the latter, *negoro-ninyo*, were carved in wood and lacquered by descendants of the priests of Negoro who invented a famous lacquering technique. In the 19th century subjects included real and mythical animals, birds, reptiles, the occupations of daily life, utensils, fruit, vegetables and the seasons. Money, medical figures, trick figures and erotica also served as subjects.

The forms of netsuke are also indicative of the age of pieces and the development of the craft. The earliest netsuke are sashi, thin pieces

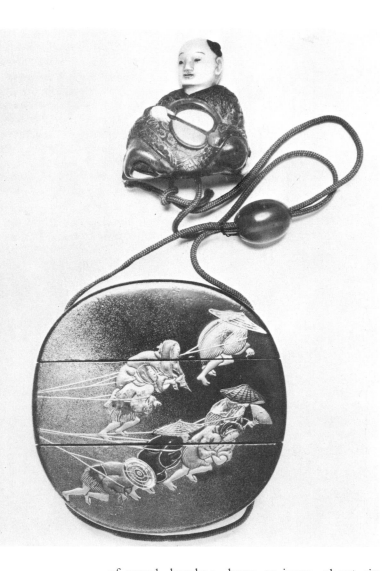

1

of wood, bamboo, bone or ivory, about six inches long with a hole at one end. *Katabori*, the largest group of netsuke, and the type next developed, include animals, insects, tools, musical instruments and human figures among their subjects. These are all about two and a half inches square. From the 17th century onwards miniature masks, carved as netsuke by Kabuki mask makers, were a popular subject.

Manju is the second largest type of netsuke. They are a flattish oval or square shape with rounded corners, resembling a Japanese cake and may consist of one or two pieces fitted together. *Manju* were mostly carved in wood during the 18th century, but by the 19th century ivory, bamboo and horn were also used. A sub-

type of *manju* is *kagamibuta*, a finely carved bowl of ivory, horn or wood which was valued for its metal lid rather than the bowl. These lids were made in iron or alloys of iron and gold, silver or copper, and some cloissonné, by craftsmen in sword furniture. *Hako*, small boxes, and *ryusa* are other forms of *manju*. *Ryusa* produced from the 18th century, are hollow forms made on a lathe, and have openwork decoration showing insects, blossoms, birds and arabesques. *Ichiraku* netsuke are relatively few in number, and are woven in thin wire or rattan cane in designs such as baskets gourds and sandals.

The fashion for wearing netsuke disappeared about 1870 when cigarettes and western dress were adopted in Japan. At the same time the demand for netsuke by western collectors led to the Japanese regarding them as works of art. A few netsuke are still carved but the craft is uneconomical.

Inro

Inro are sets of boxes which fit into each other and apart from pipes and tobacco boxes, inro were the objects most often carried by means of netsuke. The word 'inro' means seal case and the earliest examples, imported into Japan from China. were used for holding seals and an ink pad. The earliest inro were thus single or double boxes, and were kept in homes as shelf ornaments. About 1500 the most typical form of inro developed. This was a flattish, rectangular box, about $3\frac{1}{2}$ to 4 inches (9 to 10 cm) long by 2 inches (5 cm) wide with three to six compartments which was carried with a netsuke on the sash. This form of inro was in widespread use in Japan until 1876.

Inro were carried both by samurai and civilians, and were usually made in lacquered wood in black, red and gold though blue and green were also used. Some ivory inro were made but lacquered wood was particularly popular and might have been originally inspired by the early taste for Chinese forms. Emperor Yoshimara c.1500 promoted the use of lacquer for everything from inro to furniture. Lacquered netsuke were commonly used with lacquered inro to avoid damaging the latter. During the 17th century inro became regarded as art objects and were lacquered in a variety of ways in the *Makie* and *Negoro* styles. Some raised work was also done on inro.

The sections or compartments of an inro are joined by a cord and are kept together on the cord by a running bead, *ojime*, which then has a netsuke on the end. Open cases and pouches lacked a bead. The *ojime* up to $\frac{1}{2}$ in (1 cm) in diameter, appear in a variety of materials – carved wood, coral, cloissonné, metal, semi-precious stones, porcelain and rarely, gold. Since it was forbidden to wear gold as jewellery, gold ojime were sometimes lacquered to avoid detection. *Ojime* and inro may be signed, and on the latter the signature may be on the outside of the base or concealed in the design on the side. It is not usually on the lid. The characters inside usually refer to the medicines it contained.

2

1, 2 and **3** Inro are described by the number of divisions between the compartments inside one outer sheath, also some have concealed openings and divisions. The lowest compartment may be lined with foil. Decorative scenes on inro include landscapes, trees, flowers, human and mythical figures. Animals, birds and fish were also depicted, illustrating the Japanese love of the natural world.

3

Metalwork

Although many types of metalwork have been brought together in this book, they can broadly be divided into two categories, precious and base metals. The first includes silver and gold tableware and ornaments, and the second a wide range of domestic and architectural metalwork made from materials as diverse as tin, brass, copper, pewter and iron.

In simple terms, methods of metal-working do not vary greatly from one field to another although inevitably each metal has developed its particular language and technology over the years. Generally, metals are formed either by being cast into moulds when heated to a molten state, or by being hammered into shape or formed from flat sheets. Although there is a world of difference between the work of the blacksmith and the silversmith, a difference reflected by the many quite distinct metalworkers' guilds that have been active since the middle ages, the basically similar methods of metal-working have ensured that style changes have not varied greatly from one metal to another.

Compared to other fields of antique collecting, metalwork is considerably older. The technology stretches back to the Bronze Age and beyond, and so it is not surprising that metalworkers were able to achieve a high level of sophistication in their work at quite an early period. Methods of working wrought iron did not change significantly from the prehistoric times until the 18th century, while gold and silver smithing reached a level of craftsmanship during the Renaissance which has probably never been equalled. New developments occurred, such as the invention of cast iron or electroplating, and new materials and alloys became available, but these were generally taken in their stride by established metalworkers, and so did not greatly affect the general pattern of stylistic change.

This relative freedom from technical limitations allowed the metalworker to concentrate his skills on the development of styles and objects that interested him, unlike for example, the potter, whose desire to produce porcelain in the 18th century was severely hampered by his lack of knowledge of both materials and techniques. As a result, metalwork has always been an accurate mirror of the styles of any particular period, and so has been able to enjoy a close relationship with architecture and interior design generally. New styles often appeared first of all in architecture, and so architectural metalwork provides a direct link between style innovation and its eventual application on a more domestic level. Because it is really a part of architecture, much metalwork on a grander scale has survived, thus allowing a broader understanding of stylistic development. This relationship is also underlined by the relative permanence of most forms of metalwork. Although most metal can be re-worked, either in detail, or as a whole by being melted down and used again, the cheapness of the basic material rarely justifies such a course of action. This factor, combined with the ability of the material to survive the ravages of time, weather and general use, has ensured that examples from most periods have survived, from the trivial to the grand artistic creation. Metal objects can therefore be regarded in considerable detail: Roman domestic metalwork, functional Renaissance bronzes, 17th century garden ornaments, 19th century cast iron street furniture or early 20th century kitchen equipment can all be adequately studied because sufficient examples have survived.

The exception is, of course, silver and gold. Because of the intrinsic value of the material itself, it has always been the rule to consider the products of gold and silversmiths with a degree of impermanence. It was common to regard silver and gold plate almost as a form of banking, the articles being a credit balance that could be drawn upon at any time. They could either be melted down and returned to the ingots from which they were formed originally, or they could be handed back to the craftsman to be reworked in a more economical or up-to-date style. This practice has obviously affected adversely the survival of objects, and so there are many periods or types of ware, such as the 17th century in France or silver furniture, where surviving examples are not sufficient to give a complete picture of the period or style. Reworking could be prompted by a need for economy, by a desire to remain in fashion or in response to changes in the political or social climate. For example, it would clearly not have been sensible to remain in possession of ostentatious or extravagant items after the French Revolution, or after the Civil War in England. Sometimes it could also be provoked by State rather than individual requirements. When governmental exchequers needed replenishing, as at time of war, it was a common practice to call in vast quantities of silver and gold plate for remelting. This practice was justified by the existing close links between gold and silversmiths' work and the currency of the country.

The other important feature of metalwork is that it is generally by definition functional. Most items have a clearly defined purpose, although this may sometimes be clouded by the quality of the materials used or the details of the ornamentation. In this, metal has much in common with woodwork, where the style of the object is no more than a veneer laid over its essential purpose. In fact, this style veneer is made more obvious by the facility of reworking metal. Although collectors tend to concentrate on the maker of the object, or the details of its shape and decoration, it can often be just as interesting to consider the essential function of the object, and the degree to which this has been hindered or improved by the application of the style or period veneer. Thus the study of the development of any one object, whether it be a coffee pot, tea spoon, door knocker, candlestick or can-opener, over a long period and in a variety of metals, can be both an enjoyable exercise and an interesting introduction to the history of changing styles, fashions and taste.

Bronze Aquamanile in the shape of a lion, 12th or 13th century.

Gold & silver

Milestones in the history of precious metals

1492–97	Voyages of discovery to America and India resulted in gold, silver and precious stones reaching Europe in increasing quantities.
1526	The Sack of Rome – Italian artists dispersed furthering the spread of High Renaissance influence to other European countries.
from 1660	European maritime countries formed companies to trade with the Far East, which brought Japanese and Chinese influences to Europe.
1685	Louis XIV revoked the Edict of Nantes and the Huguenot emigrés took the French classical Baroque style to Protestant countries.
1697	Higher Britannia standard of silver introduced into Britain to replace sterling.
from 1719	Both Britannia and Sterling standards permitted.
1742	Sheffield plate discovered and developed.
1814	Paul Storr in London made The Galvanic Goblet of silver, electrogilt.
1840	Elkingtons of Birmingham, England, took out first patents for electroplating processes.
1859	Silver discovered in U.S.A.
1899	Liberty & Co. London, launch their Art Nouveau style of 'Cymric' silver.

Characteristics of Gold and Silver

catch the sun, is still a partial source of both materials.

Both gold and silver are malleable and can be beaten into shape; they are also ductile, that is, they can be melted and cast in a mould. However, gold melts at about 1065°C and silver at 1000°C, so until kilns capable of reaching these heats had been developed (originally for the making of glass and pottery) casting was not possible.

In their pure state, both gold and silver are too soft for practical use, so they have to be hardened by alloying them with another metal, usually copper. The purity of gold is measured in carats, 24 carats representing pure gold. The word carat derives from the Arabic name for the little seeds of the carob tree, which were once used as weights. Gold of 22 carats is usually the highest quality worked, and this is expressed nowadays as the proportion 916.6 to the 1,000 and the article is stamped 916.6 accordingly. Similarly,

Gold and silver, unlike other materials used in the decorative arts, have, until this century, had two distinct and easily reversible functions: they could be made into coin of the realm or into objects of use and beauty. For example, in 1540, Francis I of France gave the Italian goldsmith Benvenuto Cellini 1000 gold crowns to be melted down and made into the magnificent salt-cellar which is now in the Kunsthistoriches Museum in Vienna. Conversely, at the end of the 17th century Louis XIV of France, in an attempt to pay for his disastrous wars, enforced sumptuary laws which called in all objects made of precious metal and ordered their melting into coin. This included all the silver furniture that glittered at Versailles when the court was first installed there in 1682.

Designs, influenced by the architecture and fine art of a period, can follow fashion more quickly in metalwork than in any other material used in the applied arts. Silver and gold are the easiest of materials in which the rich, the smart, and the influential can show off their wealth, impress their neighbours and set a trend. Where silver and gold have survived they are more durable than objects made in other materials, such as wood or textile, and they can therefore give a truer representation of a past style.

Gold can be mined or found alluvially. Silver is usually found in conjunction with other metals, most often lead, and probably its qualities were first realized as a by-product of lead extraction in Asia Minor 5,000 years ago. Gold does not tarnish, nor does silver in clean air and this exceptional and seemingly magical property encouraged their use as money and for making beautiful things. Electrum, the naturally occurring mixture of gold and silver that was used by the Egyptians to cap obelisks so that they might

1 The design of bulrushes (c 1845) shown in this detail was achieved by flat-chasing, a technique which does not remove any silver from the work. During the 19th century both hand and machine techniques were used in lavish decoration.

2 Towards the end of the 17th century English silver was usually embossed; sometimes, however, it was flat-chased with chinoiserie decoration deriving from Oriental architecture.

18 carat gold is stamped 750, and 14 carat 585.

Silver is usually alloyed with copper in proportions that vary from country to country. In Germany and Italy, 800 parts to the 1,000 are used; in Sweden, 813 to the 1,000; in Britain, North America and many other countries, the 'sterling' standard is 925 to the 1,000. The highest practical proportion is 958.4 parts of silver to the 1,000. This standard is used in France and also in Britain for the alternative Britannia standard silver. It has been suggested that the origin of the widely used word 'sterling' comes from a contraction of the name 'Esterling', an East German tribe who in the 12th and 13th centuries used a particularly fine and reliable silver alloy in their financial dealings.

Originally, silver was beaten, but since the Industrial Revolution it has been rolled by machine into sheets of suitable thickness for articles to be raised by hammering. Objects can also be cast in moulds and the component parts soldered together. During the hammering process the crystals of metal will distort, harden, lose their malleability and crack unless the silversmith anneals the work, that is, softens the crystals by heating the metal until it glows a dull red, at about 700°C, then quenching it quickly in a cold liquid. He has to repeat the process as often as is necessary during the raising of the work.

Mechanical aids have now taken some of the difficulty out of this work, but in the past the silversmith's skill showed in his control of the annealing process. After the silversmith has made up the shape he requires, imperfections are filed away and the surface is burnished, nowadays by using a mechanical polisher but in the past an agate stone or a dog's tooth were used. The surface can then be modelled by 'chasing' it with hammered punches. In 'flat chasing' the pattern is pressed in without removing any metal. In 'engraving', a tool called a burin is pushed across the surface, lifting away a shaving of silver. In 'bright cut engraving', popular at the end of the 18th century, an angled scorper makes an asymmetrical groove like a tick ($\checkmark$), which gives greater reflection. When a piece is 'embossed', the work is done from the back and the decoration is raised from the wrong side to make a three-dimensional design; embossing is only possible on thin silver and has the effect of strengthening it. Repoussé decoration is embossed from the back and chased from the front. In objects made of heavier gauge silver, three-dimensional decoration, handles, feet and so on, are cast separately and applied with solder.

Engraved ornament can be filled with 'niello', a black alloy which fuses with silver on heating, making strong emphasis, or with coloured enamels. Enamels are used in various ways. 'Cloisonné enamelling' is achieved by fusing little wire fences or 'cloisons' to a metal base to keep the enamels in compartments. In 'champlevé enamelling' the coloured enamels are fused to a metal base which has had compartments made in it to receive them by chiselling, stamping or casting. 'Basse-taille enamelling', a development of champlevé, uses translucent enamels so that a low relief design chased on the metal base shows through to great effect. Wires, or sheet silver stamped or cut out (predictably called 'cut-card' work) can be applied with solder to strengthen and to decorate.

Silver can be 'etched' or 'oxidized' to make a matt surface in effective contrast with burnished areas. 'Parcel-gilt' silver is the phrase used to describe an object that has been partially gilded, so that both white and yellow areas of metal may be seen. 'Silver-gilt' is silver that has been gilded all over (until the 1840s by the mercury process), to give the effect of gold at a lower cost. Throughout the centuries, wherever a desire for opulent display was paramount, silver-gilt was used in preference to 'white' silver.

Quatre couleur describes golds of differing colours used to decorate a gold piece and was particularly popular with 18th-century French gold box makers. Subtle shades can be obtained by alloying for example, with copper for red gold, with steel or arsenic for blue or grey, with silver in varying quantities for white or green. The technique is called *quatre couleur* even when more or less than four colours are used.

The connection between goldsmithing and banking is an obvious one and it has always been important that the proportions of gold and silver to alloy should be properly regulated. A system of marking finished work was used in republican Rome and ever since that time safeguards have been devised and used, sometimes with varying success, by the powerful guilds and companies of goldsmiths and also by governments. Before work could be sold a goldsmith would have to send it to be assayed by his guild where, in one of the methods used, a small scraping of metal would be taken from the underside of the piece and its quality tested. If it were proved not to be 'up to scratch' penalties could be high. Even now, in France and in England, a piece found to be made in substandard silver is returned to its maker, crushed flat. The goldsmith himself had to serve a long and testing apprenticeship. To become a master in France he had to produce his 'master piece' in a set time and his sponsor had to leave caution money with the guild as a surety for him before he was allowed to 'make his mark' and register it.

Additional marks were devised, whereby the town and year of origin might also be stamped on a piece and the quality of silver used shown, so that not only the maker could be traced but also the guild which had approved it; in this way the quality of the material used was preserved. In addition, governments found taxes on gold and silver to be a convenient source of revenue and marks would be stamped to show that tax had been paid.

Illuminated medieval manuscripts frequently show how displaying articles of silver and gold was regarded as an essential demonstration of the wealth, and the taste of a powerful person. Ostentatious plate, impressively displayed on a range of shelved cupboards beside the high table and guarded by men at arms, not only emphasized the power and wealth of the host but the amount of display was in direct proportion to the degree of honour due to the social position of an important guest.

In the 15th century, both an Ambassador reporting home about his reception at a foreign court and a Pope commenting on his entertainment by one of his cardinals, measured power, success and honour by the amount of plate on display and in no way thought it vulgar to be very showy. Little secular medieval gold and silver now remains, but from manuscripts and tapestries and from the ecclesiastical pieces which survive in slightly greater numbers, we may infer that throughout the Holy Roman Empire, from the time of the crowning of Charlemagne in A.D. 800, designs deriving from the old Roman Empire began to be augmented with flat, interlacing arabesque patterns of Near Eastern origin. These were brought in by return-

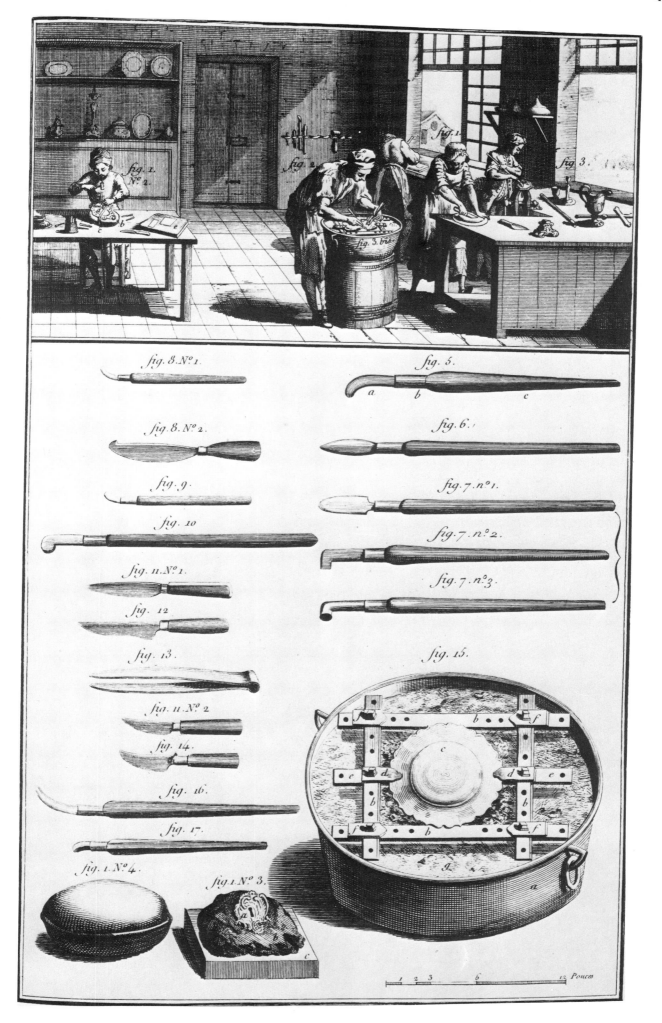

ing Crusaders and by trade through Venice. From this same source, new techniques were assimilated. Vertical architectural features were incorporated in gold and silver vessels, which might also be decorated with human or animal figures or with inscriptions in Lombardic or Gothic script, imitating the use of Kufic script in pattern making.

Mazers are the commonest surviving drinking vessels, made of dense, impervious wood, decorated with a silver lip band and a disc in the middle of the shallow bowl. Later, the low and wide mazer shape became deeper and gradually raised up on a foot and a stem. There was also a fitted cover. Such cups became objects of great ceremony and the customs associated with passing round such cups at banquets still exist in some societies today. Exotic objects like coconuts (which supposedly had magical properties), ostrich eggs, shells, precious rarities like imported Chinese and Turkish ceramics, minerals

1 This late Bronze Age (12th century B.C.) gold vessel consists of three spoon shaped cups joined by electrum tubes through which liquid passes from one cup to the next. The electrum handle is decorated with niello. The cup forms part of the Vulchitrun hoard which was found in the walls of the palace of a Thracian chieftain and it is to be seen in the Museum of Antiquities, Sofia.

dence was regulated by position above and below it. In France, this place was marked by a model of a ship called a 'nef', and existing ones show 15th century goldsmiths work at its best. In England, a great salt stood in the centre of the high table, the piece itself was often tiered and always impressive, but the salt container was relatively small.

Ewers and basins were much in use, because their decorative shapes made them suitable for display and diners had frequently to rinse their fingers in the course of a meal eaten only with spoons. Attendants took the ewer – filled with warmed and scented water – the basin and a napkin round to each guest and in this way the lavish beauty of the plate was shown off.

In 15th century Florence the verticality of former designs began in all the decorative arts, to be replaced by a greater horizontal emphasis and by decoration taken from the Greek and Roman precedents. The Renaissance spread outwards

like serpentine and rock crystal, were converted into drinking vessels by mounting them in silver gilt. They have often survived because too little silver had been used in their mounting to warrant it being melted later on. Highly prized Venetian glasses were also mounted sometimes, and this goblet shape was copied in silver.

Mediaeval etiquette placed the greatest importance on the use of a vessel of silver gilt to mark the place at the table of the most honoured person at the gathering, and prece-

from Tuscany, and putti, masks and trophies, acanthus, anthemion and rinceaux gradually superseded the older style.

By the beginning of the 16th century, increasing quantities of silver began to be mined in Germany, Austria and Hungary. The mines of India and the Americas further increased the supply. This coincided with a turbulent period in Italy, when in 1526 Rome was sacked, and the consequent dispersal of artists carried ideas to other centres, both in Northern Italy and beyond.

2 The Burghley Nef was made in Paris in 1482–3 by Pierre le Flamand. On a base imitating waves a siren supports an exotic nautilus shell which forms the hull of a ship. Among the tiny figures aboard are Tristan and Isolde sitting at a chess board below the main mast. Guns guard all points of the compass and a sinister dragon figure head enhances the war-like effect. The small depression for salt is in the poop deck at the stern. The piece was acquired by the Victoria and Albert Museum in 1959, having previously been in the collection of the Marquess of Exeter.

3 The Studley Bowl dates from the late 14th century and was probably used for a porridge-like food. Its principal decoration, chased and engraved, consists of the black letter alphabet branching from a stylized leafy girdle. The sober beauty of its proportion is increased by the manner in which the decoration is thrown into relief. Victoria and Albert Museum.

Rulers all over Europe now began to vie with each other in the culture and the magnificence of their courts, setting themselves up as patrons and collectors in the manner of 15th-century Italian princes and embracing the new style learnt from Italy, which everywhere gradually drove out Gothic motifs in favour of classical decoration.

Court artists were employed to create designs for goldsmiths to follow, an arrangement which can occasionally be detected in the unsuitability of a design for the material in which it is nevertheless superbly executed. Important centres of goldsmiths work at this time were Paris, Augsburg and Nürnberg. But as the artists who worked in these and other centres came from all over Europe and used designs by Court artists such as Guilio Romano, J. A. Ducereau, Hans Holbein and Cornelis Floris – which were subsequently engraved and passed round lesser workshops – it is difficult to detect any particularly national flavour in work of this period.

The power and prestige of Hapsburg Spain (which also included the Kingdom of Naples) and of the Hapsburg Holy Roman Empire, with a sphere of influence which stretched from Antwerp across Europe to Prague, was enhanced by Spanish control over the rich imports of bullion from the New World into Andalusia. Much of the treasure coming into the Iberian peninsula was used to make objects for ecclesiastical use. Gold brought back from India by Vasco de Gama, who first rounded the Cape of Good Hope in 1497, was used to make a monstrance. Although the goldsmiths of southern Spain were the first to receive the increased supplies of gold, silver and precious stones, it was not until the 1570s that a national Spanish style evolved out of the varied work that had previously been carried on in the many regional centres. From the 1570s, however, the richness and austerity associated with Philip II's building of the Escorial continued to be associated with silver, until the Baroque

3

style emerged in the next century. In the greater part of Europe the clarity of Italian renaissance forms gradually became obscured because Northern artists, frightened of empty spaces, tended to overload a design with detail. At the same time, a complete mastery of his craft by the goldsmith led to ever greater display of virtuosity. Wenzel Jaminitzer of Nüremberg (1508–85), for example, is renowned in part for his dazzling technique, learnt from Paduan artists, in which he added natural objects cast from life to his decoration.

In politically restless Northern Italy, a style of decoration evolved from the beginning of the 1520s in which interlacing leather-like straps, ending in curls resembling wood shavings, were used at first to frame, then to decorate and finally to dominate interior decoration. This strapwork

was pushed to its extreme in designs for metalwork and all through the 16th century its influence was felt throughout northern Europe. Its nervous uneasiness was allied with grotesques derived from late 15th century Italian revivals of Imperial Roman decoration. Mannerist designers continued to use Renaissance decorative ideas, but gradually the stylish way in which a theme was expressed became more important than the theme itself. To express an idea in *una bella maniera*, to use the then current phrase, could become the only goal of an impoverished mind and brilliant technique might slickly embody a worn out theme.

It would seem logical to assume that the plainer, less decorative style of the early 17th century arose as a result of growing Protestant

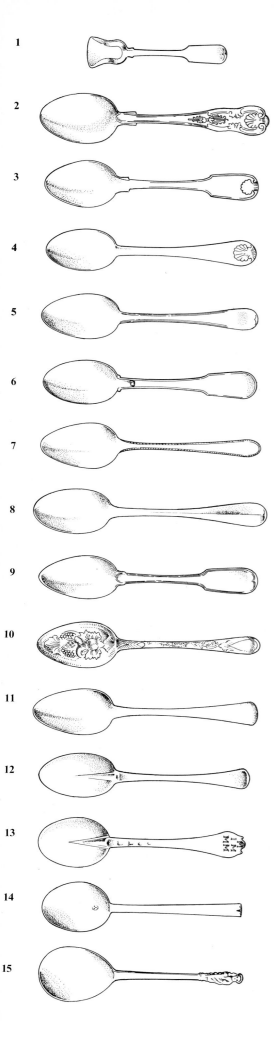

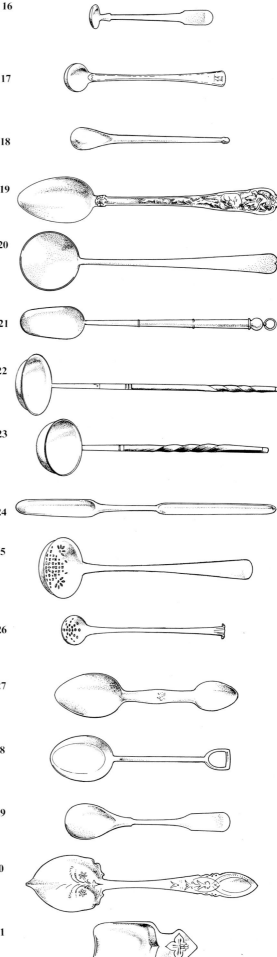

1 Salt shovel, upturned fiddle back; English or American 19th century.
2 Tablespoon; King's pattern, London 1837.
3 Fiddle thread shell pattern.
4 Old English shell pattern.
5 Old English thread pattern.
6 Military fiddle thread pattern spoon (back) late 19th century.
7 Old English pattern, bright cut *c.*1770s.
8 Hanoverian pattern *c.*1740s
9 French fiddle-thread or modèle à filets, early 19th century.
10 1793 Old English tablespoon by Peter and Anne Bateman 'converted' *c.*1970 into a berry spoon.
11 Hanoverian spoon.
12 Rat tail Hanoverian (back) 1st quarter 18th century.
13 Rat tail trifid (back) third quarter 17th century.
14 Notched end Puritan; third quarter 17th century.
15 Apostle spoon, St James the Greater *c.*1650.
16 Miniature ladle, fiddle back, downturned end, flaring shoulder *c.*1830.
17 Mustard ladle, Old English thread design; G W Adams, London 1847.
18 Mustard end set with chrysoprase; designed Christopher Arwee, made Guild of Handicrafts Ltd, London, 1901.
19 Gravy spoon, stag hunt pattern; designed Thomas Stothard, RA, made Paul Storr, London, 1816.
20 Soup ladle, notched end.
21 Basting spoon, long handled; Dublin 1724.
22 Punch ladle, twisted whalebone handle.
23 Toddy ladle, twisted whalebone handle.
24 Marrow scoop; G. Smith, London 1780.
25 Sugar sifter or old English handle, bowl pierced in decorative pattern; London 1790.
26 Pepper ladle, Onslow pattern; London third quarter 18th century.
27 Medicine spoon, English, mid 19th century.
28 Ice spade; early 20th century, E.P.N.S.
29 Mustard spoon, fiddle back.
30 Berry spoon; L. Ladomus & Co, Philadelphia *c.*1860–70.
31 Pewter caddy spoon; designed Rex Silver, early 20th century.

1

2

1 The treatment of the chased auricular central mark and of the figure of Bacchus on the rim of this vessel made by Adam van Vianen in 1622 shows the virtuoso quality of this Utrecht master's work. Adam van Vianen's son, Charles, worked in England for Charles I; Adam's brother, Paulus, was goldsmith to the Hapsburg Emperor Rudolf II, in Prague.

2 Silver-gilt, trochus shell and mother-of-pearl wager cup by Meinrach Bauch, Nuremburg, 1590. Double cups, which had to be emptied without the contents of either being spilt, were often made in the shape illustrated, where the figure inverts to form the second cup.

taste following the Reformation and the polarizing of religious attitudes with the counter-Reformations of the 16th century, but this does not seem to have been the reason. Plain styles began to be used for people who were chary of spending too much money on the fashioning of plate, over and above the cost of the material, lest it soon would have to be melted again for cash. The Thirty Years' war in Germany of 1618–48, the Civil War in England in the 1640s and the Fronde in France of 1647–53 made people shrink from commissioning expensively decorated plate in large parts of Europe.

Only Holland, at this time, triumphant in having liberated herself from Spain – which now began to decline in power – and expanding her empire overseas, enjoyed a confident prosperity. Throwing off the mannerist grotesques of the 16th century a new Dutch style of silverware arose, a style of sinuous fluidity and erotic sensuousness, most characterized by the use of cartilaginous and marine motifs, whose chief exponents were members of the van Vianen family of silversmiths of Utrecht and their pupils. This molten, 'auricular' style, as it became known, spread to Germany and to English court circles before the Civil War. It was followed in Holland by an expression of the prevalent interest in botanical studies in a profusion of embossed flowers, often tulips. This style, too, was taken to England, at the restoration of Charles II in 1660. Dutch interest in pictorial representation showed itself in embossed and engraved plaques and dishes with a religious or classical theme, following engravings of paintings by 17th century artists.

The middle years of the 17th century saw the introduction to Europe of new tastes in drinking; chocolate, coffee and tea brought from overseas, cooled white wine and hot punches all led to the invention of vessels for their service. Ever since the first years of the century there had been increasing contact with the Far East, following the establishment of trading companies by the maritime nations of Europe. A lightening of Baroque European taste came about, by means of pseudo Indian, Chinese or Japanese decoration, called *chinoiserie*, regardless of its exact provenance. *Chinoiserie* entered all branches of the decorative arts and, with fluctuations in popularity, remained there. Temporarily submerged by the neo-classical movement of the second half of the 18th century, it was revived again, in an altered form, in the 19th century.

The second half of the 17th century saw the

3 When Charles II was restored to the throne from exile in Holland in 1660, the influence of Dutch culture began to be felt in England. The Dutch interest in botany is seen here in the naturalistic flowers embossed in thin gauge metal. This silver-gilt two handled cup and cover was made in the year of Charles's return. A drink of warm wine, spice and sugar called 'caudle' would be served in a vessel such as this. The cast caryatid handles may be compared with the supports of the standing salt of 1549 illustrated previously. Victoria and Albert Museum.

gradual spread of a 'politer way of living'. It now became the custom to use forks at every course in a meal. Previously, two-pronged 'sucket' forks had been used for sweetmeats at banquets, but the rest of the meal had always been eaten with a spoon and fingers. Changed methods of cooking and changed menus encouraged the idea – which came from Italy – of using forks all the time and this made ewers and basins unnecessary, although their decorative function continued.

Strong lead glass was now developed, which displaced both the fragile and highly prized Venetian goblet and the silver wine cup. Glass was preferred because it did not affect the taste of wine, as did silver. Beer was drunk out of tankards in northern countries and the Scandinavian tankard mounted on three feet was popular. Plain beakers were also used for drinking and the Dutch type of beaker was taken to New England and used in some non-conformist churches as a communion cup. Flagons were used for serving beer and wine and the pattern, like an extended tankard without a lip, was com-

3

1 Parcel gilt sauceboat by François Joubert, Paris 1754–5 Musée des Arts Décoratifs. Paris. The arms decorating this sauceboat are those of Mme de Pompadour (1721–1764) who, from her arrival at the Court of Louis XV in 1745, exercised a strong and beneficient influence on the development of the arts.

2 Chocolate pots are distinguishable from coffee pots because they are provided with a hinged cover on the hinged lid through which a stick called a 'molinet' may be inserted to stir the thick chocolate. This example, made in London in 1704 by Anthony Nelme, has a hinged flap on the spout and a handle set at right-angles to the tapering body. Anthony Nelme's workshop was at the sign of the Golden Bottle, Amen Corner, Ave Maria Lane.

mon for both secular and ecclesiastical purposes.

Greater prosperity led to a proliferation of silver objects being made in Europe and in America, and quantities of teapots, kettles and kettle stands, tea caddies, coffee and chocolate pots, sugar boxes and creamers, waters, salvers and trays were needed for the less formal and more intimate gatherings preferred in the early 18th century. On the dining table would now be placed small, individual salts, casters for spices and sugar, candlesticks, tureens and sauceboats. At the beginning of the 18th century, sauces were served cold and piquant; double lipped, two-handled sauceboats were put directly on the table. Later, sauces were served hot and so sauceboats were raised off the table on a base or on three feet, so that the polished surface would not be scorched.

Heavy drinking habits called for wine coolers and occasional wine fountains. On the centre of the table would be placed an epergne, an arrangement of branches holding assorted sweetmeats in a number of baskets or on small trays – the French called this object a *surtout de table*, which accurately describes its function.

The dressing tables and writing desks of the wealthy all over Europe and America were graced with toilet sets, ink stands and tapersticks. Silver furniture may still be seen at Rosenborg Castle and at various places in Germany, although French examples have perished.

From the 1660s and all through the 18th century the encouragement given by French royal patronage to the arts led to French taste dominating Europe. Reference has already been made to the disappearance of French silver of the

3

period. In 1685, Louis XIV revoked the Edict of Nantes, which since 1598 had guaranteed freedom of worship in France. This led to a consequent exodus of Huguenot workers, chiefly from the French provinces, into the Protestant countries of Europe, where the extreme elegance and sober and refined monumentality of French classical Baroque taste was assimilated.

In England, the fusion of native and Huguenot taste made this the period of, perhaps, the country's greatest glory in silversmithing. Second generation Huguenots, such as Paul de Lamerie (1688–1751), were capable of producing work of the greatest distinction and simplicity, in which the shape itself constituted decoration enough. They also made pieces in silver-gilt of the utmost elaboration, with cast and applied decoration, skilfully conceived and modelled in the highest sculptural tradition. English plate displayed engraving and flat chasing of great virtuosity.

The first quarter of the 18th century in France marked a period of transition from the majestic style associated with the building of Versailles, into a style now called 'Régence'. This new trend showed a swing away from sobriety.

Gradually, in response to the ideas of French architects, designers and goldsmiths – who once more took their inspiration from Italian sources – the whole of Europe shed the static weight of the Baroque style in favour of a lighter, Rococo mood, which used ideas taken from rockwork and shells in graceful, undulating curves and reversed C-scrolls. The spirit of playfulness was also expressed in the continual use of *chinoiserie*, to which the asymmetrical nature of this new style was particularly suited.

4 Two-handled cup and cover by John Boddington London, 1697. A fine example of the sober classicism introduced to English silver by the French ex-patriot Huguenot workers.

3 Silversmiths in New England in the 17th and 18th centuries used styles familiar to their European counterparts. This two handled cup was made in Boston in 1692 by Jeremiah Dumner.

1 Tea kettles were necessary when the price of tea was high and teapots small in consequence. This splendid marine confection, made in London about 1735 by Charles Kandler, is exceptional in still possessing its matching tray. Kandler seems to have arrived in England shortly before 1727, the year he registered his mark; he was perhaps the finest silversmith of the Rococo period in England. His work is rare; the most remarkable piece by him is a vast wine cistern capable of holding 60 gallons. It weighed over 7,221 oz troy and had to be disposed of by lottery in 1737; soon after it went to Russia.

2 This Sheffield Plate coffee pot, made in about 1760, betrays the uncertainty of a transitional style. It is Rococo in shape, in decoration, however, it looks forward to the chilly austerity of Neo classicism.

1 previous pages. Silver basket by Paul de Lamerie, London, 1747. Ashmolean Museum, Oxford. A scallop shaped basket is in the full Rococo style. Cast dolphin feet and a flying scroll female term handle, together with fanciful pierced work demonstrate the skill of second generation Huguenot silversmiths. Paul de Lamerie was trained in England: he began his apprenticeship under Pierre Platel in London in 1703.

2 In contrast with the Lamerie basket this pair of wine coolers made in Paris in 1781 by Robert Joseph Auguste are wholly Neo-classical. The ram's head handles, the laurel wreath rim, the swags encircling the vase shaped body and the palm leaf decoration above the moulded foot are all inspired by antique Roman and Renaissance prototypes.

The Rococo style appeared early in silverware in the use of *bombé* shapes, full of swaying movement because they contained no straight lines. The effect of asymmetry was achieved by applying cast decoration in such a way as to disguise the basic regularity of shape. Some of the finest works ever made appeared in this style, for which 'white' silver was preferred to the majestic quality of silver gilt.

In France, where the Rococo style originated, the designs of J. A. Meissonnier (1695–1750) show a complete mastery. Much silver was melted during the Revolution, but it is still possible to see some of the superb work of Thomas Germain (1673–1748), the greatest French silversmith of the first half of the 18th century. He was the son and the father of highly talented workers, and in addition to his work for Louis XIV and Louis XV, executed pieces for the Portuguese Royal Family, many of which were lost in the catastrophic Lisbon earthquake of 1755.

J. M. Dinglinger (1664–1731) is justly renowned for the works of art he created from 1698 in Dresden for his patron Augustus the Strong, Elector of Saxony and King of Poland. Incredible wealth in precious and semi-precious stones and metals came from Saxon mines and Dinglinger used them to make objects of extraordinary fantasy.

Housed in the Green Vaults in Dresden, Dinglinger's cabinet pieces are perhaps the most famous of his works and they show an early interest in Eastern subjects, of which the Gold Coffee Set and the Great Moguls Birthday Party, a metre square stage set with over a hundred figures of guests, attendants bearing gifts and exotic animals in gold, silver-gilt and precious stones, are examples. The Apis Altar, his last work, has an Egyptian subject which was not pursued elsewhere in Europe until later in the 18th century.

A portrait of Dinglinger exists, in which he is painted holding his Bath of Diana, an elaborate confection based on a stag's head whose antlers support a chalcedony bowl framed with gold and above which rests an ivory Diana carved by the court sculptor, Permoser. Dinglinger also made jewelry, which was housed in the Jewelry Room of the Green Vaults, on which the great Meissen porcelain modeller J. Kaendler worked as a wood carver. This connection between metalwork and porcelain has an interesting parallel in London, where in 1742 the Liège goldsmith, Nicholas Sprimont, registered his mark and a few years later founded the Chelsea porcelain factory.

The 18th century was a period of great industrial change in Europe with machine processes gradually taking over from the craftsman – and in this England led the way. Until this time, workshops had been small, with a master and some assistants working for commission and for stock. This system was gradually superseded by one in which large general firms collected their stock from a number of specialists who did not need to deal with the public themselves, but could also work on their own account if they wished. Not only did the introduction of machinery make silver production cheaper from the mid-18th century onwards, but the invention of substitutes allowed more people to have what had previously been a luxury. The first of these substitutes for silver was Sheffield plate.

In about 1742 it was discovered that a sheet

3

3 The only object bearing the maker's mark of J.A. Meissonnier known to survive is a gold and lapis lazuli snuffbox. The candelabrum reproduced here was made by Claude Duvivier from a candlestick design by Meisonnier.

4 Meissonnier's fame rests on his influential engravings one of which is seen here, a *surtout de table* and two tureens designed for the second Duke of Kingston.

of copper could be fused by heat to a thin skin of silver and that when put through a rolling mill the two metals would expand in unison and could be used in the same way as sheet silver at a fifth of the cost. Horse powered rolling mills gave way to water power and then to steam. Die-stamping and swaging machines made patterns, copper wire was plated with silver and then drawn out and used to strengthen and to decorate pieces.

At first, one side only of the copper sheet was plated, but later both sides were covered and the edge of the piece where the copper layer was exposed was disguised by soldering on a grooved silver wire, by soldering on stamped out silver mounts or by lapping over the edge. Matthew Boulton (1728–1809) at his Soho factory in Birmingham, England, ensured the highest standards of design and workmanship in this new medium, as well as in silver, by commissioning the best designers. Boulton, like his potter friend, Josiah Wedgwood, was one of the first to use industrial processes on a large scale. Subsequently fused plate, as it was called, was made in France and in Russia, though less successfully.

The new industrial methods were particularly suited to the expression of Neo-classical taste, which spread throughout Europe and America from the 1760s. Once more the artistic impulse

4

came from Italy – architects and artists studying there were influenced by the Roman architect, Piranesi, and by the archaeological treasures then being uncovered. For the first time, the artistic initiative which began the new style did not come from court circles, but from intellectual ones. Monarchs, fearful for their thrones, suspiciously regarded it at first as liberal and revolutionary. Again, for the first time, the style was accepted very quickly and within 30 years all over Europe and north America the swaying, Rococo shape was replaced by the chaste, classical vase. Contemporaries refer to this style, which we call Neo-classical, as the 'true' and 'correct' style. Matthew Boulton's description

1 Paul Storr, apprentice to Andrew Fogelberg in the 1780s became the best known silversmith in the Regency style. He carried out work based on designs from publications like *Designs for Ornamental Plate.*

2 This tureen exemplifies the early Neo-classical desire to return to the classicism of 15th century Italy and the majesty of 17th century France.

of it cannot be bettered – it evolved, he said "by adapting the elegant ornaments of the most refined Greek artists and humbly conforming to their style and making new combinations of old ornaments without presuming to invent new ones".

The publication of numerous engraved designs in this simplified style enabled manufacturers rapidly to produce classical designs in silver and in Sheffield plate for an ever-increasing and prosperous middle-class clientèle.

Sweden had, in the past, been influenced first from German and then from French artistic sources, but at this period in London there was working a Swedish silversmith of great talent,

Andrew Fogelberg. His work and that of the English late 18th-century silversmith, John Schofield, expressed in the purest fashion the first phase of Neo-classical taste. However, the finest silver produced in this style was still recognized to come from France and work was commissioned from Jacques Roettiers (1707–84) and R. J. Auguste (*c*.1730–1805) by many Royal patrons, including Catherine the Great of Russia.

In the second phase of the classical revival, about 1800, large firms in England such as the Royal Goldsmiths, Rundell and Bridge, were using designs by sculptors and architects like Flaxman and Tatham which were made up by Paul Storr (1771–1844) and others. The Rundell firm had agencies all over Europe, India and in South America. Silver gilt was much used in work at this time – it exhibited the highly cultivated taste of the Prince Regent, later George IV. In France, the firm founded by M. G. Biennais (1764–1843) rose to success in the service of Napoleon's Imperial dream and here again the use of silver-gilt was preferred. So highly regarded was Garrards, the firm that succeeded Rundells as Royal Goldsmiths, that in the 1820s the Paris goldsmith Odiot sent his son to work there and ordered English machines for his Paris workshop.

England continued to dominate the industrial world by producing in 1820 a steam-powered

3 During the 18th century the idea slowly evolved of having matching items in toilet, tea, coffee or dinner services all made by one maker. This tea and coffee service of 1790–1800 which was made by Joseph Richardson of Philadelphia and which may be seen in the Winterthur Museum, Delaware, shows full Neo-classical influence in the square foot and in the vase shape of the coffee pot, sugar bowl and creamer. The pieces are also linked visually by the use of a fretted gallery decoration.

4 Candlestick by John Carter, London, 1767. Worshipful Company of Goldsmiths. This candlestick was designed by Robert Adam (the design may be seen in the Sir John Soane Museum, London); it was made up by other silversmiths besides John Carter. It is a good example of the Neo-classicists' desire, in Matthew Boulton's words, 'to make new combinations of old ornaments without presuming to invent new ones.'

5 Candelabrum by Georg Jensen, Copenhagen, 1921 This candelabrum, with its heavily encrusted branches lethargically drooping, is characteristic of Jensen's style. It was made in the year before the firm was taken over by the Pedersen family and is still being reproduced.

lathe for spinning shapes and by the discovery of the electroplating process. As early as 1814 Paul Storr had made an electrogilt silver goblet, but not until 1840 did the Elkington cousins of Birmingham take out the first patents which led to their revolutionizing and monopolizing the plating industry.

When articles were made in Sheffield plate the copper sheet was silver plated before the object was shaped. In electroplating the object was completed in base metal before being put into the plating vat to be covered with a thin skin of precious metal by means of an electrical current passing through. At first the electroplaters used a copper base which gradually showed through with wear, as it had done with Sheffield

1 This christening mug, decorated with a frieze of angels and a kneeling child was designed by the painter Richard Redgrave in 1848 for 'Felix Summerley's Art Manufactures' an organization which strove to produce goods of 'superior utility' decorated with 'appropriate ornament.' The design was popular and continued to be used for many years. The mug illustrated was made in 1849 by S.H. and D. Glass.

had produced a lasting effect of great beauty it was lethal to the workmen who often used it incautiously.

Electrotyping was a further development of the electroplating process, in which objects could be copied in copper and plated. This was popular with the growing public for revived styles, and who were satisfied with electroplate. Usually, a mould was taken from the object to be reproduced, but in the 1840s there was a revival of interest in natural forms and objects which led to the electrotyping of real flowers, leaves and plants and also of small animals and insects – an interesting return to the work of the 16th-century mannerist goldsmiths.

From 1842 G. Christofle (1805–63) in Paris

plate, then a layer of whitish alloy was interposed between the copper and the silver. This was 'German' or nickel silver, a mixture of copper, zinc and nickel, invented in China and introduced into England in the 18th century. By 1836 the copper base was replaced entirely by improved nickel silver, now called 'Argentine' silver.

Another metal, a mixture of copper, antimony and tin which originated in the 18th century and had been used by the Sheffield platers was also electroplated. This was called 'Britannia' metal. The great advantages of using a 'white' base metal and of the electroplating process itself was that when the silver wore away the colour of the exposed base layer was less obvious, and also that the object could be put in the vat for replating as often as was necessary.

Electrogilding was a merciful improvement on the gilding technique which had been used until this time, since although mercury gilding

began making electroplated goods under licence from Elkingtons of Birmingham. All his designs were available both in silver and electroplate, an important selling point, and his use of an 18th-century style was greatly to the taste of Second Empire France.

American silver of the 18th century had always reflected its European origins and the work of John Coney of Boston (1655–1722), Philip Syng of Philadelphia (1703–89) and William Faris of Annapolis (1728–1804) betrayed their transatlantic heritage. One of Coney's apprentices was a Huguenot emigré, less famous on his own account than because he was the father of Paul Revere (1734–1818). Revere's style ranged from articles made in admirably sober Huguenot shapes before the War of Independence to lighter-weight articles produced in the delicate Adam-inspired London taste of the closing years of the 18th century.

The company of Reed and Barton, heirs in the 19th century to the Taunton (Massachusetts) Britannia Manufacturing Company, did not at first make articles in silver at all, but concentrated on the market for electroplated goods. Silver was discovered in the USA in 1859 and the success of the Gorham Manufacturing

2 Tea urn by Paul Storr 1809–10, made for Rundell and Bridge in their Dean Street workshops. The tea kettle of the first half of the 18th century was succeeded by the tea urn, heated by inserting a hot iron rod into a central sleeve. At this time matching coffee and tea urns were made, the tea urn having twice the capacity of the coffee urn. This tea urn is to be seen in the Victoria and Albert Museum, London.

styles which continued to be popular with the general public.

In 1876, the English designer, Christopher Dresser (1834–1904) visited Japan, buying both for Tiffany and for the South Kensington Museum (now the Victoria and Albert) in London. Dresser's functional designs, drawn with the machine in mind, and made to be executed in either silver or silver plate, were marked by their beauty and simplicity of shape, no decoration blurred the burnished surface. Japanese influence appeared in the shapes he used and the positioning of the handles on his objects.

Artists in many fields were by now concerned to eliminate the grosser evils resulting from the Industrial Revolution. The many popular exhi-

3

Company was derived from the consequent lowering in price and the increased supply.

Unhampered by the rigid assay systems of European rivals, the firm of C. F. Tiffany (1812–1902) was able to show at the 1867 exhibition in Paris work which reflected the simpler style stimulated by the resumption, after many years, of trade with Japan. The 'Aesthetic Movement' as the Japan inspired style began to be called, was more palatable to the Western intellectual elite than were the eclectic revivals of previous

3 Silver parcel gilt fan shaped tray with frosted background: part of a tea service in the Japanese taste. Elkingtons, Birmingham 1879.

bitions from 1851 onwards unwittingly demonstrated supreme technical control allied with appalling design. Throughout the rest of the century designers and artists tried constantly to revert to what was thought to be the golden age of the craftsman when, it was felt, the worker, unsullied by contact with machines, was inspired by joy in the work of his hand and mind.

Christopher Ashbee (1863–1942) was one such thinking artist. He was probably influenced by philanthropic classes organized in Philadelphia

by Charles Leland. He founded a Guild and 1
School of Handicraft in 1888 at Toynbee Hall in
London, where unskilled workers were taught
age-old crafts and where an amateur, hand-made
look was cultivated in opposition to the cheaper,
characterless, slick finish of the factory.

The firm of Liberty and Co. of London exploited the appeal of Ashbee's Guild style. It was
in keeping with the general Art Nouveau taste of
the 1880s and also with Liberty's original reputation as importers of oriental goods. From
1899, Liberty's 'Cymric' silver and 'Tudric' pew-
·ter fused the influence of Dresser with that of
Ashbee. Made by using factory die-stamping
and spinning processes, Liberty silver still bore
hammer marks which made the work look as
though it was completely hand made. In fact, the
hammer marks were either included in the die-
stamp or added to a spun piece after it was
finished. Liberty silver was not cheap, but the
use of machine process and hand finish enabled
it to undercut firms which would have no
involvement with machines.

The designs of the Glasgow architect, Charles
Rennie Mackintosh (1868–1928), more influential in continental Art Nouveau than they were
in Britain, clearly showed a development from
sappy, tendril-like hothouse curves to a tauter,
more purposeful and energetic style appropriate
to the 20th century.

Russia has not been previously mentioned,
because in general silver designs were derived
from those prevailing in Western Europe. Since
the mid-17th century Russian rulers had encouraged architects and artists from outside to
go there to work. Russian museums now hold
many superb examples of the best European
silver which over the years had been presented to
successive Tsars as ambassadorial gifts. Not all
Russian silver, however, was derivative – certain
objects developed along their own lines in a
particularly national tradition. An example of
this was the kovsh, a flat-based boat-shaped 2
vessel with a prow-like handle, which was used
as a cup or a ladle. Another was the charka, a
small spirit cup of more conventional shape.
Both could be decorated in 'niello' or in 'cloisonné' enamel – neither the shape of these cups
nor the techniques used to decorate them were
to be found elsewhere in contemporary Europe.

The work of Carl Fabergé (1867–1920) in
silverware, derived from French precedents
combined with traditional Russian forms and
decoration, used predictably eclectic late 19th
century designs. Some cabinet objects, however,
obviously harked back to the goldsmith's work
of Jamnitzer of Nüremberg in the 16th century
and of Dinglinger of Dresden in the early 18th
century. Fabergé's work was much patronized
by Russian Court circles and was not generally
known outside Russia until discussed in Diaghilev's art journal *Mir Iskusstva* and exhibited at
the 1900 Paris exhibition. Since the closure of
the firm during the Russian Revolution, its
products have been admired for craftsmanship
in the French 18th century manner. The works
themselves remain tinged with a melancholy

associated with the doomed society for which they were created.

Diaghilev brought the 'Ballets Russes' to Paris for the first time in 1909 and the artistic world of the West was immediately influenced by the barbaric and primitive splendour of work by the Russian painters and composers he employed. Remaining in the West, the 'Ballets Russes' naturally lost its particularly national flavour, but because Diaghilev employed *avant garde* artists to design his costumes and sets all branches of the decorative arts became more responsive to the latest artistic movements. The section of the public which would not have visited a gallery to look at contemporary painting was influenced through seeing the work of Picasso, Bakst, Derain, Matisse, Braque and others on stage.

The Danish silversmith, Georg Jensen (1866–1935), produced silverware which continued the craftsman's approach made popular in the 1890s, and was also responsive to the latest artistic movement, Post-impressionism. His designs for tableware and cutlery brought a new look to traditional, useful silver and the hammered look decorated and with a slightly oxidized surface, may still be seen at branches of his firm. The appeal of his original designs may be gauged by the manner in which they have been plagiarized.

During the 1920s there was a revival of Egyptian influence in the decorative arts, following the discovery in 1922 of Tutenkhamen's tomb and much has lately been made of the effects of the 1925 Paris 'Exposition Internationale des Arts Décoratifs et Industriels Modernes'. More fundamental, perhaps, and in the long run more influential, was the philosophical approach to living of those associated with the Bauhaus from 1906 to 1932, such as van der Velde, Gropius and Mies van der Rohe.

Jean Puirforcat (1897–1945), the Paris silversmith whose work showed a monumental smoothness and a simplicity of the most luxurious kind, ascribed his creed of 'beauty in usefulness' to a return to the harmonic values expressed in Platonic theory, and although other silversmiths were less consciously intellectual in their approach the appeal of much silver made since World War II shows that an agreeable synthesis of craftsmanship and technology has taken place. Although the world of the 20th century looks askance at luxurious display in a way which would have been incomprehensible to any Renaissance prince, there is no dearth of inspiration in silverware designs nor lack of craftsmanship in the silversmith.

1 The Magnolia Vase was made by the firm of C.F. Tiffany for the World's Colombian Exhibition of 1893 and reflects purely American ideas. Eight handles deriving from Toltec art represent early Americans; flowers and plants symbolize the four points of the compass. Metropolitan Museum, New York.

3

2 Tureen, cover and ladle designed by Christopher Dresser in 1880 and made in electroplate by Hukin and Heath of Birmingham. Japanese influence is strongly felt in the shape and in the plain ebony handles.

4 Eugene Feuillâtre designed and made this cup in silver gilt decorated with *pique à jour* enamel in about 1900.

3 This christening set, made for Mappin and Webb in 1903 by William Hutton and Sons, shows a pleasing use of Art Nouveau forms by a commercial firm.

Base metals

Milestones in the history of base metals

c.2700 B.C. Domestic work in most metals and alloys already in use, with finely developed designs. Bronze, copper and other non-ferrous metals and alloys already in architectural use in both East and West.

11th century A.D. Forged wrought ironwork in wide use in Europe for grilles, door hinges and other architectural details.

12th century Widespread application of metals and alloys, especially bronze and brass, but also wrought iron, to many artifacts – especially for ecclesiastical use.

13th century Commencement of the application of brilliant benchwork to numerous artifacts especially locks and keys. Casting much used for brass and bronze domestic utensils, church lecterns and memorial brasses. Brass and bronze used for tomb effigies, cathedral doors and similar applications. Lead also used for architectural purposes.

15th century Benchwork became fashionable throughout Europe.

16th century Commencement of widespread use of cast-iron for firebacks, firedogs, grave slabs, holloware, and so on. Pewter came into general use.

17th century Beginning of widespread use of lead for cisterns. In ironwork a general return to forging (though sometimes combined with benchwork) with elaborate scrollwork and false perspective. Second half of century saw development of wrought iron gates and screens to enclose courtyards of chateaux and similar buildings. Beginning of application of cast-iron to architecture. New developments in the design of fireplaces to meet more general use of coal. Cast-iron, polished steel and other alloys much in evidence for these. Japanned steel, copper and other metals and alloys, in fashion and made in large quantities. Development of the design of fine bronzework. Mid-century saw apogee of wrought iron gates and screens.

19th century General application of cast-iron to domestic metalwork. Application of historic and exotic styles to the design of all architectural metalwork. Mid-century saw apogee of architectural cast ironwork, especially in the Crystal Palace, London (1851). Application of Art Nouveau, Art Deco and other 'modern' styles to all metalwork. General use of aluminium and stainless-steel.

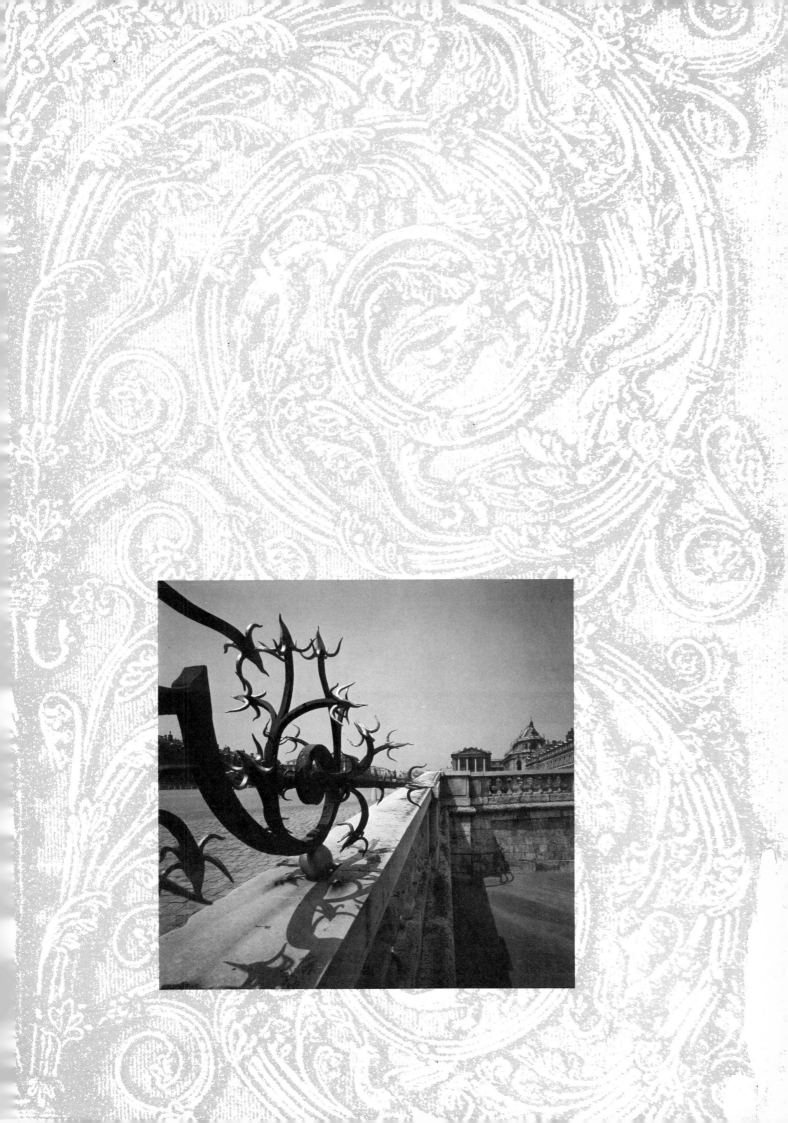

Architectural Metalwork

The metals most frequently used in both architectural and domestic metalwork are iron, copper, lead, and their alloys. Of these the commonest in architectural metalwork is iron, but in domestic work it is closely rivalled, if not exceeded, by the copper group.

Iron is the most useful and plentiful metal on earth, and the fourth most abundant element. Yet in early times it was considered a precious, indeed magical metal, being known only in meteorites which were thought to have been flung down by the gods.

There are two main forms of iron, wrought iron and cast iron. Initially all iron is smelted from ore in blast furnaces, and run into ingots or pigs. If it is to be used for casting it is left in this state. If wrought iron is required (iron that can be shaped by forging or cutting) the pig iron is put through a further process known as puddling, which consists of boiling and stirring the molten metal in a vessel until most of its impurities have been burnt away. After cooling, the mass is squeezed to drive out any remaining impurities and shaped into solid blocks of iron (blooms). These are subsequently reheated and rolled (in earlier times they were hammered) into bars, sheets or plates. Hammering produced bars of less consistent section than rolling, and it is this which helps to give early wrought ironwork its character.

Steel is an alloy of iron, containing more carbon than wrought iron, but less than cast iron. For a long time it was made only with great difficulty, and it was not until the middle of the 19th century that industrial processes made its manufacture easy.

Copper occurs both in a free state and in over 300 copper-bearing minerals, of which only a few are used for smelting. It has many applications, not least (in the form of sheet) for covering roofs and domes. When exposed it gradually acquires a beautiful bright green colour, which provides a protective chemical film. Until the 15th century it was the most plentiful metal, since when this position has been taken by iron.

Its widest use is in alloys. Some of these were used for short periods and in limited applications. An alloy known by the Chinese name Paktong, a silver-coloured amalgam of copper, zinc and nickel, was much used during the 18th and 19th centuries for grates, fenders and fire irons. But the most widely used alloys of copper have for many centuries been brass and bronze.

Brass has been known since 1000 B.C. The term also embraces various sub-divisions of the alloy used in the Middle Ages – laton or latten, for example, for the brass plate from which such things as monumental brasses were made. It came into general use in Roman times and has been common ever since. There are many types containing between 38 and 46 per cent zinc.

Bronze has been used since prehistory. Like brass it has many forms, but it always contains tin in addition to zinc and copper. Among widely used bronzes are the corrosion-resisting gunmetal (up to 88 per cent copper, 10 per cent tin and 4 per cent zinc), the hard and brittle bell metal (up to 25 per cent tin) and statue bronze (approximately 85 per cent copper, 11 per cent zinc and 4 per cent tin). Ormolu is gilded bronze; in classical times brass and bronze were differentiated by the fact that bronze could be gilded, whereas brass could not.

Lead has a long history, extending over thousands of years. It is made by smelting mainly from the most important lead ore, galena or sulphide of lead. It has a low melting point and is of enormous density. Yet it is weak and ductile, despite which its applications are widespread. Like copper it has for centuries been used for roofing, but it has also been widely used for such things as statuary, cisterns, seats and urns, and the Romans used it for conduits in their water systems.

There are many alloys of lead, most of which are of industrial application and therefore outside our present context. But an important exception is pewter, much used in domestic metalwork, and is an alloy of lead and tin, sometimes with small amounts of copper. In some cases antimony was also added, and on occasion was used instead of copper. Coffin metal is also worthy of mention, being used for many years for making coffins. It contains about 45 per cent lead, 40 per cent tin and 15 per cent copper, and the famous Glastonbury cross, now lost but once thought to have marked King Arthur's grave, was probably made from this alloy.

The most important techniques by which metal is shaped are casting, forging (called blacksmithery when applied to iron), benchwork or locksmithery, and sheet metalwork.

All the metals and alloys previously mentioned may be cast. Usually the metal is melted in a crucible (a bigger tower-like structure called a cupola is necessary for melting iron) and poured into moulds.

There are various ways in which moulds are made. Irregularly shaped objects like statuary are made with a wax pattern, but the commonest type of mould is a two-part metal box in which sand is rammed around a wooden pattern; after this, the box is split, and the pattern removed, leaving an aperture which, when the box is closed, is of the size and shape of the pattern. Holes are made for the introduction of the metal.

Forging is most commonly applied to iron and steel, but certain bronzes may be forged, as may copper, but it is rarely used in this way. Brass is too brittle to be forged while lead is too soft and weak. There are several basic processes in forging. Bending, twisting and perforating are self explanatory; drawing out consists of heating the metal and increasing its length. Jumping up or upsetting consists of heating it and decreasing its length and/or increasing its girth. Both of

1 Wrought-iron chantry gates and screen in St George's Chapel, Windsor, by Master John Tresilian (English, late 15th century). This was made almost throughout in cold-worked metal, and constructed from hundreds of small units precisely fitted together. It is one of the supreme masterpieces of ironwork in the Gothic style.

these processes are used to alter its section. Finally, wrought iron may be welded by heating the pieces to be joined at the point of fusion and hammering them into one solid piece; wrought iron is formed by tiny laminae, and welding helps to consolidate them. If bronze and brass require joining, they are usually brazed, a form of soft soldering.

Benchwork of locksmithery, as its name implies, is the technique of the locksmith. But at times, particularly during the late medieval period, the term covered making everything from tiny finger rings to large gates. Iron, steel, bronze and brass were used, and the cold metal was shaped by means of hammers and chisels, saws, drills, files and punches.

Any of the metals and alloys mentioned above may be worked in the sheet metal technique, a blend of whitesmithery or tinplate work (tin-plate being iron or steel sheet coated with molten tin), with elements derived from plumbing and from the armourer's craft.

The sheet metalworker must reduce the shape of the object he is to make so that it may be marked out on a flat sheet of metal, and then, by the use of various shears, tools, hammers, anvils and blocks, cut it out and raise it to the three-dimensional form required. Sometimes, if the object is complex, several developments (as the foregoing process is called) may be necessary, which, after being raised, are joined together by various kinds of folded or brazed joints, or, in the case of lead, by welding with a blowpipe. Sometimes, sheet metal is spun into shape on a lathe.

An important type of sheet metalwork is repoussé, of the decoration of sheet metal by hammering shapes from the back. Repoussé is a specialized craft in its own right, and some craftsmen demonstrate amazing virtuosity – three-dimensional masks and flowers, heraldry and animals to name but a few. Repoussé is restricted to iron, copper and occasionally bronze. Brass and lead are unsuitable – too brittle in the first case too soft in the other.

The early history of artistic metalwork is almost entirely occupied by non-ferrous metals (those not containing iron) and their alloys. Apart from a few isolated examples, ironwork as an art did not flourish before the 12th century, for iron was a rare metal and not so highly valued as copper and bronze. In Egypt there is little or no evidence of its use until about 1300 B.C., after which it was used to some extent, though only functionally. Soon its use spread to Greece and Asia Minor, and later to the Italian peninsula and to Central Europe; but here again, its use was almost exclusively utilitarian. Yet in places, at Pompeii for instance, some artefacts have been found showing that classical antiquity was not unaware of the artistic possibilities of the metal.

In China the use of iron was not firmly established until about 200 B.C.

With copper and bronze the story is different. In Egypt bronze was known by about 2550 B.C., its artistic possibilities were soon realized. Objects such as cast ornamented bronze ewers and bowls soon began to appear. At about the same time, bronzeworking began in Asia Minor and shortly after in Western Europe, especially among the Greeks, Romans and Celts. Nor was the architectural use of copper and bronze neglected. This is exemplified by two well-known works in the British Museum, London, England: a frieze from Ur made of sheet copper hammered over a wooden foundation, secured by copper nails and with wrought copper details (about 2700 B.C.); and the Assyrian fragmentary bronze gates of Shalmaneser III which illustrate his campaigns (about 845 B.C.). But some of the most notable examples of classical metalwork are the life-size Greek horses of hand-beaten copper sheet over the entrance of St Mark's basilica, Venice, Italy (4th century B.C.).

Lead was well known in antiquity, but it was used less widely than bronze, and its applications were often utilitarian. Herodotus mentions its use, with iron, to bind together stone on a bridge at Babylon, but it was also used decoratively.

1

1 and 2 Wrought-iron pulpit in the Cathedral of Avila, Spain (1525) with (right) a detail. It was made using a combination of techniques, and shows the refinement which Spanish smiths of the period were capable.

The arts of metalwork were practised throughout the Dark Ages, although there was little important development in design. Yet in places metalworking centres flourished, such as those in Spain and Sicily during the rule of the caliphs, in Persia, and in Ireland.

By the 11th and 12th centuries, good ironwork was beginning to make its appearance, yet little enough belonging to this date survives – rust and neglect having taken their toll. Ironwork of this early period is small in scale, the best pieces being door hinges and small grills. Great choir screens such as those made in Spain two or three hundred years later, were unknown, indeed impossible because of the absence of long bars. The early medieval blacksmith had perforce to assemble his works from small pieces hammered out from blooms and welded together, thus giving the profile of the work an interesting inconsistency.

The usual form of grille at this time was a framework of verticals, to the sides of which were welded sprigs, each convoluted into a scroll, secured to the next vertical bar or to the next scroll by a band. Such grilles are on the entrance to the chapel of Santa Cruz in the cloister of Pamplona cathedral, Spain, at Le Puy-en-Velay, Languedoc, France (about 1200), at the Monastery of Bobbio, Italy (about 1210) and, the earliest of all, the fragmentary St Swithin grille, in Winchester cathedral, England (about 1093).

In the church of Conques, France, is a sanctuary grille erected at the end of the 12th century which shows a further development – a line of spikes along the top serving both as prickets for candles and as a protection against climbers. The grille on the tomb of Queen Eleanor in Westminster Abbey by Thomas de Leghtone (1294) has similar spikes and its form and scroll-work are more elaborate than those of grilles made at the beginning of the century.

The terminations of the scrolls in all the grilles are beautifully finished, those on the St Swithin (Winchester) grille being forged into cinquefoil and trefoil clusters. In St Mark's basilica, Venice, some of the doorways and windows have bronze grilles, but although they are of about the same period as the iron grilles, they are of more sophisticated design and construction, as is to be expected when it is remembered that bronze working had already had a long tradition.

The hinges of this period are often even more beautiful than the grilles. Apart from providing pivots on which the door could swing, they were elaborated into scrolls and patterns that meandered all over the door, not merely to provide decoration, but also to strengthen and provide support for the often indifferently constructed woodwork.

Early hinges have survived better that most other ironwork of the time because they were useful and were therefore kept in good repair. For the same reason they survived periods of iconoclasm. At first they were quite simple, but they soon came to be elaborately decorated with flowers, clusters, buttons, leaves, gargoyles' heads and many other motifs. Examples abound, but of special interest are those at Orcival, Noyon and in the cathedral of Sens in France, and in the church of Sindelfingen in Württemberg (all 12th century).

In more northern parts of Europe development was somewhat different, and little change came until well into the 17th century. Here the work though elaborate is less sophisticated. Much of this northern hinge-work has details derived from Viking and Norse motifs. There are examples on doors in the churches of Gronbaek, Jutland, Skonberga and Vänga, Ostergötland, Sweden, and at Stillingfleet, Yorkshire, England.

A masterpiece of hinge-work adorns the doors of St Anne and of the Virgin on the cathedral of Notre Dame, Paris, France. A mixture of blacksmithery and benchwork, it is incredibly rich. Each hinge, made of deeply fluted sections, blossoms into great scrolls that contain a mass of lesser scrolls of astonishing variety, with leaves, flowers, human heads, birds and monsters, whirling and overlapping one another and filling out every area of space on the underlying woodwork, yet all organized into an overall and coherent design. They probably belong to the 12th or 13th centuries, although there is a tradition, little more than a legend, that they are the work of a 16th century Burgundian smith, Biscornet – a claim which may be put in the same class as that which suggests that they are the work of the devil!

In the 14th and 15th centuries simplicity was often discarded, as is evident from the 15th-century choir grille of Toulouse cathedral, France, with its decorations of dragons' heads and flowers, made possible by the use of small plates of iron welded to bars of larger section and then forged into shape.

Much brilliant development was taking place at this period in Italian ironwork, a noteworthy example being the grille of the chapel of the Pubblico Palace, Siena, finished about 1445. The main structure is divided into squares filled with elegant quatrefoils joined to the main structure and to one another by collars. Above these are rectangular panels containing elaborate floral arabesques and devices, and along the top rail is a frieze of prickets interspersed with vases, bouquets of flowers and leaves, all of iron. The main structure is realized largely in benchwork, the border of each panel being decorated with chiselled crenellations.

At this time, benchwork became very fashionable all over Europe. As we shall see in the section on domestic metalwork, it was particularly suitable for small domestic artefacts, but larger work was also made, an important example of which is the grille of the Rinuccini chapel in the church of St Croce, Florence, Italy (1371). This contains much forging, but the main structure is of benchwork and, most impressive of all, so are its little Gothic arcades and decorations which include, at their apex, a roundel as elaborately detailed as a great rose window in a cathedral.

One of the most spectacular specimens of architectural benchwork is in St George's chapel, Windsor, England. The chantry gates and screen were made by Master John Tresilian (late 15th century). It measures 3.5 × 2.7 m (11 ft 6 in × 8 ft 10 in) to the top of its flanking pillars. It is amazing that this work was minutely and painstakingly filed, chiselled and dovetailed together like a vast Chinese puzzle with no more equipment than the simplest hand-tools.

Similar work was being produced at the same period in Germany and in Spain. In the cathedral at Avila, Spain, is a pulpit of Gothic design made by benchwork; it is one of the supreme masterpieces of the technique (1525). Of hexagonal shape, it measures 1 m (3 ft 3 in) in height and

stands on a stone base of about 3 m (9 ft 10 in). It is composed of panels, each carved with Gothic motifs: roses, arcades and friezes, while on the principal panel are the arms of the basilica. There are many such pulpits in Spain, but this one is surely supreme.

Another is situated beside the choir grille in Seville cathedral (about 1519–24), but in this case it is the grille which dominates, a vast structure consisting of panels of elaborately upset and drawn-out Corinthian balusters with two horizontal bands of rectangular panels containing scrollwork, devices, angles and portraits of saints and of Christ. The work is crested with tall finials bearing flame tufts and prickets and angels surmounting them, interspersed with scrollwork and more figures and a large rectangle at the centre which contains a representation of the Entombment. This grille was the work of Sancho Muñoz de Cuenca, and his collaborators, Brother John and Brother Francis of Salamanca.

Spanish ironwork of this period marks the zenith of medieval forging combined with benchwork. The sheer brilliance of technique of the Spanish smiths is manifest even in such minor works as the small gates from Guadalajara, now in Chester cathedral, England (1558), and in the

1 A wrought-iron choir-screen in Seville Cathedral by Brother Francisco de Salamanca (c.1530). It was made with a combination of forged and benchwork. This vast work, the size of which may be judged by the altar standing behind it, is one of the world's finest wrought-iron screens.

2 The bronze North Doors of the Baptistry at Florence by Lorenzo Ghiberti (1403–4). Ghiberti also made the East Doors, while the South Doors were the work of Andrea Pisano, with framing decorations by Vittorio Ghiberti and figures by Vincenzo Danti.

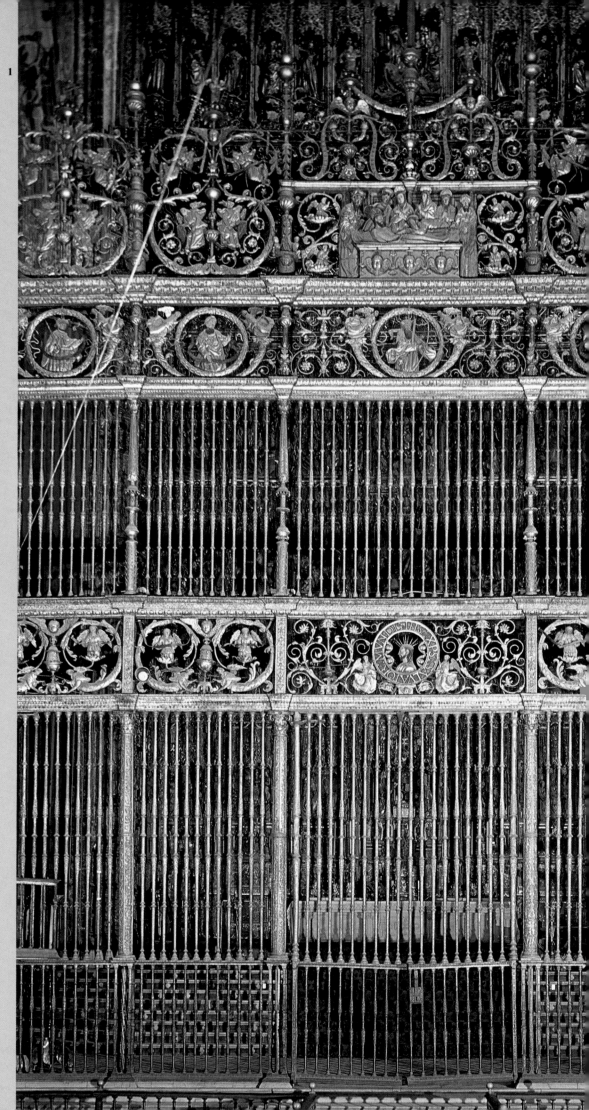

1

2

elegant little window grilles of similar but simpler construction on small houses in Seville, Salamanca and elsewhere.

In the meantime the use and application of bronze and brass were being widely developed, in such works as the gilded bronze tomb effigies on certain important Gothic tombs. They were cast by the *cire-perdue* process. Such are the effigies of King Henry III and Queen Eleanor in Westminster Abbey, England, cast by the goldsmith William Torel (1291), and also those in the church of Notre Dame at Bruges in Belgium, representing Mary of Burgundy and her father, Charles the Bold, each showing the subject in a recumbent position, head resting on a cushion, and hands lightly joined in an attitude of prayer (late 15th century).

The more beautiful of the two is that of Mary, with her prim girlish face, richly embroidered cloak, wimple and coronet. This effigy was cast by P. de Beckere who received 14,000 florins for it, out of which he had to allow 40 florins compensation to each of his workmen for the loss of teeth caused by the mercury used in gilding the bronze.

Bronze effigies were cast in the Far East, centuries before these Gothic works appeared. At Nara, in Japan, to take a phenomenal example, there is a cast effigy of Buddha over 16 m (52 ft) high which was made in A.D. 749.

In Europe it was Italy that was pre-eminent in medieval bronzework. One of the most notable examples is the two pairs of gilded bronze doors by Lorenzo Ghiberti (1378–1455) on the baptistry at Florence. A competition was held for the design of these doors, in which such artists as Filippo Brunelleschi and Jacopo della Quercia took part, but the work of Ghiberti was preferred. The north doors are divided into 28 compartments with scenes from the lives of Christ, of the Evangelists and of the Doctors, enclosed by figurative framing and surmounted by figures by Giovanni Rustici. The more famous work is the pair of east doors in which Ghiberti was assisted by Bennozo Gozzoli, Michelozzo and other craftsmen and which Michelangelo so admired that he called them the 'Gate of Paradise'. They contain 10 panels depicting Old Testament scenes, and they are surrounded by framing with 24 statuettes and 24 medallions.

These doors, which date from about 1440, are in complete contrast to the Gothic metalwork being made farther north at the same time. They are true Renaissance work in which the artist has overcome all the problems of perspective, grouping, depth and plasticity. Yet it must not be thought that such work was made only in Italy, for baptismal fonts, doors (simpler it is true, than those of Ghiberti), and grilles, all in cast bronze and sometimes gilded, were made in places as far afield as Spain, Flanders and Germany. Nevertheless, on the whole, Italy was the land of the Renaissance while the north was still Gothic.

In Italy also, bronze sculpture as an architectural embellishment was highly developed, such as on the Tortoises fountain in the Piazza Mattei, Rome (1581–4), with its life-size naked bronze youths holding tortoises over the edge of the marble basin. These were made by the Florentine sculptor Taddeo di Leonardo Landini (about 1550–96).

Bronze was to take an ever more important part in Italian architecture, reaching one of its most brilliant manifestations in the gilded bronze baldacchino in St Peter's basilica, Rome, which was designed by Giovanni Lorenzo Bernini and unveiled by Urban VIII in June 1633. It is 29 m (95 ft) high and was cast from bronze taken from the Pantheon. The four tortile columns, which are set on marble plinths, are decorated with laurel and genii. They support the festooned and tasselled canopy on which are figures of angels and children by François Duquesnoy, and on the apex of which is a globe and a cross.

The three bronze flagpole pedestals in front of St Mark's basilica, Venice, should also be mentioned. These are embellished with reliefs and were made by Alessandro Leopardi in 1505.

Lead also was used for architectural statuary. As it is a soft, heavy metal, liable to distortion or even collapse if unsupported, it was often reinforced by an internal wrought-iron armature, or even hammered out in thin sheets and soldered together on the surface of a wooden model, which was thus totally enclosed. In France, such statues were known as *embouties* (from *emboutir*, to beat out or to plate). There is a fine lead statue of St John the Evangelist at the Cluny Museum, Paris; it is 2.4 m (7 ft 10 in) high (14th century). Lead tombs were also made, such as the 15th century cast specimen at Moissac, France, which carries a representation of the Entombment of Christ.

Gothic architectural leadwork worthy of note includes roof finials, crestings and spires made by sheet metalwork and casting. These features were once common in England, but little now remains there, although they are still quite common in France. Some of the finials are really sculpture, for example the figure of the Virgin and Child over the Lady chapel at Rouen, and the large Virgin at Clermont-Ferrand. Most roof decorations still remaining, however, are either abstract, with Gothic or other motifs, or based on flowers and leaves.

With the Renaissance, ironwork was again dominated by forging and, while benchwork was still used for small artefacts, its widespread architectural application declined. Moreover, the centres for the finest work became firmly situated in Italy, Spain and Germany, where fine scrollwork again appeared on architectural ironwork, as on the grilles at the Contini Palace, Venice, on the balcony of the Belvilacqua palace, Bologna, and on the grille at the Farnese Palace, Piacenza. In addition to the Spanish examples already cited, there are the brilliant screens to the Main Chapel, Palencia, by Christobal de Andino (1520) and in the same church the choir screen by Gaspard Rodriguez of Segovia (1550–9), also that of the Royal Chapel, in Granada cathedral by Master Bartolomeo.

German ironwork of the period is the finest of all, having unequalled grace, lightness and

fantasy. Much of its effect was achieved by the
use of scrollwork made of bar of round section,
elaborately crossed, interlaced and passed
through one another as on the grille to the Fugger
tomb in the church of St Ulrich, Augsburg, by
Hans Mezger (1553–1612), with its leaves,
flowers and heraldry prettily enlivening the composition. And yet contemporary German ironwork is often still mixed with benchwork, as
illustrated by three grilles at Freiburg in Breisgau
(1538–70). On the other hand, at Augsberg and
Nuremburg, in central Germany, at Innsbruck,
in Austria, and at Prague, in Bohemia, the
new technique had taken over completely, as is
shown by Jörg Schmidhammer's grilles to the
princely tombs at the church of St Vit, Prague,
and that to the tomb of the Emperor Maximilian
in the court church, Innsbruck (1568–73).

German blacksmiths of this period known by
name include, in addition to those previously
mentioned, Simon Laubener and Simon Schmidt
who made a grille to the baptismal fonts in the
church of St Mary Magdalene, Breslau (1576),
Mathieu Andrès, who made the grille in the
church of Our Lady, Ingolstadt (1561), and
George Scheff of Heilbronn, maker of a charming balustrade around the fountain of Auguste,
Augsburg (1574).

2

1 Detail of wrought-iron
Spanish gates (Guadalajara,
1558) in Chester Cathedral.
Two pairs of these gates
have stood at the entrance
of the North and South
aisles of the Cathedral since
1876. They are mainly of
forged work combined
with some benchwork.

2 Bronze door-knocker in
the manner of Tiziano
Aspetti (Venetian, early
17th century), decorated
with a sea-nymph and boys
on dolphins.

Some architectural ironwork was also being made at this time in Switzerland, a first-class example being the grille in German style from the Cistercian abbey at Wettingen, in the National Museum at Zurich (end of the 16th century).

During the 17th century there was in architectural ironwork a tendency towards heavier design, albeit expressed through fluent virtuoso technique. Such are the gates made for the garden of the Chateau de Maisons, near Paris, France, (1642), now at the entrance of the Apollo Gallery in the Louvre at Paris. With their framework they are a *chef d'oeuvre*, a combination of forging, benchwork and repoussé. So inclusive is the design that the details are not at first apparent, but on closer inspection roses, acanthus leaves, birds' wings, caducei, rosettes innumerable interlaced rings and other decorative details become apparent.

In the second half of the century a fashion arose in France for magnificent screens and gates to enclose the vast courtyards of the great chateaux. In these, the main decorations are generally reserved for the overthrow of the gates, the railings themselves providing a *clair-voyée* through which the buildings, parterres and prospects could be seen with minimal obstruction to the viewer.

This style is exemplified by the gates and screens made by Gabriel Luchet for the Royal Court at Versailles (1678), in which the comparatively plain verticals are provided with spearheaded finials, and with an arrangement of S-scrolls at the base. These areas of plain verticals are punctuated by decorative panels containing lyre-shaped motifs crested by a sun (a compliment to Louis XIV, the 'Sun King') and with three fleurs-de-lys on the top rail. The gates are plain, but are surrounded with a frame of C-scrolls and are surmounted by a magnificent pyramid-shaped repoussé overthrow containing the shield of France within a wreath, surmounted by the royal crown, and flanked by symbols of pomp and plenty. Nothing could give a more powerful impression, and lavishness is added by a generous application of gold leaf.

Further splendid ironwork is in the Marble Court at Versailles, which contains a grand balcony decorated with crowned interlacing Ls (for Louis), cloths of estate, fleurs-de-lys, flambeaux, thunderbolts and brilliant scrollwork. This was made by Nicolas Delobel.

This new French style dominated work made in many other countries in the 17th century. In Italy it was mixed with national styles. The screens in the cathedral of St John Lateran in Rome show how at this time the older quatrefoil type of construction was dropped in favour of the plain verticals framed in borders of C-scrolls very similar to those made by Gabriel Luchet for the Royal Court at Versailles.

In Spain choir grilles continued to be made, but their greatest period had passed. Yet works like the sanctuary-chapter grilles in Toledo were created (1607); these were made by Bartolomeo Rodriguez under the direction of the sculptor and architect Juan Bautista Monegro.

In Germany the 16th-century style remained dominant; interlacing scrollwork continued to provide the central theme around which everything else was arranged. But there was one important development, in the introduction of *trompe l'oiel* perspective, two of the finest early example of which are the grilles in the minster at Constance (1628 and 1646). In these the smith has introduced straight lines into the scheme of scrollwork in order to arrive at his effect, one essentially baroque in that it instils extra perspective and movement as well as illusion into the work.

Further 17th-century examples are to be seen in the Collegium Clementinum, Prague, and in Lucerne cathedral, the central perspective of which is used to display a large crucifixion. The Lucerne screen took three years to make (1641–4) and cost 5,890 guilden; it was the work of Johann Reifell, formerly of Constance. German influence was felt throughout Switzerland and also in other neighbouring countries like Denmark and the Low Countries.

The later years of the 17th century witnessed the dawning of the finest period of English wrought ironwork. This development was due to one man in particular, the Huguenot blacksmith Jean Tijou, who was probably brought to England from Holland by William III and Mary. Before the advent of Tijou and since the close of the Middle Ages, British ironwork had been well made, of simple design, but on the whole uninspired. It is true some attractive works had been created, such as the gates at Traquair Castle, Peebleshire (about 1664) with a simple overthrow of scrolls, tulips and shields, and the staircase balustrade at Caroline Park, Midlothian (about 1695), but it lacked the sophistication and elegance of contemporary Continental work, such as that seen in France.

1 Wrought-iron gates to the Belevedere Palace. Vienna (about 1720), showing the characteristically heavy overthrow.

2 Detail from the wrought-iron screen at Hampton Court by Jean Tijou (about 1700). This is an example of wrought-iron repoussé work at its finest, combined with splendid blacksmithery.

1

Tijou was in England only from about 1690 to 1712, but those few years were sufficient for him to influence, indeed to create, a whole school of British smiths, many of whom worked for him when he was making the ironwork in St Paul's cathedral, London, under Sir Christopher Wren. It was becoming fashionable at this time for designers to publish books of engravings of their work. Tijou followed suit. In his *New Booke of Drawings* (1693) we may see the original conceptions of some of the finest extant ironwork in England, and also of some now swept away.

Tijou's masterpiece is his screen at Hampton Court, a magnificent set piece of wrought iron repoussé on an underlying framework of straight bars and volutes. Repoussé like Tijou's had not been seen in England before and little enough like it existed on the Continent; one has only to examine one of his masks to wonder how such a hard and intractable material as sheet iron could be raised to such splendid three-dimensional form.

None of his followers was able to emulate his repoussé work, but they did develop his black-smithery into something very English. Robert Bakewell's garden arbour at Melbourne, near Derby (about 1710), Thomas Robinson's gate and screen at New College, Oxford (1711), and John Warren's gates at Clare College, Cambridge (1714), are all examples of this.

The work of Robert Davies of Croes Foel, North Wales, shows more Continental influence than that of any other contemporary British blacksmith. This is particularly noticeable in the white gates and screen at Leeswood Hall, Mold, Flintshire, with its cresting of broken pediments and other details that might be found in contemporary German work (first quarter of the 18th century).

The first English architectural application of cast-iron was made in the early 18th century. This occurred in London on the fencing and gates around St Paul's cathedral (about 1710–11), and around the church of St Martin-in-the-Fields

1

(about 1726), and, in Cambridge, around the Senate House (about 1720). Lightness is accomplished by alternating cast and wrought iron balusters. Cast-iron was used also for the capitals and bases of Robert Davies's gates at Chirk Castle (early 1720s).

The 18th century was not only the golden age of British ironwork, it was also the age of French blacksmithery. In France, no building, public or private, was complete without its gates, screens, grilles, balconies or stair balustrades. Moreover, the severe verticality of such works as the screens and gates at Versailles gave way to sinuousness and Rococo flamboyance, achieved with much repoussé embellishment and with exploitation of the blacksmith's ability to produce a curvaceous framework of scrolled bars. Nowhere is this new departure better illustrated than in the work made in Nancy by Jean Lamour (1698–1771), blacksmith to the King of Poland. Of Lamour's output, his *magnum opus*, unique in Europe, is the system of iron screens and decorations in the Place Royale (now Place Stanislas) in that city.

In 1737 King Stanislas Leczinski of Poland, by the Treaty of Vienna, took possession of the duchies of Lorraine and Bar, and he wished to make Nancy, his capital, as imposing as possible. As part of this plan, he engaged Lamour to decorate various buildings with iron balconies, grilles and other embellishments. The summit of Lamour's work was the ironwork in the Place Royale, made in the middle of the century. This magnificent venue, measuring over 124 m × 106 m (406 ft × 347 ft), provided a splendid setting for iron screens, and Lamour (probably under the guidance of the architect Emmanuel Héré) made the most of the opportunity by providing a perfect system of Rococo decoration. The grilles and porticos, decorated with pilasters, capitals, cornices, crowns, vases of flowers, leaves and lanterns and brackets, are captivating. Although classical verticality is not eschewed, most of the bars curve and writhe where square corners hitherto would have been expected, the whole structure seeming to have been arrested in the midst of energetic movement. The climax of the system occurs at the fountain, where statuary, stonework and running water unite with ironwork to make an unforgettable spectacle.

Lamour's work marks the zenith of 18th-century ironwork, but there was much other superlative work in France at the same time, although styles varied somewhat. The fine communion rail in the church of St Roch, Paris (about 1760), for example, is thoroughly Baroque, and that in the church of St Germain l'Auxerrois in the same city (about 1767), is almost severely classical in a way that seems to adumbrate the taste of the Empire. It was made by Pierre Deumier. The Rococo again makes its appearance in gates in the cathedral at Lyons, but this lacks the inspired lightness of the work of Lamour. Work reminiscent in construction and design of the 17th-century ironwork at Versailles was erected in Paris during the second half of the 18th century, but its detail was much more complicated than that of its exemplar. Such are the

1 Sheet-metal 'Turkish' tent at Drottningholm, Sweden (about 1781).

2 Wrought-iron stair-balustrade in the main hall at Schloss Bruhl, Bonn, by Balthasar Newmann (after 1740).

2

gates and screens of the Military School and of the Palace of Justice.

In view of the splendid ironwork which was being made all over France it is surprising that the surge of craftsmanship did not outlast the century. The Revolution was doubtless a contributory factor to its decline, but so also was the chasteness of the rising classical style, which did not altogether lend itself to the natural tectonic properties of forged iron, and was in fact expressed better in bronze. Nevertheless, for a time during the 18th century, French ironwork reached a point of achievement never surpassed and rarely equalled.

Ironwork in 18th-century Germany, while of the highest quality in craftsmanship, was exaggerated in design. The *trompe l'oeil* treatment of gates and screens for instance was overdone, even though one may marvel at its virtuosity. Yet there is something admirable in such brilliant specimens of the style as the grille in the church of St Ulrich, Augsburg (1712) and that at the monastic church at Zwiefalten Württenburg, by Joseph Büssel of Rankweil (1751–56).

German Rococo ironwork is not so light as French work, yet it is not without charm. This may be seen on the staircase balustrades at Brühl Castle, near Cologne, designed by Balthasar Neumann and made by the smiths Köbst and Müller (after 1740), and the grilles in the Jesuit church at Mannheim (1753–56). To take a small example of Baroque work, there are the iron lanterns in the Belvedere, Vienna (about 1720), richly decorated with repoussé leaves, and supported by groups of marble *putti* on a staircase of the same material. It would be difficult to imagine a more typical example of German Baroque expressed in iron and stone than this. Ironwork of simpler but graceful design is on the exquisitely beautiful spiral staircase in the collegiate church at Melk in Austria.

National tradition survived alongside these works with their degree of foreign influence, and ranged from work such as the great grille at Schöntal, Westphalia (1727) to the marvellous piece of late benchwork, the small jewel-like grille in the chapel of St John, Vienna (1744). In Switzerland, too, the German influence was strong, as is evident on gates in the Rittergasse, Basle, and on the fanlight of the house of the Little Stone Bench, Zurich (1726).

The 18th century was notable for ironwork in many other parts of Europe. Among Italian smiths was Giovanni-Battista Malagoli of Modena (1729–97), work by whom may be seen in many parts of that city, including the University and on several palaces. At Bologna, in the church of St Petronio, is a sumptuous Baroque grille. Throughout Veneto there are many good specimens, outstanding among which are a pair of pretty little garden gates at the Freia House, Asolo, Treviso, which show German influence; gates and screens of severe French-inspired design at Villa Cordellino-Bissarro, Montevecchio Maggiore, Vicenza, and a grille and gates of complicated scrollwork at the Villa Pisani, Strà, Venezia. Finally, an Italian adaptation of German interlaced scrollwork appears on the extraordinarily beautiful gates at the Villa Manin at Passariano.

Spanish ironwork of the 18th century is on the whole unpleasing, being overcomplicated and much influenced by the Churrigueresque. On the other hand, some good work was done in Portugal, such as cathedral grilles at Lisbon, Vera Cruz and Braga.

The influence of French, English and German ironwork penetrated northern Europe. The Scottish architect and decorator, Charles Cameron, under the patronage of Catherine the Great of Russia, was responsible for ironwork of classical inspiration at the palace of Tsarskoe-Selo, not far from Leningrad. In Leningrad itself, magnificent though heavily designed ironwork abounds; at the Summer Garden, for example, where panels of cast and wrought iron reminiscent of the Versailles railings, are flanked by huge urn-surmounted granite pillars, designed by the architects Y. Felten and Egerov (1784). Lighter

3 A garden arbour, called 'The Birdcage' by Robert Bakewell (early 18th century) at Melbourne Hall, Derby – great *jeu d'espirit* by an English blacksmith.

and simpler railings of wrought iron surround the tombs of Emperors and Empresses from Peter the Great onwards in the Fortress Cathedral of SS. Peter and Paul (1712). Italian influence on ironwork was introduced into Russia by the architect Bartolomeo Francesco Rastrelli, designer of the Winter palace (1762).

An interesting development occurred in another northern country, Sweden, not far from the royal palace of Drottningholm, in four pavilions in the *chinoiserie* taste (about 1760). The ironwork on these is of pleasing but conventional design, but in the grounds a metal tent for the pavilion guards was erected, a structure of sheet iron on a framework of wood (1781). A similar one was erected near to the palace of Haga. These, with the pavilions, are precursors of much exotic metalwork that was to be erected elsewhere early in the 19th century, as at the Brighton pavilion, England, and at the Chinese palace, Palermo, Italy.

Bronzework in the 18th century followed a pattern similar to that of iron, except of course

1 Brass candelabra and chandeliers in the Singers' Hall, Neuschwanstein, Bavaria (German, 19th century), showing the influence of Gothic-inspired Romanticism on contemporary metalwork.

that it was mainly cast. The most important bronzework in this century, however, was domestic rather than architectural, and will be dealt with in that section. Nevertheless, some interesting architectural work was made, like the Baroque lantern groups on the west staircase in the Royal palace, Stockholm, Sweden, by the French craftsman Jacques-Phillipe Bouchardon (1762). Supported by *putti* and surmounted with crowns, these lanterns are among the most delightful examples of the bronze founder's craft.

The bronze gates of the Loggetta in St Mark's Piazza, Venice, are of more complex design. Made by Antonio Gaïa (1684–1769) in 1750, they consist of two square leaves containing allegorical figures, trophies and *putti*, surmounted with further similar figures and devices and two winged lions of St Mark. Again in Venice are the Rococo balustrades in the School of St Rocco, perhaps the work of E. Molinier, one of the founders at the ordnance foundry in the Arsenal.

Much contemporary German work was influenced by French design. Such are the bronze

1

2 Cast-tin tomb of the
Emperor Francis I in the
crypt of the Kapuziner-
kirche, Vienna (18th
century) which is an example
of the rare application of
this metal to large work.

mouldings and decorations on the library of
Frederick II at Sanssouci, designed by Johann
August Nahl the elder (1710–81). Excellent work
was also produced in the Low Countries, including choir grilles at the great church of Dordrecht
(1711–5), and the doors of the church of St
Bavon, Ghent, by Guillaume de Vos (1708–11).
In England, large-scale bronzework of this period
was mainly restricted to statuary.

A powerful group of works are the tombs of
cast tin in the Imperial vault of the Capuchin
church in Vienna. Pure tin, because of its brittle-
ness, is very rarely used for architectural work,
except as a component of bronze and other
alloys. But here it has been used to great effect
for huge tombs of Baroque magnificence for the
Emperors of Austria.

In the 19th century, design became more universal and less national, so that work made in
France, Italy, England or Germany might have
originated almost anywhere. The beginning of
the 19th century was also marked by a great extension of the use of cast-iron, as well as a

3 Wrought-iron stair-
balustrade in the Hotel
Solvay, Brussels, Belgium
(late 19th century), showing the adaptation of
traditional smithcraft to
Art Nouveau design.

4 Detail of wrought-iron
railings at the Houses of
Parliament, Westminster,
London (about 1850). An
English example of
Romantic Gothic design.

flowering of exotic design in all metalwork. Often the exotic design was assisted by the ease with which cast-iron could be adapted to reproduce any desired shape or pattern. Typical of this are the cast iron balustrades of simulated bamboo in the Royal pavilion, Brighton, England. The balustrades on the Hindu gateway at Dromana, Co. Waterford, Ireland (about 1830) are more abstract, being reminiscent of the designs on encaustic tiles from the Middle East.

A different kind of exoticism is apparent in the grotto of Venus (1876–7) at Linderhof, Bavaria, the fantastic castle built by Ludwig II. This grotto consists largely of cast-iron stalactites coated with cement, and contains a lake and a stage, set for the first act of *Tannhäuser*.

Wrought iron was exotic too, yet with more restraint than cast-iron. The staircase balustrade in the Chinese palace at Palermo, Italy, is a typical example, combining a kind of Chinese fret pattern with classical moderation.

But the most typical expression of ironwork at the beginning of the 19th century was the combination of cast and wrought iron in the same work, the wrought iron supplying the basic framework and the cast-iron the decorative element. Often the decorative embellishments were cast on to the wrought iron framework, that is the wrought iron bar was introduced into the mould and the molten metal poured around it so that the two were actually united. Such work may be seen on iron balustrades, balconies and verandahs on terraces and houses in Brighton, Cheltenham, Edinburgh and London in Great Britain, and in Paris, Brussels and many other places on the Continent. Some of the finest work of this kind was made in France during the first Empire, before styles became more internationalized. Examples can be seen at Malmaison.

Later, wrought iron (and cast-iron too) reflected the confusion of contemporary architects, obsessed as they were by historical styles. In England, the wrought-iron gates and screens on the Law Courts in the Strand, London, and the screen beside the chapel at St John's College, Cambridge, try hard to be like the 13th-century Eleanor grille in Westminster Abbey, but due to the standard sections from which they were made, they have a hardness that more effectively reflects the industrial age of the 19th century.

In a different way, the same thing was happening to ironwork made in France during the second Empire with its somewhat pompous classical splendour. Yet there was good work also, including the heavy wrought iron balustrade of the grand staircase at Chantilly by A. G. Moreau. But the most original French smith of the late 19th century was Émile Robert (1860–1924), who laid the foundation for many of the better ateliers of blacksmithery in the 20th century. Among his works are the entrance grille to the Museum of Decorative Arts, Paris, based on a motif of spikes, and that at the French Consulate at Brussels, decorated with cast glass by Lalique, an interesting combination. Robert broke with tradition by discarding scrolls, acanthus leaves and the other motifs of earlier black-smithery, and relied instead upon a restrained use of natural forms.

One of the most elegant late 19th-century developments in wrought iron was the application of the Art Nouveau style, with its sinuous and involved curvaceousness. This was superbly adapted to work made from heated iron, beaten into shape by a hammer; examples vary from the almost stark simplicity of the balustrading and balconies by Charles Rennie Mackintosh on the Glasgow School of Art in Scotland (1897–99), to the balconies, as lush as tropical plants, by Antoni Gaudí on the Milà House, Barcelona, Spain (1905–10), and from the pretty decorations by Joseph Maria Olbrich on the Vienna Secession building at Vienna, Austria (1899), to the overripe curves of the balconies by Victor Horta on the Horta residence in Brussels, Belgium, (1898–1900). Cast-iron, too, was used by Art Nouveau designers in many places, including the façade of the Carson Pirie Scott and Co. Department Store, Chicago, USA, by Louis Sullivan (1899–1904) and on Paris *Métro* stations, by Hector Guimard (about 1900).

As to cast-iron in the second half of the century, whole buildings were made of it, the Crystal Palace, erected in Hyde Park, London, England, for the International Exhibition of 1851, being the greatest functional example. Designed by Sir Joseph Paxton, it consisted of units of cast-iron repeated hundreds of times and filled with glass. The result was superb and it adumbrated an approach to prefabricated building, the effects of which are still apparent in present-day architecture.

The application of cast-iron to building was worldwide, even if its design was not always as original as the Crystal Palace. It was much used in the USA, for façades of shops or stores, and also for complete buildings. One of the greatest centres for highly decorated architectural cast-ironwork, ranging from balustrading to whole buildings, was Melbourne, Australia, where much still survives. Mainly of British origin, it went thence in ships sent to collect grain or wool that would otherwise have sailed empty, and thus acted as ballast as well as merchandise.

Much highly finished cast-ironwork was made in 19th-century Belgium. An example of a work which probably originated there is the enormous pheasant aviary at Waddesdon, Buckinghamshire, England. Of countries other than those mentioned previously, little architectural work of originality was made in the 19th century either in wrought or cast-iron.

Bronze followed much the same path as iron, but there was less of it. Only rarely, in France, was fine work done, this especially during the first Empire. A superb example is the bronze-clad Vendôme column in Paris, which is 43.5 m (over 142 ft) high, based on the style of Trajan's column in Rome. It was designed by Pierre Bergeret and made from captured Russian and Austrian cannon. It was constructed 1806–10 and celebrated Napoleon's victories in the campaigns of 1805–07.

The use of lead on architecture has continued

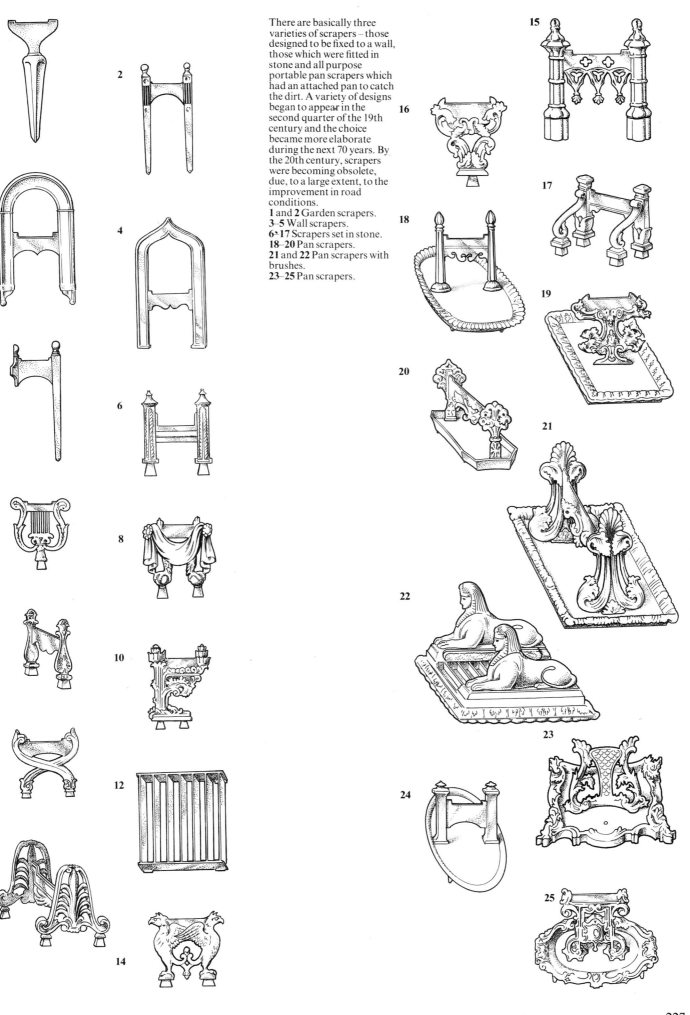

There are basically three varieties of scrapers – those designed to be fixed to a wall, those which were fitted in stone and all purpose portable pan scrapers which had an attached pan to catch the dirt. A variety of designs began to appear in the second quarter of the 19th century and the choice became more elaborate during the next 70 years. By the 20th century, scrapers were becoming obsolete, due, to a large extent, to the improvement in road conditions.

1 and **2** Garden scrapers.
3–5 Wall scrapers.
6–17 Scrapers set in stone.
18–20 Pan scrapers.
21 and **22** Pan scrapers with brushes.
23–25 Pan scrapers.

1

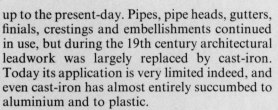

1 An illustration showing
the method of erecting the
framework of the Crystal
Palace in 1851.

2

up to the present-day. Pipes, pipe heads, gutters, finials, crestings and embellishments continued in use, but during the 19th century architectural leadwork was largely replaced by cast-iron. Today its application is very limited indeed, and even cast-iron has almost entirely succumbed to aluminium and to plastic.

Present day wrought ironwork, or what is often passed off for it, is on the whole poor stuff. The cheap, light-steel gates sold by some ironmongers and which are seen throughout suburbia are little better than rubbish, not one bit of them has been touched by a hammer, let alone heated in a fire. Yet good work does exist, particularly in Germany, where the work of Fritz Kühn provides an outstanding instance of how traditionalism and modernism may be successfully united. In France, too, the work of Edgar Brandt and of Raymond Subes, pupil of Robert, is masterly. These smiths successfully evoked in their work the spirit of Art Deco, an element of which is also present in the work of the Hungarian smith Szabo. Some English work also is good, some of it however being taken over from the smith by the skilled machine-operator and fitter, working, in a sense, in the tradition of benchwork. Such are the steel gates to the American Military Cemetery at Madingley, Cambridgeshire, which were made by the mechanic Ernest W. Fox at a Cambridge factory. Finally, it should be noted that stainless-steel has been used to some extent in 20th-century architecture.

Architectural bronzework has been made in the 20th century, in particular doors and grilles for public buildings, banks and insurance offices. A cast-bronze entrance grille is on the University Library, Cambridge, England, designed by Sir Giles Gilbert Scott (1931–34). Similar work, much of it depressingly pompous, is to be found in almost every large town throughout Europe and America, with little evidence to show in what county it was either designed or made.

Aluminium, so rare at the time of the second

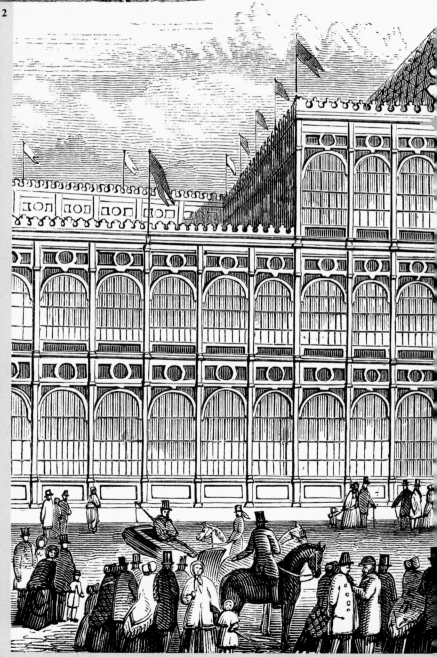

Empire that it was considered a precious metal, has come into its own in the present century. It was used to some extent in the 19th century (Alfred Gilbert's statue of Eros in Piccadilly Circus, London, England, is an aluminium casting) but it was not until well into the 20th century that its architectural use became widespread. Anodizing, an electro-chemical treatment, has been widely used since 1945 to colour sheets of the metal used for cladding buildings. One of the most impressive examples of the architectural applications of aluminium is on the Brussels Atomium designed by the Belgian architects André and Jean Polak for the 1958 exhibition. It is 109 m (over 357 ft) high and has a steel framework covered in polished aluminium sheet.

2 The Crystal Palace was designed by Joseph Paxton, who had been gardener to the sixth Duke of Devonshire. The design of the Palace grew out of a waterlily glasshouse designed by Paxton for the Duke.

Domestic Metalwork

The development of domestic metalwork is quite similar to that of architectural metalwork, except that in many cases it was the smaller objects of domestic use that preceded the larger architectural applications.

The ancient world was dominated by bronze, and some of the objects made in the first two millenniums B.C. remain unsurpassed for beauty. Examples of these are many of the hand mirrors made in Egypt, Greece and the Roman world. The basic design, wherever the mirror happened to be made, was largely the same as that of a modern mirror: a highly polished disc to provide the reflecting surface, sometimes decorated on its reverse, with a handle which was also usually decorated. The handles of mirrors were sometimes cast in the form of a figure, human or divine and sometimes the periphery of the disc had cast figures of cupids or animals. Occasionally the reverse side of the disc was engraved with an allegorical scene, as in some Etruscan examples.

But bronze was used for all kinds of things: for votive objects by the Celts, for throne decorations by the Assyrians, for vases, lamps and boxes by the Greeks and Romans, for plaquettes by the Byzantines. The list could be extended almost indefinitely. In China, fine cast bronze was in extensive use by the second millenium B.C. for objects as varied as those made in the West, from hollow vessels to statuettes.

Oriental Bronzes

Bronze working in eastern Asia started about 1500 B.C., during the Shang dynasty in China (1766–1122 B.C.).

The sophisticated style of Shang bronzes suggests a long tradition of metal working, yet there is little evidence of this in China. The development of bronze metallurgy about 2500 B.C. in western Asia also suggests that the original ideas came from there. However, Chinese bronze work, like other Chinese crafts, followed its own distinctive evolution.

Shang bronzes were primarily ritual vessels and weapons. The vessels are of specific and named shapes, each with its own function. They served as containers of food, wine and water, and were included in burials to provide nourishment for the soul. Some forms had been made during the earlier Stone Age cultures of China, such as the tripod, li, a shape unique to China. Ting, a food cauldron with three or four solid legs is the best known vessel, and, with bronze bells, chung was the most highly valued by the Chinese.

During the Shang Dynasty (1600–1027 B.C.) some of the enduring features of Chinese culture were established. The social system was feudalistic, fiefs were held from the ruler and neighbouring states paid tribute. A small, city-dwelling elite, supported by peasantry, fostered craft specialization. Bronze workers formed secret societies, and such 'brotherhoods' have been a significant social factor throughout Chinese history from earliest times.

There was a concern for man's fate after death, and society was integrated by ritual practices which particularly involved the ruler. The focus of these rituals was sacrifice, the means to gain power and to attune the ruler to the Will of Heaven. As a result bronze vessels were used to contain both animal and human offerings. Lesser men than the ruler also gave sacrifices to their ancestors.

The control of bronze working was recognized as an essential to the mythology surrounding the ancestors of the ruling house (which legitimated the rule of the living king) before the five legendary Shang Emperors brought the arts of civilization to the Chinese. The third Emperor, Yu, mapped the universe and mastered the arts of water control and metalwork. Yu cast nine cauldrons as symbols of his power. Succeeding rulers held such cauldrons as well as axes, being further symbols of the ruler's power to punish. The bronze dagger-axe, ko, was another typically Chinese shape.

Shang vessels are decorated in high relief. Animals, wild, domesticated and imaginary, are common motifs, including horses, water buffalo, rams, tigers, elephants, deer and dragons. These may be shown in part or combination, in naturalistic or stylized form. The dominant motif is the tao-thieh, the 'glutton', a horned dragon who averts evil, and may derive from shamanistic beliefs current before Chinese civilization formed.

Other motifs are of owls and parrots, fish,

1 Shang bronze-rams and t'ao-thieh. The t'ao-thieh is a composite creature which was interpreted in various ways at different times: as a sky god, as the head and skin of a bear such as shamans wore before the development of Taoism, its description as 'glutton' is an attribution made much later in the Sung period.

snakes and cicadas; hunting scenes and human features are sometimes depicted. Typical abstract decoration, either in the raised areas or as background, includes catherine wheels, fretted patterns and geometric shapes: diamonds and lozenges.

During the following Chou Dynasty (1027–249 B.C.) the forms of bronzes changed. Spouted vessels and stylized birds were made, the ting and li shapes were modified, and modelling was often coarser with shallower relief. Some motifs were discarded, such as the tao-thieh and cicadas, and more commonplace articles such as ladles and spoons were made. About 600 B.C. the influence of nomadic peoples from central Asia and the Ordos region begins to show in the animal

The fine workmanship of Shang and early Chou bronzes was helped by their high lead content – 15 per cent or even 30 per cent in some cases. designs which can be found on bronze vessels. This reduced the melting point, improved the flow in casting and reduced the risk of surface flaws. The softness of high lead bronze also made it easier to chisel and cold finish the articles. Bronzes were cast in fired clay moulds and, towards the end of the Chou, by the lost wax or *cire perdue* method.

When the Chou Dynasty ended, bronze working declined and some of the associated rituals were forgotten, although the ruler's prestige still depended on his possession of cauldrons and bells.

2 Sung wine vessel in the form of a phoenix. From the start of the Sung dynasty, the phoenix was the emblem of the empress; this ruler of the birds was a composite creature consisting of the cock, duck, peacock, pheasant and crane. In later folk art the phoenix symbolized a bride.

3 Six Dynasties dragon. The dragon, lung, was the chief of all creatures and always a major symbol in Chinese thought. It was a benevolent creature which brought prosperity and represented many ideas: the power of the emperor, the Taoist Way, adaptability, the force of Yang.

In the Han Dynasty (206 B.C.–A.D. 220) the increasing use of iron tools and cast-iron moulds led to a revival in bronze working. Fine figures of humans and animals were produced, for example bears and horses, model chariots, horse harness, belt hooks and some swords and knives, although most weapons were now made of iron. Vessels generally had simple, functional shapes and might be decorated with gold and silver inlay. This wider use of bronze for domestic and decorative purposes coincided with the end of feudalism and the adoption of a bureaucratic form of government. Nevertheless, the Han emperors were still concerned with the ritual aspects of bronzes, the remaining traditional lore of ritual vessels was recorded and it was decreed that all discovered antique bronzes were to be presented to the emperor.

With the establishment of Taoism, about 500 B.C., the decorations on bronzes were regarded as having magical significance and providing a means for the harmonious flow of energy in the observer, the gold markings in bronzes symbolizing the paths of Tao. Taoist communities were especially involved in technological activities and preceded metalworking with rituals of abstention and purification. Bronze mirrors, a notable feature of the Han period, often symbolize Taoist beliefs in their decoration and design: the Five Elements, Yang and Yin and the ultimate source T'ai-chi.

Bronze mirrors and exceptionally fine figures,

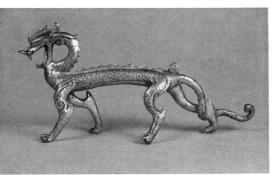

such as horses and owls, were also produced about A.D. 600–800 during the T'ang Dynasty, at which time another peak in Chinese arts occurred. After this, Buddhism provided the main stimulus for bronzework in China, as elsewhere in Asia.

During the Sung Dynasty (A.D. 960–1279) many copies of earlier bronzes were made, often decorated by stamping rather than carving the mould. This method produced blunt-edged designs. Taoist, Confucian and Buddhist symbols were popular decorations. At the same time antique bronzes were collected and studied, and the patina was particularly admired. In 1098 a ten volume catalogue *Pictures for the Study of Antiquity* illustrated 211 bronzes in the Imperial collection; one of these bronzes was from the last Shang capital near An-Yang, and was then more than 2000 years old.

1

European Metalwork

Iron in antiquity was probably used for domestic objects to a greater extent than is now evident, for rust and other corrosives must have destroyed much, with the result that, apart from a few fragments of various artefacts, there is nothing to indicate how widely it was used.

Lead, too, is only represented by a handful of objects, though these are varied in form, among them Egyptian votive slabs, Roman cups and lamps. Greek weights, vases, and plummets.

The same pattern of usage for these metals and alloys continued from the fall of the Roman empire until the dawn of the Middle Ages. Artistically, as may be expected, design was cruder in the early part of this period, yet it often has a barbaric strength and compelling spontaneity. It varies from the relatively simple design and decoration on bronze stewpots made by Huns, to highly decorated cruciform brooches made by Anglo-Saxons. Such a splendid specimen as the wonderful shrine of St Patrick's bell or Bell of the Will appears later (about 1100). This was made to the order of Donal O'Loughlin, King of Ireland (National Museum, Dublin), and consists of bronze worked in a combination of casting, sheet metalwork and forging, decorated with gemstones. Another important work is the font decorated with three-dimensional figures illustrating the life of John the Baptist and supported

1 Chola bronze – Siva. Indian figures are usually carried in religious processions or serve as holders for temple lamps. Southern Indian bronzes are usually Hindu figures, northern Indian figures are usually Buddhist and Jain and are associated with monastic usage. Bronzes are made on commission by guilds of professional metalworkers based in towns and cities or by hereditary village craftsmen. From the 7th century onwards, bronze sculptures were made by the lost wax method.

2 Lokapala Virupaksa. The Lokapalas guard the four points of the compass. Virupaksa is the Guardian of the West, King of the Nagas – snakes with magical powers who live in treasure laden palaces at the bottoms of lakes. Virupaksa is also attendant upon Maitreya, the future Buddha, and carries a reliquary in the form of a stupa and a serpent.

2

by bulls, in the church of St Barthélémy, Liège, Belgium (12th century).

The Gloucester candelabrum made about 1112 and dedicated to the Abbey of St Peter at Gloucester, England, is of almost oriental splendour (Victoria and Albert Museum, London). Another handsome 12th-century candelabrum, this one having seven·branches, and measuring 5 m (over 16 ft) in height, is in Brunswick cathedral, Germany; it is said to have been the gift of Henry the Lion, Duke of Saxony. A 12th-century bronze door-knocker in the form of a lion and a ring is in Lausanne cathedral, Switzerland. A bronze thurible of the same century, architectural in form, inscribed with the name Gosbertus, is in

vives. Two examples will suffice. A lead sheet in the British Museum inscribed with an edict of Charlemagne, in which he assumes the title of Emperor of the West, and bearing the date 18 September 801. And a 12th-century casket in the form of two boxes, one inside the other, which once contained the heart of Richard Coeur-de-Lion, discovered in 1838 in the choir of Rouen cathedral, France, and bearing the inscription: HIC . JACET . COR . RICARDI . REGIS . ANGLORUM (Here rests the heart of Richard King of the English).

With the 13th century came the beginning, especially in France, of a period of brilliant domestic ironwork dominated by the technique

3

3 This bronze head of a queen mother is said to have been instituted in Benin by King Besigie who reigned in the early 16th century. It was cast by the *cire perdue* method and placed on an altar dedicated to the deceased queen mother. The distinctive hairstyle represents a cap or coral beads.

4 The shrine of St Patrick's bell, about 1100, is a remarkable specimen for its period. It consists of bronze worked in a combination of casting, sheet metalwork and forging. It is decorated with gemstones.

4

the cathedral of Trier (Rhineland-Palatinate, Germany). Among its architectural details it embodies busts of Moses, Aaron, Isaac and Jeremiah, with Solomon enthroned at its apex. Laton or latten was also used at this time, especially for such utensils as ewers, like the 13th-century German specimen in the form of a lion in the British Museum, London.

Little domestic ironwork survives from before the 12th century. As suggested in the architectural metalwork section, little enough large work remains, so it is hardly to be expected that smaller works will have survived. However, there are a few fragments which remain; one or two early locks and furniture fittings, and here and there a horse shoe, but little more.

Lead was widely used, mines being operated in France, England, Saxony, Silesia, Bohemia and Andalusia, yet an insignificant amount sur-

of the locksmith and closely influenced by that of the armourer. Such objects made at this early date are very rare, but those that do remain illustrate the virtuosity of which craftsmen were already capable. One such is a pair of wafering irons – a pair of tongs with its terminations in the form of two engraved plates, between which batter is poured, and which are then heated so that wafers for communion hosts are made. Later the irons were adapted for household purposes, such as making waffles. This pair of irons is so elaborately engraved that it is a *tour de force* in this alone, and is in Cluny Museum, Paris.

Despite the rarity of actual specimens of 13th-century benchwork, one or two pattern books survive which give some idea of the scope of the work made at this period. One series of designs by the architect Alessandro Romani, is in the Public Library at Siena, Italy.

In the next two centuries, and indeed until the 18th century, the objects made by benchwork multiplied enormously. It would be difficult to imagine greater refinement in ironwork than that which was achieved in this work. The vast amount of labour involved, to say nothing of the loving care in making a lock, is almost impossible to assess. There is, on a miniature scale, as much carving in a few square inches as would be present on many a cathedral wall or reredos. The

minute, jewel-like precision attained in such an uncompromising material, well matches the mathematical construction of Gothic architecture in general. And although the lock is a marvellous specimen, it is by no means unique. Such locks, large and small, are the pride of the fine collections at the Cluny Museum, Paris, at the Le Secq des Tournelles Museum, Rouen, and at the Victoria and Albert Museum, London. They were made right up to the latter part of the 18th century, reflecting the taste of the period in which they were made. Sometimes, in the later periods, they were decorated with *putti* and other allegorical figures. Padlocks also were made throughout these centuries.

As with the locks, so with the keys. The bows (handles) of some 15th- and 16th-century examples are decorated with arms or monograms, while the bits (the parts that move the wards in the lock) are cut with such complication and precision that they look like gatherings of Gothic lace. Later there was a tendency for the bows to be cast, but the decoration did not diminish.

Apart from locks and keys, the benchworker made many other objects, including furniture fittings (hinges, bolts and key-escutcheons), nails with ornamental heads, judas grilles (which were fitted to doors so that the householder could see who was knocking), door knockers, caskets (a very beautiful group), sewing accessories, tableware, bag frames, seals, candlesticks, lecterns, and even statuettes.

The benchworker's tools were made as beautifully as his products. Hammers, vices, chisels, hacksaws, shears, tongs, small lathes and many others were as carefully wrought and as elegantly

1 Wrought-iron casket (German, 16th century). It is locked through the lid and the key can be seen in position.

2 French and German steel keys (late 17th century). The bows, or handles, reflect the decorative fashions of the time, while some bear coronets and heraldic charges.

3 Steel alms-box (French, 16th century). The padlock, like its 20th century counterparts, is completely functional; the frilled sheet-metal cover on the other hand, is purely decorative.

decorated as the locks, keys and other artefacts that came from their owners' workshops.

The surface decoration of benchwork is finely conceived and applied. Some objects, such as jewelry (even finger rings were made) were gilded all over. But the commonest decoration was by engraving, etching or, especially in the earlier work, by sculpting. Fretwork and castings were also used, the former being sometimes underlaid with leather, velvet or cloth, when it is called *marouflage*. Some doorplates thus decorated are in King's College Chapel, Cambridge, England (early 16th century).

One of the most attractive forms of surface decoration was damascening, also used on fine armour. It originated in Asia or Asia Minor, its name being taken from Damascus, a centre for sword smiths, where it originated; it was perhaps introduced by such craftsmen into Spain during the Arab rule, whence its use must have spread over Europe. It consists of making undercut dovetailed grooves on the object to be decorated, filling them with silver, gold or copper wire and hammering it so that it fills them out, and becomes keyed in position.

Not all of the work was small. Large robust coffers with complicated locks, for containing treasure or documents, were not uncommon. Such a specimen as the 16th-century coffer in the Archaeological Museum, Madrid, Spain, must have been almost impossible to penetrate without a key. It is also superbly decorated, especially on the handles, lock escutcheon and even on the actual mechanism of the lock.

Another large object is the wrought iron chandelier in the church of Vreden, Westphalia, Germany (1489). This consists of a big ring of fretwork, around which are Gothic niches containing statuettes of saints, in front of each of which is a little crown surrounding a candleholder. Above all of this, in the centre, is a figure of the Virgin and Child standing on a crescent moon, with rays of glory surrounding them. Above this statuette is a hexagonal structure again decorated with fretwork and with applied lettering; at each corner is a little spire, and the whole is in turn surmounted by two more figures and further spires and at the apex is yet another spire and a little coronet.

Benchwork was used also in Italy, where some of its finest products were lanterns. Four, on the Strozzi Palace in Florence, are in the form of hexagonal temples; they were made by Nicolo Grosso, called Caparra, in 1500. Another, by the same craftsman, derived, with variations, from the same design is on the Guadagni Palace in the same city. This classical detailing is completely of the Renaissance, yet the lanterns were made at a time when the Gothic style still prevailed in 4 most other parts of Europe.

Forged ironwork was used for domestic utensils throughout this period, but not much is left. The expensive items made in benchwork would have received special care and therefore have had a greater chance of survival. Nevertheless, some things remain including items of furniture. Such is the 16th century gilded wrought iron four-poster bed, probably of Sicilian make, now in the Bagatti Valsecchi House, Milan, Italy. It is elaborately wrought with twisted uprights surmounted by bouquets of flowers and with great pyramids of flowers at the foot and the head. An extensive collection of similar beds is in the Sicilian Ethnographical Museum near Palermo.

During the whole of this period bronze and brass continued in use. Bronze cauldrons were cast, usually with legs, but sometimes without if they were intended for hanging from a chimney crane. They usually have two handles and are sometimes decorated with bands, either plain or patterned. The design was probably developed from bronze-age cauldrons made of riveted sheet-metal, such as had been used in the 8th or 9th centuries B.C.

Skillets and posnets or pipkins of various designs were also made. They were a kind of deep pan or saucepan with legs (usually three) and with a long handle decorated with a pattern or with the name of the owner or maker, or with a motto or text. There was a type without legs for use with a wrought iron stand. They were usually made of brass or bell metal, and later were some-

4 Wrought-iron and steel coffer (Spanish, 16th century), in the Museo Arqueologico Nacional, Madrid. The elaborate lock inside the lid is typical of such strong-boxes.

times fitted with cast-iron handles. They were used as early as the 13th century, but were made as late as the 19th century and were known in colonial America; there is one at Mount Vernon, George Washington's home.

Other cast bronze utensils made in the Middle Ages and soon after included jugs, ewers, pestles and mortars and candlesticks, some of them elaborately decorated and of beautiful shape. But as with other things, they continued to be

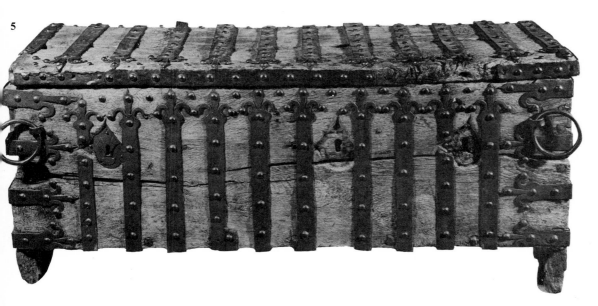

5 A German wood coffer reinforced with iron strips in Marburg University Museum. It is a less decorative, more functional example than the Spanish example above.

1 Cast-iron fireback (English, first half of the 16th century). The decorative motifs were made by pressing individual patterns into the sand of the mould.

2 Cast-iron firedogs (English, 16th and 17th centuries). The cast-iron front upright (stauke) is to prevent the logs from falling out of the fire, and the horizontal (billet) bar supports them.

3 Italian cast-bronze baptismal bowl by Giovanni Albeighetti.

made for long afterwards, and even until the present century. A Renaissance bronze ewer by Desiderio da Firenze is outstanding, with its richly moulded decorations of swags, masks, fruit and other devices. In the same class is a Venetian bronze door-knocker of the early 17th century, in the manner of Tiziano Aspetti. It depicts a sea nymph flanked by boys riding on dolphins.

Of bronze benchwork an interesting group is formed by the little brass caskets made in Germany and the Low Countries in the 16th century. Sometimes they are only 50 to 75 mm long. They are models of refinement, every decorative resource being used to heighten their *belle tournure*, including engraving.

The bronze or brass lecterns of the time are excellent. These were usually cast with elaborate benchwork added, and had as their main feature, as they still do an eagle (the symbol of St John the Evangelist) with outspread wings on which the Bible was laid for reading.

Laton was much used for memorial brasses, which originated in the Low Countries at about the first quarter of the 13th century. These plates were engraved with an effigy or with emblems

and inscriptions. Many brasses have been destroyed, especially on the Continent, but the earliest extant example is at Verden, near Hanover, Germany; it commemorates Bishop Yso Wilpe, who died in 1231. Some of the brasses in England were Continental work, like that of Thomas Pounder and his wife at Ipswich, which is Flemish (1525). But the majority are English; there are about 10,000 examples remaining in England, more in fact than in all of the rest of Europe.

Meanwhile work in cast-iron had been progressing. It was used for early ordnance, which had been made possible by the invention of gunpowder in 1325. The first ordnance was as dangerous to those who were firing it as it was to the enemy, but its use persisted, and out of the resulting cast-iron industry which developed in the Weald of England grew the manufacture of domestic cast-ironwork.

The cast-iron grave slab was one of the earliest products; it might have been suggested by the memorial brass. One or two early examples still remain. The oldest is in Burwash church, Sussex (mid 16th century), decorated with a cross and has, in Lombardic characters, the inscription in relief: ORATE P. ANNEMA JHONE COLLINS (Pray for the soul of Joan Collins). Another, much closer in design to brasses, is in Crowhurst church, Surrey; it is a memorial to Anne Forster (1591) and bears an inscription, heraldry, figures and a representation of a shrouded corpse. Cast-iron grave slabs were made until the late 19th century; one as late as 1885 is in St Leonard's churchyard, Bilston.

Closely related in form to grave slabs are firebacks, which originated at about the beginning of the 15th century. They were, it is thought, first made for use in the newly-introduced wall-fireplace, both to protect the wall and to radiate the heat of the fire. The first ones were probably simple slabs of cast-iron, but they soon became

4 Sheet-copper kitchenware in the Kitchen at Hardwick Hall, Derbyshire. These utensils were probably made in the 18th or 19th centuries, but it is often difficult to date them exactly as the types changed little over the years. The coffee-pot and fish kettle on the bottom shelf are particularly fine.

5 Dutch brass warming-pan with wrought-iron handle (1602), in the Victoria and Albert Museum. The design of the perforated lid is a particularly fine example of this type of decoration.

decorated. A plain board was used as the basic pattern, and the mould was open topped. After the pattern's removal, decoration was impressed into the sand. The commonest impressions were taken from stiffened lengths of rope, pushed into the sand to form patterns such as pentagrams, triangles, squares and borders. Sometimes the founder would push the impression of his hand or of some of his tools into the sand. Such decorations long persisted and were used alongside more sophisticated decorations on the same backs.

In time, firebacks made from patterns carved in one piece became the norm. The earliest English specimen dates from 1548. Decorations vary enormously and include heraldry, devices, flowers and scenes, allegorical, biblical and domestic. Shape also altered somewhat over the years; at first firebacks were simple horizontal rectangles, sometimes with a pointed or curved top. Later they became less elongated and had more elaborate tops; from the end of the 17th century they became roughly square, again with decorative tops, to fit into the newer, smaller type of fireplace. They were made into the 19th century, and reproductions are still cast.

Continental centres for casting firebacks included Germany and Holland, and backs from these areas, imported into England from the time of the accession of William and Mary in 1689, for a time almost completely eclipsed the English production. Dutch and German backs are usually more finely cast than the English ones. They are not so thick and are much more elaborate in design, some completely mannerist, others Baroque. Moreover, their subject matter is more varied, embracing subjects from classical mythology, allegories of virtues and ideas, and elaborate flower-pieces. French firebacks (and firecheeks for protecting the side walls of the fireplace) from Versailles are exhibited in the Museum of Decorative Arts, Paris; they depict the crowned sun, a fleur-de-lys or a royal cipher, supported by sphinxes or griffons (late 17th century). French backs were made into the 18th century and carried religious or secular scenes.

Firedogs or andirons have an even longer history than firebacks. They were used in Roman times, long before the invention of the wall fireplace, when the fire was made in the centre of the house and the smoke escaped through a hole in the roof. Their parts are known as the stauke (the front, usually decorated, upright) and the billet (horizontal) bar. The billet bar supported the logs and the stauke was to prevent them from falling out of the fireplace. The earliest firedogs were made of wrought iron, but from the middle of the 16th century the staukes were cast on to the billet bars. The greatest English centre for the production of the latter was the Weald.

From the 16th century, firedogs became more elaborate, and though the simpler types were still used in ordinary houses and the kitchens of big houses, the more flamboyant types were used in the main rooms of big houses. Before long they became no more than a decorative adjunct to the fireplace, in elaborately-wrought and highly-polished brass, bronze, steel and even silver.

237

Cast-iron holloware should also be mentioned (cauldrons, bowls and mortars for instance), which was made in the Low Countries and in England in great quantities from the 16th century onwards. Design followed that of similar bronzework, albeit more simply.

During the 17th century brass and bronzework continued along the lines already described. Some beautiful brass alms-dishes in sheet metalwork were made, especially in the Low Countries, and also items such as bedwarmers. These bedwarmers, first used in the 16th century, were often made of copper; earlier specimens had wrought iron handles, later superseded by wooden handles. The lids were decorated by engraving, by repoussé, or by piercing, sometimes with erotic subjects.

There were, too, skimmers (perforated discs) of brass or copper, and sometimes of tinned iron, used in the kitchen or dairy for operations such as separating cream from milk, and brass chestnut-roasters, in form like little warming pans, with perforations all round. Similar objects included saucepans, fish kettles, beer warmers, jugs, pails and innumerable other artefacts, made either in copper or brass, and by sheet metalworking. These objects are usually quite functional and it is therefore often impossible to judge

from which country a specimen has originated or what date should be assigned to it. They were used in most, if not all, European countries and also in the USA. Most specimens that one is likely to come across will probably be later rather than earlier in date.

Both copper and brass were used for curfews (from the French *couvre-feu* – cover fire), which were used from early in the Middle Ages to cover the embers of a fire overnight, to keep it smoul-

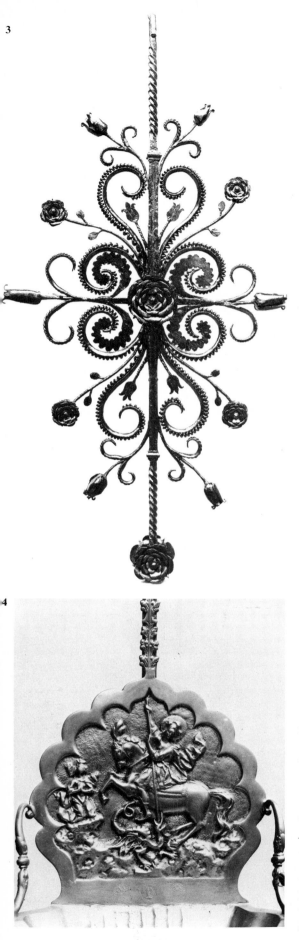

dering. The curfew was a half dome open at the back, so that it could be pushed against the wall of the fireplace, and was fitted with a handle and usually decorated with repoussé.

Holland was noted for its brass chandeliers, of a type also made in England. The usual pattern consisted of a large central brass ball from which scrolled arms radiated, carrying candle sockets at their extremities. A finial, often in the form of a bird, was provided at the apex of the structure, which was sometimes suspended by an elaborate wrought iron hanger. These chandeliers were made by a combination of casting and benchwork. In England they were most often used in churches and public buildings, whereas in Holland they were commonly found in private houses. Excellent chandeliers were also made in Germany.

Bronzework more refined than the foregoing was also made during the 17th century. In France, in the reign of Louis XIV it was used, together with mosaics and coloured stones, for the enrichment of furniture; numerous examples are displayed in the Museum of Decorative Arts, Paris. In Italy the many bronze artefacts of the time included candelabra and a profusion of other small objects, with Rococo embellishments replacing earlier decorative elements. In Spain the activity of bronze founders was not great, but some objects, especially for ecclesiastical use, were made.

Domestic ironwork in the 17th century was often attractive, as evident from the many French examples at the Cluny Museum, Paris, outstanding among which is a magnificent chandelier with heraldic embellishments. In the Le Secq des Tournelles Museum, Rouen, is a fine wrought iron lectern, consisting of a triangular shaft with scrolled feet, and ornamented with scrolls and leaves. In Italy a splendid instance of how simple forged shapes may be used to make a fine design (the very essence of good blacksmithery) is a cresset of riveted construction on the Saminiati Palace at Lucca. Comparable in conception, but considerably more ornamented, are many cemetery crosses made in Germany and Austria during the same century.

Apart from grand work, simple domestic ironwork at this time was made all over Europe: things such as gridirons, trivets, toasting irons and toasting forks, and so on. Sometimes they are completely functional, but often they are decorated with pleasing and quite rich scrollwork. As already remarked in the case of some copper and brasswork, it is often impossible to judge precisely the country of origin or the date of any given piece.

During the 17th century there was a considerable increase in the use of lead cisterns in the courtyards and paved areas of houses. Cisterns had been used since the previous century, but such early examples are of the greatest rarity. The 17th-century and later specimens are usually pleasingly decorated, a favourite scheme being an adaptation of framed strapwork, with armorial bearings, flowers, cupids, dolphins, stags or classical motifs; they nearly always bear a date.

3 Wrought-iron suspension-rod for a chandelier (English, about 1700). This was intended to carry a chandelier such as the Dutch one illustrated opposite. It is, however, unusually elaborate, and the tulips, roses and ferns are all made with great sensibility.

4 Pewter basin and cistern (South German 1742). The cast relief of St George and the Dragon is finely conceived. Note the hallmarks under this design.

1 Two pewter measures in the Victoria and Albert Museum. Scottish 18th century; English about 1700. These are two simple, yet pleasing specimens of sheet-metal pewterware. Such measures were made up until the end of the 19th century.

2 Polished steel fireplace in the dining room at Arbury Hall, Warwickshire (English, late 18th century). A Neo-classical design which also shows some evidence of the dawning fashion for more exotic styles.

the late 18th and 19th centuries, it was largely superseded by a harder alloy called Britannia metal (tin, together with about 5 to 10 per cent antimony, sometimes with a small amount of copper). Pewter was usually worked by sheet metalwork, with the addition of castings for small mountings such as handles, knobs and feet. Decoration was applied by casting, engraving and repoussé, the last less common than the others. It was widely used in Great Britain, some very fine things being made in Scotland, and on the Continent, particularly in Germany, Scandinavia, Holland, Flanders, France and Austria.

All kinds of objects were made: spoons, porringers, dishes, plates, tankards, flagons, measures, sauceboats, chalices, candlesticks, tea and coffee pots and cruets, are but a few. Usually, British pewter is more restrained in decoration than Continental pieces, relying largely on its intrinsic shape for effect. Continental work is often elaborately decorated, sometimes as much as the finest silver. American pewter is closer to the British and usually very restrained, though a few American objects have a quite baroque splendour, such as some candlesticks made by Johann Christopher Heyne, Pennsylvania (about 1756–80). But these are decorated with religious motifs and, like much of Heyne's work were intended for ecclesiastical use.

The usual type is box-shaped, but cylindrical and semi-cylindrical types exist, though they are scarcer. The sides and bottoms were cast and welded together, the cylindrical ones being, of course, first curved. Lead pumps were also made, but are now rare.

Of alloys of lead, the most important in the domestic context is pewter, but today what is passed off as modern pewter is more often tin. It has been used since Roman times, but its heyday was from the 16th to the 18th centuries. In

3 Sheet metal and enamelled tea or coffee urn decorated with a pastoral scene (Pontypool, late 18th century), in the National Museum of Wales.

4 Designs for candelabra by Matthew Boulton (1728–1809), the Birmingham inventor and metalworker.

kinds and Scottish lamps or cruses for burning oil; these were in the form of two oval, lipped cups, one above the other, the top one to hold the oil and a lighted wick, the lower one to catch the drips. Rushlight holders were another lighting appliance used in poorer English homes. They consisted of small upright tongs set in a base, usually a heavy piece of wood, which held a burning rushlight (a rush dipped in tallow) which was moved along as it burned down. They came into use after a tax was put on candles in 1709 and continued even after the repeal of the candle tax in 1831.

Among other artefacts were sheet-metal spout-lamps for burning oil, which looked somewhat like an odd-shaped kettle on a leg, the spout

French domestic ironwork of the 18th century was still dominated by benchwork. This is shown by the collection in the Le Secq des Tournelles Museum, Rouen, in which there are fire irons, firedogs, locks, knockers, comfit boxes, cane handles, *necessaires*, chatelaines, needlecases and a host of other objects, all made of chiselled iron and decorated with repoussé, damascening, etching or engraving.

Italian work of the 18th century is more representative of forging, and includes candelabra, lanterns, beds like those made in the 16th century, and well cranes. In Spain and Portugal, sanctuary lamps, candelabra, and door lamps and brackets are of particular note; there are some noteworthy large lamps in the cathedral at Lisbon. German work of the time includes chandeliers, lanterns, knockers and small sculpture in steel, many of these things being strongly influenced by French design. Signs for inns and shops of charming Rococo design, made during the 18th century, may still be seen in position in many places in Germany and Austria.

Of everyday artefacts of a kind made all over Europe in the 18th century are sugar nippers and hammers (for breaking up sugar loaves), kitchen knives and pastry jiggers (for cutting out pastry), chimney jacks, and candle snuffers of infinite variety, all made by benchwork. Forged work includes stands for warming plates in front of the fire, and goffering irons with a socket for receiving a heated iron or poker, and over which frills, ruffles and so on were prepared; later, in the 19th century, goffering irons usually had cast-iron bases. There were also various lighting appliances including candlesticks and lanterns of many

holding the wick; and sheet-metal candle-moulds and boxes, kettles, and candlesticks, some of which, for bedroom use, were fitted with cylindrical glasses. Office candlesticks with two holders and shades, all adjustable, sometimes combined wrought iron and sheet steel, the central stem and scrolled supports of iron, the base (sometimes filled with lead), holders and shades

(usually prettily perforated) of steel; these are late 18th or early 19th century.

Firegrates of polished steel and various alloys, including Paktong, were widely used in the 18th century. Made by a combination of blacksmithery and benchwork and sometimes casting, they were decorated with perforations that included Rococo and Gothic patterns, classical arcading and Chinese fret. Matching fenders were also made. The firebasket itself was usually of plain forged wrought iron.

Cast-iron was used for fireplaces, often with great imagination, as on late 18th century hob grates, which consisted of two cast-iron boxes or pillars, often delightfully decorated, connected by wrought iron firebars. Apart from these there were hundreds of different designs for framed grates.

Wrought iron fire irons – pokers, shovels, tongs, log forks – varied considerably in the elaboration of their design, but basically they have not altered much over the centuries. The more elaborate really differ from simpler ones only in their handles, which are sometimes cast

bronze, brass or iron, or of chiselled or forged steel or iron. One basic variation, however, is in the design of tongs, which may be either of the spring or hinged pattern; the former, which have a bow-shaped spring in place of a hinge, were not used until the late 18th century, but the latter were in use as early as the 17th century.

An aspect of sheet metalwork practised widely in the 18th century was the manufacture of japanned ware. It was made in Holland, France and Great Britain, and although each produced good work, that made in France was of the best general quality. The lacquer was applied and repeatedly stoved at a low temperature, and one stoving could last as long as three weeks. The metal most frequently used was tinned steel, for this helped to give great hardness to the finished surface, but other metals and alloys were also used, including copper and Britannia metal.

Japanned ware covered an enormous range of objects, including trays, urns, vases, tea and coffee pots, candlesticks and snuffers, coffee urns and coal vases. The decoration varied, much of it *chinoiserie* (for japanned work was at first made to meet a demand for real Japanese lacquer, the export of which was banned in the 17th century), but there were many other forms – flowers, rustic scenes, tortoiseshell and abstract patterning among them. Sometimes japanned work was fitted with bronze, ormolu or gilded steel mountings.

Bronze in the 18th century was frequently of a high standard, especially in France. Two of the greatest French bronze founders of the time were Jacques Caffieri (1678–1755) and his son, Philippe (1714–74), whose output was enormous and included fine chandeliers, a specimen of which is in the Mazarine library, Paris. A pair of ormolu firedogs by Jacques Caffieri is in the Wallace Collection, London, England. The works of the Caffieri are notable for their use of Rococo design. Other French bronzeworkers in the Rococo style included F.-P. Gallien, Fermier Antoine Lechaudel, Georges-Alexandre Moreau fils, who worked with the Caffieri, Feuchère, and Jacques Renard, a fine candelabrum by whom is in Autun cathedral.

1 Bronze pestle and mortar (English, early 18th century). Mortars are among the most decorative of early holloware, some of them being covered with cast lettering and devices; others like this one, are plain.

2 Ormolu (gilded bronze) *chenets* or firedogs attributed to J. Caffieri (French, 18th century) in the Wallace Collection, London. Unlike the functional firedogs illustrated on page 236, these later ones are purely decorative; some were even made of silver.

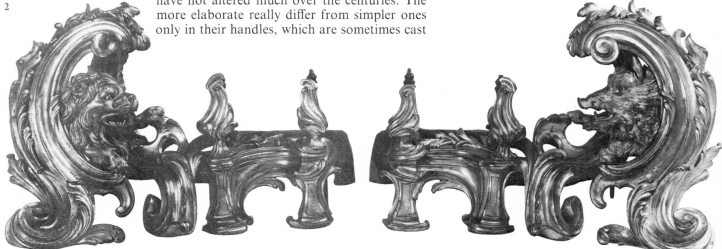

Later in the century there was a return to classical style, one of the foremost exponents of which was the bronzeworker Gouthière (1740–1806), whose patrons included Madame Dubarry. At Versailles there are chandeliers by him in the form of a central torch surrounded by four baby fauns playing trumpets; scrolled arms with rosettes and leaves grow from the bottom of the torch, and each one has a candle socket at its extremity.

In Germany, notable work was done in the Potsdam atelier of the Swiss craftsman, Jean-Melchoir Kambly, who made furniture fittings and mountings, mirror frames and clockcases, all of them in French style. In the Low Countries bronzeworkers were also busy, and their work is exemplified by several fine church lecterns, such as in the cathedral at Ypres by W. Pompe (this cathedral also contains a brass baptismal font of about 1600) and in the church of Notre Dame, Courtrai, by Jean Bernaes (1711).

During the 19th century most of the wrought iron household artefacts already described were still made with little difference, except that there was a growing tendency to supply some parts in cast-iron. In fact, the 19th century became the foundry age *par excellence* and everything possible was made in this metal. Useful objects like door knockers, boot scrapers, door porters and pavement covers for coal chutes, and useless objects like cast-iron razors; large objects like baths and kitchen ranges, and small objects like ears for roundabout horses; mechanical objects like penny-in-the-slot machines and coffee grinders, and toys like mechanical money-boxes.

One very attractive group included the Wardian case, a glass case, often with cast-iron framework and decoration, invented by Dr Nathaniel Bagshaw Ward (1791–1868) for growing plants, particularly ferns, in sealed conditions. There was an infinite variety of types, patterns and sizes. There were also hand-glass frames, a kind of cloche in cast-iron framing, and aquaria framed in cast iron and supported on cast-iron stands.

Cast-iron furniture was not uncommon, especially for the garden, where favourite designs included concoctions of Gothic motifs, fern leaves, ivy and animal life. Similar to this were tables and chairs designed especially for public houses and gin palaces. But there was also house furniture, one of the most indefatigable designers

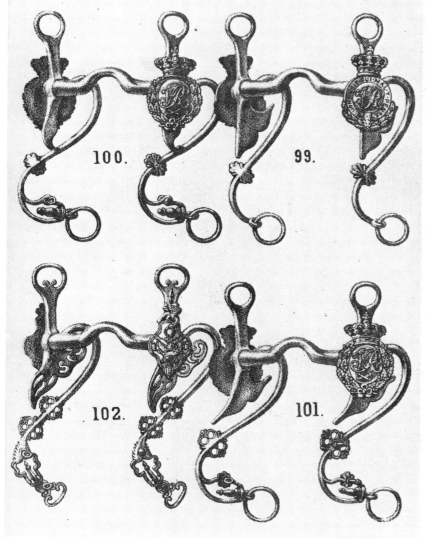

3 Designs for bits by Latchford

4 Cast-iron cooking-stove (American, 19th century), marked 'Cooks Favourite' and 'Cyrus Lamborn Chester County'.

243

of which was Mr Mallet of Dublin, Ireland, who assembled his furniture from units of easily-cast shapes. Some of it was very attractive and included Gothic, honeysuckle and purely functional designs.

Great Britain was one of the most important centres for foundrywork and products of such firms as Steven Bros. and Co. of London, S. Adams and Co. of Oldbury, Birmingham, Jobson and Co. of Sheffield, Skidmore of Clerkenwell and High Holborn, London, Macfarlane

and Co. of Glasgow, and the Coalbrookdale Co. of Shropshire were sent all over the world.

But first-class cast-ironwork was also produced elsewhere. Some very delectable things were made in the USA, wood-burning stoves and kitchen ranges providing a very vivid evocation of the American spirit in design as, in another sphere, did the cast-iron Columbian printing press with a great eagle with outspread wings on its bar.

German cast-ironwork was notable for its fine finish. Chimney ornaments, not unlike door porters, some of them illustrating biblical scenes such as Christ and the woman of Samaria, form one group. Cast-iron chessmen and chess tables were made by Zimmerman of Hanau, Berlin, and, in 1849, by Secbafs and Co. of Offenbach. Imagination was used in making the sets; some have Romans on one side, barbarians on the other, others are made up of characters from the story of Reynard the Fox.

These things might be thought to represent the ultimate refinement in cast-iron, but even finer was the cast-iron jewelry made from about 1820 by the Royal Prussian Iron Foundry, Berlin, and later given in exchange for valuable jewels handed in by Prussian ladies to help the war effort against France in 1870–71, so that to be

1 Bronze statuette 'The Bather' by E.M. Falconer (French, 1850–75), in the Wallace Collection, London. Elaborately-shaped work such as this is made by the *cire perdue* process. A model of the work is made in wax and covered in a sand mould, the wax is melted from the sand, leaving an aperture into which the molten metal is poured.

2 A selection of martingales with brasses illustrating typical classes and patterns (English, 19th century).

3 Steel Art Deco wall-light
by Edgar Brandt (French,
1925) in the Victoria and
Albert Museum. This is an
example of the adaptation
of traditional forms and
patterns to a modern style.
Brandt was one of the finest
of modern metalworkers.

seen wearing cast-iron jewelry was a sign of patriotism. The lacy quality of this jewelry has to be seen to be believed.

Cast-iron was made in France throughout the 19th century, but the best was made during the first Empire, when decorative panels, lanterns and shop signs of very pleasing quality were made. But later there was much mediocre work, and to see the best French ironwork of the second half of the century one must look to blacksmithery, although there was a second blooming of overripe and pompous cast work during the second Empire.

Most of the blacksmithery was architectural, though smaller objects of everyday use were made both in France and elsewhere, and some good benchwork was still turned out. But during the 19th century, all over the western world these things were made more cheaply and often more efficiently, though not always so beautifully, in cast-iron.

Yet wrought iron design did have something of a revival with the coming of the Art Nouveau style at the end of the century, and many small artefacts such as candlesticks, fire irons, brackets and table lamps were forged in the curvaceous, drooping-tulip lines of the style.

Jardinières, window boxes and stands made of bent steel wire and painted white are an attractive subdivision of ironwork. They were popular throughout much of the 19th century and were made up to the beginning of the Great War (1914). Shapes and sizes are of considerable variation.

There was a blooming of bronze and brass work during the 19th century, especially in the France of Napoleon I, when it was, in common with other arts and crafts, dominated by the classical style. Among the great workers of this period was Pierre-Philippe Thomire (1751–1843), who had earlier been patronized by Marie-Antoinette. His works include perfume burners in the form of a Greek tripod with winged griffins at the base and three female trumpeters at the top (Louvre, Paris). In collaboration with J.-B. Claude Odiot, Thomire made the cradle of the King of Rome (The Treasury, Hofburg, Vienna). This piece of furniture is richly constructed and decorated and has an eagle perched at its foot and above its canopy a winged Nike carrying a wreath. It is an impressive piece of craftsmanship, combining bronze casting and sculpture.

Despite the often turbulent changes of national administration, good work continued

3

1 Writing desk designed by the architect C.F.A. Voysey and made by W.H. Tingey (English, 1896), now in the Victoria and Albert Museum. The metal panel with a pastoral design in the centre of the middle cupboard hinge should be compared with the pierced warming-pan lid illustrated on page 237.

to be turned out in France throughout the 19th century. Some of the best products being smaller objects, among which we may include a pretty little bronze statuette of a bather by E. M. Falconet (1850–75) in the Wallace Collection, London. In France there were hundreds of manifestations of the craft of the bronzeworker: lighting fittings in the form of torches, chandeliers, candelabra, suspension fittings, stair rods and furniture decorations among them. As in the case of wrought iron, Art Nouveau later in the century held sway over the design of many of these things.

In Germany much bronzework was Gothic in

design. Typical of this are the enormous candelabra and chandeliers in the singers' hall of Ludwig II's castle, Neuschwanstein in Bavaria. Assemblies of Gothic units, heavy and highly polished, they are masterpieces of their kind. Much similar work was made in England, in particular in Birmingham, a great deal of it stemming from the artistic theories of Augustus Welby Pugin, but more often it was of little artistic merit.

Horse brasses, used for the decoration of harness from the middle of the 18th century until the present day, make an interesting group of English brasswork. They embrace a whole range of metalworking techniques. The earliest brasses were made by simple benchwork, but after 1800 most of them were cast in alloys that varied considerably. There was calamine brass (copper together with zinc carbonate) in use from about 1850, pinchbeck brass (half copper, half zinc), Emerson's brass (copper and zinc but more golden in colour than the others) in use from before 1840 to about 1860, and brasses of many other types in use from 1860 onwards. Early cast horse-brasses were often chased and brilliantly polished and burnished, and some of them were given an almost coppery hue by applications of heat and acid. After 1860, brasses were often made by stamping; these are lighter than the cast or hand-made specimens. Modern brasses, which are not really intended for use on a harness, but are merely curiosities, are cast and very roughly finished.

Hundreds of different types of decorative motifs and designs may be collected. One of the most pleasing – and incidentally an early pattern – is the sunflash, a rimmed and usually ribbed cone worn on the strap on the horse's face, so it flashes in the sun. Sometimes, in the later years of the 19th century, it was fitted with a glass or enamel boss. But there are others equally attractive in their way, including portraits of royalty, statesmen and heroes, stars and moons, birds, animals, devices and abstract patterns. Sometimes the horse's head-stall was surmounted by a decorative disc set in a ring, or with a polished bell, traditionally to frighten away the 'evil eye', but more practically to warn approaching traffic.

Closely related to horse brasses, is loriner's work: the metal mountings of horses' bridles, in which, for convenience, spurs are sometimes included, although strictly speaking they are the specialized products of the spurrier. This group of artefacts was made throughout most of the periods previously discussed.

The parts that are in contact with the horse's mouth, the curb chain and curb hooks and the bit, snaffle or curb, are usually made of steel. But the branches, the parts that lie beside the animal's muzzle, are frequently of other metals or alloys, such as bronze or brass, and are beautifully decorated by casting, chasing or engraving, or by all three together. Spurs, too, are made of steel or other metals and are often brilliantly decorated.

The fashions of the present century have been reflected in its domestic metalwork. At the

1

beginning, both arts and crafts and Art Nouveau styles were still in favour and such objects as wall sconces, furniture fittings, candlesticks, ashtrays, fireguards, firedogs, dishes and plates, in pewter, brass, bronze, steel and other metals and alloys were made all over the Continent, in Great Britain and in the USA. Alfred Bucknell was outstanding among English metalworkers, and even in a world context. He made many of the designs of the Cotswold designers Ernest Gimson and Sidney and Ernest Barnsley.

In the 1920s Art Deco became fashionable and much wrought iron furniture was made in the style. In this class the work of the French craftsman Paul Kiss, whose work embodies traditional techniques with great success, is brilliant. This was really the last period when good domestic ironwork was made on an extensive scale, but even then it was more limited than it had been a few decades earlier. The 1951 Festival of Britain ushered in a fashion for so-called wrought iron furniture, and to some extent this still obtains, but the design is usually feeble and the workmanship so poor as to be unworthy of attention.

So far as bronzework is concerned, its most original domestic manifestations in the 1920s and 1930s were in the form of table lamps, chromium-plated table cigarette-lighters and motor-car mascots. But the little Art Deco statuettes which combined bronze or other alloys with ivory and coloured stones, and were designed by such people as Demetre Chiparus, Otto Poertzel, B. Chariol and Frederick Preiss, evoke in a very special way the particular and unique artistic spirit of the time.

Fakes and Frauds

Finally, a word about fakes and forgeries. There are not many and it should not be difficult, with some experience, to spot them. The most important test is the surface of the work, for old work acquires a patina that time alone can give.

In the case of ironwork, it should always be remembered that bars of standard section are comparatively recent. The profile of old bars, even as late as the 18th century, always has less sharpness than that of modern ones, and however much the latter are hammered and worked this cannot be disguised. Pure wrought iron was invariably used in architectural work until well into the 19th century; the presence of steel in such work should always be treated with caution.

Wrought iron may be identified if a small part of the surface is carefully scraped to expose the metal: it has small dark hairlines in it, showing its laminae, where the surface of steel is unbroken. The presence of electric or oxyacetylene welding should also make one pause, although this may simply imply a careless repair.

Modern cast-iron is usually identifiable by the colour of its rust; on new work it is bright orange, on old work it is much darker. On firebacks and firedogs the deposit of soot and blacking should be examined; on old specimens it is thick, hard and difficult to remove, on new ones it is soft and easily rubbed away. Aluminium is now being used to reproduce many things previously made in cast-iron, especially garden furniture. But this is unlikely to mislead anyone, as it is so much lighter than iron, and its surface texture is rougher.

The surfaces of lead, copper, bronze and brass all have their special ageing characteristics which usually amount to a patina of surface marks and, in the last three, years of polish. Rough, sharp, new-looking surfaces on the inside of castings such as candlesticks and on the underside of mortars should be treated with considerable doubt and suspicion.

Regarding preservation, copper and its alloys do not require much more attention than careful

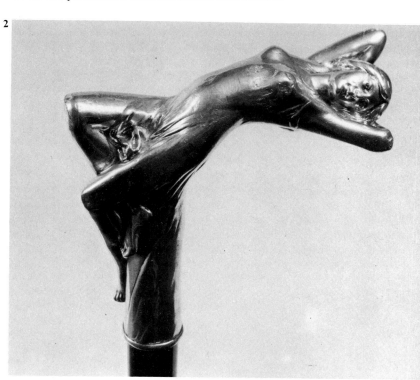

2 Cane-handle of Art Nouveau design, late 19th century. This, like the statuette on page 244, was made by the *cire perdue* process.

and regular polishing, but really abrasive polishes should be avoided. These metals may be coated with various lacquers, which is the best way of dealing with them if they are not in constant use, as polishing will then be avoided. If they are in exposed positions on buildings, it is best to apply a coating of a chemical mixture which will produce a green patina. The best coating is made of eight parts concentrated vinegar, three parts copper carbonate and one part each of sal-ammoniac, cream of tartar, copper acetate and common salt. This is applied daily until the desired effect is achieved. Gilded bronze (ormolu) requires no attention beyond a certain amount of care in handling. Lead needs little or no attention.

Iron and steel in exposed positions are best sprayed with zinc and then painted. Benchwork or other iron or steel of bright finish should be very thinly smeared with a little petroleum jelly, but if such objects are frequently handled, natural grease from the hands should keep it free of rust. Black iron may also be treated in this way, but painting is best for larger objects.

Arms & Armour

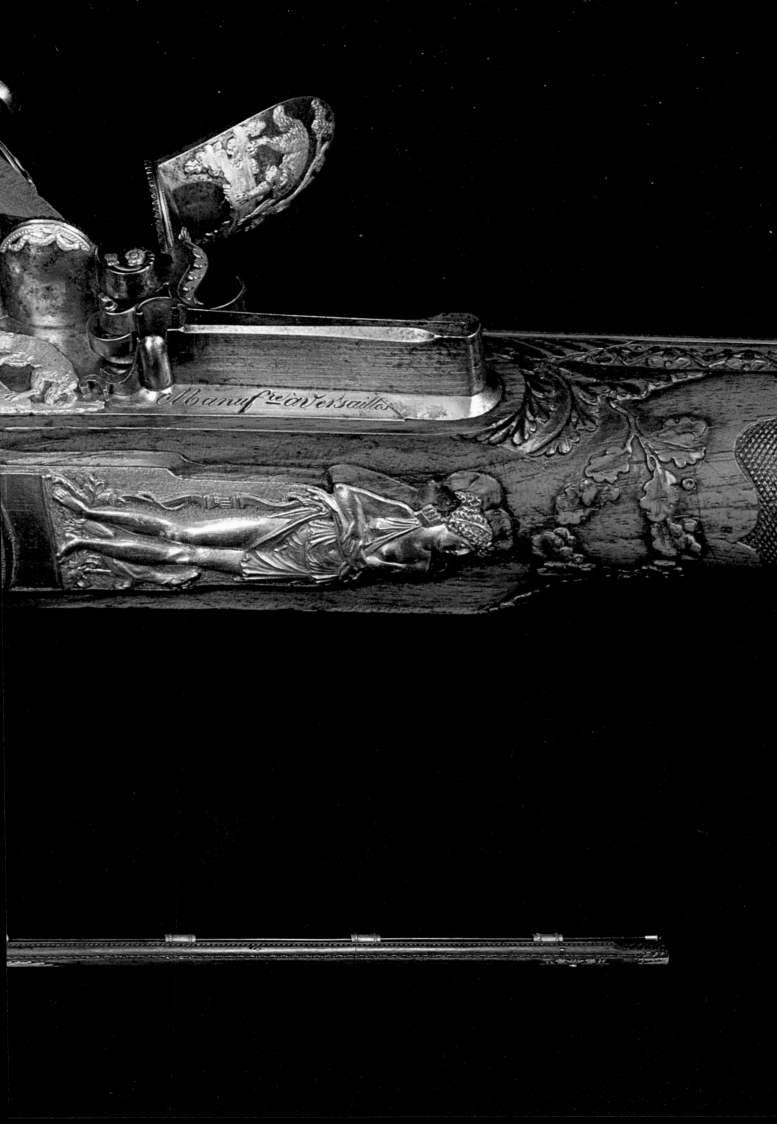

Manuf.re à Versailles

The fascination of military artefacts, weapons of all kinds, armour and general military paraphernalia is one of the more curious aspects of antique collecting. For a start, it is a fairly single-minded pursuit, and those who practise it rarely have interests in other fields. Secondly, no other field reflects so precisely the attitudes and character of the collector. To be a specialist in militaria requires a highly developed sense of fantasy, for the equipment itself can very rarely be put to any use. Swords, guns, armour and the like were all made for a very specific purpose, and have no real function once removed from that purpose. As very few collectors will have the opportunity to use the items in the manner for which they were originally designed, they have to rely on a strong fantasy factor. Sometimes this factor is obviously expressed, as in the large number of military historical societies who spend much of their time refighting famous battles and campaigns of the past (generally in a harmless way). Sometimes it is less obvious, and the mere possession of an antique weapon or piece of equipment is sufficient to transmit some of its latent power to its present owner.

Most military equipment, and its civil counterparts, was designed to prevent or provoke violence and destruction. The development of weapons was entirely determined by the need for increasing efficiency and effectiveness, a pattern still clearly apparent in the present global arms race. Most weapons are therefore machines or scientific instruments whose primary appeal lies in their efficiency. Objects are often considered to be beautiful if they perform to perfection the task for which they were designed and this applies particularly to weapons. Therefore, their purpose and function has always determined their design and appearance, for attractiveness, ornamentation and craftsmanship were of no value in themselves if the object to which they were applied was inefficient in performing its essential function. The owners of beautiful guns which did not shoot properly were rarely given an opportunity to take them back to the maker.

As a result, the technology of weapons and militaria has always been highly advanced, a fact that has appealed particularly to collectors in later ages. An awareness of the dramatic changes in technology they represent can increase rather than reduce the interest aroused by a suit of armour, a rapier or a matchlock. With the passage of time, such items become more than simple examples of outmoded technology; instead, they achieve the ability to reflect changes in society and civilization, and the increasing speed with which these changes occur. The fascination that this creates is understandable, for it is possible to possess today a weapon that is now no more than a piece of history, but which, when new, was able to alter the course of history.

Similarly, weapons or equipment associated with particular armies or individuals can acquire and carry a permanent aura of the power and impact generated by the original owners. The most recent example of this is the mystique and mythology that now surrounds the weapons and regalia of Nazi Germany, equipment which, when new, was no more than the necessary paraphernalia of a successful, modern army.

It would be wrong, however, to see militaria only in such technological and functional terms, for ornamentation has always been an important aspect of the design of weaponry. Decoration and craftsmanship were the means of identifying the status of the owner or user, a means as relevant today as in the middle ages. The wealth of a medieval knight would be judged by the quality of his armour and that of his horse, and by the ornamentation of his weapons. Apart from other considerations, in the heat of battle, little else would be visible. Today, the clear definition of rank and status survives in the differences between the uniforms of a private and a general. The ability to identify the social level of the original owner is also one of the attractions of collecting weapons and militaria, for pieces can reflect a level of craftsmanship perhaps unmatched by other fields of antiques. There is great pleasure to be drawn from the products of a craftsman who has been able to combine a complete control of materials and technology with a wonderful decorative technique. This type of decorative and technical perfection can be found most readily in the sporting weapons of the 18th century, for these were designed specifically to give pleasure, their excellent performance in the field being taken for granted.

Weapons and equipment of earlier ages have always been collected, partly out of general interest, and partly because of the power latent in them. In times of war this collecting was predominantly functional, for the weapons could always be put to good use. In times of peace, the motive was more likely the quality of the weapons themselves. Until comparatively recent times, all large houses would automatically have had a gun room or armoury as part of their equipment. With the passage of time, this has become less a defence against marauders and more a collection for its own sake, in which the exotic and the unusual might be prominently displayed. Today, essential restrictions on the possession and use of many types of weapons have been introduced, making the field of the collector more limited. Inevitably this has brought about a concentration on the material that is still freely available – military equipment, badges, buttons, pieces of uniform, and medals – which can tell the collector as much about the more recent chapters of military history, as pieces of chain mail can about the medieval period.

Third dragoon Guards officer's helmet, about 1840.

Militaria

1 (Top) Close helmet with etched and gilt decoration. The central comb has a plume holder fitted at the base. German dated about 1560.
(Bottom) Early, simpler style of close helmet made in Milan about 1510. The visor, like the German example, can be locked in position by means of a small spring catch.

2 German breastplate with etching and gilt panels dating from the second half of the 16th century. The large holes are for the attachment of extra reinforcing pieces and a lance rest. At the base are two loops for a securing strap to pass through.

Metal armour has been used by warriors for thousands of years but, apart from a very occasional excavated piece of Roman or Greek armour, very few pieces pre-dating the late 16th century are likely to be available. By this date the wearing of armour was already in decline, for firearms were changing the face of war and new tactics were making armour obsolete. In the Middle Ages the knight had been encased in a shell of metal but gradually the amount of armour was reduced – first to go were the leg pieces and then the arms. By the 17th century the majority of troops wore only a helmet and breast and back plate. Some units and individuals did retain the full suits but they were rare.

Full suits of armour are very rare and many of those which do appear on the market are composed of parts from different armours. A number of Victorian copies also exist and these will seldom deceive the collector for they are usually 'tinny', light and lack the graceful lines of the original.

Although full armours are rare there is a great deal of interest in the collecting of component parts. Helmets are probably the most desirable pieces. Early 16th century examples of the close helm have a fluted surface designed to give greater strength. This style is known by collectors as Maximilian and is very attractive. The fluting was gradually discarded and close helmets of the latter part of the 16th century have smooth, uncluttered surfaces. Both types have a one-piece skull and two pieces, the bevor and visor, pivotted at the side. Some rather crude examples of close helmets may be found and these are usually church helms which were hung above the tombs. They were often put together out of odd pieces and many have a crest fitted.

During the late 16th century there was an increased use of helmets without face pieces, and these burgonets were worn by both cavalry and infantry. Probably the commonest form is that known as the lobster tailed burgonet which was popular during the period of the Thirty Years War (1618–48) and the English Civil Wars (1642–48). It has a domed skull with a peak through which passed a curved bar, the nasal, which gave some protection to the face. The back of the neck was covered by a flared guard made of several overlapping strips or lames. Two ear flaps protected the cheeks.

By the late 17th century metal helmets were seldom worn, and during the 18th century they had disappeared to return at the turn of the century as part of the cavalryman's uniform. These cavalry helmets were more decorative than protective most being fitted with a variety of plates, crests and plumes. Brass and white metal were popular materials and some very elaborate styles were developed, especially for elite units.

Trench warfare during World War I made it

necessary to provide some protection for the ³ head, and in 1915 the French army became the first of the Allies to issue a steel helmet. Known as the Adrian it was simple and effective and was soon followed by British and German patterns. Each style was fitted with some kind of padded lining and apart from minor changes, virtually the same pattern helmets were worn during World War II. There have been variations in the basic patterns and there is scope for collectors with limited means in this field of collecting.

Gauntlets, metal gloves, are popular items since each is a complete unit. The early examples may be fitted with fingers or be mitten like in form. Some were made with the Maximilian fluting but the later versions were simpler in design. The fingerplates were rivetted to leather gloves and in many cases, since the lining glove has rotted away, the finger pieces will be lacking. One form, the elbow gauntlet, has a very long cuff which extends the full length of the forearm.

Breast and backplates are also popular and these are probably a little more readily available for they were worn long after helmets and gauntlets had been discarded. Many cavalry units retained their breastplates in the early 18th century and they were reintroduced to other units in the 19th century. Some French cavalry rode to battle at the beginning of World War I still wearing their armour, but experience pointed out that it was largely irrelevant in the face of modern firearms. Some body armour was worn during World War I, mostly by the Italians and Germans who issued it to some assault troops and those likely to be placed in exposed positions. This armour was strong enough to withstand a modern bullet and because of its very strength it has a solid, rather ugly look to it.

One oddity of modern armour was the face mask issued to some tank crews during World War I. It was a leather covered, metal mask with slits for vision and from the bottom was hung a small curtain of mail. The whole thing was tied on by tapes. The mask was designed to protect the face against the flakes of metal which were chipped off the inside wall when the armour plating was struck on the outside by a bullet.

The other odd plates and sections of armour are interesting and are collected, but lack the appeal of more complete pieces. There are also certain problems in displaying odd pieces.

Mail has a special interest since its manufacture was so tedious, a single shirt requiring several thousand links. European mail makers rivetted each individual link, but those of Asia and Africa normally only butted the links. Early examples of mail are extremely rare and the majority of shirts that appear on the market are of Sudanese origin. In Asia and Africa mail was retained in use and is still worn on occasions.

Asiatic armour is, as yet, not a popular collectors' item but it is becoming so and this trend will undoubtedly increase. Helmets attract attention and some early Turkish examples do appear but these are expensive; later Persian and Indian ones are still reasonable. They consist of a metal, domed skull fitted with a variety of

spikes and plume holders and a sliding nasal bar. They often have chiselling or applied decoration and from the rim there is a curtain of mail.

Asiatic armour is usually composed of a mixture of mail and plate combined in various styles. The body defence is commonly made up of four large plates while the arms may have a metal guard with a mail glove attached. Some pieces of Indian armour are painted while others will have chiselled surfaces.

Shields figure largely in the east and are usually round and made of hide or metal. Those of rhino hide have a pleasant, translucent appearance with four metal bosses attached. This style is repeated on the metal versions which are decorated with chiselling and, occasionally, applied metal decoration.

Armour offers an interesting range of items both old and new but it does present problems in display since many of the pieces are awkward to mount.

3 Superb quality half suit of armour designed for foot combat. It was one of twelve made by the master armourer Anton Pfeffenhauser and which carry the mark of the town of Augsburg. The armours were to be presented to the Elector Christian I of Saxony on Christmas Day 1591. (Courtesy Christies.)

Uniforms

Military uniform dates back only to the 17th century, for prior to this date there was little or no overall control of uniform, each unit dressing according to the ideas of its commander. The standardization of dress developed during the 18th century, and by the middle of the century most nations issued sets of rules, dress regulations, setting out details of the uniform.

Headdress is probably the most collected item and the range of styles is enormous. Each army developed its own fashions but most fall into recognizable groups. During the 18th century and early 19th century Grenadiers of most European armies favoured a mitre cap, so-called because of its resemblance to a bishop's hat. The shako was favoured by most armies including the British, French, German and American and usually consisted of a cylindrical, flat-topped crown and a small peak at the front. Fitted to the hat were various plumes, badges and cords varying from unit to unit. Spiked helmets were another style worn particularly by German and British troops of the late 19th century.

Favoured by the French and American forces was the kepi, which had a soft crown and a forward, stiff peak. Cavalry units tended to adopt rather more exotic forms, such as the Polish tschapka or the Hungarian busby. Most of the colourful styles were abandoned after World War I to be replaced by soft berets or simple caps.

Tunics and coats are next in order of preference, since these too have a unity of their own. The infantry ones were usually plainer than those of the cavalry which have rather more in the way of braid and other applied decoration. The majority of items on the market are of 19th century origin, but a few earlier pieces do occasionally appear. The added items such as epaulettes are often attractive pieces. In most armies distinctions between regiments was made by badges, epaulettes and by varying the colours at collars and cuffs.

Buttons on the early tunics were of pewter later changing to brass. Officers' buttons were obviously more elaborate, and gilt and silver were not uncommon. Most of the buttons can be identified with reasonable ease and frequently carry regimental markings.

Owing to the spate of television and films which have featured the events of World War II, the number of reproduction uniforms is enormous. Great care is essential when collecting such items and it is becoming increasingly difficult to distinguish genuine and reproduction.

Badges

Badges have always been vital to the soldier, for quick recognition of friend or foe could mean the difference between life and death. In the 17th century distinctions were very simple, being little more than a twig or piece of coloured cloth tucked into the hat. Sashes were commonly used for the same purpose and it seems that only early in the 18th century did regimental distinctions begin to appear

1 Selection of uniforms and headdress. The central helmet with the eagle crest was worn by a member of the German Kaiser's Bodyguard. On the right is an example of the famous German Pickelhaube.

2 Leather and metal helmet with yellow plume worn by members of the British Norfolk Yeomanry, a volunteer cavalry unit. These date from about 1905. (Private Collection.)

Prior to the latter part of the 18th century most regimental badges were either woven or painted on material. From the latter part of the 18th century metal badges became more and more common and were fitted mostly to headdress and items of equipment such as cartridge boxes.

Early specimens are extremely rare, but examples from the 19th century are not uncommon, although they have become increasingly expensive. The most common badges are probably those from military headdress, but the majority date from the mid-19th century only. Although there are obviously innumerable varieties the majority of European armies used brass for their badge material and most were large plates with a raised design often incorporating all or part of the arms of the ruling house of the country. Towards the end of the century there was a trend towards smaller styles of military headdresses, and consequently the badges were smaller. Brass remained the commonest material, although during and after World War II plastics were often substituted.

From the 19th century onwards increasing specialization and growing military technology led to the adoption of a whole range of badges worn, usually on the arm, to show the bearer's skill or technical qualification. These were originally embroidered but later many were made in metal.

Badges of the Third Reich gained tremendously in popularity as collectors' pieces and commanded very high prices on the market, but a flood of reproductions has made it extremely difficult to identify pieces as original.

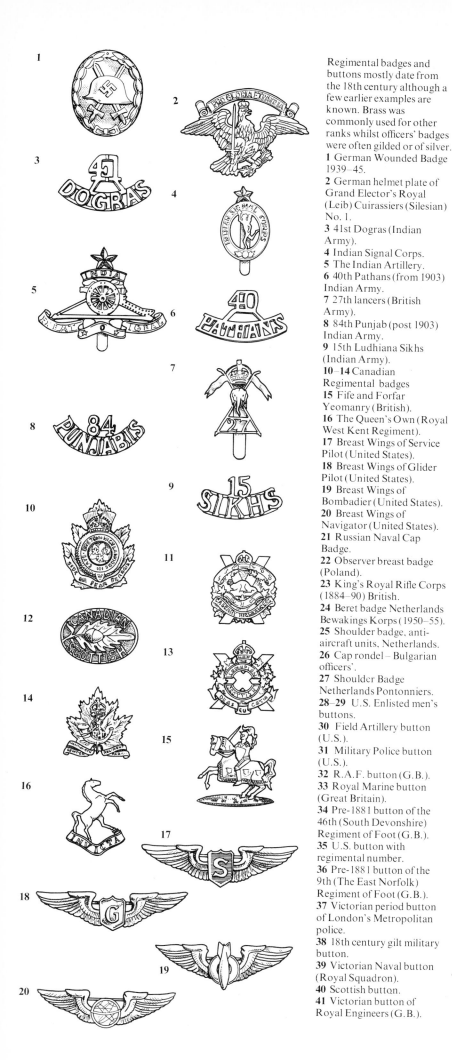

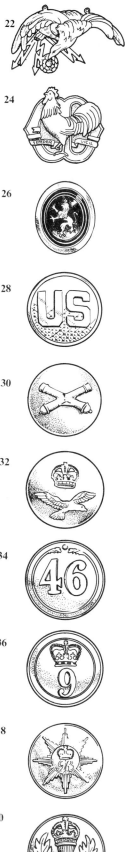

Regimental badges and buttons mostly date from the 18th century although a few earlier examples are known. Brass was commonly used for other ranks whilst officers' badges were often gilded or of silver.

1 German Wounded Badge 1939–45.
2 German helmet plate of Grand Elector's Royal (Leib) Cuirassiers (Silesian) No. 1.
3 41st Dogras (Indian Army).
4 Indian Signal Corps.
5 The Indian Artillery.
6 40th Pathans (from 1903) Indian Army.
7 27th lancers (British Army).
8 84th Punjab (post 1903) Indian Army.
9 15th Ludhiana Sikhs (Indian Army).
10–14 Canadian Regimental badges
15 Fife and Forfar Yeomanry (British).
16 The Queen's Own (Royal West Kent Regiment).
17 Breast Wings of Service Pilot (United States).
18 Breast Wings of Glider Pilot (United States).
19 Breast Wings of Bombadier (United States).
20 Breast Wings of Navigator (United States).
21 Russian Naval Cap Badge.
22 Observer breast badge (Poland).
23 King's Royal Rifle Corps (1884–90) British.
24 Beret badge Netherlands Bewakings Korps (1950–55).
25 Shoulder badge, anti-aircraft units, Netherlands.
26 Cap rondel – Bulgarian officers'.
27 Shoulder Badge Netherlands Pontonniers.
28–29 U.S. Enlisted men's buttons.
30 Field Artillery button (U.S.).
31 Military Police button (U.S.).
32 R.A.F. button (G.B.).
33 Royal Marine button (Great Britain).
34 Pre-1881 button of the 46th (South Devonshire) Regiment of Foot (G.B.).
35 U.S. button with regimental number.
36 Pre-1881 button of the 9th (The East Norfolk) Regiment of Foot (G.B.).
37 Victorian period button of London's Metropolitan police.
38 18th century gilt military button.
39 Victorian Naval button (Royal Squadron).
40 Scottish button.
41 Victorian button of Royal Engineers (G.B.).

1 (Top left) Shoulder belt plate of the 9th Regiment of Foot dated about 1820.
(Top right) Shoulder belt plate of the 17th Regiment of Foot dated about 1790.
(Centre left) Shoulder belt plate of the Loyal Chelmsford Volunteers dated about 1810.
(Centre) Helmet plate of Volunteer Battalion of The Welsh Regiment, late 19th century.
(Centre right) Shoulder belt plate of St Margaret and St Johns Association dated about 1810.
(Bottom left) Shoulder belt plate of the 2nd West India Regiment dated about 1840.
(Bottom right) Shoulder belt plate of the 884th Regiment of Foot. (Private Collection.)

2 British Campaign Medals. (Top left) East & West Africa Medal (1887–1900) with bars for 1892 and 1893–9.
(Top centre) First China War medal (1842).
(Top right) Indian General Service Medal (1854–1895) showing reverse of bars.
(Centre left) General Service Medal (Army and Royal Air Force) 1918–1964, with Malaya bar.
(Centre right) Baltic Medal (1854–1855).
(Bottom left) Queens South Africa Medal (1898–1902). with five bars.
(Bottom centre) Air Crew Europe Star (1939–1944).
(Bottom right) Military General Service Medal (1793–1814), with three bars. (Gunshots.)

Badges are still comparatively cheap, but the cost of early 19th century examples is rising rapidly. One of the joys and frustrations of badge collecting is the problem of identification, but an increasingly large number of reliable books is making this a simpler task.

Medals

Medals have been given as rewards or recognition from the earliest times but as far as the collector is concerned examples from the 17th century are the earliest available. Medals can be divided into several groups, each of which has its own interest and fascination.

Commemorative Medals These were struck to commemorate some specific event such as a battle, the opening of a building or the signing of a treaty. These were not, as a rule, issued but were available for purchase. They bear no names and can seldom be traced to any specific owner. The range of events and occasions covered by such medals is very great and in date they range from the 17th century to the present.

Campaign Medals Awarded to members of the armed forces, to those who served in a particular campaign. They usually have a bar or other means of indicating which particular battle the owner served in. Most of these medals bear the recipient's name, usually around the edge. Since they are named the details of the original owner can frequently be traced in some detail from official records. Owing to the large numbers awarded the practice of naming each medal was abandoned for Second World War medals.

Gallantry Awards As their name implies they were given for specific acts of bravery and again usually, but not always, details of the heroism and recipient can often be traced. Some, like the Iron Cross of Germany, are not named.

Decorations and Orders These too are given in recognition of services in various fields and, in general, are less easily available to the collector. Often the details of the award can be traced. In this category may also be included a range of medals for shooting and similar sports.

Ribbons Almost all medals are suspended by some form of coloured ribbon. Small oblongs of the appropriate coloured ribbon are usually worn in place of the actual medal.

The value of a medal, whatever group it falls into, is dependent on a whole range of factors. Rarity is important and can be determined by many factors. In the case of campaign medals the recipient's unit is a great importance, as is his rank. Obviously, the higher the rank the fewer there were, and consequently the value rises. The desirability of a medal is also affected by the regiment of the recipient. Those from units which saw heavy action in a particular campaign or have a reputation for bravery, are usually more sought after.

The style of naming is important and should always be examined carefully to ensure that the medal has not been tampered with. Any indication that the medal has been renamed should raise doubts about its authenticity. Some medals were renamed for various genuine reasons but, in general, such items are best avoided. British medals are usually named, but many other countries including the United States and Germany, issued the medal with a certificate of citation and, unfortunately, these were often lost or separated from the medal and consequently it is often impossible, to identify the recipient.

Condition is extremely important and this applies to all types of medals. Most auction houses and dealers have a set group of categories such as, among others, 'fine' and 'extremely fine', but the interpretation of such terms is subjective and will vary from dealer to dealer.

Equipment

The soldier has always been burdened with weapons, packs and bundles, and these have necessitated various straps and fittings to accommodate them all. Early examples of the soldier's equipment are not plentiful, but pieces from the 19th century onwards are far more available.

Waist belts are probably as plentiful as any other item and many of these had attractive buckles of various patterns. These waistbelt plates are still comparatively cheap and are collected. British examples of the 19th century often have the regimental badge and number incorporated in their design, and officers' dress belts are attractive in their own right. Unfortunately the buckles of the American Civil War period have been reproduced on a massive scale and it is extremely difficult to acquire genuine examples. Imperial and Nazi Germany examples are popular, although some of these have also been reproduced.

From the 18th century onwards most troops wore a belt crossing the shoulder which was secured on the chest by a large, decorative plate. In Britain they were abolished in 1855, but countries such as Spain and France retained them much longer. Modern collectors use the term shoulder belt plate and these very attractive pieces are becoming more and more collected, with consequent rises in price.

Packs, cartridge boxes, water bottles, haversacks and similar items are not in great demand although they are of considerable interest. Possibly the cartridge boxes carried at first on the waist belt and later on the shoulder belt, are most easily identified since they usually carry a regimental badge or marking. Sword belts of the late 18th century are to be found and there are numerous patterns.

For the collector with a taste for the unusual there are many 'fringe' interests well worth collecting such as personal issue pieces – penknives, cutlery, pipes, diaries and name plates hung above the bed in barracks. Most bear the owner's name and regiment.

During enforced idleness in prisoner of war camps, trenches or barracks many soldiers passed their time carving and model making. Often they used materials such as cartridge cases and this group of objects is known as trench art.

Edged weapons

Flint has been used by men for tools and weapons for hundreds of thousands of years. He made knives, axes and spears in great quantities. Arrow heads were expendable and were produced in particularly large numbers and, consequently, are still readily available at quite reasonable prices. Generally speaking, the earlier ones are cruder and lack finish, while those of the Neolithic period are polished and well shaped. Many are barbed and most have a short neck which was used to secure the head to the wood or reed shaft. Many primitive cultures continued to manufacture arrow heads of flint long after metal had replaced its use for other weapons. Some Red Indians of North America and the Aborigines of Australia were still making them at the beginning of this century.

Flint is brittle and is unsuitable for constructing long blades, so swords of flint were not practical. When man discovered the secret of melting tin and copper together to make bronze he was able to cast a greater variety of weapons in moulds of clay or stone. Axeheads, daggers, arrow and spear heads and swords were produced all over Europe and sufficient have survived to ensure that some still appear on the market; swords are likely to be the rarest and most expensive. Many of the bronzes available today are from Luristan in Asia Minor, and are generally of good quality although unfortunately a number of very good copies have begun to appear so care and studious attention when buying is essential.

By the 1st century A.D. iron had largely supplanted bronze as the metal for weapons. While iron was better for manufacture it was far less able to survive the centuries. Bronze could resist rust and rot, iron could not and swords dating from the 1st century until the 15th century are extremely rare and very early examples are likely to be little more than masses of blackened rust. The few good quality examples which have survived will certainly be very expensive.

Very few swords and daggers dating from the 12th–15th centuries appear on the market, but those dating from the 16th century onwards are more readily available.

Generally the medieval sword had a long, straight blade, usually double edged, fitted with a simple cruciform cross guard, a leather covered grip and a counter-balance weight (the pommel) at the end of the grip. These swords were essentially slashing weapons designed to hack at armour and mail and some were made big enough to be gripped with two hands. One, known as a hand-and-half, was small enough to be used in one hand but with a grip big enough to hold with both hands to deliver a very powerful blow. A larger version, the two-handed sword, was so large that it could only be used with a two-handed grip.

During the 16th century there was a gradual change from cutting to thrusting as the main method of attack and as armour became more and more effective the sword had to be adapted to offer the warrior any chance of penetrating this protective shell. The solution lay not in cutting through the armour but in attacking the weaker, less well protected spots by thrusting at them. As the Middle Ages progressed, so the swords became longer and more pointed. Another significant change was also taking place, and to obtain a firmer grip the first finger of the right hand was hooked over the cross-guard or quillon. In consequence the top 25 mm (1 in) or so of the blade just below the quillon, was left blunt and was known as the ricasson.

The next step was to add some form of protection for the finger which was, at first, a simple half loop extending from the quillon. The idea was gradually developed and soon metal rings and bars designed to protect the hand were commonplace.

There evolved in time one of the more common and very desirable types of sword, the rapier. At first they had long, double-edged blades; some were of inordinate length and, consequently, extremely difficult to handle. The hand was protected by an arrangement of bars which virtually enclosed the hand in a basket of metal. The art of sword play, fencing, developed and the blades were shortened and the edge was blunted and the essence of the rapier was the use of the point. An opponent's blade was diverted by means of a short, parrying dagger held in the left hand. The early ones were ordinary daggers but later specialist forms were introduced.

These left-hand daggers had fairly substantial blades with a simple cross-guard with the quillons having a slight droop towards the point, and a single side ring. A few specialized forms, known as sword breakers, had deep notches cut into the blade. These were designed to catch and possibly snap an opponent's blade.

The Spaniards and Italians developed a form of left-hand dagger which had a narrow, flat blade and long, thin quillons from which sprang a triangular shaped guard which curved up to meet the pommel. Both rapier and left-hand dagger were often decorated *en suite*. Left-hand

1 This 19th-century engraving shows differing styles of the 'On Guard' position. On the left the Italian holds a left hand dagger in a style of fencing that the Mediterranean countries retained long after it had been abandoned in the rest of Europe.

daggers were gradually abandoned and by the late 17th century were no longer used except in Spain and areas under her influence, where their use continued until the mid-18th century.

During the last quarter of the 16th century the idea of defending the hand by means of bars was extended and pierced metal plates replaced some of the bars or filled in the spaces between them. Their use was extended and by the early 17th century a single, pierced plate was popular and the size was increased until it was a full bowl with two long quillons. The cup-hilted rapier enjoyed only quite a limited spell of popularity except among the fencing schools of Spain and Italy who retained its use together with the left-hand dagger long after the rest of Europe.

1

1

1 (Left) Cup-hilted rapier, Italian 17th century. (Right) Left hand dagger by Antonia Cilento of Naples. The style of chiselled decoration on the cup and guard of the sword and dagger is typical of the rather elaborate styles favoured in Spain and areas under her domination. (Victoria and Albert Museum.)

The rapier continued in use until around the mid-17th century, but its design changed, becoming shorter and lighter. The quillons were reduced in size and curved down, the knuckle bow was dispensed with and in place of the cup or bars two small shells were fitted one on either side of the quillons. This was the early form of the smallsword. During the late 17th century the knuckle bow came back into fashion and the more usual form of small sword was developed. These were delicate weapons weighing very little and fencing with them was a fast moving skill.

The swords themselves were effective weapons but were also regarded by most gentlemen as being part of their costume, in consequence they were often quite elaborately decorated. During the 18th century the hilt was sometimes of silver and it could even be of gold. Even if of steel then the shells might be pierced, the grip enamelled and even set with precious stones. On plainer versions the grip was more often bound with wire. The style of blade varied and there were three main forms. Possibly the commonest was fairly flat, slightly oval in section. The coliche-marde blade was very wide just below the hilt (the forte) and narrowed abruptly about one-third of its length, to a very thin section which was the thrusting part of the blade. The third

was carried in a leather sheath suspended from the belt by means of a very simple hanger, usually little more than a hook to go over the belt and two chains to attach to the scabbard. The small sword continued as a popular item of dress and costume until the 1760–70s, when it was generally discarded. It was a form of sword which continued to be worn by diplomats and other officials.

From the 17th century until at least the middle of the 19th century, few military or naval officers would have considered themselves to be properly equipped without a sword. Most infantrymen, even if the firearm was their prime weapon, carried some form of edged weapon. During the 17th century the infantry often carried a form of rapier while the cavalry used a much stiffer, broad-sectioned blade. The hilt of these cavalry swords was usually simple with a single knuckle guard, two side rings sweeping out enclosing a pierced plate and uniting behind the grip, and with a small, down-curving, rear quillon. The blade was wide, double edged and fairly stiff.

The British cavalry of the Civil War 1642–49, used a more solid and substantial metal basket with a number of bars which were often chiselled with simple decoration. Some of these swords

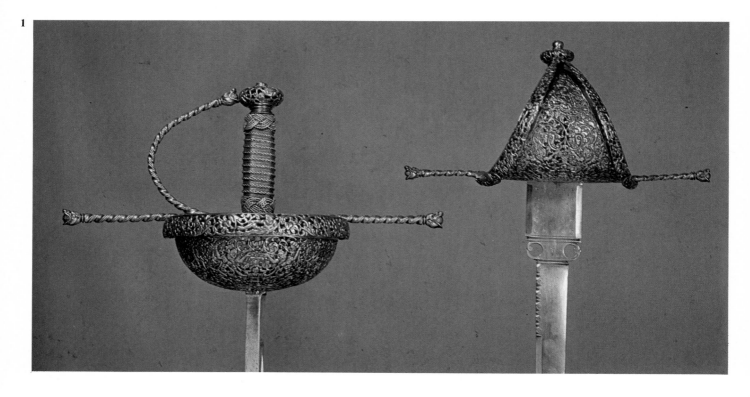

type, known as hollow ground, was triangular in section and gave rigidity with lightness.

The most common style of hilt had a knuckle bow, a small, down-curving rear quillon and two side shells. There were two loops springing from the lower end of the grip and curving over to meet the shells. The size of these is a good guide to the age, for the earlier ones are large enough to insert the fingers but later examples are very small and purely decorative. The small sword

have a head chiselled on to the basket and tradition has it that this represented Charles I who was executed in 1649; for this reason they are known by collectors as Mortuary swords.

One specialized form of basket hilted sword is that known as the Scottish claymore. Strictly the term should be used to describe only the large, two-handed sword, the claidheamh mor, but usage has meant that it is now applied to the straight-bladed sword with an eleaborate metal

basket of bars, carried by Scottish troops long
after the ordinary regiments had abandoned
theirs and still carried today by officers in some
Scottish regiments.

Later most of the infantry were armed with a
short, light sword known as a hanger. These
usually had a fairly narrow, slightly curved
blade usually only single edged and often with a
brass hilt since this was less liable to rusting.
Although Britain withdrew the sword from most
of her troops many other countries retained
some form of side arm for certain units. Many
were designed to serve both as a weapon and
tool, being fitted with saw-like teeth on the back
edge.

The 18th-century officer's sword was usually
a more substantial version of the smallsword and
had a single knuckle bow, two side rings or
possibly shells, a small rear quillon and a long,
straight, narrow blade. Until the end of the 18th
century the majority of officers were armed with
weapons of their own choice but it became increasingly common, from late in the 18th century, for governments to specify standard military patterns, a policy used more and more
during the 19th century.

The majority of military swords are simple
and robust and most have a plain hilt with either

2 The Scottish basket-hilted,
broad sword was fitted with
a characteristic metal guard
which enclosed the whole
of the hand gripping the
hilt. Late 18th century.

3 (Left) Hilt of the late 18th-
century small sword. It is
silver gilt with inset translucent enamel medallion and
bears the hallmarks for
1797–9.
(Right) English hilt of a
very late 18th-century small
sword, the whole chiselled
and set with paste.

4 Simple, practical trooper's
cavalry sword of late
1780s. The knuckle bow is
of brass and the scabbard of
steel.

a single knuckle bow or, perhaps, just one or two bars. Often the blades are etched with designs which may well include the badge of the officer's regiment. The early scabbards are almost invariably of leather although from the late 18th century metal scabbards, either plain or leather covered, were increasingly used.

While the infantry officer might well regard the sword as being only occasionally of use, the cavalry relied on it far more. Basically there were two forms of sword for cavalry; there was the straight, long, stiff, heavy blade, designed primarily for thrusting, and the curved, single edged blade, intended primarily as a slashing weapon. **1** Variations of these types were carried by most European armies of the period. There was a good deal of discussion about the virtues of each type and there were many attempts to produce a sword which could be used for both methods of attack. Some troops retained their swords during the 19th century but they were in the nature of a double purpose side arm. Artillery men, engineers and transport troops often had a broad-bladed weapon, the back edge of which was serrated. Its purpose was not to make it a more efficient or unpleasant weapon but rather to permit its use as a tool as well as a sword. The same idea was applied to bayonets.

Troops of the latter part of the 17th century onwards were increasingly armed with muskets which, once fired, had to be reloaded before another shot could be fired. The loading process took time and for this period the soldier was useless as far as fighting was concerned. He was very open to any attack at this moment and some method of giving him a means of defence was necessary. One of the most universal ideas was the bayonet. Originally it was simply a large knife and its name was derived from the French town of Bayonne famous for its cutlery. The earliest form of bayonet consisted of a short, fairly broad, tapered blade with simple cross quillons, usually quite short, and a plain wooden handle which tapered towards the tip. After the musket had been fired, should an emergency arise such as a sudden attack by cavalry, the hilt of the bayonet could be pushed down the muzzle and the musket was thus converted into a 2.13 m (7 ft) long pike, clumsy and inefficient perhaps but sufficient to hold off a cavalry attack.

The problem was that with these plug bayonets in position the musket could neither be loaded nor fired. Attempts to overcome this great problem were soon devised and the form developed in the late 17th century was the socket bayonet. This had a straight, triangular section blade attached by a curved neck to a short cylinder just wide enough to slip over the barrel of a matchlock musket and engage with a stud to prevent it slipping off. Even with the bayonet in position the musket could still be loaded or fired without trouble. This socket bayonet remained in use with virtually every European and American army until the mid-19th century and there is little to choose between the various patterns. Some had spring clips so that they could easily be clipped on or removed. During the 19th century

a firmer more positive means of attachment was developed which used a lug and spring catch. In the back of the bayonet hilt was cut a shaped slot with a spring catch fitted. This could be pushed over a correspondingly shaped lug on the barrel and the quillon was cut with a hole just large enough to slip over the muzzle. The spring catch engaged with the lug on the barrel of the musket and the bayonet was held safely in position. To release it, the catch was pressed and the bayonet could be removed.

1 In 1822 the British army introduced a new style of sword hilt for Infantry officers, the so-called Gothic hilt with a series of sweeping bars forming the guard.

An enormous variety of bayonets was produced and from the 17th century until the present day the output has continued unabated. Until recently these were a cheap collector's item but growing interest and the fact that they were so cheap, led to an increased demand which has pushed their prices up; some examples now realize quite considerable sums at auctions. However they do offer a most fruitful and entertaining field for the average collector.

Similar in size to the bayonet although less military in nature, are the various daggers pro-

stiff blades marked off with various scales. These were used by artillerymen as ready-reckoners for sundry ballistic calculations.

One dagger which was very popular with civilians, especially during the late 16th or early 17th century was the so-called ballock dagger which had a plain wooden grip and, in place of conventional quillons, had a guard of two rounded lobes. The distinct phallic shape of the grip did not escape the eye of the people – hence its name. They seem to have gone out of fashion

duced over the ages. The daggers of the Middle Ages are extremely rare and most collectors cannot hope to acquire any pieces earlier than the 17th century. Most of the daggers had a simple, cruciform hilt and were, in effect, a miniature sword. Blades were sometimes cruciform in section but more usually only slightly oval in section. One special form was the stiletto which usually had square or triangular section blade with very simple, turned steel quillons and a plain grip, the whole thing light and delicate. Some, known as gunners' stilettoes, have their

2 This engraving by W. Edsall was published about 1780 and shows 'An Irish Volunteer' withdrawing the ramrod from his Brown Bess musket.

3 Small dagger, resembling a midshipman's dirk, carried by Sir James Abbott at the time of the Indian Mutiny 1857. It is an unusual weapon to be carried by an army officer.

during the first quarter of the 17th century but at the same time in northern Britain, there developed the Scottish dirk which may have owed its origins to the ballock dagger.

The traditional grip of the dirk was of wood, was short and had a swelling at the centre, with two globose guards just like the ballock dagger. The pommel was circular and set at right angles to the blade. Often the grip was carved with intricate, typically Celtic, interwoven strapwork patterns. Dirks were often made using a broken piece of sword blade and this style became traditional and later examples have the blade made to resemble the point section of a sword blade with a false edge and a blunt back edge.

Originally dirks were fighting weapons but with the revival of interest in all things Scottish early in the 19th century, they became glamourized and were produced as costume pieces. They had ornate pieces of mineral, usually a cairngorm, fitted to the pommel, and elaborate sheaths with forks and other pieces of cutlery slotting into special pockets mounted at the side

1

of the sheath. The whole weapon and sheath was often mounted in silver and became part of the traditional costume of Scottish Highlanders.

One knife which has acquired a tremendous reputation since the early 19th century is the American Bowie knife. It was popularized by Colonel James Bowie whose life reads like an adventure story and who died at the famous battle of the Alamo in Texas in 1836. The usual blade was fairly large and widened slightly from the hilt, the edge then swept up in a curve to the point. A few inches (about 50 mm) of the back

1 Bowie knives and sheaths of mid-19th century. The majority of these weapons were made in Britain for sale on the American market. Most, but not all, have the blade cusped towards the point.

edge was sharpened and clipped to a slight curve. The cross-guard was simple, being just an elongated metal oval, and the grip was rather ornate; some quite elaborate ones had pommels made in the shape of a horse's head. A great variety of styles was produced including some with folding blades.

Bowie knives were also made in varying sizes ranging from 50 mm or so (a few inches) to giant, almost sword size. Blades were frequently etched with a variety of patriotic or partisan messages such as 'Death or Liberty'. Although this was so essentially an American weapon the great majority of them were produced in Britain, particularly by the firms of Rodgers and Son and Wolstenholme. They were normally carried in a leather sheath fitted at the belt. Genuine examples of these Bowie knives are highly prized but, unfortunately, large numbers of replicas have been produced over the past few years and it is becoming distinctly difficult to distinguish between genuine and fake.

Modern firearms rendered most edged weapons, except perhaps the bayonet, obsolete, although swords continued to be worn as part of an officer's uniform. The First World War demonstrated their useless nature and the demand for military swords fell rapidly. In Germany, Hitler came to power in 1933 and the cutlers of Solingen, a town long famous for the quality and quantity of its blades, approached the new government in the hope of getting orders. The idea of ceremonial daggers and swords for a whole range of official bodies was approved by all. In 1934 it was agreed that the political group *Sturm Abteilung* (SA) founded in 1921, should be issued with a dagger for dress wear. It was almost an exact copy of one designed by Holbein, the 16th-century artist. It had a brown wooden grip and a brown metal sheath, its wide blade tapered to a point and was engraved with the words *Alles Für Deutschland*, 'All for Germany'. The *Schutzstaffel* (SS) were given virtually the same dagger, except that it had a black wooden grip and the motto *Meine Ehre Heist Treue*, 'My Honour is Loyalty'.

Once the idea of having a decorative dress dagger was accepted other units were soon clamouring for their own patterns. Soon a great variety of daggers were being carried by members of the army, navy, airforce, police, customs, postal workers, Hitler Youth and many others. In addition to the daggers, a number of units also had dress swords of varying patterns.

Despite the fact that these daggers and swords are no more than 40 years old and most were supplied in thousands, they are still sought after by many collectors. Those issued to officers and the rarer models fetch quite high prices in auction. As a result of the increased demand and rising prices a number of manufacturers have produced some copies which are very difficult to distinguish from the genuine article and this has produced a healthy scepticism about all items.

While the daggers and swords of the Third Reich were essentially decorative, the two World Wars saw the issue of a number of daggers which were very much intended for use. The fighting knife was largely the result of trench warfare and the early examples are often home made and crude, but later official issue weapons were made available. These are collected, but again a number of copies have found their way on to the market.

Swords and daggers were not limited to Europe but continued in use in Africa, India and the Far East long after firearms had displaced them in Europe. African swords were very varied in size and shape and some, intended **2**

2 Cap, belt, tunic and dagger of an Oberleutenant in the Luftwaffe, 1933–45. Jacket of Hauptmann in 2nd Panzer Regiment with Iron Cross, wound badge and combat badge for tank battles.

primarily as throwing weapons, have a bewildering array of short blades set at different angles. Far simpler is the Sudanese Kaskara which has a straight, double edged blade and a very simple, cruciform hilt with straight, slightly flaring quillons and a leather-covered grip and flat disc pommel. They were carried in a leather sheath which had a wide section near the tip which has no function other than decoration. The simple shape of these swords led, in the past, to them being described as Crusaders' swords, left behind by the Christian warriors. Unfortunately, there is no basis for the story and most of the blades were made in Belgium during the 19th century.

African cultures also made great use of the spear, both as a missile and as a stabbing weapon. The blades vary greatly in size and shape and the best known of the missile variety is probably the assegai of the Zulus of South Africa. This has a comparatively small leaf-shaped head on a long shank with a short, leather bound wooden shaft. Another type of spear from Somalia has an extremely large blade and was intended for stabbing, not throwing.

Spears and lances played their part in the story of India, but swords were more common. The commonest form of Indian sword is known as a talwar and usually has a slightly curved blade and a simple hilt with two stubby quillons and flat, plate-like, pommel. Often the grip is decorated with simple chiselling or applied decoration and most are likely to be rather small for the average European hand. Some talwars have a knucklebow, but the Indian swordsmith seems not to have developed the idea of a basket guard, although one specialized weapon, the gauntlet sword or pata, had a complete metal cover for the hand.

The range of edged weapons from India and surrounding countries is very considerable and it is only in the last few years that the quality and interest has been appreciated, and the demand for these weapons is now increasing.

Edged weapons offer great opportunities to the collector to acquire a group of widely differing pieces or to specialize in one particular type. Whichever form of collecting is chosen, it will prove very rewarding.

Japanese Swords

The Japanese sword is the finest product of Oriental arms. Its usage is associated with a particular rank of society, the samurai, who played a major role in the history of Japan.

Early Japanese swords had straight blades, Chinese in pattern, and these were carried by warriors fighting as mounted archers. In the 9th century, Yasutsuna, with divine inspiration, developed the slightly curved, single edged blade which has remained the constant shape of Japanese swords for 1,000 years.

In the Muromachi period (1392–1573) the samurai, now using the sword as their major weapon, emerged as a distinctive class and extended their powers and privileges in numerous wars. During the Onin wars (1467–77) many samurai and their servants, chugen, were killed. The latter were replaced by peasant archers (asigan), and the samurai tended to discard their use of the bow and rely exclusively on the sword as a weapon.

At the end of the 16th century the shogun Hideyoshi encouraged metal workers, especially those making sword furniture. At the same time he instituted sword hunts to disarm non-samurai.

In 1600 the Battle of Sekigahara initiated the period of rule by the Tokugawa shoguns. The samurai victor, Ieyasu, chose to depend upon his class for political stability and issued legal

Woodcut from the Chinese novel *Shin Hu Chuan* showing a man with halberd.

codes which defined a rigid social system and forbad movement between classes. Under the emperor, a deity with absolute authority in theory, but little practical power, was the pawn – sometimes almost a slave – of powerful clans or families, and the shogun or commander-in-chief of the emperor's armies, who now enjoyed hereditary office and was the *de facto* ruler of the country. There were three distinct classes: the samurai or warrior class, who governed, carried arms and increased in numbers under the Tokugawa; a class of merchants, shopkeepers and artisans, some of whom might be very wealthy; and peasant cultivators who were a mixture of free and tenant.

About 1550 St Francis Xavier describing the Japanese said: 'they highly regard arms and trust much in them; always carrying a sword and dagger, both high and low alike, from the age of 14 onwards'. Under the Tokugawa, only samurai were allowed to carry the two swords of their rank. This warrior class included powerful

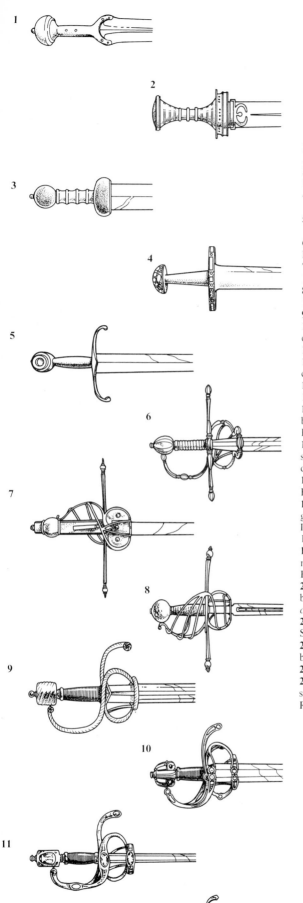

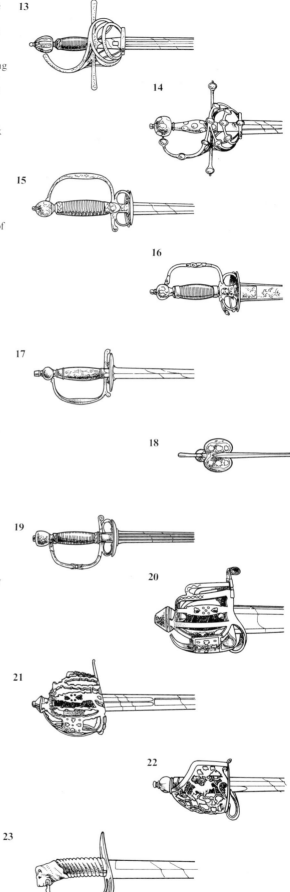

Early hilts were very simple but became increasingly complex reaching a peak in the late 16th and early 17th centuries. There was a general simplification during the 18th century and by the mid 19th century most hilts were fairly basic.

1 Bronze Age sword hilt.
2 Typical shape of the Dark Ages.
3 Hilt of a Roman legionary's gladius.
4 Cruciform hilt of early 13th century.
5 Sword of Henry V early 15th century.
6 Decorative hilt of rapier of late 16th century.
7 Spring loaded hilt of late 16th century rapier.
8 Swept hilt rapier – late 16th century.
9 Gilt hilt dated 1588.
10 Spanish hilt of late 16th century.
11 French hilt dated 1599.
12 German hilt of late 16th century.
13 French hilt of around 1580.
14 Hilt of rapier which belonged to Louis XIII of France, early 17th century.
15 Early 18th century small sword hilt with gold decoration.
16 Gilt bronze hilt of a French small sword *c*.1700.
17 and **18** Hilt with applied gold decoration made in India for Europe in the late 18th century.
19 Hilt with decoration made in Japan for the Europeans *c*.1700.
20 Basket hilt of Scottish broadsword with brass inlay *c*.1740.
21 Early 18th century Scottish basket guard.
22 U.S. Light Cavalry gilt brass hilt 1785–1800.
23 Plain 19th century hilt.
24 Brass hilt of Sapper's sword of French Revolutionary period.

Daimos (dukes) and their retainers, independent lords and penniless warriors. Samurai behaviour and ideals became codified as 'bushido' and were strongly influenced both by Zen Buddhism and Confucian ideas from China, which were promoted by the shoguns.

The relatively peaceful years of the shogunate resulted in swords becoming shorter. Swords forged before the late 16th century are known as 'koto' or old swords and include blades up to 1.8 m (6 ft) long (Nodachi), which were carried slung across the back; Tachi were shorter and were slung from the belt; a dagger (Tanto), with a 25–37 cm (10–15 in) blade and a handguard was also slung from the belt with the edge down.

Swords made from about 1600 are known as 'shinto' (new swords), and most of the blades still in existence are shinto. This class of swords includes the Katana, with a blade length of 53–76 cm (21–30 in), and the wakizashi with a blade length between 30–60 cm (12–24 in). Various knives and daggers such as yoroi-toshi, a short fighting knife used to pierce armour, were smaller versions of the swords.

The two swords of a samurai were called 'daisho'; the katana, allowed only to samurai, could be replaced with the shorter wakizashi and a dagger, tanto or yoroi-toshi. On rare occasions members of other classes could carry the short sword and dagger. Also, free peasants (goshi) might carry swords at their own risk. The sword and dirk were carried in the waist sash. Although the long hilt on Japanese swords allows two-handed use they were usually used single-handed with a slashing action rather than a thrust, though the point was used with daggers and knives.

Samurai women were not allowed to handle a sword, but they were trained in the use of other weapons such as the halberd. Samurai dominance over other classes was often despotic – sword blades were tested on criminals and even passers-by as well as on iron bars and hay bales.

All the famous swordsmiths were of samurai rank. Smiths were regarded as artists rather than artisans, and founded dynasties and rival schools of swordmakers, some of which lasted for centuries. The Japanese also invested the sword with a religious quality – it was the 'soul of the samurai'. Japanese ideas about swords reflect the mixture of Shinto, the indigenous beliefs, and imported Buddhist ideas: swords were thought to have magical qualities, and to be made of the Five Elements, earth, fire, water, wood and metal. Smiths tended to lead moderate, even ascetic lives; forging was complex and took weeks of skilful work.

When forging the hard edge on a sword blade, an almost religious ritual was followed. The smith and his assistant wore special robes indicating their social rank; the smithy was locked and Shinto rites were performed to make it into a shrine with plaited straw hangings and paper flags to prevent the entry of evil spirits.

To produce a hard edge on a sword blade it was covered with wet clay in which a line was drawn about 12 mm ($\frac{1}{2}$ in) from the edge. The clay was removed between the line and edge and

1 The unique feature of Japanese swords was their capacity to take and hold an edge without being brittle. This was achieved by repeatedly folding and welding iron and steel together in the forging process. The iron provided a soft, flexible core and the steel an edge of the finest temper. The hilt was made of two pieces of grooved wood glued together around the tang with a ferrule, fuchi, fitted to one end. A copper washer, seppa, was placed between the ferrule and the guard. A wooden peg held the tang in the hilt. A layer of sting ray or sharkskin was glued on to the wooden grip and bound with braid which held a small metal ornament, menuki, on either side and a pommel, kashira, in place.

2, 3 Sword fittings were often made in copper with a semi-matt finish, an alloy of copper and gold, shakudo, was also used. Tsuba were the most ornate part of sword furniture. Early guards were made of iron, softer metals such as bronze were used later. Decoration included relief, openwork and gold and silver inlays. A guard with three openings is usually for a wakizashi, the two off-centre holes are for the small knives, kodzuka and kogai. A samurai usually had several tsuba to allow fashionable changes on the same sword or set of swords.

the remainder allowed to harden, the blade was then placed in the furnace and watched for the right colour change. The blade was then removed, the clay taken off and the blade quenched. This process produced a hardened, decorative cutting edge (yahiba) with a milky white colour where the exposed steel had crystallized.

Characteristic designs were used when drawing the line of the yahiba. These included a jagged line signifying a horse's tooth, and a stepped line indicating a road up the mountains. These patterns (hamon) may be used to date and value a sword and place its tradition or school.

The blade was sharpened and polished over several weeks to produce a mirror finish. The effect of the repeated folding and welding of the original ingot shows in the pattern of the softer surface steel layer (jihada) away from the edge. Shinto swords were also often decorated with engraved figures (harimono). The tang might then be inscribed with the maker's name, province and the date before the sword furniture and scabbard were mounted. If the blade were to be stored it was mounted with a plain wooden grip in a plain wooden scabbard. Whether stored or worn, a collar (habachi), fitted into the top of the scabbard to provide a seal to prevent the damp climate attacking the blade.

Swords are identified by their period, the area where they were produced, and the smith's signature. However swords were not always signed, and some famous signatures were copied by later smiths. The identification of blades was a touchy subject, even among the samurai. Some 19th century smiths referred to their ancestry when signing blades, others used variations on their name and title.

Swords were mounted with various fittings. These were primarily functional, to protect, strengthen and help the grip. During the Tokugawa the decorative nature of sword furniture increased and was changed according to fashion and purse. Scabbards were usually of lacquered wood, often decorated with very small motifs in contrasting colours.

About 1800 many smiths condemned elaborate sword furniture as decadent. Samurai who followed this puritanical trend often had their sword guards inscribed with morally uplifting texts or used plain iron copies of earlier forms of guards. Apart from this trend the 19th century saw the peak of achievement in decorative sword furniture with Kano Natsuo, and a revival of swordmaking under Masahide. Popular subjects as decoration on guards (tsuba) at this time included myths, folklore and battles.

In 1867 the feudal period officially ended when the emperor was restored. After the Satsuma rebellion of 1876–77 an imperial edict forbade samurai or anyone else from carrying swords. Many smiths became unemployed and the craft almost died. From this time on swords were largely made for the military, with knuckle guards and western style scabbards. In 1937 there was a mass production of traditional type swords which were issued to the Japanese armed forces in World War II.

2

3

Firearms

Of all antique weapons, firearms are probably the most popular with collectors. They have romantic, aesthetic and mechanical qualities which appeal to so many people. Until the mid-19th century each was hand made and good quality pieces were the product of the skills of many craftsmen. Each one was unique.

Details of the early history of gunpowder are vague, but it seems fairly certain that it was in use on a limited scale in China during the 11th or 12th century. The story of European firearms begins with a reference to them in 1326 and, by coincidence, the earliest illustration of a crude gun can be dated to the same year.

The earliest firearms were essentially artillery, primarily designed to replace the older forms of missile weapon used to demolish fortifications. In a very short time the idea of hand firearms had developed and the first handguns were very simple. They were nothing more than a tube with one end closed, and near the closed end a small hole (the touchhole), was drilled through the wall of the tube. A charge of black powder, a mixture of saltpetre, sulphur and charcoal, was poured down the barrel; a ball of lead, iron or stone was then pushed down on top of the powder inside the barrel. A pinch of powder was placed over the touchhole and this priming was ignited by some means or other, perhaps a glowing ember. The priming flared and the flame passed through the touchhole to the charge inside the barrel. As the gunpowder exploded the expanding gas drove the bullet down the barrel of the gun.

The first handguns had a barrel mounted at the end of a wooden stick, although some were all-metal types with barrel and stock made in one. Examples of these early handguns are extremely rare although similar weapons made at a much later date in the Orient may occasionally be found. Soon the barrel was lengthened and fitted to a wooden stock with the end shaped to fit against the shoulder.

From around the end of the 15th century the matchlock ignition system was developed and this used a piece of cord which had been soaked in a very strong solution of saltpetre and then allowed to dry. If the end of this cord was ignited it smouldered with a glowing tip, burning down very slowly. The match was attached to a simple, mechanical arm which was fitted to a plate set into the stock. When the trigger, set under the stock, was pressed, the arm (the serpentine) which held the match, swung forward and pressed the glowing end into the priming powder and ignited the main charge.

This weapon, known as a musket, was long and heavy, and during the 17th century became the main arm of the infantry of most armies. Seventeenth century muskets rarely appear on the market, and then they are extremely expensive. Army-issue weapons were very plain but some, owned by groups known as the Trained Bands or town guard, were sometimes decorated with inlay of horn or ivory.

One great disadvantage of the match was its vulnerability to wind and weather. Rain could easily extinguish the glowing end and the wind could blow sparks about – a great danger with gunpowder near. Gunsmiths sought other means of ignition which would be less liable to the vagaries of the weather. One solution was known as the wheellock. The idea was basically simple, but the mechanism was rather complex. A steel wheel was fitted with a square-ended axle and the edge of the wheel was roughened by various cuts. This wheel was coupled by a very short linked chain, to a powerful V-spring. The edge of the wheel was so placed that it formed part of the floor of a pan set next to the touchhole. A metal arm, attached to the lockplate, had two jaws which held a piece of pyrites – a common mineral. To prepare the mechanism for firing a special key was fitted over the squared end of the spindle attached to the wheel. As this key was turned the wheel also rotated and this movement compressed the spring. When fully compressed, a small arm (the sear) engaged with a hole in the side of the wheel, locking it in place. The cock holding the pyrites was swung forward until the pyrites was presed against the wheel's edge which had been cut and roughened. A pinch of priming powder was placed in the pan and the weapon was ready to fire. When the trigger was pressed the sear was drawn clear of the wheel which, driven by the spring, rotated rapidly. The friction between wheel and pyrites produced a shower of sparks which then ignited the priming powder and so discharged the weapon. This mechanical system of ignition was a big advance on the old matchlock and offered several advantages, being far less subject to the weather. The wheellock was, however, fairly complex and expensive to produce and was, therefore, never

issued on a large scale. It was fitted to longarms and pistols, some of which were extremely ornate with the wooden stocks inlaid with mother-of-pearl, ivory, steel, gold and silver. Many of these weapons were works of art in their own right.

The wheellock was fitted to long arms often used primarily for hunting, and since this was essentially a pastime of the rich these wheellocks were often very ornate and elaborate. To ensure greater accuracy, many of these hunting wheellocks were fitted with rifled barrels. They are extremely attractive pieces but their very quality ensures that they fetch very high prices indeed.

Wheellocks were in general use from about 1550 to 1650 but their cost meant that they never ousted the matchlock musket as the standard military arm.

The matchlock was gradually displaced from the middle of the 17th century, not by the wheellock but by a much simpler system, the flintlock. In place of the pyrites a shaped piece of flint, an even more common mineral, was used. The flint was gripped between the jaws of the cock, which was connected by means of a shank to a shaped metal block, known as the tumbler, fitted on the inside of a lockplate. Bearing down on the tip of

1 Series of engravings showing some of the many movements to load and fire a wheellock pistol, normally carried in a holster at the saddle. The last two show the *cuirassier* with a carbine or *harquebus*. (National Army Museum.)

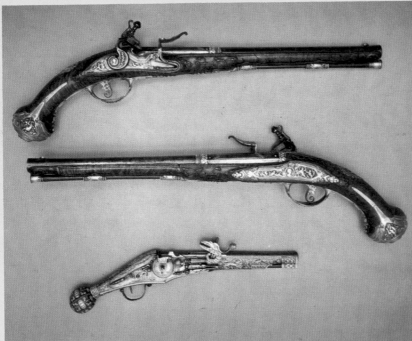

the sear. As the spring was under tension, once the sear was released, it pressed on the tip of the tumbler and caused it to turn rapidly and so swing the cock forward. The flint held in the cock scrapped down an L-shaped arm of metal known as the frizzen, to produce sparks. The short arm of the L served as a pan cover and as the flint pressed on the top section it caused the frizzen to pivot forward allowing the sparks to fall directly into the pan to ignite the priming and so fire the main charge.

There were several varieties of flintlock but the most common form was the French lock which appears to have been first constructed in France about 1610. The miguelet lock is a variant

1 (Top) Pair of fine quality early 18th-century, Italian flintlock pistols signed F. Bigioni in Brescia, a town noted for its fine quality steel chiselling.
(Bottom) Small German wheellock pistol of the late 16th century with typical ball butt and inlaid stock.

2 Detail of wheellock mechanism from military weapon of about 1640. The decoration, gilt wheel cover and studs, suggest that this was an officer's weapon. It is one of a pair. (Private Collection.)

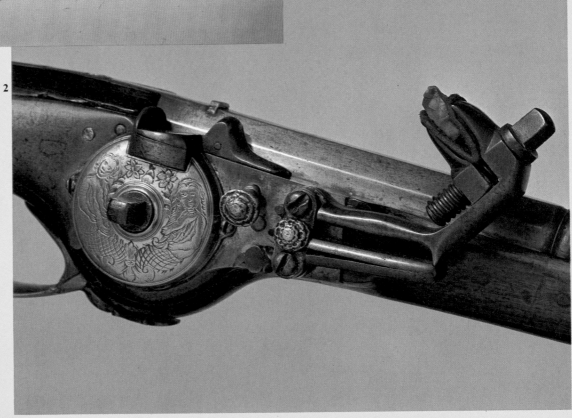

the tumbler was a strong V-spring; also pressing against the outer edge of the tumbler was a small arm known as the sear. As the cock was pulled back the tumbler turned and the sear rode over the outside edge and slipped into a small slot cut into the face of the tumbler. In this position the trigger could not disengage the sear from the slot. Known as the half-cock this position enabled the shooter to carry the loaded weapon in safety.

If the cock was pulled further back the tumbler turned and the sear automatically disengaged from the first slot and moved along the edge of the tumbler and then engaged with a second slot. This was the full cock position and in this setting pressure on the trigger disengaged

form in which the cock was locked not by a sear pressing against the tumbler, but by an arm which passed through the lock plate to engage directly with the arm of the cock. The common Spanish miguelet is characterized by a short, square frizzen and a squat, square cock.

The flintlock was simpler than the wheellock and by the end of the 17th century the only wheellock weapons still being produced were very expensive hunting arms for the leisured nobility. The matchlock was no longer the standard military issue and generally the only matchlocks still in use after the 17th century were to be found in the East. When the Portuguese explorers first reached Africa, India and, eventually, China and Japan they took with them their matchlock muskets.

The impact of these new weapons on the Asiatic cultures was very marked. The native craftsmen made copies and in Asia and Africa the matchlock was to continue in use until the very beginning of this century.

The Indian matchlocks are generally quite simple with very long barrels and plain, chunky stocks but the obvious difference between matchlocks from India and those from Europe is that the serpentine arm is set partly inside the stock, unlike the European pattern which has the lock plate mounted on the side of the stock.

Japanese matchlocks are far more ornate and, as befits the skill of their craftsmen, the Japanese produced some very fine quality pieces. Barrels on the Japanese matchlocks tend to be very thick and heavy while the wooden stock does not, like the Indian version, copy the European style. Japanese matchlocks are usually quite short and chunky and they are frequently inlaid or lacquered. The springs on these weapons are almost invariably of brass and the lock favoured by the

3 Pair of late 18th-century boxlock, flintlock pocket pistols by Wilson of London. The butts are decorated with inlaid silver wire and grotesque silver butt caps. (Tower of London Armouries XII 1667, 1668).

4 Japanese matchlocks are increasingly popular among collectors and the skill and craftsmanship of their makers command high prices in salesrooms.

have been responsible for the spread of the pistol but it was the flintlock that made the pistol commonplace. From the 17th century onwards the French style of lock was the dominant version and will be found fitted to pistols and longarms made all over Europe and America.

The shape of the lockplate can be a useful guide in dating flintlocks. The late 17th-, early 18th-century lockplate tends to be rather drooping, almost banana shaped, and is frequently convex in section. As the 18th century progressed the lockplate became straighter, losing that characteristic droop at the rear; it also became flatter in section.

The shape of the cock can also help in dating, for early ones have a very graceful S shape, later versions are less graceful. By the turn of the century many of the cocks are of the ring necked style with the lower S-section being replaced by a strengthened neck. Various improvements were made to the mechanical action of the lock – all designed to reduce friction and make the action more positive. Small metal rollers were fitted on the lock at points of maximum friction such as the tip of the frizzen where the spring pressed against it – a feature of the late 18th and early 19th century weapons.

Another useful guide, but by no means infallible, is the butt cap on the pistol. As a generalization, and it must be appreciated that there are exceptions to all these general guidelines, the earlier the pistol the larger the pommel or ball at the end of the butt, is likely to be. The pommel was usually fitted with a metal cap, and running up the side of the butt were two arms, one on either side. As the 18th century progressed these arms tended to be shorter until, by the turn of the century the butt cap was often dispensed with altogether. If, as on many military pistols, a butt cap was still fitted, the only trace of the side arms was a slight upward curve on the edge of the cap.

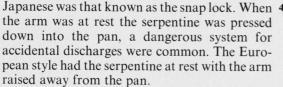

Japanese was that known as the snap lock. When **4** the arm was at rest the serpentine was pressed down into the pan, a dangerous system for accidental discharges were common. The European style had the serpentine at rest with the arm raised away from the pan.

European matchlocks are rare but those from India are fairly common and, unless of good quality, not greatly favoured by collectors. Those from Japan are more sought after and often fetch high prices in the salerooms.

One great advantage of the flintlock was that it could be produced in any size, large enough to fire a cannon or small enough to fit on a pistol to slip into a pocket or purse. The wheellock may

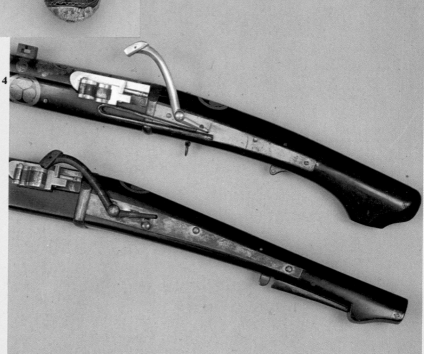

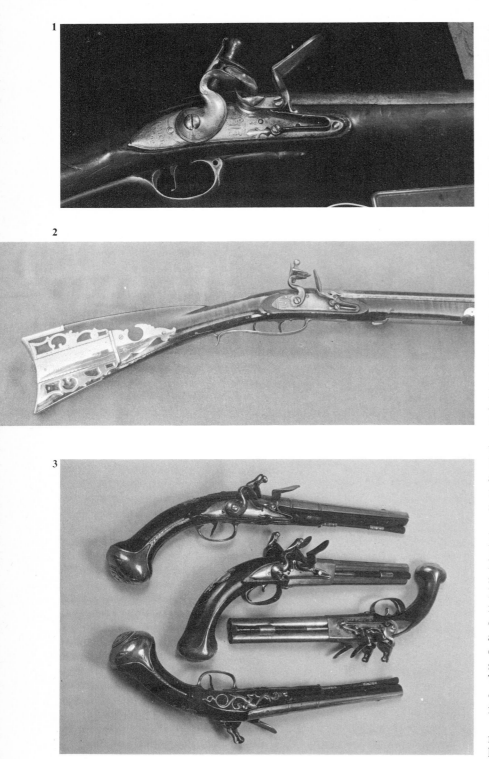

1 The flintlock of a Brown Bess musket dated 1762.

2 Butt and lock of a flintlock Pennsylvanian Long rifle.

3 Pistols by Barber of London. The pair in the centre are double-barrelled, over and under pistols with separate locks for each barrel. Those at the top and bottom are fine quality officers' or holster pistols.

until 1764, the date and name of the manufacturer. The walnut stock had a brass butt plate and trigger guard. In a slot cut in the stock beneath the barrel, was the ramrod. On the early models this was of wood but it was soon replaced by a metal one. The ramrod was held in position by small brass pipes set into the stock.

About 1768 the barrel was shortened to 106.7 cms (42 in) and in 1794 a shorter, and in many ways cruder, version of the Brown Bess, known as the India pattern, was taken into service, and this had a 99.1 cms (39 in) barrel. Later still, about 1810, the New Land Model was introduced and this reverted to a 106.7 cms (42 in) barrel.

Military muskets are occasionally to be found with identifying regimental marks engraved on the barrel or on the butt plate and these are very desirable pieces. Many Brown Besses were produced by private suppliers for the volunteer movement which flourished during the period of the Napoleonic wars. These will often bear the name of a gunsmith and, quite often, a series of initials which identify the particular volunteer unit to which they were issued. The muskets and pistols of the European powers France, Prussia, Austria and Russia conform to much the same style as that of the Brown Bess.

The pistols of the same period are fitted with walnut stocks, a 30.5 cms (12 in) or 22.9 cms (9 in) barrel and a lock plate with the word Tower and a crowned cypher and, like the musket, there may be on the barrel the initials of a regiment or ship to which they were issued.

The European military musket differed from the Brown Bess in the method of attaching the barrel to the stock. The British used a series of lugs under the barrel which were secured to the stock by pins which passed through holes in the lugs and stock. The French and other European nations favoured a simpler system using a ring or band which encircled the stock and barrel and at the muzzle end there was usually a more elaborate band. Most European weapons bear some marks, such as the name of the arsenal – Tula (Russia) or Suhl (Austria) or a proof mark or national emblem which will usually help identify the country of origin.

The flintlock pistol was produced in a tremendous range of patterns. There were tiny ones, known as muff pistols, intended for self-protection, and deriving their name from the fact that they were small enough to be secreted inside a muff or in a pocket or a purse. Pocket pistols were slightly larger and these too were intended primarily as self defence weapons. They fired a small ball and instead of the cock and frizzen being mounted on the right hand side of the stock they were fitted with a device known as a box lock. The cock and frizzen were mounted centrally in the stock, just behind the breech. These pistols are frequently decorated with inlaid silver wire or by the use of special woods to enhance the appearance with the patterning and, less often, with some other form of inlay.

Very much sought-after by collectors are duelling pistols. They appeared first towards the

The ease of manufacture, maintenance and certainly of operation made the flintlock very suitable for military weapons and from early in the 18th century most European armies were equipped with flintlock muskets and pistols.

One of the best known and widely collected of these muskets was that of the British army, known as Brown Bess. This was produced in several styles which varied in detail although the basic shape and pattern remained the same. The earliest ones have a 116.8 cms (46 in) barrel with a bore of about 1.9 cms ($\frac{3}{4}$ in). The lockplates, since they were government weapons, normally carried the Royal cypher, the word Tower and,

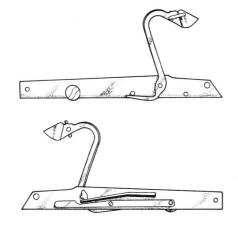

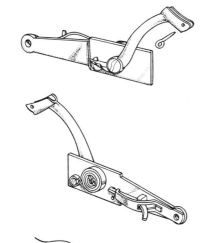

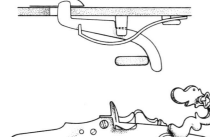

The earliest guns were fired by means of separate ignition devices but these were soon replaced by mechanisms attached to the weapon. The snaplock used a glowing match held in a spring operated arm. Later the Japanese developed a similar system with a coiled brass spring and a sear projecting through the lockplate. More common in Europe was the trigger lock in which the arm swung forward under the pressure of a trigger.

In the 16th century the match was replaced by the wheellock which produced sparks by friction between a steel wheel and a piece of pyrites. A simpler method was the snaphaunce which used a piece of flint to strike sparks from a steel plate. In the 17th century the flintlock was common and this had a combined steel and pan cover. Various designs of flintlock were used and round the Mediterranean the miquelet was popular. This lock functioned in much the same way although it differed mechanically. In 1807 Alexander Forsyth patented his scent bottle lock which produced a flash by detonating small crystals of fulminate. By the 1820s his lock had been simplified by the adoption of the percussion cap. When metal cased, centre fired cartridges were developed in the 1850s it became possible to design simple, efficient repeating weapons such as the Winchester which was operated by means of the lever beneath the butt.

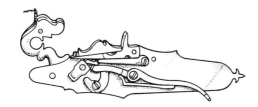

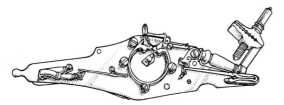

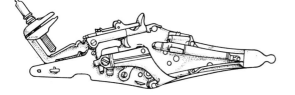

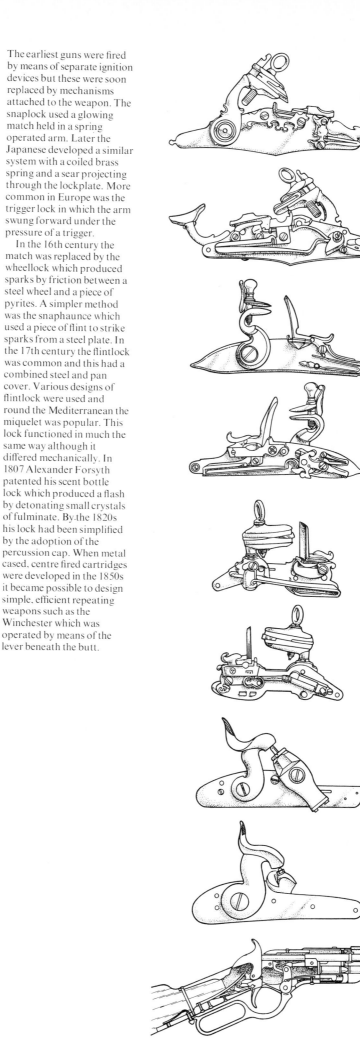

end of the 18th century when they were basically just a form of officer's holster pistol, with a fairly long barrel.

At the end of the 18th century and certainly during the first part of the 19th century, specially made pistols intended solely for duelling, were produced. These were sold in pairs complete with accessories such as a flask to hold the powder, a mould in which to cast the lead bullets, sundry cleaning rods and leather bags to hold bullets. All these were fitted inside a case of oak or mahogany, together with a pair of flintlock pistols which were, as far as possible, identical. These duelling sets are very highly prized, particularly if by one of the better known British

1 Cased pair of pocket, percussion pistols by Egg of London dated about 1830. The butts are decorated with inlay, and the accessories include a key for unscrewing the barrels, and a bullet mould.

makers such as Manton, Mortimer, Twigg or Parker. Those by Wogden are especially desirable, for he was noted for the production of very fine quality duelling pistols.

On the Continent of Europe the gunmakers of France and Belgium excelled in the production of superb percussion duelling pistols. They were usually cased in trays with contoured compartments and often included extra accessories such as small mallets for tapping down the tight-fitting ball. The pistols were usually very ornate with chiselling and carving on barrels and stocks.

The barrels of most flintlock pistols were of steel but some were of brass, especially if the weapon was likely to be exposed to sea air or constant damp since brass does not rust.

One type of flintlock weapon which has always been popular with collectors is the blunderbus. These weapons vary in detail but basically all have a bore which expands gradually from the breech towards the muzzle. The blunderbus was loaded with 10 or 20 small pistol bullets with the idea that the widening bore would ensure that the shot spread over a wider area. In fact the

widening of the muzzle only had a limited effect on the spread of shot but they were, none the less, very popular weapons. They were often fitted with a spring-operated bayonet fixed above or below the barrel. Either the trigger guard or a separate catch could be pressed so that the bayonet, which was folded back along the barrel, was driven by a spring to snap into the extended position in front of the barrel. These blunderbusses were carried by the guards on Royal Mail coaches, and those examples bearing post office markings or stage coach identification are extremely desirable. These inscriptions are normally to be found engraved round the muzzle. Although the blunderbus seems to have originated on the Continent it was most popular with the British, and comparatively few European made examples are found. Austria alone seems to have experimented in arming their troops with them.

Most of the pistols and muskets were, by modern standards, wildly inaccurate, but an improvement in accuracy could be obtained by rifling the barrel, that is cutting a number of quite shallow, spiral grooves on the inside face of the barrel. The idea was that the bullet, which was made of lead, would grip these ridges and as it moved down the length of the barrel the bullet would be forced to turn so that as it left the muzzle the ball was spinning. This spinning motion produced a gyroscopic effect which helped to cancel out the variations in shape, size and weight of the bullet, so resulting in far greater accuracy.

This basic ballistic fact had been known from the earliest days of gunpowder but the limiting factor was the difficulty of cutting the grooving or rifling on the inside surface of the barrel. It could be done and many of the wheellock guns were, in fact, rifled, but it was not until the middle of the 19th century that mass produced rifled barrels became possible.

One of the best known of all rifles was the so-called Pennsylvanian or long rifle also known, erroneously, as the Kentucky rifle. It was an American weapon which had been developed from the European hunting rifle. The distinguishing feature of these very attractive and desirable rifles was the long barrel, around 94 cms–101.6 cms (37–40 in) long, which fired quite a small diameter ball. The combination of a small bullet and a long, rifled barrel resulted in a standard of accuracy far in advance of the old, smooth-bored Brown Bess.

The Pennsylvanian rifle was frequently stocked with maple or other figured woods which gave it a very attractive appearance. Another distinguishing feature of these rifles was the graceful, down-drooping butt found on most of them, and the deep curve cut at the back of the butt where it fitted against the shoulder. During the American War of Independence these rifles were used by various volunteer units and caused a high rate in casualties among British officers. The users of these Pennsylvanian rifles were considered to be little better than murderers since they picked out specific targets.

During the American War of Independence the colonists were largely armed with British style weapons although a number of muskets were supplied by the French. When, eventually, the new colonists were able to create their own arms industry they rather copied the French style.

The flintlock mechanism worked well, indeed its long life indicates this for it was in general use from about 1650 until the 1830s, but it was not without its faults. Probably the biggest inconvenience was the so-called hangfire which was the cumulative effect of a number of quite small delays. When the trigger was pressed a small period of time passed as the tumbler turned and the cock swung forward to strike the frizzen. The priming flashed and there was a further slight delay while the flame passed through the touchhole to ignite the main charge, which then fired. These small delays all added together to produce the hangfire which was particularly irritating to the hunter whose target was moving.

The flintlock mechanism was, like the matchlock, also somewhat at the mercy of the weather. If the priming powder got damp then the chances of a misfire were very high, or a strong wind might well blow most of the priming away. There were many attempts, some very ingenious, to overcome the hangfire problem and susceptibility to damage from weather. It was eventually

2 Cased pepperbox revolver with powder flask, bullet mould, tools and other accessories. These weapons were popular during the 1840s but were supplanted by the percussion revolver.

3 Eighteenth-century blunderbusses. *Top* Early eighteenth-century example with belled brass muzzle and the lock marked "Smart". *Bottom* Late eighteenth-century blunderbuss with spring operated bayonet and made by the famous London maker H. W. Mortimer (Durrant Collection)

a Scottish clergyman, the Reverend Alexander Forsyth, who pointed the way to a solution to these problems.

Forsyth used fulminates, very unstable chemicals, to ignite the main charge. His first practical system was the so-called scent bottle, a device which deposited a few grains of the fulminate just above a touchhole communicating with the main charge. A solid nosed hammer banged a small rod down on to the grains of fulminate causing it to explode and produce a flash to fire the main charge. Forsyth patented his percussion system in 1807 but as yet it was not a really practical proposition. By the 1820s a simpler method of using the fulminate had been developed. A thin layer of fulminate was deposited on the inside of a thimble-like copper cap which was placed on top of a small pillar which had a tiny hole drilled through it to connect with the main charge. When the hammer swung forward it struck against the top of the cap forcing it down against the nipple, so causing the fulminate to explode and the flash passed through the tiny hole to ignite the charge.

The use of the percussion cap increased the efficiency of the firearms very considerably and the number of misfires was greatly reduced and priming was made so much simpler. With the matchlock, wheellock and flintlock priming had

1 A presentation Enfield percussion Artillery carbine. This British weapon was a variation on the 1853 pattern and was issued in 1858.

2 The mid-19th century saw the introduction of mass production methods into the firearms industry and the new machines made possible greater standardization. This set of gauges was used to test the size of the various components of the 1853 Enfield Rifled Musket.

3 Colt Percussion Revolvers. (Top) Cased 1851 Navy Colt, .36 calibre, six-shot. The accessories include powder flask, tin for caps and bullet mould. (Bottom) Similar cased set for the Model 1849 Pocket revolver, .31 calibre. (Private Collection.)

always been rather a slow business. After some powder had been poured down the barrel another pinch had to be deposited in the pan. Sometimes this was done using a special container known as a powder horn or powder flask which usually had some simple, automatic measuring device fitted at the nozzle.

From the mid-17th century onwards it became increasingly common to use a paper cartridge which was simply a tube of paper holding a charge of powder and a bullet. To load the weapon the end of the cartridge was bitten or torn, a pinch of powder was placed in the pan and the rest of the powder, followed by the ball and the paper case, was poured down the barrel and pushed home with the ramrod. With the percussion cap the system was simpler and the cartridge was merely torn open and the paper, powder and bullet poured down the barrel but instead of the priming powder a copper percussion cap was placed over the nipple and the weapon was then ready for firing.

One big problem for firearms makers and the military authorities brought about by the adoption of the percussion cap was that they were now left with quantities of obsolete flintlock weapons. From the 1830s onwards many of the military flintlocks were converted to the percussion system in a variety of styles. The most

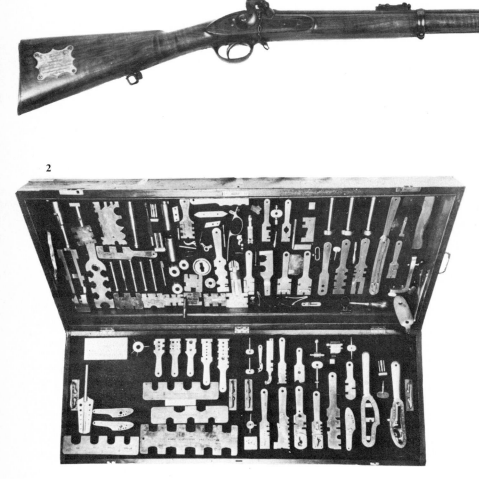

common way was to fit a nipple into the touchhole and replace the cock with a solid nosed hammer and remove the pan and frizzen. This type of conversion was quite effective and was carried out on all types of flintlocks.

Converted flintlock firearms are never as desirable as the original flintlock and some restorers will re-convert and restore the percussion weapon to its original flintlock state. Neither the flintlock converted to percussion or the reconverted weapon is as desirable as one in its original condition.

Another great virtue of the percussion cap was that it made possible a simple, practical, multishot weapon. The great majority of matchlocks, wheellocks and flintlocks were single shot weapons. There had been many attempts to make them multishot and double and triple barrelled weapons were not uncommon. Not all of them were efficient and most suffered from some limitation. The big problem with all multishot flintlock and wheellock weapons was the complexity of the mechanism needed to discharge them. However, with the adoption of the percussion cap the problem was simplified.

The pepperbox revolver consisted of a large, metal cylinder drilled with five or six bores each

3

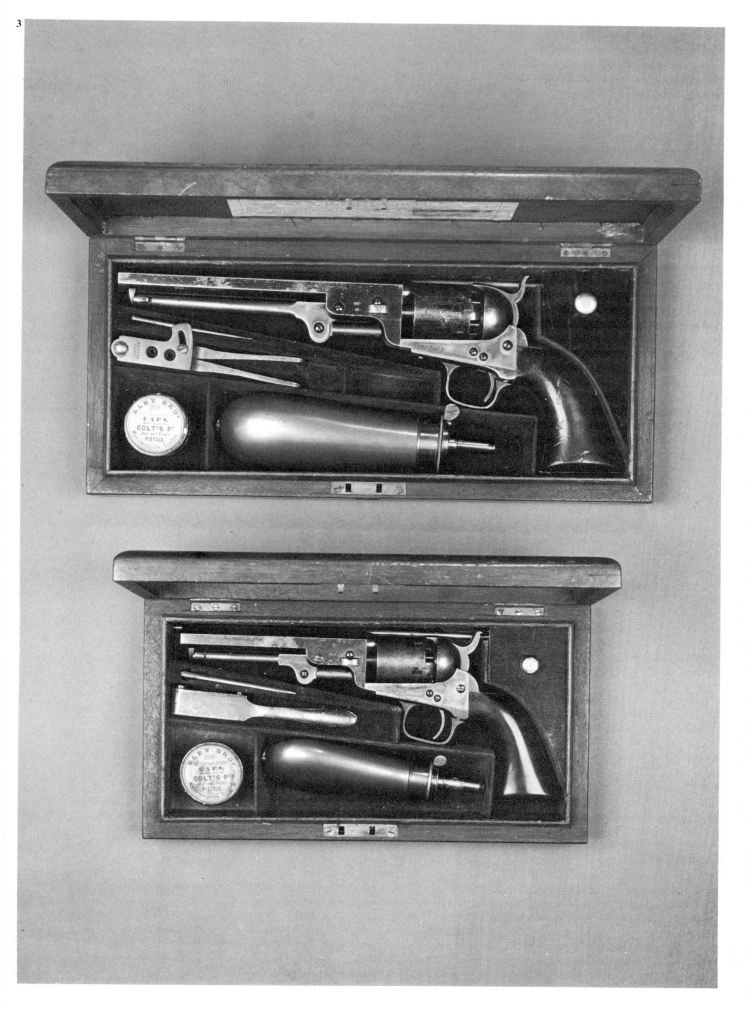

connected to a nipple. Each bore was loaded separately with powder and ball and each was primed by placing a cap on the nipple. The whole barrel assembly was mounted in a frame with a hammer operated by a trigger and, either by mechanical means or by hand, the barrel assembly was rotated so that the hammer fell on a nipple and fired one shot, then the trigger was pulled again and the next unfired chamber was brought into position for firing. These pepperboxes, so called because of a similarity between the pepper pot in the kitchen and the end view of the block with its five or six holes, are desirable – especially if cased with all accessories.

As a weapon pepperboxes were barrel-heavy, clumsy and, at best, rather inaccurate. Across the Atlantic an American, Samuel Colt, was developing a much more efficient percussion revolver. He saw the great possibilities of applying 'modern' manufacturing methods to the firearms industry. In 1848, after many ups and downs, he produced the Colt Dragoon pistol. This was a heavy weapon which weighed over 2 kgs (4½ lbs) and fired six .44 bullets.

1 (Top) Model 1851 Navy Colt with ivory grips together with combined nipple key and screwdriver. (Bottom) Walch revolver 1859. Each cylinder held two super-imposed loads. (Private Collection.)

The charges were housed in a cylinder and as the hammer was cocked with the thumb the cylinder was turned to bring an unfired charge in line with a rifled barrel. This system made for accuracy and rapid shooting and soon Colt was leading the world in the design and supplying of percussion revolvers. He produced many models, a particular favourite being the 1851 Navy Colt, which fired a 9 mm (.36) bullet, and took its name from the fact that the cylinder was decorated with the engraving of a naval battle. In 1861 he produced the Army Colt which fired an 11 mm (.44) bullet.

In 1851 Colt visited Britain to display his goods at the Great Exhibition in London. He promoted himself and his products with verve and skill and upset the majority of the British gunmakers who had nothing to offer in competition to his superb percussion revolvers. Stimulated by the impudence of this Yankee businessman British manufacturers such as Adams, Daws, Webley and Tranter, were soon producing their own models of percussion revolvers. At the time there was a great deal of controversy as

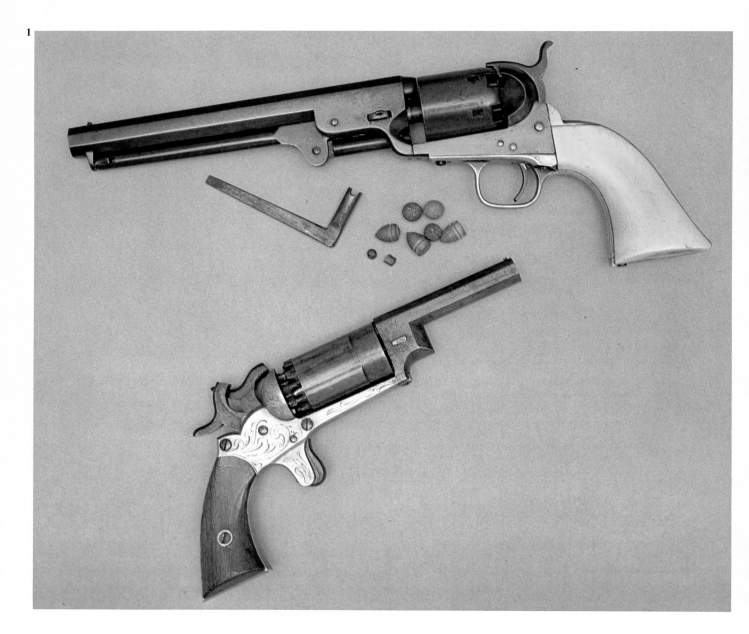

to whether the Colt or British revolver was preferable. All Colt's weapons were single action and they had to be cocked manually, that is hammer pulled back by the thumb, before each shot could be fired. The British used another system whereby the hammer was cocked by pressure on the trigger and continuing pressure fired the charge.

Later, British Manufacturers produced a double action version in which the hammer could be cocked either manually with the thumb or mechanically by means of the trigger. By the 1860s the number of percussion revolvers on the market was considerable.

Colts have long been prized by collectors, but British percussion revolvers have only recently begun to climb in price as collectors turn to their study and collection, for they are fine examples of mid-19th century British craftsmanship.

Another big innovation around the mid-19th century was the general issue of rifled weapons to the armies of the world. The British Enfield rifle was one of the best and in the United States there were rifles and carbines such as the Spencer

2 Pair of Colt cartridge revolvers made about 1895. They are a target version of the Single Action Army Model and were called the Colt Bisley Model, after the famous British shooting ranges. (Tower of London.)

and the Sharps, and many others which were excellent weapons in their own right.

Another very important development was taking place at the same time and that was the adoption of breech loading systems. The majority of flintlock, wheellock, matchlock and percussion weapons were muzzle loading, the charge and bullet being poured down from the muzzle. The idea that loading from the breech end was simpler, easier and quicker, was not new – some of the earliest weapons, for example one owned by Henry VIII, were breech loading. The main problem was that in order to gain access to the breech there had to be some opening, and when the charge was fired gas escaped through this opening unless it was very effectively sealed. This gas escape was injurious to the firer as well as reducing the velocity of the bullet. During the 1850s and 1860s there were many systems devised to overcome this problem and there is a very rich field for collectors in these capping breechloaders.

The other development which was in full flood at this time was the introduction of a metal

2

1 Lever action of the 1866 · Winchester repeating rifle. The loading gate through which the cartridges were fed into the under-barrel magazine can be seen as well as the small locking catch to secure the loading lever.

2 Colt's greatest rivals in the United States were Smith and Wesson.
(Top) The second Smith and Wesson model, a .22 seven-shot pistol, 1850s.
(Centre right) No. 3 Model 'American' .44 six-shooter, a later version of the No. 3 American model of 1870.
(Centre left) The 'Russian' model, distinguished by the spur on the guard. Many thousands of this model were sold to the Imperial Russian Government.
(Bottom) A .32 calibre version, with birdhead grips, of the pistol illustrated at the top.

cased cartridge. Paper cartridges were not a new idea, dating back to the 16th century, but what was being developed was a metal cartridge which contained the means of ignition as well as the propellant and bullet. One of the earliest was the pin-fire cartridge developed by Lefaucheux in 1835. This was a small copper case and in the base was a pinch of fulminate and touching this was a small, metal rod which projected through the wall of the case. The propellant was also inside the case and the mouth was sealed by the bullet. The pinfire cartridge was inserted into the breech and as the hammer fell it struck the pin which, in turn, hit against the fulminate exploding it and the flash fired the main charge. However this system, efficient though it was, left much to be desired, being awkward and dangerous to handle because of the projecting pins.

In 1860 the firm of Smith and Wesson produced a copper case cartridge which could be loaded into the rear of a revolver cylinder or into the breech of a rifle. The fulminate was deposited on the inside base of the case which was struck with the hammer to fire the cartridge. From then on muzzle loading was obsolete and cartridge weapons came into their own.

There was the usual problem of converting old weapons to the new system. Various stop-gap methods of converting old muzzle loading weapons to the new breech loading were adopted. In Britain the Snider system was approved; in the United States it was the Allin system. However most countries sought a completely new weapon. A system designed by an American, Henry Peabody, was popular and was taken up by several countries, including France, Switzerland and Mexico.

A great flood of breech loading cartridge weapons were produced; one of the best known was the Colt revolver introduced in 1873 and known as the Single Action Army Colt. It was extremely efficient and has continued in production, virtually unchanged, ever since. Numerous breech loading rifles were also introduced and then, in 1890, came the latest development, the introduction of self-loading pistols.

With the revolver the hammer had to be cocked either with the thumb or by pressing the trigger before another shot could be fired. In 1893 Hugo Borchardt designed one of the first, really practical, self-loading pistols. The design was later developed by George Luger who produced, in 1898, the famous Luger or Parabellum pistol. This weapon was loaded by means of a separate magazine which slipped into the butt. An ingenious recoil mechanism operated and once the first shot had been fired it would throw out the empty case, insert a fresh cartridge into the breech and make ready the action for firing. To discharge a shot all that was needed was a comparatively light pressure on the trigger, and the action could be repeated as long as there was any ammunition in the magazine.

Webley, Tranter, Mauser, Colt, Browning, Smith & Wesson were just a few of the manufacturers who produced metallic cartridge weapons, including many self-loading models.

3 Mauser automatic pistol, 7.63 calibre, with wooden holster that also served as a shoulder stock. This weapon was one of the first really practical self-loading pistols. The shape of the butt earned it the nickname of Broomhandle.

4 Browning Hi-Power Automatic 9mm pistol – a rugged handgun issued to a number of modern military forces. It has a large capacity magazine carrying 13 rounds.

The early 20th century was a period rich in mechanical devices, many of which came to nothing. But from a collector's point of view, these are still of considerable interest. However, collectors of these later weapons are at risk, for many of them are still quite capable of being fired and ammunition is still available; that means that, in many parts of the world these are viewed as modern firearms and, in consequence, fall within the scope of firearms legislation and control. Anybody planning to begin such a collection would be well advised to check the legal position.

Printed Materials

Although many aspects of printed materials have only recently attracted the attentions of collectors on any significant level, the whole field is one that warrants particular study, reflecting as it does the very nature of collecting itself.

On one level, there are those who consciously study yesterday's ephemera, and collect postcards, packaging, railway tickets, magazines, posters, photographs, objects of advertising and so on. These are prompted partly by nostalgia, and partly by an understandable fascination for temporal objects that have strayed into another age. The random survival of examples of printed ephemera is in itself an attraction, for it is only by chance that these objects become, in effect, time capsules, capable of recreating not only the atmosphere, but also the social order and whole way of life of another age.

On another level, there is the collector of books and prints, perhaps traditionally the most established, accepted and academic collector of all. Books have been collected since they were first produced, partly because of the knowledge they contain, and partly because of an interest in their appearance and means of production. The study of prints demands a similar academic approach, a combined awareness of technical processes and art movements, which has little in common with other fields of collecting. These pursuits are essentially intellectual, and so the acquisition and study of the objects is only a small part of the total activity.

An interest in printed ephemera incorporates these two extreme and apparently unrelated types of collector, who seem to have very little in common, apart from a broad understanding of similar reproductive techniques. However there is far more common ground than would appear at first sight. To collect any form of printed ephemera is to be concerned with time. Most antiques are expected, both by their creator and by their subsequent owners, to continue to exist through several decades, generations or even centuries. Although this survival is inevitably affected by chance, by accidents and by natural decay, the original hopes and aspirations of the craftsman or patron are reasonably realistic. Time is not something, therefore, to cause too much worry, and it is rarely surprising to find in a museum or private collection an example of 17th-century furniture, 18th-century porcelain or Victorian silver. These objects have been made in a way to ensure as far as possible their permanence, and their survival from one age to another. Indeed, their value is frequently based precisely on this fact, and collectors invest their money with some

degree of certainty about its likely stability. These considerations do not apply to printed ephemera, for the nature of the materials involved is that they should disappear once they have fulfilled their original purpose. Even a book, a relatively permanent object, is no more than a fairly strong container for the information enclosed within it. And this information can be as ephemeral as an example of packaging, a picture postcard, advertisements for all kinds of items, greetings cards or a photograph.

A fascination with time, and the ability of some ephemeral objects to overcome it, is probably the main attraction to collectors of printed ephemera. There are, of course, many other factors, such as an interest in printing technology, or photographic techniques, or a desire to analyze changes in artistic styles, or a straightforward pleasure in nostalgia. The collector of railway tickets can recreate in his mind the long-forgotten journeys that the tickets represent. However, even this is really no more than an attempt to reverse the passage of time and re-live an often imaginary past.

Another area of common ground is the general interest in patterns of social change. Printed ephemera accurately reflects the period that created it, and transports this period into another age. A study of the items can therefore be a useful guide to patterns of social development, revealing as they do the development of advertising and the consumer society, the changes in transport systems, patterns of leisure activity, eating habits, political beliefs, alterations in educational and professional life and the varying status of the sexes. Even books can be as revealing of these changes as the more obvious examples of ephemera.

Interest in this field will obviously expand, because of both the availability of material and the increasing value of the messages that the surviving items carry. This chapter is no more than a suggestion of some of the more obvious fields for study, but any interested collector will soon be able to find new ones. It is a very rich field and the surface has hardly been scratched. A particular area of development is likely to be the photograph, which must be one of the most probable candidates to be the antique of the future – not in terms of investment value, although this will also apply to some areas, but because of the value of the process as a universal recording system. Only the photograph can actually recreate an earlier period, because of its ability to capture and transmit perfectly a single moment in time.

Printed ephemera attracts on many levels. The whole nature of the subject can perhaps be expressed by the metaphor of canned food. This essentially unromantic product has the power, when painted by Andy Warhol, to become the ambassador of the consumer society to future ages. The same basic can, preserved in a hut at the South Pole, can bring to life Scott's doomed expedition to Antarctica or simply recall a way of life which no longer exists.

Eno's Fruit Salts poster by
E. McKnight Kauffer, 1929.

Illustrated books & bindings

Milestones in the history of printing

c.1425	Illustrations first reproduced in quantity from woodblocks.	1804	Earl Stanhope developed stereotyping.
c.1450	Gutenberg developed means of printing text with movable type.	c.1848	First steam rotary press used.
c.1470	The first Roman typeface was developed.	1852	Fox Talbot developed photogravure.
		c.1855	Colour printing first developed.
1473	The first bestseller *De Imitatione Christi* by Thomas à Kempis was published.	c.1880	Photo engraved illustrations reproduced.
mid 16th century	The use of engraved or etched copper plates for reproducing illustrations was developed.	1886	First Linotype machines in general use.
		1890	First Monotype machines in general use.
1798	First paper making machine made by Nicolas Louis Robert. Lithography developed by Alois Senefelder.	c.1910	Film setting invented.

To link together the development of printing with the spread of knowledge, and thus of civilisation, is to state a broadly accepted historical truth. Although its actual development probably took place in China during the 6th century, the printing of books first took place in Europe between 1440 and 1460. The discovery is usually credited to a Mainz goldsmith, Johann Genzfleisch zum Gutenberg, although it would be inaccurate to say that Gutenberg invented printing. The realization that the creation of a stable society could be hastened by a rapid spread of knowledge had been well understood for several centuries, especially among the members of the Church, who were generally the guardians of this knowledge.

Gutenberg brought together the results of many early attempts at mechanical reproduction, perhaps developed a means of casting large numbers of individual metal letters from one original matrix, discovered an ink that would adhere to these metal letters and then allow itself to be transferred under pressure on to paper, and adapted the familiar screw-driven wine-press into the first successful printing machine. Although Gutenberg himself made practically nothing from his efforts, he lit a fire that spread with dramatic speed. By the end of the 15th century, the mechanical reproduction of books by printing was under way in every country throughout Europe.

Prior to the development of printing, the spread of knowledge through the written word was in the hands of large numbers of scribes who painstakingly reproduced existing books and written documents by copying them by hand. This technique, of course, had existed in many earlier civilizations, such as classical Rome or ancient Egypt, but it reached a remarkably high level of sophistication and productivity during

1

288

the early medieval period. Whole workshops of scribes, usually under monastic control, toiled to produce the religious, legal and governmental works that society demanded.

The need for large-scale production of literature had been understood well before Gutenberg's time, and so the reproduction of texts had become a recognized and lucrative trade by the 15th century. Booksellers and publishers, aided by armies of scribes, strove to produce the large number of volumes requred to satisfy the ever-increasing demands of those wishing to read for education, for social development or simply for pleasure. Many of these early hand-written texts survive and so make possible the serious study of European history before the 15th century. Many were also finely made, the text meticulously written in a script specially developed for the purpose and interspersed with jewel-like illustrations that were included to clarify or illuminate the text. These manuscripts were then frequently bound with carved ivory or jewelled wooden panels to reflect the value of their contents and to safeguard them for the future.

Illuminated manuscripts are now usually only to be found in major public collections and so are accessible to study, not only for their contents, but also for their stylistic development. The changes in design, subject matter and method of illumination underline the many social upheavals of the early medieval period, making, for example, the close links between the manuscripts of Ireland and Scandinavia quite understandable. It is also important to realize that the early illuminated manuscripts established the form and style of the book as it is today. Printing merely continued the tradition, adding only speed and quantity to a well established pattern.

Although early illuminated manuscripts are outside the scope of this book, it would be wrong to assume that the production of such books and documents ceased with the coming of printing. To this day, the scribe and the illuminator are still called upon to produce the special book and the commemorative scroll. Such handmade documents frequently appear on the market once the reason for their original production has been forgotten and can often be bought quite cheaply. A royal visit, the opening of a factory, railway station or bridge, the launching of a ship, the laying of the foundation stone of a chapel, even the coming of age of the eldest son of an industrialist or landowner were the kinds of events commemorated by the special illuminated scroll, events of great importance at the time, but subsequently of little interest except to latter-day collectors.

The productions of Gutenberg and other early European printers followed closely the styles of hand-written manuscripts and so the letter forms they used were designed to resemble the formal characters used by the scribe. The full implication of the invention of printing from movable metal type was not realized until the last quarter of the 15th century and then the styles began to change dramatically. The Gothic,

2

MAXIMILIANO II·
IMPERATORI INVICTISSIMO

HIERONYMVS MERCVRIALIS
perpetuam Felicitatem. D.

J quando mecum diligentius considero, MAXIMILIANE Inuictissime, quot, quantaque Jmperatores, summiq. Principes pro hominum salute, & tranquillitate tam bello, quam pace gesserint, in eam facile descendo sententiam, merito, atque optimo iure omnes fere gentes, & nationes fecisse, quod eos dignos existimarunt qui in Deorum immortalium numerum referrentur. Jnter ea uero, quae in humanum genus innumera contulerunt beneficia magnam partem sibi uindicant artes paene omnes liberales, quas maximis propositis praemijs non excitarunt modo, atque extulerunt aliquando iacentes, sed ita etiam earum dignitatem amplificarunt, ut ipsi soli illarum auctores, & instauratores propemodum uideantur. Jd facile perspicere quiuis potest, qui militaris disciplinae, le-

★ *ij gum*

3

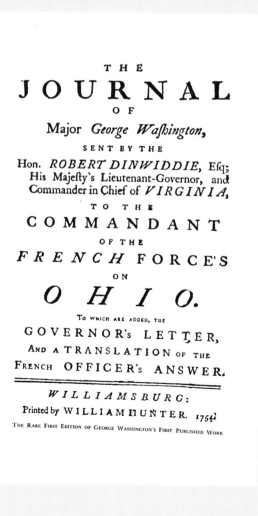

THE

JOURNAL

OF

Major *George Washington,*

SENT BY THE

Hon. *ROBERT DINWIDDIE,* Esq;
His Majesty's Lieutenant-Governor, and
Commander in Chief of *VIRGINIA,*

TO THE

COMMANDANT

OF THE

FRENCH FORCES

ON

OHIO.

To which are added, the

GOVERNOR's LETTER,

AND A TRANSLATION OF THE

FRENCH OFFICER's ANSWER.

WILLIAMSBURG:
Printed by WILLIAM HUNTER. 1754.

THE RARE FIRST EDITION OF GEORGE WASHINGTON'S FIRST PUBLISHED WORK

1 A page from the Gutenberg Bible of 1455, showing Psalms 1–4. Although the 42 line columns were set from movable type, the page format still reflects the style established by medieval illuminated manuscripts in previous centuries. This traditional approach can be seen particularly in the foliate decoration, the illuminated initials and the red horizontal guide lines.

2 In 16th century Venice, printing effectively came of age, establishing forms and styles that are still applicable today. This dedication page, from *De Arte Gymnastica,* was printed by the Guinta family in 1573. The main innovation was the Italic type-face, although the illuminated initial still reveals the link with manuscripts.

3 This title page from the first edition of George Washington's first published work, printed at Williamsburg in 1754, is a typical example of the classical styles of mid-18th century typography. The elegance of the page is created by the careful balance established by the varied type sizes and letter forms.

1

2

Goethe's

Werke.

Vollständige Ausgabe letzter Hand.

Eilfter Band.

Unter des durchlauchtigsten deutschen Bundes schützenden Privilegien.

Stuttgart und Tübingen,
in der J. G. Cotta'schen Buchhandlung.
1 8 2 9.

or blackletter, style of type was replaced by the more elegant Roman or antique form, a reflection of the humanism spreading across Europe from France and Italy. Venice and Paris became the centres of a new style of printing, epitomized by the work of Nicholas Jenson, and this style laid the foundations for modern printing. In Bologna, Francesco Griffo developed the first italic, or cursive type, and then in Paris Claude Garamond became the first to confine himself to the design and manufacture of typefaces to be used by other printers.

Aided by the demands of governments, churches, universities and private patrons, printing spread rapidly, so that by the 16th century it had already become the essential social force it is today. Because of their rarity, book collectors have traditionally specialized in the products of the 15th century printers. The term 'incunabula' is used to refer to any book printed before 1500. Although arbitrary, this division is understandable; by 1500 printing had reached a stage of

development that was then to remain unchanged for at least 300 years. The methods and the machinery did not greatly alter until the early 19th century, so much so that Gutenberg would certainly have been able to operate an 18th century press. The metal type and woodcut illustrations were produced in the same way and even the paper and the ink did not vary in any significant way during this period. In fact, the general style and form of the book was finalized to such an extent that they do not vary greatly even today.

However, many changes did take place between 1500 and 1800, mostly in the actual design and appearance of the book. In the early 16th century, type designs proliferated, especially in Rome and Venice, where printers such as Blado and Aldus developed an individuality of style lacking in the 15th century. In France, the highly personal pictorial manuscript style associated with the Books of Hours was adapted for books by printers such as Geofroy Tory.

1 and **2** During the 19th century there were many technical and stylistic developments which affected the appearance of the printed page. The steel engraving process, with its durable printing surface, enabled illustrations to be included in many popular books, printed in large editions. This frontispiece and title page from the 1829 edition of Goethe's complete works shows the continuity of 18th century styles, while the use of the traditional black letter type was probably prompted partly by a spirit of nationalism.

The spread of the Renaissance through Europe encouraged the increased use of illustration and decorative detail. Arabesques, heraldic details and floral and geometric borders were used with increasing freedom, while new methods of reproducing illustrations, such as copper plate engraving and etching, were rapidly applied to books. By the 17th century, the design of books was closely allied to general changes in artistic styles, a relationship that has not altered since. This pattern of stylistic change continued into the 18th century, when typographers such as Fournier, Bodoni and Baskerville were able to increase still further the choice of typefaces available to printers.

In his *First Principles of Typography,* Stanley Morison wrote: "The history of printing is in large measure the history of the title page". Certainly no other part of the book reflects so precisely its period or style, or indeed expresses so clearly the nature of its contents. As a result, the book collector is likely to pay as much attention to this one page as to the rest of the book. It is also by the title page that the printer or designer of a book can be recognized, either because he has put his name on it, or because his style is distinctive. The development of the title page also reflects the gradual shift of emphasis from printer to publisher. Today, a book carries boldly the name of its publisher on the title page and makes little mention of its printer. However, this is a relatively recent development, for it was only in the 19th century that the publisher emerged as the main producer of the book.

Originally, the printer published his own books and was responsible for all selling and distribution, either through book shops or by subscription. Then the printer worked in conjunction with a stationer or bookseller whose task was to sell the books, but the printer was still responsible for the origination, production and distribution of the books. As printers developed and diversified their activities, some set themselves up as publishers in order to control more precisely the production and selling of their books. However, in the 19th century, the whole system was turned round and the independent publisher appeared, his main function being to originate and sell books, this being done largely on a speculative basis.

The publisher simply contracted the production of the book to the printer and therefore felt justified in replacing the printer's name on the title page with his own.

During the 19th century, printing was totally revolutionized by a number of technical developments and so the nature of the book was changed dramatically during the same period. First, the application of mechanical power to printing presses and other machinery enabled them to work faster, on a much larger scale, and thus to produce many more books. Secondly, new papers and inks were developed to match the speed and output of the new machines, and these in turn allowed a greater flexibility to the designers and manufacturers of books. Thirdly, large numbers of new typefaces were produced,

3

many of which reflected the eclecticism and the successive fashions that followed and merged with each other throughout the 19th century. Designers and printers made free use of the Tuscans, Egyptians, Sans Serifs and other new and exotic letter forms that were put before them. Fourthly, the method of printing by lithography, developed by A. Senefelder in 1798, was rapidly adapted into an adequate and accurate method of reproducing all kinds of illustrations in large quantities to suit both commercial and artistic demands. This facility was not available to printers and publishers until the 19th century, and so before then illustrated books had only been produced in limited quantities and then only by rather laborious methods. Once the principle of lithography was generally established, it was soon developed into a means of reproducing illustrations in colour. From the middle of the century, chromolithography was in general use, and so for the first time large quantities of books, illustrated throughout in

3 *The Well at The World's End* was written by William Morris and printed by him at the Kelmscott Press in 1896, with illustrations and page decorations by E. Burne-Jones. This consciously archaic style, based loosely on medieval illuminated manuscripts, greatly affected book design and typography generally at the end of the 19th century. However, as this very decorative style deliberately used old-fashioned methods, it did little to advance the art of printing.

1 Advances in technology in the late 19th and early 20th centuries made possible the widespread use of colour printing. This affected particularly the design and production of children's books, and many leading artists and designers in Europe and America worked in this new field. Although best known for his book illustrations, Walter Crane also designed and decorated pottery, tiles, textiles and furniture.

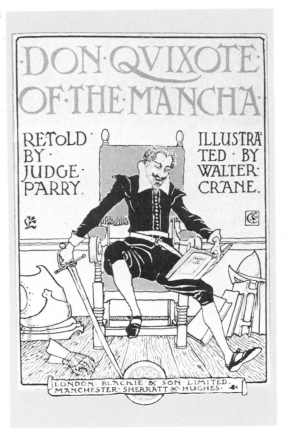

full colour, could be quickly and cheaply produced.

There were also changes in marketing. The production of large numbers of books was dependent upon there being already in existence a market ready to absorb them, and so various changes in selling and distribution took place, most of which were aimed at reducing the cost of books. Publishers began to advertise their products more widely and developed new ways of selling. For example, books were produced in paper covers, or were sold in instalments in magazine style. At the same time, the gradual spread of education throughout the 19th century ensured that new markets were continuously becoming available. Ultimately, the establishment of a general standard of education and literacy in one country after another throughout the world only became possible because the books were available to act as bricks upon which this concept of civilization could be firmly based.

In the 20th century, further changes have taken place in the methods of book production, but their impact has been rather less than those of the previous century. Book production has been advanced by technical developments such as computer-aided typesetting and the metal type itself has largely been replaced by film. Photographs in colour and black-and-white can now be reproduced in any book, almost regardless of its price. International co-editions have increased both the range and the quantity of published material. However, despite developments such as these, the book is still produced in the form ultimately finalized by the publishers and printers of the 19th century.

Of all collectors, the book collector is perhaps the oldest. The tradition was well established in classical Greece and Rome, and by the Middle Ages was generally accepted as a suitable activity for learned or wealthy gentlemen.

Many of the illuminated manuscripts produced during this period were immediately hoarded by collectors, both private and public. Indeed, the fruits of these early collectors are still to be seen, such as in the university libraries throughout Europe. The development of printing merely encouraged the enthusiasm of early collectors, who seized the new books as they came from the presses.

Many scholars of this period, for example Erasmus, were known as much for their libraries as for their actual writing. Even in this early period, there is evidence of collectors specializing in the work of particular printers and paying less attention to the subject matter of the books they were collecting than to the typography. Once established, the habit rapidly spread and developed, aided by the efforts of the booksellers, who were as willing to keep old books in circulation as to sell the new. By the 18th century, the antiquarian and second-hand bookseller was an essential part of any civilized community, a pattern that has not really altered since then.

The development of an interest in old books was felt to be a necessary part of any young man's education and the acquisition of the interest was made as easy as possible. Auction houses were established which specialized in the sale and resale of old books, ensuring that as soon as one library was broken up others would be formed to take its place. The broad acceptability of book collecting made it stand apart from other forms of collecting, which by comparison were made to seem less necessary and rather underhand. To collect books was to collect knowledge, even though the collector may have in fact paid little attention to the words within the covers.

As a result, the famous book collectors of the 18th and 19th centuries were far better known, both during and after their lifetimes, than collectors in other fields. To give one example, the collection of Sir Horace Walpole at Strawberry Hill was known throughout Europe. When it was dispersed at auction, its contents were judiciously scattered through the libraries of Europe, having been made more attractive by their connection with Walpole. Even today, a book known to have come from Walpole's library will command an interest greater than that aroused by its contents or typography alone. Indeed, the association of books with famous collectors of the past is one of their permanent attractions. To own a book with such associations is to own a part of that person, albeit temporarily.

Book collectors have a rich choice before them. They can concentrate on particular printers and so develop a knowledge of the changes in typographic styles. They can collect the works of particular authors in all their var-

2 Grolier binding of the 16th century, showing the styles traditionally associated with the craft. The Renaissance strapwork and arabesques inlaid and embossed into the leather and typical of the period, show the close relationship with other art forms, such as furniture and metalwork.

4 Late 19th century printed bindings are a rich and decorative field still hardly exploited by collectors. These designs, with their strong colours and richly embossed patterns, not only reflect contemporary artistic styles such as Japanism, but also under-line the variety that was lost with the introduction of the printed paper wrapper or book jacket – which, of course immediately adopted the same styles.

3 The art of bookbinding was revived in France during the 1930s. This binding, made of coloured inlaid calf leathers in 1952 by Paul Bonet, shows the typical bravura of the period, when bindings were closely related to contemporary art styles. This example reflects the work of Matisse.

second-hand bookshops is a universally attractive pastime and can be practised at any time and on any level of the market. Whether the collector is buying incunabula at auction, or old paperbacks in junk markets, it is still fascinating.

One particular aspect of the book which is often overlooked by collectors is the binding. The cover of a book is often taken for granted, simply as a means of protecting the more delicate material inside, but in fact a study of bindings can be as rewarding as the books themselves. Manuscripts were frequently given splendid bindings, both to protect them and reflect the sacred significance of the contents. With the development of printing, this pattern was altered, for early printers rarely made any attempt to bind their books themselves. Most books were bought on subscription by a limited number of purchasers, all of whom would expect the books to conform with the styles already established in their libraries or collections. The books were therefore supplied unbound by the printer and the purchaser would arrange for his own binder to complete the work. This pattern continued until the early 19th century, when changes in marketing and production methods completely altered the nature of the book.

Traditionally, leather has been the usual material for book binding, as it combines the necessary qualities of flexibility and permanence. Anyone with only a general interest in books will be aware that old books are likely to be bound in leather and decorated with embossed gold tooling, but they may not understand the complexities of style and technique that these bindings can conceal. In terms of

ious editions. They can pursue a particular subject or theme, which is perhaps the widest choice of all, because there is no subject that has not been written about at one time or another. They can study a particular technique of illustration, or the work of a particular illustrator. They can collect books associated with famous people. They can collect author's presentation copies, or first editions of 20th century novels. The choice is literally infinite and it is made even richer by its ability to fit any size of pocket. Browsing in

1 Mid-Victorian embossed and printed book binding, reflecting a variety of stylistic influences, from the Gothic revival to the Arts and Crafts movement.

2 Printed book jacket for Henry Miller's *Black Spring*, published in Paris in 1936. This continues the powerful imagery used on the earlier printed bindings.

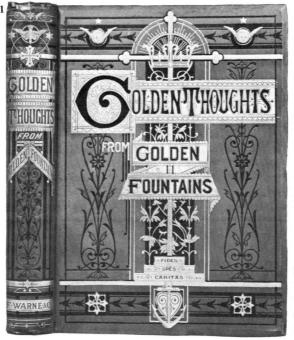

rise of the independent publisher meant that books were now required to have their own binding, for the public would no longer be willing or able to pay for individual custom-made binding. Printers therefore developed binderies and mechanized equipment to produce the new kind of book. Secondly, the far greater quantities of books being produced meant that leather had to be replaced by cheaper materials and so the technique still practised today of binding with stiff cloth-covered cardboard was developed. New materials did not, however, mean a reduction in standards or inventiveness, for during the 19th century book binding shows a greater use of imagination than at any earlier period. Imitation and substitute leathers were used with great freedom, many of which were embossed and blocked in sharp relief. The Gothic styles of the 1840s and 1850s were particularly suitable for this kind of treatment. Cloth bindings could be printed and decorated in a variety of ways, some of the most interesting and exciting being those used on children's books during the latter part of the century. Bindings could range from simple paper covers to elaborate confections inlaid with exotic materials such as ivory or tortoiseshell, while lacquer and papier-mâché could produce a finish beyond the wildest dreams of the early binders.

However, even in this period of expansion and novelty, the traditional methods of binding survived. There was a continuing demand for the work of the specialist book-binder who was able to produce an individually designed and made binding in the finest materials. Like the tools and the materials, the styles were also now quite old-fashioned and so it was rare for a Victorian binder to match the inventiveness of his newer and cheaper rivals.

The quality and the craftsmanship was as powerful as ever, but the designs had been gradually weakened by constant repetition.

During the last quarter of the 19th century, there were some attempts at revitalizing the designs by returning to the early medieval sources, but the real change did not occur until the 1920s and 1930s, when there was a total renaissance of craft book binding in France. There, for the first time, avant-garde design was applied to book binding and whole new techniques of leather working, matching and embossing were developed to interpret correctly the designs of artists such as Matisse.

From France the techniques and the dynamic modern styles spread to other countries, bringing about an international revival in book binding. This movement also brought together the design of the book and the design of the binding, which now combined to produce a unified whole. The influence of these avant-garde designers was not limited to craft book binding, but affected equally the cheaper mass-produced bindings. These and the paper book jackets, which did not come into common use until the 1920s, helped to revitalize typography and graphic design in Europe and America during the interwar period.

style, binding has generally followed the fashions of contemporary typography and so the Renaissance arabesques of the 16th-century printers would also be echoed in the gold blocking on the binding. Similarly, the typographic elegance of the 18th century and the stylistic eclecticism of the 19th century were reflected in the book bindings of those periods. Collectors should not forget, however, that books have frequently been rebound, in which case the binding is likely to have followed its own period style rather than that of the original book.

The bindings of the 19th century are particularly interesting and are well worth collecting because they are both varied and available. The

FRY'S ORNAMENTED

SAN SERIF SHADED

Garamon
Italic

GARAMOND OLD STYLE & ITALIC

Windsor

WINDSOR

Futura
INLINE

FUTURA LIGHT & INLINE

Gill Sans
Ultra

GILL SANS MEDIUM & ULTRA

Optima

OPTIMA

LAPIDAIRE MONSTRÉ

Rockwell

ROCKWELL MEDIUM

Although frequently taken for granted, and therefore not immediately obvious to many people, typefaces can be helpful in dating printed material. The faces used can be dated either from the period when they were first designed, or by the fashion they reflect. Those selected in this feature illustrate both the development of typographic styles, and the role played by fashion.

Cloister Black, although a 19th century design, is in the style of the early blackletters of the 15th and 16th centuries, and therefore reflects the Gothic revival of the Victorian period. Windsor and Uncial are later echoes of the same medieval fashion. Garamond and Bodoni represent the elegant and revolutionary styles of 16th century Venice, styles very popular during the Neo-classical movement of the 18th century. Century is a 20th century interpretation of the same philosophy. In the early 19th century type-designers became more adventurous and introduced more ornamental faces, such as Clarendon, Thorogood, Rockwell and San Serif Shaded; this move became more extreme later in the century, producing faces that were often ridiculously over-decorated.

In the 20th century, a form of typographic puritanism has dominated styles, with simple faces like Gill Sans and Optima being greatly preferred to the excesses of the Victorian period.

Clarend

CLARENDON BOLD

AMERICAN UNCIAL

LETTERS ORNEES

Cloister

CLOISTER BLACK

Century

CENTURY SCHOOLBOOK

ANTIQUE TUSCAN

ARNOLD BOCKLIN

AUGUSTEA INLINE

Bodoni
Ultra
Heavy

BODONI BOOK, HEAVY & ULTRA

THOROWGOOD ITALIC

Photographs

1 Portrait of Rachel and Laura Gurney, by Mrs Julia Margaret Cameron.

The study of the history of photography and the collecting of old photographs is a relatively recent development and yet an extensive range of specialist books has already been produced to help the collector.

The invention of photography in the early 19th century, and particularly the contributions made by the Frenchman Joseph Nicéphore Niepce to its development during the 1820s, has been studied at length. Equally, most amateur photographers are aware of the dependence of the process upon the old idea of the *camera obscura*, a means of transmitting an actual scene on to the wall of a specially constructed dark chamber by a rudimentary lens. However, the vast number of apparently similar and closely related processes that have combined to form the technical and historical background to present-day photography have only recently been studied on a popular level. With this increase in knowledge, collectors have turned their attention towards old photographs, old cameras and old albums, hoping to find rare examples of early techniques. Many of the personalities behind the processes have been identified and so the history of photography is now adorned with as many names as any other collecting field. Closely related is an increasing interest in early or unusual cameras and photographic equipment, such as exposure meters. The popularity of the whole field of photography is reflected by the number of photographic museums now open in America, Britain, France and Germany, the countries that have contributed the most to the development of the photographic process.

Following experimental work by Niepce and others, the first practical steps towards modern photography were taken during the 1830s – in France by Louis Jacques Daguerre and in England by Henry Fox Talbot. The Daguerreo-type, effectively the first practical form of photography, was used extensively for portraiture and other work for about 20 years, but its disadvantage was that each photograph was unique. There was no way of making extra copies, and it was also expensive. The real breakthrough was made by Fox Talbot, who developed the first negative-positive process, thereby establishing the future pattern of photography. The Fox Talbot Calotype was a slow and laborious process, but it made possible the production of multiple prints from one original negative. Improvements rapidly followed. The wet plate collodion process, with its vital portable darkroom, was replaced by the gelatin dry plate, which gave the photographer far greater freedom of action. It also made possible the taking of 'instant' photographs, because of the short exposure times involved.

By the 1860s photography was established in a form that would be recognizable today. The souvenir portrait, the views of popular scenes, the *carte de visite* showing an image of the presenter, all became commonplace, while the roving photographer was able to record events and scenes as they occurred, such as the Crimean War and the American Civil War. The artistic implications of photography were also being slowly realized. Painters began to use photographs as instant sketch books, but it was a long time before photographers could free themselves from the need to copy the traditional rules of pictorial composition. Most important, there was a general understanding that photography could be a valuable sociological and historical recording device, a means of presenting the past to the future as it had actually occurred, and so leading to a greater understanding.

These developments also affected the actual equipment. Cameras became smaller and com-

pact and were separated from the developing and printing processes which were left behind in the darkroom. In 1888 George Eastman developed the first Kodak portable camera; its roll film freed the photographer from the paraphernalia of glass and paper negative plates. He launched it on the market with the slogan 'You press the button, we do the rest', having realized that the future of popular photography lay in the provision of a complete developing and printing service for the amateur. The Kodak, so named because the word had no actual meaning and therefore could be used universally in all languages, was an immediate success. In 1900 the Brownie camera was produced: with its very cheap price, its easily accessible and quickly processed roll film, the Brownie launched the era of the snapshot. Since 1900 equipment has become more complex and precise, but effectively no significant developments have altered the pattern of popular photography established by Eastman and the other pioneers. Even the first colour photographs date back to 1861. Moving pictures and sound have, of course, added extra dimensions, but these are beyond the scope of this article.

The collector of photographs may be concerned with particular processes, such as Daguerreotypes, wet plate collodions, and so on. Alternatively, he may concentrate on the work of a particular photographer, such as the portraits by Hill and Adamson or Julia Margaret Cameron, the war pictures of Matthew Brady, or the landscapes of Sutcliffe, Emerson, Stieglitz and, more recently, Bill Brandt. Other interests include art photography, special effects, miniaturization and the application of photography to glass, porcelain and other materials. Cameras and photographic equipment provide an endless variety of stimuli for the collector.

Perhaps the most popular field, and certainly the most accessible, is the vast number of early snapshots that are still to be found, often packed into old photograph albums. These range from the totally trivial to the historically important, mostly taken for the moment by forgotten photographers, and are often of vanished scenes and people. Their accidental survival into another age gives them an immediacy and a direct link with the past that few collectors can resist. Another field of great interest is provided by stereoscopic photographs. This early attempt at three dimensional effects was extremely popular from about 1860 to comparatively recent times and so there is a vast choice of material. The photographic slides, with the two images mounted side by side, were frequently sold in sets and covered a range of topics that included travel scenes, war scenes, popular events, famous people, theatre, exhibitions, sport, art and history, plants and wildlife, and a great many others. These stereoscopic slides and sets, and the simple, adjustable viewers are still readily available.

Photography is, of course, a continuing process. The collecting of work by contemporary photographers is still something of a rarity, but this will certainly develop, helped by the many galleries that now specialize in photography. This shares many of the risks inherent in the collecting of any kind of contemporary material, but it can be profitable. The appeal of the photograph is that it is simply a record of a moment in time, however carefully or carelessly it has been taken. So the fashion plates, reportage, sporting pictures, portraits and snapshots of today will inevitably be of interest from the early parts of the 21st century.

2 Card photograph, about 1865–70, of the Empress Elizabeth of Austria, taken by the Vienna firm of Rabending and Monckhoven.

3 The Building of the Forth Bridge, 1888, taken by G.W. Wilson.

Prints & posters

The possibilities of reproducing their work by mechanical means have always intrigued artists, and there is ample evidence of experimentation in many early civilizations. However, it was not until the Middle Ages that this possibility became a reality in the West.

The development of mechanical reproduction was closely related to the invention of printing from movable type, a technique pioneered in Germany by Johann Gutenberg during the late 1440s. The realization that an impression, or print, could be taken from carved letters in relief was quickly applied to illustrations carved in similar three dimensional forms, and so engraving developed. Although an inaccurate term, engraving has come to be accepted as a generic title for all kinds of mechanical reproduction of illustrative material. In fact, there are three main types of engraving: the relief, or cameo, process; the intaglio process and the surface, or planographic process.

In its simplest form, the relief or cameo process can be expressed as a potato-cut or a linocut. A design can be carved on to a soft, flat material in such a way that it is left standing in relief, all the surplus surrounding material having been cut away. The carved design can then be covered with ink and its image transferred by pressure on to paper or some other equally flexible and absorbent surface. The process can then be repeated as many times as required to produce a number of identical impressions, or prints, from the original carved design.

The material most suitable for this process is wood, especially the hard fruit woods such as pear, lime and box. The technique of wood-cutting dates from the 14th century. With a strong, close-grained wood, the design left standing in relief could be quite fine and, at the same time, the carved block would be strong enough to produce hundreds, or even thousands, of impressions. The woodcut was developed extensively during the medieval period, and in the hands of artists such as Durer attained a level of artistic quality that has rarely been equalled. It was widely used for illustrating the predominantly religious publications of the period and some secular designs were also produced. The best known example is probably the manual on chess printed by William Caxton during the early 1470s. As technique and style improved, so the tools used by the woodcutter became more sophisticated, which in turn allowed a greater artistic freedom to develop.

At the start of the history of mechanical reproduction there was already a kind of division of labour between the artist who was also capable of cutting his own designs on to wood and the professional engraver who simply used his technical skills to cut and print the designs of others. This division has remained a feature of print-making ever since, regardless of technique or style. From the point of view of the collector, prints made by the artist himself have always been more desirable than those produced by the professional engraver.

From the wood cut there developed the wood engraving, which is effectively the reverse process. Here, the design is cut into the wood, leaving all the surplus material untouched. When printed, this produces a white design on a solid black ground, and so gives both artist and engraver a far finer control of line. Although developed at the same time as the wood cut, the wood engraving was not used extensively until the 18th century, when the combination of fine detail and a slow rate of wear of the block when in use made it suitable for book, magazine and newspaper illustrations. The most effective use of wood engraving can be seen either in the late 18th century natural history illustrations by Thomas Bewick, or in the great variety of large scale illustrations in Victorian magazines and newspapers, whose immediacy, impact and speed of production could ultimately be bettered only by the photograph.

The second process, intaglio, is infinitely more flexible, although it also developed at about the same time as the woodcut. Here the design is cut into a metal plate with a series of small, sharp chisels, or burins. Until the develop-

1

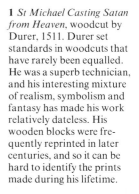
1 *St Michael Casting Satan from Heaven*, woodcut by Durer, 1511. Durer set standards in woodcuts that have rarely been equalled. He was a superb technician, and his interesting mixture of realism, symbolism and fantasy has made his work relatively dateless. His wooden blocks were frequently reprinted in later centuries, and so it can be hard to identify the prints made during his lifetime.

ment of the steel plate in the 19th century, the metal generally used was copper, as it was soft enough to be engraved by hand, and firm enough to withstand the pressures of printing. When the engraving of the plate is complete, it is rolled all over with a stiff ink. The surface of the plate is then wiped clean, leaving ink only in the engraved lines. A damped piece of paper is then laid carefully on the plate and both are forced through a press, rather like a domestic mangle. The great pressure transfers the ink from the grooves in the plate on to the surface of the paper. This technique produces a far more precise result, with an infinitely greater range of tonal control. By the use of cross-hatching, a variable range of mid tones can be created, allowing the engraver to impart a surprising amount of 'colour' into his work and giving greater flexibility than the simple black and white of the woodcut. However, because of the pressure of the printing, engraved copper plates wear out quickly, so only a limited number of impressions can be taken. In many cases the deterioration of the plate is quite apparent, the lines becoming softer and more blurred as the run progresses. Collectors should always look closely at the sharpness of the printed line, as this can be a useful guide to the age of the plate when the print was actually produced.

The most common form is the line engraving, so called because the design is formed entirely of lines. However, many other engraving techniques were developed during the 17th and 18th centuries, mostly designed to improve the reproductive quality of the process. These included the stipple engraving, in which the design

2 *The Hour of the Boar*, by Utamaro, 1790. Japanese prints were hardly known in Europe until the 1860s, but their appearance in Europe at that time created a wave of interest that affected all aspects of artistic production. Their impact can be measured in Impressionist painting, in furniture, metalwork, tiling, wallpapers and textiles and in most other late 19th century fine and applied arts.

3 *Chairing the Members*, plate four from the *The Election*, a set of engravings by William Hogarth, published in 1758. Hogarth, one of the greatest satirical cartoonists, produced a number of series of engravings in this style, of which *The Rake's Progress* and *Marriage à la Mode* are probably the best known.

General Nap turned Methodist Preacher,

A

NEW ATTEMPT TO GULL THE CREDULOUS;

DEDICATED TO MR. WHITBREAD.

"Dear Sam, repeat my Words, but not my Actions."

DEARLY beloved brethren, Honour, Country, Liberty! this is the order of the day; far from us all idea of conquest, blood-shed and war. Religion and true Philosophy must ever be our maxim. Liberty, a free Constitution, and no Taxes, that is our cry. No Slave-trade; humanity shudders at the very thought of it!! The brave, the excellent English detest it. Yea we shall all be happy. Commerce, Plenty, and all sorts of pretty things will be our lot. Good Jacobins' rise and assert your right's. And you, brave Soldiers, the honour of France, Plunder and Blood shall once more be your cry. Double pay and cities burnt will come down in showers upon you. Yea! ye shall all be Generals, all be Members of the Legion of Honour! The Eagles will once more cover the world. Now is the time to destroy Great Britain, that treacherous country, which always seeks our ruin, Honour and Victory will lead us.

Dear Countrymen, without good faith there is no tie in this world. Dear Jacobins, we all acknowledge no God, and nothing else. Let the altars be lighted up, and your organs play the Marseillois, that sacred air, which fires every Frenchman's breast. Yea, I swear by this holy cross I now hold in my hands, and in this sacred place, where you are all free and without restraint, that my intentions are pure, and that I wish for nothing else but Peace, Plunder, and Liberty. Amen!!

was created in dots rather than lines, a technique stylistically similar to that used for the reproduction of photographs in many newspapers today, and the mezzotint. In the latter, the whole surface of the copper plate is covered by a fine mesh of burred dots. The design is then created by alternatively smoothing or roughening areas of the plate to produce tonal contrasts of light and shade. This process was popular during the late 18th century because it was capable of reproducing many of the tonal qualities of paint. These techniques were often used in combination and so, by the end of the 18th century, engravings were in universal use for both artistic and reproductive purposes.

Other processes, such as etching and aquatint, involved the use of acid to etch or bite the design into the plate, instead of the tools and muscle power of the engraver. In this, the design is drawn with a needle on the surface of a plate coated with an acid-resistant wax. The plate is then immersed in an acid bath and the acid attacks only the areas exposed by the needle. Using his skill and control over a series of immersions in the acid, the etcher could produce a remarkably precise design with a far greater tonal range than the engraving and with a far softer quality. Etching was devloped early in the 16th century, but its greatest period was in the 17th century, in the hands of artists such as Rembrandt. There was also a significant etching revival during the late 19th and early 20th centuries, expressed particularly by the work of the

American, J. M. Whistler. Variations of the etching process, such as aquatint and soft ground, were developed during the late 18th century as part of the move towards greater realism and tonal control, especially in landscape work. Most of these developments were designed to remove the hard outlines of etched or engraved work, bringing print-making nearer to painting.

The 18th century was the greatest period of the engraver, for the great explosion of technique at this time allowed him to work on so many levels. First there were the trade engravers, reproducing designs for catalogues, visiting and trade cards, magazines and books and for transfer printing on to ceramics, and producing copies of popular paintings of the day. Highly professional and technically skilled, these engravers rarely produced original designs of their own. However, they frequently signed their work in the plate and so they are relatively easy to

1 Etching reached its apogee in the hands of 17th century artists, such as Rembrandt.

2 Early 19th century satirical print, *General Nap turned Methodist Preacher.*

3 *Crossing the Rockies,* a lithograph by Currier and Ives, a partnership instrumental in establishing the popularity of the topographical form in America.

4 The Oriole, a plate from J.J. Audubon's *Birds of America.* This monumental work, one of the most desirable of 19th century books, reflected a new scientific approach.

collect. Then there were the engravers of fashion plates, comic and satirical designs and miscellaneous sporting, social and topographical scenes. Some of these were artists of great originality, while others were content for their work to be largely reproductive. The output and range of this type of engraver was enormous and many examples are still available quite cheaply to present-day collectors. The third category were the artist engravers, who simply used the print-making processes as an extension of their work. This type of print has always been keenly collected, so the collector needs both money and judgment, plus a thorough understanding of the refinements of the techniques involved.

It is essential to remember that wood blocks or copper plates can often outlive the artist or engraver who originally produced them, and so can be reprinted many years later. There is no technical reason to prevent a block cut by Durer being printed today. It takes considerable experience to judge the actual age of a print, experience that should include an understanding of ink and paper technology as well as the ability to judge the degree of wear on the plate. Many prints include the name of both engraver and artist cut into the plate, but these are of no use as a guide unless the names are actual signatures in pencil or ink. During the 19th century it became a common practice for artist engravers to sign their work and give some indication of the number of prints produced, a practice that is

widely used today. These details obviously help the collector. Many artists also now insist that a plate be destroyed or defaced on the completion of the planned print run to make reprinting impossible. In the past these rules did not often apply and so the practice has developed among collectors of referring to prints by states. First state indicates a first proof printed by the artist or engraver, or at least one of the first edition to be produced, while second, third and successive states refer to subsequent or later editions of the print, often after alterations have been made by the engraver to the design. These alterations, combined with the sharpness of the line, are the best ways of distinguishing the states from each other. With popular or well-known artists, further editions of their work were frequently issued after their death, but with experience these later editions can usually be distinguished.

Another feature of the late 18th century was the search for a means of reproducing designs in colour. During this period there were many experiments in colour printing in France and elsewhere, most of which used the principle of printing several successive plates on top of each other. Each plate was inked with a separate colour, a technique that produced a fully coloured result when the plates were printed precisely in register. However, this process was both laborious and slow and, until the development of chromolithography in the mid-19th century prints were usually coloured by hand. This was done simply with flat washes of colour, all the tones and shadows already being present on the print. Many engravings were designed to be so coloured; others, intended to be left in the black, often acquired colour at a later date.

The third main process, the planographic, is not really engraving at all. In 1798, A. Senefelder first developed lithography, and thereby set in train all the various techniques that have revolutionized mechanical reproduction. The high speed colour printing that is generally taken for granted today could not exist without the early experiments in lithography and the development of trichromatics, that is to say, the realization that all colours can be formed from combinations of the three primaries, red, blue and yellow.

The lithographic process is based on the mutual antagonism of oil and water. The design is drawn with a greasy chalk on a smooth surface, originally stone, but generally a zinc plate today. The surface is then wetted and rolled with a greasy ink. The wet surface repels the ink, which adheres only to the areas drawn with the greasy chalk. A print is then taken and the process can be repeated, with almost no limit to the number of prints that can be made from one original. A lithograph also accurately reproduces very fine detail, and so could imitate closely the soft quality of drawing. It is therefore not surprising that its rapid development in the early 19th century was in part due to its popularity with artists such as Goya, Daumier and Turner.

It was not long before the colour lithograph was also developed, which clearly changed dramatically both fine and applied, or commercial, art. Once again, artists played a major part in this development, bringing about a general change in the status of the print maker. Although the commercial possibilities of chromolithography were startling, the artistic potential was

1 Cordiform world map, the *Carte Cosmographique*, a woodcut published in Paris in 1544 by P. Apianus.

2 *Sheerness Dockyard*, 1755, from a set of Views of Royal Dockyards, engraved by P.C. Canot after T. Milton.

3 *Stellatum Planisphaerium*, engraved by Louis Vlasbloem, and published in Amsterdam in 1695.

even more exciting, for here was a development that gave the print-maker a position in the artistic hierarchy that was higher than any he had achieved since the invention of engraving in the Middle Ages.

This change has naturally affected also the collector of prints, as he now has a greater choice than ever before. He can specialize in art prints, either of the present or dating from the early years of this century. He can pursue particular artists, particular periods, unusual techniques, or simply specialize by subject, such as sport, topography, marine, architecture or natural history prints. He can buy cheaply from the folders of the print dealers in antique markets, hoping for a rare find, or buy extravagant rarities at the top of the market, such as plates from Audubon's *Birds of America*. There is still a wealth of 18th century prints available at cheap prices and earlier examples are generally cheaper than other antiques of similar age. Equally, there are many interesting fields, most of them still scarcely considered by collectors, such as early 19th-century steel engravings. Taken as a whole, it can be seen that print collecting is still really in its infancy.

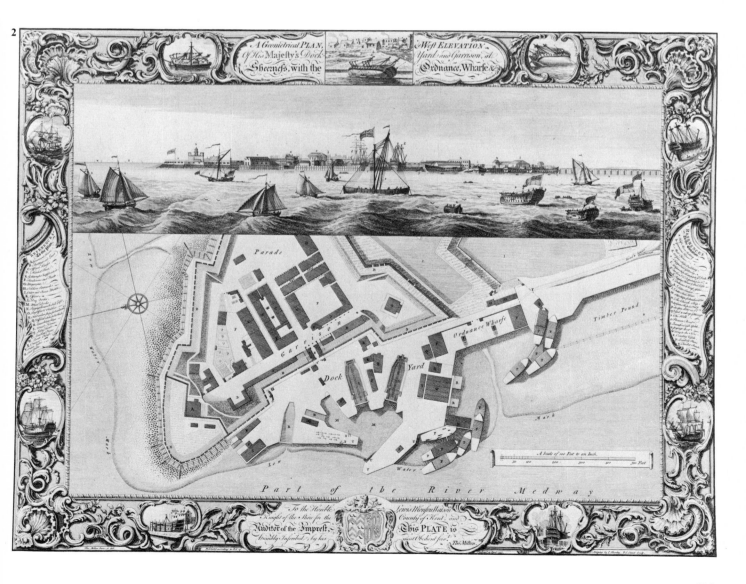

Posters

1 Typographic playbill, 1826, a form that created its impact by the dynamic use of contrasting typefaces.

2 Shimbashi Station, by Kuniteru II, 1871. 19th century Japanese prints had a direct influence upon European posters, especially those printed by chromo-lithography.

Although poster collecting has achieved considerable popularity, the development of the poster itself is a comparatively modern phenomenon. Today, it is not uncommon for posters to be produced specifically to appeal to collectors, the design and decorative aspects often being more important than the message they have to carry. Similarly, many old posters have been reprinted to sell as modern wall decorations and have achieved a longevity and fame far beyond the wildest dreams of their creators. In fact, they now have the sort of recognition more usually associated with the formal arts.

Posters, placards and playbills date back to the 18th century and beyond, but they did not become commonplace until the latter half of the 19th century. Early posters tend to be wholly typographical, relying on the size and variety of letterforms used by the printer to make their impact. Illustrations are rare, largely because of the technical problems involved in their reproduction, and colours are limited. The best known is probably the theatrical playbill, in which the diverse qualities of the entertainments advertised were expressed by the mixed styles and sizes of the typography. However, these displays of the printer's virtuosity inevitably have a limited appeal, partly because of their rarity and partly because of their lack of visual detail and the added interest of colour.

The change came in the Victorian period. Firstly, technical developments such as chromolithography, high speed printing and photography gave the poster designer a new freedom. Chromolithography, or colour printing, was in regular use by about 1860, while the steam-powered printing press could produce up to 10,000 sheets an hour by the same date. Secondly, the rise of what is now called 'the consumer society' inspired a dramatic growth in advertising, affecting both its use and the subtlety of its presentation. More people were able to afford more and more things, and so they had to be increasingly persuaded that they actually needed them. Equally, the increasing availability of advertising sites on walls, hoardings and particularly in the new railway stations, encouraged competitiveness among manufacturers and suppliers of information. Thirdly, increased demand and the greater availability of money encouraged artists of greater skill and reputation to try their hands at poster designing; this was a change that immediately made posters more acceptable, and more memorable, to the rapidly increasing educated middle classes.

The fourth, and in some ways the most important, factor was the revolution in artistic styles prompted by the reopening of the Japanese frontiers in the 1850s. Having been totally closed to the West for so long, Japan had acquired a magic and a fascination that knew no bounds within Europe. When the doors finally opened, they released Japanese artefacts into Europe that provoked an astonishing response affecting every field of artistic production. Spreading from France, the *Japonisme* movement swept across Europe, led by advanced designers such as the French engraver and artist F. Bracquemond and the English industrial designer and critic Dr Christopher Dresser. While all aspects of Japanese art and production made an impact, none was so immediate and dynamic as the discovery of Japanese colour prints. These magnificent designs, so simply drawn with their flat areas of bright colour, created a new style in European art. They affected particularly the French Impressionists and painters such as the American painters Whistler and Sargent, but their most direct and striking influence was on poster design.

3 Early chromolithograph theatre playbill.

4 May Belfort, poster by H. Toulouse-Lautrec, 1885.

1

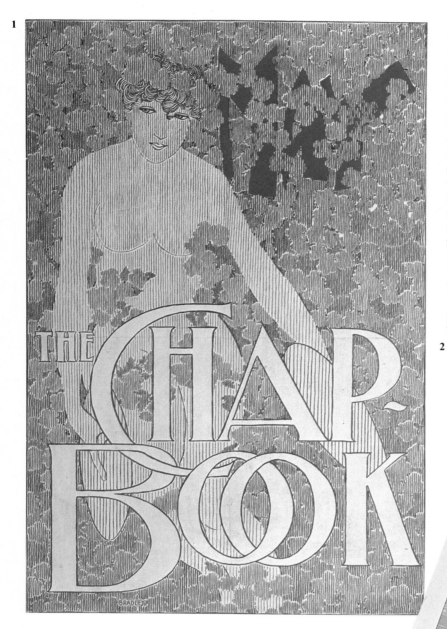

This pattern continued until the First World War. Because the war was fought at first by volunteers, the poster became an important means of encouraging recruitment and returned to its original role as the bearer of messages, slogans and information. However, the artistic aspects were not forgotten and all sides engaged in the conflict made extensive use of powerful propaganda posters, many of which were remarkably similar. After the war the gradual economic recovery inspired a return to conventional advertising, but this time the designers had to consider the marketing demands of the product. Despite this, many designs of the 1920s and 1930s are very remarkable, reflecting contemporary developments in art. Particularly memorable are the abstract designs of McKnight Kauffer and the modernist transport posters of the Frenchman Cassandre.

Since the 19th century impact of *Japonisme*, posters have always been closely allied to contemporary art movements. Leading avant-garde

2

These elements combined to produce a wholly new sort of poster, in which colour and drama were vital elements. This developed first of all in France, in the work of Toulouse-Lautrec, Chéret, Grasset, Steinlen and de Faure, but spread rapidly to other countries. In England, Beardsley and Dudley Hardy followed the French lead, in America it was Will Bradley, while the Czech Mucha made his colourful and sinuous women familiar all over Europe.

As *Japonisme* turned into Art Nouveau, the poster came of age. It had become a totally decorative artistic medium, brightly coloured, often garish, rich in pattern and sensuous drawing and universally applicable. The object being advertised, or the message to be broadcast, almost ceased to matter, the same decorative approach being applied freely to bicycles, cigarettes, theatres, cooking oil, sewing machines and politics. Posters had now achieved the status of works of art and so were able to outlive the ephemeral quality of actual advertising.

artists have often become poster designers, and so throughout this century posters have tended to mirror their period very precisely. While most examples can be dated by the product and their style of advertising, the relationship with art can be a more accurate guide. This is still true today, although more recently posters have fallen into groups determined by their subject matter. War, politics, protest, pop, as well as conventional advertising, all impose their own language and symbols, many of which are now international. These can limit decorative freedom in a way that 19th century designers would have found quite unacceptable. Despite this, the relationship between art and poster design continued to expand, especially in America, where contemporary artists have been quick to see the value of the poster in spreading their own message or style. A poster for national distribution is far more effective than a number of gallery shows.

It is probably this element, plus the obvious decorative and ephemeral qualities, that make poster collecting so appealing today. The continuing impact of the poster, regardless of its period, and its value as a living memorial to a past age has made it hard to collect. Originals by any of the great names will be as expensive as paintings, even though the quantity produced at the time may have been considerable, and so most collectors will have to content themselves with reproductions. However, it is a field where luck and perseverance can produce the most unexpected results. Many old posters have turned up unrecognized on market stalls, or framed into the backing for pictures. There is also such a wide choice of subject matter. The obvious themes, such as war or transport, will always be in demand, but it is not hard to find less popular areas for study.

1 Poster advertising *The Chap Book* by Will Bradley.

2 American propaganda poster by H.R. Hopps, typical of the hundreds produced by both sides involved in World War I.

3 *Nord Express*, poster by Cassandre, 1927.

4 *Bank*, a modern artist poster by Andy Warhol, first issued in 1969.

Printed ephemera

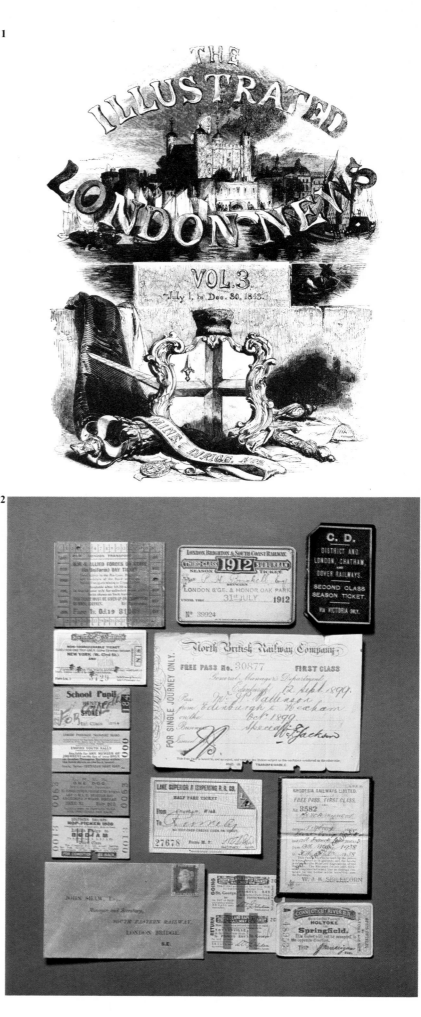

The development of printing dates from the Middle Ages and since then it has played an ever increasing role in the spread of Western civilization. For several centuries, printing and the publication of knowledge was associated largely with books, but since the 18th century it has come to affect every aspect of our lives. This spread has been assisted by advances in technology and by changes in social patterns. The concept of universal literacy has ensured that our lives are increasingly determined and regulated by printed material, most of which is, by its nature, ephemeral. This, in turn, has encouraged a new pattern of collecting based on an interest in printed material for its own sake. Many now wish to preserve printed material precisely because of its ephemeral nature.

Although printed ephemera has been collected since the 18th century, it is only in recent years that it has emerged as a major collecting field. Although it is beyond the scope of this book, stamp collecting is probably the earliest large scale interest in ephemera. Following this lead, specialist collectors turned their attention towards other areas of printed ephemera such as early trade cards, book plates and political or theatrical posters. Some specialized on the products of early jobbing printers, which included advertising matter, theatre, travel and sports tickets, invoices, labels, paper bags and other forms of packaging.

These collections were inspired partly by an interest in typography and styles of printing, and partly by an awareness of the changes in social and domestic life provoked by the development of advertising. From the efforts of these early enthusiasts there emerged the internationally famous collections of ephemera at the New York Public Library, the American Antiquarian Society, the Bibliotheque Nationale in Paris and the St Bride's Library in London.

Almanacs and calendars represent the earliest fields of interest, partly because the material itself can be of considerable age. In America, Benjamin Franklin's *Poor Richard's Almanack* was first produced in 1732, while the English *Old Moore's Almanac* dates from 1700. A similar French almanac, first produced in 1679, is still published today. Almanacs reflect the religious, social and political life of a community, as do magazines, newspapers and journals, and so the interest they arouse today is understandable. Old magazines and newspapers not only bring the past to life in a very direct way, but also reflect the changing impact of advertising on the public. It is also interesting to study the style and structure of newspapers in an age when there was no means of reproducing illustrations. Children's comics are a recent development in this field, reflecting changing attitudes to education and leisure and interesting applications of contemporary styles of drawing, the range extending from Kate Greenaway to Captain Marvel.

were designed to increase sales of cigarettes by encouraging the collection of a series of related cards. This cultivation of the collection of the ephemera of the present soon developed into a general interest in the ephemera of the past, which was encouraged no doubt by the romantic nostalgia that is a part and parcel of all kinds of collecting.

Some collectors have highly specialized interests and the specialist in matchbox covers, cigarette cards, beer mats or railway tickets is often interested in little else. Such collectors concentrate on the narrow but well-defined limits of their field of study, aided and guided by the societies, conferences and specialist publications that have grown up to serve them. Many of these very obscure publications will in turn become valuable examples of printed ephemera in the future, reflecting an interest that may then be quite incomprehensible. Others specialize in playing cards, Valentine cards, Christmas cards, funerary memorial cards and decorative music covers. The latter two are closely related to the colourful pictorial posters of the late 19th century and both express the decorative freedom enjoyed by artists and designers after the development of chromolithography.

Much printed ephemera is related to the history of advertising, and so such a collection can express very graphically the development of the consumer society. Since its growth in the 19th century, the styles and psychology of advertising have undergone dramatic changes, many of which can be expressed perfectly by surviving printed material. To collect all the paraphernalia of advertising – packaging, labels, free offers, wrappers as well as the actual posters and advertisements – is to bring together an interesting and valuable record of the changes in society. Such items also reflect contemporary styles in typography and design quite forcefully, as they are prone to demonstrate the extremes of any particular period. Thus an enthusiasm for old cigarette packets, chocolate boxes, tea cartons and advertisements for Guinness, Pears Soap or Singer sewing machines is quite understandable, although to have to eat several packets of breakfast cereal each week in order to keep up with changes in packaging may be taking an interest in ephemera too far.

Perhaps the most popular of all ephemeral fields is the picture postcard. These have been collected as souvenirs, as nostalgia and as decoration since their development in the latter part of the 19th century. There are cards with views, cards with travel scenes, cards with religious, political or romantic themes, cards for children and, most popular of all, cards adorned with a seemingly endless range of comic, salacious and generally rude subjects. Designed for the moment, and often decorated with a message to match, most of these cards were quickly forgotten and put away to await their discovery years later in some album, attic, old trunk or buried among the clutter of a jumble sale or junk shop. They are probably the most collectable form of printed ephemera.

1 The Illustrated London News, 1843, one of the many mass-circulation newspapers and magazines made possible by the advanced printing technology of the early 19th century.

2 Railway tickets and labels, one of the most popular forms of ephemera among collectors because of their immediate nostalgic appeal.

3 Match box labels drawn from many countries of the world.

Equally, bookmarks, book plates, trade and sale catalogues are keenly collected for similar reasons. Trade catalogues are direct records of a vanished way of life and so can connect the past with the present in a very tangible way, while old sale catalogues permit the tracing of the history of objects and collections that might still be accessible today. Collectors of book plates can be inspired either by the connection with the famous person who once owned the book, or by a general interest in typography. In fact, a general interest in typography, graphic design and printing technology can produce a collection of broad scope and popular appeal.

The interest in printed ephemera was greatly encouraged by the production of material specifically designed to appeal to the collector, the most obvious example being the apparently endless variety of special issue postage stamps. Others include souvenir programmes and tickets and popular items such as cigarette cards which

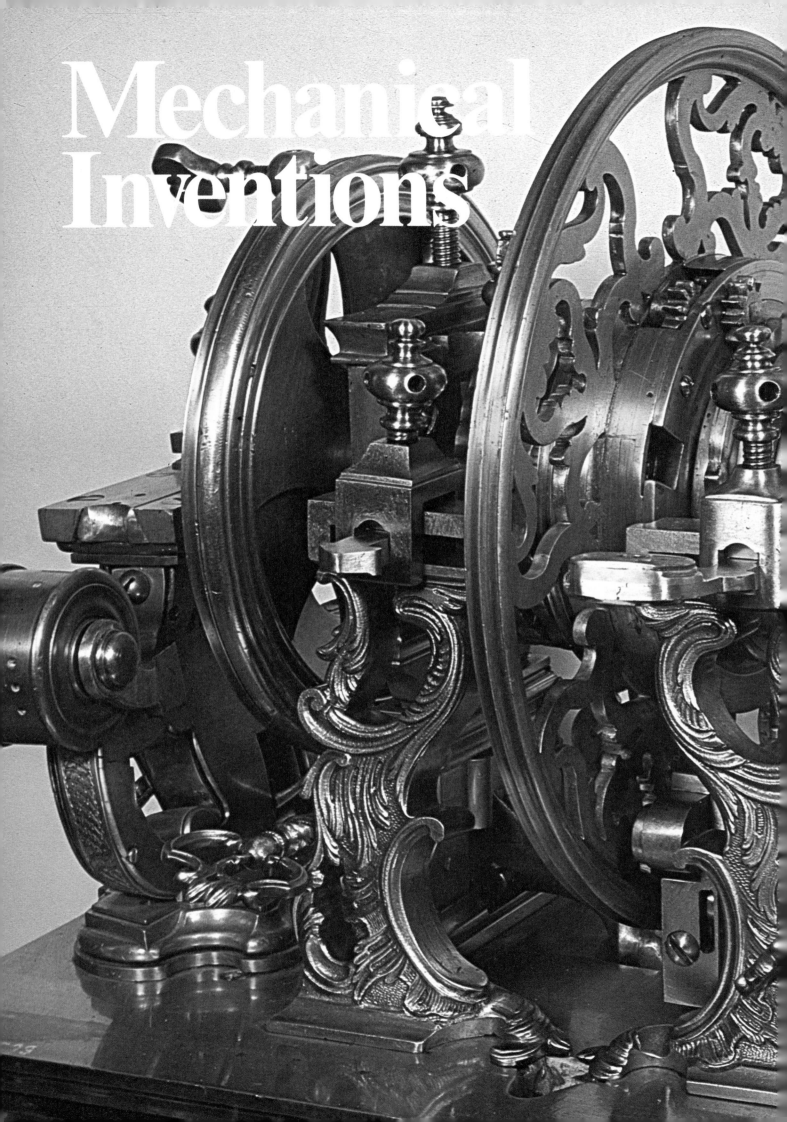

Mechanical Inventions

The interest among collectors in the out-of-date products of applied technology is comparatively recent, mainly because it is only in the last hundred years or so that the consumer society has become dominant. In previous ages, when domestic or industrial equipment was produced to last indefinitely, there was no point in collecting it. It is only when these items have in turn become the victims of consumer-dominated fashion that they can be elevated to the ranks of the antique.

In the past, development was related entirely to advances in technology, ensuring that replacement would only be prompted by the greater efficiency of the new model. There was clearly no point in keeping the old model, as it was quite simply less efficient. Sentiment did not enter into it. Today, items are rapidly replaced, more for reasons of fashion than for technical advances, and so out-of-date things are rejected much more quickly – a rejection often having little to do with their actual condition. Ironically, it is this habit of rapid and continuous replacement that has, in turn, generated a great interest in the artefacts of the recent past, prompted partly by nostalgia and sentiment, and partly by a genuine desire to preserve the products of vanishing skills and technologies.

Within this field can be included watches, clocks, domestic and social equipment, scientific and industrial machines and instruments, toys and models and musical instruments. With the exception of clocks, watches and musical instruments, few of these aroused much interest among collectors until this century. Watches and clocks have always been collected, partly because of an eternal fascination with time and our attempts at controlling it, and partly because their structure has only ever been in part technological. Until this century, the ownership of a watch or clock implied some degree of wealth, and so the decoration of the parts and cases has been a part of the mainstream of stylistic development. Indeed, it is not out of place to consider many clocks simply as furniture, for their outward appearance is often more important than their machinery or means of operation. In some cases, new items of furniture have evolved, such as the long case clock, simply to absorb and exploit mechanical developments. Today, clocks and watches are freely available throughout the world and only rarely have any direct social significance. As a result they have become more transitory, no more than fashion accessories, a change which has, inevitably, provoked a greater interest in antique examples.

The development of musical instruments has been a similar mixture of technological advance and stylistic change. These have also been long collected, partly because age has not always affected their performing ability. Like weapons, they are essentially functional, and so any decoration must be secondary. A violin is always a violin whatever the style of decoration applied to it. It will only cease to be a violin when its development has turned it into another instrument altogether.

Both timepieces and musical instruments have also been long collected because of the craftsmanship involved in their creation. It is possible to own and appreciate examples purely on the grounds of their decorative qualities. This interest in craftsmanship has encouraged many collectors to turn to other fields in this area. Domestic and social equipment is a recent field, but already such things as typewriters, gramophones, radios, sewing machines, vacuum cleaners, washing machines, fountain pens, corkscrews and can openers, cookers and stoves are being amassed and studied with all the efforts hitherto granted only to more established branches of antiques. Industrial and scientific equipment is now similarly regarded and there are many museums, private collections and auction sales devoted to agricultural and industrial machinery, scientific instruments, street furniture and relics of outmoded systems of transport.

However, perhaps the most significant field today is that devoted to the collecting of toys, models and games, where the playthings of yesterday's children have become the currency of today's adults. The interest in dolls, early clockwork pressed tin and die-cast toys, model railways and games is now so widespread that these items run the risk of being priced out of the reach of the average collector. Others, such as model soldiers, have always been intended to be as much for the entertainment of adults as children.

It is perhaps relevant to consider further the background to the development of these new collector fields. Craftsmanship apart, the main reason seems to be nostalgia, a desire to recreate the conditions and environment of the past through its surviving artefacts. Since the emergence of the consumer society, there has been an increasing desire to preserve the consumer products of the previous generations. As these products were generally designed for the moment, and to be largely expendable, their survival into another age makes them all the more interesting. While we have come to expect the

survival of 18th century watches, we are surprised to see an Edwardian vacuum cleaner or a 1920s gas cooker. This can help to explain the rapid growth throughout the world of museums of technology and transport, for these memorials to a very recent, but frequently quite vanished past have an immediate appeal based on a successful mixture of memory and nostalgia. This mixture can rarely be created so effectively in other collector fields. The other determining factor is availability. The items now being collected and displayed in museums are often still available to the collector of modest means. The chance discovery of some rare item is always a possibility, and so, for this reason if for no other, these new collector interests will continue to develop and expand.

Bracket clock by Knibb, about 1700.

Clocks & watches

Milestones in the history of clocks and watches

1380	First domestic clock (Italian).	1807	Eli Terry of Connecticut accepted an order for 4,000 shelf clocks initiating the mass-production of clocks in America.
1500	Invention of the mainspring by Peter Henlein.		
1511	First small portable clocks (watches).		
1657	First practical application of the pendulum to a clock made by Salomon Coster in Holland to designs of Christiaan Huygens.	1840	First electric clock invented by Alexander Bain of Scotland. Earlier attempts had been unsuccessful.
1671	First long pendulum clock made in England by William Clements.	1900	First serious attempts to introduce a wrist watch.
1730	First cuckoo clock constructed by Anton Ketterer in Germany.	1921	The beginning of the development of the quartz crystal clock by Dr Warren Marrison of America.
1775	Abraham Louis Bregnet set up business in Paris, establishing his reputation within five years.		

1 Early Italian Gothic clock

2 A German 16th century gilt metal circular striking table clock. This is an exceptionally fine example and includes complicated calendar and astronomical work.

The origin of the first mechanical timepiece is obscure. Although scholars have studied manuscripts dating from the 5th century, it has not been possible to reach any dogmatic conclusions. One difficulty lies in the fact that any references to 'horologia' can also allude to a sundial or water-clock and not necessarily to a mechanical clock. One commonly held belief is that the clockwork mechanism originated in the Islamic World where the sciences of astronomy and mathematics were far in advance of those in the Western Hemisphere. Whether this is correct and that descriptions carried back to Europe by the Crusaders engendered experimentation is uncertain, but strong evidence indicates that it was during the 11th century that mechanical clocks began to appear on the Continent, spreading at a later date to England. The earliest examples were large, iron and weight driven, with a verge and foliot escapement. A large bell struck the hours. Apart from small hour markings on the motion wheel and a fixed pointer this was the only method used to indicate the hour. It was not until further technical advancements had been made and the process reversed (the pointer to traverse a fixed dial), that dials were added.

Initially, clocks were made by blacksmiths under the supervision of monks. It must be remembered that prior to the Reformation all learning was the prerogative of the Church and the monasteries the only seats of learning. It was also the monks with their strict hours of devotion both day and night that had the greatest need for a mechanically regulated timekeeper with an alarm bell. However, by the 14th century large public clocks were appearing on churches, palaces and other buildings throughout Europe. References can be found in contemporary literature to clocks on the Church in Milan (1335), the Carrara Palace at Padua (1344), at Rouen (1389) and many other locations. Many of these are no longer extant but one of the oldest clocks in England – that from Salisbury Cathedral (1386) – can still be seen in the North Transept of the Cathedral.

Large dials embodying astronomical data as well as indicating the time of day began to appear as skills grew, while others incorporated automata – a feature especially popular on the Continent of Europe to this day.

The earliest domestic clocks were also of iron and were weight driven with a verge and foliot escapement. The movements were held by an open four-posted frame, but although the posts and dials were decorated, the sides were left open. As well as striking on the hour, some had provision for quarter striking or alarm mechanisms. They were intended to be hung on a hook or stood on a wall bracket to enable the free fall of the weights. These early Gothic clocks, as they are generally called, first appeared in Italy and some fine examples have survived to this day. It was, however, only a short time before the craft passed to South Germany with the towns of Nuremberg, Augsburg, Cassel and Ulm becoming recognized centres. Similar clocks were also made in France and Switzerland, but England produced few domestic clocks at this period.

The next milestone in the history of horology was the invention, in 1500 by Peter Henlein of Nuremberg, of the spring. The problem caused by the unevenness of the power of the spring depending upon whether it is tightly or loosely coiled, was overcome to some extent by the invention in 1510 of a stackfreed. This device was used extensively on the Continent for many centuries, while the alternative solution of the fusee (perfected by Zacob the Czech in 1525), came to be the choice of the English clockmakers. These various innovations, together with the introduction of the use of brass as opposed to iron, offered considerably more scope to the casemakers.

The first spring driven clocks were horizontal

3 This example of an Augsburg astronomical clock in a water gilt tabernacle case was made about 1650.

with the cases either drum shaped, square or later hexagonal. The sides were now fully enclosed and frequently highly engraved. Progress was rapid and soon highly ornate and more complicated clocks appeared. Greater accuracy was possible and so minute hands were added. Automata and astronomical dials appeared, together with complicated strike and chime mechanisms. The previously mentioned centres in South Germany produced the finest clocks at this date. Organized guilds in these areas were particularly strict and by now distinct from those of the blacksmiths, locksmiths and gunsmiths. The Parisian Clockmakers Guild had also been granted a charter by Francis I, but the Company of Clockmakers was not established in England until 1631. Until the turn of the 16th century clockmaking in England had not been widespread. At the beginning of the 17th century there emerged the characteristic English lantern clock. Made of brass, these were weight driven, with a verge and balance foliot rather than a bar foliot. This was to remain virtually unchanged until about 1660 when the latter was slowly replaced by the short pendulum.

The introduction of the use of the pendulum revolutionized clockmaking. The first practical application was to a clock made in Holland by Salomon Coster in 1657 to designs by Christiaan Huygens. It was now possible to achieve far higher standard of timekeeping. Portable spring-driven clocks made by Coster at this time were enclosed in wooden cases, with the dials covered in velvet upon which a gilded or silvered chapter ring prominently appeared. France adopted a similar style.

Clocks using this device were introduced into England during 1658 by the Fromanteel family, the Fromanteels having come from Holland some two generations previously and settled in Norwich. This advent heralded the Golden Age for English clockmakers. The main factors contributing to this was the upsurge of awakened interest in the new ideas and concepts carried back to England by Charles II, returning from his exile on the Continent, combined with the many advances made in the field of mathematics which enabled further technological progress, and the masterly skills of such clockmakers as Edward East, Daniel Quare, Joseph Knibb, Thomas Tompion and George Graham, to mention but a few. Their superb craftsmanship and attention to detail has rarely been excelled.

In 1671 William Clements produced a clock with a new escapement – the anchor or recoil escapement. It is generally accepted that its invention should be accredited to Dr Robert Hooke (1635–1703). With this escapement the short bob pendulum, as used with the verge escapement, could be abandoned and a longer pendulum with a heavier bob could be introduced. The weights of the weight-driven pendulum clocks were by now encased in a slender wooden trunk, standing upon a wooden plinth, so it needed but a slight modification to make the trunk sufficiently wide to accommodate the arc of the swing of the long seconds pendulum. This combination of anchor escapement and seconds pendulum became and remained the standard design for English longcase or coffin clocks as they were initially called.

Later inventions were the deadbeat escapement in 1715 by George Graham, followed by two important methods of overcoming the problems of the adverse affect of changes of temperature on the pendulum (the gridiron pendulum by John Harrison in 1725 and the mercurial pendulum of George Graham in 1721); these added to the advances being made towards producing precision timepieces. Accuracy of timekeeping was now of imperative importance both to the

1 A brass 17th century English striking lantern clock signed 'Jeffrey Baylie at ye Holborn fecit'. The original verge escapement with balance foliot has been converted at a later date to a verge escapement with pendulum; a not uncommon occurrence in clocks of this type.

2 A 17th century English eight day table clock by Samuel Knibb of London. He was a cousin of Joseph and John Knibb. Only three clocks by Samuel are known – the example illustrated here, a longcase clock formerly in the Royal collection at Windsor Castle and an ebony veneered table clock in an architecture design case with gilt metal mounts.

astronomers and to the seafaring nations. Supremacy at sea both for purposes of exploration and trade depended upon the ability of a clockmaker to produce an extremely accurate portable timekeeper which would enable the sailors to chart their longtitudinal position accurately. Both French and English Governments were actively encouraging their craftsmen towards this goal at the beginning of the 18th century. However, although Le Roy and Berthoud of France produced some extremely accurate timepieces, John Harrison (1693–1776) must go down in history as the man responsible for conquering the problem.

The making of the cases now came under the care of the cabinet makers and naturally reflected the current fashions in their respective countries. The English longcase styles changing from the early ebonized, architectural examples with gilt mounts and twist or barley sugar columns to high domed tops (from 1705), broken arch (from 1760) made of oak veneered in walnut or other decorative woods to the pedimented tops (from 1780) of the lacquered or marquetry cases of the next century. Mahogany only came into use in England in the later half of the century.

The longcase clock did not achieve the same degree of popularity on the Continent that it

3 A two-day marine chronometer

4 An English Act of Parliament clock by Thomas Moore of Ipswich (1720–89), made about 1750.

5 Eight-day oak longcase clock, about 1760 and signed J. Dixon.

4

5

3

enjoyed in England. The Dutch examples were the most similar, but their cases were more elaborate with bombe bases, outcurving feet and hoods surmounted with carved figures. Marquetry was extremely popular. Colourful scenes with automata in the dial arch or musical mechanisms were more common. The French examples either emulated bracket clocks standing on matching pedestals or had trunks that curved outwards towards the base with an aperture through which an ornate pendulum was visible. Locally made cases would be simple, but those intended for the more sophisticated town dwellers would be elaborately decorated with exotic woods, veneering and ormulu but becoming more classical in design towards the end of the century. Many of the movements, especially those originating from the Franche Comte district, were totally unlike those of the Dutch and English.

Spring-driven bracket clocks were also produced in abundance during this period and followed much the same changes in case and dial styles as the longcase clocks, as well as including many of the same technical innovations. In many instances they achieved an equally high standard of accuracy. English bracket clock cases tended to be relatively plain, although there were more elaborately cased clocks with ingenious mechanisms. These were frequently intended for the Eastern market, as was the extraordinary collec-

tion made by James Cox of Shoe Lane, London. Unfortunately, through local unrest these were never exported and after being placed on display and a fee charged to view them, they were disposed of in 1775 by lottery.

The Dutch cases also tended to be more elaborate, but for the most exotic and extravagantly decorated cases it is necessary to turn to the French clocks of the 18th century. During the reign of Louis XV (1723–1774) there is little doubt that the clockmaker played a subservient role to that of the casemaker. The movements had to be adapted to fit the cases and not vice versa. Although there are exceptions (the work of makers such as Julien Le Roy and Ferdinand Berthoud), the consequence was that movements of this period tended to be of a fairly standard pattern. The current Rococo style of furnishings

1 English water clock, signed and dated Arnold Finchett, Cheapside, 1735.

2 This mid-18th century French mantel clock is made in the form of a bronze elephant standing on a rectangular base. It supports on its back a clock movement housed in a chased ormulu case which in turn is surmounted by a small monkey holding a shade.

3 This is a Dutch 30 hour clock of the 18th century, with a verge and foliot. Note the ornate matching bracket.

4

was carried over to the clock cases and master-pieces, often signed by their makers, of boulle work, lacquer or intricate veneering embellished with fine ormulu appeared in abundance. Towards the end of the century many fine porcelain cases appeared. During the reign of Louis XVI cases were still superb but there was a general return to more classical lines and themes and more emphasis on complicated movements.

Clockmaking in Germany declined during the 18th century. Obviously, clocks continued to be made both of the spring-driven and weight-driven variety, but it was the wooden movements of the Black Forest area that came to the fore at this time. These simple weight-driven clocks

4 Early 18th century French pedestal clock with movement by Mynuël known to have been working 1693 to about 1750.

5

5 French 19th century ormulu mantel clock with the allegorical figure of a Muse strumming a lyre. A common feature of these clocks was a silk suspension to the pendulum.

with a verge escapement and foliot were made by the farmers during the winter months while outdoor work was impracticable. Tradition has it that the familiar cuckoo clock originated from this area and was first constructed by Franz Anton Ketterer about 1740, and by the end of the century these clocks were being exported throughout Europe. Slowly the anchor escapement replaced the verge and first the escape wheel and the train wheels became of brass, but it was not until the end of the 19th century that wooden plates were finally dispensed with. A few bracket cuckoo clocks were made towards the end of the century, with some examples including a fusee, but generally they retained their simple design and resulting low cost. Their manufacture, although now by factory methods, has continued to this day.

319

The 19th century saw many changes in the craft of clockmaking. The demand was growing for a cheaper priced clock for the masses instead of being costly possessions of the élite. The French in the preceeding century had realized that sub-division of labour and specialization could achieve a greater output without necessarily destroying the quality of the product. It was, however, the Americans who took this concept a stage further. Many of the 18th century settlers had been or became skilled clockmakers. They had one major problem – a lack of metal from which to manufacture their movements. By laborious methods some of them managed to overcome this problem and some fine long case clocks were made in and around Philadelphia. In their attempts to overcome the difficulty, the clockmakers of the New England area slowly developed a characteristic style of their own.

Simon Willard of Grafton, Massachusetts was an outstanding maker of this period and examples of his work and the longcase clocks made in Pennsylvania at this time can be seen as museum pieces today. The Connecticut makers with their abundant supply of local wood, decided to produce wooden movements. Eli Terry stands out as an important pioneer in this stage in the history of American clockmaking. After accepting an order to make 4,000 movements he had through necessity to devise some labour and time saving conveniences. Part of his solution was the standardization of parts and in 1816 he patented details of a weight-driven wooden or brass movement for a shelf clock. Further designs by other makers and the technological improvements after 1837 in the making and handling of brass meant that the earlier wooden movements could be replaced by this metal.

Typical of this era was the weight-driven movement housed in an Ogee case. The fully glazed front door often had the lower half filled by a painted tablet, mirror or gold tracery. In 1842 Chauncey Jerome shaped history by sending a shipment of his cheap mass produced spring-driven shelf clocks to England. The cases were of cheap veneered wood, painted zinc dials, glazed doors with either straightforward movements or with the additional features of alarm or striking on the hour. These clocks flooded the market and sounded the death knell for the more conservative English clockmakers.

The Germans, however, had been quick to realize that, if they were to survive, their cottage industry must adopt new methods. One family, the Junghans, were particularly progressive, and in the mid-1860s the business skills of one brother and the knowledge gleaned of 'the American Way' by other members of the family while working in America, resulted in the opening of a factory making mass-produced clocks with American machinery. Some of their designs followed those of the Americans so closely that it is in many instances difficult to tell them apart. However, they also continued with their traditional cuckoo clocks, postman alarms, and various clocks for which they were famous.

The French clockmakers, who had long

1 American 19th century clock made by Seth Thomas of Thomaston. The case is veneered rosewood with gilt columns and painted tablets depicting birds and flowers. This particular example has an eight-day movement.

2 19th century English skeleton timepiece on white marble base and typical fretted plates and dial.

3 Prior to 1873, the Japanese retained a method of timetelling peculiar to themselves. This Pillar Clock has an iron movement and is controlled by a foliot balance. The time is shown by means of the pointer moving past the vertical scale of hours.

realized the potential of mass production continued, notably in factories run by the Japy Frères, to produce movements to a standard pattern for the 'makers' to case as they wished. These roulants appear in every conceivable style of French clock: four glass clocks, the typical Victorian black marble clock, and many elaborate cases and garnitures (the designs of which were copied from earlier styles) and also the carriage clock. The carriage clock was tremendously popular. Possibly its attraction lay in its compactness, wide diversity of quality and style of case decoration, together with variations of simple or complicated strike and chime.

The English clock industry dwindled. While other countries accepted the new ideas, the English makers insisted on continuing their now out-dated methods which could not meet either the demand or price range of their new customers. A few small factories opened in the mid-1800s, one being the British United Clock Company, but they failed to realize how completely competitive they needed to be. Although struggling at the lower end of the market, the Victorian clockmakers did produce some magnificent pieces of quality workmanship for those who could afford them. The brass skeleton clock under its glass shade with its varying escapements, frame designs and strike enjoyed tremendous popularity.

In 1851 Lord Grimthorpe and Edward John Dent devised the Great Clock of Westminster, which came to be known after its installation as Big Ben – the most famous public clock in the world – an event that no doubt was a contributory factor to the numerous orders received by the turret clock manufacturers of that day from many foreign parts. The order books of Potts of Leeds, Smith of Derby, and Gillet and Johnston of Croydon make fascinating reading. No doubt this also influenced the making of the huge longcase and bracket clocks made about the turn of the century with their multiple choice of chimes on bells, tubes or gongs. The Westminster chimes, Whittington chimes and St Michael chimes were the most commonly heard.

It would appear that the age of the mechanical clock is nearing its end and will be entirely replaced by those utilizing the quartz oscillator. This has been a natural evolution from the first successful application of electricity to clocks by the Scotsman, Alexander Bain, in 1842. From that date we have seen the progress of many systems of master clocks controlling slave dials (that of Synchronome first patented 1895, and Lowne patented 1901) and domestic battery clocks (the Eureka first patented 1906 and the Bulle of 1921), followed by the synchronous mains clocks of the 1920s and 1930s.

4 Three Bulle electric clocks of this century. The example in the centre is of an earlier date than the other two.

5 French carriage clock, the movement with platform lever escapement, and striking on a gong.

Clock Hands

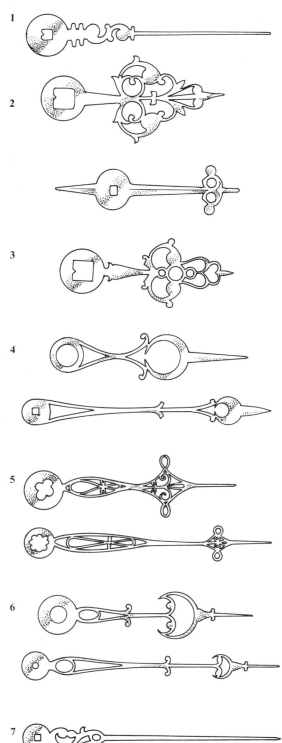

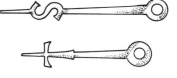

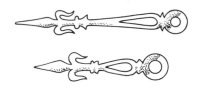

By the end of the 19th century most of the clock hands were stamped out by machinery. Prior to this date the quality would depend to a large extent upon the skills of the craftsman involved and cost to the customer. Many were superb pieces of work – the piercing and hand finishing of which would have taken several days. It is rarely possible to give exact dates for specific designs, although one may differentiate between early and late examples of a pattern. Makers in large cities would follow more closely contemporary designs in other fields, while provincial makers would be more readily influenced by local tastes, personal ability and so on.

1 An example from an early single handed clock (an English lantern clock).

2–8 Further examples to be found on English clocks of the 17th, 18th and 19th centuries.

9 Readily identifiable as being a design used by the American manufacturer, Seth Thomas during the 19th century.

10–13 A small selection of French clock hand designs popular between 1850 and 1875.

14 and **15** would be found on 20th century cuckoo clocks from the Black Forest, Germany. Made of bone they would be either left plain or carved.

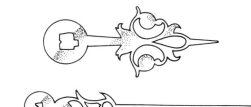

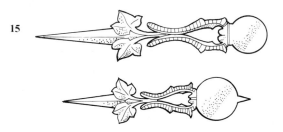

Watches

The first pocket watch was a miniature spring-driven clock movement placed in a spherical case which was then worn suspended by a cord around the neck or from a belt. Peter Henlein, the Nuremberg locksmith reputedly responsible for the introduction of the spring in place of weights as a motive power, is recorded as having made watches of this type early in the 16th century. Through a translator's error these are quite often incorrectly referred to as 'Nuremberg Eggs'. Other examples of early watchmaking are known to be of Italian or French origin.

These early German movements were made of iron, with a verge escapement and foliot with a stackfreed to equalize the power of the spring. French and English watchmakers, however, favoured the use of a fusee for this purpose. Initially these were of a gut line, but this was replaced by the fusee chain, the invention of which is attributed to a Swiss called Gruet. Brass was more commonly used after 1575.

About the turn of the century case styles altered dramatically. The drum shape favoured by the Germans gave way to the oval, round, square and more exotic 'form' cases. One of the most noted examples of the latter is a case in the shape of a skull that is known to have been in the possession of Mary, Queen of Scots. Others took the shape of stars, crosses, shells, flowers and birds. Casemaking had now become the task of the lapidist, enameller and a little later the gold and silversmiths. Apart from the *cloisonné* and *champlevé* work already seen on dials and cases, there now appeared other forms of enamelwork. Beautiful examples can be seen with scenes painted in enamel following the methods introduced by Jean Toutin working in Blois about

1630, or the school of enamelling founded by Jean Petitot (1607–91) in Geneva about 1650. It is generally acknowledged that the fine enamel work of this period was never surpassed.

By now cases were hinged to the movement with a 'glass' cover enclosing the dial (1626). The relatively fragile enamelled cases necessitated some form of protection. Originally made of stiffened leather, by mid-century these outer cases were of metal covered with leather, shagreen, tortoiseshell and often decorated with pique work. Perversely the inner case became plainer with the outer case receiving more attention. Although highly decorative cases continued to be made towards the middle of the century there was introduced in England a

simple watch with both outer and inner silver cases completely devoid of any form of embellishment. This innovation is generally attributed to firstly the Puritan influence and then to the introduction of the pocketed waistcoat.

The lead in the field of watchmaking had initially been held by the German makers, but at a time when watches were regarded not as serious timekeepers but merely beautiful baubles, the French with their natural flair for artistic work rapidly overtook and passed them. The English makers, although somewhat tardy in the 16th century, were to dominate in the 17th with what in modern parlance would be described as a technical breakthrough. This was the successful application of the balance spring to a watch by Thomas Tompion in 1675. There are several claimants to the invention of this device, but in this particular watch by Tompion, tribute is paid to Robert Hooke as the inventor. Although the use of a balance spring did not solve all the problems that needed to be overcome before the watch became a precision timekeeper it most certainly did change its role. Cases became much plainer and simpler; the improved accuracy warranted the addition of a minute hand, and shortly after this a seconds hand. Much experimentation both on the Continent and in England was carried out in attempts to improve upon the verge escapement. George Graham perfected the cylinder escapement about 1725. Although used in a few English watches, it was not used extensively until the end of the 18th century when the Swiss and French makers dispensed with the fusee and utilized this escapement in their endeavours to meet the demand for thinner more elegant watches. Through persisting with the use of the fusee even in their cylinder watches and declining to adapt the verge watches in order to

meet this new fad, the English slowly lost their lead in the overseas markets.

The advantage thus given them was eagerly grasped by the French, who also had the advantage of having at this time an exceptionally artistic as well as technically brilliant horologist – Abraham Louis Breguet (1747–1816). Born in Neuchatel in Switzerland he spent most of his working life in France. Movements of the watches produced during this century included many complicated mechanisms, namely automata, striking, chiming, repeating work, perpetual calendars and so on, as well as incorporating technical improvements needed to achieve precision timekeeping. Although using many of the previously introduced techniques of enamelling and so forth, the application to cases altered. The paintings were now confined to panels set into a gold case, with the metal being pierced, chased or set with half-pearls or brilliants. The former were characteristic of many Swiss cases, although the French and Swiss designs tended to be similar in most instances. Guilloche or Engine-Turning became widely used towards the end of the century and frequently was further embellished with a coloured translucent enamel. Repoussé work was at its peak mid-century but continued in varying degrees of quality for a further 25 years. The general aim of the case designer at this period was one of restrained elegance and a quality of quiet, good taste.

The 19th century saw many changes. Possibly the most noticeable technical achievement was the advent of the keyless watch. The difficulty encountered when attempting to incorporate this feature into a watch with a fusee, heralded the finale demise on the Continent of the fusee, although many English makers clung to the key wound verge watch until as late as the 1880s.

The Swiss industry began to emerge from its previous state of quiescence to become one of the major manufacturers. With a widening market the form watch was reintroduced. Now intended primarily for use by the fair sex, these small movements were housed in finger rings, bodies of butterflies, bracelets, and so forth. Although Frederic Japy had begun making watches in France by machine tools as early as 1776, it was during this century that true factory methods were generally adopted. The Americans, who had hitherto made few watches, were swift to realize the potential of mass production. The Waltham Watch Company (1850–1950) made some watches of excellent quality, while other firms such as Waterbury (1880–1896) and Ingersoll concentrated on the rapidly growing need for cheaper watches. These cheap watches – the products of advancing technology and acceptance of new ideas – were eventually to crush the more conservative English watch trade. The Swiss makers survived, however, by adopting and improving upon the best of the 'new' methods of production. Many of the names appearing on watches of modern manufacture bear names of eminent makers of this century – Jurgensen, Frodsham, Bonniksen, Vacheron,

1 (Left) Sun and moon dialled watch by Windmills, London, silver champlevé, about 1700. (Right) Pocket chronometer by Barraud, London, the silver case is hall-marked 1797.

2 (Right) English silver-cased verge watch by William Feltham of Stowmarket, about 1844. The engraving round the dial reads 'keep me clean and use me well and I to you the truth will tell.' (Left) Small fob watch by Ingersoll converted for wearing as a wrist watch by a leather pocketed strap.

2

Constantin for example – their work having been continued by their various successors.

As the century progressed the emphasis changed, with cases becoming plainer. The demand was now for a technically interesting watch that was highly accurate, or for a simple inexpensive model with an adequate degree of accuracy.

The demise of the pocket watch for general use was comparatively swift. Although there are a few recorded instances of watches worn on the wrist at earlier dates, it was not until the turn of the 19th century that serious attempts were made to introduce them commercially. This met with violent opposition from the general public who regarded them as effeminate affectations. The fact that they had been made and supplied to Officers in the German Army in the late 1800s made no impact on this opinion. However, when their practicality had been further demonstrated by their use during the First World War (1914–18) they began to be more widely accepted. The first examples were small pocket watches placed in various wristlets, but by 1926, manufacturers such as the Rolex Watch Company had moved the winding button to its present position, added lugs to which straps were attached and overcome the problems of shock proofing and the exclusion of dust and water. The wrist watch was here to stay and the owners of pocket watches most definitely form a minority group today although they are now slowly becoming fashionable again.

3 This lady's fob-watch from Geneva has an ornate gilt dial and cylinder movement, 20th century.

3

Scientific instruments

Living in a world where the all pervading authority of science is increasingly resented, it may seem paradoxical that collectors are eager to acquire examples of the early apparatus and instruments which helped to create that domination. Yet the layman's fascination for the artifacts of science is almost as old as science itself. Neither Jean de Berry, Duke of Normandy in the 14th century, nor Emperor Rudolph II at Prague in the 16th century, nor the English monarch George III in the 18th century was a scientist, but each one of them collected instruments. It is difficult to imagine any present-day patron of the arts emulating that example and acquiring an electron microscope or a geiger counter, and the reason is not hard to find. Not only has science changed radically in the present century, but scientific instrument manufacture has also changed. Mass production techniques have led to an inexorable decline in individual craft skills, while the apparatus has been stripped of all decoration. At the same time the growing complexity of science has led to an elaboration of almost every instrument. In this manner the inherent attraction of form showing function has been dissipated as the critical instrumentation becomes hidden behind an anonymous facia panel.

In stark contrast, almost all scientific instruments of former eras possess some aesthetic appeal. In them, mechanical ingenuity and technical prowess are combined with the loving skill of the master craftsman and even the most utilitarian artifacts show the dextrous proficiency of their makers. In these early instruments science has combined with art to produce objects of lasting beauty.

Because the pace of change has varied between one science and another, and even between the various branches of the individual sciences, it is not possible to give a single cut-off date beyond which scientific instruments are no longer of interest to the antique collector. Certainly the exigencies of the First World War caused a major upheaval in the scientific instrument manufacturing industry; nevertheless even after that cataclysm certain instruments continued to be made in a form that had been unchanged for a century or more. One classic example is the Sikes's hydrometer, used to test the strength of spirituous liquours for revenue purposes in the British Isles from 1816. The design hardly changed through more than a century of manufacture and the instrument itself was only replaced by more sophisticated methods during the last decade.

The brass hydrometer, covered with a fine film of gold to prevent corrosion, is frequently seen in antique shops sitting in an attractive velvet-lined case with a set of small gilt weights, an ivory backed thermometer and a slide rule in boxwood or ivory. As with any scientific instrument the maker's name is the most reliable guide to date, though where a firm has been in business for two or three generations or more, other pointers are required. A practiced eye will know real ivory from the various synthetic ivorines that replaced it, while silver and brass should be readily distinguished from polished nickel and chrome plate. Those with a knowledge of furniture may rely on the way that the case is made and finished. The centre piece, the hydrometer itself, gives few clues to its age. The calligraphic style of the callibration and other engraved lettering can be helpful, but frequently, as with other instruments whose design was long lived, it is the sum of the evidence drawn from the object, its accessories, the case lock and hinge, that provides the experienced observer with evidence of the date of origin.

A contrasting example is the sextant. It has remained an essential tool of the navigator since its introduction in about 1758. It was an improvement on the octant or reflecting quadrant invented in 1730 quite independently by John Hadley in London and Thomas Godfrey in Philadelphia. Unlike the Sikes hydrometer, the marine sextant has run through a series of variations to the basic idea. On design features alone it is possible to date individual instruments to within 30 years or so as a matter of course, and frequently to much closer limits. From an aesthetic point of view the most desirable sextants are those made in the last quarter of the 18th century, solely from brass, their surfaces protected by a clear lacquer.

Of all the sciences it is astronomy which has the longest history of an appreciation of the vital role played by precision instruments. Not surprisingly the archetypal and most desirable of all scientific instruments, the astrolabe, was used in astronomy. Primarily the astrolabe is a mechanical analogue device replacing the written calculations used to predict star and planetary positions. It could also be used to measure solar elevation, compute the latitude, tell the time and undertake basic surveying. The theory of the stereographic projection, on which the instrument was based, was known in classical antiquity, but the earliest surviving astrolabes were made during the 11th century by Islamic craftsmen living in southern Spain. By the late 17th century the astrolabe had become obsolete in Europe. However these classic instruments continued to be made in the Islamic world, and are still made in Isfahan by craftsmen who follow the traditional techniques of construction. Such is its attraction that scholars have been studying European and Islamic astrolabes for more than a century.

The fine metal work, delicate engraving and graceful lines of an astrolabe have an immediate and lasting appeal. An eye catching feature is the intricately pierced rête whose pointers represent important stars. Products of the Flemish workshops of the Arsenius family are particularly prized for a very high standard of craftsmanship. Indeed an astrolabe made in 1556 by Gemma Frisius, the uncle and teacher of Walther and Regner Arsenius, holds the world record price for an antique instrument sold at auction, fetching 310,000 Swiss Francs in 1975. This was an exceptionally beautiful astrolabe, a presentation piece engraved with the arms of Phillip II of Spain and Mary Tudor of England.

The one single device which greatly influenced future instrumentation in astronomy was the telescope. Invented in the early years of the 17th century by an unknown spectacle maker, the telescope was given immense publicity by the startling discoveries of the great Galileo. Scientist and layman alike were eager to own and use the new instrument. Initially they were both rare and expensive, and only a handful of telescopes made before 1650 have survived. The second half of the century is better represented. The typical late-17th-century hand-held telescope has a number of cardboard draw-tubes. For portability they all slide into an outer tube or barrel which is normally highly decorated. English instruments of the period are characterized by patches of green and orange on the white vellum cover of the barrel, with a pattern of gold stampings providing further embellishment.

In the next century brass draw-tubes with wood or leather-covered barrels commonly occur. The intermediate stage when vellum-covered pasteboard was combined with a polished shagreen stained red or green is particularly attractive, especially if the lens mounts and reinforcing ferrules are made of silver rather than horn, ebony or brass. By the latter part of the 19th century nickel, aluminium and chrome plate are used and these hand-held telescopes hold little attraction. At this late date, however,

Technically this beautiful French octant, made about 1786, incorporates a most unusual feature, a magnetic compass set in the centre of the all brass frame. Above the compass are engraved the words 'DEDIE A SA MAIESTE LOUIS XV' indicating a presentation piece. In contrast to the utilitarian and typically chaste ebony-framed mariner's octant, this example has been elaborately decorated by its maker. Functionally and aesthetically this is indeed an instrument fit for a King, and it proudly bears the maker's signature 'FAIT PAR MAGNIE A DUNKERQUE'.

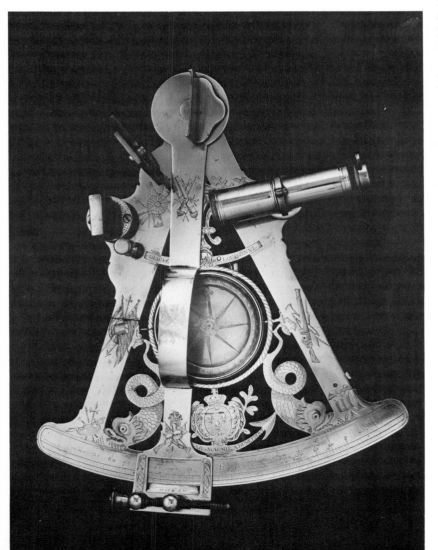

1 Dated 1632, this astrolabe was made in the Nuremberg workshop of Georg Hartmann. After studying mathematics and theology at Cologne Hartmann travelled to Italy to continue his mathematical education. In 1518 he settled in Nuremberg, a City State which was fast becoming the leading European centre for the manufacture of scientific instruments. For over 20 years a Vicar at the Sebalduskirche, Hartmann was also a prolific instrument-maker. On his astrolabes the design of the pierced rête which carries the pointers representing the important stars, is reminiscent of the window tracery which is such a visually exciting feature of gothic architecture. Also typical of Hartmann's work is the rose ornament on the bracket.

astronomical instruments using the telescope only as a sighting device still retain a strong aesthetic appeal. It is the sheer ingenuity and complexity of the mounting, be it transit, equatorial or altazimuth that overcomes the drab but hard-wearing finish then applied.

In the 18th century the leading makers of precision astronomical instruments all worked in London. The names of Graham, Bird, Short, Troughton and Ramsden were familiar to astronomers throughout the world. But by the turn of the century German workshop began to compete and then overtake their English rivals. The Mathematical-Mechanical Institute of Reichenbach, Utzschneider and Leibherr, a Munich consortium, led the way, followed by the equally illustrious names of Frauenhofer, Ertel, Merz and Repsold.

The visual attraction of pieces from German workshops during the early decades of the century was attained by the use of brass with various colour characteristics; a copper-rich alloy highlighting the more usual yellow brass, while the whole instrument was enlivened by the inset circles of silver on which the fine divisions of degrees were marked and calibrated. In the middle years of the 19th century a dark blue/green or black oxide finish was applied to

astronomical instruments. This provided a practical and durable finish but the price paid was an immediate reduction in visual impact. Surveying instruments of the period were similarly treated. They are far more common and less intricate than astronomical instruments. In a search to uncover supposed former glories quite a number have been 'restored' by the removal of the original lustreless finish and buffed-up to an unnatural sheen. The total effect is disastrous.

Just as the telescope opened new worlds in the heavens so too did the microscope uncover for the 17th century an unimagined kingdom of the minutiae. For 250 years the microscope was the most loved of all the instruments available to the amateur. To be sure, professional scientists used the instrument and made many important discoveries, but from the publication of Robert Hooke's *Micrographia* in 1664 until the end of the Victorian era, ladies, gentlemen and children discovered microscopy as a recreation.

From 1650–1830 the optical performance of the microscope improved only marginally. Through the same period the stand was redesigned and improved by a host of makers. Some specialized in miniaturization, others in elaborate mechanical gimcracks. One of the most long lasting designs is that the London mathematical instrument-maker Edmund Culpeper.

The first form of the 'Culpeper' microscope was introduced about 1725 as a modification of the tripod microscope developed by English opticians after an Italian design manufactured by the renowned lens polisher Giuseppe Campani of Rome. As with telescopes of the period, the body tube is pasteboard covered with shagreen, the stained and polished skin of the sting ray. The eyepiece is turned in ebony, the stage, legs and fittings are brass. Culpeper's significant technical innovation was the concave sub-stage mirror that gave improved illumination of the object. For this reason the instrument was known as the 'double reflecting microscope'. There were almost a dozen design variations in 50 years; the final all brass form of about 1770 was in production for over 70 years as the 'three pillar microscope'. If fully equipped the 'Culpeper' microscope has a range of accessories stored either in the octagonal foot or in the drawer of the tapering case. Culpeper's own work invariably has an oak case, and the attribution to the maker is made from the engraved trade-label pasted in the back of the case. Later models have mahogany cases and less than half of those that survive have the maker's name engraved on the stage or the body-tube. Lately some unsigned instruments have been 'doctored' with the signatures of reputable makers to enhance their value. With a keen eye and a powerful hand lens such fraudulant activity can usually be uncovered.

The recent engraving of signatures should not be confused with contemporary attempts to reap financial benefit from the reputation of a well known maker. The firm of P. & J. Dollond of London were renowned for the achromatic telescopes, indeed for some years they had a

1

monopoly of the manufacture of telescopes with the doublet objective for reduction of colour abberation patented by John Dollond in 1758. Unwary buyers at the end of the 18th century bought telescopes signed '*Dolland*' in the fond belief that they were acquiring a product of the house of Dollond. Almost a century earlier the expatriate English instrument-maker Michael Butterfield suffered similar plagiarism from unscrupulous colleagues in Paris, whose substandard sundials were engraved '*BVTERFIELD APARIS*'.

During the 18th century, Continental microscope makers took up and modified the designs of the market-leading London Opticians. The Parisian atelier married brass, silver, wood and shagreen with confidence and to far greater aesthetic effect than their rivals across the channel. There is no English counterpart to the French 'Box' microscope, where the body of the instrument is set on a handsome cabinet inlaid with marquetry, decorated with ormolu mounts, or merely faced with carefully chosen veneers.

On the few occasions when a London optician set out to make an overtly decorative microscope the effect was unconvincing. The great silver microscope made by George Adams for George III in 1761 is certainly a fine and impressive example of mechanical skill, but is also in monumental bad taste. In contrast Alexis Magny, a Parisian maker who worked for clients like Bonnier de la Mosson, owner of one of the most extensive cabinets of instruments in France, produced microscopes that incorporated not only all the latest technical features, but were also of considerable beauty. They were celebrated with the Rococo decorations in gilded bronze, and a highly decorated shaped leather casket. These mechanical and aesthetic triumphs of Magny were proudly owned by members of the French aristocracy like Louis XV, the Marquis de Pompadour and the Duc de Chaulnes.

In the 3rd decade of the 19th century, with the development of the compound achromatic objective, the microscope came of age as a scientific instrument. From this date development based on sound mechanical and optical principles was undertaken both in Europe and the United States. The workshops of Ploessel of Vienna, Norbert of Barth, Oberhauser of Paris, Nachet of Paris, Powell and Lealand of London, Ross of London, Dancer of Manchester, Spenser of New York, Grunow Brothers of New Haven and Zentmayer of Philadelphia produced excellent instruments. By 1870 the English makers had been overtaken in eminence by American and German firms who continued to adapt and innovate rather than rely on well tried models. Zeiss of Jena led the field, their designs stimulated by the theoretician Ernst Abbe. The 'Jug-Handled' Zeiss remains a classic instrument among microscopists today. A number of French and American firms also produced advanced work. The Bausch and Lomb Optical Company of Rochester are worth particular mention, and it is interesting to note that the leading American microscope makers of the latter part of the 19th

2 Italian tripod microscope dating from the second half of the seventeenth century. The collar and tripod are a restoration, but the rest of the instrument, including the optical system, is original. To focus on the object the whole body of the microscope is screwed in or out of the collar. Some variation in magnification with any given objective lens can be achieved by pulling out the draw-tube within which are mounted a field lens and a biconvex doublet eye-piece. The field lens was first used by the English physician Henry Power in 1661 while an Italian optician Eustachio Divini is credited with the introduction of the doublet eye-piece and the microscope used in the now conventional manner. To view a transparent object the white ground would be removed and the microscope held like a hand telescope to allow observation by transmitted light.

3 An unusual inverted achromatic microscope, first manufactured by the Parisian optical firm Maison Nachet et Fils in 1886. The objective is placed beneath the stage. This peculiar arrangement would otherwise distort the image seen through a conventional microscope.

1

1 and 2 Vacuum tube made to the design published by William Crookes in 1879 to demonstrate the proposition that 'Radiant Matter' proceeds in straight lines independent of the position of the positive poles. The engraving is from a broadsheet issued about 1710 by John Patrick the leading London barometer-maker. On the right is a diagonal barometer incorporated in the frame of a mirror, 'whereby gentlemen and ladies at the same time they dress, may accommodate their habit to the weather.'

century were almost all refugees who had left Germany during the political upheavals of the 1850s.

The development of the American instrument-making industry has a history which is quite well represented by surviving instruments. The first colonists had to rely on European instruments, but by the mid-18th century indigenous craftsmen were able to satisfy the desperate local demand for the utilitarian instruments used by surveyors and navigators. The earliest recorded maker of instruments in North America, James Halsey of Boston, is from a navigator's backstaff dated 1676. Since brass had to be imported from England until the second quarter of the 19th century, the colonial makers turned to the native hardwoods. In New England black-walnut, rock maple, pear, wild cherry and apple were used. These woods were neither sufficiently close-grained nor resinous enough to survive the rigours of shipboard use, so that for octants ebony and mahogany imported from the West Indies was preferred.

The classic American instrument is the surveyor's compass, which in the 18th century was made totally of native wood. Like all colonial work, this instrument had no superfluous decoration. The one exception to this general rule is the engraved paper compass card at the centre of the surveyor's compass. It is frequently found with an elaborate design in the central roundel. In the early examples, the style and motifs of the decoration followed English traditions, using, for example, the crown and tudor rose. Not unnaturally, Old World themes were rapidly abandoned after 1776. A common post-independence design has a marine scene as the central vignette. This is an unexpected iconographic feature to

find on a surveying instrument, but is explained by the economic desire to use the same copper plate to print compass cards for the surveyor and the navigator.

One area where the colonists had to rely on imported instruments was in the supply of apparatus for college teaching. The apparatus of natural philosophy as it was called in the 18th century, embraces a very wide subject area. It includes such items as air pumps, with the associated pneumatic apparatus like Magdeburg hemispheres and guinea and feather apparatus; there are hydrostatic balances, inclined planes and a host of mechanical models to demonstrate the operation and principles of the gear, pulley and lever, also loadstones, magnets and the very wide range of electrical apparatus out of which modern physics evolved.

Not until the third and fourth decades of the 19th century were American instrument-makers, like Benjamin Pike of New York, able to produce all these instruments. Before that time London makers, such as Martin, Adams and the brothers William and Samuel Jones, supplied Colleges like Harvard and Dartmouth. This is not to imply that London held a monopoly of the manufacture of demonstrative apparatus. In Holland, France, Italy, Germany and even Sweden there were men who manufactured a range of instruments used to explain and illustrate scientific ideas. Much of the Dutch work is of a very high standard with the woodwork echoing contemporary styles of furniture, while the French makers adorned some pieces with gaily painted patterns of flowers and foliage. The barometer, for all its being a meteorological instrument invented by Toricelli about 1640, is the extreme example of this trend to turn the laboratory into a salon. Indeed the vast majority of mercury barometers that survive were made and sold as items of domestic furniture rather than as scientific instruments.

The electrostatic generator, which was developed during the latter half of the 18th century, is an attractive example of an instrument of natural philosophy. The glass cylinder or disc, which is turned against leather rubbing cushions to generate a static charge, is mounted in a mahogany frame. There are large brass condensers set on insulating pillars of glass. It is an impressive artifact, as is its later 19th century equivalent, the influence machine. This was developed by Holz and Töpler and is familiarly known under the name Wimshurst machine, after a common late 19th century design.

The invention of the voltaic cell and the development of electromagnetism and current electricity led to many new instruments like the induction coil, the tangent galvanometer and the multi-cellular voltmeter, with the electric telegraph providing both a new means of communication and a large market for receivers and transmitters. The delicate workmanship of the later electrical instruments used for precision measurement is often hidden inside a protective case. Those without some technical insight might not appreciate the subtlety of the design.

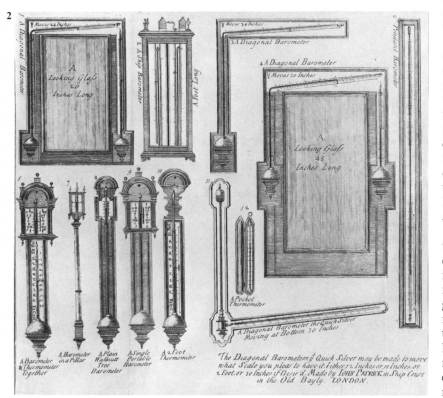

However, the layman cannot fail to be attracted by the various forms of vacuum tubes with which 19th century physicists studied the effect of high voltage discharge through gases at a high degree of exhaustion. Geissler, Plücker, Hittorf and Crookes all gave their names to vacuum tubes of particular types. If we can no longer be dazzled by the fluorescence of uranium glass in a Geissler tube, we can still be impressed by the skill of the glassblower who was able to insert a small paddle wheel inside a Crookes tube so that it would spin and run along a glass railway when bombarded by rays of 'radiant matter'.

Here was the birth of particle physics, and at a more directly useful level it was with a pear-shaped Crookes tube that W. T. Röntegen discovered X-rays in 1895, and so opened the way to radiotherapy. Most early medical instruments being almost solely concerned with surgical applications have macabre associations that tend to swamp any aesthetic attractions. In contrast the early X-ray tube has a functional form of considerable strength, and would not be out of place in a gallery of 20th-century sculpture. For the collector of scientific instruments, perhaps the most desirable are those made in Germany by firms like Müller of Hamburg, where the etched signature includes the word 'Rontegenrohr' commemorating the discoverer.

By the beginning of the present century, physics had outgrown descriptive natural philosophy and become a highly mathematical subject. Mathematics itself had advanced considerably and in combination with electrical technology was soon to spawn that master of all our destinies, the electronic computer. In its earlier history, the tools of mathematics were far less awesome artifacts. Indeed an ability to use mathematical instruments was at one time one of the essential skills of an educated gentleman. For wealthy clients, craftsmen like Giacomo Lusuergh of Modena, who worked in Rome from the late 1660s, produced comprehensive sets of mathematical instruments. Such compendia includes all the tools necessary for architectural drawing, surveying, gunnery and computation.

Domenico Lusuergh produced similar work for at least 50 years after succeeding his uncle in 1697. Like other Italian craftsmen of the period, the Lusuerghs produced lavish compendia of mathematical instruments in which technical expertise was complemented by engraving.

French, Dutch and English makers of this time tended to produce only pocket cases of drawing instruments, including a sector for computational purposes. Decoration is not found as a matter of course, though there are some notable exceptions. For example, during the first four decades of the 18th century, London makers often engraved an oak leaf border pattern on sectors, protractors and plain scales. This can be very effective on silver instruments.

Another exception is the practice of French makers well into the 19th century, to engrave a floral decoration on the hinge of sectors and folding rules. Parisian makers like Butterfield,

LeMaire (both father and son) and Canivet produced elegant etui or pocket-cases of instruments in brass and silver. Nicholas Bion (1653–1733) who held the title. 'Ingenieur du Roy pour les Instrumens de Mathematique' made at least one set in gold. Its case is covered in shagreen decorated with pique work in gold headed nails. Bion was the author of the classic and comprehensive text *Traité de la construction et des principaux Usages des Instrumens de Mathematique*. Six French editions were published between 1709 and 1752, with German and English translations in 1713 and 1723 respectively.

One of the most intriguing of all early mathematical instruments is an aid to calculation called Napier's Rods, or 'Bones', since the earliest examples were made from ivory. Boxes of 10 or 20 rods no bigger than a cigarette packet, were used by those who found multiplication difficult – the face of each rod has the multiplication table of a digit from one to nine. The design was published by John Napier in Edinburgh in 1616, and it rapidly became widely known. Few sets are signed and it may be as difficult to ascertain their origin as their date.

Another computational instrument is the slide rule which utilizes Napier's better known invention of the logarithm. This is a very specialized area with a bewildering number of slide rule designs for use in gauging, ullaging, joinery, navigation and engineering, to name just a handful of areas. Boxwood was the preferred material, though ivory is quite common for hydrometer rules, while brass and more rarely silver are known to have been used for circular slide rules by French, German and English makers. There are rather more signed slide rules than is generally appreciated; the

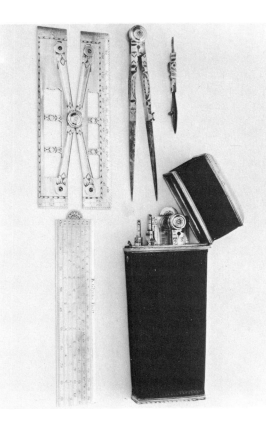

3 Pocket case of drawing instruments made in silver. The oak leaf decoration, which is a typical feature of English work of the early 18th century, can be seen on the combined protractor and parallel rule. It is less usual to find this motif appearing on the dividers and compasses. Normally such small pieces are undecorated and a careful comparison of design details is necessary to ensure that a 'complete' set has not been made-up with the odd contemporary item by another maker. Richard Glynne, who made these elegant instruments, completed his apprenticeship in 1705. From Glynn the succession can be traced through five generations to Augustine Ryther (flourished 1576–95), one of the first of a dynasty of craftsmen who practised the art of instrument-making in England.

1 and 2 A presentation set of
navigational instruments;
back-staff, cross-staff with
four vanes and two Gunter
scales. Made in ivory by
Thomas Tuttell of London,
about 1700. The half-hour
sand-glass is contemporary
but not Tuttell's work.
Below a cometarium made
by W & S Jones of London.
This is a device used to
demonstrate how the speed
of a comet varies according
to Kepler's law of equal
areas.

signature is often hidden on the stock beneath one of the slides and can easily be overlooked.

The area which is best represented in number and diversity of surviving instruments is gnomics; the science of dialling, or the designing and making of sundials. The various instruments used to set out and calibrate sundials, such as the declinatory, dialling scale, and movable horizontal dial, are rare and frequently pass unrecognized. The sundial itself is, however, immediately appreciated as an instrument for telling the time by the sun. That there are a profusion of dials of all sizes, periods, materials and designs, surprises those who have forgotten that

watches and clocks need to be regulated to a standard time. Until well into the 19th century, and the spread of the electric telegraph, the sundial was the only way of finding the time once your mechanical timepiece stopped.

Archeologists have recorded Greek and Roman dials carved in stone, but if we exclude these and other mural dials, the earliest sundials by European instrument-makers are the horary quadrants made in the late medieval period.

The most frequently seen horary quadrant is that named after Edmund Gunter, whose design was published in 1623. London makers like Allen, Bedford and Hayes in the 17th century, produced fine examples of the Gunter quadrant. Some have a celestial planisphere on the reverse face which permitted the time to be found at night from the circumpolar rotation of the stars. Rather than using silver, brass or boxwood, cheap horary quadrants were printed on paper from a copper plate, and pasted on to wooden boards. There are some nice early 19th century examples of this type, printed in Italy with letterpress instructions on the reverse: *Spiegazione per l'uso dell' Orologio a Quadrante Solare.*

In the 16th and 17th centuries Nuremburg craftsmen supplied Europe with a distinctive form of sundial, the diptych dial. Formed from two hinged plates of ivory, the diptych may contain just vertical and horizontal dials on the two inner leaves. More usually it supplements those dials with polar, equinoctial and scaphe dials. In addition there may be tables of epacts (to calculate the date of Easter) lunar and solar volvelles, and dials that indicate the length of the day and the season of the year. Most Nuremburg dials are fully signed – though some bear only the master-sign of the maker. Many are also dated. One craftsman with a distinguished style was Paulus Reinman, active from 1575 to 1609. Reinman's work is often decorated with attractive vignettes, a pair of musicians, lovers talking, hunting hounds. As was the fashion his calibration and decoration is picked out in red, blue and black. Reinman's master-sign was used by Michael Lesel from 1609 to 1629, making it difficult to give firm attributions to some pieces.

In terms of quantity, the Nuremburg dial makers were succeeded from the mid-17th century by the *Kompassmacher* of Augsburg, whose typical product was the universal equinoctial dial. Working in brass, in the early period often gilded, the Augsburg craftsmen had a flourishing trade, printing instruction sheets in German, French and Spanish. Men like Johann Martin and his half-brother Johann Willibrand set very high standards. In the latter part of the 18th century the quality of workmanship declined. Floral patterns in the decoration became hurried and stereotyped. The work of the last of the Augsburg Kompassmacher, Johann Schretteger, who died in 1843, compares very poorly with that of his predecessors.

Possibly the highest point of Augsburg craftmanship was attained in the 16th century and is best represented by instruments produced by family dynasties of craftsmen like the Kliebers

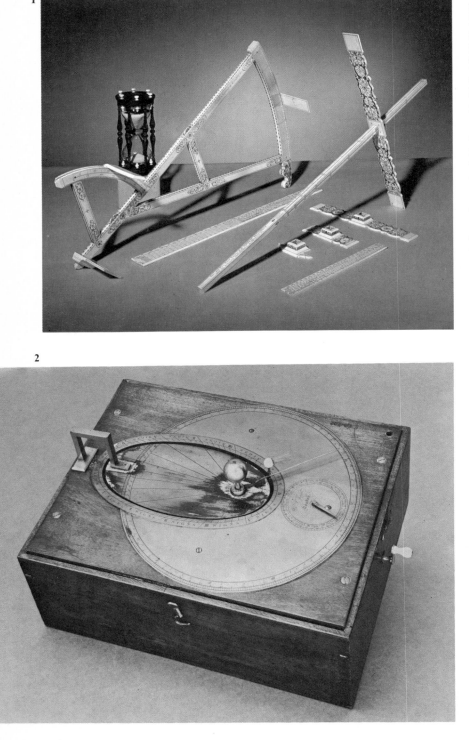

1

2

(1487–1619 in three generations) and the Schisslers (1531–1625 in two generations). Both these families produced wonderful pocket compendia in gilded brass. These dials open out to reveal various universal sundials, nocturnals, astrolabes and perpetual calendars. The compendium allows the instrument-maker to show all his constructional skills in one masterpiece. Italian, Flemish and less often French and English makers produced fine compendia, but none reached the standards of the 16th century Augsburg masters.

Two distinctly French sundials are those named after Michael Butterfield and Charles Bloud. The 'Butterfield' dial is a pseudo-universal horizontal dial adjustable for use over the latitude range 40° to 60° north. The archetypal form has an octagonal dialplate and a characteristic bird decoration on the adjustable gnomon – the beak of the bird indicates the latitude. Made in brass or silver the Butterfield dial was a typical product of the Parisian instrument-makers from about 1675 to 1750. The quality of the craftsmanship is variable, though that of Butterfield himself is consistently good, and is comparable to his contemporaries Bion and Chapotot, and, in the later period, Langlois.

The 'Bloud' dial is one of the few examples of a French instrument of the 17th century made outside Paris. From the 14th century the Ivoirier of Dieppe held an international reputation. In the 17th century a distinct school of diptych dial makers appeared. About 1650 Charles Bloud designed a form of magnetic azimuth dial incorporating a perpetual calendar. He proudly signed his dials *Fait et Invente par Charles Bloud A Dieppe*. Other Dieppe makers like Senecal, Guerard, and Gabriel, Jacques and Jean Bloud produced similar dials. In the Dieppe style they decorated their work with a characteristic border of pecked crenelations.

In its time the universal equinoctial ring dial was very popular, primarily because it is self-orienting and requires no compass to align it. The design was inspired by the astronomical ring of Gemma Frisius and it is most frequently found in the form published by Oughtred in 1652, with two rings set at right angles. There is a pin-hole gnomon on a diametrical bridge, casting a spot of sunlight on to the hour ring. This was the design used by the leading London instruments-makers for over 150 years. French and German makers produced similar instruments, together with the three ring variety which is, however, quite uncommon.

Most long-lasting of all pocket sundials is the cylinder, pillar or shepherd's dial; this latter name refers to its use in the present century by the Basque people of the Pyrenees. The design is known from 13th century manuscripts, and from that period Continental workshops made them in silver, ivory and wood. One 19th century Parisian clockmaker even marketed cylinder dials made of porcelain; it is a most cumbersome timepiece and cannot compare with the elegant silverware of Schissler of Augsburg, whose cylinder dials contained a set of writing imple-

ments, and incorporated an ink well and a sand caster.

Scientific instruments epitomize man's long struggle to understand and then control his environment. That attempt has been seen to achieve a measure of physical success since the 16th century. In the 17th century Isaac Barrow could confidently claim that it was through science that we receive 'the principal delights of life, securities of health, increase of fortune . . . that we dwell elegantly and commodiously, are protected from the incursions of the enemy and have safe traffic through the deceitful billows of the sea', all thanks to the benefits of science. And as Edmund Stone pointed out in 1723, it is instruments which permit the sciences to be 'rendered useful in the affairs of life'. In the present century, science has piled material success or material success, but at the same time it has become less and less comprehended by the layman. Indeed the culture of the scientist has drifted away from that of his fellow men. A Nuremburg instrument-maker of the 16th century would proudly emblazon a piece of finished work *Soli Deo Gloria*, to God alone by the Glory. No wonder; these early instruments represented the mechanical skills and aesthetic standards of their age. The imponderables have little place in modern science. Its instruments may be of technical interest, but there is no soul, and consequently, no art.

3 Early 19th century Italian unequal arm, or 'steelyard' balance. The balance arm is steel, the pan and its hangers, the suspension hook and the counter-weight are brass. This type of balance was used for every day commercial weighing. The design dates back to classical Roman times and a large number of examples have been excavated from the ruins of Pompeii. In France the steelyard balance, which can still be seen in use at country markets, is called 'Balance Romaine'.

The engraving in the background is from the great French *Encyclopédie* edited by Denis Diderot. It shows two equal arm balances and a selection of weights. The most attractive item is the nest of cup weights with the distinctive sea-horse clasp and mermen handle which was a typical decorative feature of Nuremberg work of the 17th and 18th centuries.

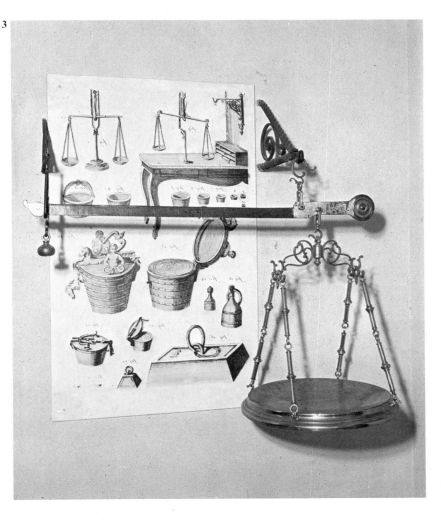

Musical instruments

1

1 Often the main, or even the only, source of information about early musical instruments and the ways in which they were played is contemporary painting. Stringed instruments (cordophones) such as the lute and the violin became very popular in the 16th century.

Musical instruments are fascinating objects. They range from the simplest instruments, which are designed to be solely utilitarian, to the most sophisticated ones, made and decorated by highly skilled craftsmen. The story of the development of musical instruments is fascinating, and many subsequently discussed were used in folk music as well as in orchestras today.

The early history of instruments in Europe relies largely on musical representations in painting, sculpture and other branches of the visual arts, for few instruments have survived from early periods, due to their fragility. Also, they were often remodelled into other instruments as soon as they became unfashionable; lutes were often rebuilt into hurdy-gurdies.

In the medieval period, manuscripts form a very valuable source of historical information. When illustrating biblical scenes, artists often depicted the instruments they knew. Grotesques and other amusing creatures were featured in the margins, playing the instruments. Sometimes these representations are not reliable evidence to the music historian. The length of a trumpet might be exaggerated to provide a complete border to the page, or a bagpipe drone lengthened for a joke or caricature.

Instruments were also used in still-life paintings; those by Baschenis were composed entirely of musical instruments. Italian wood intarsias of the 15th and 16th centuries included them, and in the 19th century inlaid work to decorate cabinets again used them. Often, this inlaid work was used to decorate the cabinets of musical-boxes. In the designs, lyres, lutes, sheet-music scrolls, aeolian harps, violins, oboes, trumpets and military drums are found. Pottery figurines also make use of musicians and their instruments. In paintings, a pastoral atmosphere is sometimes created by the inclusion of a bagpiper, or in a portrait the sitter might be posed by or with a much-prized instrument.

Instruments from the 18th century onwards are to be found in greater numbers; they sometimes are to be found in small music shops, antique markets or auctions. This survey traces the development of the instruments from the 17th century, together with some mention of contemporary folk instruments. The instruments can be grouped together, according to the manner in which the sounds they make are produced—percussion (bells and gongs), drums, strings, and wind instruments.

The first groups of instruments are the idiophones, these include rattles, bells, gongs, musical-boxes and musical glasses. These are all the instruments which, when struck, produce sound by vibrating themselves. The most familiar of this group are bells, gongs and musical-boxes. Bells can be made out of many materials, the most common being metal. Using casting methods such as *cire perdu* it is possible to design them with very ornate decoration; bells from Tibet and Burma use this technique. In England, large pellet and clapper bells were used on harness for horses. Some of these were made at Robert Wells foundry at Aldbourne, Wiltshire, England; they were justly famed in the 18th century for their fine tone.

Bells have also been made of pottery. For example, those used in festivities in Naples at the feast of Piedigrotta. Glass bells became very popular in the last century.

Wooden bells and gongs are found in many countries. Some of the bells used on cattle are quite simple in design. The Chinese mu-ju which became popular in dance bands is a very beautiful instrument. The curved fish is to represent wakeful attention and it was originally used as a temple bell. Also from China is the tamtam. This is a large, flat gong with a shallow rim. Only a few of the best quality came from China to the West; they were expensive to produce and the secrets of their manufacture were known only to a few. The best of these were engraved with a dragon, the rank of the owner shown by the number of the creature's claws.

Musical-boxes have a great fascination for collectors. In the centre of the box is a metal comb which is plucked. Early examples had each tooth fastened individually, but by 1820–30 most combs were formed as a single unit. The 19th century saw the greatest development of new effects; the instruments were also given more elaborate boxes and cabinets. In the early 19th century, the boxes were quite plain, the tone of the movement soft and sweet, but later a harsher tone with greater brilliance was achieved. Principal areas of manufacture in the period 1790 to 1820 were Geneva and St Croix. From 1830 to 1860 some of the finest boxes were made by Nicole Frères, Lecoultre and Duconmum Girod.

The international expositions resulted in a large number of inlaid box cases from 1860 to 1870, and the 1870s saw the period of greatest elegance and use of mechanical devices. Makers of that era were Paillard, Bremond, Allard, Baker-Troll and Greiner. The end of the century marked the end of popularity of the large cylinder movements, and the subsequent use of discs. The disc movement was first developed in the 1880s, by the firms of Polyphon, Symphonion and Regina.

The second group of instruments is the membranophones – those having a skin which vibrates when struck, drums being the main example. The orchestral side-drum developed from the drums used by the Regiments of Foot. The ancestor of this was the medieval double-skinned drum, called a tabor or tabret. Across one of the skins, the lower one in the case of the side-drum, is stretched a snare which causes a

rattling sound. Tabors, which are still used in popular music, vary considerably in diameter and depth. The strings used to tighten the skin make criss-cross patterns, often emphasized when the instrument is used decoratively. The orchestral timpani were preceded by the cavalry's kettle drums.

Instruments in the group of chordophones produce sounds through strings which vibrate. In some, the strings are plucked, such as lutes and harpsichords. In others they are hit—dulcimers and pianos—while with the violin family a bow causes the strings to vibrate.

The lute was introduced to Europe at the end of the 13th century from the Arab civilization. Good lutes are extremely fragile, as the best sound is obtained from instruments of very thin wood. This means that early examples of lutes are very rare. The most famous school of luthiers was at Bologna, where the makers Laux Maler, and his son Sigismund, flourished in the early 16th century. In the second half of the 16th century a large form, the theorbo was invented. Bass theorbos were over 1.52 m (5 ft) long, and they continued in use in song accompaniment

and continuo until the end of the 18th century. A small lute was developed from the mandora. It was called the mandoline and based on the Neapolitan form, and was very popular in the late 18th century and then again at the end of the 19th century. These are often found in antique shops and are frequently highly decorated with inlay, using mother-of-pearl and tortoiseshell.

The guitar flourished by the side of the lute in the 16th century and remained popular for a long period, especially in Spain. Being sturdier and easier to keep in tune it had great popularity with the less competent players of that period. Guitars of the 18th century were ornately finished with inlays of mother-of-pearl and ivory. Intricate work is used to decorate the wood

2 Bells, gongs and rattles (idiophones) are perhaps the most widespread of all musical instruments, probably because they can be so easily produced in their most rudimentary form. This selection includes Chinese mu ju, Tibetan temple bells, an Italian pottery bell and an English number bell.

1

1 Musical boxes have a special fascination for collectors, perhaps because of the diversity and ingenuity of their designs. The 19th century saw the greatest development with many mechanical contrivances such as dancing figures and singing birds.

2

2 Girl with Guitar by Jan Vermeer (1632–75). The guitar enjoyed great popularity in Europe in the 17th century. Note the elaborate decoration on the sound-hole.

inside the sound-hole. And at either end of the bridge there often is an elaborate scroll. By the end of the 18th century the six-stringed instrument was used, and many' of these continued to be played until the present day. These later instruments have less flamboyant decoration, limited to the purfling round the edge of the belly and simpler patterns of inlay round the sound-hole. In the Regency period, there were a number of experimental instruments – guitars designed like lyres, others called harp-lute-guitars, and harp guitars; not surprisingly none of these achieved lasting success.

The earliest four-stringed surviving violins date from the mid-16th century. Centres of manufacture were round Gasparo da Salo in Brescia and the Amatis in Cremona, both in Italy. The highest point in their development came with the makers Stradivari and Guiseppe Guarneri del Gesu. The beautiful design of the violin is functional, the body designed to amplify the sound, the narrow waist enabling the bow to pass easily across the high and low strings, and the inlaid wood at the edges of the belly and back to minimize damage to the body. The T-shaped holes in the belly have an ornamental appearance, but these are absolutely necessary for the good production of sound.

By 1800 the violin was being used to display the great virtuosity of solo performers. The age of the public concert demanded a more brilliant tone than could be met by the early design. This was obtained by raising the playing pitch, heightening the bridge, lengthening the playing string and neck, and shaping the fingerboard to facilitate maximum dexterity.

In the 19th century another development was the making of cheap 'factory fiddles', from Mirecourt in France, Mittenwald and Markneukirchen in Germany.

The 18th and 19th century dancing master's fiddle, or kit, was an adapted form of the violin that was very portable, sometimes fitting into the master's walking stick. The French pochette, a long and narrow instrument with a rounded back was even tinier.

The Norwegian Hardanger fiddle is a beautiful example of the folk violin. The oldest is dated 1651, and they are still used to accompany dancing. Like the viola d'amore it has sympathetic strings. This instrument is usually beautifully decorated with inlay work.

Keyboard instruments which have strings also fall into this category. They include the clavichord, harpsichord, spinet and virginal, where the strings are plucked, and the piano whose strings are hit by hammers. The largest of the first group is the harpsichord. It was the principal keyboard instrument in the 16th and 17th centuries, until it reached the highest point of its development in the 18th century. In the second half of the century it was gradually superseded by the piano.

The piano as we know it was invented by Bartolomeo Christofori in 1709. His work did not become really popular in his lifetime, although Pistoia wrote music for it in 1731. It

1 Early Egyptian stringed instrument.
2 Vihuela, 16th century.
3 Italian guitarra battente, 16th century.
4 Italian guitar with five double strings, early 17th century.
5 Czechoslovakian guitar, mid 17th century.
6 Stradivarius guitar, late 17th century.
7 Italian guitar, mid 18th century.
8 French guitar with 'C' holes, late 18th century.
9 Guitar with cut-out soundbox, 19th century.
10 Guitar with oval soundbox, 19th century.
11 French guitar, 19th century.
12 Spanish guitar, 19th century.

1 For centuries military music has been important. The exact composition of a military band varies from country to country and even regiment to regiment. However, it usually includes some woodwind, traditionally the piccolo and flute and often clarinets and oboes, a number of horns, trumpets and trombones and two drummers and a variety of percussion instruments.

2 The viola d'amore has no frets and was held upwards like the violin. It's name literally means 'love-viol' and this probably derives from its tone which was much affected by the sympathetic strings. These are additional strings which are not played upon by vibrate resonantly. This specimen was made by Jean Nicolas Lambert in Paris in 1772.

was the work of Johann Andreas Stein, who invented the different action known as the 'Viennese', that was to direct notice to the instrument. Hearing a Stein piano in 1777 Mozart wrote to his father saying that he liked it far better than the piano by Spathe, and subsequently composed for it. By 1800 the piano has established itself as a solo instrument, although it had to obtain greater power for use in public concert halls. By 1855 the instrument reached the modern form – Broadwood produced his first complete iron-frame for the Great Exhibition of 1851. Square pianos were used until 1860, but by that date the 'upright' had virtually replaced them in popularity for use at home in small rooms.

The last group of instruments are the aerophones – those instruments which produce sound by the vibration of a column of air. In the 16th century this group included recorders, flutes, crumhorns, curtals, shawms, cornetts, sackbuts and trumpets. This group is best described by taking the woodwind first, then the brass. Small wooden instruments in the 16th century were made of boxwood and the large ones of maple.

There was little ornamental turnery, this being limited for the most part to bagpipe design. The 17th century marks the period during which the instruments we know today developed. Many of these early changes began in France, where the wind instruments had continued to be popular. The maker Hotterre is thought to have been responsible for many of these. Originally a bagpipe maker, he adapted the jointed construction to the flute, oboe and bassoon, at the same time using ornamental turnery to strengthen the joints of these instruments.

As well as the change of design from instruments made in one piece to those constructed of several pieces, keys began to be added. The Hotteterre flute, with three joints and one key, became the standard 18th-century form. The problem of only having one key was that it was very difficult to get notes in tune in view of the complicated cross fingerings used. The flute was the first instrument to have chromatic keywork, when London flute makers added three closed keys of the type earlier used on the musette. This served to not only improve the tuning, but also to extend the range.

INSTRUMENTS OF MILITARY MUSICK.

The clarinet was an important 18th-century German development by Denner. It was originally introduced into France to be played in partnership with the horn. After 1750 the bell was elongated, and from 1770 there were five keys.

The 19th century saw the great period of mechanization of the woodwind. Firstly through the introduction of the 'simple system', by which each instrument had a set of simple closed keys. These provided accurate notes for each semitone. Instruments were made of boxwood or ebony, with brass and silver keys; from the 1850s

German silver was sometimes used. Subsequent methods of construction made keys more reliable and less sluggish. Innovations by Theobald Boehm (1793–1881) made use of ring keys in the clarinet and flute. Although Buffet worked on the design of the oboe using a Boehm system, the eventual arrangement of the modern oboe was the result of improvements on the older models. In Germany, new techniques were used by Heckel on the bassoon, without spoiling its tone.

Horns, trumpets and trombones form today's brass instruments. Horns and trumpets have been used as signalling instruments from time immemorial. Early horns were made from a variety of materials – animal horns often being used. These were sometimes decorated with silver mounts, and mouthpiece for foresters and were often held as symbols of office. Long trumpets of metal also have a long history. A pair of trumpets were one of the customary gifts to impress a king. Such trumpets were used in ceremonial and would have been straight with flags suspended from their length. Because of this ceremonial connection, composers have often used their sound to portray battles and pageantry in music.

The great innovation in the history of brass instruments was the valve. Horns in the 17th century were in the form of a hoop, and different horns had to be used for playing in different keys.

4 (Left) Oboe by W. Mullhouse, London, 19th century. (Right) Oboe by Richard Potte, London, late 18th century.

4

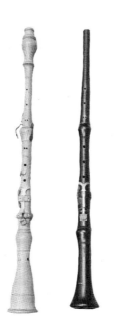

3 18th century gilded and painted harpsichord with single manual. It was the most popular domestic keyboard instrument from the 16th to the end of the 18th centuries when it was superseded by the pianoforte.

But by 1715 crooks (different lengths of metal tubing) had been adapted which could be slotted into the instrument when a new length was needed. In 1815, with the invention of the true valve principle, it became possible to play a chromatic scale without even changing crooks.

The valve was also applied successfully to the trumpet, which otherwise had reached its typical form by 1500. The trombone, and its precursor the sackbut, have been less changed, for the slide meant that it was comparatively easy to change the tube length.

Toy instruments can be looked at as a group. They sometimes reflect developments of the rest of the instrument world but they more often show a continuity which is astonishing. One of the first toys given to a child was the silver coral and bells. This is a rattle made up of a handle of coral (or occasionally mother-of-pearl), the centre part to which rows of bells are attached, and a whistle at the top. This was fastened by a link to a ribbon or chain and to the child's belt. Many 17th-century portraits of tiny children show one, an example being the portrait of Elizabeth of Bohemia, daughter of James I. Rattles like this continued to be given until the present century.

Many instruments such as May whistles and bull roarers were made by children themselves, or by their parents. Whistles were used both as toys and as signalling devices. In the 19th century they were used in speaking tubes, and also as dog whistles. Many beautiful whistles were made in the shapes of dogs' heads, from bone, ivory, metal and even occasionally slate. The potteries produced whistles from clay using the conventional design, but they also produced cheap whistles in the shapes of birds and other novelties that were to be won as prizes at fairs.

3

Toys, dolls, games & models

Milestones in the history of toys

1740	Papier mâché toys made.	1877	Phonographs invented by Edison.
1763	Dissected maps produced.	1893	Electrical trolley cars made in
1815	Pressed tin-plate introduced.		Germany.
1826	Thaumatrope invented by Dr Paris.	1903	Clockwork trains made in England,
1844	Rubber toys cast in moulds.		Bassett Lowke.
1848	Nuremberg scale defined, Infantry men 3 cm (1.25 in), cavalry 4 cm (1.6 in) high.	1905	Teddy bears invented in United States. Dolls eyes made to close by means of weights.
1860	Dolls made with swivel necks.	1907	The name Meccano registered.
	Zoetrope invented. Musical boxes introduced.	1934	Modelled Miniatures re-christened Dinky Toys.
1870	Toys became mass-produced by the mechanical lathe. Lithographed paper used.		

Strange how a toy invokes childhood, yet all toys were not made for children. Clappers were originally designed to drive away evil spirits, dolls to encourage fertility, corn-husk figures to promote a good harvest, and intricate moving toys were invented to amuse rich men at their banquets. African rattles were mere seedpods, Greek knucklebones were real bones, natural forked twigs were used in Australia while in England wishing-bones and old clothes-pegs became dolls when dressed.

Clay was modelled very early on, especially by folk living near rivers, where plenty of mud is available. Minute pots and humped-back clay animals came from regions north of India, jointed dolls from Greece; there were also many birds which, when blown into, made a hollow sound.

Sticks and brooms ridden astride were the forerunners of the hobby horse, hoops came from discarded barrels, and in South America a little wheel on a toy cart came before real wheels were used as a means of locomotion.

About 2,500 years ago kites were flown in the East and eventually it was a kite which led to the first suspension bridge over the river Niagara. Now they take the shape of huge birds, tortoises or flying bats and are beautifully coloured.

During the 5th century B.C., many little figures were made depicting the daily life of the inhabitants of Greece and Rome. Some were made of a mixture of lead, tin and antimony, others from bronze or from clay. Tin was added to harden the bronze and was in great demand, the Phoenicians even coming as far as Cornwall in their search for materials. During the Middle Ages, treasures retrieved from sunken ships have included miniature domestic items, and during the 12th century boys played with toy knights manipulated by strings.

Copies of pilgrims badges were made as playthings for children, and lead soldiers stood upright by means of boards with holes. These figures were made in moulds, many of which have survived. Trees were often sold flat and later bent into position. The Hilpert family in Germany were famous for their animals and soldiers. Other makers were Gottschalk and Beck, both from Switzerland. Ernst Heinrichsen was busy in Nuremburg, and it was he who introduced the size of 3 cm (1.25 in) for the metal figures and soldiers. Another well-known toy maker, Allgeyer of Fürth, also conformed to this scale from about 1848.

Early soldiers are flat and known as flats, though later ones are solid, like the Churchill soldiers in Blenheim Palace which were made by a Frenchman called Lucotte. The first hollow metal soldiers were made in 1893 by William Britain, an Englishman.

Toy vehicles of all kinds, whether road or rail, are useful historic indicators of how means of travel have altered. The first metal trains were coloured by hand, though later the rather brittle colouring was applied by heat. Little tin-plate German cars were assembled by means of tabs and slots, whereas those from France had the joints soldered. The more expensive cars of about 1908 had doors made to open and shut. Childrens' pedal cars came as early as 1906.

Rubber was an ideal substance for balls and solid rubber balls were played with in Mexico about A.D. 700. Hollow animals and dolls were made in two halves and often contained a squeaker, but rubber dolls have never become popular being apt to fade and heavy to hold. Toy aeroplanes were propelled by rubber bands.

Celluloid was used for bath toys and for ping-pong balls. It was made famous by the little Kewpie dolls designed by Rose O'Neill Wilson

1 Early in the 19th century many wooden arks were made in the form of a house on a flat-bottomed barge. When the gabled roof was lifted, inside were sometimes as many as 150 pairs of wooden animals, all sizes, both wild and tame. After 1875 the animals were made to a 'just proportion'. Beetles were no longer as large as elephants. Noah and his family were also inside. London Museum.

2 Home-made toys were hawked at local fairs and markets especially around Nuremberg in the Old World and New England and Pennsylvania in the New. Bulk-buying began when the toys were collected by agents. Novelties were shown at industrial fairs and toys could be purchased in small haberdashery shops. Stores arrived in the U.S.A. about 1840 and the famous Schwarz toy store opened in 1849. Drawn by Francis Bedford, c 1898.

3 17th century Nuremberg kitchens were made on the principle of three-sided rooms with a floor but no ceiling. Iron and tin utensils hung on the side walls which were set at an obtuse angle for display. Metal stoves which actually worked were popular in the U.S.A. about 1860. American kitchen. Museum of the City of New York.

of the United States in 1913. With their shiny
tummies, wide open eyes and tiny blue wings
they were instantly appealing. In the heyday of
celluloid, pretty goldfish from Japan floated in
many baths, but eventually all celluloid toys
were banned because they were too inflammable.
The material did, however, lead to the present-
day plastics.

Buzz toys were introduced into the United
States by British soldiers towards the end of the
18th century. German immigrants introduced
arks, rocking horses and some of their dolls.
Now, over the years, various toys have gradually
become associated with specific countries. These
include nest toys and pecking toys from Russia,
creche figures and marionettes from Italy, silver
toys, wooden dolls and dolls' houses from the
Netherlands, and arks from Bohemia. Early
dolls' houses were known as baby houses.

Germany is noted for its toy soldiers and
engines, France for fashion dolls and strangely
for cheap clockwork toys, Switzerland for intricate automata and England for wax dolls and
paper cut-outs. The United States became known
for cast-iron toys, intricate fire-engines, cap pistols and Daisy guns. Also from America came
the first teddy bears, but gollywogs remain exclusively English.

Not only toys are collected, now their boxes
are collected also. Little oval pinewood boxes
are especially pretty and contain wooden animals
and figures. Cardboard boxes can also be attractive; both oval and rectangular kinds appeared
in the 1880s, many with interesting labels. In
times of scarcity, even net bags take their place.

Dolls

The wooden dolls of the mid-18th century had
their heads particularly well made, though with
most dolls it is the head that receives the greatest

1 Two dolls here, one in white, one in pale blue are wax dolls. They have painted eyebrows, tinted lips, inset glass eyes and hair wigs. Doll heads could be of solid wax or of poured wax made in moulds and hollow. Others could be over a foundation of wood or composition.

The doll in the pink dress has a very fine bisque head and yoke with a swivel neck. She also has blue eyes supposedly popular because of blue-eyed Queen Victoria.

Strong bodies of kid over a wooden foundation were made but many dolls had calico bodies stuffed firmly with sawdust or straw, including the legs. Forearms were often of wax but these two dolls have arms of white porcelain.

2 This elaborate bazaar stall is covered with minute trinkets. The vendor is dressed in the latest fashion, so she probably represents a grand lady at a charity bazaar rather than a saleswoman from such a place as the Lowther Arcade. She has jewel cases, workboxes, dolls from the East; many, many things but no licence. She is German with a wooden body and a composition head, and is beautifully dressed in the fashion of 1835. The more usual pedlar dolls carry a tray with a cord to go round the neck and often wore scarlet cloaks and hoods. Some even have shrivelled faces as their heads have been made from apples. Pedlars travel on foot, hawkers have carts.

3 Dolls made from cloth can be home-made, perhaps from paper patterns, but are often commercial with not very attractive faces. However present-day dolls which catch the eye are those made by Sasha Morganthaler, the Swiss doll-maker whose dolls have become famous all over the world. Girl dolls with pensive faces, boy dolls with a tomboy appearance, all have straight hair and are completely washable. Sasha Morgenthaler-von-Sinner of Zurich died in February, 1975, but the dolls live on in the tradition of Käthe Kruse and Marion Kaulitz.

attention, while the rest of the body can be positively crude and may be of rough wood or merely a bundle of stuffed calico with straw to stiffen the limbs. Care is normally only taken on the parts which show after the doll has been dressed. If the doll wears a cap, then only wisps of hair poke out, if a low neck is the fashion then this is finished smooth to match the face; two ragged shoes on wooden sticks may protrude beneath a silken gown, and on jointed dolls it was not until their dresses were short that the joints were put above the knees and not below.

England was noted for wooden dolls and later excelled in making dolls of wax. Madame Montanari became famous after the Exhibition in London in 1855. Pierotti, Charles Marsh, Meech, and Lucy Peck all worked in London and Meech claimed to be the maker of dolls for the English royal family. Unlike their wooden sisters these dolls had well-modelled lower arms and lower legs of poured wax. Their calico bodies fitted tightly into the hollow limbs, the glass eyes were inset and strands of real hair inserted carefully into the warm wax. As well as these the Italians also excelled in making wax figures and babies for their cribs.

Rag dolls, often home made, have always been popular and two famous examples are the early Roman doll in the British Museum (who has now lost her remaining blue bead eye), and 'Bangwell Putt' of the United States who now sits comfortably in Deerfield, Massachusetts.

China-headed dolls came from the Continent of Europe. The majority had white glazed heads, tinted pink cheeks, little scarlet mouths, eyes usually blue, and highly glazed black hair, which was sometimes ornamented with pretty wreaths of coloured flowers and leaves. Tiny hands and tiny feet wearing shoes were also made of porce-

2

furnishings of dolls' houses. Their occupants too, especially the men, are much sought after.

Automata

In the 2nd century B.C. complicated moving figures and singing birds were designed for the amusement of grown-ups, but some are definitely toys. A little Egyptian lion, now in the British Museum, has a moveable jaw worked by a string and is surely a toy. It was made in 30 B.C. Far older is the Egyptian toy of 2000 B.C. in which a wooden man rolls a piece of dough up and down a board, worked by means of string. Pecking chicks from Russia and India, Eskimo buzz toys, and even the thaumatrope, are all worked by the same method.

The thaumatrope is the simplest of all optical toys as it consists of a circular piece of card about 7.5 cm (3 in) across and some thread. If a picture of a bird is drawn on one side in the centre of the card, and an empty birdcage on the other side, the bird will appear to be in the cage if the string is held taut and the disc rotated quickly.

The wind provides another simple way of producing movement, and numerous toys such as windmills from Holland, bird scarers from Germany, and cuckoo whistles from Switzerland all work by blowing or by means of bellows.

There are various toys in which weights are

lain, but with soft bodies the dolls could lie down 3 or sit up. As the dolls were sold by length, often they would be taller than one would expect from the size of the head.

To obtain a more natural appearance china-heads would be left in the unglazed state known as biscuit, and in the doll world as bisque. The bisque heads being hollow were soon fitted with weights to enable the eyes to close when the doll was laid down, the lids being painted directly on to the glass eye-ball. When hollow bodies arrived, these also were fitted with gadgets so that the doll could walk, talk or cry and even to perform other movements.

Well-known French manufacturers of the past are Jumeau, Bru, the S.F.B.J., and Jules Nicolas Steiner. Famous German names include Heubach, Handwerck, Schilling, Kämmer & Reinhardt, Kestner, Simon & Halbig, and Edmund Ulrich Steiner. There are many more, but the maker who produced the most dolls seems to be Armand Marseille from Kopplesdorf. His mark A M is incised on the back of the bisque heads, a place where the majority of marks are found. After 1890 the name of the country of origin was marked by law.

Not only dolls but all the things which go with them are collectible items: beds, prams, cradles, beautiful tea-sets, and all the other

1 This animated party shows various small figures which come to life by the turning of a wheel. The base consists of a box made of thin wood and covered with patterned paper, varnished. The 'works' are inside, the whole effect is that of a stage.

More elaborate scenes will contain a musical box and the figures animated by clockwork. These are wound up with a key.

Very few mechanical toys made of wood have survived. These were known as 'Leyern' and came from Altdorf. To the 19th century belong the 'scopes', Thaumatropes, Stroboscopes, Zoetropes and so on, followed by the Magic Lantern.

Many early 20th century clock work tin toys are still in good working order, particularly those marked EPL for Ernst Paul Lehmann. Comic cars, three wheeled carriages in which people raise their hats and toys with exotic themes all abound. Also Martin's conjurors, jugglers and dancers, with figures attired in crude cotton clothes.

The early trains, trams and motor cars have all been made in tin, in fact the history of the vehicle can be followed by studying the toys of the day.

used, such as the tumbler dolls from Japan and Russia, the movable eyes of dolls, walking mechanisms and so on, and the interesting moving scenes in picture frames where the movement is caused by sand trickling down complicated slopes hidden at the back.

Magnets and springs, as in the Jack-in-the-box, were all used before the coming of clockwork, but towards the end of the 15th century the many intricate striking clocks in Europe led to the making of simple clockwork toys and a new era began. At first these toys were expensive but the use of discarded pressed tin-plate later made them cheap to produce.

To prevent walking figures falling they were made to push or pull carts, others to ride tricycles or other vehicles.

One of the first walking dolls came from the United States. This doll had the extraordinary name of the Autoperipatetikos and was patented in 1862. Examples turn up now and again in salerooms and most are in working order, the key hidden under their ample skirts.

In 1872 came Bru's musical doll from France, in 1878 the swimming doll of Charles Bertran, then in 1890 the talking doll of Thomas Edison was produced in America.

Around the 1860s the best known makers of musical boxes were the Nicole Frères of Switzerland. Little round musical boxes for children worked by simply turning a handle. About 30 years later, polyphons arrived from Germany. These used perforated discs instead of cylinders and amused children well into the 20th century. Other pretty things were the singing bird musical boxes made by Lucien Bontemps.

Pictures with animated views showed castles and bridges, peasants working and fountains playing; the realistic-looking flowing water was made from thin rods of twisted glass.

At the end of the 19th century the best-known makers of simple clockwork toys were William Britain in England, Fernand Martin in France, and Ernst Paul Lehmann in Germany. Ives was famous for his wind-up toys in the U.S.A.

Famous makers of engines were Märklin in Goppingen, Bing and Planck from Nuremburg, and Carette from France. In the United States

Carlisle and Finch were well established, while in England the names of Bassett Lowke and years later Frank Hornby, the inventor of Meccano, were important.

Games

Games with balls have a long history. The balls themselves are made of various materials, but are usually of a size to hold conveniently in the hand or large enough to kick. They are not, however, always round. From Samoa come square balls woven from palm leaves.

Some of the prettiest balls are the porcelain carpet balls which were rolled along the corridors of stately homes in the 17th century. However, a ball often requires something else with it and in medieval games one finds a trap and ball, cup and ball, and bat and ball.

Hoops were mostly for boys in medieval days, but battledore and shuttlecock was played by both boys and girls, the same with diabolo and the much more ancient game of yoyo.

At the end of the 18th century small books appeared extolling obedience to one's parents, and picture cards issued in 1788 also had a moral purpose, for it had been said that many indoor games promoted cunning. In 1815 alphabet cards appeared, and there were sets of ivory letters to help with reading. Some books were less than 5 cm (2 in) high and 35 mm (1½ in) wide.

Picture cards were cut in halves, the picture being complete when the correct half had been found. Children learnt natural history and geography by these means. The cards were hand-coloured engravings and after 1835 could be hand-coloured lithographs. At first they were pale but later they were printed in bright colours.

The Victorians and Edwardians enjoyed playing cards and other indoor pastimes. Board games were numerous on both sides of the Atlantic and lucky children shared improving games with their parents. Jig-saw puzzles and picture alphabets taught them much, and many historical facts were learned effortlessly. It was quite usual for a five-year-old child to read.

These early board games, jig-saws, building bricks and puzzles came in wooden boxes with sliding lids and attractive labels. Inside would be

the instructions and the counters. Instead of dice which were considered to promote gambling, a teetotum was introduced which could be of various shapes and size. Moral games were still the thing in which virtue was rewarded and vice punished.

The first dissected puzzles were maps. The pieces were large, often being cut around the actual county or country and there was a guide sheet to follow.

The first board game published by Milton Bradley in the United States also had a moral tone. This was The Checkered Game of Life, which came in 1860. Many of the later games were based on banking and earning money such as The Business of Going to Work, and later still Monopoly. This continued to be a highly popular subject for such games.

Puzzles were popular in the United States, Charles Crandall's Pigs in Clover being one of the best sellers. This was in 1889 and their popularity continued till after the World War I, then gradually disappeared with the coming of radio and other similar recreations.

2 This tin plate model ship is German and dates from the period before World War I. R. McCrindell Collection.

3 Puzzles of various kinds became popular pastimes from the mid-19th century and have remained firm favourites with children ever since. Girls's amusements, Victoria and Albert Museum.

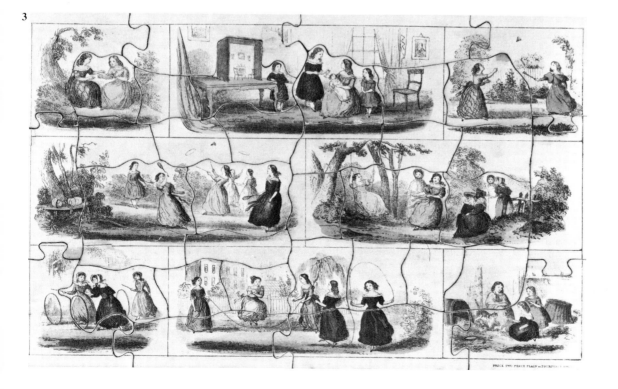

Engineering Models

Fine ship models have been collectors' items for a century and more, and so have the far rarer but generally less valuable fine dolls' houses and some of the models of furniture, staircases, musical instruments, and other artifacts made by apprentices as their 'masterpieces'. But it has only been in the last 10 years or so that engineering models and the high class toys of the recent past have begun to fetch high prices in the salerooms.

A collector in this field is likely to need to collect manufacturers' catalogues (many of which are now fortunately available as reprints) as well as the saleroom catalogues which all serious collectors in all fields find indispensable. In addition, a small reference library dealing with the prototypes will be necessary if unique models are to be acquired.

Most collectors specialize, and many collect only catalogued toys, of all kinds, of one kind, or of one manufacturer. The great toymakers of the late 19th and early 20th centuries, notably Georges Carette and the Bing Brothers (both Nuremberg firms) produced an extraordinary range of excellent toy versions of all forms of transport; of steam, gas, and hot air engines; of productive machinery such as machine tools, threshing machines, brewery equipment, cranes, watermills and windmills; of electrical apparatus and scientific experimental kits; as well as such things as magic lanterns and toy gramophones.

A collection of such objects is not only an illustration of the quality of the manufacturers, but also a fascinating reflection of the history of technology. This is less true of the toys for younger children, more simply made, but no less ingenious; among these we find the village blacksmith wielding his hammer when a small crank is turned, and many mechanical animals, including a gaudy tinplate butterfly which flutters its wings and pursues an irregular path across the floor, driven by clockwork.

It is probably railway models that attract the greatest number of specialized collectors, and offer the greatest range of commercial products. There are hundreds of different types of locomotives, carriages and wagons, and there is an enormous range of accessories such as stations, rails, signals and there is even a platform refreshment trolley complete with two magnums of champagne. The great names in this field are Bing, Carette, Märklin, Bassett Lowke and Hornby (for European Models) and Ives, Lionel, and American Flyer in the United States. But some of the most highly prized collectors' items are from smaller manufacturers: for example, anything by Jean Schönner of Nuremberg is eagerly sought after, and the finest and most realistic tinplate train in 'O' gauge – 32 mm ($1\frac{1}{4}$ in) between the rails – was made in the mid-1920s by the small firm of Marescot in Paris.

A special word should be said about Bassett Lowke, most of whose beautiful productions were made for them by German firms: Carette at first, then Bing for very many years, and finally some by Märklin. As most of these items do not appear in the real manufacturer's catalogues, it follows that a collector of, say, Bing products has to know which items from the Bassett Lowke catalogue were made by Bing. And no firm made anything finer than their elaborately liveried models of early 20th century British locomotives, for which some of the credit is due to W. J. Bassett Lowke for providing the demand, and to Henry Greenly for providing the designs.

For commercial models of continental railways, Märklin was pre-eminent until the very recent appearance of very expensive models made in small series. Between the wars a range of fine locomotives, carriages and wagons appeared for gauges 0 and 1 – 45 mm ($1\frac{3}{4}$ in) between the rails – which were very close to the real thing, yet possessed a slight, enjoyable, toylike quality in the brightness of their colouring and the splendour of their nickel plate. The locomotives were mostly electrically driven, but a few steam versions were made which worked admirably. The range included models of Swiss electric locomotives, of which the big double-motored 'Crocodile' is perhaps the most coveted. Märklin was never in the cheap market, but has produced at the opposite extreme some of the most elaborate commercial models of all, including a stationary steam engine with a base about 1 m (1 yd) square, and standing over 1.21 m (4 ft) high.

Much that has been said about railway models can also be said about ship models. The largest catalogued models of warships and of ocean liners came from Märklin, closely followed by Bing. Steam or clockwork propulsion was the rule, and some of the clockwork motors were of the size of those fitted to gramophones. All these models had to be grossly distorted below the waterline to provide enough buoyancy to support their solid tinplate structures and large power units. Aesthetically, the smaller boats, up to 0.60 m (2 ft) long, are more pleasing and

1 Railway models are the most popular childhood items among adult collectors. Locomotives, such as this fine tin plate specimen, are in the greatest demand but carriages, wagons, stations and all the various accessories are also widely collected.

1

easier to display, and because they were made in greater quantities there is a better chance of finding them. There is a great variety of types, including submarines (some actually representing fish – a tinplate pike being one example). One of the most charming is a small Bing steam launch, about 30 cm (1 ft) long, which has a tiny working steam turbine; and Märklin made a clockwork windjammer.

All toy manufacturers produced road vehicles, but by far the greater number of these were cheap pieces of which only fairly recent examples are likely to be found. Because road vehicles do not lend themselves to a system they are more likely to be in constant use – as compared with a train set which has to be laid out or a boat which is taken out to a pond on special occasions – and few have survived in good order.

The older and more elaborate road vehicles are highly prized, evoking as they do the early days of motoring – the pre-1914 taxi, the Paris omnibus or the electric tram. The French firm of JEP made some of the largest and most sought after. Among the attractions of such old toys are plate glass windows, upholstery and curtains, uniformed chauffeurs, and moving parts under the bonnet. Propulsion was usually by clockwork, but sometimes by steam, and in either case there might be battery-worked or oil headlamps.

The materials used in making high class toys have changed greatly in the last 100 years, but all the most sought-after items up to now have been made of metal. Generically this class of model is often referred to as 'tinplate' and their collectors as 'tinplate collectors'. Strictly speaking, tinplate is tinned steel plate – a light, strong, crisp material which lends itself to joining by soft soldering or clipping, which can be decorated by printing or transfers while in the flat, and also takes paint better than non-ferrous metals. But iron and brass castings, brass and copper pipe and

sheet, German silver rods and stampings, and a certain amount of steel have always been used. Between the wars the use of zinc die-castings became common for details, and for complete small non-powered models of cars, and it was applied to the bodywork of locomotives for the small sizes then becoming popular. This technique, like the plastic moulding which is almost universal today, precludes elaborate decoration, because this would have to be done by hand. Fortunately for the manufacturers, the present age does not favour elaborate liveries on real trains or cars, so a high degree of realism is possible, particularly in view of the ease with which fine details of surface can be moulded, so that the grain of timber, the heads of rivets and such things as ventilation grilles can all be faithfully copied.

The recent appearance of fine commercial models made in series of a few hundred only marks the attention that the model trade is now paying to the adult collector. This is something quite new. While the products work admirably, there is little doubt that few of them are ever called upon to do so, and the chances are that very few of these models will ever be lost to the world of the collector, so they will never be very rare. Predominant among these are the so-called 'Japanese brass models' which provide a collection of almost museum quality representing the history of American steam locomotives. They are made in the 'O' and 'HO' gauges, the larger size being, of course, the finer. They are electrically driven, but something similar with steam propulsion, in the larger gauge '1', has recently begun to appear from Europe and Japan. Matching rolling stock has never been made in equivalent quantities and is likely to achieve a greater scarcity value.

Also somewhere between the model proper and the catalogued toy there is the 19th century

2 Large overtype twin cylinder steam engine and generator, manufactured by Märklin and dating from about 1925.

2

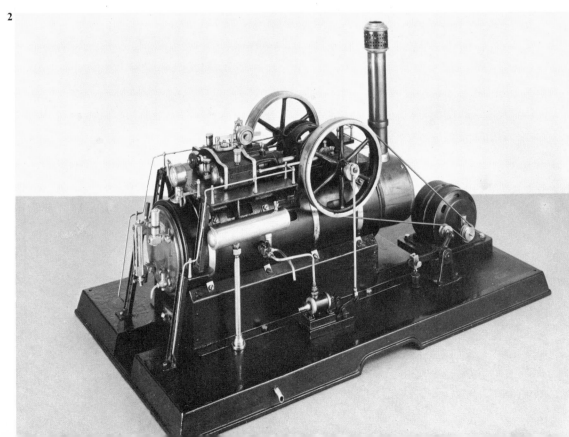

1 Model ships, although still very popular are not such a rich field for collectors as other kinds of models. They are easily damaged over the years and few survive in really good condition. This 90-gun ship (1706 establishment) is typical.

1

2

model built largely of brass castings. These are mostly locomotives and stationary engines, but they may appear as marine plant in wooden hulls. The 'Birmingham dribbler' type of locomotive, usually with four wheels and always with oscillating cylinders, is the poorest specimen of the kind, but higher up the scale are some elegant productions of scientific instrument makers and the originally educational models produced by Radiguet of Paris. These things are never exact models of real prototypes, though they sometimes resemble some prototype rather crudely. Very seldom does one see two exactly alike. Visual appeal and quality of workmanship sometimes lead to high prices.

Where the unique craftsman-built model is concerned it becomes difficult to map out the field. Almost the only criterion of worth is fidelity to the chosen prototype, and this demands great knowledge on the part of the collector. There can occasionally be other reasons for valuing a model highly, such as intrinsic historic importance (if the model is associated with a great man, perhaps) or, in the case of a passenger hauling locomotive, its virtues as a useful machine, but accuracy and fine workmanship are an unfailing recommendation. However, the popularity of the prototype or its visual appeal has a large effect upon the price a model will fetch in the saleroom, other things being equal, and it is also evident that buyers are extraordinarily susceptible to paint. An ill-proportioned locomotive, beautifully painted, will sometimes fetch a price well beyond its true worth, and this simply reflects a buyer's ignorance. The other side of this coin is that a superb model will often be undervalued just because it is very dirty and in need of paint restoration or a complete repaint.

The financial side of collecting does not always operate in the interest of the model or of history. For instance, a fine old model of a sailing vessel which has suffered years of neglect may have broken spars and decayed rigging, as well as much dirt and loose detail on the hull. In that state it will fetch little, because the cost of proper restoration is great. But if the rigging is removed entirely, the hull cleaned up and polished or painted, and the loose pieces discarded, the result is likely to be a highly decorative object which will be bought for a good price purely as such. But much of the original model, and any historical value it may have had, is gone for ever.

Among unique models coming on to the market, ships undoubtedly predominate. Very few models of power driven ships are of high quality, because they are mostly working models and suffer in some measure that distortion below the waterline which has been mentioned. These are not for collectors. There is, however, a steady trickle of builder's or owner's models of fine quality, some dating from the last century, which have been in boardrooms or offices, and these are generally rather underpriced in relation to the amount and quality of work put into their making. One trouble is that they are mostly rather large: few are less than 1.8 m (6 ft) long. There are also a very few amateur built working models which are not distorted and which may have finely made (though not true to prototype) steam machinery.

The élite of sailing ship models are the contemporary dockyard models built for the British Admiralty. Most of these are now in museums, but a few come on to the market. These are mainly models of the hulls only, and are not planked all over, but on the other hand the carved decorations of the 17th and 18th centuries are beautifully modelled. These things are exquisitely made antiques, and their prices reflect that fact. Also very expensive, but not at all in the same class, are the bone and ivory 'prisoner of war' models said to date from the Napoleonic period. The historic interest attaching to these rather numerous pieces may inflate their prices, but price is generally proportionate to accuracy

2 With the development and progress of flight in the 20th century, model aircraft have become the most popular models for today's children and perhaps for tomorrow's collectors. This is a model of a Hawker Hart fighter.

and workmanship, and this goes for the whole vast field of sailing ship models made by sailors and other amateurs in the last three centuries. But it is also true that many of these are almost art objects, possessed of great aesthetic appeal.

Contemporary models of old locomotives are exceedingly rare and almost all are now in museums. Modern models of old locomotives are among the best things offered in the sale-rooms, because they are not built primarily for hauling large loads of passengers on club tracks. Even so, they mostly seem to be fitted with super-heaters, which is an absurd anachronism. In the small sizes, electrically driven models can command high prices if their external accuracy is photographic, and especially if they are known to be the work of a famous builder of such things, or have been fully described in some journal and perhaps won prizes. The best way to display a small model of a locomotive is at the head of a train, but it is generally far more difficult to find four or five coaches, or wagons, of matching quality than it is to find the locomotive.

The whole field of stationary and marine engines has been extensively modelled, and there are good models in existence of almost every imaginable machine: looms, pumps, bicycles, aircraft and their engines, lathes, presses, cranes and combine harvesters. But apart from station-ary steam engines, the opportunities for collect-ing these things are limited.

It is one of the surprises of model collecting that so few fine models of aircraft are made. The reason is no doubt that most models are made to fly, and such things cannot measure up to the standards of accuracy required of a collector's piece. On the other hand, there is an increasing supply of good models of horse drawn vehicles. Prices of these are still quite low, and their special blend of technical interest, visible crafts-manship and aesthetic appeal must make them appear a very attractive starting point for a collection of models of the once familiar things now passing out of living memory.

Model Soldiers

The present high value of toy soldiers is due not only to antiquarian scarcity but also in part to nostalgia of collectors who seek relics of their childhood. However, many of these ancient warriors are also sought as examples of vanished craftsmanship. In fact poor quality lead, plastic and even tin soldiers are not desired unless very old.

The silver soldiers of the 17th and 18th cen-turies made for French royalty are not to be seen in the salerooms but the tin soldiers of the 18th and later centuries do appear. Made by pew-terers, silversmiths and goldsmiths as a 'side-line', by 1760 tin soldiers were a common play-thing for small boys. The rise of Napoleon brought forth many model armies by makers in Germany, Switzerland and France. The flat tin soldier, which varied in height from 24.5 cm (9¾ in) to 8.5 cm (3⅜ in), continued to be made on the Continent of Europe, reaching the highest standards of engraving and painting though they

are now connoisseur's items and quite beyond the reach of a child.

The cut-out paper soldier had beginnings in the mid-18th century and was most popular in Strasbourg, expanding as may be expected in the Napoleonic era. Production continued in France and Germany, with some English sheets about 1840. This branch of toy soldiers flourished up to the turn of the century but became poor in quality, and as they are now produced in Italy and some Continental nations they are simply cheap products for small children.

The rising cost of tin brought about the pro-duction of soldiers with a higher lead content, made as the 'half-round' type or the large 'solid' figure. The former group were produced mainly in Germany, where they were made until the end of Queen Victoria's reign, and the solid troops of Heyde were popular until after the First World War. The former have a limited demand but solid soldiers, especially from Haffner, are much desired – as are, to a lesser degree, those of Lucotte and Mignot from Paris.

It was the development of the hollow-cast lead soldier by William Britain about 1892 that enabled this cheaper soldier to capture a world market and to oust the expensive German soldier. Unfortunately in recent years the rising cost of metal made Messrs. Britain turn to the plastic figure and about a decade ago the old hollow-cast figure ceased production.

3 These tin soldiers were made between 1830 and 1880 from moulds engraved in Germany and France.

Wooden soldiers were made in Frederick the Great's period and workers in Germany's forests still make the lathe-turned soldier, so well known in Victorian times.

The modern plastic, even made well with minute detail, is not yet sought but in the future will no doubt command a market, as will the expensive 'military miniature' when the present processes are obsolete.

Industrial
& domestic artefacts

1 A typical sewing machine of the 1860's, this was built by the English firm of William Jones, a Lancashire company still making machines today. It sews lock stitch and is shown here without its treadle base.

2 Spinning wheels are popular items among collectors both because of their attractive appearance and because of their long history. They have remained unchanged in their basic form since the early 16th century, although different kinds of decoration have appeared at various times.

The labour-saving devices of yesterday have a vast amount of charm, often due to functionally superfluous embellishment, later to be discarded in the name of design and rationalization. Though their condition may vary, domestic artifacts are getting fewer and further between on the junk stalls and have of late been promoted to the province of the antique markets. Many objects, particularly those made of cast-iron, have stood the test of time very well, so in areas of vast mass production, it is as well to look for quality. Though many of these objects have earlier origins, the 19th century American influence is strong, due mainly to a shortage of labour which undoubtedly created a receptive environment for almost any improvement. From about the 1850s Europe woke up and followed this frantic style of invention, which resulted in a proliferation of gadgets and appliances which still has not ended.

Spinning wheels While cloth has been woven for over 6,000 years, the spinning wheel as we know it is only about 450 years old. It already looked familiar by the 1480s when the 'flyer' was added, and even more like the present-day object when the treadle was introduced in the 1520s. Since then all developments to the cottage machine have been basically decorative. The flyer, or U-shaped piece round the bobbin, is a simple device, usually attributed to Leonardo da Vinci, which imparts a twist to the thread, while the treadle allows one to turn the wheel keeping both hands free for spinning. An attractive machine with turned wooden legs and spokes, it is known as a Saxony wheel, and was common all over Europe from the mid-16th century.

The function of a spinning wheel is to stretch and twist a handful of flax of wool into a weav-able thread; in its heyday during the mid-18th century a spinster could produce about 347 m (380 yards) an hour. It was a chore traditionally done by women and hence the word spinster being associated more with an unmarried woman than with 'one who spins'. A spell at the spinning wheel was part of the housework for a farmer's wife. But she was working at a disadvantage, because the 18th-century weaver making cloth would consume the full-time output of two or more spinsters if he were to keep his loom busy all day, and this discrepancy was seized upon by the budding inventors of the early Industrial Revolution.

Hargreave's spinning jenny of 1764 was in fact a type of spinning wheel which produced 16 bobbins of yarn in the time it had previously taken to spin one. When similar machines were installed in a factory, they had as many as 120 spindles each and were driven almost non-stop by power derived from a water wheel. These machines shifted the art of spinning away from the cottage to the factories of the new textile industry. Near centres of population this effectively wiped out the simple spinning wheel, though it continued in use in remote parts into the 20th century.

Sewing machines By the mid-19th century industrialization was well advanced in Europe and America, and though the housewife may no longer have spun her own yarn or woven her own cloth, she still did a lot of sewing. The first practical domestic sewing machine to ease her work was made in 1858 by Isaac Merritt Singer of Boston, Massachusetts. It grew from an industrial forerunner invented by him in 1851, but was lighter in weight, smaller in scale and made more attractive by the addition of transfer

decorations. This was the first complex machine
in the home apart from the clock, and paved the
way for a host of other intricate gadgets.

Singer's methods were sound, and after a
slow start were copied by many rival sewing
machine manufacturers. In one of the earliest
model factories, Singer's machines were built on
a production line as early as 1856 with mass produced and interchangeable parts. He also introduced the first ever Hire Purchase system to try
to reach a larger market, and his success was
such that he was able to set up factories in
Europe, making machines in Paris from 1855,
Hamburg from 1863 and Glasgow from 1876.

Most early sewing machines were mounted
on ornate cast-iron treadle frames which now
seem to be far scarcer than the machines themselves. This is perhaps due to the later addition
of small electric motors making the heavy tables
obsolete. Though pretty sewing machines are
not too hard to find, one in good condition on
its original stand is a rare animal. Electrically-
driven machines date from the 1920s, though
Singer did produce one very early domestic
model with an electric motor in 1889.

Typewriters Though originally intended for use in an office, the typewriter found its way into the home once it had been developed into a cheap and reliable machine. It was a hybrid of many existing patents put together between 1866 and 1873 by Christopher Scholes and Carlos Glidden of Milwaukee, and its success stems mainly from the fact it allowed rapid typing without the keys jamming, and so in the hands of an experienced operator was quicker and cleaner than using a pen and ink.

Early typewriters are reminiscent of early sewing machines, both in artistic embellishment, and size and complexity of mechanism. This is no coincidence, for Scholes and Glidden took their demonstration model to the Small Arms firm of E. Remington, who had diversified into sewing machines over a decade before. With spare capacity in the sewing machine department, the pre-production development and subsequent manufacture was naturally placed here with the result that the same skills, craftsmen and machines were used to make the new machine. It was put on sale by 1876 and the techniques and style were much copied. Rivals in this lucrative market encouraged the adoption of modifications and improvements, the notable ones being the introduction of upper and lower case letters (the first typewriter had only written in capitals), and a paper-feed which allowed the user to see what had been written straight away without it being obscured by the machine.

Charcoal box irons A maid of the 1880s would not appreciate our desire to collect those appliances that were the bane of her life. Irons, which before the advent of the lightweight electric and steam irons of the 1950s, seemed designed to keep the servant uncomfortably hot. The box iron, for instance, was filled with glowing charcoal embers and fanned hot by the insertion of a pair of bellows through a hole in the back. Over-zealous bellowing was liable to send soot up the chimney and all over the clean washing.

Charcoal box irons were known in Holland in the late 17th century and were made of brass, but became much more common all over Europe and America in the period 1800–1900 in their cast-iron form. It is interesting to note they were made in China in the 1940s, and were still being manufactured in Germany in the 1960s who exported them at the rate of 10,000 a month to those vast areas of the populated world still without electricity.

Various shapes of chimney are typical to certain countries. Those made in Spain, England and America had a right-angled bend, level with the top of the wooden handle; the traditional German iron, called a *Kamineisen* had a chimney with a smooth curve forming a quadrant, while the French model had the chimney at the back instead of the front. But all of them had the crescent-shaped heat deflecting shield to protect the hand. It was made of brass and embossed with the maker's name or trade mark. The high sides of the charcoal box were usually smooth, but some models had a corrugated plate fixed to one side. This was a fluter attachment for ironing frills. To use it the iron had to be layed on its side and the cloth had to be pushed into the grooves with a fluted rocker. One ingenious model of the late 1880s had a rocker-come-handle built on to the underside of the removable brass heat shield.

Mrs Potts sad-irons A sad-iron was a solid piece of cast-iron with a metal handle which was heated up over a stove and used until it cooled down. Three were usually used in rotation.

With no insulation from the sole plate, the great disadvantage was that the handle got uncomfortably hot until the solution was found by a Mrs Mary Florence Potts of Ottumwa, Ohio. In 1871 she designed a double ended solid iron with a detachable wooden handle. They were sold in boxes containing three irons with only one detachable walnut handle, through there were sets of four, five and six irons, which being several different sizes, needed one or two extra handles. It can now be seen why there are frequent offers of irons without handles, though the interesting item for collectors is a complete set of irons, preferably in its original wooden box.

These types of irons are usually dated on the flat part directly below the removable handle, but besides being made in the United States, Germany, Denmark, United Kingdom and Canada in the 1890s, one American company (the Coalbrookdale Iron Foundry of Pennsylvania) was still making them in 1953, and a German firm, the Grossag Co., was still advertising them in 1955.

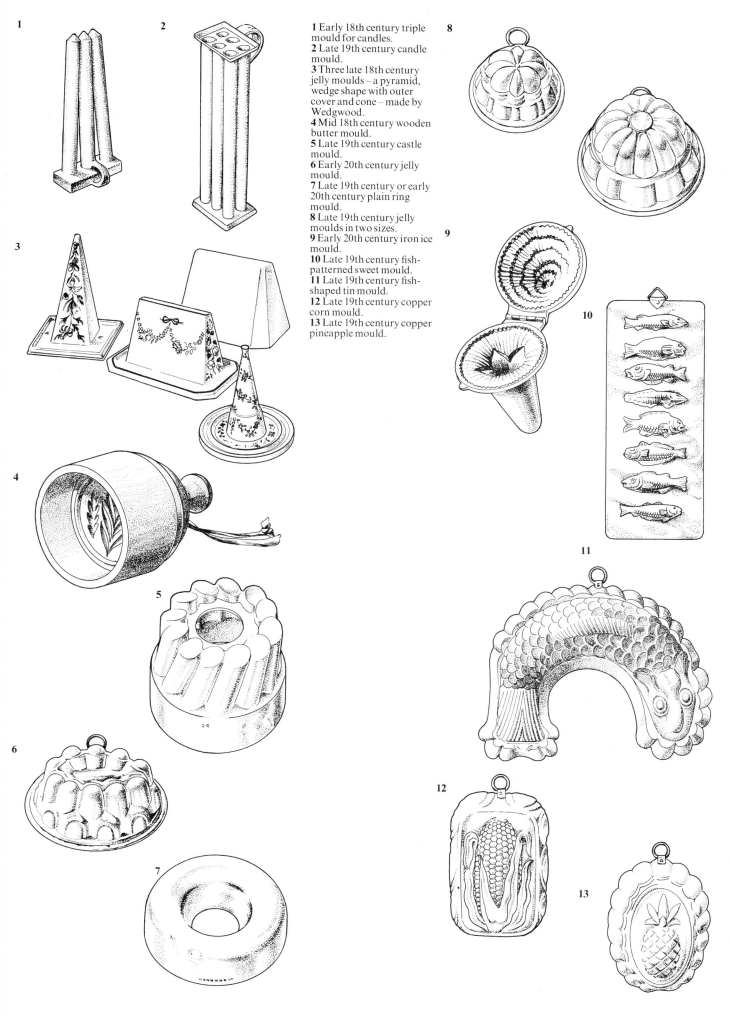

1 Early 18th century triple mould for candles.
2 Late 19th century candle mould.
3 Three late 18th century jelly moulds – a pyramid, wedge shape with outer cover and cone – made by Wedgwood.
4 Mid 18th century wooden butter mould.
5 Late 19th century castle mould.
6 Early 20th century jelly mould.
7 Late 19th century or early 20th century plain ring mould.
8 Late 19th century jelly moulds in two sizes.
9 Early 20th century iron ice mould.
10 Late 19th century fish-patterned sweet mould.
11 Late 19th century fish-shaped tin mould.
12 Late 19th century copper corn mould.
13 Late 19th century copper pineapple mould.

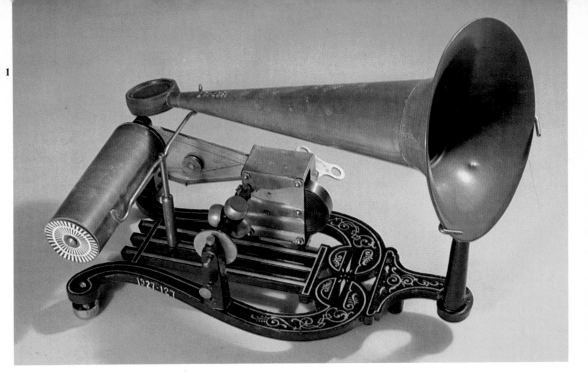

1 The Puck phonograph of c.1900 was made in Germany in vast quantities and sold at very low prices to stimulate the sale of cylinders.

2 A pair of rotary knife-cleaners by Kent and Spong from the turn of the century. They were for cleaning steel knives, but became obsolete once knives were made of stainless steel.

3 This Columbia gramophone was sold by the American Graphophone Co in 1902. Its 18 cm (7 in) turntable is clockwork driven, wound by the crank handle on the wooden top. The horn is fixed to the needle and swivels on its extended arm as it tracks the disc.

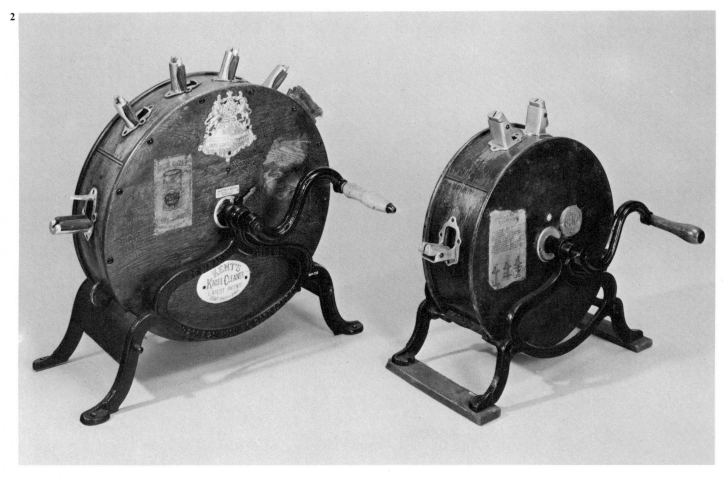

4 This attractive table telephone of 1890–5 used a magneto generator to provide the necessary power, which was built into the set. The curved legs are in fact the two magnets for the magneto.

Rotary knife cleaners Before the advent of cheap stainless steel cutlery in the 1920s, knives were made of ordinary steel with bone or ivory handles. The steel was naturally prone to rusting and so needed careful wiping and polishing after being washed up. The rotary knife cleaner was a welcome solution to this tedious chore as a few turns of a handle scrubbed and buffed several knives at the same time. In England they were manufactured by Kent's and also by Spong's from 1882 till around 1915. The drums were wooden, mounted vertically on a cast-iron stand, and took anything from two to six knives depending on the model.

An already washed knife was put into each slot round the rim of the drum, and an abrasive powder such as Oakey's Britannia Polish was poured in through a hole. This was then closed with a lid or bung, and a turn of the crank handle would push alternate stiff brushes and felt pads past both sides of each blade.

Phonographs One of the brainwaves of full-time inventor Thomas Alva Edison, the phonograph was developed primarily as an office dictating machine in 1877. Unlike the gramophone by E. Berliner, which followed 11 years later and which only played back existing records, Edison's original talking machine was designed to record as well as play. Apart from this basic difference, phonographs played cylinders, while gramophones played discs.

Berliner's success in producing a machine for home entertainment encouraged Edison to give up the office machine, which anyway had been a commercial failure, and with the new clockwork motor (an Edison invention of 1895) concentrated in bringing enjoyment into people's homes, and incidentally cornering the lion's share of the market. As a result the players were simplified and the recording facility gradually dropped. In Germany cheap players were made, cutting the manufacturers profit to a bare minimum, but stimulating enormous sales of cylinders. Prices were so low that cheap phonographs enjoyed a wide market in Europe until about 1910. Being clockwork driven it is not surprising that Germany and Switzerland produced the bulk of European manufacture.

In an attempt to recapture the market – which they ultimately succeeded in doing – disc player manufacturers introduced various developments, including increased disc diameters and hence playing time, from the early 18 cm (7 in) up to 25, 30 and even the massive 50 cm (10, 12 and 20 in) records. In France Pathé Frères produced a gramophone which only played Pathé recordings. These started in the centre and the needle tracked towards the outer edge. Despite the obviously limiting factor of not being able to play any other discs, these machines were made from 1906 to 1920!

Telephones In March 1876 Alexander Graham Bell prophesied '... the day is coming when telegraph wires will be laid on to houses just like water or gass – and friends converse with each other without leaving home'. Later that year his first successful telephone was exhibited at the World Exhibition in Philadelphia. Initially it was used as a business instrument and only found its way into the homes of either the wealthy or the home-based professional such as the doctor or dentist. Power to send the signal was derived firstly from batteries and later a magneto generator in the user's home, but later on these were located at the exchange. Nevertheless, many pre-1900 telephones still had batteries to provide the speech current, small though it was. This same power supply allowed the subscriber to attract the attention of the operator.

The classic Ericsson table telephone was first available in 1890, and the familiar pedestal telephone (with the mouthpiece on the stand, and the earpiece on the end of a wire) appeared in a nickel-plated form in 1901. The cheaper ebonite model followed later, though without the automatic dial for a while, which had first become available in 1901.

3

4

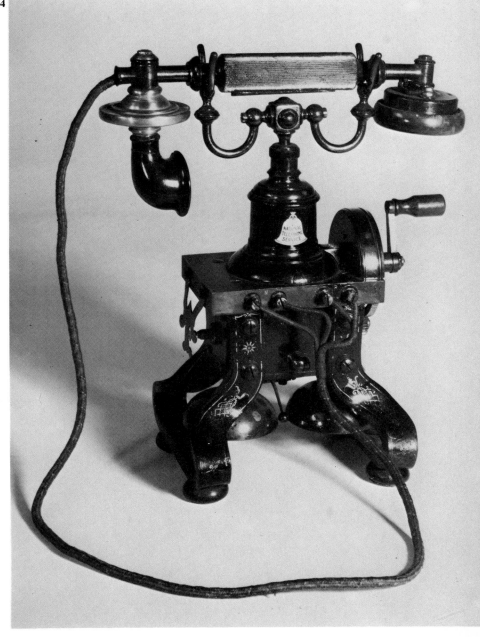

Repair & restoration

Restoration of antiques and works of art is usually concerned with returning the object to its original state. This sometimes involves removing later additions which alter the original appearance, or replacing parts which have been damaged or lost. Restoration may go a step further and attempt to regain the original structural strength to prolong usage and life.

1 Iron rivots, used by African craftsmen to arrest a shrinkage split in a wooden bowl from Uganda, form a typical 'field repair'. It is of great interest in itself and, unless it were to cause actual damage or be considered too unsightly, an effort would be made to preserve it.

2 The rich patina of the nineteenth century Japanese incense burner was deliberately produced in its final stages of manufacture as part of the artistic design concept. The restorer must seriously consider all patinas before allowing any surface treatments or alterations.

Conservation, in its purest sense, aims at keeping as much of the original as possible and preventing further deterioration. Restoration and conservation should be compatible, indeed restoration performed without regard to conservation can prove a disastrous waste of time and money. In many cases, preventative conservation makes it possible to avoid the need for restoration altogether.

When viewing an antique, it is important to remember that it is a product of ageing and of history. Careless restoration can remove this quality. Repairs and even blatant additions must be considered historical evidence of usage and may, therefore, be an integral part of the object. Sometimes a repair can be of great interest in itself by exhibiting technical ingenuity or by showing the importance an antique may have held throughout its history. With ethnographic material, this concept of history is vital. The form in most recent use is just as valid as the original, and legitimate 'field repairs' tend to be left.

Often, however, one is faced with bad and disfiguring repairs of no historical significance, or damage or deterioration of a piece that make

restoration inevitable.

It is important to bear in mind the effect of natural ageing and usage. Normal handling over time produces signs of wear, while environmental factors produce colour changes, cracks and splits. There may be evidence of insect and mould attack, and corroded metals. And, of course, there is the almost inevitable accumulation of dirt and grime. All this produces what is known as age-related surface, or patina.

Patina lends authenticity to an antique, and it can have an attractive mellowing effect. It can just as easily be unsightly and obscure or alter the appearance completely. It is often a question of degree – too much or the wrong type.

Any restoration must take the patina into consideration. What has taken centuries to form can be removed by the restorer in seconds, and all antique quality erased. Re-patination can be achieved, but it is rarely completely successful and is often obvious. Cleaning should be a compromise. Enough patina should remain to keep the feeling of age, yet the original should be allowed to show without disfigurement.

In certain cases, patinas are very important in themselves. Some are a deliberate part of the manufacture and design. With antiquities, patinas may be so prized that great attempts are made to preserve and enhance them.

Underneath the old restorations, the alterations, and the patina, lies the often much disguised original. How can it be recognized? Experience and a knowledge of antiques are obviously important guides in knowing what to expect. Research and comparisons are also helpful.

Visual examination can yield a lot of information. Most restoration ages at a different rate from the original and this may be obvious through a variation in colour, tone, texture or depth. Joins in repairs or additions may be noticeable. Examination should include the backs, undersides and in the crevices of objects, where less careful faking and matching is likely. Signs of wear and patina should be consistent. Restoration materials may be different from the original and thus show up under ultra-violet light, on X-rays, or through solubility tests.

Whenever possible, restoration should be reversible. It may be necessary to get back to the original in order to correct a misconception in restoration. Made-up areas and colours age at a different rate from the original and may become too obvious in time. The restorer may also wish to make changes while working and re-do certain steps. New materials or methods may prove unsatisfactory and need to be removed. So, it is a good principle to ensure that all restoration can be removed without harming the original. Sometimes though, strength and permanence cannot be achieved without resorting to irreversible methods.

Another important aspect of any restoration to be undertaken is that of sympathetic media and materials. All restoration must be compatible with the original – when it is not, restoration becomes destructive. Materials added must respond to the environment in the same way as the original, moving with a similar coefficient of expansion. Adhesives should also be selected with this in mind. For example, it would be unwise to stick a flexible object together with a rigid adhesive. Chemical compatibility is equally important since a support, lacquer, or anything in contact with the original may be or become unstable and cause damage. Materials which would attract problems such as insects or mould growth should also be avoided.

Restoration may be needed on purely aesthetic grounds to remove falsifying additions or bad restoration or to improve the appearance where damage has been extensive. Action may be necessary when weakness or damage threaten the safety and existence of a specimen.

The question of 'do-it-yourself' versus the professional restorer must be considered. There is much published information on every aspect of restoration which should indicate exactly what is involved and the degree of difficulty and skill to be expected. Even if it then appears to be a job for the professional, armed with some knowledge of the subject and what is involved, it is easier to negotiate with the restorer.

Obviously, value helps to justify the expense of professional attention, and good restoration can often enhance the value of an object. In some cases, the expense involved in purchasing the materials and equipment needed for a single restoration job at home may be greater than that charged by the professional restorer. However, if a professional restorer is used, it is essential that he is ethical and reliable.

Preventative conservation. The best approach to restoration is to avoid the need for it altogether. In many cases, damage and deterioration can be prevented by measures designed to eliminate the causes. This may involve dealing with environmental factors or those of use and handling. The approach might best be called 'preventative conservation'. It may appear perfectly obvious and simple, but its importance and understanding are fundamentally vital to any collector.

Relative Humidity

Perhaps the most important single factor in deterioration is humidity. It is the controlling factor for most deterioration processes, and it can be destructive in itself through fluctuations and extremes.

Relative humidity is a measure of the amount of moisture present in the air, expressed as a percentage of the amount of possible moisture in the air at a given temperature. A high relative humidity would mean a high moisture content while a low value would reflect a drier atmosphere. Most organic materials attempt to stay in equilibrium with the environment and respond to changes in relative humidity by releasing or absorbing moisture. Extremes and rapid fluctuations cause problems. There is a range of relative humidity and moisture content best suited to each material, and reasonably constant

3 Materials used in restoration must prove compatible with those in the object under treatment. Plaster, used to fill a shrinkage split in the face and neck of a wooden figure from the Nicobar Islands, has actually increased the damage. As a hard substance, unable to move with the wood, it has acted like a wedge and forced the split wider.

4 Fluctuating and low levels of relative humidity can produce stresses and cause wood to split. The shrinkage split in the wooden fetish figure from Nigeria is now a virtually permanent disfigurement. Stable and safe environments for antiques and works of art prevent most damage and make costly restoration unnecessary.

values within this safe limit can be achieved either by keeping the temperature constant and altering the moisture content of the atmosphere with humidifiers and dehumidifiers or by changing the temperature. Any change, however, should be achieved slowly to avoid stresses. Absolute values of relative humidity can be read with a hygrometer.

Light

Damage by light takes two forms. The most obvious is usually a colour change which can be a colour loss or fading or a change in hue and tone. The second form is fibre deterioration in which light has an acceleratory influence on normal chemical degradation, and fibre strength is lost at a rate related to the amount of light and length of exposure. Obviously, different dyes and types of fibres are affected in different ways.

There are basically two factors in light which cause this deterioration. The first is related to the brightness or intensity of light present. Absolute values are read in lux from a device called a lux meter. Particularly light-sensitive materials need low levels of illumination. The *type* of light is also critical, as it is the ultra-violet content which is destructive. Daylight and most fluorescent light is high in ultra-violet rays.

Light can be controlled by filters, shades and baffles, dimmers, and by careful selection of light-fittings and their placement. Certain bulbs and tubes are less harmful than others.

Insect and Mould Attack

Organic materials are potential food for both insects and moulds. Such environmental components as temperature and moisture are contributory and controlling factors. Unfortunately, those conditions ideal for the well-being of most organic materials and often found in the home are equally suitable for insects. Woollen textiles, furs and feathers can be attacked while in storage by the larvae of the clothes moth. Carpet-beetle and fur beetle can also be a problem.

The larvae of the furniture beetle, *Anobium punctatum*, commonly known as woodworm, is the main culprit where wood is concerned, though termites and powder-post beetles can also be destructive in certain parts of the world. Insecticides are available for their control, but professional advice should be sought as treatment can be dangerous and ineffective unless done correctly.

Moulds prefer a dark and moist environment with little air movement, but once established, can tolerate normal domestic conditions. Fungicides are available and are especially useful where dampness persists. The usual treatment is to increase ventilation and dry out the atmosphere slowly to an acceptable level. After airing and drying, the mould can be brushed off.

Dust and Chemical Pollution

Air-borne pollution in the form of dust and the chemical pollutants of an industrial atmosphere are other destructive agents. Not only is dust unsightly, it can work its way into textile fibres

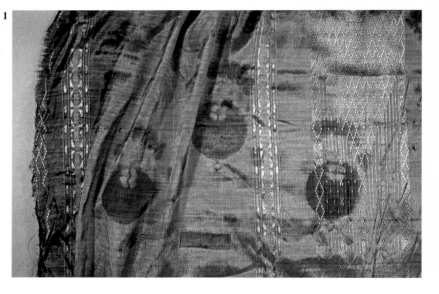

1 A silk textile from North Africa, used as a background for a jewelry display, was exposed to moderate daylight and fluorescent light over a period of fifteen years. Except where specimens protected the light-sensitive dyes, all colour has permanently faded. Had correct lighting been used, this destruction could have been avoided.

2 Woodworm and other wood-boring insects can cause great damage to furniture and art objects of wood. Although the surface of the wooden tankard from Norway is greatly disfigured by insect flight holes, this is only a superficial indication of the real destruction. Extensive tunneling by the larvae within the wood itself greatly reduces structural strength and can lead to breakage or collapse. In instances of severe infestation, virtually all internal wood can be reduced to powder. Treatment is available to arrest insect activity and, in many cases, consolidation can restore lost strength.

where it can act as an abrasive to make the fibres brittle and weak. It can also be hygroscopic and, by attracting moisture, encourage metal corrosion.

Chemical pollutants may use dust particles as nuclei of activity. Most industrial and urban atmospheres are high in sulphides which can combine with moisture and form sulphuric acid. Sulphides also tarnish silver. Ozone may be present in some situations and accelerate chemical reactions of deterioration. Air-conditioning is the best solution to the problem, though obviously this is not always possible. Alternatives that can be used are dust sheets, polythene bags, acid-free tissue and tarnish-resistant tissues, all of which help to isolate articles from the atmosphere.

Water

The affects of atmospheric moisture are related to levels of relative humidity and this has already been described. Aside from the obvious destruction caused by flooding or soaking, one of the most frequent instances of water damage in the home is that caused by wet objects being set on wooden furniture, with the resulting formation of bloom or rings. These are caused by moisture getting under the polish. In some cases, it dries out, but often only refinishing will remove it. Water, being a solvent, can dissolve gesso, size, dyes, and some paints. Most adhesives and varnishes will also absorb water, and many will break down and lose their adhesion after prolonged soaking. Before using any water treatment in cleaning, it is essential to test first in some inconspicuous place.

Abrasion and Over-cleaning

Most normal abrasion or wear can be minimized by sensible care and handling. Where necessary, surfaces can be protected. Cleaning agents which are too strong or abrasive and objects likely to cause scratches are easily avoided.

3 Poor storage or display conditions can ruin most antiques. This is especially true with textiles. The woven banana-fibre mat from Santa Cruz has been folded and crushed with the result that fibres have broken along crease lines. Insect and mould activity is free to develop undetected in the inner folds.

4 Using a New Hebridian woven fibre mat as an example for proper storage methods, creases can often be avoided by rolling a flat textile around a supporting tube. In this instance, acid-free tissue has been used for cushioning and to minimize contact with any chemically unstable materials such as cardboard.

Over-zealous cleaning can remove patinas and finishes, so routine cleaning is best done using the mildest methods available which still manage the job. Cleaning as part of restoration should be approached with caution, testing first and perhaps cleaning in stages to reach the final appearance.

Storage and Handling

The more an antique is handled, the greater the risk of damage. Even while a piece is in storage, where handling is minimal, safety cannot be assumed. Poor storage conditions such as adverse relative humidity or light may also be a problem, and insect and mould damage may develop undetected. Certain packing materials such as newspapers, standard cardboard, coloured tissue paper, plastic and foam rubber can deteriorate and release harmful chemicals.

Adequate support and protection is important for pieces in store – they can prevent crushing and distortion which may be irreversible.

Heat

The relationship between temperature and relative humidity has been mentioned, and the low relative humidity caused by excessive heat can be especially damaging. However, heat itself can cause problems. Resins and waxes can melt or distort. Furniture finishes and paint layers can be blistered and ruined. Heat can accelerate both the process of ageing and deterioration which has been induced by chemicals.

Restoration and Conservation of Organic Material

Wood and furniture. Wood is probably the most common of the organic materials in the home and a likely component of most collections. Its wide usage is based not only on beauty and versatility, but also on its strength and resilience. However, it is extremely prone to damage through abuse and environmental factors.

The moisture content of wood is self adjusting to reach equilibrium with the environment. Seasoned wood is deliberately brought to a moisture content compatible with its intended atmosphere. The ideal relative humidity generally accepted for wood is in the range 50–60 per cent at 20°C (68°F). Trouble occurs when adjustments are required which are too extreme or occur too quickly. Under very dry conditions, as may be caused by central heating, sufficient moisture may be lost to cause wood cells to collapse, then splits and cracks appear. Swelling is the opposite phenomenon, and is caused by high humidity. Rapid fluctuations increase the risk of stresses being formed which can result in splitting, lifting veneers, and so on. Warping is caused by a number of factors including long-term support faults, but more especially, by uneven exposure to moisture. This can occur when one surface is polished, painted or covered while its opposite surface is free to swell or shrink to produce curling.

Insect damage is common and the pests vary with the district. The type of destruction usually consists of a network of tunnels eaten away under the surface with the result that structural strength can be lost. Flight holes can be unsightly.

The usual indication of infestation is the formation of fresh frass, resembling sawdust, falling from flight holes. Such obvious activity is most likely in late spring when the adult emerges from the wood. Fumigation can be extremely dangerous and is best done professionally, but there are several insecticides on the market which can be applied either by injection or by surface application. Care should be taken with these poisons. Many insecticides have strong solvent properties and can dissolve finishes and paint. Instructions should be followed carefully and

tests made for solubility and colour change before treatment.

Finishes can be damaged in other ways. Abrasion through scratches or coarse cleaning agents is common. Some are affected by alcohol, and most by water. Heat can cause blistering. Excessive light can accelerate deterioration and discoloration.

Breaks can usually be repaired simply. Joins may break down and veneers lift due to glue embrittlement, insect and mould activity, or wood movement. It is generally advisable to remain consistent with adhesives throughout a piece so that all joins react in the same manner to stresses and future restoration efforts will be simplified. All traces of old glue should be removed before resticking, to produce a strong and clean join.

Adhesive should be applied to both surfaces to be joined and the pieces stuck together. Taking

care not to bruise the wood, clamps, weight, or tourniquets can be applied to squeeze out excess adhesive and ensure a tight fit. Extruded adhesive should be carefully removed at this stage. Animal glue, soluble in warm water, is the adhesive generally found in antique pieces and used for repairs, but later restoration may have been done with synthetic adhesives. Where the repair is a break rather than resticking a join, stronger

synthetic adhesives may be advisable. Dowelling or new pieces of wood may be required.

Splits present an interesting problem. In some cases, small splits can be permanently closed by correcting the humidity or by pressing the split together and holding it with an adhesive. However there is a risk that the stress will seek an outlet elsewhere, and a new split form.

An alternative is to fill the split, though fillers harder than wood should be avoided as they will not react to normal wood movement and can act like a solid wedge and so create more problems. Wood is the ideal filler, and it is possible to insert slivers of similar wood shaped to fit the split and held in place with an adhesive. This can be brought to the same surface plane, colour matched, and finished to be virtually invisible. Often, splits are better watched and left alone.

Careful cleaning can return a newly acquired antique to its original appearance and yet leave enough patina. Any cleaning method should be carefully tested in an inconspicuous area. This is very important where solvents are to be used. Finishes and varnishes are of various compositions and a method of cleaning should be sought which will remove accumulated wax, dirt, and grime without harming the original finish. In

1 Active woodworm in a wooden spoon rack from Eastern Europe is shown being treated with a liquid insecticide. A hypodermic needle is used to inject the liquid into the flight holes and the insect's own tunnels serve to carry the insecticide deep into the wood. A small piece of ruuber near the tip of the needle prevents the liquid flowing back. If done properly, a residual poison is left in the wood to give protection for several years.

2 Often, simple cleaning will reveal the original finish to be in reasonable condition and 'refinishing' will prove to be unnecessary. Cleaning should always be done cautiously and any method considered should be tested first in an inconspicious place. Ideally, cleaning will remove the accumulated layer of grime and not affect the surface beneath.

some cases, a good quality paste wax can be massaged into the surface and will remove the top wax layers and grime and replace it with fresh wax. Gentle abrasives such as metal polishes may be useful in other instances.

A good standard cleaner can be made from an emulsion of two parts turpentine, two parts white vinegar, two parts methylated spirit, and one part linseed oil. The strength can be reduced by using less methylated spirit in the solution. This is not, however, intended for regular use on the same piece.

Where total refinishing is necessary, the old polish or varnish and, in some cases paint, must be removed. This can be done with various solvents ranging in strength from water through alcohols and the organic solvents, white spirit, toluene and xylene, to paint strippers. Alternatively, mechanical methods such as sandpaper or steel-wool could be used.

A new finish should be selected which is in character with the original appearance. French polish is the most common finish encountered in antiques, but it is difficult to apply without a great deal of practice. Varnishes can be simpler to apply though the result can be disappointing. Pumice powder or jeweller's rouge applied with a soft brush helps reduce a new high gloss to a softer sheen. A good coat of wax will help to protect the final finish as well as improve its appearance.

Basketry and vegetable fibres. With the increase in interest and value in ethnography, basketry and articles made of natural fibre are finding a place in collections. The problems are much the same as those encountered in both wood and textiles. Most damage would seem to occur in storage, where crushing is likely. Desiccation features heavily as a problem and increases the risk of breakage.

Reshaping is usually accomplished by damping with distilled water applied by spray and, when flexible, gently manipulating into shape. Adequate ventilation must be available for drying to avoid the formation of mould.

Leather and skin. Leather is made up of protein fibres, and its flexibility is dependent on the ability of these fibres to move in relation to each other. When allowed to become too dry or when lubricants have been soaked out or become rigid, this ability is lost, and the leather becomes brittle and stiff. The ideal relative humidity is 50–60 per cent.

3 and **4** Basketry, like textiles, can be crushed in storage to produce distortion and breakage. A Nigerian basket which has been folded for several years is being re-shaped for safer storage. The first step in re-shaping is to relax the fibres with distilled water. This is usually best applied as a fine spray. The basket can then be gradually unfolded.

When the fibres have become flexible, the basket can be re-shaped. Stuffing with non-reactive polythene and acid-free tissue will keep this shape until the basket has dried. Re-shaping may require several such stages. Stuffing to give adequate support is a sensible precaution for storage.

Under damp conditions mould can form. Insects can also be a problem. Liquid insecticides are best avoided, but small-scale and safe fumigation is possible by enclosing the infected article in a plastic bag with paradichlorobenzene crystals for a few weeks.

Some dyes are extremely light sensitive and require a low intensity of light, and the exclusion of ultra-violet rays. Leather dressings are available which can be massaged into the skin to replace lost lubricants. Too liberal an application can cause subsequent weeping and a sticky surface.

Paper. The repair and restoration of paper is a specialist's field. Tempting home remedies such as adhesive tapes, bleaches and glues can have disastrous results. It is far better to recognize and avoid, if possible, the problems involved.

3

1

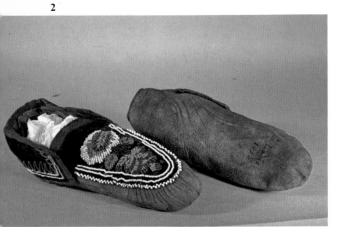

2

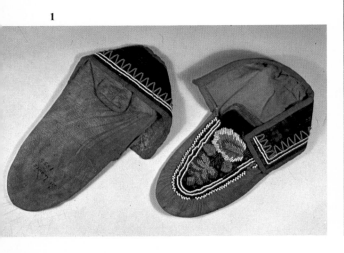

The formation of brown spots or 'foxing' is common with paper behind glass. This is caused by the paper's close proximity to the glass, which encourages mould to develop. A mount would increase this space and reduce the problems. All mounts and supports should be of acid-free conservation board.

Paper can also be attacked by wood-eating insects and by silver-fish. Fumigation is preferable to liquid insecticides, and paradichlorobenzene crystals can be used as a fumigant by enclosing the article with the crystals for several weeks in a plastic bag.

Light can cause dyes and pigments to fade, and where watercolours are concerned very low levels of light in the range of 50 lux would be sensible.

Atmospheres high in sulphides are destructive. Also dry environments cause paper embrittlement, while mould can develop in the opposite extreme; a relative humidity of 50–60 per cent is about right.

Ivory and bone. Ivory is very much affected by moisture and relative humidity fluctuations, and is prone to splitting and warping under dry conditions. If a split is forced together and stuck, there is a considerable danger that the split will occur elsewhere. Generally, it is better to fill splits with a plastic adhesive such as a polyvinyl acetate with a marble flour filler. Such treatment may prevent the split from getting larger yet be plastic enough to give with any expansion or contraction. An ideal relative humidity for ivory and bone is about 60–65 per cent.

Textiles. Of all the organic materials commonly encountered in antiques, textiles are probably the most subject to environmental damage in the home. They are also especially beset by inherent problems which make them seem almost self-destructive. Some dyes can become acidic, and, in time, whole areas of the textile so coloured can disintegrate. Fabrics of mixed thread com-

1 and **2** Leather can also suffer from bad storage and display. These North American Indian moccasins have been crushed, producing folds and weakness along these lines. Excess light has caused fading.

The moccasins have been cleaned and the creases were relaxed and then gently opened by stuffing with acid-free tissue paper. Some form of internal support is necessary for both storage and display.

3 Textiles can deteriorate to the point where all strength is lost. This fragment of Chinese silk is being 'couched down' or sewn to a supporting piece of cloth so that it can be preserved.

position can suffer from different responses to the environment and rates of deterioration. In many cases, the unsupported weight of the textile can cause it to split and tear.

To these inherent fabric faults must be added the problems of dust and pollution which can be abrasive and cause the physical breakdown of individual fibres. Conditions of low relative humidity accelerate this deterioration by drying out the fibres and making them brittle, while the opposite extreme produces conditions ideal for mould growth. Again, a range of 50–60 per cent should be acceptable.

Insects can be a real threat to fabrics. Moths can ruin wool and fur unless prevented by frequent inspection and the use of naphthalene or paradichlorobenzene crystals.

Restoration is rarely straightforward or simple. Short-cuts are few. Even washing is complicated by fugitive dyes and differential swelling and shrinking of fibres. Textiles may be so fragile that they need to be attached to supports to be washed or handled and, indeed, to survive at all. Even in storage, it may be necessary to pad and support to prevent folds and creases breaking delicate fibres.

Restoration and Conservation of Inorganic Material

Archaeological metals may be a part of a collection of antiques, which can lead to problems. During periods of burial, chlorides from the soil form compounds with the metals which are stable in anaerobic conditions, but once excavated can enter into chemical cycles using oxygen and moisture to form acids that will destroy the metal. With iron, droplets of brown liquid form on the surface which indicate the problem, while with copper and its alloys, a pale green powdery substance, 'bronze disease', is formed. Because atmospheric moisture is required, archaeological metals should be kept dry and never allowed in conditions of high humidity. Ideally, chlorides should be removed in the laboratory.

Iron. Cleaning is usually involved with the removal of layers of oxides commonly called rust. There are instances where most of the metal has been replaced with products of corrosion and their total removal would destroy or disfigure too much. Examination with a magnet or by X-ray is a first step in determining the type of treatment.

Chemical rust removers, based on phosphoric acid, are fast and involve little labour. However, since they remove all rust, a pitted and etched surface is likely, and the protective layer of phosphates formed alters the colour of the metal.

Mechanical cleaning methods are generally to be preferred because of the control possible. Corrosion is physically abraded away down to the surface of the metal or, in instances of extensive corrosion, to the original surface. Pits and crevices can be left filled with corrosion to leave a smooth surface. The abrasive used depends on the extent of corrosion and on the desired finish and vary in degree of coarseness from metal polishes through wire-wool and finally to emery

paper. It is often advisable to work through a series of emery papers from coarse to fine, using a light machine oil as a lubricant.

Future formation of rust can be inhibited by degreasing the metal with acetone and then lacquering with a good nitro-cellulose lacquer. Graphite powder can be mixed with the lacquer to offer additional protection and to intensify black patination. A microcrystalline-based wax applied over or instead of the lacquer is also helpful and reduces the shine. Relative humidity should not exceed 60 per cent.

Copper and its alloys. One of the most frequently encountered metals in antiques and in antiquities is copper. It may appear in its pure form or in alloys such as bronze and brass. Even silver and gold often contain copper for hardness and strength. The behaviour of copper and its deterioration should be understood. Alloys, even those of low copper content, can show a dominant activity on the part of copper and suffer the effects of its corrosion.

'Bronze disease' is an active corrosion which forms a powdery, pale green corrosion in a relative humidity greater than about 50 per cent. This is best treated by a specialist. Copper acetate or verdigris can have a similar appearance but is more wax-like in texture. It is organic in origin, usually more unsightly than harmful and easily removed by the appropriate solvent or by light mechanical treatment. Copper carbonates may also be formed under burial conditions. These are usually highly prized as green patinas, but some degree of expert mechanical cleaning may be needed to form a good surface.

Surface oxides or tarnish can be removed to reveal a bright metal surface. Cleaning with a mild abrasive is generally best as it can be controlled to leave varying amounts of patina and yet polish the metal. Too coarse an abrasive can scratch and wear away the surface. Chemical cleaners can also be very helpful, especially when tackling very tarnished metals but these can over-clean and plate copper on to the surface. A reversible clear lacquer, such as a nitro-cellulose lacquer, can be applied to prevent the need for repeated future cleaning in the case of objects not subjected to much handling.

Silver. For the most part a stable metal, silver in the home is subject to two forms of corrosion. Copper, alloyed with silver for hardness and used as a base metal in silver plate, can be attacked by organic acids and produce copper corrosion products which can disrupt or cover the surface. These can be removed by cleaning with mild abrasives in most cases, but swabbing with dilute ammonia or formic acid may be necessary. Avoid prolonged contact with vinegar, pickles, or salt and the like.

The second and by far more common form of corrosion is that caused by sulphides – tarnish or silver sulphide. Though relatively harmless in itself, the danger lies more in repeated cleaning. The more abrasive the cleaning agent and the more often cleaning is required, and the more rapidly the silver is worn away.

Air-borne sulphides, prevalent in urban and

4 and **5** Silver, brass and copper have been used by nineteenth century Indian craftsmen to produce this small lidded pot. Unfortunately, tarnish has reduced the intended contrasts of metal colours and textures.

Controlled cleaning, in this case with a wadding type of metal polish, has revealed the colours and brilliance of the different metals involved. Sufficient patina has been left to intensify the engraved work, texture, and antique quality. An even coat of a reversible lacquer will keep this appearance for years.

4

5

industrial atmospheric pollution, can be removed through air-conditioning. Some paints and textiles, rubber, linoleum and eggs can be avoidable sources. Silver in storage can often be effectively protected by using storage bags and shelf liners of fabric treated to prevent tarnish. Objects intended for display alone can be lacquered with a sulphur-free, reversible, and non-yellowing lacquer manufactured specially for silver.

Chemical cleaners are available which remove tarnish on immersion. They are easy to use and ideal for cleaning areas impossible to reach. However, it must be realized that they remove all tarnish and thus patina, and contrast in engraved and raised surface decoration is reduced. Some objects cannot take immersion in a liquid. Chemical cleaners contain acid which can destroy coral and pearls and may etch the silver. After repeated usage, enough silver finds its way into the solution to begin plating back on to the surface, giving a frosted and quickly tarnished surface.

The alternative is mechanically cleaning with commercially prepared silver cleaners. These contain mild abrasives and usually have certain chemical additives. Paste cleaners and creams must be carefully and completely removed to avoid a build up of dried deposits in decorated areas. Impregnated waddings and cloths may be preferable from this point of view. The mildest effective method should be used.

Gold. Pure gold is virtually non-reactive and free from deterioration. Where alloyed with copper, tarnishing and even copper corrosion can occur. For the most part, the problem is one of accumulated dirt, which can be removed by gentle swabbing with cotton or a soft cloth dampened with a soap solution.

Lead, pewter and tin. The amphoteric metals, lead, tin and zinc, are attacked by acids, but,

unlike iron, copper and silver, are also corroded by alkalis. Pewter, an alloy of lead and tin, is also amphoteric. Vinegar and acidic wines can corrode pewter food containers. Prolonged contact with poor quality paper and card, certain paints, and indeed anything likely to be acidic or alkaline, should be avoided. Some detergents therefore can create problems.

Cleaning is straightforward unless corrosion is extensive or active in which case professional advice should be sought. Mechanical cleaning with a mild abrasive cream or wadding or just polishing with a soft cloth should be sufficient. Chemical cleaners should be avoided. A light coat of microcrystalline wax often improves the final appearance.

Ceramics. Most damage to ceramics is through mishandling and should be avoidable. In some cases, inherent problems do exist. Through burial or usage, pottery can contain soluble salts which are affected by changes in relative humidity and crystallize on the surface pushing glazes and surface away. Intensive and prolonged washing under laboratory control is the usual treatment.

Generally though, ceramics are stable and not noticeably affected by normal environmental factors. However, repairs and some glazes are sensitive to light and heat. Except with unfired pottery, cleaning should simply be a matter of washing or gentle swabbing with mild soap and water. It is best to use lukewarm water because sudden temperature changes can cause glazes to craze and crack. Restored areas and adhesives can react badly to water and especially stronger solvents, such as acetone or methylated spirit, which may sometimes be needed. Concretions and heavy deposits may require abrasive metal polishes or even acid for removal. Gilding and luster glazes are less able to stand abrasion and strong cleaning.

1 Clean dry edges are essential for good joins in ceramic restoration. An adhesive is being applied to both edges of pieces of a Rumanian dish to be stuck. These pieces will be pressed together and carefully aligned, excess glue removed and finally they will be balanced in a sand tray to dry.

The first step in ceramic restoration is to ensure that joins are clean and all old glue and adhesives removed. Sometimes it is necessary to take apart an old restoration. Most old adhesives come down on soaking in water. Methylated spirit or acetone may prove to be the solvent in other cases. Epoxy resins and other resistant adhesives may be broken down in commercial paint strippers.

Clean edges will help produce tight and less visible joins. Bleaching cracks and edges before sticking is also advisable. Clean dry pieces can be stuck with a suitable adhesive. Epoxy resins and other non-reversible adhesives, although strong, are difficult to work with and are best left to those with experience. A clear non-yellowing and reversible adhesive such as a nitrocellulose adhesive is best for most purposes. A sand tray is helpful for positioning pieces for drying. It is important to work out the logical sequence of sticking. Normally, a small amount of adhesive is applied to both edges to be stuck to ensure good coverage and then the pieces pressed together. Excess glue extruded from the join can be cleaned away with an appropriate solvent.

Missing pieces and gaps can be completed after sticking. The choice of gap-filler depends on the size, type and texture of the material to be replaced and the strength required. Gap-fillers may include plaster, wax, proprietory fillers, and epoxy fillers. Reversibility is usually advisable. Fillers should be modelled or sanded down to the correct level and textured and coloured to match. Varnishes and resins are available to reproduce a glazed appearance.

Glass. Repairs to broken glass can be very unrewarding. Strength is difficult to achieve because the edges of broken glass are too smooth to allow an adhesive to key well. And the adhesive must have the same refractive index as the glass or the join will show. Also it must be an exact colour match.

Adhesives which set on drying, shrink on loss of solvent and draw air into the join producing visible bubbles. Contact adhesives for glass repair are being used, but these seem to lose strength in time. The most successful adhesive to date would seem to be a two-part resin adhesive manufactured for glass restoration.

Painted surfaces. The first step in treating any painted surface must be examination to determine the cause of deterioration. This must be put right or all restoration will be a pointless exercise.

Often a layer of dirt or grease or a layer of discoloured varnish may be obscuring the paint beneath. Should it be necessary to remove these superficial layers, it must be done so that no solvent is used which adversely affects the paint layer, ground, or support, and abrasion must be avoided.

The paint film itself should be examined for deterioration due to excess light, heat, and damage through pollution, solvents, and abrasion. Flaking may be caused by a loss of adhesion, and a suitable binding medium must be introduced between the appropriate layers. Heat and a vacuum may be required to make the flakes and blisters return to the correct level. The fault often lies in the support where deterioration can lead to a loss of structural strength. Excess movement in the support may also be contributory.

Before retouching can be carried out, areas of paint loss must be filled to a similar level and texture to the existing paint film. Wax with various fillers is commonly used. Pigments in water colours, tempera, acrylic or oil media may be used to replace lost areas of colour. Care should be taken to avoid over-painting original paint. Where varnishes are to be replaced, reversible varnishes should be used.

2 Paint often flakes on the surface of wood because the wood underneath is liable to expansion and contraction while the paint layer tends to be more rigid. A thermoplastic adhesive has been used to re-lay paint flakes on this painted barrel from Eastern Europe. The adhesive is allowed to flow under the lifting flakes, and when dry, a heated spatula can be used to iron the flakes into position.

3 Chips, missing pieces and cracks can be filled after the ceramic has been stuck together. Many types of fillers are available ranging from resins to the more simple plaster-like forms. These can be moulded, modelled, and shaped to the correct level, form and texture and then coloured to match. Even glazes can be reproduced with synthetic resins or lacquers.

Antiques at auction

All the objects illustrated on these four pages were sold at auction during 1978. They fall into two categories: they either fetched record or extremely high prices in their particular field, or they were sold for about £50 ($100). All were sold at major sale rooms, and so have been selected to show the wide range of items that are regularly sold at auction. Record prices may make the headlines, but there are still plenty of bargains to be picked up by the discerning collector.

1 Elizabethan presentation glass goblet, dated 1584, made in England by Giacomo Verzelini, sold for £75,000, approximately $150,000. This record price was the result of the extreme rarity of glass of this period, particularly by Verzelini. In addition, the fine engraving made this a very unusual example.

Antique collecting can give endless pleasure and entertainment. It is also quite a sociable habit and can be financially rewarding. However, anyone thinking of taking it up should realize that it is a disease which, once caught, can develop into a mania. Over the last few years the disease has reached epidemic proportions, spread in part by the publication of books such as this. The rare and strong individuals who never suffer from the disease are in many ways the lucky ones, for, once caught, it is likely to take over and control the victim utterly, affecting every aspect of normal life. The collecting disease can be caught in a number of ways. First, it can be inherited) many future collectors were as children dragged complaining around antique shops and museums by their collector parents, acquiring thereby the latent germ that would blossom later. Second, it can be passed from one person to another by close contact, shared interests being extremely catching. Third, and most dangerous of all, it can suddenly seize a victim without warning, inspired by a radio or television programme, by a newspaper or magazine article, or even by a casual and unplanned encounter with a collector.

The collecting disease is frequently fuelled by nostalgia, a romantic longing for a past that only exists in the imagination of the present. Objects have an ability to bring this to life, simply because they can survive from one age to another. Much popular collecting is inspired by such fantasies, particularly where the main aim of the collector is the recreation of a period or epoch beyond his actual experience. However, on this level the disease can be comparatively trivial, for this type of collector is inspired more by the whims of fashion than by a genuine, deep-seated acquisitiveness.

2 Important marquetry coiffeuse, made by Abraham Roentgen and dated 1769, sold for £200,000, approximately $400,000. Roentgen is one of the most desirable of the European cabinet makers of the 18th century, and good examples of his work are rarely sold. This desk, or dressing table, with its elaborate marquetry, bronze mounts and its variety of concealed drawers and compartments, is a quite remarkable example.

Far more serious is the other main type of collector, the one who collects for investment or financial gain. Although this type has always been a traditional feature of the antique trade, it is only recently that the financial and investment drive has spread down to affect the lower and more amateur levels of collecting. This new pattern has actually changed the nature of collecting as a disease, for an ailment that used to cause minor inconvenience often takes the form now of a virulent and all-consuming plague. Aesthetics and pleasure are cast aside in the quest for profit, and even the most tawdry and trivial objects, such as old bottles, are collected on the basis of an investment for the future. Investment collecting is a serious pursuit, to be pursued only with professional guidance, and so it obviously lacks the casual pleasure traditionally to be gained from tracking down or discovering by chance a varied collection of either related or unrelated objects. Business and pleasure are, after all, generally incompatible.

While the motives and background to collecting are quite varied, the methods of actually forming a collection are fairly universal. The casual collector, even one with a degree of specialized interest, will spend most of his time exploring antique and junk shops, enjoying the search as much as the finds. Some shops will be visited on a regular basis, to establish a relationship with the dealer, while others will be visited only in passing. For most collectors, the lure of an unexplored shop will be hard to resist, and whole days can happily be spent in casual searching, days that will still count as valuable and enjoyable even if nothing is discovered. To carry treasures home in triumph is effectively a bonus pleasure, the icing on the cake. Antique shops of course vary greatly, from the very smart to the really junky. Finds can be made at every level, although the real junk shop tends today to live up to its title and be fairly unrewarding. The popularity of antique collecting, and the resultant spread of knowledge has inevitably made the searching all the harder. The most rewarding areas are now the fairly grand antique shops, for a careful browsing through their extensive and varied stock can be both pleasurable and instructive, even if no hidden treasures come to light.

Street markets are another traditional source. Many markets, however small, contain stalls dealing in second hand goods of all kinds, while most cities have regular markets devoted to the sale of antiques, often held at weekends. In London, for example, there is quite a choice – Bermondsey on Friday mornings, Portobello Road on Saturdays, Culter Street and Petticoat Lane on Sundays. Here large numbers of dealers from all over the country gather together to display and sell their stock, often only for a few hours at a time. So collectors are faced by a large number of stalls to be explored, loaded with every conceivable antique and collectable – and some inconceivable ones. The best markets always start early, and regular visiting is essential. However, at 5am on a cold, dark, wet

3

3 T'ang horse, sold for £110,000, approximately $220,000. Although the coloured glazed earthenware tomb figures of the T'ang dynasty are not rare, this example, a harnessed fereghan horse, fetched a record price. It is a particularly fine model, with many unusual features, such as the striped mane, and it was also one of the largest (25½ in high) to be sold for many years.

4

4 Violin, made by Joseph Guarneri del Gesu Cremona in 1734, sold for £115,000, approximately $230,000. This price, an auction record for any musical instrument, reflects both the rarity and quality of instruments of that period, and the investment potential in certain antiques and works of art. This is a field in which prices have risen dramatically over the last few years.

5

5 Automaton of the man in the moon, sold for £2,300, approximately $4,600. This unusual continental automaton and musical box reflects the high prices that the best examples of these late Victorian and Edwardian children's toys can now command.

367

1 Ivory netsuke of two sedan chairmen resting for a smoke under their burden, 4.5cm (1¾ in) high, dated about 1900. This was sold for £45, approximately $90.

2 The charm of nostalgia is immediately apparent in this piece of Christmas sentimentality, sold for less than £50, about $100.

3 An oak joint stool, the hinged seat opening to reveal a compartment, with carved side panels on turned legs joined by a stretcher. Dated about 1930, this sold for less than £50, approximately $100.

winter's morning the dedication and enthusiasm of the collector face their most severe test. A large breakfast is always a consolation, and finds made in such extreme conditions seem more memorable in comfortable retrospect. Recent developments are the indoor markets and the occasional flea markets and antiques fairs; in the former, a number of dealers come together to rent stalls under one roof and so achieve more permanence and comfort than the street offers, while the latter, held frequently in town halls, village or church halls or hotels give the collector a chance to see a wide range of wares brought together for a one day event. Many dealers travel regularly from fair to fair, and so it is not necessary to travel to fairs outside your normal area in order to see varied stock.

Buying at auction is the most traditional form of antique collecting, and one that is still extremely popular. There are now more auction sales than ever before, held in towns and villages the length and breadth of the country. Some are general, some specialize, but all advertise in local newspapers. The major salerooms may attract most of the attention in the press, but many provincial sales can be just as exciting. However, buying at auction always requires considerable self-control, and it can take up a lot of time. For a sale must always be viewed very carefully, to make sure that the items are as described in the catalogue and to look out for damage; it is necessary also to decide in advance the value of an item, and then to stick to that value and not be carried away in the heat of the moment by excitement and enthusiasm. However, sales are rarely a waste of time because they provide an accurate guide to contemporary pricing, and they enable the collector to see and handle a wide range of antiques. The major salerooms are in many ways the equivalent of museums, with the great difference that the objects can be handled and examined.

Many collectors, particularly those with specialist interests buy privately, from advertisements in newspapers and magazines. This can be very rewarding, for visits to private collections often reveal undreamt of treasures. However, the private buyer must be very knowledgeable, and must have a good idea of the value of the items under offer. Prices in the private sector can be highly erratic, and so can be unfair to either buyer or seller.

Knowledge is important for every collector, for the whole basis of collecting is to try to find something that everyone else has missed. Collecting is frequently the exploitation of mistakes made by others, and a bargain or discovery for the buyer is simply an error on the part of the seller. Knowledge and experience are therefore crucial, and a good memory very helpful. Knowledge can be acquired from books, lectures, evening classes, museums and other public collections, magazine articles, TV and radio programmes and from general conversation, but the best way to learn is simply to see and handle as much as possible. The best collectors and dealers are looking and learning

all the time. Many collectors' societies have also **4**
been established in recent years, to serve both
general and specialized interests, and these can
be both valuable and entertaining. They range
from the grand and academic to the decidedly
amateur and so every collector can find his own
level.

Essentially, there are several basic rules that
collectors should follow, regardless of their
experience or knowledge:

First, antique collecting is for pleasure. It is
unpredictable, erratic and time-consuming, but
highly enjoyable. There are always new discoveries just around the corner.

Second, decide at an early stage the level of
collecting to be pursued, and whether or not to
specialize. The collector following a highly
specialized line will have to develop a different
approach to collecting as a whole, for the
specialist can easily develop into the total
fanatic.

Third, decide the price level to be followed and
collect accordingly. There is no point in being
extravagant, and it is a mistake to think that
antiques are better just because they cost more
money. Errors are most frequently made by
collectors who step out of their knowledge and
price level.

Fourth, buy what you like and can live with, not
what you think you ought to buy. Taste is a
personal matter, and so there are no rules. Some
antiques are more socially acceptable than
others, but the best collectors always put their
personal taste to the fore.

Fifth, buy for pleasure or buy for investment,
but do not try to mix the two. It rarely works out.
Sixth, having decided the field and price level,
always buy the best available within your limit.
Be prepared to back your own judgment.

4 Prints, posters,
advertisements, and all
kinds of printed materials
are still a rich field for
collectors. Many fine
examples are available at
all ranges of prices, such
as this one sold for less
than £50, about $100.

5 Children's tin toys are
becoming increasingly
popular among collectors.
These sold for less than £50,
approximately $100.

Great houses

Although pictures of great houses may seem out of place in a book about antiques, a general understanding of the development of architectural style can be very valuable. Changes in style frequently appear first in architecture and painting, and then are gradually absorbed by other art forms. The style of furniture, silver, ceramics or any other applied art inevitably follow the fashions created by architects and painters.

The great houses illustrated in the following pages have been selected because they indicate clearly the major changes in style that occured between the 15th century and the present day and their international impact. These styles are also echoed by the antiques illustrated throughout the book, and so an appreciation of the main stylistic features of each period, as reflected by architecture, can only help the collector.

1 Ca' d'Oro, Venice, built 1421–36. The Italian Gothic style is one of the most elegant of the medieval period, representing a mixture of many cultures, including the Middle East.

2 Azay-le-Rideau, 1524. This picturesque chateau, with its blend of gothic and Renaissance details, represents the transition between moated fortified castles and elegant private mansions.

3 Little Moreton Hall, Cheshire, 1559–80. In England, the traditional timber-frame style of building survived well into the 16th century often exploited with great imagination.

4 The long gallery at Little Moreton Hall. Running the whole length of the building, the gallery shows in its structure and panelling the versatility of oak as a building material.

5 Villa Capra, Vicenza, built about 1560 by Andrea Palladio. One of the foremost architects of the Renaissance, Palladio based his designs on classical Roman architecture.

371

1 Palace of the Marqués de Dos Aguas, Valencia, 1740–44. The classical styles took many forms during the 18th century, but none was more extreme than the confections of the Rococo. The entrance portals in white alabaster by Ignacio Vergara shows the frenetic activity and fluidity of the style.

2 Mereworth Castle, Kent, by Colen Campbell. The Palladian style became very popular in England during the early part of the 18th century, so much so that many 16th century buildings were copied by architects such as Campbell and Lord Burlington. Mereworth is closely based on the Villa Capra.

3

3 Palace of Jacques Coeur, Bourges, built 1443–51. This medieval house built in traditional fortified style around a central courtyard, has many of the typical features of the Middle Ages.

4 Hotel Soubise, Paris, built 1732–39. The medieval courtyard plan of building, as in the illustration above, was continued well into the 18th century. However, by now, the style combined the formality of classicism with the rather frivolous details of Rococo.

4

1 Saloon, Saltram House, Devonshire. In England, the greatest exponents of the classical style during the second half of the 18th century were the Adam brothers. Robert Adam was able to combine the skills of architect and interior designer, making himself responsible for all the details.

2 Ropes Mansion, Salem, Massachusetts, built 1720. In America, a quite individual style of classicism had developed by the 18th century. Many elegant small scale houses survive from this period, which share some of the features of the contemporary Queen Anne style in England–dormer windows, tall chimneys etc.

3 Pingree House, Salem, Massachusetts, built 1804. Throughout the 18th century, American domestic architecture followed a similar pattern of development to English, but it retained nevertheless, its own distinctive features, for example, a purer use of classical proportions and details.

4 Palace of Sanssouci, Potzdam, built 1744–47. In the rest of Europe, styles of interior decoration were often more extreme than in England. In Germany the Baroque and Rococo styles were very popular and so the elaborate and exotic plasterwork decoration of this music room was fairly typical.

1

1 Royal Pavilion, Brighton.
The extraordinary Moorish
details of the Pavilion, built
during the Regency period
by John Nash, make it
unique in European
architecture. However, it
well represents the
contemporary interest in the
exotic, when styles from
Egypt, Rome, China, India
and the Middle East were
commonly used together,
frequently with bizarre
results.

2 Mark Twain House,
Hartford, Connecticut,
built 1874. The 19th century
was a period of extreme
styles, particularly in
America. This unusual house
was built in a mixture of
gothic and local vernacular
traditions, and the result was
something that was far more
inventive than many
Victorian revivalist styles.

2

3 State Government House, Melbourne. This large formal mansion was built in a revived Italianate style, popular in England during the 1840s and 1850s. Although not precisely from any particular building, many features, such as the bell tower and the asymmetrical layout, are broadly drawn from the Renaissance.

4 Duntry League House, Orange, New South Wales. This 19th century building, with its ornamental verandas in oriental style, shows many of the characteristics of colonial architecture of the period.

1 Chateau-sur-Mer, Newport, Rhode Island, built 1872. The extravagance and splendour of American 19th century architecture is well expressed by this staircase, showing so many varied materials and styles.

2 Bryanston House, Dorset, built by R. Norman Shaw. In England, in the late 19th and early 20th centuries, many architects looked back to the purity and simplicity of earlier classical-inspired styles. Although this house was based on the ideas of Wren, it is still a highly original creation, making the most of formality and contrasting materials.

3

3 La Pedrera, Barcelona, by Gaudi. In Europe, the Art Nouveau style dominated the early 20th century. With its sinuous curves and organic structure, this style echoed some of the features of the Rococo, but managed still to be new and original. Architects such as the Spaniard Gaudi were able to use materials in totally new decorative ways.

4 Palais Stocklet, Brussels, 1911, by Joseph Hoffman. In this century architecture has gone in many new directions, but this has only been possible because of revolutionary buildings such as this. With his extreme modernism, Hoffman was able to break away from all the architectural and styles of the past.

Glossary

Acanthus motif A classical ornament based on a stylized representation of the scalloped leaves of the acanthus plant.

Altazimuth An instrument for determining the azimuth which is the arc of the heavens extending from the zenith to the horizon.

Anthemion or Honeysuckle motif A Greek ornamental motif based on stylized palmettes or the similar honeysuckle flower forms. It was widely used in the 18th century and 19th century when the classical style was in vogue.

Appliqué work A needlework technique where one material is applied to another by means of decorative stitches.

Apron An ornamental member on furniture situated under the seat rails of chairs, and beneath the frieze rails of stands and tables.

Arabesque A rhythmic linear ornament of intricately interlaced foliage fruit and scrolls. It was a popular motif in Islamic decoration and has been widely used since then.

Arcanist A workman who knows the secret of porcelain making and other processes, for instance, faience making.

Armoire A wardrobe or cupboard of a monumental nature, usually sumptuously decorated and often incorporating architectural motifs.

Arts and Crafts Movement A concerted effort to improve standards of design in the late Victorian period by reviving handcrafts. The romantic socialist ideals of William Morris and John Ruskin were the main inspiration. C. R. Ashbee, Walter Crane, William Lethaby and Ernest Gimson were distinguished members. Initially they developed individual styles but by the 1890's a solid austere style was in evidence which became the characteristic style of the movement.

Art Deco The modernist style of the inter-war years 1918–39 which catered for the new demands for machine like forms and mechanized production. It was characterized by geometrical forms and strident colour combinations.

Art Nouveau An extravagant decorative style which was popular in the West about 1880–1914. It is characterized by the ubiquitous use of curvilinear motifs, elongated figures, exotic flower and leaf designs.

Aurene glass A type of iridescent glass developed by Frederick Carder at the Steuben Glass Works USA.

Auricular, cartilagenous, Dutch grotesque or lobate style A 17th century Dutch decorative style characterized by undulating forms which resemble the ear lobe or cartilage. Its most important development was in silver where it was often combined with fantastic motifs, eg, monsters, dolphins.

Automata Mechanically animated figures. In medieval times they were usually associated with clocks. From the 14th century onwards they were popular as table ornaments.

Baldachino An ornamental canopy projecting over an altar or throne.

Baluster A short pillar with a pear shaped bulge at the base. It is usually one of a series which supports a rail or coping known as a balustrade. The name, baluster is given to similar shapes in many media, eg, table legs, drinking glass stems, vases, candlesticks etc.

Baroque style A heavy and flamboyant style developed in 17th century Italy. Baroque motifs include putti, flowers, fruit, helmets, shields and musical instruments. The style was popular throughout Europe in the late 17th century and early 18th century and was applied to furniture and silver work in particular.

Basse-taille A refined enamelling technique where translucent enamels are applied to sculpted gold or silver reliefs. The different density of the enamel on the high and low areas of the relief produces an effect of light and shade.

Beds By the 18th century the canopy was the dominant feature of the bed. The French gave names to the different sorts of structures.

à la duchesse: the canopy was attached to the wall or ceiling above the head.

à colonnes: the canopy was supported on four wooden pillars.

à la polonnaise: the canopy was in the form of a dome draped with curtains. The framework was curved iron.

Berlin woolwork A type of needlework executed in coloured wools on square meshed canvas. Designs, published in Berlin, were printed on squared paper corresponding to canvas and could thus be copied exactly.

Bezel Part of the setting on a ring which encloses a precious stone. It is also the oblique face of a cut gem.

Biedermeyer style A German decorative style which developed during the 1820's–40's as a reaction to the excessively ornate styles of the 18th century. It is most apparent in furniture which is of simple classical form designed for comfort rather than ostentation.

Birdcage Hinged construction on tables, found particularly during the 18th century, which allows the top to tip vertically or revolve when not in use.

Bocage The background to a porcelain figure or group usually in the form of a small tree or flowering shrub.

Bombé A convex swelling shape very popular in the Rococo period for furniture facades and ceramic and silver forms.

Boso A circular protuberant ornament often richly carved in a leaf or floral design, applied on the surface of an object. In architecture, it is the projection at the intersecting point of vault ribs.

Boulle work Marquetry of tortoiseshell and brass or other metals. The technique was perfected by A. C. Boulle (1642–1732) the most celebrated of Louis XIV furniture makers and designers.

Bun foot A ball foot, flattened at top and bottom which was introduced in the late 17th century.

Bureau à cylinder or roll top desk Desk with the writing and storage area hidden, when not in use, by a cylindrical section which slides back into the body of the desk on opening.

Burr or Burl A diseased growth on the trunk of a tree which, when cut, produces unusual but attractive markings. Wood in this condition, especially from the walnut, elm and yew was very popular for veneering.

Butterfly table A drop leaf table with outward slanting legs which was popular in America from early 18th century. The brackets which supported the raised leaves were butterfly shaped hence the name.

Cabaret A porcelain tea or coffee service complete with matching tray made by many European factories in the 18th century. When it is designed for two people it is called a tête à tête, a solitaire is a set for one.

Cabochon A rounded stone of natural form which has been polished but not cut.

Cabriole leg A curving tall furniture leg inspired by an animal form and terminating in a club, hoof, scroll or claw and ball foot. It was popular during the first half of the 18th century.

Calcareous glaze A glaze incorporating calcium bearing materials which provide the main source of flux.

Calcined flint Flint is a hard siliceous material which is calcined, ie, heated to dispel water and organic impurities and then ground to a fine powder for use in the preparation of bodies and glazes.

Calibration The act of determining the diameter of the bore of a gun or cannon.

Cameo A gem, hardstone or shell carved to form a design in relief.

Cameo glass Ornamental glass composed of two or more different coloured layers, areas of which have been cut away to form a pattern in relief and to reveal the colour contrasts. Developed by the Romans, the technique was revived in the 19th century.

Canapé The French name for a settee or a sofa used in the 18th century.

Cartouche A fanciful scroll ornament used as a border decoration or to surround a panel which bears an inscription coat of arms or emblems. It was a popular device in the Rococo period.

Caryatid A column in the form of a sculptured female figure. Originally an architectural motif it also appears on furniture and other decorative arts.

Celadon A name of French derivation given to Chinese stoneware and porcelain with soft green to grey blue glazes. This colouring was much admired for its resemblance to green jade.

Champlevé enamelling A design is engraved on the surface of the metal and the grooves are filled with enamel. After firing the enamel is polished to the same level as the surrounding metal. The technique has been known since the 6th century B.C.

Chasing Surface modelling of metal with hammer and punches of various shapes. It is widely used along with other decorative techniques.

Chatelaine A set of decorative chains worn at the waist to support keys, trinkets or a watch.

Chinoiseries Western interpretations of Chinese decorative shapes and motifs popular for ornamenting furniture, silver, ceramics etc, in the 17th and 18th centuries.

Churrigueresque style Named after José Churriguera who was the leading exponent of the Spanish Baroque style. It is characterized in furniture by elaborate carving, gilding floral inlay and spiral turning.

Cire-perdu An ancient method of bronze casting where a clay core is covered with a layer of wax which is intricately carved. This is then coated with clay and allowed to dry. The wax is removed by heating and replaced with molten metal. When the metal has cooled the clay is removed leaving a replica of the wax carving in metal.

Claw and ball foot A termination, based on an eagle's claw, for furniture legs which was popular in the 18th century. It is probably an adaptation of the Chinese bronze motif of a dragon's claw clutching a pearl

Cloisonné enamelling Thin metal strips are soldered to the surface of a metal object to form enclosures for different coloured enamels. The tops of the strips remain exposed in the design. It is one of the oldest enamelling techniques.

Cloud band or pattern A motif in carpet design derived from the Chinese symbol of immortality, the chi, which takes the form of variously shaped clouds or bands of clouds.

Coffer A deep sunken panel.

Collet The part of a ring which contains the stone.

Comfit or sweetmeat box A very small box popular in the 17th and 18th centuries for holding sweets or cachous. They were made in a variety of materials and shapes.

Commode The French term for a chest of drawers. It was one of the most fashionable pieces of 18th century French furniture and became an important piece of English furniture in the second half of the 18th century.

Console An ornamental bracket usually made of gilt wood carved in scroll forms. It might support a vase, clock or ornament.

Console table A side table with a bracket support of console form attaching it to the wall. It was a fashionable piece of furniture in the late 17th century and the 18th century and was often made with a matching mirror to hang above.

Copper-plate engraving A method of printing from a plate on which a design has been incised with an engraving tool. Ink is rubbed on to the surface and pressed into the incisions. The surplus is then removed and the plate is ready for printing on dampened paper.

Cornice A projecting decorative moulding, originally a feature on Classical architecture.

Cornucopia An emblem of abundance consisting of a goat's horn overflowing with fruit and flowers. The motif was very popular in the Rococo period and was frequently modelled as an earthenware or porcelain flower holder.

Corsage The bodice of a lady's dress.

Crenellation A pattern with indentations like a battlement.

Cresset A metal vessel for holding oil or grease for light or wood for fuel. It is usually mounted on a rod.

Cresting A medieval ornament, often leaf-shaped which is found on metal-work and also on furniture where it is carved along the top of horizontal members, eg, headboards, picture frames.

Crewelwork A type of embroidery in coloured wools on linen or cotton twill, made mainly for bed furnishings. The patterns were usually floral, of Indian derivation.

Cross-banding Decorative use of thin strips of veneer, cut across the grain, on furniture or panelling.

Curule chair The curule or magistrates of ancient Rome sat on this style of seat which has arms but no back.

Cusp A projecting point in the ornamentation of arches or panels.

Diaper A pattern consisting of repeated small geometrical shapes like lozenges, squares or stars. Sometimes dots are included.

Die stamping A method of shaping small metal objects by pressing them between engraved metal blocks or dies. The process was cheaper than casting or engraving and was used to decorate foot rings of beakers, medals and buttons etc.

Directoire style A French style which developed from the Louis XVI style reaching its peak in the Directoire period 1795–99. It still featured Neo-classical forms and ornament but in a more austere manner.

Distaff The stick which holds the fibres, wool or flax etc from which thread is made in spinning.

Dovetailing A technique of joining two pieces of wood by putting pieces shaped like a wedge or dove's tail spread out (tenons) into like cavities (mortises).

Draw table An extending table with flaps which may be drawn out from beneath the top. Dates from the 16th century.

Ebonized Stained to look like ebony, an expensive jet-black wood.

Empire style The late Neo-classical style developed in France about 1804–30 which reflected the tastes of Napoleon I. Classical forms were mixed with Egyptian ornament, popularized after the Emperor's campaigns, and also Napoleonic motifs, eg, crowns surmounted by the initial N. Chief exponents of the style were Charles Percier and P. Fontaine.

Enamel A vitreous compound which can be coloured by melting with metallic oxides and then fused to a metal surface under heat. It has been used for decorating metal since antiquity. A similar substance is used to decorate ceramics and glass.

Encaustic tile A clay tile inlaid with a design in a different coloured clay. This method was used frequently in the Middle Ages and became popular again in the 19th century.

Encoigneur A free standing corner cupboard. A popular 18th century piece of furniture often made in matching pairs.

Engine turned decoration Decoration applied to ceramics and metals by turning on a lathe. Patterns include chevrons fluting and chequers.

Escapement The mechanism, in clocks and watches, controlling the rate of unwinding of the train and the movement of the hands. It also gives energy to the pendulum or balance.

Escutcheon The metal plate, often highly ornamented, which surrounds the keyhole on a piece of furniture.

Etching The process of creating a pattern on metal or glass by the action of acid. The surface is covered with a resisting layer of varnish and the design is drawn through the coating with a fine tool exposing the surface to acid. It was originally used to decorate armour in the 15th century. The technique was applied to glass about 1670. It has been extensively used as a print making technique since the 16th century.

Etui A small case usually for carrying sewing necessities. It was designed either to be hung on a chatelaine or carried in a pocket.

Felspathic glaze A high temperature glaze for stoneware and porcelain in which felspar is the main flux.

Ferrule A metal ring or cap strengthening the end of a stick or tube. Also a band strengthening or forming a joint.

Filigree Delicate and decorative wirework used for jewelry and open work panels on boxes, baskets etc.

Filigree glass A decorative technique where interlaced threads of white, coloured and gold glass beneath the surface create a delicate tracery effect.

Finial An ornamental projection found on architecture, furniture and also the covers of vessels where it is used as a knob. Various forms are featured, eg, urns, acorns, balls and flowers.

Firedogs Iron appliances, made in pairs to support the logs in a fire. Originally they were shaped as seated hounds but later took various forms often highly ornamented.

Fluting A form of ornament consisting of parallel shallow grooves which are semi-circular in section. They can be arranged vertically or in an oblique or curved pattern.

Fob chain A chain for attaching the watch to clothing used since the 17th century. In the 19th century the popular form held the watch key and seal as well.

Foliate ornament or design Leaf shaped ornament.

Foliot A timekeeping element in earliest clocks which consists of a metal bar pivoted at the centre which swings back and forward at roughly constant intervals. It was replaced by the balance and pendulum.

Frass Refuse left by wood boring insects.

Fresco A method of wall painting in which powdered colours mixed with water are applied to a damp, freshly laid plaster ground. As the colours dry they become integrated with the wall itself.

Fret or key pattern A geometrical repeat pattern of horizontal and vertical straight lines usually set at right angles to each other. It is derived from classical Greek architecture.

Fretwork Fret patterns carved in relief or pierced. In the 19th century the term was used to describe open work patterns in thin wood cut by a fret-saw.

Fusee A spirally grooved cone shaped pulley in clock or watch train to equalize uneven force of spring as it unwinds. Catgut or a chain is used to connect the fusee with the mainstream barrel.

Gadrooning A pattern of parallel convex curves frequently applied as an edging on furniture, metalware, ceramics, glass etc.

Galloon A narrow braid or trimming woven from silk, gold or silver thread.

Garniture de cheminée A set of vases for the decoration of a mantlepiece made for export in China during the late 17th century and 18th century. Usually five vases were made, three baluster shapes and two flared beakers. European porcelain factories made imitations.

Gate-leg table Table with one or two hinged flaps which may be supported on gate like legs which swing out from the central support. Dates from 16th century.

Gesso A composition of plaster of Paris and size which, when applied to furniture and picture frames can be modelled into decorative reliefs then painted and gilded.

Girandole See Sconce

Glastonbury chair A folding oak chair of 16th century design which has an X frame base and a solid back, frequently decoratively carved. The arms run diagonally from the front of the seat to the top corners of the back.

Gnomon The rod, pin or plate which casts the shadow on a sundial.

Goffering iron An iron implement used in the 16th and 17th centuries for crimping fashionable neck ruffs.

Gothic Revival The Gothic style was revived in England in the 18th century for superficial decoration. Gothic motifs were applied to otherwise normal Georgian forms. In the 19th century however, A. W. N. Pugin advocated the correct use of medieval precedents.

Gothic style The Gothic architectural style developed in Europe from the 12th century to 16th century. Characteristic motifs are painted arches, tracery, fabulous beasts, fleur de lys and leaf and vine designs. Its form and ornament were reflected in furniture and other decorative arts.

Grisaille Painting in various tones of grey to depict solid bodies in relief.

Grotesque Decoration composed of human figures, animals, mythical beasts with entwined foliage and arabesques. It was derived from decorations in Roman subterranean ruins or 'grottes' which were rediscovered in the early 16th century, hence the name.

Guéridon A decorative candle stand or small table designed to hold a candelabrum. It generally consists of a circular tray supported by a column or the more exotic form, a Moor or Negro.

Guilloche A repetitive pattern of two or more interlaced bands widely used in architecture, furniture and metal work.

Halberd A combined spear and battle axe.

Hippocamp A seahorse, a type of small fish with a head and neck similar to those of a horse.

Hurdy-gurdy A stringed musical instrument with a mechanical bow known from the 11th century. Initially it was used in churches but after the 13th century it became smaller and was adopted as a folk instrument.

Husk ornament A stylized representation of a corn husk much used as a decorative motif on furniture and metalwork of the Neo classical period.

Hygrometer An instrument for measuring moisture in the air.

Hygroscopic Sensitive to moisture.

Iconoclasm The act of destroying images.

Inlay A decorative technique used on furniture and other wooden objects, in which pieces of coloured wood or other materials like ivory or mother of pearl are laid into chiselled out areas of the wood ground to form a pattern.

Intaglio The opposite of cameo, the design being cut into the surface of gemstones or glass.

Intarsia An Italian term for inlay usually of a geometric or pictorial nature, eg, architectural perspectives and still life subjects.

Istoratio An Italian term meaning 'to tell a story' which is applied to Italian majolica decoration of a narrative nature.

Japanning Western imitation of Oriental lacquering. True oriental lacquer ingredients were not available in the west so substitutes like gum lac and shell lac were used. The technique became popular in late 17th century England for the decoration of furniture, trays and small boxes, usually in a Chinoiserie style.

Japonisme A 19th century style inspired by Japanese art which had been introduced to the West after the opening of Japan in the 1850's.

Klismos A classical Greek chair type much favoured during the Neo-classical period. The front legs curve forwards and the back ones, backwards. The back has a concave top rail attached to verticals.

Knop A decorative swelling on the stem of a goblet or glass; also a decorative feature at the end of spoon handles. A variety of forms are used including acorn, ball, baluster etc.

Lambrequin A name originally used for pendant draperies, it is also applied to pendant lace-like ornament on ceramics.

Lapidary One who is skilled in the cutting, polishing and engraving of precious stones.

Latten A metallic alloy of copper and zinc which has the appearance of brass. The term is also often applied to brass.

Lattice A network of wood or metal formed by strips or bars crossing each other diagonally.

Lead silicate Lead oxide fused with silica to form a glaze and thereby overcoming the toxic nature of the lead.

Linenfold Carved decoration which resembles linen arranged in stylized vertical folds. It was much used by 15th century wood-carvers for the decoration of furniture and panelling.

Lithography A printing process invented in 1798 based on the principle that water repels grease. A design is drawn with greasy chalk on a slab or stone or a sheet of zinc. The ink, also greasy is rolled on and will only adhere to the greasy areas. The image is then transferred to paper.

Louis XV style The French version of the Rococo style, which is associated with the reign of Louis XV (1715–74) as it reached its peak of popularity during that period.

Louis XVI style The French style current during Louis XVI reign (1774–92) when Rococo exuberance was being replaced by a restrained Neo-classical style.

Majolica A term originating in Italy in the 14th century which referred to the Italian tin-glazed earthenware which was made in like manner to the Hispano-Moresque wares imported from Majorca, hence the name. It is sometimes applied to all European tin-glazed earthenware.

Mannerist style Primarily a court style, Mannerism developed from the Renaissance style in the 16th century. It is characterized by fanciful treatment of Renaissance motifs.

Marlborough leg A square leg used on furniture from the mid-18th century onwards. It can be straight or tapering and sometimes has a plinth foot.

Marquetry A surface decoration for furniture where shaped veneers of wood or other materials like ivory or mother of pearl, are arranged in a design. If the pattern is geometrical it is called Parquetry.

Merese Flat, disc shaped knob in the stem of a drinking glass.

Mezzatint A technique of engraving in which the plate is roughened all over and then smoothed out in areas according to the required design. The roughest parts retain the most ink. Subtle gradations of tone can be achieved by this method.

Mihrab A prayer niche in a mosque usually designed with a pointed arch. It is used as a decorative motif on the centre of prayer rugs and Islamic tiles.

Mille fleur tapestries A group of tapestries where the backdrop to the figure groups is an arrangement of numerous flowers, small animals and birds. They were woven in France in the late 15th and 16th centuries.

Monstrance A glass or crystal cylinder set into a gold or silver structure in which the Host is displayed in religious ceremonies.

Moresque A term used generally to describe any ornamental design of a Moorish or Arabian nature.

Mortar A vessel in which foodstuffs or chemicals can be pounded with a pestle. It was usually made of cast bronze, bell metal and sometimes marble. It was in common use throughout Europe from the 14th century–18th century.

Mosaic The art of arranging coloured marble, glass and other suitable materials in a pattern or picture and securing them in a bed of cement.

Nankin porcelain Blue and white Chinese porcelain made for the export market at Ching tê chên.

Necessaire A portable box for toilet or household paraphernalia like cutlery, sewing needs etc. They varied greatly in size and decorative finish.

Neo-classical style A style inspired by decorative motifs of classical Greece and Rome which developed in mid-18th century France after excavations at Pompeii and Herculaneum and soon spread throughout Europe and America. Classical motifs were treated in a light delicate manner.

Niello The process of engraving metal and filling the incisions with a black coloured alloy of silver and other metals.

Objects of vertu A term for small luxury items intricately worked in gold, silver, enamel, gems, glass, lacquer, etc. Articles described thus include snuff boxes, étuis, necessaires, chatelaines, fob seals, scent bottles etc.

Ogee A double continuous curve in cross section concave below convex above. It is used as a moulding for furniture and silver.

Ogival arch A pointed arch.

Ormolu Brass or bronze which has been gilded and used to make decorative objects, especially mounts for furniture.

Paktong An alloy of copper, zinc and nickel which looks like yellow tinged silver. It was often used by Chinese furniture makers for hinges etc.

Palladian style An architectural style based on strict classical principles defined by the 16th century Venetian architect Andrea Palladio. It was introduced into England in the 17th century by Inigo Jones. Later furniture designers adopted the style, producing massive pieces embellished with antique ornament.

Pâpier maché A material, thought to be of Oriental origin made from pulped paper or whole sheets of paper mixed with chalk size and sand. It appeared in Europe in the 17th century where it was moulded into boxes, trays and furniture. When baked it provided an excellent surface for japanning and inlay.

Parcel Gilt Furniture or silver gilded in parts.

Parian Ware Hand paste porcelain with a fine grain, usually unglazed, which resembles marble. It was first produced in 1844 at the Copeland factory and was used chiefly to make figures, often after the work of famous contemporary sculptors. Tableware was also made.

Parquetry See Marquetry.

Parure A set of matching jewelry which consisted usually of a brooch, a necklace, earrings and a bracelet.

Pastille burner A small container for burning pastilles, an aromatic substance mixed with charcoal used to diffuse a pleasant odour in the room. They were made in silver pottery and porcelain in a variety of shapes.

Patera A low relief circular or oval ornament usually in the form of an acanthus or flower which was much used on Neo-classical furniture and silver.

Patina The green surface on bronze caused by oxidation. The term is also used generally to describe the surface texture of old furniture and silver.

Pediment The triangular low pitched gable above the portico of a classical temple. It became a popular finish for the tops of pieces of furniture often diverging from the basic triangular shape, extra scrolls and mouldings being applied, eg, swan neck, which is a broken pediment with sides in the form of sloping C scrolls.

Pelican in her Piety The motif of a pelican making a wound in its breast to produce blood to nourish its young. It became a symbol of Christ's sacrifice on the cross.

Pembroke table A drop leaf table with bracket supports at both ends. It was made from the mid-18th century and was possibly named after a Countess of Pembroke who may have ordered the first one.

Petit-Point Open mesh material such as canvas which is entirely covered in wool or silk embroidery. Tent stitch is generally used, a short slanting stitch done in parallel lines from left to right. This needlework was used mostly for chair and cushion covers.

Pie-crust table A tea table popular in the 18th century and late 19th century which has a scalloped top like the edge of a piecrust, supported on a tripod base. It is usually made of mahogany.

Pier glass A tall narrow mirror which was hung in the wall spaces, between the windows, known as piers. It was a popular form of mirror in the 18th century.

Pietre dure An Italian term for hard or semi-precious stones fashioned into decorative objects. In the 16th century a popular technique was to work the stones into mosaics for the surfaces of tables or altar fronts.

Pilaster A shallow pier or rectangular column. It is often used as a motif on furniture.

Pique work Tortoiseshell or ivory inlaid with gold or silver-wire or studs usually fashioned into a variety of small articles, eg, snuff boxes.

Plaquette A medallion of square or oblong format made of bronze lead or silver used to ornament furniture and household implements. They were decorated with religious, historical or mythological scenes and were made throughout Europe from the 15th century.

Plique á jour enamelling A technique where unbacked metal cells are filled with translucent enamel so that light can shine through producing a stained glass window effect.

Porcelain A white highly vitrified and translucent ceramic substance discovered in China and made later in Europe during the 18th century. Hard paste 'true porcelain' is made from china clay (kaolin) and petuntse. Soft paste varieties were created in Europe during attempts to copy true porcelain. Several materials were used but the most usual were white clay and ground glass.

Porringer A small eating or drinking bowl with one or two handles and with or without a lid. It was generally made of pewter or silver and was a popular form from the 17th century–19th century.

Posset pot A drinking vessel for posset which is hot milk curdled with wine or ale and seasoned with spices. It was made in either pottery or glass in the 17th century and 18th century.

Prunt A blob of molten glass modelled into various forms, in particular a raspberry or a lion mask, and applied to a glass vessel for decorative effect.

Purfling An inlaid ornamental border on the edges of stringed instruments.

Putti Winged infants commonly found in Renaissance and Baroque art. They feature as angels in religious works and attendants of Cupid in secular subjects.

Quincunx An arrangement of five objects, one at each of the four corners of a square or rectangle, the other at its centre.

Régence style The French style which was popular around the time of Louis XV regency (1715–23). The classical motifs of the preceding Baroque style were given a lighter more elegant treatment, heralding the Rococo style. Subject matter became more romantic.

Regency style The predominant style in England from the 1790's until the 1840's. A period longer than George, Prince of Wales' regency (1811–20). It was a reaction to the elegant Adam style which relied on antique motifs for decoration but not antique forms. Regency furniture copied antique forms, the result being solid and heavy. Regency silver was massive and sculptural. The chief exponent was C. H. Tatham.

Renaissance style A style influenced by classical ideals and models which emerged in Italy during the 14th century–16th century and spread throughout Europe. Decorative motifs were derived mainly from Roman architecture and sarcophagi, eg, columns and capitals, draped figures, medallions, urns and putti.

Repoussé A metalwork technique where the design is hammered out from the back of a thin sheet of metal which is supported on a bed of pitch or wax. The front surface is then worked to sharpen the detail.

Reredos The decorative screen covering the wall at the back of the altar.

Rhomb Diamond or lozenge shape.

Rinceau A French name for ornamental foliage, usually acanthus leaves, which has been moulded, carved or painted.

Rocaille An ornament much favoured in the Rococo period composed of scroll, foliage and shell shapes.

Rococo style Decorative curvilinear style characterized by delicate asymmetrical motifs based mainly on rock, shell and floral forms. The style evolved in France early in the 18th century and spread rapidly throughout Europe and England where it reached its peak 1750–70 and America 1760–80.

Rollwork See Strapwork.

Sampler An embroidered panel originally made as a source of reference for various stitches and patterns. Later it was an exercise sheet for a young embroidress.

Sans-serif A type face without fine strokes or serifs at the termination of lines.

Scagliola A material, used to imitate marble, which consists of marble chips, isinglass, plaster of Paris and colouring substances. It was used originally for floors, columns and other architectural features, and later also for table tops.

Sconce An ornamental bracket candlestick for one or more candles attached to the wall with a polished back plate or mirror to reflect the light. Highly elaborate Rococo sconces are often called girandoles.

Sea weed marquetry The name given to English marquetry decoration of the 17th century and 18th century where the grain of the wood is reminiscent of sea weed.

Secrétaire French desk which dates from the 18th century.

Sèvres French national porcelain factory which led European ceramic fashions from 1760–1815. It catered mostly for the luxury trade.

Sgraffito A method of decorating pottery by scratching a design through a coating of slip in order to reveal the contrasting body underneath.

Shagreen A type of untanned leather with an artificially granulated surface made from the hide of a horse, ass or camel. Also the rough skin of a shark or sting-ray ground flat to make a granulated pattern. The substance has been used since the 17th century to cover small boxes.

Singerie Decoration consisting of monkeys often dressed in human clothes and aping human occupations and sports. The motif was most popular in the 18th century and embraced all the decorative arts and painting.

Slip Fine clay and water mixed to the consistency of cream and used either for the decoration or casting of pottery.

Stijl, De A Dutch magazine founded by Theo van Doesteeng and Piet Mondrian in 1917, devoted to the principles of Neo-Plasticism a style of geometric abstraction. The name was applied to the group of artists and architects associated with the periodical. The style can be characterized by the use of austere lines, flat surfaces and primary colours.

Strapwork or Rollwork An ornamental pattern consisting of interlacing bands or straps reminiscent of cut leather or carved fretwork. It was a popular design in Northern Europe in the late 16th century and early 17th century. Later it became a Chippendale motif.

Stucco A mixture of plaster or cement suitable for coating wall and ceiling surfaces and moulding into architectural decorations.

Stumpwork A form of needlework where much of the ornament is in relief having been worked over shaped blocks of wood or padding.

Spandrel The space between an arch or circle and the surrounding rectangle or square. On prayer rugs it is the area above the mihrals.

Spindle A slim turned shaft of either constant width or with tapering ends much used in chair backs.

Stackfreed A device in early watches which roughly equalizes the decrease in power of the spring as it unwinds. It consists of a curved spring pressing against a shaped cam attached to the mainspring. It was replaced by the more efficient fusee.

Stipple engraving A decorative glass technique where the design consists of tiny dots of varying density which have been applied to the surface by a diamond point, struck lightly against the glass.

Stretchers Strengthening rails which run horizontally between the legs of chairs, tables etc. A variety of designs and shapes were employed, sometimes plain, sometimes highly decorative.

Sucket fork An implement used for eating fruit which has a spoon at one end and a two or three pronged fork at the other.

Tambour desk A desk with a roll top made of a series of narrow strips of wood glued side by side to a canvas backing.

Tambour work A type of chain stitch which was embroidered on fabric stretched over a round frame known as a tambour. It was popular in England and France during the late 18th and 19th centuries.

Tatting A delicate knotted lace made with fine linen or cotton thread wound on a small shuttle.

Tazza A drinking vessel with a wide, shallow circular bowl mounted on a foot. The form was popular throughout Europe in the 16th and 17th centuries.

Tesselated tiles Small square tiles arranged in a chequered pattern.

Thumble A censer, a vessel in which incense is burnt.

Transfer printing A method of decorating ceramics by taking a print on transfer paper from an engraved copper plate and transferring the image from the paper to the ceramic body either before or after glazing.

Trembleuse A French name for a saucer which has a raised ring to hold the cup.

Trivet An iron tripod stand for holding cooking vessels by the fire. The term is also used generally to cover many types of stand.

Trompe l'oeil The use of pictorial techniques to deceive the eye as to the reality of the objects represented.

Turkey work The name given to English knotted pile fabrics made in the same way as Turkish and other Oriental pile fabrics. The technique was popular in the 17th and 18th centuries principally for upholstery and cushions.

Turning A method of carving furniture members by revolving the wood on a lathe and shaping with a chisel or some other instrument. There are various kinds of turning – baluster, bead and reel, bobbin, spiral and ball which usually take their name from their resemblance to these forms.

Vandykes A border ornamentation of points and indentations as seen in paintings by the Flemish painter Sir Anthony Van Dyck (1599–1641).

Vase splat The central, vertical member of a chair back shaped to form a silhouette of a vase.

Veneer and Veneering A veneer is a thin sheet of fine wood. In veneering, thin sheets of expensive wood like mahogany or rosewood are used to cover furniture made of coarser wood.

Verre églomisé Glass decorated on the back with a layer of engraved gold. The design sometimes pictorial, sometimes decorative, is protected by the addition of another layer of glass.

Vignette The name for a running ornament of vine leaves and tendrils. Also, a small ornamental design not enclosed within a definite border. In printing a vignette is often used as a heading or tail piece.

Vitruvian scroll A classical ornament of convoluted scrolls resembling waves. It was used in 18th century architecture and furniture and as a border decoration on silver.

Volute The spiral scroll on the capital of an Ionic column. The motif was later used to decorate silver, furniture etc.

Wainscot Term used in England and America for solid wooden panelling or furniture built of solid wood.

Warp In weaving, threads stretched lengthwise in a loom to be crossed by the weft threads.

Willow Pattern A chinoiserie design incorporating a pagoda, a willow tree, two flying birds and a bridge with people on it. Many speculations have been made about the significance, if any, of the scene. The pattern was used in England from the late 18th century onwards to decorate blue transfer-printed ceramics.

Windsor chair A traditional English chair which has a spindle back dowelled into a shaped wooden seat. Early examples were made by primitive assembly line production, each part shaped from different suitable woods. They were in general use in the 17th century but since the late 18th century they were considered to be rustic furniture.

Wood-block printing A printing method using a block of wood on which a design has been cut in relief.

X Chair A chair supported on an X-shaped frame, a popular form in the medieval period.

Biography

Adam, Robert (1728–92) British Neo-classical architect and designer of applied arts who emphasized unity of conception in interior decoration. The Adam style created in partnership with his brother, James, spread to Europe and America. It is characterized by classical motifs and forms used in an elegant, delicate and novel manner. His major architectural venture was The Adelphi, an area of houses between the Strand and the Thames started in 1768.

Affleck, Thomas (1740–95) An outstanding Philadelphia cabinet maker. He was born in Scotland and emigrated to America in 1763. He worked primarily in the Queen Anne and early Chippendale styles and was known for his well-proportioned highboys, lowboys and chairs.

Ashbee, Charles Robert (1863–1942) English architect, designer and writer who became the leader of the Arts and Crafts movement. His work was exhibited widely in Britain and abroad. His furniture design was influenced by William Morris while his metalwork and jewelry are in an Art Nouveau style, though he would have denied any association with the movement. In 1909 he published *Modern English Silverwork* and in 1911 he wrote an introduction to the work of Frank Lloyd Wright, the American architect whom he greatly admired.

Bakst, Leon (1886–1925) Russian painter, stage and costume designer whose ballet decors created a sensation between 1910 and 1912. His exciting use of oriental and 19th century Persian art in his designs had a great impact on the decorative arts in Europe.

Belter, John H An eminent New York cabinet maker who was working from c.1840–60. He designed very ornate furniture in the High Victorian taste.

Bennet, E & W In 1846 Edwin Bennet started a pottery in Baltimore with his brother William and produced both useful and decorative ware. Of note are pitchers made in various forms which derived their name from the relief decoration such as stag, hunt pitcher, and hound handle pitcher.

Boucher, François (1703–70) French court painter in the Rococo style whose decorative, romantic and pastoral compositions greatly influenced the decorative arts in Europe. They were painted on and modelled in porcelain, copied in marquetry and printed on textiles. He was directly involved in the decorative arts when he was a designer at the Beauvais then the Gobelins tapestry factories.

Burges, William (1827–81) English architect and designer working in a Gothic Revival style. His approach reveals more of a feeling for fantasy and colour than his contemporaries whose designs were influenced by archeological accuracy.

Burgkmair, Hans the elder (1473–1531) German painter and designer of woodcuts who formed his style by contact with Venetian art. His woodcuts show the influence of Durer in their sensitive and expressive use of line and tone.

Burne-Jones, Edward (1833–98) English painter and designer who produced many tapestry and stained glass designs for William Morris' firm. His subject matter was literary and romantic executed in a pre-Raphaelite style. He also designed furniture in the Gothic Revival style.

Callot, Jaques (1592/3–1635) French engraver who made many etchings of fairs, festivals, courtiers, hunchbacks, etc, combining a late Mannerist style with witty and acute observation.

Cellini, Benevenuto (1500–71) Important Italian Mannerist sculptor and goldsmith whose celebrated autobiography *The Life of Benvenuto Cellini Written by Himself* gives us insight into the life of an artist in the 16th century. It also describes the many pieces he made in gold but only one survives – an exquisitely modelled salt cellar (now in the Kunsthistorisches Museum, Vienna) of gold enriched with enamel, consisting of many figures in elegant postures.

Chippendale, Thomas (1718–19) Well known furniture maker whose workshop undertook the complete furnishing and decoration of large houses. He published *The Gentleman* and *Cabinet Maker's Director* (1754, 1755 and additional plates in 1762) which was the first comprehensive book of furniture designs. Most of the designs are in a fanciful Rococo manner with Neo-Gothic and chinoiserie motifs. His finest furniture however was made in the Neo-classical style.

Cogswell, John (1760–1818) Leading furniture maker working in Boston, USA. His fine bombé shaped pieces in the American Rococo style are particularly notable.

Cole, Sir Henry (1808–82) A designer and writer dedicated to improving industrial design and public taste in Britain. He founded 'Summerly's Art Manufactures' (1847–50) and commissioned painters and sculptors to design household articles to be produced by the large manufacturers. He was an organizer of the Great Exhibition in 1851 and was the first director of the South Kensington Museum now the Victoria and Albert Museum.

Coney, John (1655–1722) Early New England silversmith working in the 17th Century English style. Many fine pieces of his work survive mostly drinking vessels and sweetmeat boxes. He was also a skilled engraver and is thought to have worked the plates from which the first American bank notes were printed.

Crane, Walter (1845–1915) English painter, book illustrator and designer of textiles, wallpapers and pottery. His style was influenced by William Morris and Art Nouveau. He was the leading propagandist of the Arts and Crafts Movement.

Davis, Alexander Jackson (1803–92) A leading American architect who worked in the Greek Revival and Neo-Gothic style. He designed some of the best Neo-Gothic furniture produced in America in the 1830s and 40s.

Dresser, Christopher (1834–1904) English designer and writer on the decorative arts who worked in close co-operation with industry unlike his contemporary, William Morris. He designed wallpaper, furniture, pottery, glass, textiles and metalwork. Most of his work reflects his great interest in botany and Japanese art but his designs for silver were ahead of their time using functional, undecorated geometrical forms. His publications include *Botany as adapted to the Arts and Art Manufactures* and *Principles of Design*.

Duche, Andrew (1709–78) A potter from Savannah, Georgia who is credited with the early discovery of porcelain predating any documented English porcelain. He visited England to sell his discovery and is thought to have made contact first with the Bow porcelain factory who patented a recipe in 1744. On his return to America he amassed quite a fortune, presumably from the success of his discovery.

Fabergé, Peter Carl (1846–1920) Russian goldsmith and jeweller who was the director of the leading firm of goldsmiths in St Petersburg, receiving the Imperial appointment in 1881. Fabergé designed the most important pieces like the intricately worked Easter eggs given as royal gifts. French 18th century design supplied many of the decorative motifs for their varied range of products. Later work was influenced by the Art Nouveau style. The concern was nationalized after the revolution.

Faris, William (1728–1804) He began his career as a clockmaker but turned to silversmithing after 1768. It is thought he was a merchant rather than a craftsman and is known mainly on account of his diaries which are informative about the life of an 18th century silversmith, rather than the products of his workshop, only a few of which are known.

Flaxman, John (1755–1826) Draughtsman, sculptor and designer in the Neo-classical style. He worked as a modeller for Josiah Wedgwood producing elegant jasper and basaltes ware reliefs and figures. He also designed silver both domestic and presentation pieces which were executed by Paul Starr. He studied in Rome (1787–94) financed by Wedgwood and afterwards worked mainly as a marble sculptor.

Fragonard, Jean Honoré (1732–1806) French painter, pupil of Boucher whose work reflects the taste for frivolity and gallantry in the mid-18th century. He first exhibited historical subjects then more intimate scenes but he is chiefly known for his small erotic canvases.

Graf, Urs (c1485–1527/8) Swiss draughtsman, goldsmith and engraver. He produced numerous designs for stained glass, woodcuts and gold pieces. He is also noted for his drawings of mercenaries, peasants and ladies of easy virtue.

Grueby Faience Co. William H. Grueby set up this company in 1894 to produce tiles and plaques in many fashionable styles. From 1898 he made his best known ware, vases of sculptural form with relief leaf patterns and decorated with subtle matt glazes showing the influence of the French potters Delaherene and Chaplet. His wares were favourably reviewed and popular with the public but the business was never successful financially and was forced to close in 1908.

Holbein, Hans the younger (1498–1543) Henry VIII's court painter from Germany who also designed costumes, gold and silver ware, weapons, jewelry and stained glass. He worked in an elabroate Renaissance style. Many of his designs survive but only one actual piece, a rock crystal bowl in an intricately enamelled and jewelled gold setting.

Kauffman, Angelica (1741–1807) Swiss decorative painter and portraitist. Her allegorical and historical subject matter was painted in the Neo-classical style. Her work was widely engraved and copied on porcelain. She often collaborated with Robert Adam on house decoration.

Lalique, René (1860–1945) French jeweller and glass maker who worked in an Art Nouveau style. In his jewelry he used asymmetric patterns and Art Nouveau motifs. After 1902 he worked with clear crystal glass engraving it with frosted patterns of figures, flowers and animals. He designed scent-bottles, vases, statuettes, panels for furniture etc.

Linnel, John (d 1796) Accomplished English cabinet maker, furniture designer and carver who worked in the Palladian, Rococo and Neo-classical styles.

Mackintosh, Charles Rennie (1868–1928) Scottish architect and designer, an influential figure in the European Art Nouveau movement and a pioneer of 20th century architectural design. His buildings, the most revolutionary being Glasgow School of Art, are boldly geometrical with little ornament. His interior decoration and furniture avoided the exaggerated forms of European Art Nouveau and are based on simple combinations of straight lines and gentle curves.

Meeks, Joseph & Sons A leading firm of cabinetmakers working in New York from 1796 to 1968 whose furniture was distributed throughout the U.S.A. They made pieces in the English Regency style and also in the Gothic Revival style when that was in vogue in the 1840s. Their later furniture shows a Neo-Rococo influence.

Mondrian, Piet (1872–1944) Dutch painter who worked in a geometrical abstract style. His mature paintings were arrangements of horizontal and vertical lines marking rectangles of primary colours with black, white and grey. He had a profound influence on art and taste of the 1930's.

Morris, William (1834–96) English designer, poet and social theorist who applied himself to reforming the applied arts advocating a rejection of machine made form and a return to craftsmanship. He founded a firm Morris, Marshall, Faulkner & Co., reorganized in 1875 as Morris & Co. where he and his fellow craftsmen designed and executed wallpapers, stained glass, textiles and furniture. He created numerous highly original patterns based on a study of natural forms and historical designs. In 1890 he founded the Kelmscot Press for the production of exquisitely printed books.

Phyfe, Duncan (1768–1854) American cabinet maker, initially from Scotland. He worked in the fashionable styles of the 19th century namely the Sheraton, Directoire and Empire styles. His best work is in mahogany, graceful in form with fine decorative detail.

Pugin, Augustus Welby Northmore (1812–52) English architect and designer of furniture, silver, textiles, stained glass and jewelry. He was a propagandist for the Gothic revival which had its first impetus in his book *Contrasts* (1836) where he advocates Gothic as a truly Christian style. Other publications include *Gothic Furniture in the style of the 15th century* (1835) and *The True Principle of Painted or Christian Architecture* (1841).

Randolph, Benjamin A Philadelphia cabinet maker working around 1762–92. He was a very skilful carver and produced some very fine furniture in the Chippendale style.

Roux, Alexandre (1837–81) Furniture maker from France who operated a successful business in New York. He worked in a variety of styles, Gothic, Elizabethan, French Renaissance, Rococo, Louis XVI and Grecian, according to the current vogue.

Sargent, John Singer (1856–1925) American portrait painter who lived in London and painted fashionable society in Edwardian and Georgian times. He frequently visited the USA and painted large scale works in Boston Public Library (1890) and the Museum of Fine Arts (1916–25)

Seymour, John (1738–1818) Leading furniture maker who learnt his craft in England before emigrating to Boston. His designs were strongly influenced by the design books of Hepplewhite and Sheraton. His furniture is noted for its fine finish and rich patterned veneers.

Syng, Philip (1703–89) Son of an Irish goldsmith, he emigrated with his family to Annapolis in 1714. He continued the business which his father had started in Philadelphia and became one of the leading silversmiths of his day. His few surviving pieces are in early to mid-18th century English taste with delicate Rococo decorations. His most famous work is a standish which was used for the signing of the Declaration of Independence in 1776.

Tassie, James (1735–99) Tassie was renowned for his process for effectively reproducing antique cameos. He developed a vitreous paste which was pressed into moulds after wax casts of the originals. Josiah Wedgwood bought many casts from 1770 onwards. In 1775 he published *A Catalogue of Impressions in Sulpher of Antique and Modern Gems*. After his death his nephew William Tassie continued to make the reproductions.

Tatham, Charles Heathcote (1772–1842) English architect and designer, whose study and archeologically accurate drawings of the antiques made in Rome 1794–7, had a profound influence on the formation of the Regency style. He published etchings of Roman architectural ornament and also *Designs for Ornamental Plate* which became a source book for decorative artists.

Teniers, David the Younger (1610–90) Flemish court painter renowned for his peasant scenes and rustic landscapes which were widely reproduced on tapestries and also in miniature on small boxes and porcelain.

Townsend-Goddard family Two American families of furniture makers united through marriage. Twenty members of these families spanning three generations were involved in furniture making in a variety of fashionable styles. e.g. Queen Anne, American Chippendale and Neo-classical styles.

Tucker, William Ellis In 1825/26 Tucker started a pottery in Philadelphia to produce hard-paste porcelain. Several workers were employed from Europe and many wares were produced in the Sèvres style.

Watteau, Jean Antoine (1684–1721) French 18th century painter who influenced early Rococo decorative arts mainly through engravings of his work published after his death. His subjects consisted of grotesques, widely reproduced on tapestries, and fete galantes, scenes of dalliance in park settings which served as models for porcelain statuettes and painting on porcelain.

Wedgwood, Josiah (1730–95) English potter and industrialist who enjoyed an international reputation unusual in the 18th century. His success can be attributed to a combination of artistic sense, technical knowledge and a flair for business. His major productions were ornamental and tablewares inspired by Neo-classical designs. He developed new ceramic bodies Jasper ware, Bassaltes ware and the most influential, a high quality cream coloured earthenware which competed with porcelain.

Weller, Samuel (1850–1925) Weller was producing hand thrown wares in Zanesville,Ohio where he ran an art pottery in addition to his commercial manufactory. One of his notable artists was a Frenchman, J. Sicard, who finished his vases in an iridescent glaze similar to Tiffany glass in effect.

Whistler, James Abbott McNeil (1834–1903) American born painter and etcher who worked mainly in England. His mature style in the 1870's which distills Japanese and realist elements into a harmonious relationship of tone and colour, had an influence on decorative arts. His own work as a decorative artist, anticipated aspects of the Art Nouveau style especially in his use of elongated forms. The Peacock room created for E. R. Leyland is a notable example.

Wright, Frank Lloyd (1867–1959) Internationally famous American architect who developed a highly personal style of architecture. His Prairie Houses, low built rugged buildings with spacious interior units, influenced American domestic architecture for over half a century. He believed that the whole building should be conceived as an integral unit and consequently designed furniture, stained glass and metal fittings for his interiors. Amongst his most revolutionary achievements in large scale building are the Midway Gardens, Chicago, the S.C. Johnson Building, Wisconsin and the Guggenheim Museum, New York.

Museums & collections

The following list of museums and collections have been listed alphabetically under town or city. The list is obviously highly selective, and has generally been limited to those museums which contain collections covering the main fields of antiques.

Where specialist museums have been included, their specialization is either apparent in their title, e.g. the Buten Museum of Wedgwood, or has been given below their name.

Adelaide, Australia
Art Gallery of South Australia
North Terrace, Adelaide, South Australia

Amsterdam, Holland
Rijksmuseum
Stadhouderskade 42, Amsterdam

Athens, Greece
Benaki Museum
1 Odos Koumbari, Athens

Auckland, New Zealand
Auckland City Art Gallery
Kitchener Street, Auckland

Bangkok, Thailand
National Museum, Bangkok

Barlaston, Great Britain
Wedgwood Museum
Barlaston, Stoke-on-Trent, Staffordshire

Bath, Great Britain
Museum of Costume
Assembly Rooms, Bath, Avon

Bath, Great Britain
American Museum in Britain
Claverton Manor, nr Bath, Avon

Bedford, Great Britain
Cecil Higgins Museum
Castle Close, Bedford

Belgrade, Yugoslavia
National Museum
Republike Sq, Belgrade

Berlin (East), German Democratic Republic
Bode Museum
Monbijoubrucke am Kupfergraben, Berlin

Berlin (West), German Federal Republic
Charlottenburg Palace Museums
Schloss Strasse 70, D-1 Berlin

Berlin (West), German Federal Republic
Dahlem Museum
Arnimallee 23/27, D-1 Berlin

Birmingham, Great Britain
City Museum and Art Gallery
Congreve Street, Birmingham B33

Boston, United States of America
Fine Arts Museum
479 Huntington Ave, Boston, Mass

Brighton, Great Britain
Museum & Art Gallery
Church Street, Brighton, East Sussex

Bristol, Great Britain
Bristol Art Gallery
Queen's Road, Bristol BS8 1RL

Bristol, United States of America
American Clock & Watch Museum
Bristol, Conn

Brunswick, German Federal Republic
Herzog Anton Ulrich Museum
33 Braunschweig, Museumstrasse 1

Brussels, Belgium
Royal Museums of Art & History
Ave des Nreviens, Brussels 4

Budapest, Hungary
Francis Hopp Museum of Eastern Asiatic Arts
Nepkoztarsasag u. 103, Budapest 6

Budapest, Hungary
Hungarian National Museum
Muzeum krt 14016, Budapest 8

Cambridge, Great Britain
Fitzwilliam Museum
Trumpington Street, Cambridge

Cambridge, United States of America
Fogg Art Museum
Harvard University, Cambridge, Mass

Cape Town, South Africa
South African National Gallery
Government Avenue, Cape Town

Cardiff, Great Britain
National Museum of Wales
Cardiff, South Glamorgan

Chantilly, France
Conde Museum
Chateau de Chantilly, Chantilly, Oise

Chicago, United States of America
Art Institute
Michigan Avenue, Chicago, Illinois

Cincinnati, United States of America
Art Museum
Cincinnati, Ohio

Cleveland, United States of America
Museum of Art
11150 East Boulevard, Cleveland, Ohio

Copenhagen, Denmark
Rosenberg Castle Museum
Ostervoldegade 4a, 1350 Copenhagen

Copenhagen, Denmark
National Museum

Copenhagen, Denmark
Kunstindustrimuseet

Corning, United States of America
Corning Glass Museum
Corning, New York

Cracow, Poland
Wawelu Castle State Art Collections
Crakow

Darmstadt, German Federal Republic
Hessisches Landes Museum

Dearborn, United States of America
Henry Ford Museum

Detroit, United States of America
Institute of Fine Arts
5200 Woodward, Detroit, Michigan

Dresden, German Democratic Republic
Porzellan Galerie

Dublin, Eire
National Museum of Ireland
Merrion Square, Dublin

Dusseldorf, German Federal Republic
Art Museum
4 Dusseldorf-Nord, Ehrenhof 5

Edinburgh, Great Britain
Royal Scottish Museum
Chambers Street, Edinburgh EH1 1JF

Faenza, Italy
National Ceramic Museum

Florence, Italy
Bargello National Museum
via del proconsolo 4, Florence

Florence, Italy
Pitti Gallery
Piazza Pitti, Florence

Glasgow, Great Britain
Art Gallery & Museum
Kelvingrove, Glasgow

Haarlem, Holland
Frans Hals Museum
Groot Heiligland 62, Haarlem

Hamburg, German Federal Republic
Museum fur Kunst und Gewerbe

Hartford, United States of America
600 Main Street, Hartford, Conn

Houston, United States of America
Bayou Bend Collection of Americana
1 Westcott Street, Houston, Texas

Istanbul, Turkey
Topkapi Palace Museum

Jablonc, Czechoslovakia
Museum of Glass

Johannesburg, South Africa
Art Gallery
Joubert Park, Johannesburg

Kansas City, United States of America
William Rockhill Nelson Collection
4525 Oak Street, Kansas City

Leeds, Great Britain
Temple Newsam House

Leningrad, USSR
Hermitage Museum
Leningrad D-65

Lisbon, Portugal
Gulbenkian Foundation
Calouste Gulbenkian Park, Avenida Berne,
Lisbon

Liverpool, Great Britain
Merseyside County Museums
William Brown Street, Liverpool 3

London, Great Britain
Bethnal Green Museum, Museum of Childhood
London, E8

389

London, Great Britain
British Museum
Great Russell Street, London WC1

London, Great Britain
Clockmakers' Company Collection
Guildhall, London EC2

London, Great Britain
London Museum

London, Great Britain
Percival David Foundation of Chinese Art
53 Gordon Sq, London WC1

London, Great Britain
Science Museum
South Kensington, London SW7

London, Great Britain
Victoria & Albert Museum
Brompton Road, London SW7

London, Great Britain
Wallace Collection
Manchester Sq, London W1

London, Great Britain
William Morris Gallery
Water House, Forest Road, Walthamstow E17

Los Angeles, United States of America
L A County Museum of Art
5905 Wiltshire Boulevard, Los Angeles,
California

Los Angeles, United States of America
John Paul Getty Musuem

Manchester, Great Britain
City Art Gallery
Moseley Street, Manchester

Melbourne, Australia
National Gallery of Victoria
180 St Kilda Road, Melbourne, Victoria

Merion, United States of America
Buten Museum of Wedgwood
Merion, Pennsylvania

Milan, Italy
Poldi Pezzoli Museum
via Manzoni 12, Milan

Minneapolis, United States of America
Walker Art Center

Moscow, USSR
Tretiakov Gallery
Lavrushinski per 10, Moscow

Munich, German Federal Rupublic
Residenz Museum

Munich, German Federal Republic
Bayerisches National Museum

Nancy, France
Museum of the School of Nancy
(Glass Museum)

Naples, Italy
Capodimonte National Museum
Parco di Capodimonte, Naples

New Haven, United States of America
Yale University Art Collection
New Haven, Conn

New York, United States of America
Frick Collection
1 East 70th Street, New York 10021

New York, United States of America
Metropolitan Museum
82nd Street, New York

Oslo, Norway
Kunstindustrimuseet
(Applied Arts Museum)

Oxford, Great Britain
Ashmolean Museum
Beaumont Street, Oxford

Paris, France
Louvre Museum
Palais du Louvre, Paris

Paris, France
Musée des Arts Décoratifs

Paris, France
Musée Guimet

Philadelphia, United States of America
Museum of Art
26th Street, Philadelphia, Penn

Prague, Czechoslovakia
Museum of Applied Art

Pretoria, South Africa
Art Museum
Arcadia Park, Pretoria

Rome, Italy
National Museum
viale delle Terme di Diocleziano, Rome

Rotterdam, Holland
Boymans-van Beuningen Museum
Mathenesserlaan 18–20, Rotterdam

Rouen, France
Musée des Beaux Arts

San Francisco, United States of America
Avery Brundage Asian Art Collection
Golden Gate Park, San Francisco, California

San Francisco, United States of America
M H de Young Memorial Museum Palace of
the Legion of Honor
Golden Gate Park, San Francisco, California

San Marino, United States of America
Henry E Huntington Art Gallery
San Marino, California

Sèvres, France
National Ceramic Museum
Sèvres, Paris

Shaker Heights, United States
Shaker Historical Society
Shaker Heights, Ohio

St Helens, Great Britain
Pilkington Glass Museum
Prescot Road, St Helens, Lancs

Stockholm, Sweden
Ostasiatiska Museet

Stoke-on-Trent, Great Britain
City Museum and Art Gallery
Broad Street, Hanley, Stoke-on-Trent, Staffs

Sydney, Australia
Museum of Applied Arts & Sciences
659–695 Harris Street
Broadway, Sydney

Taiwan, Formosa
National Palace Museum
Taipei (Taiwan)

Tokyo, Japan
National Museum
Ueno Park, Tokyo

Toledo, United States of America
Museum of Arts
Toledo, Ohio

Toronto, Canada
Royal Ontario Museum
Queen's Park, Toronto 5

Turin, Italy
Civic Museum of Ancient Art
Palazzo Madama, Piazzo Castello, Turin

Venice, Italy
Correr Museum
Piazza San Marco 52, Venice

Victoria, Canada
Art Gallery of Greater Victoria
1040 Moss Street, Victoria, British Columbia

Vienna, Austria
Kunsthistorisches Museum
Maria Theresienplatz, Vienna

Washington, United States of America
Freer Gallery of Art (Smithsonian Institution)
Jefferson Drive SW, Washington DC

Washington, United States of America
National Gallery of Art
Constitution Avenue, Washington DC

Wellington, New Zealand
National Art Gallery
Buckle Street, Wellington

Williamsburg, United States of America
Colonial Williamsburg

Winnipeg, Canada
Winnipeg Art Gallery
Memorial Boulevard, Winnipeg, Manitoba

Winterthur, United States of America
H F Dupont Museum

Worcester, Great Britain
Dyson Perrins Museum of Worcester Porcelain
Severn Street, Worcester